LAROUSSE

Dictionary of

WORLD
FOLKLORE

LAROUSSE

Dictionary of

WORLD FOLKLORE

Alison Jones

LAROUSSE

LAROUSSE
Larousse plc
43-45 Annandale Street, Edinburgh EH7 4AZ
Larousse Kingfisher Chambers Inc.
95 Madison Avenue, New York, New York 10016

First published by Larousse plc 1995
Paperback edition 1996

Copyright © Larousse plc 1995

10 9 8 7 6 5 4 3 2 1

British Library Cataloging in Publication Data for this
book is available from the British Library

Library of Congress Catalog Card Number:
95-082382

ISBN 0 7523 00 43 1

The publisher would like to thank Gail Wood,
Director of Libraries and Instructional Technologies
at SUNY College of Technology at Alfred, New York,
for her invaluable assistance in reviewing the material
for this volume.

Illustrations by John Beaumont, © Larousse plc
Typeset by Pillans & Wilson Ltd, Edinburgh
Printed in Great Britain by Clays Ltd, St Ives plc

Contents

Introduction	vii
Dictionary	1
Further Reading	469
Biographical Notes on Prominent Folklorists	475
List of Ethnographical and Folklore Museums throughout the World	481
A Calendar of Festivals and Folkloric Events throughout the World	488

Introduction

Of all the fields of modern scholarship, folklore remains one of the most notoriously difficult to define. Yet if the exact boundaries of folk culture are unclear, it is at least certain that the term is a meaningful and useful one; most of us would have little difficulty in thinking of a story, song or superstition which we would consider to be a folk item.

To arrive at a workable definition of folklore, we can begin with the most general and least contentious definition: folklore is what is handed down through the generations in a culture by oral transmission—the tales, skills, rituals, music and so on that are repeated among members of that society. Although similar in this respect to mythology, folklore is not primarily concerned with sacred or religious beliefs but with the everyday life of the people and their tales of heroes, animals or people like themselves. Neither is it strictly legend, which attaches to historical figures and events. In general, myth is what is believed to be sacred and true, legend is what is at least half-believed to be based on history, and folktales are narratives received as fiction or fantasy. Where the supernatural enters folklore, as in most fairy tales or in the stories of spirits or ghosts, it does so on a level far below the divine; the heroes are humans, albeit marvellously endowed or aided, and not deities. Since folk culture is no respecter of boundaries—temporal, geographical or conceptual—items from mythology and legend are incorporated where they demonstrate the themes and workings of folklore; hence Perseus is included as an archetypal dragonslayer, and Charlemagne appears as a sleeper.

Folklore is essentially an oral form; its two key features are variation and repetition. This apparent paradox is what gives folklore its dynamic tension: it is simultaneously artistic and functional; a fluid, creative process and a conservative repository; innovation and tradition. If a tale is 'frozen' by writing it down so that it can only be told in one form, it ceases to be true folklore. Even in the highly literate West, many fairy tales, such as Sleeping Beauty, exist in various different forms. In folk culture, each telling of a tale is an individual experience, fusing the accumulated tradition and familiar form of the tale with the experience of the speaker, the listeners and of the society at that time. The result is a diffused body of lore that preserves its central features with astonishing consistency, while permitting an endless variety of embellishment and modulation.

If the subject area of folklore is open to debate, the means of approaching that area are even more diverse. The body of material is so vast and overlaps with so many other academic disciplines that it has over the years been subjected to a wide range of theories on how best to tackle it, some conflicting, others complementary. As in any academic field, no theory has progressed in isolation, and much productive work has been done by combining a number of approaches, such as the anthropological with a more aesthetic school. Various theories are discussed within the text of the dictionary, and further insight into their practitioners can be gained from the biographical listing of folklorists.

Before it was a field of scholarship, of course, folklore was and still is the preserve of the people. Since it is found in every culture, from the most primitive to the most sophisticated, it may be assumed to fulfil a universal need among society. In pre-literate groups folklore may be primarily the transmission of learned information, a vital part of group survival. This in itself is insufficient as a definition; the prevalence of imaginative tales and the importance accorded to them demonstrate that folklore fulfils a deeper function, giving shape to the beliefs and value systems of a society, rationalizing its preoccupations and institutions, and perpetuating a sense of identity and continuity throughout time. Tales are frequently told as a means of entertainment appealing to the common sense of humour within the group and thereby strengthening the relationships within it; this role is as vital as that of the work chants which synchronize the efforts of the group and maximize its effectiveness.

Folklore is of course very much alive in many rural or primitive areas of the world, but in Western materialistic society many assume that it survives only in fragmentary superstitions, less than half-believed (such as the taboo against walking under ladders) or in children's stories. In fact, urban society has developed its own folklore; stories and customs which are not written down but yet which circulate with surprising ease among the various communities and social groups created by modern industrial society, establishing rules for entry and participation within the group and also a common bond of experience and entertainment.

For these reasons, folklore has never died out, even among societies with sophisticated communication. The weight of tradition and habit of generations still has a pull on the modern mind, and some fundamental part of us rejects scientific reductionism for the richness of a lore that credits our everyday surroundings with the power to influence our lives, creates imaginative and satisfying fiction, and invests the whole business of living with a mysterious, humane significance.

Alison Jones
January 1995

Using the Dictionary

It is a difficult task to mould the vast scope of folk culture into a one-volume A–Z dictionary, but I have tried to locate each entry at the most intuitively obvious position, with cross-references supplied where there might be confusion (eg **ague tree** see **sassafras**) or where variant spellings exist (eg **silkie** see **selkie**). Biographical entries for historical figures are to be found at the surname where applicable (eg **Crockett**, Davy), while legendary or fictional characters are listed under their full names (eg **Johnny Appleseed**). In addition, where the text of one entry contains a reference to another this has been highlighted in bold type, and related topics are indicated at the end of entries by the symbol ▷ to guide the reader to additional information on a given subject. It is hoped that this extensive cross-referencing system will not only improve access to information, but also encourage browsing. One of the central tenets of the book is that folklore is a network of threads that not only bind generations of one cultural group together, but also run throughout centuries and civilizations, and the interconnectedness of the information within it reflects that philosophy.

abandonment

MOTIF OF FOLKLORE, appearing in a variety of forms in tales throughout the world. One of the most common devices of European **fairy tales** is the abandonment of children by parents; this may be because there is not enough food (as in **Hansel and Gretel**) or because the child is ill-omened in some way, either born of an illicit—often incestuous—union (eg St **Kentigern**), suspected of supernatural parentage (see **twins**), or the subject of a prophecy that says he or she will destroy the parents (most famously **Oedipus**). This form of abandonment, especially of new-born babies (when it is known as exposure), reflects actual practices in many areas of the world; folk beliefs and social and economic pressures often dictate that a particular child or even a number of children could not be either supported or tolerated by the group. For example, in societies where high dowries are usual, female babies are frequently exposed. Abandoned children in folktales however, unlike their real life counterparts, typically survive and thrive. They are generally taken in by **animal nurses** or a kindly peasant, although if older they may make their own way in the wilderness. Usually they end up in the court of a king who brings them up as nobles (eg Moses, Oedipus, **Havelock the Dane**). Invariably such children live to fulfil the prophecy spoken at their birth, or they become heroes with supernatural powers (see **Bear's Son cycle**) who shame their aged parents by their good qualities and compassion. In Native American and especially Inuit tales however the abandoned children often become great hunters, who feed the still-starving group that abandoned them but may take their revenge by killing their parents.

Many societies also practise abandonment of the old and sick, those who no longer help to support the group usefully and have become instead a drain on valuable resources; in nomadic groups, where an infirm individual slows down the group and may jeopardize its chances of finding prey, abandonment is particularly common. As late as the 19th century, pioneer wagons in North America left those unfit to continue the journey by the side of the trail with a small fire to ease their last hours. A sight common until relatively recently in parts of Africa and North America was an enclosure of stakes containing a skeleton—someone abandoned by the group and left with just a little food and some protection from wild animals. An additional motive for such abandonment is the widespread superstitious fear of disease-causing demons, and the common belief that ill health is an unlucky omen bringing ill fortune to those associated with it, whether or not the disease is itself contagious.

The abandoned wife is another common motif, found particularly in the Eurasian tale-type *The Maiden Without Hands*. Typically, the woman has her hands cut off and is abandoned by her husband or family, often for an illegitimate pregnancy (mutilation to prevent abandoned persons fending for themselves was common—Oedipus's name derives from the laming he received when exposed). She may be abandoned in an open boat, on an island, or down a well, but is eventually found by a king who marries her. After bearing his children she is again cast out, when jealous rivals slander her, claiming that she has killed or eaten her child. She is finally reconciled to her husband, often after drinking from the **water of life** which restores her beauty.

In folktales abandonment may be for none of these reasons, but simply a villainous act over which the hero

1

triumphs. Hence **Aladdin** escapes from the cave of wonders after the magician abandons him there, and in a Finnish tale the hero abandoned on a golden mountain, where he has been taken to cut the gold and throw it down to his master, succeeds in escaping and wreaking his revenge.

abatwa

FAIRY RACE of the south of Africa, a tiny, peaceable people dwelling among the anthills. They are miniature humans in form and have a similar social structure to the tribesmen, with clan and family loyalties. Like many other **fairy** folk, they are very shy and thus seldom seen by humans; they will only show themselves to young infants, shamans or, occasionally, pregnant women. If a woman sees a male abatwa in the seventh month of her pregnancy, she is certain to bear a son.

Abbot of Misrule see Lord of Misrule

Abbot's Bromley Horn dance

ANCIENT ANIMAL DANCE, one of the very few to survive in performance to the present. It is also known as the Abbot's Bromley Antler dance, and now takes

Abbot's Bromley Horn dance

place at Abbot's Bromley in Staffordshire, England, on the first Monday after 4 September (its original date was Twelfth Day, **Epiphany**). Six men dance to the sound of an accordion holding antlers to their heads, accompanied by a series of other characters including Maid Marian and a fool. The antlers are brightly painted, three red and three white. The troop visits local farms before the dance, which suggests that the dance originally had great ritual significance, probably as a bringer of luck to the community for fertility or good hunting.
▷ **folk dance**; **Morris dance**

Abe No Yasuna

JAPANESE POET AND LEGENDARY HERO. Abe one day saved a white fox from a hunting-party of noblemen by concealing it in the folds of his gown. The next year he met and fell in love with Kuzunoha; they married and she bore him a son, Abe No Seimei, who grew up to become a poet and magician, astrologer to the Emperor. However Kuzunoha died soon after the birth, leaving Abe distraught. Three days after her death she appeared to him in a dream and revealed that she was the fox he had saved.

Beast marriage between humans and foxes is common in folktales, but this tale is notable in the Japanese tradition, as it presents the **fox maiden** as a faithful, virtuous wife and not a sly enchantress.

abiku

TERRIFYING NIGHT DEMON of the Yoruba people of West Africa. Abiku have no stomach, and are therefore continually ravenous, and always on the lookout for children either to eat them or to enter their bodies in order to procure food and drink. If a child is possessed by an abiku, its parents may try to drive the demon out by causing pain or by ringing **bells,** a noise peculiarly distasteful to abiku, as the child eats.

Among the Dahomeans, the abiku is a forest spirit born within a newborn human child and precautions must be taken to prevent the spirits calling him back to the forest. Parents may scar their child's face to make him or her less desirable, dress a boy in girls' clothes in an attempt at disguise, or bind the child to the human community with **iron** ankle bands or belled bracelets.

The fear of the abiku reflects a general belief of world folklore, that prepubescent children are especially vulnerable to evil and can be protected by disguise or mutilation, or by the deliberately disparaging attitude of the parents.
▷ **evil eye**

abominable snowman see **Yeti**

Abou Hassan
RICH MERCHANT, victim of a trick, whose tale is told in the *Arabian Nights*. He is translated in his sleep to the bed of the Caliph, Haroun al-Raschid, and when he awakens is treated as the Caliph, much to his confusion. Shakespeare uses the same idea in *The Taming of the Shrew*, in which Christopher Sly undergoes a similarly disorienting experience.

abracadabra
CABBALISTIC CHARM, a magical formula efficacious for relieving sickness, particularly toothache, and occasionally for ensuring luck. The word was generally inscribed as follows on an **amulet** worn around the neck:

abracadabra

Just as the word dwindled away, so the illness was thought to subside. Some scholars opine that the word is derived from the Hebrew words for the persons of the Trinity, *ab* (father), *ben* (son) and *ruach acadsch* (holy spirit), but others think the word may originally have been the name of a demon of disease, whose influence was thought to wane by this ritual diminishing. It seems clear that the

charm reflects the primeval belief in the power of true names (see **name taboo**). The exotic resonance of the word won it currency among medieval magic-workers, and it has become a byword for mysterious, magical mumbo-jumbo.
▷ **charms**

achacila
SPIRITS OF THE AYMORA PEOPLE of Bolivia, who sometimes appear to humans disguised as old men. They are thought to control rain, hail and frost from their underground homes deep in the mountains.

Acheflour
FIGURE OF ARTHURIAN LEGEND, sister of **Arthur** and mother of Sir **Perceval**. After her husband Sir Bliocadrans was killed fighting in a tournament, she resolved that her son should have nothing to do with chivalric combat. On the pretext of leaving on pilgrimage to see St Brendan in Scotland, Acheflour withdrew to the Waste Forest and brought up Perceval to distrust fighting and fighting men.

acheri
NATIVE AMERICAN GHOST, the spirit of a young girl who lives in the mountains but descends by night to human habitations to dance and sing in her lonely revels. To hear her plaintive voice is an omen of death or disease. The colour red, however, is a protective **talisman** against her power, and hence many peoples wear clothes fringed, embroidered or beaded with red, and a red thread is tied round the neck of new babies to ward off the disease she brings in her shadow.

Achikar
COUNSELLOR OF THE KING OF ASSYRIA, archetype of the wise old man who emerges from hiding to save his country in a widespread tale-type. With no son in his old age, despite his 60 wives, Achikar adopts his nephew Nadan, who promptly conspires against him and succeeds in exacting the death penalty. Achikar escapes into hiding, and is reported dead. At this moment the Pharaoh of Egypt demands of Sennacherib, King of Assyria, that he produce a castle in the air. If he succeeds, a

fabulous reward will befall him; should he fail, Sennacherib will owe the same amount to Pharaoh. All seems lost, until

Achikar

Achikar reappears, constructs the marvellous castle and claims the prize for his king from Pharaoh.

The earliest appearance of the tale is in a fifth-century manuscript, but it is thought to be even more ancient, probably Macedonian in origin, and the prototype of a series of similar tales throughout the world using the motifs of impossible **tasks** and despised helpers. Other tales tell of a famine in which the ruler orders all old, therefore useless, men to be killed, and only one escapes, hidden by his son. This one then emerges in a crisis to save the land by his old wisdom.

aconite

PERENNIAL HERBS of the buttercup family (Ranunculaceae), divided into two genera, *Aconitum* and *Eranthis*. The summer-flowering *Aconitum* plants, for example monkshood (also known as wolfbane), are extremely poisonous and, especially in Nepal where the most deadly variety is found, have been used to tip arrows or harpoons, or to poison the water supplies of enemies. An Italian tale tells of two lovers who died after the father of the girl persuaded her to apply an ointment containing aconite as a love-charm. In skilful hands, however, aconites can be used as pain-relievers or tonics.

acorn

NUT produced by the oak tree (*Quercus*). Because of their unusually long period of maturation (up to three years) and the fact that they only appear on mature trees, acorns have traditionally represented the fruition of labour and patience and have symbolized, in convenient folkloric shorthand, a long period of time. An example is the common proverb 'Great oaks from little acorns grow', urging the listener to take the long view, that seemingly insignificant labours will bear much fruit in the future.

One German folktale tells how a peasant outwits the **Devil** in a Faustian soul bargain by promising to deliver himself when his first crop should be harvested, and by planting acorns wins himself a considerable respite.

▷ **oak**

act of truth

A MOTIF OF FOLKTALES, found especially in Asian lore but common throughout the world. It denotes any supernatural event which occurs specifically to confirm (or occasionally refute) a character's declaration. One of its most popular uses is in conjunction with the **chastity test**, for example in the Indian tale of a white **elephant** belonging to the king which sickened and seemed about to die. The king was distraught, until it was revealed to him that his elephant could be cured by the touch of a chaste woman. All 80 000 of his wives were called upon to perform the healing, but the elephant responded to none until a servant girl named Silavati came forward to touch him, whereupon he rose and began to eat. **Sita** demonstrates her faithfulness to **Rama** by calling on the earth to swallow her up, in a somewhat extreme form of the motif.

There are many other functions for the act of truth; it can be used to establish paternity, or save oneself from execution as a criminal or witch. Sometimes it works against those who falsely invoke it. It survives in **children's lore** in the oath typically rendered as 'Cross my heart and hope to die, Never never tell a lie'.

Adachigahara

CANNIBALISTIC JAPANESE DEMON, a woman armed with a knife who is often portrayed as a child-killer. There are various legends told of her origins; according to one popular tale she was a servant in the imperial court who killed children to obtain blood to effect a magical cure for the prince, and her crimes were subsequently pardoned. She is thought also to be a menace to those, especially pilgrims, who unwarily seek shelter in her home.
▷ **ogre**

Adam Bell

LEGENDARY ENGLISH ARCHER, immortalized in the **ballad** of that name. His companions were fellow outlaws **William of Cloudesly** and **Clym of the Clough**, and all three were outstanding marksmen. When William of Cloudesly was brought to execution in Caerlel,

having been apprehended on a clandestine visit to his wife, his friends brought off a daring and flamboyant rescue and immediately rode for London, to secure the favour of the king before outraged justice could forestall them. Aided by the intervention of the sympathetic queen, William won the king's pardon, and the three performed such marvels of archery that they and their families enjoyed royal favour for generations.
▷ **William Tell**

adaro

MELANESIAN SPIRITS, half fish, half human. They travel from their home in the sun by means of **rainbows**, and on earth they ride on waterspouts. If the sun shines during a rain shower it is certain

adaro

that adaro are on the move. They can be harmful to humans, shooting them with flying fish and causing unconsciousness which, if not treated by stronger magic, can result in death.

Addanc of the Lake

WATER MONSTER, the fabulous beast slain by Peredur in the *Mabinogion*. He is overcome by the use of a magic stone which renders Peredur invisible.

adh sidhe

IRISH SPIRITS of uncertain appearance, seen only by those with a murky con-

science. They are said by some to be
sharp-toothed hags who tear at their
victims' flesh, and by others to be
beautiful temptresses or even terrifying
black horses. This uncertainty is a result
of the natural reticence of those who
may have seen them, unwilling to admit
to a sighting. The real danger from the
adh sidhe is the fear of running insane
with terror during their midnight
visitations.

Adlet

DOG PEOPLE, a fabulous race believed by
the Inuits to be the descendants of an
enormous red dog. They are said to be
the result of a **beast marriage** between
the dog and an Inuit woman, which
produced five monstrous children and
five dogs. The dogs were set adrift on a
raft by their mother and drifted across
the sea to beget between them the white
races, but the monsters produced a
terrible race of bloodthirsty, cannibalistic warriors. Called Adlet by Labrador
groups and Erqigdlit by those west of
Hudson's Bay, this mythical people is
also recognized by tribes in Greenland
and Baffinland.

adultery

ILLICIT SEXUAL INTERCOURSE, in
European and modern American tradition generally outside marriage, but
elsewhere in the world outwith specific
social or kinship groups. There is startling variation even among closely related
ethnic groups in attitudes to adultery,
ranging from death for the disgraced
woman, her lover and the shamed
husband to the tradition of the maritime
Koryaks, whose husbands regard their
wives' infidelities as a point of honour
and thank their rivals if a child results
from the affair.

Where a prohibition against adultery
exists, it is generally enforced against the
woman only, as an extension of the
man's sexual jealousy and the principle
of ownership (see **marriage**, **dowry**). In
such cases the most usual form of
punishment for a woman caught *in
flagrante* is mutilation or execution by
the outraged husband for both her and
her lover; even when this primitive
justice is not expressly condoned in law it

is usually accepted as an unwritten code
of honour. A woman might typically
have her nose cut off, her head shaved,
or a public display made of her as an
adulteress. Her lover would more probably be killed outright rather than
humiliated, although depending on his
social class he might escape with no harm
or have his genitals mutilated or
removed. Among highly sophisticated
societies, the fashionable classes sometimes underline their chicness by coun-
tenancing, or even approving of, extra-
marital affairs, which is an interesting
ethnological phenomenon.

Unfaithfulness has frequently been
invested with a mystical aspect, partly
due to the Paulian teachings of Christianity which stress the importance of
bodily purity. Just as **virginity** endows a
woman with spiritual power, such as the
means of attracting the **unicorn**, so
unfaithfulness disperses her mystique
and can bring harm to her wronged
husband, as witness the legend of
Guinevere and the effect of her liaison
with **Lancelot of the Lake** upon **Arthur**.
Hebrew tradition likened the condition
of an Israel unfaithful to her God's
commandments to an unfaithful wife,
dramatized in the life of the prophet
Hosea who was commanded by God to
take an adulterous wife and continue to
love her to demonstrate God's love for
his people.

In cultures which do not subscribe to
such tenets, however, and even to some
extent in those that do, adultery is more
a matter of social standing and custom
than religious principle. It is practised
widely as a charm for fertility at the
sowing of the harvest, or to encourage
the livestock to breed, around the world.

The unfaithful spouse punished is a
motif in a number of modern **urban
legends**; one American tale tells of the
general consternation and the husband's
humiliation when a white woman gives
birth to a black child. It later emerges
that her white husband had, nine months
earlier, slept with a prostitute who had
recently slept with a black customer.
This tale recalls traditional tales of
immaculate conception, in which sperm
is transferred from the male to the
female in an unlikely, and entirely
innocent, way (see **virginity**). Another

popular legend tells of an outraged wife who superglues her husband's erect member to his chest after learning of his adultery.

Aedh

PRINCE OF LEINSTER, a captive in **fairy-land**. As a child playing with his friends he was kidnapped by two amorous **sidhe** women and borne off to a palace in fairyland, where he remained a captive for three years. Finally he contrived to escape, and ran into St **Patrick**, who smuggled him in disguise into the Leinster court and reunited him with his father as a whole human boy, free from the **glamour** of the fairies. This is one of the earliest examples of the 'captives in fairyland' tale-type, appearing in the *Silva Godelica*.

aes sidhe see sidhe

Aesop's fables

ALLEGORICAL ANIMAL TALES, the archetypes of this popular genre of didactic folktale. The nub of the tales is typically pragmatic rather than lofty; in the fable of the **fox** and the **cat**, the fox boasts of his thousand wily tricks while the cat confesses that he knows only one, the ability to climb a tree quickly, but when the dogs attack it is this one trick that saves him while the fox is killed in his panic. The moral: those who boast of their wisdom are often very great fools.

Aesop's fables however are remarkable not only for their moral but also their political weight. It seems clear that even early Greeks such as Hesiod recognized that one of the main purposes of such tales was social criticism; the device of using animals as characters seems innocent but may provide a disguise beneath which topical issues can be discussed and a clear moral conclusion drawn, usually criticizing the powerful for injustice to the weak without offending the rulers or endangering the moralist's own person. The capacity of the fables for political content has been strikingly demonstrated in more recent times: it is said that the first translation of the fables into Chinese was suppressed by the authorities who suspected that they were a form of contemporary political commentary.

The first recorded collection of fables attributed to Aesop was produced by Demetrius Phalareus in the fourth century BC, but all extant fragments date from considerably later. The most famous collection is that of Phaedrus who wrote a series of fables as Latin elegiacs in the first century AD. A prose version of this collection, attributed to Romulus, was current in the Middle Ages in Europe and adapted by the German scholar Heinrich Steinhöwel, who believed that the fables were Aesop's. It was this collection, in French translation, that was used by William Caxton when he began printing his English version in 1483. Another famous treatment of the fables was that of La Fontaine, the 17th-century French poet and fabulist.

The fables of Aesop have now passed into the literary canon, but it seems clear that their roots were in the folktales of Greece and Asia, and their simplicity and memorable dramatic style illustrate the enormous capacity of the folktale for entertainment and instruction.

afreet

TERRIFYING SPIRIT OF ISLAMIC LORE, the second most powerful of the five classes of **jinn**.

African folklore

THE BIRTHPLACE OF FOLK CULTURE, the continent of Africa is second only to Asia in size. It is also a land of great mineral resources, and has attracted many to its shores. Although the vast majority of the population is native-born, there have been significant outside influences; white Europeans, particularly in South Africa, Arabs in West Africa, and Asians in the south and east.

The traditional culture of Africa is based around the ethnic group, distinct from its neighbours not in economic or political terms but in the sense of having a unique cultural identity, and often a unique language. Very few languages have an indigenous written form, although many attempts to transcribe the languages were made by European missionaries in the 18th and 19th centuries. All communication and continuation of knowledge and tradition is therefore necessarily oral, and it is within this context that the folktale has gained such popularity and significance in Africa. There is in African lore an astonishing number of tales, proverbs, songs and so on already recorded, but the collection is far from complete. The storyteller of any one tribe will probably have a repertoire of a couple of hundred tales, and it is estimated that there are about 3 000 such groups in Africa.

Rather than fables, the moral values of the culture tend to be expressed more naturally in proverbs. Often a tale with moral content will end with a proverb designed to make the allegorical point quite clear. Researchers have noted a clear pattern in the way folklore is used in children's education: young children are told monster stories, to pleasurably frighten them but also to instil in them the need to be obedient and to remain attached to the family or social group. These are replaced by moral tales, punctuated by proverbs, in the case of older children, and among adults this fund of common wisdom forms a large part of conversation and everyday thought. In West Africa, a legal case may even be decided on the weight of an apposite proverb cited by a lawyer.

A related form is that of the **riddle**, common throughout Africa and usually phrased as a statement rather than a question, eg 'Elephant dies, Mangudu eats him; buffalo dies, Mangudu eats him; Mangudu dies, there is no one who wants to eat him'. The implicit question is 'who or what is Mangudu?', the answer is 'cooking pot'. This playful use of words is characteristic of African folklore: the **tongue twister** too is a common form, but usually untranslatable.

Tales are almost always told at night, usually to a group by the tribe's recognized story-teller. There is a general feeling that folktales belong in some sense to the spirits of the dead, and it would be both dangerous and offensive to tell stories in daylight. Darkness also heightens the magical and dramatic aspects of the story-teller's art. There is usually much interaction between the narrator and his audience, who may respond to his questions, add encouragement and especially join in with the songs. Most tales include songs, often with many repetitions, and this is a hallmark of a popular and communal oral form.

African songs tend to have rhythmic rather than rhyming structure, and listeners will usually support the song by beating time. They function not as components of folktales, but in their own right as a means of recording and transmitting news. Songs created at historic occasions may survive for centuries, others of less note die out and are replaced by more topical songs or new songs on the age-old themes of love, rejection and hardship.

Between the 16th and 19th centuries, the slave trade to the New World transported millions of Africans, mainly from West Africa, across the Atlantic. Blacks in the New World succeeded to a remarkable degree in retaining their traditional folklore, and developed a distinct lore and culture of their own. Typical examples are the **Brer Rabbit** tales told to white American children by their black nurses, taken from the trickster tales of their homeland, and the haunting rhythmic spirituals created as enslaved African consciousness met Christianity.

▷ **North American folklore**; **trickster**

afterbirth

A VITAL ELEMENT OF THE HEALTHY BABY in many cultures world-wide. Customs relating to the treatment of the afterbirth are closely bound up with the notion of the **separable soul**, by which token the disposal made of the placenta has enormous ramifications for the life which it nourished in the womb for so many months. In some cultures this mysterious identification takes the form of twinship; in most the bond is a looser, more mystical kinship. Often a tree is planted where the afterbirth is buried, and the health of this tree in the future will be bound up with that of the child.

Miniature tools or tokens, for example a bow and **arrows**, tiny needles and thread, cooking pots or animal pelts, may be attached to the afterbirth, to bestow the appropriate skills on the baby by **sympathetic magic**.

Sympathetic magic also operates to prohibit the feeding of the afterbirth to any animal; should a wild creature dig up the placenta and eat it the child would develop the undesirable qualities of that animal. Occasionally this principle is reversed; some Native Americans of British Columbia feed their afterbirths to **ravens**, to ensure the gift of true foresight for the child. Several cultures take the practical step of encouraging the mother to eat the placenta, which provides a valuable source of nutrition for her.

The afterbirth is regarded almost exclusively as a positive force, a precious repository of the child's own or his guardian's spirit, and even when ritual disposal is not practised charms made from its elements are frequently used for protection, for example the sailor's **amulet** against drowning is an unbroken caul.

▷ **childbirth**; **sailors' lore**

afterlife

LIFE BEYOND THE GRAVE. Although strictly belonging in the province of mythology, belief in an afterworld is relevant to folklore since it determines many of the folk customs and legends associated with **death**. Most cultures have some concept of a land for the dead, located under the earth, in the sky, across the water or simply 'in the West'. These typically involve a system of reward and punishment, a beautiful world for the blessed and a dark, usually underground, place for the rest, and often there are lands in between. Many rituals are designed to help the soul reach the state of happiness; the Roman Catholic Mass is one example, the sacrifices of primitive tribes and the inclusion of food, drink and money for the journey in an Egyptian tomb are others. Cremation is considered by some cultures as a means of releasing the spirit for reincarnation, for example among Hindus, whereas many Native North Americans believe that a soul cannot achieve peace if the body is destroyed or dismembered. It is considered very dangerous for the living to enter the world of the dead, although **Orpheus** in Greek mythology and others have accomplished it.

▷ **funeral customs**; **otherworld**

afterworld see **otherworld**

Agastya

HINDU HOLY MAN, traditionally one of the authors of the sacred Vedas. The group of seven sages who composed the Vedic hymns and fathered the Brahmans, known collectively as the *rishi*, accrued an enormous amount of popular legend. Agastya (also known as Agasti) was said to have sprung from the water into which the semen of the gods Mitra and Varuna had fallen as they watched the lovely nymph Urvasi. The *Mahabharata* tells how he drank the ocean to expose a group of demons plotting against the gods, and he came to the gods' aid a second time by tricking Mount Vindya into halting his growth, which had threatened to impede the progress of the sun.

He is now said to live on the hill named after him in old Travancore state (now part of Kerala) in south-west India, and is regarded as the patron saint of southern India.

Agnes, St (d.c.304)

VIRGIN MARTYR, a powerful symbol of Christian chastity and innocence. The various legends of St Agnes offer conflicting evidence, but most are agreed that she was born of a wealthy Roman family and, although exceptionally beautiful, consecrated herself to chastity as a child. When she was betrayed to the Roman authorities as a Christian by a rejected suitor, at the age of 12 or 13, she endured martyrdom rather than compromise her faith or her **virginity**.

To this basic story many traditions add elaborations, such as the story of the soldier who looked on her in her imprisonment with impure thoughts and immediately lost his eyesight; it was only restored by the prayers of Agnes. During her arrest she is said to have been unmoved by the governor's range of torture implements, until in desperation and enraged by her radiant purity he sent her to a house of prostitution in Rome. But Agnes was impervious to the corruption around her. She returned to the governor as virginal and as intractable as ever, and finally he ordered her execution.

She is variously supposed to have been beheaded, pierced through the throat, and burned to death. These conflicting accounts of her martyrdom suggest that the details of her story were lost in myth by the time of her *Acts*. From the sixth century at least Agnes's emblem has been that of a lamb, from the similarity of her name to the Latin *agnus* ('lamb'). At St Agnes in Rome, where the nuns weave the pallia for archbishops, the lambs which provide the wool are specially blessed on her feast-day. Her cult gained immediate popularity, with influential figures such as Ambrose, Prudentius and Jerome singling her out for praise, and several early English churches were dedicated to her. In art she is usually depicted with long hair and a lamb, sometimes with the sword of her martyrdom at her throat. Her feast-day is 21 January, and she is the patron saint of betrothed couples, gardeners and virgins, invoked for chastity.

The night before St Agnes' feast-day is traditionally regarded as propitious for love divination by young women in Britain. A popular incantation to be said while preparing the spell (eg by sprinkling grain on the ground), which has numerous variations, is:

Agnes sweet, Agnes fair,
Hither, hither now repair;
Bonny Agnes, let me see
The lad who is to marry me.

ague tree see sassafras

Ahl al-trab

MISCHIEVOUS SPIRITS OF ISLAMIC FOLKLORE. Emerging from their homes just below the surface of the Saharan sand, these tiny spirits make miserable the lives of travellers in the desert, drinking pools of water before they can reach them, plaguing camels and whipping up the sand into the eyes of human and beast.

Ahmed

PRINCE OF THE *ARABIAN NIGHTS*, best known for his marvellous tent. This **magic object**, given to him by the fairy Paribanou, was so small that it could be carried in a pocket, but when erected became large enough to shelter the entire army. He also possessed a magic **apple**, bought at Samarkand, which had the virtue of curing every illness known to humankind. His brother **Houssain** possessed a **magic carpet**.

ahuizotl

CENTRAL AMERICAN WATER-MONSTER. Known to us through several appearances in Aztec carvings, the ahuizotl is a grotesque creature some way between a dog and a monkey with a startling appendage: a hand on the end of its sinuous tail.

Should an unwary person venture too close to the water's edge, the ahuizotl would simply reach out with its tail and seize its victim, whose body would be found some time later, minus the eyes, teeth and nails, all coveted by the creature. When it became impatient, it would lure fishermen by causing fish to leap enticingly, or sit on the bank keening until pity overcame caution and a human approached close enough for the creature to grab. Those seized by the

Ahl al-trab

ahuizotl were thought to be blessed inasmuch as their souls would certainly go straight to Paradise; they had been chosen by the rain gods whose servant the ahuizotl was.

Aido Hwendo

RAINBOW SERPENT OF AFRICA, supporter of the earth. In Dahomean legend Aido Hwendo carried the creator goddess Mawn around as she brought the universe into being, and when it was complete he lay coiled beneath it to support its great weight. Mawn surrounded him with sea to allay the fierce heat, but Aido Hwendo is still far from happy; earthquakes occur as he shifts around in discomfort, and he is one day likely to become so hungry that he will begin to eat his own tail, at which point the earth will surely collapse.

In Haiti his volatility is renowned, and it is customary to make offerings to him at marriage ceremonies and beseech him not to harm the young couple out of envy.
▷ **Atlas motif; dragon; sea-serpent; snake**

Aigamuxo

FABULOUS AND MONSTROUS RACE, a cannibalistic people with eyes in their heels who delight in shredding humans with their long teeth. The tales told by the Hottentot people about this race are similar to European **ogre** tales, in which the hero uses his cunning to outwit the stronger but more stupid villain.

Aiken Drum

FIGURE OF NURSERY RHYME AND BALLAD LORE. He is variously regarded as the man who came 'to oor toun' in the Scottish version or 'lived in the moon' elsewhere in Britain. This Aiken Drum is whimsically dressed entirely in edible garments, sporting a coat of roast beef and a hat of cream cheese, for example. The name was given in 1878 to the Brownie of Blednoch in William Nicholson's *Poetical Works* (third edition). Here Aiken Drum wears nothing but a skirt of rushes, and finally disappears, in typical **brownie** fashion, when a gift of clothes is offered in thanks for his help.

Ailill Mac Matach

OLD IRISH KING OF CONNACHT, husband of the formidable **Medb**. In the tale of the Ulster cycle, *Táin Bó Cuailnge*, Ailill's insistence that his possessions out-value those of his wife provokes Medb into the famous cattle-raid which led to war against **Cuchulainn** and Ulster.

He appears also in the *Táin Bó Fraech* as the father of the beautiful **Findabair**, deceitfully promising his daughter to every hero who would fight with him against Cuchulainn. He opposed Fraech's courtship of Findabair, even attempting to have him killed, and relented only when Fraech agreed to oppose Cuchulainn. Some legends tell how Findabair later died of a broken heart after Fraèch was slain in battle by Cuchulainn.

Aillen Mac Midhna

OLD IRISH MUSICIAN, a fairy figure of the **Tuatha de Danann**. Each year on All Hallow's Eve (Samhain) he would emerge from Sidhe Finnachaid and make his way to Tara and the court of the High King, playing marvellous music on his tambourine or *timpan*. Anyone who heard the music was irresistibly lulled into a magic sleep, and while its defenders slumbered the castle was consumed by three fiery blasts from the nostrils of Aillen Mac Midhna. After 23 years of this destruction, **Finn Mac Cumhal** finally conquered him by breathing the fumes of his magic spear, the point of which was so poisonous that it overcame the spell of Aillen's music and roused him; he drove off the creature and beheaded him.
▷ **Beowulf**

Aine

OLD IRISH FAIRY WOMAN, originally a goddess who revenged her rape by a Munster king by slaying him with magic. In popular folklore she survived as a **swan maiden** type, the daughter of King Egogabal of the **Tuatha de Danann**, who was spotted by the Earl of Desmond as she sat combing her hair by Lough Gur. He seized her cloak, thereby effectively trapping her in mortal shape, and made her his wife. She bore him a son, Earl

Fitzgerald, and all went well until the first Earl Gerald broke the taboo laid upon him by uttering a shout of surprise at his supernatural son's tricks. The boy immediately disappeared under the waters of Lough Gur, where he is still said to inhabit an enchanted castle from which he occasionally emerges, and Aine vanished into Knock Aine, on the shores of the lough. She is associated with fertility rites performed until quite recently there on **Midsummer** Eve.

airi

MOUNTAIN SPIRIT OF INDIA, said to be the ghost of a hunter who now roams wild places with his ghostly pack of hounds. His saliva is highly poisonous, but usually a mortal will die of fright having merely seen the airi. To those robust enough to survive such an encounter, the airi may show marvellous caves of hidden treasure.

aitvaras

LITHUANIAN HOUSE SPIRIT, appearing as a **cock** when inside the house and a fiery **dragon** on his excursions outside. Like most house spirits, the aitvaras is something of a mixed blessing. He supplies the house with grain and wealth, but as this is generally stolen it often brings trouble with it, and it is almost impossible to persuade him to leave once settled. For those who feel the deal is worthwhile, the aitvaras can usually be purchased from the Devil for the price of one's soul.
▷ **household spirits; mischievous spirits**

aiza

PROTECTIVE SPIRIT OF AFRICAN FOLKLORE. Among the peoples of Dahomey, aiza are classes of spirits which protect the various groups of society: regions, villages, households and so on. Shrines to the various types of aiza are built, incorporating elements symbolic of the group to be protected such as materials bartered at a market. The sense of belonging to an aiza is a vital part of the sense of communal identity, and they are held responsible for the prosperity or otherwise of the group.

Ajatar

FINNISH EVIL SPIRIT, the Devil of the Woods. She is a fearsome creature in the shape of a **dragon**, who suckles snakes and causes pestilence and diseases. It is possible that she is related to the Lithuanian **aitvaras**, who also appears in the shape of a dragon but is altogether less demonic. In some areas her name is a curse, and she is spoken of as the mother of the **Devil**.

akalo

SPIRIT OF THE DEAD, a benevolent ghost of Solomon Island folklore. Whenever a clan member dies he is thought to become an akalo, able to aid his people; his relatives ensure that the soul remains in the house by catching it with a special rod after the individual dies, and then keeping the soul in a shrine containing an item from the corpse such as teeth, hair, fingernails or even the whole skull. This is a form of ancestor worship, in which the dead person becomes a **guardian spirit** for the house.
▷ **death; fingers; separable soul**

akuma

TERRIFYING EVIL SPIRIT OF JAPAN, also known as *toori akuma* or *ma*. To see an akuma is considered extremely unlucky, and is also a terrifying experience; it has an enormous, flaming head with eyes like live coals and carries a sword borne aloft as it sweeps through the air. One tale tells how a Japanese nobleman hid in terror as he saw an akuma approaching and, peeking out from his hiding place, saw the creature enter his neighbour's house, from whence came a dreadful shrieking. When he dared to emerge, the man found that his neighbour, in attempting to battle with the demon, had inadvertently slain his entire household.

al

PERSIAN DEMON, found in Islamic, Christian and particularly Armenian lore. Originally associated with disease in general, als became specifically linked with **childbirth**. They can be male or female, and appear half human and half beast, covered with shaggy hair, with eyes like fire, nails of brass, teeth of iron and a tusk like a wild boar. Boggy ground is their favourite habitat, but unswept corners of houses or stables will serve them as a home.

The al preys on the mother in child-birth, causing miscarriage, and its favourite trick is to steal babies a month or two before term to supply it with its favourite food. The best way to protect both mother and unborn child is to surround the bed with **iron** weapons, and to keep her awake and alert after the birth.

In Afghanistan, als are young women with floating hair and long nails who feed on corpses.

Aladdin

ASIAN FOLKTALE, 'the most famous story in the world'. In the *Arabian Nights*, Scheherazade describes Aladdin, son of a poor tailor in a city in China, as a good-for-nothing who refused to apply himself to his father's trade. Worn down by grief and worry when the tailor dies, his widow tries to support herself and her wayward son alone. But Aladdin is discovered by an African magician who has been searching for him, the only one who can enter the magical cave in which the magician's treasure is buried. The magician wins the trust of the boy and his mother by posing as the brother of the dead tailor and by his apparent kindness and generosity, and he persuades Aladdin to come with him to the cave and open it for him. He gives the boy a ring to protect him and tells him to fetch a copper lamp. When Aladdin arrives back, laden with jewels he has found in the cave, he asks his 'uncle' to help him out before handing over the lamp and the magician, suspecting some trickery, shuts the cave on him in fury.

Wringing his hands in despair, Aladdin is startled to see a jinni appear before him demanding to know his wish. He escapes the cave, and returns to his mother a changed boy. Aladdin's mother frees the jinni of the lamp when she tries to clean it, and they live in comfort for some time.

Aladdin catches a glimpse of the hidden Princess Badr al-Budur, and with the jinni's help he fulfils the various impossible tasks demanded by her father and wins her as his bride. They live in a

Aladdin

magnificent pavilion built by the jinni in front of the king's palace, with windows made of precious stones.

By posing as a lamp seller, the Moroccan magician tricks the princess into parting with the magic lamp. He immediately transports both her and the pavilion to Africa, but with the aid of the jinni of the ring Aladdin follows and succeeds in regaining the lamp and returning the palace. The magician tries once more to trick the princess, but is defeated and killed by Aladdin and the two remain happily married, with Aladdin succeeding the Sultan (his father-in-law) to the throne of China.

The story is a typical Asian folktale, with its emphasis on fantastic adventures, supernatural jinn and opulent detail. It is a little unusual in its concentration upon the hero; for example, in this tale Aladdin recovers his palace and princess by his own resourcefulness, aided by the jinni of the ring, but often in such tales the restoration of the **talisman** or lost object is brought about by helpful

13

animals. The motifs of the **magic object** in an underground room and the object which magically fulfils wishes are common throughout Asian and European lore. The basic principle of the poor boy making good, the lowliest member of society bettering the ruler, is one of the fundamental themes of world folklore. Where Aladdin differs from much European tradition is his very worthlessness at the start of the story; in more romantic Western fairy tales the moral point is usually clarified by having the hero poor but good-hearted, as in the **Cinderella**-type.

alan

MISCHIEVOUS SPIRITS OF THE PHILIPPINES, generally friendly towards humans. They are half-human and half-bird in appearance, and spend much of their time hanging upside down from trees by their feet in their forest homes (which practice is aided by the peculiarity of their digits, the usual toes and fingers being reversed). In folktales however they frequently inhabit halls of gold, and act as foster-parents to the heroes of the tales.

Alasita

FESTIVAL OF THE AYMARA NATIVE AMERI-CANS of South America. It is a celebra-tion in honour of Eq'eq'o, the fertility god and bringer of good luck, who is thought to watch over all sexual activity. At his festival people bring miniature replicas of goods such as clothes, live-stock, tools and so on to be bartered for stones in a mock market. This ensures that Eq'eq'o will provide these needful things the following year. Afterwards the children are given the miniatures as toys. Sexual activity is encouraged during the festival as a form of fertility rite, and the fiesta derives its name from the call of the vendors in the pantomime market, '*alasita*!', 'buy from me!'

Alasnam

CHARACTER OF THE *ARABIAN NIGHTS*, who possessed eight marvellous dia-mond statues but required a ninth, yet more precious, to fill his final pedestal. He discovered a worthy solution to his dilemma in his wife, the most beautiful

albatross

and flawless woman in the world. He achieved this prize with the aid of a magic **mirror** given to him by a genie; if he gazed into the mirror thinking of a woman and it were to cloud, he would know that she would be unfaithful to him, but if it remained clear, her virtue was beyond doubt.

albatross

PORTENTOUS SEA-BIRD, capable of astonishing endurance and distance in flight, around which many legends have grown up. One of the most famous of these legendary accretions is that the albatross is able to predict bad weather, or in some versions that the presence of an albatross near a ship is enough to bring on a storm. Because of its seem-ingly motionless flight, the bird is said to sleep on the wing, and it is thought to raise its brood on a floating raft rather than solid ground. In Japan the albatross, servant of the great Sea God, is considered a particularly auspicious omen.

As Coleridge's *Rime of the Ancient Mariner* attests, the **taboo** against killing an albatross is a common and powerful one.
▷ **birds**

Alberich

DWARF KING OF NORSE LEGEND, who held court in a marvellous underground palace hewn from rocks and studded with precious stones. In the *Nibelungenlied* he was the guardian of the Nibelung hoard. He was renowned for the **magic objects** crafted by his subjects, which he on occasion gave to deserving humans; Siegfried received from him the marvellous sword **Balmung** and a cloak of **invisibility**. The gods too benefited from his munificence; Freya's troublesome necklace **Brisingamen** was **dwarf**-made by Alberich's subjects, as was Draupnir (the ring of Odin) and **Tyrfing**, the magical sword.

Albion

ANCIENT NAME FOR BRITAIN, derived either from the white cliffs facing Gaul (*albus* is Latin for white) or from the Celtic *alp*. A plethora of legends grew up to explain the meaning and history of the name. A son of Neptune named Algion was said to have founded his kingdom in the country, and in the 17th century Drayton claimed that Albion was a Roman Christian who became Britain's first martyr. More imaginatively, it was said that the king of Syria had 50 daughters, all of whom were married on the same day and all of whom murdered their husbands on their wedding night. Instead of execution they were sentenced to drift in an open boat; they found themselves in Britain where they married natives and gave the name of the eldest sister, Albia, to their new home.

Yet another legend tells how **Brut**, a survivor of Troy's siege, led a band of Trojans to Albion where they defeated the terrible giant Gogmagog and set about populating the land with Britons (named from Brut).
▷ **Gogmagog**

alchemy

THE SCIENCE OF THE SEARCH FOR GOLD. Alchemists, who sought to create gold from base metals by means of the fabulous **philosopher's stone**, practised a primitive kind of chemistry which in fact laid the foundations for the modern science. Alchemists flourished in ancient Greece and Egypt, in medieval Arabia and in Europe from the 16th century, but all their labours came no closer to success than might the methods of the

alchemy

folktale, the stealing of a goose which lays golden eggs or finding the pot of fairy gold at the end of the rainbow.
▷ **lodestone**

alchera

MYTHICAL PERIOD OF AUSTRALIAN ABORIGINAL LORE, more commonly known as the **Dreamtime** or Dreaming. The term, popular among central groups, is flexible, and can also be used for anything relating to an individual or clan totem (see **totemism**).

alder

A TREE OR SHRUB OF THE BIRCH FAMILY (Betulaceae), genus *Alnus*, found throughout the northern hemisphere and in cooler, elevated areas of South America. In Brythonic mythology it is closely associated with the gigantic **Bran the Blessed**, who was recognized at the Battle of the Trees by the alder branch he carried. For Bran and many others, the alder was a symbol of regeneration and resurrection, and in Norse mythology the first human couple were created from the **ash** and alder. Part of its mystical significance may be due to the fact that the wood turns from white to purple when it is cut, suggestive of blood. Irish foresters try not to chop down alder trees, and in fact to fell an alder was historically a punishable offence.

In Newfoundland the alder is valued primarily for its medicinal uses; as an infusion it is used to combat rheumatism and itching, and the bark is used in a salve to soothe burns.

alectorian stone

MAGICAL STONE, a **talisman** allegedly found in the belly of a **cock**. It brings health, strength and wealth to the one who possesses it. An ancient Greek athlete, Milo of Cortona, was said to owe the secret of his legendary feats of strength to an alectorian stone he always carried with him.

alectryomancy

DIVINATION by means of a **cock** bird. Some authorities specify that the cock must be white to make this method truly effective. A circle is drawn on the ground and the letters of the alphabet written around it. A grain of corn is placed on each letter, and the cock is then asked a question and placed in the centre of the circle. Careful note is taken of the letters corresponding to the grains eaten by the cock, which will spell out the answer to the diviner's question. This technique is an ancient one, known to have been practised in Ancient Rome at least.

aleuromancy

FORM OF DIVINATION FROM FLOUR. Scraps of paper bearing messages are concealed within balls of dough which are then distributed randomly to those present. The modern Chinese fortune cookie testifies to the enduring popularity of this method of divination.

alfar

ELVES OF NORSE lore. They were divided into two types: **svartálfar**, the dark elves who inhabited an underground kingdom, and *liosálfar*, the light elves whose home was **Alfheim** under the kingship of the sun god Frey. Svartálfar were later confused with the subterranean **dwarfs**, despite their differences in temperament and appearance, and in medieval legends often appear as subjects of **Alberich**. The alfar retained close links with the Teutonic gods, often aiding them against their enemies.

Alfheim

OTHERWORLD OF SCANDINAVIAN LORE, home of the light **elves**, ruled by the god Frey. In contrast to that of the dark elves (Döckálfar, often confused with the home of the **dwarfs**), this kingdom is located well above ground, somewhere between earth and heaven.

Alfred the Great (849–99)

KING OF WESSEX (871–99). Although his main achievements as a ruler were military (notably against the Danes invading Wessex in 871 and 878), constitutional and literary, he is best remembered in popular lore as the king who burned the cakes. In a tale dating from the 11th century or perhaps even later, Alfred takes shelter in a cowherd's hut during a campaign against the Danes and sits by the fire tending his equipment and warming himself, quite unrecognized by his hosts. The cowherd's wife leaves him in charge of her baking while she goes about her chores, and on returning finds her cakes charred while the absent-minded king sits dreaming. Alfred bears her scolding humbly.

Ali Baba

A MASTER THIEF OF ASIAN FOLKLORE, he is one of the most famous characters in the *Arabian Nights*, whose story displays many familiar folklore motifs. The origins of the tale are uncertain; like *Aladdin and the Wonderful Lamp* it was only included in the *Arabian Nights' Entertainment* in the 18th century by Galland, who heard it from an Arab in Paris.

Ali Baba is a poor woodchopper, living humbly with his wife and children by selling firewood. In the forest one day he hides from a band of robbers and watches as their leader opens a rock face with the words 'Open Sesame!'. The robbers stash their booty in the cave, the captain commands the rock to close, and the group rides off. Emerging cautiously from his hiding place, Ali Baba speaks the words of opening and enters a vast store-house of treasure. He fills his pockets and loads his asses with gold pieces and returns home to his wife.

To count the gold, she borrows a measure from the wife of Kassim, brother of Ali Baba, who, curious to know what her poor relations could be weighing, coats the underside of the measure with wax or suet. When Kassim sees a gold coin stuck there, he threatens to bring Ali Baba before the governor for theft if he will not share his secret.

Reluctantly, Ali Baba tells Kassim of the cave and his brother immediately sets off with a train of mules. Kassim speaks the magic formula and enters the cave, where he delightedly sets about collecting treasure with which to load his mules. When he comes to leave, however, he realizes that he has forgotten the words of opening. The robbers return and Kassim is caught and cut into pieces which are then piled inside the cave as a deterrent to other would-be thieves. There Ali Baba finds the body, and brings it back home secretly.

So that his brother's death should not excite suspicion, Ali Baba's servant girl **Morgiana** pays a local cobbler to secretly stitch the body together, blindfolding him on his way to and from the house, and it is buried with the usual rites.

Although sworn to secrecy, the cobbler cannot resist bragging of his skill, and is heard by one of the robbers. He bribes the old cobbler to lead him back to Ali Baba's house, wearing a blindfold as he had the first time, and marks the door with chalk and leaves, but Morgiana notices the suspicious mark and prudently duplicates it on every door in the neighbourhood. The thieves are baffled when they arrive to take their revenge, the spy is killed and another goes to bribe the cobbler to lead him to the house. This spy makes a less obvious mark on the door, but again Morgiana notices it and marks the other doors in the same way. Once again the thieves are frustrated and the spy put to death for his incompetence. The next robber to be led there by the cobbler makes no marks but fixes the house in his memory and is then able to lead his comrades back to it.

The captain returns to the house posing as an oil merchant, with his men hidden in 37 of his 38 jars. He begs hospitality of Ali Baba, planning to signal his men to attack in the night, but Morgiana discovers the ruse and kills the robbers in their jars by pouring boiling oil from the 38th jar over them all in

Ali Baba

turn. Finding his comrades dead, the captain flees the house and Morgiana tells her master of the plot the next morning.

Alone now, the chief robber swears revenge and next enters Ali Baba's house disguised as a cloth merchant who has befriended his son. Morgiana however sees through the disguise and kills him, and in gratitude Ali Baba frees her and marries her to his son.

The tale contains many common motifs; that of thieves hidden in jars or sacks is found in Eastern European, African and Native American tales, and the hidden treasure chamber is a common Asian device. Although the tale is normally considered as an Asian fairy tale, apart from the 'Open Sesame' device there is very little supernatural or marvellous content in the plot. With its emphasis on believable characters and motivation, in fact, it has almost as much in common with a modern crime story as with an ancient fairy tale.
▷ **Open Sesame**

All Hallows' or All Saints' Day

FEAST-DAY OF THE CHRISTIAN CALENDAR, commemorating all the saints. Also known as All-hallowmas, it was originally celebrated on 13 May after its introduction by St Boniface in the seventh century, but in the next century Pope Gregory III changed its date to 1 November.

The inception of the festival was an attempt to convert the ancient Roman pantheon, the temple of all gods, into its Christian equivalent, and there is much speculation that the shift in dates from May to November was intended to coincide with an ancient Germanic festival in honour of all the gods. Certainly in modern times folk tradition emphasizes the pagan aspects of the festival, with most of the celebrations taking place on **Hallowe'en**, the eve of the feast.
▷ **All Souls' Day**

All Souls' Day

CHRISTIAN HOLY DAY, instituted by St Odilo of Cluny in the 10th century as a festival for prayer releasing souls from Purgatory. According to legend, Odilo was persuaded by a pilgrim returning from the Holy Land that on a particular island the plaintive moans of souls in Purgatory could be heard, begging for prayers to release them. Folk traditions observed during this period include the decorating of gravestones and the leaving out of food for hungry returning spirits. The feast is celebrated on 2 November, and is closely associated with the potent magic of **Hallowe'en**.

The feast in honour of the dead is well established in religion and folklore throughout human history, found in ancient Babylon, Greece and Rome. In China and Japan the Feast of **Lanterns** fulfilled a similar purpose, and Buddhists celebrate the date of Buddha's attainment of Buddhahood (15 April) as a feast for all the dead. Most feasts for the dead in the northern hemisphere occur towards the end of the year, associated with winter and the need to safeguard life.

Allan-a-Dale

MINSTREL OF BRITISH LEGEND, a friend of **Robin Hood** who also makes an appearance in Sir Walter Scott's *Ivanhoe*. His most notable adventure was the rescue of his sweetheart, who was being constrained to marry a foul, aged but wealthy knight. Robin Hood aided him in this enterprise.

Allen, Ethan (1738–89)

AMERICAN SOLDIER, a folk hero who fought against the British for the freedom of the Green Mountain area, now Vermont. His troops were called the Green Mountain Boys, and their exploits passed into the folk history of Vermont.

alligator

LARGE REPTILE of the *Crocodilia* family, found in the south-eastern United States and formerly in the Yangtze River, China. It differs from its **crocodile** cousins in its blunt snout and its lower teeth, all of which fit snugly into sockets within the snout rather than protruding outside. It inspires a general reverence and is frequently worshipped and propitiated. It plays a large part in Native American and African American trickster tales, usually as the gull of **Rabbit**'s audacious tricks. In one typical tale-type, Rabbit contrives to cross the river dry-shod by persuading Alligator to line up his family to allow Rabbit to count

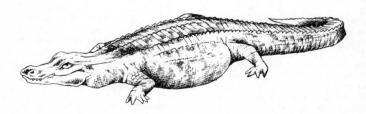

alligator

them, which he accomplishes by walking from one back to the next over to dry land. The last alligator, however, realizing what had happened, nipped off Rabbit's tail. **Brer Rabbit** is said to have trapped an alligator in a dry field and set it alight, which explains the reptile's scaly skin.

Alligator teeth are prized charms, especially potent against **witches** and poison. A necklace of them around a child's neck will alleviate the pain of teething while protecting against predatory witches.

In recent years a popular urban myth has grown up asserting that a race of giant alligators lives under the streets of New York in the sewer system. They are said to have originated with an unwanted baby alligator (a fashionable pet in some circles) flushed down a toilet. This is an interesting reworking of the monster race and underworld themes.

Allison Gross

'THE UGLIEST WITCH I' THE NORTH COUNTRY', who hankers after the love of a comely young man in a popular Scottish ballad (Child no 35). Despite the earnestness of her amorous advances, and the many rich gifts she promises him, the hero rejects her in no uncertain terms ('Awa, awa, ye ugly witch, Haud far awa, an lat me be'). Enraged, Allison Gross transforms him into an ugly worm and he is compelled to 'toddle about the tree' until freed from his enchantment by the queen of the fairies passing in the fairy ride.

The ballad contains many familiar strands of Scottish and European lore, but is unusual in depicting a fairy undoing the spell of a witch. The worm shape assumed by the unfortunate hero was that of the Celtic **dragon**-type, a wingless, usually poisonous rather than fiery beast.

almanac

BOOK OF THE YEAR, a repository of miscellaneous information and folklore. The word derives from medieval Arabic, originally meaning the place at which the camels kneel. This developed to signify a resting-place or campsite, and finally the weather at that site. The earliest almanacs contained weather forecasts based on astrological survey, since in seasonal Arabic countries the positions of **stars** was a reasonably consistent guide to **weather**. It was natural for predictions to be incorporated into such a format, following the pervasive influence credited to the heavenly bodies at the time, and such prophecies were a feature of almanacs for centuries.

The almanac's history then is closely related to that of **astrology**, but as the form developed it encompassed wider issues such as farming, cookery, medicine, humorous tales and tables of information as well as the traditional calenderical data (tides, moons, holidays and so on). In the 17th and 18th centuries the almanac became the prototype magazine, and these now provide a valuable source for social historians and folklorists alike. The jest-book characteristics of the early American almanacs in particular, for example Ben Franklin's *Poor Richard's Almanac*, evolved into fully comic almanacs, such as those featuring Davy **Crockett** in the 19th century, which ridiculed the improbable prognostications of their more earnest ancestors. Modern almanacs, which are usually reference works of miscellaneous information, still often retain the characteristic 'Man of the Signs': a human figure surrounded by the signs of the **zodiac** linked to their respective parts of the body by connecting spokes as of a wheel.

almond

SMALL TREE AND ITS FRUIT, native to south-west Asia but found in warm temperate climatic zones throughout the world. The edible nut is produced by the sweet almond, *Prunus dulcis* (family Rosaceae). It is loaded with significance in folklore; in Hebrew lore it was a symbol of watchfulness and promise, because of its early blossoming, and this has an interesting symbolic development in Christian iconography, where the Virgin's womb is often represented by branches of almonds enclosing the Christ-child, the fulfilment of God's promise. In many Christian countries the almond is closely associated with **Mary**.

Aaron was chosen from among the other tribes of Israel by the sign of the rod that put forth almond blossom, and this is paralleled in the tale of **Tannhäuser**, when Pope Urban declares that his wooden staff would live again and bloom before Tannhäuser could receive forgiveness. Three days later the staff is found to be bearing almond blossom and fruit, and messengers are sent after Tannhäuser, to no avail (see **act of truth**).

One interesting claim advanced for almonds is their efficacy against drunkenness; Pliny avows in his *Natural History* that five almonds consumed before alcohol will preserve one's sobriety. Foxes, however, should never eat the almonds as they will perforce die unless they can quickly find water. In Chinese lore, the almond is a symbol of endurance through sorrow, associated particularly with suffering female beauty.

Alnaschar

CHARACTER OF THE *ARABIAN NIGHTS*, whose tale is a lesson in not counting one's chickens before they hatch. He is the fifth brother of the Barber who spends his last penny on a basket of fine glassware, which he intends to sell at a profit to buy more, and so on until he has made his fortune. In his dreams of the splendid life he will lead as a wealthy man he envisages marrying the daughter of the Vizier, whom he will lord it over. He gives his imaginary wife a kick to illustrate the point, connects instead with the precious basket, and smashes the basis of his airy fortune.

A similar European tale tells how a young girl walking to market with butter or eggs balanced on her head to sell there begins to dream of how she will invest the money, and the grand life she will lead as a lady. She tosses her head to indicate her disdain for the young men who will pursue her, and the butter falls and is spoilt.

alomancy

DIVINATION BY MEANS OF SALT. In this ancient technique, a handful of salt is thrown onto a fire and the resulting flames are scrutinized for messages.

alphabet rhymes

MNEMONIC VERSE, designed to teach children the letters and their order in the alphabet. The concept is an ancient one—there are similar acrostics in Hebrew Scripture (Psalm 119)—and the earliest extant English rhyme, dating from c.1375, is Chaucer's *ABC*, a homage to the Blessed Virgin. Chaucer based this on a French poem at least 50 years older. English rhymes of 300 years' standing are still used as models today, most memorably *The Tragical Death of A, Apple Pye Who was Cut in Pieces and Eat by Twenty-Five Gentlemen with whom All Little People Ought to be Very well acquainted*, the text of which is scarcely longer than the title:

A was an Apple pye
B bit it
C cut it
D dealt it
E eat it etc.

The verse's vintage is betrayed by the use of 'eat' (*et*) for modern English past tense 'ate'.

Early rhymes such as these are appealingly unselfconscious in their subject matter; *Thumb's Alphabet*, traced in print to the early 18th century, celebrates I the Innkeeper who loved to bouse [booze]. More serious-minded guardians replaced these with more moralistic rhymes, such as that in Benjamin Harris's late 17th-century *New England Primer* which piously begins:

In Adam's fall
We sinned all

and ends with the tale of Zaccheus.

The popular **tongue twister** 'Peter Piper picked a peck of pickl'd peppers' is in fact a stanza of an alphabet rhyme current in England and America in the 18th century, which included such characters as Andrew Airpump who asked his Aunt her Ailment and Needy Noodle, who Nipp'd a Naybour's Nutmeg. In the last two centuries, the alphabet rhyme has proved fertile ground for such writers as W M Thackeray, Edward Lear and Hilaire Belloc, as well as a plethora of lesser-known children's writers, but the enduring popularity of the earliest forms testifies to the effectiveness of oral transmission in the nursery.

▷ **children's lore**; **nursery rhymes**

alphorn

alphorn

LONG WOODEN HORN, traditionally sounded by Alpine herdsmen to summon their beasts and also for communication over distances and in ceremonies and rituals. The horn can be anything up to 4m/12ft long; since the last century such long straight horns have developed an upturned bell end. Eastern alphorns are often trumpet-shaped, and there are occasional S-shaped designs. There are no stops, and pitch is determined by lips and variation in breath. The strong, resonant tone of the alphorn was believed to prolong daylight as it ebbed away with the sunset, and also to protect humans at this dangerous time of transition between day and night. It was natural then that Christian practice should involve the alphorn as a signal for evening prayers. The instrument is ancient, mentioned by the Roman historian Tacitus, and such sunset rituals are common in folklore modern and ancient throughout the world.

Amadán

FAIRY FOOL OF IRISH FOLKLORE, greatly feared by humans for his crippling touch. He is sometimes called the **stroke** lad; if he touches anyone's face or side that person will be paralysed down that side or crippled for ever after. He strikes seemingly where the whim takes him, but those who have committed crimes or who foolishly linger by fairy haunts in the moonlight are especially vulnerable. June is his favourite month for mischief-making. The only way to avoid harm if you see him is to call out for protection from God.

Amadán Mór is the best known of this type, the Great Fool of the **sidhe** in tales and verse. Another such figure is Amadán na Bruidne, fool of the fairy mounds.

Amadis

GALLIC HERO, whose tale is told in the prose romance *Amadis of Gaul*. The tale is thought to be Portuguese in origin, dating from the early 14th century, and many of the characters are based on figures of Celtic lore; as it developed it incorporated elements from Arthurian legend and other popular romance. The first extant version is that of Garci Ordóñez de Montalvo (1508).

Amadis, Child of the Sun, was the illegitimate son of Preion, King of Wales, and Elizena, Princess of Brittany. Abandoned at birth, he grew up to become the archetypal chivalric ruler, accomplished, chaste, gallant and fearless. His many adventures culminated in the prize of the fair Oriana, daughter of the King of England. The high-flown, idealized tone of the book became a byword for style among fashion-conscious members of polite society, especially in France, in the 16th century. It spawned numerous imitations, until Cervantes's brilliant parody *Don Quixote* deflated the fashion successfully in the early 17th century.

Amadis rejoiced in an astonishing number of sobriquets, including Lion-

Knight, Beltenebros (beautiful in darkness), Lovely Obscure, Knight of the Green Sword and Knight of the Dwarf.

Amaethon

BRYTHONIC HERO, brother of **Gwydion**. The Celtic tale *Kulhwch and Olwen* tells how he succeeded in tilling an untillable field, and in a later tale he is the one who precipitates the **Battle of the Trees** by bringing back from the underworld a **dog**, **lapwing** and roebuck, the property of **Arawn**.

It seems clear that Amaethon, whose name derives from the Cymric meaning 'the plowman', was originally a god of agriculture or a **culture hero** (this latter is suggested particularly by his role in bringing back objects from the underworld).

Amala

TSIMSHIAN CULTURE HERO. Youngest of his brothers, Amala was mocked and despised as a child, given the nickname Very Dirty and excluded from the family games. But he secretly developed superhuman strength, and eventually proved himself by rescuing various relatives and defeating the forces of the animals, birds, trees and mountains. His fame spread to the old chief who lay and supported the world, and felt himself to be near death: he called Amala to him and transferred the end of the pole from his own chest to Amala's, where it now turns smoothly in a spoonful of duck-grease.

Amazons

FABULOUS RACE OF WARRIOR WOMEN, said by the Greeks to inhabit the regions around Scythia (modern Turkey). The etymology of the word is doubtful; a common explanation is that it means without (Greek prefix *a-*) breasts (Greek *mazos*), and that each girl had her right breast cut or burned off to enable her to wield a bow more effectively, but no early representations in art support this.

Under the leadership of their elected queen (Hippolyta among others), the Amazons raided much of Asia Minor and the surrounding islands, using their skill in archery and riding to devastating effect. In peace they hunted, cultivated

Amazons

the land and built a gracious capital, Themiscyra.

Bowing to biological necessity, a group of Amazonian virgins would journey each year to the nearby Gargareans and mate with men there, returning to bear their children. Any male babies were returned to their fathers or slaughtered.

Other cultures have similar tales of female warriors, for example the Makurap of Brazil, who tell of a neighbouring village, Arapinjatschäküp, inhabited exclusively by hostile women.

amber

FOSSILIZED TREE RESIN, generally yellow with varying shades of orange and brown. It is especially notable for the wide variety of fossilized insect life preserved intact within it. A poetic Greek legend, recorded by Ovid in his *Metamorphoses*, attributes amber's origins to the tears of **Meleager**'s sisters, who wept ceaselessly after his death.

Amfortas see Fisher King

Amis and Amiles

HEROES OF OLD FRENCH ROMANCE, also known as Amys and Amylion, archetypes of the **Two Brothers** motif. They are perfect friends and fellow-knights, but when Amiles takes Amis's place at a combat trial he is punished with leprosy. Amis is told in a dream that the blood of his two children will heal his friend; on wakening he kills them both without demur. Amiles is healed, and the children are restored to life.

The story is probably Oriental in origin, closely related to European fairy tales such as **Faithful John**, and reflects a worldwide preoccupation with the themes of death-defying friendship and the potency of blood. In the 12th century it was incorporated into the **Charlemagne** tale cycles, as a *chanson de geste*, *Amis et Amiles*, which was much admired and imitated throughout Europe. A Middle English version, *Amis and Amiloun*, appeared in the late 13th century.

Amleth

DANISH HERO, the mad prince. According to Saxo Grammaticus, Amleth's father Horvendil, king of Jutland, was murdered by his brother Feng who then claimed the throne and married his erstwhile sister-in-law, Amleth's mother, Gerutha. To avoid his uncle's murderous intentions, Amleth feigned madness. Feng's counsellor tried to test his veracity (and therefore whether he was harmless or not) by eavesdropping on Amleth's private conversation with Gerutha; playing mad still, Amleth ran through his hiding place with a sword.

Feng then sent his nephew to Britain with a message charging the king there to kill the bearer; Amleth altered this astutely, with the result that Feng's two courtiers were executed and Amleth himself received the king's daughter in marriage. He returned to Denmark and killed Feng with the usurper's own sword and became king amidst great rejoicing. He later returned to Britain, where his father-in-law tried to avenge his old friend by giving Amleth a sealed note for the queen of Scotland, commanding his death. Hermutrude however changed the note herself and declared that it directed her to marry the bearer. Amleth defeated the king by propping dead men upright on the battlefield to look like a vast army and returned to Denmark with both wives, where he was later killed in battle.

A strong element of this story is the northern European concept of justice, with the characteristically Danish detail of the villain being killed by his own sword.

amulets

FORM OF CHARM, usually an object carried on the person or placed in the house to protect oneself and one's possessions from all manner of danger. This type of **charm** is known among virtually all peoples, world-wide. An amulet is generally passive and protective, having no inherent power. In modern societies examples such as the rabbit's foot and **horseshoe** abound, and many Westerners have individual superstitions regarding objects which they believe bring them luck.

A common type of amulet is that made from part of an animal, usually to transfer a quality of that animal to the bearer. Inuits in Greenland for example may sew the head or foot of a **hawk** into the clothing of a child to ensure that he will be a great hunter. In India most amulets are made from plants, especially from holy trees, and many kinds of vegetables and fruit are used world-wide to protect the bearer (for example, **garlic** is supposed to defend against **vampires** or, in Japan, against infectious diseases).

As well as these natural amulets, however, even the most ancient societies were accustomed to manufacturing charms. Tiny figurines representing gods, sacred animals or artefacts such as canoes or bows and arrows are used around the world depending on the needs and preoccupations of the people. These amulets are often very ornamental, and it has been suggested that all decorative jewellery originated with the

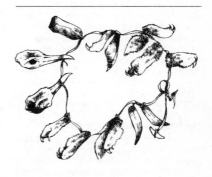

Netsilik Inuit amulet belt

fashioning of amulets, although this significance is now retained only in such items as the charm bracelet or St **Christopher** medallion. Certainly, much jewellery is still worn amuletically today; Chinese parents use jade to protect their children, and metal rings in India are believed to defend the wearer against evil magic.

Amulets often contain writings of a religious or magical nature, most famously the Mezuzah of the Jews, which contains sentences from the Scriptures. In Tibet, a sentence written to the Buddha is commonly used as an amulet, and geometric figures or magic squares, in which a sequence of numbers is arranged to give the same result if added along the rows in any direction, have been popular since ancient times.

▷ **scarab**; **tattoo**

Amys and Amylion see Amis and Amiles

anchanchu

DEMON OF THE NATIVE NORTH AMERICAN AYMARA. He is thought to inhabit desolate places, especially by rivers, and generally travels in a **whirlwind**. His appearance is initially reassuring, but he deceives his victims with smiles before smiting them with terrible diseases and afflictions, sucking their blood during sleep and draining their strength.

▷ **vampires**

anchunga

SPIRIT OF THE TAPIRAPE GROUP, central Brazil. Anchunga may be either benevolent spirits of the dead or demons intent on working harm to humans. Ware, a great shaman and **culture hero**, rid the southern Tapirape of evil anchunga by setting alight their long hair, but the demons of the north survive. Anchunga are thought to appear to shamans in dreams.

Androcles and the Lion

EXAMPLE OF THE HELPFUL BEAST TALE-TYPE. A runaway slave hiding in a cave is approached by a **lion** who, instead of attacking him, holds up a paw in which a thorn is painfully embedded. Androcles pulls out the thorn, but he is then

Androcles and the Lion

recaptured and sentenced to death by fighting with a lion in the public arena. His opponent is of course the lion he has helped, and on recognizing him refuses to fight. At such a miraculous sign the order is given that the slave should be freed. This is a common tale-type; the legend later attached itself to St **Jerome**, who is often portrayed in company with the lion who followed him everywhere in gratitude for such a service. Many such tales of kindness and affinity with animals grew up around the **saints** in medieval lore, as instances of their goodness and harmony with nature, and the associations of the lion with nobility and fierceness made it an especially suitable subject.

Andromeda motif

MOTIF OF THE DRAGON-SLAYING TALE-TYPE, named after the classical tale of **Perseus** who saves Andromeda and wins her hand. Here and elsewhere the maiden is about to be sacrificed to the monster and is rescued by the hero who slays the beast and claims her as his prize. Its ubiquity may reflect a widespread ancient practice of offering sacrifices to the water-gods. The original Andromeda was the daughter of Cassiopeia, who angered the Nereids (Greek sea-nymphs) by boasting of her daughter's beauty. The Nereids induced Neptune to send a sea-monster against Ethiopia to which Andromeda must be sacrificed.

Andvaranaut

MAGIC RING OF NORDIC MYTHOLOGY, with the power of attracting gold ore, stolen from Andvari by the trickster god Loki. Andvari cursed both it and his stolen treasure, bringing ill fortune to all those who subsequently came into contact with it. Loki gave the ring and treasure to Hreidmar, king of the **dwarfs**, in recompense for the murder of his son Otter (unwittingly slain by Loki), but **Fafnir** later took both when he killed his father.

Wagner's great operatic cycle, *Der Ring des Nibelungen*, charts the progress of the ring and the misfortune befalling those who possess it.

Angang

OMEN OF MEETING, a German word applied to a form of **divination** common throughout Europe with parallels throughout the world. In its most usual form, Angang refers to the first person or creature encountered on the road when setting out on or returning from a journey. Some general principles seem to hold fast—it is considered unlucky in almost any undertaking to meet an old woman, symbol of barrenness, or a **raven**—but the nature of the journey is also a factor, so for example a hunting-party would be loath to meet even the most prepossessing woman, hunting being considered a specifically male activity.

A similar concept appears in folktales such as **Beauty and the Beast**, in which the first being to meet the traveller becomes forfeit to the monster.
▷ **Jephthah's vow**

Angus Og

OLD IRISH HERO of the **Ulster cycle**. He meets in his dreams a beautiful woman, with whom he falls madly in love but whose name he cannot discover. After a year she stops appearing to him in his dreams, and he searches the world frenziedly for a year without success.

Angus Og

Finally **Bodb**, king of the **sidhe** in Tipperary, discovers her identity and reports to Angus that his lover is Caer, daughter of Ethal Anoual and one of the sidhe. Her father is summoned, and he admits that Caer is under an enchantment which forces her to spend alternate years as swan and woman. Angus promptly sets out to find her as a swan, is himself transformed, and the two fly off together, joined in otherworldly harmony.
▷ **swan maiden**

anhanga

DEMON OF BRAZIL and the Amazon basin, a forest spirit much given to tormenting travellers and hunters and occasionally to stealing children. He has no clear form, and often appears in dreams as a troublesome, shadowy presence.

animal fable

WELL-ATTESTED PRIMITIVE TYPE OF FOLKTALE, probably deriving from early civilizations in South Asia. The main characters are animals, who act in more or less human fashion, speaking, holding councils, plotting against each other and even carrying out tasks such as planting, cooking and spinning. In Western cultures, the animal fable is nearly always didactic, using the animals to illustrate human truths and the values of the group. In other cultures animal fables also function as explanatory tales (how

animal nurse—Romulus and Remus suckled by a she-wolf

Spider became flattened) and in connection with totemic beliefs as sacred tales.
▷ **animal tale**

animal nurse

WORLD-WIDE TALE-TYPE, an animal, usually female, who raises a human baby. The human is thereby endowed with the characteristics of that animal, usually superhuman strength, and may retain a special relationship of mutual support with the species after his reintegration into human society. A striking example of this tale-type in recent lore is the popularity of **Tarzan**, Lord of the Apes, created by Edgar Rice Burroughs. Perhaps because the practice of abandoning **twins** was widespread, tales of animals nursing twins who then grow up to be heroes are common. Examples include **Romulus and Remus**, the famous founders of Rome who were suckled by a she-wolf, and the Twins of South American lore who were brought up by the **jaguars** that killed their pregnant mother.

animals

A CENTRAL PREOCCUPATION of our consciousness from prehistory has been the relationship of humans with the animals that share their world. As both predators and prey, animals have been central to human existence and speculation about their origins and behaviour is one of the most fundamental themes of folklore throughout the world. Of particular interest is the degree to which animals and humans may be said to interact, whether they may interbreed, share souls, or feel similar emotions.

In many societies the line between human and animal, in folklore at least, appears to be an indefinite one. The **culture heroes** of the Native Americans may be animals who speak and act like humans, or they may appear to be humans but act like particular animals in the tales. Many primitive cultures trace their origin back to an animal species, with whose properties they identify, and the species is revered and protected by taboos on eating the flesh. Sometimes the animal may be eaten, but in a very ritualistic manner. Hunting too may often be governed by ritual, recognising the greatness of the prey (especially formidable prey such as **buffalo** or **bear**) and begging pardon from its soul while requiring the meat to live (see **hunting magic**).

This sense of identity with animals, and mutual dependency, is illustrated also by the belief in **sympathetic magic** prevalent among Native North Americans especially. Members of the Hopi tribe will sleep wearing an animal **amulet**, believing that the animal's spirit will warn them of any approaching danger.

Certain animals, particularly the **lion** or **crocodile**, are believed to contain the souls of ancestors, and offerings may be made to them by the living.

Animals are usually credited with a fund of superhuman knowledge. In primitive mythologies they are generally supposed to have existed before man and to have acquired from the gods wisdom of healing and the ability to cause disease, hence they are frequently used to cure illness.

Another common function of the animal in folklore is the transferral of specific properties. Sometimes this correspondence is direct (pregnant Zulu women will traditionally abstain from pigmeat in case they produce ugly children), in other cases it is a conceptual link, such as the ease with which a snail emerges from its shell as a benefit to women in **childbirth**. The most common means of transferring animal properties is that of eating the animal. Other links between humans and animals are less literal, but arise through identification of apparently human traits in animal behaviour.

The idea of communicating with animals emerges in many different forms; primitive myths tend to assume that animals speak exactly as humans do, and in many fairy tales animals and humans are able to converse when the animal is magically given the power of human speech. Occasionally human beings are blessed with the ability to understand animals, for example the Peruvian hero, **Huathicuri**, who won his bride by listening to a **fox** and was helped in his further adventures by other animals. The literary figure of Doctor Doolittle is a more modern example.

Closely linked with the idea of a speaking animal is that of the **helpful beast**, found especially in European folklore (eg **Puss in Boots**).

Another common type of animal tale is explanatory, giving the origins of a species or, more frequently, telling how an animal came by a certain characteristic. Mice, for example, are said to have been created by the **Devil** in the ark (or alternatively to have been the Devil in disguise), to gnaw through the wood; to have dropped from the sky during a storm; or alternatively, in Germany, to be made from scraps of cloth by **witches**. Many Native American trickster tales, in which the hero gulls another animal, claim to explain the characteristics of animals (these are known as aetiological tales).

▷ **animal tale**

animal tale

FORM OF FOLK NARRATIVE, probably the oldest found throughout the world and just as popular today as ever. Of all the tales having animals as main characters, the aetiological type, explaining the characteristic appearance and behaviour of animals, is probably the most basic. Into this category fall a vast variety of **trickster** tales, such as the **alligator** developing its scaly skin from being caught in a burning field or the **bear** losing his tail in the ice.

A second type of animal tale is the moralistic **animal fable**, best known in the West through the collection of Aesop. Although almost wholly a literary tradition today, this was originally an oral form told as entertainment as well as to educate children or make an oblique political point.

The most sophisticated form of animal tale is the **beast epic**, particularly common in medieval Europe, as demonstrated in the enormously popular **Reynard the Fox** tales. These are cycles of tales more or less loosely grouped around a central figure, and the hero will vary from place to place depending on the dominant trickster figure in the area.

A common characteristic of all such animal tales is a disregard for realism; the listeners are expected to accept the premise of animals speaking and behaving as humans without question, and no attempt is made to site the tale in historical time (although local places may well be used). Related tales in which animals interact with humans (eg the **helpful beast** type) do not properly belong to this class.

ankh

ANCIENT EGYPTIAN SYMBOL, a tau **cross** with a looped top arm, also known as *crux anstata*. As a hieroglyph it represents the life principle, used in combinations representing health and happiness, and it is frequently held in the hand of a deity or king. Gods may hold an ankh to the nostrils of the dead to bring them back to life. Various attempts have been made to explain the symbol's origin; it seems to resemble the sandals of the time, frequently painted on tombs, or it may represent a magical

knot or a phallus. It was adopted and widely used by the Coptic Christian church.

Anne, St

THE MOTHER OF MARY. Although no historical details are known about the grandmother of Christ, including her name, her popular cult is based on the apocryphal *Protoevangelicum* of James. According to this unreliable second-century document, Anne was the childless wife of Joachim, but she was visited by an angel as she prayed and was promised that she would have a child. Anne vowed to dedicate the child to God, and so the Virgin **Mary** was born. There is a strong resemblance to the Old Testament story of Hannah and the birth of Samuel (1 Samuel 1), and the identity in Hebrew of 'Anne' and 'Hannah' (both meaning 'grace') suggests that this may be the source of the legend and not merely an illuminating parallel. Other versions of the legend name Anne's father, a nomad called Akar, and claim that she was born in Nazareth, married Joachim at the age of 20 and gave birth to **Mary** aged 40. Joachim is supposed to have died soon after the birth of his grandson, Jesus Christ.

As veneration of Mary became increasingly popular in the 12th century, so too did interest in her parents, with various churches throughout Europe laying claim to Anne's relics. She was especially popular as a patron of religious guilds in medieval England. The observance of her feast was made obligatory throughout England in response to a petition of 1382 by Pope Urbanus VI, and many have speculated that this was arranged to coincide fortuitously with the marriage of Richard II to Anne of Bohemia in the same year. A major reason for the startling popularity of her cult is that the relationship between Joachim and Anne served as a model for Christian marriage in a more accessible way than did that of Mary and Joseph.

Anne is frequently pictured holding Mary and Jesus (on her lap or in her arms), at her betrothal to Joachim, or teaching the young Mary to read Scripture. A famous picture by Dürer shows Anne and Joachim embracing at the Golden Gate after both had been divinely informed of the coming birth, and this is generally recognized as an iconographic representation of the conception of Mary. Her feast-day is 26 July and she is the patron saint of miners.

Annie Christmas

BLACK HEROINE OF NORTH AMERICAN FOLKLORE, over six and a half feet tall, the proprietor of a floating brothel. She was a formidable lady, able to drink any challenger under the table, habitually dressed in scarlet satin and feathers. She had 12 sons all taller than herself, and finally killed herself through unrequited love.

Annwn

CELTIC OTHERWORLD, the realm of **Arawn**. Brythonic mythology seems uncertain of its exact location; most commonly, as in the *Book of Taliesin*, it is located beneath the earth, but it is also portrayed as a floating castle or fortified island, or simply as a neighbouring country, as in the *Mabinogion* where **Pwyll** and Arawn exchange realms. It is generally agreed to be a delightful Elysium where death and sickness are unknown and endless days are spent hunting and feasting.

One of its features is the inexhaustible **cauldron**, a **magic object** which, on earth, would have various marvellous properties, such as curing the sick or injured and conferring long life. However, the many attempts of mortals to steal this cauldron have been foiled by the ever-watchful Arawn.

ant

INSECT OF FOLKLORE, symbol of industry. The concept of the industrious ant is widespread; **sympathetic magic** leads Moroccan shamans to feed them to lethargic patients, and to dream of ants is generally a sign of coming prosperity. The Hopi Indians of North America believe that the first people were ants.

Like **bee** stings, ant bites are widely considered to have healing properties, and they are also widely used as a test of endurance in **initiation** ceremonies, for example among the native tribes of California. Like bees too, ants are sometimes portrayed as messengers of

ant

the gods (for example in West Africa). Perhaps because of their fearsome sting, ants are popularly believed to be dangerous and vindictive; to offend them by urinating on an ant-hill is in some cultures to court disaster.

antelope

GRACEFUL, PLAIN-DWELLING MAMMAL, found mainly in Africa with some species in Eurasia (the North American pronghorn is not strictly an antelope). The antelope's horn is prized for its medicinal powers and as a magical tool for confining spirits (Congo).

Because of their fleetness, they are depicted in the *Rig Veda* as the bearers of the Maruts, Vedic storm gods, and the Indian wind god Vaya is also pictured riding astride an antelope. Its two horns led medieval Christians to utilize it as an allegory for mankind, armed with the twin spiritual weapons of the Old and New Testaments.

Antero Vipunen

FINNISH GIANT, a primeval being who lay asleep beneath the earth until awoken by **Väinämöinen**. Väinämöinen had been trying to build a magic boat but lacked the knowledge of the necessary spells and chants, which were known only to Vipunen. When Vipunen opened his mouth, however, it was not to speak but to swallow the troublesome intruder who had disturbed his rest. Undaunted, Väinämöinen set about causing such agonizing pains inside the giant by burning, piercing and hacking at him that Vipunen was obliged to relent. His song of ancient wisdom is written in the *Kalevala*, song 17.

Antero Vipunen's name illustrates the veneer of Christianity laid over the most ancient of the Finns; it is thought to derive from 'the cross of St Andreus'.

anthropological theory

THEORY OF FOLKLORE SCHOLARSHIP, based on the premise that folktales should be seen as relics of ancient cultures. The movement's bottom-up approach began as a reaction to the prevailing 19th-century view of the folktale as collapsed myth, and its exponents, including Sir James George Frazer (1854–1941) and Andrew Lang (1844–1912), aimed to trace motifs and details of tales back to long-lost practices, customs and beliefs. **Polygenesis**, the multiple origins of one type of tale, is one of the central tenets of this school; the similarity of tales across the world is primarily explained by similar development among different peoples rather than by cross-influence through trading, migration and so on.

Anthropologists tend to bring the tools of social science rather than aesthetics to their material. The group rather than the lore itself is the end of the study, their cultural norms, value systems and ancient practices, but this method of study tends to lose sight of the life of the tale itself and its wider development, and to underestimate the inventive imaginations of generations of tellers and the cross-fertilization that inevitably takes place across cultural frontiers.

Apakura

PACIFIC ISLAND HEROINE, found particularly in New Zealand, Samoa and the Marquesas where she is known as Apekua. She is essentially a mother seeking revenge for her lost child, although the details of her adventures vary from place to place and from teller to teller. Her son seeks the daughter of Hatea-motua as his bride, and is killed by the chief, who refuses to acknowledge his identity and the legitimacy of his request. Apakura enlists the help of her brothers to secure her revenge; with them she overcomes such obstacles as the tree that will not be felled and a vine that would drag down their canoes, and finally slays Hatea-motua.

Apakura is unusual although not unique in world folklore as a pro-active heroine; this is probably due in part to the structure of Pacific society as a whole, which is less patriarchal than most.

apalala

BUDDHIST WATER-MONSTER, a **dragon** or serpent dwelling at the source of the Swat River, whose conversion by Buddha is a popular subject for artists. There are parallels with St **Patrick**'s and St Columba's dealings with Celtic dragons.

ape

MANLIKE PRIMATE, any species of the families Hylobatidae and Pongidae. Because of their resemblance to humans and the apparent intelligence of their behaviour, apes share with **monkeys** a common fund of superstition, including the belief among some groups that they are perfectly well able to speak but refrain from doing so lest they be compelled to work. A Jewish folktale claims that one of the races involved in building the impious Tower of Babel was transformed into apes by God as punishment, while an Islamic tale relates that Allah transformed many Jews of Elath into apes for daring to fish on the Sabbath. In Hindu lore the ape tends to be portrayed as a human-like **helpful beast**, for example **Hanuman** in the *Ramayana*. Christians held that the ape was a symbol of lust, the bestial and base aspects of human nature. One tale has them as the creation of the **Devil** in answer to God's creation of mankind.

apple

TREE AND ITS FRUIT, one of about 25 species in the genus *Malus* (family Rosaceae), which features widely in mythology, legend, folktales and folk belief. One of its chief functions is as a symbol of immortality; **Heracles** sought the golden apples of the Hesperides which conferred eternal life, and in Norse myth Idhunn tends the apples of perpetual youth in **Asgard**. It is also a symbol of sexual desire and fertility in many areas; Paris presented the prize of the golden apple to Aphrodite, goddess of sexual love, in Greek mythology, and although the forbidden fruit of Genesis is not named it has been widely interpreted in the Christian world as an apple, hence the fruit represents temptation and seduction. In Teutonic lore eating an apple often results in pregnancy. An apple tossed to an object of one's admiration in ancient Greece seems to have been interpreted as an invitation to bed. Such beliefs are relevant too in tales where apples are used as distractions—as when Hippomenes wins Atalanta by defeating her in a race with the aid of three golden apples tossed at her feet. In Celtic lore a fairy woman gives an apple to Conle which he fed from for a year without lessening its size, but which implanted in him a deep and irresistible longing for the pleasures of **fairyland**.

Unsurprisingly, the apple is extensively used in **love magic** and love divination in many areas, including Haiti, Scandinavia, Britain, Germany and North America. In one typical example of such beliefs, apple peel taken off in one continuous ribbon and thrown over the shoulder will land in the shape of the initial of one's future husband. The tradition of ducking for apples at **Hallowe'en** is a remnant of ancient Druidic divination rites. An apple can serve as a **chastity test** in Danish lore, withering if the giver is unfaithful.

In common folk belief apples are regarded as health-giving fruits (a belief supported by modern dieticians)—'an apple a day keeps the doctor away'. They can be rubbed on the skin to remove birthmarks, and the apple is of course recommended for women wishing to conceive a child.

Apple-Tree Man

SOMERSET SPIRIT, the embodiment of fertility in the apple orchard. The Apple-Tree Man is the oldest tree in the orchard, and should be treated with respect to ensure a healthy and healthful supply of apples. **Wassailling** is recommended for this purpose, recalling ancient fertility practices of libations to vegetative spirits.

apricot

SWEET STONE FRUIT, similar to a peach, of a tree native to China but flourishing in many temperate regions of the world, *Prunus armeniaca* of the famliy Rosaceae. It was reputed in European lore to be a strong sexual stimulant, as shown in Shakespeare's *A Midsummer Night's Dream*, when **Titania** orders her attendant to give apricots to her beloved Bottom, and in Webster's *The Duchess of Malfi*, when the Duchess's illicit pregnancy is discovered by her enormous appetite for the fruit.

Probably because of this link with fertility, it is considered very good luck in England to dream of apricots. In China, however, the fruit represents cowardice and death.

April fool

A PERSON TRICKED OR MADE A FOOL OF on 1 April (All Fools' Day or April Fools' Day). It is thought that this may originally have been the final day of the festivities celebrating the spring equinox, which began on Old New Year's Day (25 Mar until 1564). The tradition, found throughout Europe, may have originated in France; outside Europe, there is an example of similar fooling during the Huli Festival in India (ending 31 Mar). In Scotland hunting the gowk (Gaelic *La'na cubhag*), gowk meaning

Apple-Tree Man

fool or cuckoo, is the rural tradition of gulling a simpleton by sending him on a fool's errand which may be extended until someone takes pity on the poor gull and undeceives him. The French April Fool, *poisson d'Avril*, may have influenced Scottish traditions after the return of **Mary**, Queen of Scots from her French exile in 1561. It is commonly thought here and elsewhere that all tricks should be played before noon, and after that time any trick will rebound upon its perpetrator.
▷ **Gwydion**

Arabian Nights, The, fully *The Arabian Nights' Entertainment*

ASIAN FOLKTALE CYCLE, also known as *The Thousand and One Nights*. This famous cycle of tales was originally written in Arabic sometime before the eighth century. It uses the form common in Medieval Europe, used by Chaucer and Boccaccio, of one tale forming a framework to explain the telling of a series of largely unrelated narratives. In this case the over-arching tale is probably of Indian origin. King Shahryar, a ruler in Central Asia, discovers that his wife has regularly been unfaithful to him and after executing her with all her lovers his anger and bitterness lead him to take revenge on all women; he marries a new wife every day, kills her the next morning and immediately takes another. This continues until the only women left in the kingdom are the two daughters of the Vizier. The eldest, Scheherazade, insists on being married to the king despite her father's objections, and succeeds in keeping her neck intact by telling her husband wonderful stories. Each evening she breaks off in the middle of a new one, and the king is so eager to hear the end that he continually puts off her execution. Finally, after three children have been born to them, he acknowledges her worth and his love for her.

The many tales told within this framework are of diverse origin, and it seems unlikely that the whole work was compiled by one author, but that it expanded and developed with time, absorbing further oral tradition down the centuries, to become the work known today. The layers of this work have been analysed by scholars, who have identified material grafted on to the structure from Baghdad and Egypt. The Arabic name for the collection is *Alf Laylah Wa Laylah*, and the earliest form to have been identified is an eighth century Arabic translation of a Persian work, *Hazar Isfana*, called *Alf Laylah*, which was rewritten in expanded form in the ninth century to incorporate further tales. The first European translation was that of Antoine Galland in 1704 and later versions added other tales, often in an attempt to make up the 1 001 referred to in the title which was probably no more than a formula to denote an unspecified high number.

Like the Aesopic fables, the tales in the *Arabian Nights* are now literary but were originally drawn from oral tradition. This is clear from the wide varieties of style, the prevalence of colloquialisms and the conversational tone which is apparent despite later attempts to make the style more literary and correct. Several later translators have been embarrassed by the forthright nature of some of the more graphic oaths and impregnations.

The tales are Asian in character, full of fantastic action, unimaginable wealth and splendid supernatural beings. A common theme is the unpredictable reversal of fortune, for better or worse, which reveals a fatalism characteristic of Asian and Oriental tales; 'All was written by Allah' is a recurring phrase.

The influence of the *Arabian Nights* on Western culture has been enormous; these great imaginative narratives epitomize the exotic appeal of the East for the less fantastical culture of Europe, and figures such as **Ali Baba**, **Aladdin** and **Sinbad** are favourites with story-tellers, writers and film-makers the world over.

àràk

BENEVOLENT SPIRIT OF CAMBODIA, guardian of the family. The àràk is thought to live in the house or inside a nearby tree. When there is sickness in the house the àràk is summoned by the shaman, who allows the àràk to possess him in order to discover what evil spirit is affecting the sufferer and therefore what exorcism or healing is required. The spirit is generally thought of as that of a distant ancestor, which confirms the general belief around the world that although the recently dead are potentially dangerous, those who have been dead a long time, who have no strong link with living persons and no urgent envy of life, are well-disposed towards their descendants.

Arawn

PRINCE OF THE UNDERWORLD in Welsh tradition. The annual conflict of Arawn and Hafgar is generally interpreted as a survival of a personified struggle between winter and summer.
▷ **Annwn**; *Mabinogion*; **Pwyll**

Arianrhod

'SILVER WHEEL', a Celtic goddess of remarkable beauty and sister and lover of the magician **Gwydion**, who appears in the *Mabinogion*. She was the mother by him of **Lleu Llaw Gyffes** and the sea-god Dylan, who plunged into the sea after his birth. Pregnant with these two, she failed the **chastity test** imposed on her by Math, and after Dylan's disappearance tried to blight the life of her remaining son in every way. She was thwarted however when Gwydion tricked her into bestowing arms upon the boy herself, the only condition on which he would ever bear them.

Arimaspians

MYTHICAL RACE OF SCYTHIA, a one-eyed people best known in classical lore for their on-going battle with the **griffins**, whose hoarded gold they sought to steal.

Arkansas Traveller

HUMOROUS SONG OF THE UNITED STATES, based on a question-and-answer dialogue between a lost Traveller and an unhelpful Squatter. The Traveller approaches the Squatter, who sits fiddling outside his log cabin, in quest of information and accommodation, but is baffled by his whimsical, witty answers. Finally, he offers to play the rest of the tune that the Squatter is sawing on his fiddle, and gains a welcome. Various attributes have been claimed for the original Traveller, including Colonel Sandy Faulkner who claimed the encounter took place in 1840 while he was lost in the Boston mountains.

It seems clear however that the song is a collection of pre-existent riddles and jokes, arranged in a format closely related to earlier British types such as the 'Whimsical Dialogue between an Irish Innkeeper and an Englishman' in a London journal of 1853. It was highly popular, and widely diffused in print and as oral lore.

arrows

AMONG THE MOST BASIC OF WEAPONS, featuring in much native lore. The use of the bow and arrow for hunting is one of the earliest skills developed by primitive man, practised world-wide, with the exception of some tribes in Oceania, Australia and a very few in Africa. Some groups use a blow-pipe to project the arrows rather than a bow. For all these cultures, the arrow has tended to become invested with a significance above the purely functional.

In ancient Greek lore the deities of love and hunting (Eros and Artemis) were both represented with bow and arrow, as was the sun-god Apollo, and mythological beings of many other cultures are portrayed in a similar way, as a sign of their potency. For many Native American and African groups, the knowledge of arrow-making was a gift from the **culture hero**, again conveying the belief that the arrow has a mythical, powerful quality. The Cheyenne possess four medicine arrows, thought to have belonged to the tribe since the creation of the world, around which most of their religious rituals centre. For example, they are brought out to cleanse a member of the tribe who has killed another member of the tribe from blood-guilt.

Arrows often serve as offerings to appease deities or ancestral spirits: the Ostyaks of Finland would shoot at a sacred tree as they passed as a mark of reverence, while Filipino tribes would offer arrows to gain the blessing of Abog, god of the hunt. When man finds himself beset by his environment, he may use the arrow to attack rather than propitiate. Several South American groups shoot burning arrows skyward during an **eclipse** in an attempt to drive

arrows

off the monster which is eating the sun, or alternatively to rekindle its light. Because of its significance in primitive life, the arrow is often used as a charm, either to impart the gift of good marksmanship or to protect from harm. They are said to protect Italian peasants from the **evil eye**, and guard defenceless Zuñi women who travel at night.

Maybe because of its phallic connotations, and probably also because hunting is generally regarded as a male pastime, the arrow is often associated closely with manhood. A pregnant Kwakiutl woman who wishes to bear a son will place an arrow or two under her bed, and many tribes place a bow and arrow on a new-born baby to ensure that he will become a good hunter. Alternatively, an arrow may be shot into the **afterbirth**, which is widely believed to be mystically twinned with the body itself.

In folktales, arrows often feature as magical objects. In Arabia they may serve to transport the hero swiftly, especially to the upper world, and a very common motif in America and the Pacific is the arrow chain, where a series of arrows fired swiftly and successively

33

by the hero become a ladder enabling him to climb to the upper world to take his revenge among the **sky people**. A famous example of this motif is found in the Coos (Native American) story of the canoe-builder whose brother was murdered by sky people; he climbed a ladder of arrows and disguised himself as a woman to gain their trust and then murdered his host in the night and escaped bearing his brother's head, which he then sewed back on to the body.

Another common theme in European folklore is the arrow which gives direction, marking the spot where the hero must build a city or a church, or seek his bride.

The importance of the arrow in primitive society, the fact that it is both dangerous and beautiful, and the skill required to use it effectively, have all contributed to the potent symbolism of the arrow in so many areas.

▷ **belomancy**

Artavazd

EVIL FIGURE OF ARMENIAN LORE. He was the son of King Artaxias, but at his father's funeral he expressed his resentment that the many rich sacrifices and suicides in honour of the dead king were depleting the kingdom to which he was succeeding. Artaxias, dead but still taking an interest, cursed his unfilial son from the grave, and Artavazd was killed soon after. He is said to dwell under Mount Mossis, bound by iron fetters in a cave, and should he ever break free he will emerge to destroy the world. Blacksmiths give a few hammer-blows to their anvils every day, even when there is no work to be done, as this is thought to strengthen the bonds that restrain him.

Arthur

CELTIC FOLK HERO, legendary king of Britain. He is portrayed as the champion of Christian chivalry, as well as a military hero who united the disparate British tribes against the threat of pagan invaders. Most legends centre on the exploits of his company of warriors, the knights of the **Round Table**, and particularly the adulterous intrigue between Sir **Lancelot of the Lake** and **Guinevere**

(Arthur's queen) and the quest for the Holy **Grail**.

If Arthur existed at all as a historical personage, he lived in the 6th or possibly 7th century AD, as a leader of the Welsh against the encroaching West Saxons in the shadowy period between the collapse of Roman rule and the chronicled Saxon kingdoms. He is mentioned only briefly by name, and never explicitly as a king or even as a noble, in early sources such as the *Annals of Wales* and the *History of the Britons*, traditionally ascribed to Nennius, but it seems likely that the heroic figure of Arthur had its roots more deeply embedded in literary rather than factual history. It may be that his very obscurity has helped the development of the legends that have become attached to him: the ancient bards could well have elaborated upon the bare facts of an obscure historical figure to produce a hero for nationalistic as well as artistic purposes.

It has been suggested that the Arthurian legend came about through the breakdown of ancient mythologies, and that he himself was originally a deity (see **euhemerism**), but Arthur appears to have few supernatural attributes. It seems more likely that he may have replaced other ancient heroes in Welsh consciousness, being a convenient peg on which to hang the dramatic story of civilization's battle against barbarians and pagans (Arthur's name appears to be derived from Latin rather than Celtic).

By the time the name of Arthur first appears in history (in Nennius's work), it is clear that a significant body of folklore is already attached to it, such as the marvellous tomb of his son Amir that could never be measured. The earliest work of all to mention him by name is the Welsh *Gododdin* of the late 6th century, an elegiac poem lamenting the heroic defeat of a Celtic force from Scotland in their battle against the Saxons. It was written by Aneirin, a poet who escaped the bloodshed. He compares the exploits of one of his companions, Gwawrddur, to Arthur and although the reference is only brief it is clear that Arthur is already regarded as a peerless hero who would instantly be recognized by the poem's readers. The reference has also given poetic epic, includes other perennial themes of folklore, such as Arthur's fight against a giant said to have taken place in Mont Saint Michel. From the 12th century on, Arthur's fame spread from Celtic lore to become a theme of European literature, his court the archetype of Christian chivalry and the epitome of a lost 'golden age' of history. Chrétien de Troyes introduced the quest for the Holy Grail (a sacred chalice said to have held Christ's blood at the crucifixion, or to have been used at the Last Supper) in the late 12th century, and this, together with the love interest of Guinevere and Lancelot and the Merlin story, became the main focus of interest for medieval writers. A vast amount of English literature relates to the Arthurian legends, which can hardly be said to remain folklore at all after the Middle Ages, yet it is undoubtedly from the rich and ancient traditions of Celtic lore that the figure of Arthur and the beginnings of his wonderful court emerged.

▷ **Dubricius**; **Merlin**

Arthur

rise to some speculation that Arthur may originally have been a Scottish leader.

The most famous Arthurian legends are mainly medieval: the Round Table; Arthur's chivalrous court at **Camelot**; his faithless wife Guinevere loved by Lancelot; the quest for the Holy Grail; the magical sword **Excalibur**; the wounding at the battle of Camlan and his final departure to **Avalon** to be healed by **Morgan le Fay** and await the time when England should have need of him. Before all these, however, there were several more primitive, folkloric tales associated with Arthur. In the 13th-century work *The Black Book of Carmathen*, Arthur is shown at the head of a marvellous train of followers, including some familiar figures like Cei the Fair (Sir **Kay**) and others less familiar, clearly figures derived from early Celtic deities. In *The Book of Taliesin* of the same period, there is a poem relating Arthur's epic journey to the underworld, **Annwn**, which is a common folkloric theme.

Geoffrey of Monmouth's *Historia regnum Britanniae* (Histories of the kings of Britain, 1137), although written more in the traditions of chronicles than

Ascension Day

CHRISTIAN FESTIVAL, celebrating the ascension of Christ to heaven after 40 days on earth following the Resurrection. In some Catholic traditions this was graphically symbolized by a ritual in which a statue of Christ was lifted through a hole in the church roof and the flaming straw figure of Satan was cast down through it. This casting-down of the **Devil** is also dramatized in some European traditions of the human scapegoat; Munich was renowned until last century for a ceremony in which a man dressed as the Devil was pursued through the streets and rolled in puddles and dung heaps the night before the feast. The disguise was burned publicly the next day.

Asgard

OTHERWORLD OF NORSE MYTHOLOGY, the home of the gods. The gods were thought to inhabit magnificent palaces, each in one of the 12 or more realms of Asgard. One such realm was Odin's hall **Valhalla**, another was Thrudheim, home of Thor. Asgard was said to be linked to earth by the rainbow bridge, *Bifrost*.

Asgardsreid see **Wild Hunt**

ash

TREE OF THE NORTHERN HEMISPHERE, any of about 70 species of the genus *Fraxinus*, of the olive family (Oleaceae), regarded since ancient days as sacred. **Yggdrasil**, the Scandinavian World Tree, was an ash, and the first man Ask was formed by the gods from an uprooted ash tree. Pliny claimed that the ash is particularly effective against snakes, and in some Western lore the belief persists that a snake will not cross ash leaves, or a circle drawn with an ash twig. In Ireland belief in the power of the ash is particularly strong, and its shadow is said to damage crops.

A cure for warts in Cheshire was to rub them with a piece of bacon which was then tucked under the bark of an ash tree, or to stick a pin into the tree, into the wart, then back into the tree where it stayed. In both cases the warts are said to be transferred to the tree, seen as rough lumps on its bark. A cleft ash tree was often used as a cure for rickets in England in a similar way to the oak in other parts of Europe. Another means of transferring disease to the tree was to bore a hole in its trunk, insert a live mouse, and plug the hole again.

▷ **oak**; **trees**

Ash Wednesday

CHRISTIAN FESTIVAL, the first day of Lent (the 40-day period leading up to **Easter**). Its name derives from the traditional ceremonies of the Roman church, in which penitents were sprinkled with **ashes** and dressed in sackcloth to symbolize their separation from the community until reconciliation on Maundy Thursday. By the 10th century the palms used on **Palm Sunday** were burned and the ashes sprinkled on the heads of the entire congregation. The modern Catholic church observes the day by marking a cross in ashes on the forehead of each member of the congregation. The day marks the beginning of the long period of fasting, prayer and penitence after the riotous spring **carnivals** preceding it, and in areas such as Italy, Spain, France and Greece an effigy of the carnival is ritually burned to emphasize the transition.

Ash Wednesday was not originally a part of Lent, but in the seventh century four days were added to the beginning of the Lenten period to bring the total number of fasting days (ie excluding Sundays) up to 40, the period of time Jesus is said to have spent fasting in the desert at the beginning of his ministry.

Ashenputtle

FAIRY-TALE CHARACTER, heroine of the Highland version of the **Cinderella** tale-type.

ashes

RELICS OF FIRE, and thus considered potent for various purposes. In many religions ashes are associated with purification rituals: Brahmans for example prepare for sacred ceremonies by rubbing ashes into the skin, and Aztec priests are known to have smeared their faces with ashes before leading religious celebrations. Alongside this emphasis on purity is the connection with humility, shown particularly in Judaeo-Christian lore, where sackcloths and ashes are symbols of repentance.

In folk custom, ashes can function in more pragmatic ways. Scattered around a cradle or bed they can be used to detect any night-time visitors, and they have a wide range of medicinal uses from an application to cure sore eyes (in North Africa particularly) to a concoction to cure headaches (India). They can also be used in **divination**, especially on **Hallowe'en**. Ashes appear in folktales too; an Inca tale tells how the sun, jealous of her brighter rival, threw ashes into the moon's face to dull her brilliance. In Bushman lore the Milky Way is a strewn handful of ashes, and in a Jamaican tale ashes speak to reveal the truth to the hero.

▷ **Ash Wednesday**

Asking Festival

AN ALASKAN ESKIMO FESTIVAL, during which each household of the community has a chance both to fulfil its own desires and meet the requirements of another. One member of the group travels between all the houses with a stick, the Ai-yá-g'ûk, from which are suspended three globes. The head of each house in turn is asked to name his own wish, and is then told of the wishes of others. He must give something that another has asked for, as the Ai-yá-g'ûk cannot be refused.

aspen

POPLAR TREE, any of three species of that genus (*Populus*), of the willow family (Salicaceae). It is found throughout Europe and North America, characterized by its quivering leaves. In Christian lore, this trembling is attributed to the aspen's arrogance at Christ's crucifixion; while he suffered all trees bowed their heads and trembled except for the aspen, which is now condemned to do so until Judgement Day. In other versions, especially in Germany, the aspen alone refused to bow or acknowledge the young Jesus as the Holy Family fled from Herod into Egypt, and was cursed by the Christ-child. It is said that the aspen trembles with guilt as its wood was used to make the cross on which Jesus hung.

Other less pious theories include the conjecture that aspen leaves are made from women's tongues and are therefore incapable of remaining still.

▷ **poplar**

ass

ANIMAL OF FOLKLORE. Few animals feature so prominently in world folklore as this humble beast of burden, domesticated since ancient times, especially in the Mediterranean world. The reputation of the ass has ranged from sacred animal to sturdy, faithful beast to the definitive symbol of stubborn stupidity.

In ancient Egypt, the ass was identified with the sun-god Ra, in Greece it was sacred to Dionysus, and after Jesus's entry into Jerusalem on its back the ass has been considered sacred by Christians. The dark cross across the animal's shoulders was thought by medieval Christians to be a symbol of its role in Christ's passion.

Alongside this respect however is a more enduring folk-tradition of the ass as a stupid creature, presumably based on its intractable behaviour and characteristic bray. In the collections of **Aesop's fables** alone there are 27 stories

relating to the ass, mostly demonstrating its stupidity. For example, one tells how an ass tried to imitate the sporting of a young dog with his master in an attempt to win his affection: the master, furious at the cavorting beast and in danger from its clumsy hooves and teeth, ordered the ass to be beaten. The ass here illustrates the folly of trying to become something unnatural to himself in order to please.

Probably the most famous tale showing this view of the ass as purely ridiculous is that of **Midas**, whose ears were changed to those of an ass by Apollo when he unwisely judged against him in favour of Pan in a flute-playing competition. The story goes on to tell of how the king's barber (or in some versions his wife), sworn to secrecy, eventually found he could not keep in his tremendous secret any longer, and relieved himself by whispering it to the reeds by the river. Unfortunately, the reeds caught the secret and whispered it aloud in the wind, and so the king was humiliated.

In one Indian tale, an ass is covered with a panther skin by its owner, who then sets it to graze in a neighbour's corn. No-one dares to approach the fearsome creature, but when it spots a farmer creeping away on all fours, the ass supposes he has found a fellow ass and brays, thus revealing the truth. A popular alternative form of this story is an Aesopic fable in which the ass, dressed in a lion's skin, was so delighted at the terror he caused that he gave himself away by braying loudly. In German folklore, a proverb reminds us that when the donkey wears a lion's skin its ears will stick out and betray it, meaning that the stupid cannot pass undetected as the noble and brave.

Two English proverbs express the wisdom of humility by referring to the lowly ass in terms of resignation; 'Better ride on an ass that carries me home than a horse that throws me' and 'Better be the head of an ass than the tail of a horse'. The distinction between the humble, silly ass and the more highly valued horse is brought out again in the proverb 'If an ass goes a-travelling, he'll not come back a horse'.

In Europe especially the ass was thought to have great curative powers.

Hairs from the cross on its back were said to act as a charm to cure whooping cough, and the pain of a scorpion sting could be transferred from the sufferer into the ass if he sat on the beast's back and whispered into its ear 'A scorpion has stung me'. In Scotland and Ireland, the passing of a child beneath the belly of an ass was thought to be a strong charm against illness, especially whooping cough.

Assipattle

ORCADIAN FOLKTALE HERO. Assipattle (the name is equivalent to Ashenputtle, a Highland name for **Cinderella**) is a Jack type insofar as he is an indolent, lowly dreamer, although his family is respectable. He is his father's seventh son and is scorned by all his brothers, who named him from his habit of sleeping among the **ashes**. But his sister listens trustingly to his tales of the marvellous deeds he will one day perform. These tales are fulfilled when the Princess Gemdelovely is in danger from a Stoorworm, the terrible Scandinavian **dragon**, and Assipattle slays the beast and rescues her.
▷ **Jack tales**

Astolat, Maid of see **Elaine**

astrology

DIVINATION FROM THE BEHAVIOUR OF HEAVENLY BODIES, one of the earliest of all sciences. In a geocentric cosmological system astrology was a science inseparable from astronomy; it was only with the Copernican revolution that the theory of stars circling the earth and influencing it by their relative positions became divorced from science and even now its influence in popular culture is strong. In early astrology, the stars were regarded as omens in much the same way as other portentous events like **dreams** or births, but in the Middle East and especially in Babylon astrology moved away from popular superstition and folktale to become a more mathematical science, used to create a calendar and later a **zodiac**, a measurement of time which was later developed as a means of attributing character and prophesying events. The Chinese zodiac is particularly complex, with numerous permutations of animal, element and time, and here and elsewhere it is common practice to draw up an astrological chart for each new child.

Recent science has tended to reject completely the theories of astrology, that the movements of the planets can affect individual lives and world events. The great psychologist C G Jung however suggested that the zodiac signs were archetypal components of the human psyche, linked to his theory of the collective unconscious. More recently, scientific research has been applied to astrological theory, as yet inconclusively. In the meantime, horoscopes remain an important element of Western popular culture.
▷ **stars**; **zodiac**

Atlantis

THE LOST CIVILIZATION, archetype of a legend which recurs frequently in folklore. Despite the volume of scholarly and literary writings about Atlantis, the only certain independent source of the story is found in Plato's Socratic dialogues, the *Timaeus* and the *Critias*. The *Timaeus* takes its name from the main speaker (Socrates himself plays quite a passive role in both of these dialogues) and although written much later, is set on the day following the discussion famously known as the *Republic*, in which Plato through Socrates describes his vision of an ideal state, and it is in this context that Critias is urged to tell his story.

In the *Timaeus* Critias claims that Solon first heard the story he is about to tell from a priest in the court of King Aahmes II of Egypt, where ancient records had survived the Great Flood, and then told Critias' great-grandfather Dropides. Critias himself heard it from his grandfather, Critias.

The story tells of a great island in the Atlantic, beyond the straits known as the Pillars of Hercules, which was the size of Africa and Asia put together (by Asia was probably meant what we now know as the Middle East). This island was the seat of an empire extending across many Atlantic archipelagos and over much of Africa and Europe. Aiming to expand eastwards into Greece and Egypt, the forces of Atlantis were engaged and defeated by the Athenians. It is interesting to note that while Atlantis has caught the imagination of later generations, the heroes of the original story were the early Athenians, whose culture is compared to that ideal put forward in the *Republic*. Some time afterwards, this ancient, idealised Athens was overwhelmed by floods and earthquakes, and Atlantis itself sank below the sea, leaving mud shallows which rendered the sea unnavigable.

Although only a fragment of the *Critias* survives, it reveals some interesting details of the lost continent. Its kings were believed to be descended from **Atlas**, son of Poseidon, and they were credited with marvellous works of engineering and architecture. The details of government are listed, the nine provinces ruled over by sub-kings, the complex system of impartial justice and the rituals to honour the gods. But even in this beautiful and ordered island-state, greed and ambition corrupted the inhabitants.

There are several factual discrepancies in the legend; in 9500BC, around the time Plato claims for the glorious Athens that defeated Atlantis, Greece was still populated by cave dwellers. It seems likely that Plato used the legend to demonstrate an example of his ideal Republic in practice, placing it in an Athens made distant and therefore more credible by time. One of Plato's pupils, Aristotle, seems to have held this view, but others accepted the story as historical fact, and the debate has raged ever since.

The flood legend at the heart of the Atlantis story is an almost universal motif derived from prehistoric Mesopotamian cultures, and it seems that Plato may have adapted an ancient myth for the purposes of political philosophy. This theory is supported by the hint at the end of the fragment of the *Critias* that the Atlanteans had become proud and greedy, and that Zeus was planning to chastise them. The motif of the flood as punishment is common to most forms of the tale.

Atlas BEARER OF THE HEAVENS, the archetype of a common mythical type.

Son of the great Titan Iapetus and the nymph Clymene (sister of Prometheus, creator of mankind), in the tradition recorded by Hesiod he was said to have led the Titans in their rebellion against Zeus, and as punishment was condemned to hold up the heavens forever. Later tradition held that Atlas was a man who had ungraciously refused **Perseus** hospitality after the hero had killed the Medusa. Furious, Perseus showed him the Gorgon's head and he was turned to stone, becoming a mountain which bore the weight of the sky. At first this mountain was believed to be located to the west of the known world, but as knowledge and travel expanded and new mountain ranges were discovered, a consensus grew that the true Atlas mountain was to be found in north-west Africa, in the range that bears the name today. In art Atlas was generally represented holding aloft the celestial sphere, and in time this was understood to represent the world itself. The modern use of the word to refer to a bound collection of maps derives from the practice of using a picture of Atlas supporting the globe on the frontispiece, begun by Gerardus Mercator in the 16th century.

Atlas motif

CENTRAL CONCEPT OF FOLKLORE. One of the most fundamental questions to be answered in any mythological system is the means by which the sky, which hangs poised just overhead, is prevented from crashing down upon the earth. It is unsurprising then that such a wealth of folkloric material has gathered around the subject. Probably the best-known answer to this troubling dilemma is the ancient Greek myth of **Atlas**, but there are many examples world-wide of belief in a similar figure. The Tlingit Indians of North America speak of **Hayicanako**, 'the-old-woman-beneath-us', and a similar figure features in Finno-Ugric myth. In Tsimshian mythology, the world is flat and circular, supported on the end of a long pole held on the chest of **Amala**.

Other mythologies have non-human Atlas figures; some Native American and Siberian tribes speak of the world being supported on the back of a giant **turtle**, for example, and the motif of four

Atlas motif

gods or pillars at the corners of the world which hold up the sky is a common one. A variation on this theme by the Cherokee tribes has the earth suspended from the sky at its four corners by ropes.

Atli

KING OF THE HUNS and brother of **Brynhild** in the *Volsungasaga*, elsewhere known as Attila. After Brynhild's death Gudrun, sister of the Nibelungs, was married to Atli in atonement. The king, hungry for the riches and power described by Gudrun as she unthinkingly spoke of her brothers, invited the princes to visit his court and then had them killed treacherously. Gunnar and Hogi, who survived the initial massacre, were executed when they too refused to reveal the secret of the treasure. Distraught, Gudrun slaughtered first her children by Atli then their father in revenge. In the *Nibelungenlied* Atli is known as Etzel.

atua

POLYNESIAN SPIRIT, a general term encompassing natural forces, ancestors and living souls. They are manifest in all aspects of nature and activity: creatures, vegetation, weather, group rituals and dances. The focus of authority in a group was the ancestral atua located in the leader. The atua are considered very sacred, and it is often **taboo** to speak their names out loud.

auki

MOUNTAIN SPIRIT OF PERU, thought to inhabit hidden estates among the peaks of the Andes complete with household servants and herds of animals. One of the most feared of the auki's retainers is its cat, Ccoa. Local shamans call upon the auki to aid in healing and **divination**.

Auld Lang Syne

TRADITIONAL SCOTTISH SONG, sung at the end of social meetings and particularly at **New Year**. Its original author is unknown—the song appeared in broadside **ballads** in the late 17th century—but the most famous version is the 1788 reworking of Robert Burns. The first verse, chorus and last verse are traditionally sung by the entire company holding hands in a circle, with arms crossed in front of the body for the last verse:

Should auld aquaintance be forgot,
And never brought to mind?
Should auld aquaintance be forgot,
And auld lang syne?

For auld lang syne, my dear,
For auld lang syne,
We'll tak a cup o' kindness yet
For auld lang syne.

And there's a hand my trusty fiere!
And gi'es a hand o' thine!
And we'll tak a richt gude-willie waught,
For auld lang syne.

aurora BRILLIANT, LUMINOUS ATMOS-
PHERIC PHENOMENON, caused by electrical and magnetic impulses near the
two magnetic poles and hence visible
most commonly in the high latitudes of
both northern and southern hemispheres. The auroras may appear as
ribbons of multi-coloured light, or
sheets, arcs or folds. Various explanations have been attributed to this
phenomenon, particularly the aurora
borealis, or northern lights, which are
more easily witnessed by humans than
their Antarctic counterpart, the aurora
australis.

Inuits claim that the light results from
the celebrations of the spirits of the
dead, and occurs most frequently after a
large number of people have died. Norse
wisdom held that the display was produced by light reflecting from the shields
of the **Valkyries**, as they assembled those
slain in battle for bliss in **Valhalla**. In one
Estonian tale the lights come from a
celestial wedding feast, the sledges and
horses of the guests glowing luminous.
Pragmatic Scots use the dazzling
phenomenon to forecast weather; a high
display means the approach of storms.

Australian Aborigine folklore

ONE OF THE MOST POETIC FOLK CULTURES
OF THE WORLD. Historically, Australian
Aboriginal culture was semi-nomadic;
the tribe's food-gathering groups tended
to be small and widespread but cooperation between groups was necessary
for survival. Even more basic than this
however was the dependency of the
Aborigine upon his environment, and
from this relationship grew a mythology
and folklore deeply concerned with the
people's relationship to the land and to
its other inhabitants. Their creation
myths, especially in the central and
northern areas of the continent, tell of
the Dreaming or **Dreamtime**, the bringing into being of the land by the
movement of the singing ancestors.
These ancestors had human and animal
characteristics, and depending upon the
songline (the route travelled by a particular ancestor as he sang the world into
being) on which the Aborigine is born,
he associates himself closely with one
species which is then taboo for him to

kill. The tales of the ancestors are told
for entertainment, but they also define
the territory and explain the environment of the group. Land ownership was
governed by the routes of the Dreaming
and could never be sold or transferred.
Each group knew only the story of the
Dreamtime journey taken on its own
land, and an Aborigine who goes beyond
the area travelled by his totemic ancestor
feels insecure; if he dies in unfamiliar
territory his spirit will be unable to find
its path and will wander forever without
being reborn. Usually, however, the
concept of the Dreaming provides a
continuum of life-force in the face of the
individual's death: the spiritual life harnessed in the death/rebirth symbolism of
the **initiation** rites passes back into the
Dreaming to be reborn in another. This
idea of death and resurrection is a
common one in Australian mythology.
A common motif is a revival of a dead
body brought about by stinging ants.

The tales told of the Ancestors resemble the North American trickster tales in
many respects, dealing as they do with
anthropomorphized animal types in a
pre-human environment. If the
ancestors are equivalent to culture
heroes, they also demonstrate the characteristics of the trickster figure in many
tales. The Ancestors however were
believed to have died, returned to the
earth or sky or to have transformed
themselves into geographical features or
animals before the arrival of humans,
their 'spirit children'.

Australian folklore

AUSTRALIA, ISOLATED AND SELF-CON-
TAINED, stood for centuries as a repository of the idiosyncratic, including
several unique species of flora and fauna
and an Aboriginal culture little touched
by outside influence until the settlers
from Europe arrived in the late 18th
century (although there was some earlier
contact with Indonesian traders from the
north). The population is now almost
entirely of European, mainly British,
stock, with few non-white immigrant
groups due to the strict migration policy
practised through most of the 20th
century. The Aborigines now form a
minority, living mainly in communities

on government reserves or mission stations, characterized by unemployment, alcoholism and poverty. A very few tribes still live in the Northern Territories, and a few of them follow their ancestors' traditional nomadic hunting way of life. After many years of repression and neglect, the rights of Aborigines are now beginning to be recognised and a respect for their culture is developing among the immigrant population.

When British colonization of New South Wales began in 1788, the first settlers were almost exclusively convicts and marines: after landing briefly at Botany Bay they sailed north to settle in the more hospitable harbour of Port Jackson. The settlers quickly became pioneers, and their records are the first literary works of Australia, but as they spread over the land, and especially with the development of sheep farming, conflict with the Aborigines inevitably led to tension and sometimes to massacre. It was when Australia's great mineral wealth, particularly its gold mines, came to European attention that the trickle of exiled immigrants turned into a flood of adventurous Westerners. By the late 19th century the settlers had a heroic ideal of their own, the forthright, laconic and independent man of the bush, tough, pioneering but a loyal mate. The growth of nationalism and a greater sense of independence from Britain has characterized Australian culture over the last century. The folklore that grew up among the settlers was of European origin, but it was enlarged by accounts of heroic feats in the hostile bush and a fund of knowledge about the new plant and animal life, and of course the hostile Aborigines, encountered by the pioneers.
▷ **Australian Aborigine folklore**

Autolycus

GREEK MASTER THIEF, the son of Hermes (Roman Mercury), who delighted in thieving his neighbours' livestock to enlarge his own flocks. Despite his skill, and his ability to transform both his own form and that of his stolen animals, he was outwitted by Sisyphus, who marked his sheep (or in some versions cattle) on the soles of their feet. Autolycus's daughter was Anticleia, mother of Odysseus by Sisyphus who seduced her on his mission to regain his lost livestock. Shakespeare used the name in *The Winter's Tale* for a rogue.

Avalon

BLESSED ISLAND OF ARTHURIAN LEGEND, the island of apples on which the sword **Excalibur** was forged, and to which the wounded **Arthur** was taken for healing after his battle with **Mordred**. Geoffrey of Monmouth is the first to mention it, in his *Historia regum Britanniae* (c.1136). Geoffrey described it in a later work as an Elysium inhabited by the beautiful enchantress **Morgan le Fay** and her sisters, covered with lush vegetation, where men could live in health and happiness beyond a hundred years old. This is clearly linked to the ancient Celtic **otherworld** of the Blessed Isles, inhabited by attentive women, traced in the Old Irish voyage tales down to that of **Brendan the Navigator**. Some scholars have suggested that the name originally derived from that of a Celtic deity, Aballach or Avallach, and was later confused with the similar-sounding Welsh word for apple, *afal*. The name reached its present form among the bards of Breton, who were almost certainly influenced by the existing town in Burgundy of that name.

The mythical Isle of Glass of Welsh lore, the resting place of heroes, seems to have been equated with the Isle of Apples in the popular imagination, and the monastic community at Glastonbury seized on the happy linguistic coincidence to proclaim itself the Isle of Glass and hence also Avalon, a claim given credence by the surrounding marshes and the local preponderance of orchards. In the late 12th century, the monks of Glastonbury claimed to have found the bones of both Arthur and **Guinevere**, and the tomb proved a prestigious and lucrative addition to the monastic estate until its dissolution.

axe

WEAPON AND TOOL, possibly the earliest devised by humans. Its ubiquity in

axe

history is reflected in the diversity of the lore surrounding it worldwide. There is archaeological evidence to suggest that the axe has been worshipped by groups in Crete and Assyria, and it was the attribute of many gods, including the Mexican Tlaloc and Greek Apollo, Artemis and Athena. A Mixtec tale has a copper axe as an **Atlas motif**, balancing the sky on its edge.

In early black American culture, it was considered unlucky for the occupants to bear an axe on one's shoulder in a house, and to dream of an axe indicated approaching danger. On the other hand, it was thought to be useful in a storm, as an axe taken to the ground would chop up and disperse the bad weather by **sympathetic magic**. In Prussia axes were used against **witchcraft**, reflecting the widespread belief in the efficacy of **iron** against enchantment. Livestock would be made to step over an axe to protect the animals from **curses** and witchcraft, and axes were used as **amulets** for the same purpose.

In the **ogre** tales of Europe, one ploy by which the **trickster** hero triumphs is to ask for an axe big enough to cut down an entire forest when the ogre challenges him to bring down a tree. In an Aesopic fable found in Lithuania, France and Poland, with versions in China and Japan, a woodcutter loses an axe in the river and is offered a golden axe by a water spirit. He replies honestly that the axe is not his, but an unscrupulous onlooker deliberately throws his axe in the water to claim the golden treasure and loses both.
▷ **axiomancy**

axiomancy

DIVINATION BY MEANS OF AN AXE, also known as axinomancy. A semi-precious stone such as an agate is placed on a red-hot axe blade and watched carefully, as its movements indicate the identity of a guilty person. This method was used by the ancient Greeks. Other forms of divination include driving the axe into wood and examining the result to gain an oracular answer, or throwing the axe into water to establish an answer by its floating or sinking.

Aymon, Four Sons of

HEROES OF A MEDIEVAL FRENCH ROMANCE, the 12th- or 13th-century *chanson de geste* of *Doon de Mayence*. **Renauld** (also known as Rinaldo), Alard, Guichard and Richard are the sons of Aymon of Dordone, and their exploits against **Charlemagne** became legendary. As renowned as its masters was their legendary horse **Bayard**. The tale became a staple of European heroic literature, with Dutch, Spanish and Italian versions throughout the late Middle Ages, and the brothers featured in many literary works including Ariosto's *Orlando Furioso* and Tasso's *Rinaldo* and *Jerusalem Delivered*.

azeman

VAMPIRE OF SOUTH AMERICA, found especially in the north-east region once known as Surinam. The azeman appears as a woman by day, but at night she is transformed into a **bat** or another animal and prowls in search of blood. Those whose blood she drinks wake feeling drained; their energy has passed into the azeman. The azeman can be diverted from her ghastly purpose by a handful of grains or seeds scattered on the floor, which she is compelled to count. Similarly, she must stop and count all the bristles in a broom left in the room, and a broom placed across the door will debar her altogether.

▷ **succubus**; **sukuyan**; **vampire**

aziza

FAIRY RACE OF DAHOMEY, beneficent spirits who teach humans practical knowledge and reveal the things of the gods. They inhabit the forest, and are closely associated with **hunting magic** for which they provide the power.

Baba Yaga

OGRESS OF RUSSIAN FOLKLORE, a cannibal whose favourite dish is children. She kidnaps her victims and takes them back to cook them in her magical hut, which turns around on legs like chickens' and can move from spot to spot. In some tales this hut is surrounded by a picket fence with a human skull atop each post containing a candle as a grisly nightlight. She is said to swoop through the air in a **cauldron** or a mortar and pestle, sweeping away all traces of her passage with a broom, and to tear her victims apart with teeth of stone and crush them against her stone breasts. She guards the fountain of the **water of life**, but few are foolhardy enough to seek it.
▷ **Berchta**

Baba Yaga

Babe

MARVELLOUS BLUE OX, the companion and fellow-logger of Paul **Bunyan**. His unusual colour was due to the astonishingly harsh Winter of the Blue Snow, in the course of which the white Babe himself turned blue. He was of immense proportions—his eyes were set apart the length of 42 axe-handles and his bulk was so enormous that with each step he sank into solid rock (this caused the formation of Lakes Michigan and Oregon, among others). His prodigious strength was legendary; he could clear a whole forest in one haul, and he was said to have straightened a twisted river by giving it a hearty tug. Ultimately however it was his gargantuan appetite that was his undoing, when he mistakenly gulped down an entire stove in his haste to devour a fresh batch of hotcakes. Paul was said to have piled up the Black Hills of South Dakota as a marker for his grave.

Babes in the Wood

ENGLISH LITERARY FOLKTALE, based on a ballad included in Percy's *Reliques of Ancient English Poetry—Children in the Wood*. The eponymous babes are the children of a Norfolk aristocrat, master of Wayland Hall, who leaves them in the care of his brother-in-law after his death. Should the children die, their inheritance was to pass on to their uncle. After a year, the uncle can wait no longer, and he contracts two assassins to take the children out into the wood and murder them there. One of these men, touched by the children's innocence, balks at the last moment, kills his companion and leaves the children to fend for themselves in the wood. In the true ballad tradition, with its emphasis on pathos, the children die of exposure and are covered gently with fallen leaves by Robin Redbreast. The wicked uncle now finds that everything goes amiss; his sons are killed, his livelihood destroyed, and he himself imprisoned. He finally dies in jail, wretched. The assassin who had relented is apprehended seven years later for highway robbery and confesses the whole story.

The story also served as the plot for a melodrama of 1599 by Robert Farrington, and it is unclear whether this predated the ballad or not.

▷ **abandonment**

badal

ISLAMIC SPIRIT, a form of **doppelgänger**. When a very holy man dies, his place is immediately filled by his badal and the transformation is known only to Allah. Only a very few humans have this capacity for spiritual regeneration.

Badb

OLD IRISH SPIRIT, the goddess of war, appearing in the form of a hooded **crow**. It is she who incites armies against each other and encourages destruction, carnage and war-madness. She is often identified with **Morrigan** (or Morrigu), and these two share the distinction of having driven the **Fomorians** out of Ireland.

In later folklore, she came to be known as a **banshee**-type figure, distinguished by always appearing as a crow, whose presence and shrieks presage death to someone in the family. Badb is often used to refer to a scold or a witch.

badger

NOCTURNAL CARNIVORE, of the family Mustelidae, characterized by the powerful claws on their forefeet. Since it is so adept at digging its way out of the ground, the badger is held by many Native Americans to be propitious in **childbirth** and a badger paw is often used as a **talisman** worn by the mother in labour or placed near her. Among Pueblo tribes in America, the badger is believed to possess great skill in herb and plant lore, and the medicine chief is usually a badger clansman. In Japanese folklore, the badger is regarded as a powerful **shapeshifter**.

badi

DEMONS OF MALAYAN LORE, who take possession of people, animals and objects. They can be exorcised or kept at bay by **charms** and rituals. They are said by some to be the offspring of **jinn**, but in other accounts they sprang from three drops of Adam's **blood**, or were engendered by the radiance of the sunset.

Badoura

HEROINE OF THE ARABIAN NIGHTS, said to be the most beautiful woman in the world. She appears in the story of Camaralzaman and Badoura.

baginis

AUSTRALIAN MONSTERS, predatory female beasts in half-human, half-animal form. The beauty of their faces belies their rapacious, claw-like fingers and toes. They capture men and rape them, but their victims are usually allowed to go free afterwards.

bajang

EVIL SPIRIT OF MALAYSIAN FOLKLORE, an omen presaging disaster and sickness. It usually appears as a great polecat. Children are especially vulnerable to its attacks, and should be protected with special bracelets woven from black silk.

In some areas, the bajang is said to be

bajang

the spirit of a still-born child which can be captured in a midnight ritual by one brave enough to attempt it, and kept in a *tabong*, a special cage of **bamboo** closed with leaves which has been prepared with **spells** beforehand. A bajang kept in this way and fed conscientiously on milk and eggs will serves as its master's familiar, seeking out and possessing those selected by its master for attack. If it is not well looked after, however, it will turn on its captor.

bajbín

MEXICAN DRUM, formed by stretching hide across a pottery jar which may by filled with water or grain. They are considered sacred objects, guarded by two specially selected keepers who must offer incense and worship regularly and prepare them for use in the **carnival**, by ritual washing, libations and dance. A bajbín is used only at carnival times, when it accompanies the dancing.

bakemono

JAPANESE EVIL SPIRITS, a wide-ranging term covering all forms of **goblins** and **ghosts**. In art they are often represented with long straight hair, which does not however conceal the tell-tale fact that they have no feet.

bakru

SOUTH AMERICAN RACE OF LITTLE PEOPLE, created by evil magicians. Belief in them is concentrated mainly in the north-east, in old Surinam and Dutch Guyana. They always appear in couples, and are roughly the size of a human child although their heads are disproportionately large. They are composed half of flesh and half of wood. A human may obtain a pair from a magician, but the wealth they bring must be carefully weighed against the exigent demands they make upon their owner. Ultimately it is impossible to profit from them, as the gods will surely punish anyone who attempts to put such evil creations to his own use.
▷ **bottle imp**

Balan and Balin

BROTHERS OF ARTHURIAN LEGEND, who meet in battle and mistakenly kill each other, each unaware of the other's identity. **Merlin** buried them together in one grave. Their story is told in Malory's *Morte d'Arthur* and in Tennyson's *Idylls of the King*. Balan features in many romances as a kindly and courteous **giant**; he was defeated by **Charlemagne** in one cycle.

ballads

NARRATIVE FOLKSONG, telling a story of drama, adventure or love. The form characteristically focuses upon one specific incident in a sensational manner. The narrative tends to be stark; emotional impact is gained from the story itself and stylistically by the repetition of certain key phrases rather than from any sophistication of language. The form developed in Europe in the late Middle Ages but drew on much older traditions of theme and content. It differs from epic poetry in its concentration on one situation, often stripped of explanatory or expository details, and from lyric folksong in its emphasis on plot; the music is subordinate, aiding memory and increasing the emotional impact of the performance. Where folktales tend to move episodically, the ballad gives isolated moments of dramatic action.

A true ballad is undateable, since it is a constant reworking by performance of a preceding tradition. Some scholars hold that each ballad is a product of collective composition by a cultural group, others point to one creative voice shaping the original form of the ballad which was then passed on and changed through the generations. The complexity and artistic awareness of the form do seem to suggest the hand of an individual artist in an advanced society, often drawing on the material of ancient lore and tradition, but using more sophisticated techniques to compose his ballads. Once performed, of course, the ballad would become the property of the folk, to be repeated and adapted as suited the memory and the preoccupations of each performer.

The ballad form is found mainly in Europe, most especially in Scotland, England, Scandinavia, Germany, Russia, Yugoslavia and Spain. The narrative form and content remain similar throughout, but the accompanying music varies widely.

The definitive collection of the ballads of Scotland and England is that compiled by F J Child, *The English and Scottish Popular Ballads* (1882–98), which contains 305 distinct ballads. The two national forms are similar, and in many cases the same ballad is found in both English and Scottish versions, but there is a general trend towards realism and romance in the English ballads while the Scottish ones often concentrate more on supernatural elements and fairy-lore, such as *Tam Lin*, which tells how Tam is held spellbound by the fairies but is rescued by his sweetheart. Similarly, *Thomas Rhymer* tells of the hero's visit to fairy-land. The best known of the English ballads deal with the adventures of the folk hero **Robin Hood**. *A Geste of Robin Hood* is the only cyclic ballad in English literature, and it is almost certainly a consciously literary product, composed by linking together several existing ballads. Robin Hood and his band of men in Lincoln Green stand as archetypes of the heroic outlaw, and this is a favourite subject of English balladry, for example *The Outlaw Murray*, *Johnnie Cock* and *Adam Bell and William of Cloudesly*. In both English and Scottish tradition, but especially Scottish, some of the finest ballads are the early tragic tales, such as the *Twa Sisters*, *Lord Randal* and *Sir Patrick Spens*. Many of these are to be found across Europe; they deal in a haunting way with the universal themes of love, despair, fate and death.

The famous Border ballads are more realistic and literary, recording the fighting between English and Scots. Such a theme might once have been treated in an epic manner, but in the late Middle Ages and beyond their natural form was the lively ballad. They include *Johnnie Armstrong*, *The Battle of Otterburn* and *The Hunting of the Cheviot*.

Many varieties of ballad can also be found in Danish folklore, including both realistic and supernatural themes, battle-songs and love-songs, and many reflect ballads of England and Scotland. The historical ballads tend to group naturally into cycles, unlike those of Britain. They deal mainly with the exploits of the brave warrior Stig Hvide, King Waldmar, and the freedom fighter Neils Ebbeson. The supernatural element is very strong; ballads tell of **trolls**, **mermaids** and magical transformations rather than the ethereal fairy world of English balladry, eg *Agnes and the Merman*, *The Lady and the Dwarf King* and *The Maiden Hind*, in which a young boy shoots a hind despite his mother's warning and discovers that he has slain his transformed sister.

There are many ballads in the epic mood telling of **giants**, **dragons** and other monsters, such as *King Diderich and the Dragon* and *Child Orm and the Berm Giant*. The tone of nearly all the Scandinavian ballads is intense and often tragic; there are few of the light-hearted ballads found in the rest of Europe.

Germanic folksong generally takes a lyric rather than a narrative form, although isolated exceptions can be found. The *Pied Piper of Hamelin* is a famous example, and *King Ermanaric's Death* is probably a reworking of ancient epic romance. Stories of supernatural creatures appear in ballad form too, especially ghosts and mermaids.

The Russian form, the **byliny**, shares many characteristics of the ballad. A more traditional type of ballad, dealing with love, death and the everyday business of living, is the **dumi** form of the Ukranians, which shows much Western influence.

In Bulgaria ballads are plentiful, dealing with all the supernatural beings of Bulgarian folklore, including the sun and moon as characters, dragons, talking beasts and entrancing music. There is also much emphasis on tragic love tales.

In Croatia women traditionally sing lyric songs while men perform heroic narrative folk-poems, again with an epic undertone. These men's songs are known as Junačke Pesme; they tend to focus on one hero so that, like the Russian byliny, they can often be grouped together to form a cycle. Several songs centre around the semi-historical figure of Marco Kraljević or the famous battle against the Serbs at Kosovo in 1389.

Neither France nor Italy has much in the way of indigenous narrative folksong, both countries tending more naturally towards the lyric form, but Italy does have a few late historical ballads. The only real body of ballad material is found in Spain, the *romancero*.

The ballad is one of the most widespread forms of folk poetry, and its literary influence has been enormous. The development of broadside ballads in 16th-century England as a means of entertainment and of spreading current news is an example of a literate and therefore stable use of the form, which makes it no longer truly folksong. Nevertheless, the true ballad form has survived until very recently in isolated areas, bearing witness to its enduring popularity as the poetry and drama of the folk.

Balmung

MAGICAL SWORD OF NORSE LORE, also known as Gram, forged by the elf-king **Wayland the Smith**. Odin thrust the sword into the Branstock tree, the great oak in the Volsung palace, and issued a general challenge, saying that the sword, which assured its owner victory in battle, belonged only to the one who could pull it free. Nine Volsung princes were among those who tried to remove the sword, but none succeeded until the youngest of them, Sigmund, laid his hand on the hilt and drew it out with ease.

Odin later destroyed Balmung in battle, but the pieces were restored and reforged, and Siegfried was able to use it against **Fafnir**, the **dragon**.

▷ **Arthur**; **Excalibur**; **Sigurd**

Balor

OLD IRISH KING of the **Fomorians**, famed for his single, deadly eye. As a child he peeked at the Druids as they prepared their charms; the noxious fumes poisoned his eye and thereafter it killed anything it looked upon. This proved very effective on the battle-field, where he was attended by four men who prised open his eye with a special handle on his command. His end came at the hand of his grandson, **Lugh**, who during the second battle of Mag Tured fired a slingshot into Balor's eye just as it was

Balor

opening, and killed not only his grandfather but a number of men standing behind him as the fatal eye was pushed out of the back of Balor's head. Balor had been warned of the danger from Lugh, and had attempted to have his grandson exposed at birth; this worldwide motif is given classical expression in the **Oedipus** myth.

▷ **abandonment**; **evil eye**

bamboo

HOLLOW, TREE-LIKE GRASS, any of the numerous species comprising the subfamily Bambusoideae, family Poaceae, found especially in south-east Asia and the Pacific and Indian islands. Because of its longevity and perpetual foliage, it is regarded in Chinese lore as a symbol of long life and in India as a symbol of friendship. It flowers only after many years, and then generally only once in its lifetime, and so a flowering bamboo is widely regarded as portentous, signifying a coming famine.

The motif of a human emerging from a bamboo stem is common in folktales of the region; in the Andaman Islands the first man, Jutpu, is said to have emerged from a bamboo joint. In a Malaysian tale, a hunter falls asleep under a bamboo and dreams of a beautiful princess, who cooks his food and tells him that she is to be found in the bamboo before disappearing as dawn breaks. He awakens, succeeds in breaking open the bamboo, and releases the princess.

Crosses made from bamboo are used on the Philippine Islands as charms placed in the field to encourage the crops to grow.

Ban

KING OF ARTHURIAN ROMANCE, father of Sir **Lancelot of the Lake**. He ruled over Benoic but died from a broken heart after he was betrayed by his steward and saw his castle taken and torched.

Banba

OLD IRISH QUEEN, one of the three encountered by the invading **Milesians**, who gave her name to Ireland.
▷ **Ériu**; **Fodla**

Banbury Cross

THE ORIGINAL CROSS OF BANBURY, celebrated in the nursery rhyme 'Ride a cock-horse to Banbury Cross', was destroyed by Puritans in 1602, although a replacement was re-erected in 1858. The rhyme appears to date from the 15th century, when 'bells on her toes' would have been a common enough fashion accessory, and there has been much speculation about the identity of the 'fine lady upon a fine [or white] horse'. In some early versions the woman is old and the horse is black. A strong contender for the role in popular opinion is Lady **Godiva**, especially as one 19th-century version of the rhyme ran 'Ride a cock-horse to Coventry Cross', but Queen Elizabeth I has also been suggested. It has been popular since the 16th century as a rhyme for children bounced on an adult knee, or riding astride a **hobby-horse**.

banjo

MUSICAL INSTRUMENT, resembling a **guitar** but with a characteristically round body. The number of strings can vary, but the most popular model has five. Its origins are African; it was brought over to America by slaves in the 19th century and popularized there particularly as a folk instrument but also for **jazz** music. One legend associated with it claims that the banjo was invented by Ham, one of the sons of Noah, killing time on the

Ark. In early black American superstition it was said that a skilled banjo player had obtained his gift from the **Devil** at a midnight meeting at a crossroads.

bannik

RUSSIAN HOUSEHOLD SPIRIT, the spirit of the bathhouse. The bannik is an unpredictable companion for anyone visiting a bathhouse; he may take it into his head to plague some bathers, splashing them with scalding water or even killing them, while others he leaves unmolested. He can occasionally be glimpsed through

bannik

the steam, but more usually signals his presence by a touch on a bather's back. If this is soft, it is a good omen, but a scratch from a bannik's claw bodes evil for the recipient. It is wise to leave a little water in the tub and some soap lying out for the bannik to use if the whim takes him.
▷ **domovik**; **mischievous spirits**

banshee

CELTIC FAIRY BEING, an anglicized form of Gaelic *bean sidhe*, 'woman of the fairies' (*ban sith* in Scots Gaelic). She is variously described as a young and beautiful or an old and haggard woman, but her function is always to foretell the death of a member of the family that hears her by her dreadful, mournful

wailing. This half-human cry is unmistakable, and cannot be shut out by the softest, thickest blankets. She is said to attach herself to a particular family, whose deaths she will foretell through the generations.
▷ **Washer of the Ford**

Barbara Allen

LITERARY BALLAD, composed by Allan Ramsey (1724), telling of a beautiful but pitiless woman whose indifference kills the young man enamoured of her. Despite her apparent heartlessness, she is remorseful after his death and dies herself soon afterwards. The theme is an ancient one in Scottish and English balladry, and it was received eagerly in America where many variations now exist.

Barbarossa, properly Frederick I (c.1123–90)

'REDBEARD', THE GREAT HOLY ROMAN EMPEROR and a national hero of Germany. His conquests ranged over much of central Europe and Italy, and in 1189 at the height of his powers he led the Third Crusade against Saladin. He was drowned the following year, but like many other rulers is said to be awaiting the call of his country in need as a **sleeper** in a cave inside the Kyffhäuser Mountain, Thuringia. He is seated at a marble table, and his **beard** continues to grow around it. In some versions he will awaken when his beard has circled the mighty table three times.

barbegazi

MOUNTAIN SPIRITS OF THE FRENCH–SWISS ALPS, a **gnome**-like race inhabiting the high peaks and caves above the snowline. The name is probably a corruption of French *barbe glacée*, 'frozen beard'. They emerge from summer hibernation to spend the winter sporting in sub-zero temperatures, their white fur garments and the long icicles on their hair and beards effectively camouflaging them amidst the snow. If alarmed they can tunnel into snowdrifts at lightning speeds. They can travel at high speeds across the snowfields using their big feet as sturdy skis, and enjoy riding avalanches down the mountainside. Although

very shy, they are thought to be well-disposed towards humans, calling to warn them of avalanches and digging them out of snowdrifts. Some climbers have claimed to have found and captured barbegazi, but they cannot survive long at low altitude and in warmer temperatures, and no specimens have lived long enough to be analyzed.

bard

CELTIC MINSTREL AND POET, originally a composer of eulogies and **satires**; more generally any poet-performer who sings of legendary heroes of the group and their deeds. Bards were also a feature of the early Gauls, but the tradition endured most strongly in Ireland and Wales. Bards had practical purposes, beyond merely preserving the legendary history of the group; they drew on such history to give timely lessons to the leaders of the present, to inspire men to battle, and were used to herald news. Festivals were often held at which bards competed; in Wales particularly the art was formalized into distinct orders during the 10th century, and the legacy survives in the annual *eisteddfod*, a national gathering of musicians and poets.

Barlaam and Josaphat

INDIAN FOLKTALE AND POPULAR MEDIEVAL ROMANCE. Barlaam was an ascetic monk of Sinai who converted the Hindu prince Josaphat to Christianity. It is thought to have been translated into Greek by the sixth century. It has many similarities with tales of Buddha's youth, and contains also the test motif of the three caskets, only one of which contains the prize, later utilized by Shakespeare in *The Merchant of Venice*.

Barmecide's feast

TALE OF THE ARABIAN NIGHTS, a byword for any disappointing illusion or a trial that must be undergone with composure and gravity in the face of a laughable reality. In the Barber's tale of his sixth brother, a prince of Baghdad, a member of the great Barmecide family, plays a somewhat heartless joke on the poor beggar Schacabac. He invites his starving guest in for a meal, then proceeds to

Barmecide's feast

set before him a succession of empty dishes and cups, all the time praising the incomparable quality of these non-existent victuals. Schacabac humours him, claiming never to have tasted the like, but revenges himself by feigning drunkenness from all the fine wine he has not been served and punching his host. The prince acknowledges the justice of the situation, and gives Schacabac all the fine food he can eat.

Bartek and Pies

POLISH FOLKTALE, in which a king and his clown exchange roles to discover the virtue of the king's prospective bride, Bialka. Bialka gives her attention to Pies, believing him to be the king by his royal robes, and treats Bartek in his lowly dress with contempt, but her sister Spiewna is courteous and tender towards the apparent jester. Ultimately of course Bartek weds Spiewna, and Bialka is left to match herself with an elderly organist.

The themes of disguise and deception to discover the truth are keynotes of folktales around the world, and particularly of the European Märchen.

basil

AROMATIC HERB, the dried leaves of the annual herb (*Ocimum basilicum*), a member of the Lamiaceae family, native to India and Iran but found widely in temperate areas. Its name derives from the ancient belief that it was an antidote to the poison of the **basilisk**, although according to some scholars the name is the more ancient and the superstition developed because of it. In India it is considered a sacred plant, although some European traditions assign it to the **Devil**.

Its heart-shaped leaves make it a symbol of love in Italy, although in Greece it is symbolic of hate and will not grow unless its planting is accompanied by curses. Its use in healing has been tempered by a tenacious belief that it is poisonous; Culpepper drew this conclusion from the observation that basil would not grow alongside **rue**, the antidote to poisons. However, in Africa it is said to protect against scorpion stings, and in some areas of Europe its smell is said to purify the heart and head and improve the mood of the user. It is used widely in cooking throughout Europe.

basilisk

FABULOUS MONSTER, a reptilian cross between a **cock** and a serpent, whose breath and gaze were fatal to humans. Also known as a cockatrice, the creature has been feared since classical times, when Pliny described it in his *Historia Naturalis* as emerging from the egg of a cock that had been hatched by a snake or toad. it is depicted in art upright, with a crest symbolizing its status in the animal kingdom, often with wings, and generally with the feet and head of a cock and the tail of a serpent.

Humans could protect themselves from the basilisk's glance by carrying a mirror—were the basilisk to see its reflection in the mirror it would itself die—and some theories state that if a traveller spots the basilisk before being spotted by it the creature will die. The sound of a cock crow is fatal to a basilisk, and its only other natural enemy is the **weasel**. It is thought that the hooded **cobra** may be the origin of the legend.
▷**basil**; **Gorgon**

bat

ANIMAL OF FOLKLORE, the only flying mammal. In its many species, the bat is found worldwide and its distinctive habits and appearance have made it a favourite subject of folklore, evoking a range of reactions across the world, as an emblem of doom or of luck.

Aesop suggested that the bat took to flying by night in order to avoid its creditors, but many cultures have proposed rather more sinister theories. The bat is closely linked with the idea of the **separable soul**, as are birds and flying insects in general (and in West Africa, Australia, Bosnia, Tonga and England the bat is considered sacred because of this), but in the case of the bat this idea has been developed in association with the belief in **vampires**, malevolent undead spirits which prey on the blood of the living. It is widely held that the bat is one of the **Devil**'s favourite disguises. In Europe and America bats, especially in ruined houses, are generally supposed to indicate the presence of ghosts, and this association is found among several South American groups. In primitive medicine, the bat was often thought to carry disease or to foretell death.

Bat features in the folktales of several Native North American groups, including the Apache, Creek and Cherokee. In one popular cycle of the Plains tribes, Bat is a thwarted trickster figure, whose two wives run away when they catch sight of his ugliness by day. His wings are believed by the Lipou Apache to have been used in the making of the first horse, and so they invoke the bat against falling from a running horse. The Creek and Cherokee tell how Bat was refused by both the animals and the birds when he wished to join in their game, but when he was finally allowed to join the side of the animals, on the grounds that he possessed teeth, he won the game for them.

The bat is not universally regarded as an ominous or ghostly sign; in China it is a symbol of long life and happiness with the five-fold blessings of wealth, health, virtue, old age and a natural death. In Poland too the bat is considered a lucky sign, and a popular European jingle, 'Bat, bat, come under my hat', reflects the belief that it is lucky to trap a bat in this way. In Macedonia too the bat is considered particularly lucky, and its bones may be carried as protective

bat

charms. The Kwakiutl place a bat in a child's cradle to impart to him the gift of sleeping all day, and similarly the Arabs recommend a bat's eye as a cure for insomnia.

The range of belief centring on the bat is an interesting study, revealing at the same time the variations and similarities of folk cultures around the world. The relationship of the people to their dead and the cultural connotations of darkness seem to be the strongest elements in the development of bat-lore in each society.

Battle of the Trees

BATTLE OF CELTIC MYTHOLOGY, known as Câd Goddeu. **Arawn** led his forces against **Amaethon**, who had stolen from **Annwn** his roebuck, whelp and **lapwing**. The long poem *Câd Goddeu* is contained in *The Book of Taliesin*. It was won by Amaethon, whose brother **Gwydion** correctly guessed the name of **Bran the Blessed** from the **alder** twigs he carried (see **name taboo**); none of Arawn's side could guess the name of Achren, a woman fighting for Amaethon.

It appears from the somewhat rambling poem that Gwydion transformed all manner of trees into warriors, but more recent scholars have taken the view that the poem represents a convoluted code of letters and learning, drawn from the ancient Celtic tree alphabet, and that its message is bound up with druidic magic practices.

bay tree

MEDITERRANEAN SHRUB, *Laurus nobilis* of the family Lauraceae, the laurel from which victory wreaths were woven in classical times. This use persists in modern proverb lore—to look to one's laurels is to strive to maintain one's preeminence whereas to rest on one's laurels is to be complacent about success. It was thought by the Greeks to be sacred to the sun god Apollo (his pursuit of Daphne ended in her transformation into this tree), and hence to partake of his oracular qualities; prophecy and poetic inspiration. These associations are due also to its intoxicating narcotic effects. Since Apollo killed the Cyclops, makers of the thunderbolt, it was said that the tree would never be struck by lightning; it was hence considered effective against lightning when worn as an **amulet**. The connection with the sun persisted among medieval herbalists, and the herb was regarded as a powerful protector against storms, **witchcraft** and the **Devil**.

A withered bay is considered an evil omen, but in Britain the tree is considered a symbol of new life since even when dried out it is able to grow back from the roots.

The bay has uses in both **medicine** and **divination**; bay roots are beneficial in clearing out the digestive system and its berries work against poison and insanity and cure epilepsy, rheumatism, coughs and consumption. Bay leaves placed under one's pillow on **Valentine**'s night ensure pleasant **dreams** of a future lover, and the noise of the crackle they make while burning corresponds to the level of good fortune in the year ahead. In Holland laurel is used to deck the house of a newly-married couple. In folktales laurel is taken to induce forgetfulness.

Bayard

MARVELLOUS HORSE, given to the Four Sons of **Aymon** by **Charlemagne**. It seemed a normal horse if it had only one rider, but it was able to lengthen its back to accommodate all four of its masters comfortably if required and sweep them off on a journey of astonishing speed. It was also alleged to have the power of human speech.

baykok

EVIL SPIRIT OF THE CHIPPEWA, NORTH AMERICA. It appears by night as a skeletal figure with red, fiery eyes, and the creaking and grinding of bones as it approaches is a warning to its victims. The baykok preys only on warriors, attacking them with invisible arrows or the club that it carries.

bean-nighe see Washer of the Ford

beans

STAPLE FOOD, put to a variety of uses in addition to simple nutrition. There is an immense variety of bean species throughout the world, and this variety has been incorporated into ritual, superstition and folk narrative throughout the world.

Voters in the classical world used beans in ballots; a white bean indicated a yes vote, a black one a no. Beans were especially significant in ancient Rome, as food for the dead and an offering to be made at the end of the annual feast of the dead, the Lemuria. In Japan too beans were used ceremonially to pacify and expel demons and ghosts. At the other end of the life-cycle, Zuñi women are given a bean to swallow during **childbirth**, so that the ease with which it slips down the throat might be transferred by **sympathetic magic** to the passage of the baby.

Probably the most famous beans in Western folklore are those given to Jack that later became the marvellous beanstalk reaching to the upperworld (see **Jack and the Beanstalk**). A similar motif is found in the Latvian tale of the **cock** and **hen** who plant a bean which shoots up to a remarkable height. The cock climbs up to collect all the ripe beans, but the hen below keeps calling to him, and he eventually falls down and is killed. The bean is also a protagonist in a tale collected by Grimm (No 18), in which the bean splits its sides laughing at the fate of the coal and straw (the straw invited the coal to cross a river by walking across him, but the coal hesitated in the middle and burnt through his straw bridge; both went tumbling into the water).

In European lore it was considered good luck to plant beans on Good Friday, and at any time by the light of the moon. To dream of beans indicates an argument is brewing, or the approach of an unknown enemy. Although Pliny recommended beans as laxatives, they are said by many to be the cause of bad dreams because they are difficult to digest.

bear

MASSIVE SHORT-LEGGED MAMMAL, belonging to the family Ursidae. Despite the enormous bulk of most species (excepting the more diminutive members of the group, such as the sun or Malay bear), bears are capable of walking, running, climbing and swimming with ease. The animal has been regarded with reverence from earliest times—bear remains have been discovered ritually interred in Neanderthal graves—and is regarded as an ancestor by many primitive groups. Bear-hunters will prepare carefully for the hunt with rituals (see **hunting magic**) and, having caught their prey, take elaborate measures to prevent retaliation by the angered spirit, explaining that the death was necessary, smoking a placatory pipe, and formally requesting pardon using a respectful title such as 'Grandfather'. **Shape-shifting** shamans often took the form of a bear, since it was associated with supernatural power and healing, and there are many tales in North America of **beast marriages** between humans and bears (see **Bear's Son cycle**).

Many superstitions and beliefs are associated with the bear. Medieval Christians (following the teaching of Aristotle and Pliny among others) believed that bear cubs were born as shapeless furry balls, which their mother shaped into an infant bear with her tongue, hence the common idiom 'to lick into shape'. The bear is frequently associated with the **Devil** in medieval bestiaries, because of its ferocity, and it frequently appears in folktales as a clumsy, greedy gull, bettered by the quick wits of men and **trickster** animals. In a European folktale found also among some Native Americans, the bear's legendary appetite for honey proves his downfall when the **fox** leads him to a nest of wasps rather than the promised beehive. In another tale the fox frees himself from the bear's jaws by convincing him that he is gnawing at a tree root and not the fox. The bear features as the butt of the boast in many **tall tales**, such as that of the settler returning home drunk from the saloon and having a wresting match with a 'big fellow in a fur coat' who wouldn't give way on the road. One common motif of bear lore is the belief that a bear will not attack its prey if it lies down faking death; a popular tale tells of a man journeying with his guide through the forest when they come upon a bear. The guide rushes up a tree, the man lies down motionless. The bear comes and sniffs him before lumbering away, and the guide descends and asks what the bear whispered in the man's ear. 'Never trust a coward like you' replies the man.

The winter slumber (it is not a true hibernation) of the bear is regarded as a weather portent in many areas—if the bear retires early, it will be a harsh winter. The superstition now attached to the groundhog, that it will return to its burrow to sleep if it sees its shadow on emerging and winter will continue for another six weeks (see **Groundhog Day**), is thought to have originated with the bear.

The bear is widely credited with great beneficent curative powers; Native Americans used mimetic dance to acquire such healing powers, and in India a bear's hair is frequently worn as an **amulet** to ward off disease.

▷ **berserk**; **bogle**; **Three Bears**

Bear's Son cycle

ANCIENT EURASIAN FOLKTALE PATTERN, also found among Native North Americans. In its basic form, it tells of a child whose human mother has been abducted by a **bear**; the bear may be his father, or the mother may have been stolen while already pregnant. The child acquires bear characteristics and superhuman strength as he grows, and on his return to human society proves himself by a series of extraordinary feats. In such tales it is common for the hero to battle with a monster, wound it, then follow it to its underwater lair to defeat it completely. In the Old English epic **Beowulf** this developed into a dual battle with **Grendel** and his mother. The slaying of the **dragon**, either to obtain its treasure or to save a maiden, and the desertion by companions are motifs characteristic of this type.

Many famous tales can be traced to the same root; some scholars have claimed that the *Odyssey* derives largely from the Bear's Son type, and certainly the vast group of **dragonslayer** tales, including *Beowulf*, seems to be closely related. The killing of the monster probably arose from early forms in which the hero avenges his mother by slaying the bear that abducted her; in oral tradition the origins of the hero became obscure as the tales focused on his adventures and so the monster evolved into a different being.

▷ **Gnome, The**

beard

SYMBOL OF MANHOOD, and thus regarded with fierce pride and significance by many races throughout the world. Since the beard is a feature common only to adult males, the historic power-base of most cultures, it has served as a convenient shorthand for all the qualities associated with that group (in reality and in imagination): strength, wisdom, authority and, by extension, royalty and even divinity. Smooth-chinned races were despised as effeminate by their hirsute neighbours; the beard was regarded in both Judaeo-Christian and Muslim traditions as a God-given distinction to separate man from inferior woman.

beard

Hence some of the most humiliating insults that could be given to a man centred on his beard; to pluck it was disrespectful, and to cut it off or mutilate it, as Hanun of the Ammonites did to David's ambassadors (2 Samuel 10:4–5), was an international incident.

Christian representations of God have almost unfailingly attributed a beard to him, and a common Muslim oath, one of the most binding that can be made, is to swear by one's own beard and that of Allah. The wolf in the nursery story of the Three Little Pigs echoes this ancient oath in an attenuated form when he swears 'by the hairs on my chinny-chin-chin' to blow the pigs' houses down. Egyptian rulers recognized the intuitive link between divinity and the hairy chin and, when they could not grow a satisfactory beard of their own, would resort to false beards for state business; even Queen Hatshepsut is known to have donned a beard on occasion.

The significance accorded to the beard derives from wider ancient beliefs in magic; hair, like other detachable parts of the body such as toenails, contains part of a man's soul and therefore makes him vulnerable to attack if it comes into the possession of an enemy with magical skills. As in tales of the **separable soul**, Hebrew legend tells how Samson's strength resided in his hair and departed when he was treacherously shorn by Delilah. The beard gained specific importance within this wider context as it was a feature of masculinity.

▷ **Blackbeard; Bluebeard; Cid, El**

beast epic

COMMON GENRE OF LITERATURE, found throughout the world but particularly in medieval Europe. It typically consists of a cycle of **animal fables**, usually making a satiric comment on contemporary society. Although primarily a literary form, the beast epic draws much of its material from oral tradition. Among the best-known examples is the epic of **Reynard the Fox**.

beast marriage

THE MOTIF OF A HUMAN MARRIED TO A BEAST is found in folktales across the world, with many variants. Sometimes, especially in Native American mythology, it is the union of an animal with a human that produces the tribe, or in folktales the animal is anthropomorphized but remains unambiguously an animal, for example the Fox-wife of the Eskimos or the Bear Husband of the Plains groups. Often in classical mythology a god takes an animal form to seduce a human, for example Zeus transforms himself into a **swan** to win **Leda**, a bullock to carry away Europa. Another common variation is the lover who is a beast by day and human by night, or can otherwise change between the two shapes. In European lore, the supposed beast is more commonly a bewitched human, who can only be released when the love of another human becomes stronger than the spell which binds him or her, and it is to this type, of course, that **Beauty and the Beast** belongs. A related body of tales deals with the adventures of the heroic or monstrous offspring of such unions. The legend of the **Minotaur** is an ancient classical example of a universal type.

A common feature of all beast marriage tales is the **taboo**; in the case of Beauty and the Beast this is a magically significant period of time beyond which Beauty cannot remain away, but in many other tales it takes the form of a ban on referring to the origin of the animal-wife, or against striking her or speaking angrily. If the taboo is broken the beast-partner will invariably disappear, and in most non-European lore, where the romantic element is less important, will never be found.

There is a general distinction between Beauty and the Beast tale-types, in which the male is imprisoned in animal form to be freed by the love of the human woman, and the **swan maiden** type in which the woman represents the supernatural, the animal temporarily transformed into human shape. Occasionally this pattern may be reversed to give the type 'search for the lost husband' or a tale of the **loathly lady**.

beating the bounds

ENGLISH CUSTOM, taking place during Rogationtide (the days preceding Ascension Day), involving a ceremonial procession around the boundaries of the parish. The boundary stones were literally 'beaten' with peeled willow switches to confirm their position and fix them in the communal memory, an important function in days before maps. The prayers for blessing on the crops that accompanied this ritual recall the ancient Roman festivals, Ambarvalia and Terminalia, which took place in May or June, at which sacrificial beasts were driven around the limits of the cultivated land while intercessions to Mars for safety for the crops were made. Although the procession was intended by the Church to be a solemn, orderly affair, it was sometimes taken at an enthusiastic gallop, and troublesome youths were occasionally 'bumped' or beaten at the boundaries, imparting to the ceremony an additional function of social control. Any house built over a boundary line was obliged to permit the procession to pass through it.

In Scotland, especially in the Borders, the custom was known as 'riding the marches', and survives in several Border towns today as the summer **Common Ridings** festivals.

Beauty and the Beast

FAIRY TALE, one of the best known of all **beast marriage** tales.

The most famous text of Beauty and the Beast is that recorded by Mme Leprince de Beaumont in her *Magasin des Enfans* (1756). According to this version, Beauty is the youngest of three daughters of a merchant fallen on hard times. One day he leaves the cottage to go into town on business which he hoped might restore his fortunes; his two eldest daughters clamour for pretty gowns and laces but Beauty, when pressed to name the gift she desires, asks for a **rose**.

The merchant's hopes come to nothing and on the way back to his cottage, lost in a fierce storm, he takes shelter in a splendid castle. He is well provided for but sees nobody, and the next morning as he leaves he remembers his promise to Beauty and picks a rose from the garden. The Beast appears, outraged, but on hearing the merchant's explanation he allows him to go free, on condition that one of his daughters should return to the castle, or his life would be forfeit, and Beauty volunteers

Beauty and the Beast

herself. In other versions the sacrifice is to be the first living thing that advances to greet the merchant, which is not the dog, as he had expected, but Beauty.

The Beast treats Beauty with courtesy and generosity, but on seeing in a magic glass how lonely her father is she begs to return to him for one week. The Beast agrees, and gives her a magic token (a ring or a **mirror**) by which she can return to him. The weeks go by and Beauty stays with her father, but in a dream one night (or in the magic mirror) she sees the Beast dying and immediately returns to the palace to find him nearly dead. Broken-hearted, Beauty promises to become his wife and the spell is broken. The Beast returns to his original comely shape, and Beauty's two sisters (who had conspired against her throughout) are transformed into statues who must view their sister's happiness until they change their hearts.

Many variations of the tale exist: the Beast is a white **wolf** in Lithuanian, and a pig in Magyar, folklore, and in one Basque version he is a serpent. In a Kaffir tale the heroine agrees to lick the face of a **crocodile**, whereupon the handsome prince duly emerges.
▷ **Cupid and Psyche; Jephthah's vow**

bedclothes

THE IMPRINT LEFT BY THE BODY IN BEDCLOTHES can be used by unscrupulous magi-cians or evil spirits to cause the sleeper harm, since some of his or her soul seeps into it. Many superstitious people shake out the sheets and smooth the mattress on rising, to prevent an enemy from using the bedclothes to gain power over them.
▷ **Holle, Mother**

Bedivere

KNIGHT OF THE ROUND TABLE, companion and loyal butler of **Arthur**. He was the one to obey the wounded king's request to throw **Excalibur** into the lake after the battle with **Mordred**, and he carried Arthur to the waiting women and the boat that were to bear him off to **Avalon**.

bee

TRADITIONALLY A SYMBOL OF WISDOM AND INDUSTRY in European belief. In Egyptian mythology and Christian lore the bee is said to have sprung from the tears of Ra the sun god and Christ respectively. In ancient mythology bees were known as messengers of the gods, and in some places the tradition survives of telling the bees of a death in the household, so they can report it to the gods. In Ireland especially, bees are taken into confidence over any new enterprise, a superstition which presumably originated with the desire to secure divine aid, and in Scotland bees are proverbially wise. In medieval lore, bees became a symbol of eloquence, and in the iconography of **saints** such as Ambrose a swarm of bees as emblem denotes great verbal skill. In folktales bees often display a remnant of their ancient role, acting as God's spies. Like some birds, they are often regarded as portents of death or disaster, particularly when they come in a swarm. A single bee in the house is more usually interpreted as a sign that a visitor is on the way, although if it does not fly straight but dies in the house, bad luck is imminent. Where belief in the **separable soul** is strong, bees are often considered to be manifestations of the soul absent from the body.

The nutritional properties of honey have long been known, and the sticky propolis with which they repair their nests has been used medicinally for over 2 000 years. Primitive homeopathic practices have promoted bee-stings as a cure for arthritis, gout and rheumatism.

▷ **wasp**

beetle

INSECT SPECIES OF FOLKLORE. There are many thousands of species of beetle throughout the world, and the folklore of some is highly specific. The ladybird, for example, was considered lucky in Europe since it was the 'little bird' sacred to the Virgin **Mary**, and the long black dharbhdaol of Ireland is known as the Devil's coach horse, or even as the Devil himself, eating the bodies of sinners. In Egyptian mythology, the **scarab**'s habit of forming a ball of dung around its egg led to a belief in spontaneous generation and to the adoption of the scarab beetle as the symbol of life itself, the force that moved the sun across the sky and the principle of reincarnation (since only one egg was laid at a time it was assumed that the emerging beetle was a new incarnation). Scarab **amulets** were commonly buried with the dead and carried by the living. Some native South American tribes regard the Great Beetle as their creator figure.

The death-watch beetle is the focus of much popular superstition; to hear one in the house is an omen of death, and when it stops ticking a sick person will die. A beetle flying in and out of the house portends unexpected news, and it is thought lucky to righten a beetle which is helpless upon its back. Although most beetles tend to be regarded as symbols of corruption, associated with death, darkness and dankness, the earwig is used medicinally, either pulped and applied to the ear or beheaded and held so that the drop of blood falls into the ear. This common folk remedy for earache seems to derive wholly from the insect's name, which by folk etymology is explained as a result of its propensity for invading human ears.

Befana

BENEFICENT SPIRIT OF ITALIAN LORE, an old fairy woman who fills children's stockings with presents during Twelfth Night, the eve of the **Epiphany** (her name is said to derive from Latin *epiphania*). In many areas celebrations are organized for her coming, with music filling the streets and Befana-dolls placed in the windows of houses hoping to receive a visit.

According to Christian legend, Befana was invited by the wise men seeking the baby Jesus to join them in their quest, but refused because she was so busy with household tasks, and said

Befana

Béfind

that she would see them and attend to them more fully when they passed again. However the magi travelled home by a different route, and each year since Befana has looked for them to join in the worship of the Christchild.

Although she leaves toys and sweetmeats in the stockings of good children, their naughty siblings can expect nothing but pebbles and lumps of charcoal. She is also known as St Befana, la Strega and la Vecchia.

▷ **Christmas**; **Santa Claus**; **Nicholas, St**; **Wandering Jew**

Béfind

CELTIC BENEFICENT FAIRY, one of the three attendant spirits at the birth of a child, who predict the child's future and endow it with fairy gifts. To win their favour, as such gifts could often be of doubtful value (see **Sleeping Beauty**), a table would often be laid for them in the birth room. Béfind was said to be the wife of the mortal Idath, by whom she gave birth to Fraech, and her sister was **Bóann**, queen of the Irish **sidhe**. Her role is closely linked to the classical concept of the three female fates, or Parcae.

▷ **three**

Beggar of Bethnal Green

THE SUBJECT OF AN OLD ENGLISH BALLAD, recorded in Percy's *Reliques of Ancient English Poetry*. Bessee, the beggar's beautiful daughter, was the object of four men's attentions; a rich gentleman, a knight, a wealthy London merchant and the son of an innkeeper. To test their devotion she required of them all that they ask the permission of her father, the 'poor blind beggar of Bednall Green'. Only the knight had the constancy and humility to perform this task, upon which he was given by the seeming beggar a substantial **dowry** and the money for a wedding dress. Bessee's father is revealed as a lord who has disguised himself to procure a worthy husband for his daughter.

Behemoth

FABULOUS CREATURE, the king of the animals in Jewish lore. Scholars have disputed whether the original creature referred to in Job 11:15 is a **hippo-**potamus or an **elephant**. In later lore the creature was conceived of as a fabulous monster, whose capacity for food was so prodigious that God wisely provided him with no urges towards reproduction, since the earth's resources can barely support one such creature. He is the land-dwelling counterpart of **Leviathan**, who will be defeated at the coming of the Messiah and whose meat will serve the chosen people at the great feast of that day. Behemoth is also the name of a fearsome demon in Jewish lore.

Behemoth also appears in a rather different form in Muslim legend, where he is a cosmic fish on whose back stands the great bull supporting the **ruby** on which the earth is founded.

▷ **Atlas motif**

bell

HOLLOW VESSEL, USUALLY OF METAL, struck by a clapper or hammer to produce a ringing noise by vibration. Found throughout the world, bells have as their consistent primary function the driving away of evil spirits. Ancient Hebrew priests wore robes fringed with gold bells to protect them as they entered and left the temple, medieval churches rang bells to fend off the **Devil**, and those demons not scared off by the gargoyles, and Native South American shamans used bells to protect themselves from evil influence as they worked their magic. The hand-held bells of the **Morris dance** were originally designed to drive away malevolent spirits and ensure health and fertility in the fields, and animals wore bells around their necks for protection primarily and only secondarily as a means of locating them. The bells rung to mark the death of an individual protect the mourners from envious ghosts, while the joyful peals at a wedding serve to drive away spirits jealous of the general happiness and that of the couple in particular. The Christian rite of **exorcism** is a clear indication of the potency ascribed to the bell; bell book and candle, all highly symbolic, are the priest's only tools. Medieval witch hunts were generally accompanied by frenzied clanging of bells.

As well as demons and evil spirits, **fairy** folk find the ringing of bells hard to bear. Teutonic legend holds that it was

60

Chou dynasty bell

the ringing of church bells that drove the **dwarfs**, **trolls** and other mountain people out of Germany and Scandinavia, and fairies often complain of the disturbance to their sport and rest caused by church bells. However the Celtic **seelie court** are renowned for the tinkling bells on bridles and gowns that mark their passage in the hunt, which reinforces the antipathetic link between bells and evil spirits.

The function of bells as warning devices, used to communicate over great distances, has bred a variety of tales in which bells ring spontaneously as omens of coming disaster. One European tale tells of the bell cast from the 30 pieces of silver Judas received for betraying Jesus which rang itself before calamitous events. In **ballad** lore Sir Hugh of Lincoln's fate is mourned by the bells of Lincoln without human assistance. The many buried or underground bells of Europe (see **drowned civilizations**) are also said to ring at ominous moments or occasions such as Christmas Eve. Some bells even speak, pealing out the name of the benefactor who subsidized them or revealing an injustice to the townsfolk.

Bells have been used in healing as objects capable of driving away evil influence and of purifying the air. In early African–American belief, a stutter could be cured by drinking from a bell and thereby transferring to oneself its clear, pure tone.

Several European folktales tell of founders who purloin the precious metals charged to them for the casting of bells, replacing them with inferior materials, and are inevitably discovered and punished. St Agatha's close association with bell-founding arose from a misinterpretation of medieval iconography, which showed the saint holding on a tray before her her two amputated breasts, which do indeed resemble bells.

belladonna

DEADY NIGHTSHADE, *Atropa belladonna*, of the family Solanaceae. The leaves and roots of this highly poisonous plant can be dried to give a toxic drug with medicinal applications. Its name, which is Italian for 'beautiful woman', is explained either by the common practice of using belladonna in the eyes to enlarge and brighten the pupils, or by a legend that a villain named Leucota used it to murder beautiful women.

belling the cat

FOLKTALE MOTIF, found throughout Europe and in parts of Africa, best known in the West in the form of **Aesop**'s fable. A counsel of mice is called to address the intractable problem of the cat that preys on their community. A suggestion is made that if someone were to attach a bell to the cat's neck, the mice would always know the whereabouts of their enemy and could never be surprised. The plan receives universal approval, until an elderly mouse points out that a volunteer is needed to approach the cat in the first place and tie on the bell, at which point all enthusiasm wanes. The phrase has become proverbial for any impossible solution, or a situation in which one person must sacrifice himself for the ultimate benefit of others.

Belly and its Members, The

FABLE OF AESOP, belonging to a widespread family of folk narratives dealing with conversation and debate between the various parts of the body. Aesop's version tells how the various parts of the body began one day to express their resentment of the Belly, which did no work but guzzled everything they spent

61

their time acquiring, and finally decided that they would no longer slave for this idle, thankless member. The Hands refused to carry food to the Mouth, the Mouth refused to admit food to the Belly, and the Legs refused to carry the Belly's weight a step further. In time of course all the parts began to fail, and they realized that the Belly's role was in fact a vital one, and that all parts are mutually dependent and must work together.

Moralistic tales with this theme occur in many different cultures, including Buddhist, Bantu, Indian, Jewish and Indonesian. It is probable that the Apostle Paul had this ancient tale in mind when he exhorted the Corinthians to see themselves as the body of Christ, in which all parts are useful.

belomancy

DIVINATION BY MEANS OF ARROWS. This ancient custom, known to have been practised by Babylonians, Scythians, Arabs and others, consisted of messages attached to a number of arrows, all of which were fired. The inscription on the arrow travelling the furthest was accepted as the answer, and its advice acted upon.

Other techniques include the use of lettered arrows, fired to spell out the oracular message by the way in which they land, and a Gold Coast trial of innocence, analogous to the ducking of **witches** in Europe, was performed with poisoned arrows.

Belphegor

ORIGINALLY A GOD OF THE MOABITES, whose name was attached in medieval times to a misogynistic demon. Concerned about the rumours reaching them of the bliss of the married state, the demons dispatched one of their number to test its truth. Belphegor spent some time trying out the role of husband, and after several different experiences of wedded life he retired in some haste back to Hell, where he was free at least of the torment of a nagging wife. Later writers such as Machiavelli and Ben Jonson alluded to the experiment knowingly in their works, and the name became a byword for a misogynistic, licentious fellow.

Beltane

CELTIC MAY FESTIVAL. The start of spring was celebrated with a great bonfire, through which people and animals passed to secure good fortune. One unfortunate person, to whom fell the charred portion of the ritual cake, would be symbolically sacrificed and treated as though dead thereafter for the next year, probably a survival of early human sacrificial rituals.
▷ **May day**

bendith y mamau see tylwyth teg

Bengodi

LITERARY OTHERWORLD, described in Boccaccio's *Decameron*, akin to the Land of **Cockaigne**, having mountains of cheese and rivers of finest-quality wine, with vines tied back with strings of sausages. Its inhabitants have nothing to do all day long, other than enjoy this sumptuous richness.

Ben-Varrey

THE MANX MERMAID, a rather more affable creature than her cousins in other waters. Although she, like other mermaids, is said to lure men to their deaths by her beauty and her siren song, there are many tales of the Ben-Varrey warning sailors of coming storms, and rewarding humans who show kindness. One unusual tale tells how a baby Ben-Varrey stole the doll of a human child, but was commanded by her mother to take the child a beautiful necklace of pearls in payment for her prize.
▷ **mermaid**

Beowulf

ANGLO-SAXON HERO, one of the most famous of all the ancient **dragonslayers**. *Beowulf* was probably composed in about AD700, the earliest vernacular epic of Europe. The earliest extant manuscript, which is anonymous, dates from c.1000. The story is a blend of legend based on history and pure folkloric invention, with many floating motifs attached to the hero Beowulf.

The tale is set around modern Jutland; Beowulf is the leader of the Geats of southern Sweden who sails to the aid of his kinsman Hrothgar, King of the

Beowulf

Danes. Hrothgar's hall, Heorot, has been plagued for twelve years by a monster called **Grendel** who attacks by night and devours Hrothgar's warriors. Beowulf's offer of help is received courteously by the king and with scepticism by some others, but that night when Grendel attacks the hall Beowulf engages him in combat, gripping him so powerfully that, although the beast escapes, his arm is torn off and he later dies. There is much rejoicing in the Danish court when Beowulf tells what has happened, but the next night Grendel's mother comes to the hall seeking revenge and seizes one of the king's best-loved warriors. Beowulf follows her to her underwater cave and battles with her there. He defeats her, and returns to Hrothgar's hall bearing the head of Grendel.

As King of the Geats, Beowulf faces his third and final conflict. An enormous **dragon** is roused from its centuries-long torpor when a slave steals a precious cup from its hoard, and in fury begins to terrorize the land. Beowulf attacks the monster in a long and painful battle; most of his trusted followers desert him but one, the young Wiglaf, rushes to his aid and together they kill the dragon. Mortally wounded, Beowulf lives only long enough to see the treasure he has secured for his people. The rest of the poem is elegiac, telling of his funeral and lamenting the passing of so great a king.

It seems clear that the battles with Grendel and his mother derive from the ancient **Bear's Son cycle**, although the death of the hero is one of the elements which lifts the poem into the epic mode. The details of *Beowulf* are closely connected with Scandinavian sagas such as the *Samsonsaga* and the *Grettisaga*, in both of which the hero fights in an underwater cave and defeats a troll wife. Some Christianizing of the lore is apparent: Grendel and his mother are said to be descendants of Cain, the first murderer, and the poem is full of Christian allusion. But the ancient Germanic values of loyalty and vengeance are the deepest source of the action. It seems that the composer of *Beowulf* drew his material from a stock of North Germanic lore, added historical details of name and place, and, over what is essentially a pagan epic, a thin veneer of Christianity.

Berchta

HAG OF SOUTHERN GERMAN FOLKLORE, an ugly old woman invoked as a **bogey** to frighten children into good behaviour. She is thought to have originally been a goddess, like her northern counterpart Hulda, perhaps the earth-goddess Erda, but her mythical aspect declined with the advent of Christianity and she was transformed into a witch or hobgoblin.

Despite Berchta's personal slovenliness, her chief concern is cleanliness and hard work in the houses that she visits particularly in the period between Christmas and her feast-day, Twelfth Night. If all is not spick and span, if there is old flax on the spinning wheel or dirty straw on the floor, she will inflict diseases on the occupants or terrify the livestock. Despite her harshness however she has a special fondness for good children, and has been known to slip into the nursery to rock the cradle when the mother is absent. In some tales she is said to have a trail of children following her, either unborn infant spirits or the souls of dead children.

Food must be left out for Berchta on Twelfth Night, else she will cut open a human stomach to get at the food and sew it up using a plowshare as a needle and iron chains as thread. She is sometimes depicted as having a single foot and a nose made from iron.
▷ **Baba Yaga**

berries in winter

FOLKTALE TYPE, a form of the impossible **tasks and tests** tale in which the protagonist is typically sent out to collect berries (in some versions roses or fruit) in winter, often in an attempt to kill him or her. Grimm collected the best-known Western example, *The Three Little Men in the Wood*; in it a cruel stepmother sends out a child dressed in a paper frock to collect **strawberries**, telling her not to return until she has the fruit. The girl is taken in by three little men who live in the forest who warm her by their fire. She offers them a share of the crust she has to eat, and they give her a broom and tell her to clear the snow from the doorstep. She does so, and discovers a pile of beautifully ripe strawberries beneath it, which she takes back to her astonished stepmother. This is often incorporated into a larger **Cinderella**-type tale.

The motif occurs also in Native American tales, particularly among groups of the North Pacific coast, as one of a series of tests imposed by a jealous father-in-law (or occasionally brother) on a suitor. In one ingenious version, the hero is challenged to perform this task but he excuses himself by claiming that his father is suffering from a snakebite, an impossible occurrence in winter. This motif, absurdity rebukes absurdity, is a popular one in Native American and African lore.

berserker

NORSE WARRIOR, one possessed by ferocious battle-madness. The name means 'bear-shirt', and indeed the berserkers were almost shapeshifters, changing their peace-time human forms for that of a maddened bear or wolf, howling and foaming at the mouth. They wore no armour but were impervious to their enemies' attacks, and were said to be possessed by Odin.

Berchta

Bertha see **Berchta**

bestiaries

REPOSITORIES OF ANIMAL LORE, encompassing both real and fabulous beasts, a literary vogue of the Middle Ages in particular. The origins of the genre are usually traced back to the anonymous second-century AD *Physiologus*, a work of scholarship combining biblical passages, philosophy, animal fables and primitive natural science. The text circulated widely in medieval Western Europe, along with St Ambrose's *Hexameron* (fourth century) and St Isidore of Seville's *Etymology* (early seventh century). Translations of such texts circulated widely and medieval Continental writers took up the form

'The True Face of the Lamia' from The Historie of Foure-Footed Beastes *(1607)*

with enthusiasm, including Guillaume de Clerc and Richard de Fournival, who in the 14th century pressed it into service as a satirical allegory for love in his *Bestiaire d'Amour*.

The enormous popularity and diffusion of these texts ensured that the stories associated with the animals (often themselves derived from ancient oral tradition) passed ultimately into literary convention and folk wisdom. Popular conceptions of the **unicorn** and the **phoenix**, among others, derive from medieval bestiaries, and their lavish illustrations helped to dignify the most spurious tales with credibility.

Bhagavadgita

SANSKRIT LYRIC POEM, the 'Song of God'. Found in Book VI of the *Mahabharata*,

this beautiful poem takes the form of a dialogue in which Krishna reveals himself to Arjuna, leader of the Pandava princes who has called upon him for guidance. The god, who had until this point been serving as Arjuna's charioteer and companion, eloquently instructs the prince in the obligations of caste and the nature of faith and duty. The poem is considered one of the greatest texts of the Hindu religion, and certainly one of the best loved, embracing not only the human dilemma of Arjuna, faced with the unwelcome prospect of a bloody war, but the nature of spirituality and of man's relationship to God.

The poem is thought to be a later addition to the *Mahabharata*, composed perhaps in the first or second century AD. It consists of three sections, each of which contains six chapters; in total 700 Sanskrit verses. Worshippers of Ganesha, the elephant-headed god, composed a version of the poem known as the Ganesha-gita.

bhuta

MALEVOLENT SPIRITS OF HINDU FOLKLORE. The term is a wide one, used to refer to troublesome **ghosts** of those who have died with unfinished business or at their own hand, as well as supernatural **goblins**. They are said to inhabit graveyards and forests, lurking to prey on the flesh of the living, and can possess the bodies of the dead to trick their victims. They cast no shadow. The best method of protection from a bhuta is simply to lie prone, as they cannot settle on the ground, and burning **turmeric** is a useful **charm** to ward them off.

bibliomancy

DIVINATION BY MEANS OF BOOKS, particularly a sacred text, also known as *sortes*. Virgil's *Aeneid* was the favoured book in classical times and in the Middle Ages (*sortes Vergilianae*), but the Bible and the Koran have also been utilized, among others. In essence, this technique involves opening a book at random and selecting a verse by pointing at it blindly; the advice, prophecy or warning contained in that passage is then the oracular truth to be applied to the state of the one seeking guidance. The practice has given rise to its own folklore; Gordianus is said to have lighted on 'Fate only showed him this earth, and suffered him not to tarry' shortly before his death, and the anecdote of the man who read of Judas's suicide, 'He went out and hanged himself' (Matthew 27:5) and then turned to the phrase 'Go then and do likewise' (Luke 10:37) is widely circulated as a humorous warning against such random divination.

In a rather different form of divination by the Bible, a suspected person was weighed in the balance against the Great Bible, and if (as must invariably have happened) he or she was found to be heavier, it was considered an indication of guilt.

Bicorn

MYTHICAL CREATURE, a cow of medieval French lore that was said to achieve corpulence and satisfaction by feasting on patient, virtuous husbands. Its antithetical twin, the skeletal Chichevache, fed only on good and patient wives.

biersal

GERMAN SPIRIT OF THE BEER-CELLAR, a mischievous **kobold** that inhabits the cellar and will keep the mugs and bottles sparking clean as long as his host provides him with a jug of beer for himself each day. If this courtesy is forgotten, the biersal, like so many other **mischievous spirits**, can become more of a nuisance than a blessing.
▷ **cluricaun**

Bigfoot

FABULOUS CREATURE OF NORTH AMERICAN MOUNTAINEERING FOLKLORE, also known as Sasquatch. It is the equivalent of the abominable snowman or **Yeti**, said to be 2–3m/7–10ft tall; its footprints are reported to be 43cm/17in long.

Big Owl

MONSTER OF THE APACHES, an evil, cannibalistic giant, usually in the form of an owl, who transfixes his victims with a glance from his hideous eye and takes them home to consume. In many Apache tales he is the child of the Sun, who after wreaking devastation among

humans is killed by his **culture hero** brother.
▷ **evil eye**

Billy Blind

HOUSEHOLD SPIRIT OF ENGLAND AND SCOTLAND, a popular figure of **ballad** lore but oddly absent in other narrative forms. His role is generally a benevolent one; he protects the house and family, and is quick to offer helpful advice and practical assistance. In *Willie's Lady* for example, a ballad collected by Child, Billy Blind informs the hero that his mother, a witch, is working spells against the birth of his son. By following the spirit's advice Willie tricks his mother into thinking that the baby has been safely delivered (holding a christening service for a dummy) and by the astonished witch's soliloquy he discovers the spells that have been laid on his wife and the means by which to remove them.

Billy Blind is also referred to as Billy Blin, Belly Blin and Blind Barlow.

Billy the Kid

AMERICAN FOLK HERO, real name William H Bonney Jnr (1859–81). He was in fact a ruthless bandit, said to have murdered 16 men by the time he was so many years old. Born in New York City, the young Bonney moved to Kansas with his family and then on to New Mexico, where he began his brief but memorable life of crime. He was shot by Sheriff Patrick Floyd Garrett after escaping from jail and the death sentence several months earlier. His lawlessness chimed with the pioneering spirit, and his daring and ingenuity won him the respect and posthumous affection of many Americans, including those who had clamoured for his execution.

birch

TREE OR SHRUB of the genus *Betula* family Betulaceae, found in cool areas of the Northern hemisphere. The birch is notable particularly for its bark, which may be grey, silvery-white or coloured, and characteristically peels from the young tree in thin horizontal sheets. It is widely used in folk medicine to treat nearly every ill; it heals wounds, prevents infertility, cures consumption and dissolves kidney stones, and it is powerful as a **charm** against the **evil eye**, lightning and gout.

Brushes made from birch twigs have been used across Europe for centuries; Roman magistrates sent their officers ahead of them to clear the way with bundles of birch twigs; Russian bathers used birch branches to scourge and cleanse the body in the steam baths; and in England the 'besom broom' of birch was a highly respected means of beating a witch out of the house. Supposed madmen were often thrashed with birch branches as a means of expelling the demons that had possession of them. Christian legend tells how a branch of the dwarf birch was used to scourge the back of Christ at the Crucifixion, and that it has ever since been unable to hold up its head.

In the Old Irish tree alphabet, *beth* (B, meaning birch) is the first letter and therefore the symbol of the start of the year. The birch is particularly significant in Estonia, as the national tree, and in Scandinavia it was said to be sacred to Thor.

▷ **alder**; **hazel**

birds

WARM-BLOODED FLYING VERTEBRATES, whose capacity for flight has earned them a central place in human folk consciousness. Birds often represent the disembodied soul, especially the **separable soul** absent from the body during sleep or illness, or the escaped soul released after death. Souls in the form of birds are distinct from the soulmate of a living human, the **bush soul**, occurring when a human child and a bird are born simultaneously and share a common destiny. Sailors revere stormy petrels (known as Mother Carey's chickens) as the embodiment of the souls of their dead comrades. In various mythologies gods have been represented with bird characteristics, from the **hawk** as Horus in ancient Egypt to the Holy Spirit appearing as a **dove** in Christian tradition. In many legends birds are messengers of the gods, bringing news from heaven to earth and back, and as an extension of this role they are often represented in folklore as figures bearing truth (see **raven**). The 'bird of truth' is a common folktale motif.

A whole array of mythical creatures shares the characteristics of birds with those of humans or other animals, from flying beings such as angels and fairies to composite figures such as the winged **Gorgon** and **Sphinx**. Although in most European folktales birds are helpful bringers of truth, they are a favourite guise (particularly as black **crows**) for **witches**, and can often work unwittingly or mischievously to bring trouble to the human protagonists. Birds devour the crumbs dropped by Hansel to mark the path home in **Hansel and Gretel**, and a common folktale motif is the bird that steals a jewel thereby causing an innocent servant to be accused. This is particularly common in Asian tales, found in the *Panchatantra* and the *Arabian Nights*.

In most tales the ability of birds to converse with humans is taken for granted, but the acquisition of bird language is a feature of many Celtic, European and Asian tales. Particularly holy **saints** were said in Christian legend to speak with the birds, for example St **Francis of Assisi** and St Rose of Lima. St Cuthbert too was renowned for his kinship with the eider ducks of Lindisfarne. In *The White Snake*, a folktale collected by Grimm, a servant eats part of his master the king's dinner and finds himself able to understand animals and birds; the eating of a snake is a common European method for acquiring the gift of bird-language. Another method is to aid a bird in need, who may then grant the gift as a reward.

birds

Birds appear widely in superstitions; a bird in the house is thought to be ominous by many, an sign of important news on the way or an imminent death. A **wren** nesting near the house is a good sign, and the call of the whip-poor-will is particularly lucky if you have the presence of mind to make a wish on the first time of hearing it that year, but the **owl's** hoot is more ominous. Bird behaviour is whimsically explained in legend; the **wagtail** spends its life attempting to shake off three drops of the Devil's blood from its tail, and the nightingale's achingly beautiful song escapes as it presses its breast onto a thorn to stay awake all night, for fear of snakes. Images of birds are inappropriate at wedding celebrations, lest they fly away with the couple's luck. Birds celebrate their own wedding feast in a popular European folk song, *The Birds' Wedding*. Here all the different birds species and some animal ones intermarry (Edward Lear's Owl and Pussycat are relics of such a match).
▷ **bat; Faithful John**

birth see **childbirth**

birthdays

ANNUAL RITE OF PASSAGE, the charting of the progress of the individual. Birthdays are by no means a universal concept; some Australian Aborigines designate their children by generation, encoded in the name, and keep no further count of age, and similar practices have been reported among some Native North American and African groups, amongst whom counting is considered evil.

Like any period of transition in life, birthdays are hedged around with danger. The celebrant is particularly vulnerable to evil spirits and envious ghosts, and the custom of surrounding oneself with well-wishers and loud noise may derive from this need for protection. As the 'bless you' spoken after a **sneeze**, the good wishes of friends are thought to combat any evil influences. The giving of presents and the shared meal are a reconfirmation of the individual's accepted place within the larger society.

As a mark of transition, the birthday is a logical occasion for rites of **initiation** and demonstrations of achievement; these may be as simple as the challenge to blow out all the candles on the birthday cake or as elaborate as the religious initiations of Christian confirmation or Jewish bar-mitzvah in adolescence.

The date of birth is the starting-point of astrological prediction and analysis, and the month of one's birthday determines the **birthstone** that should be worn.

birthstones

AMULETIC GEMS, said to bring luck depending on their magical sympathy with the month of the wearer's birth. There are many local and historical variations, but this is a standard table of birthstones by month:

January	garnet
February	amethyst
March	aquamarine, jasper, bloodstone
April	diamond, sapphire
May	emerald, agate, carnelian
June	pearl, moonstone
July	ruby, onyx, turquoise
August	sardonyx, peridot
September	sapphire
October	opal, tourmaline, beryl
November	topaz
December	turquoise, lapis lazuli

black

COLOUR OF FOLKLORE. Because of its natural association with darkness and night, traditionally the domain of spirits, and also because of the ethnocentricity of white European groups dominant in politics and colonization for much of history, black has come to be used as symbolic shorthand for anything mysterious, evil or ugly. Hence **witches** were thought to keep black cats as familiars, the Black Mass was a sacrilegious travesty of the Christian rite performed by Satanists, and the Black Dwarfs are less kindly to humans than their lighter counterparts. This is not invariable however; in Scottish lore the blackfoot was a matchmaker or pander, who if he betrayed his trust would be termed a whitefoot.

Black is also in Western tradition the

colour of mourning, and this has been utilized in folktales in the motif of black and white sails. In the classical tale, Theseus returns home victorious having defeated the **Minotaur** but forgets in his haste the promise extracted from him by his father Aegeus, that he will signal his victory by changing the black sails that had borne the Minotaur's victims to Crete to white. His watching father assumes that Theseus is dead, and in anguish throws himself into the sea (see also **Tristam and Iseult**).
▷ **colour**

Black Annis

CANNIBALISTIC MONSTER, a **hag** with a blue face, long white teeth, a single eye and claws of iron, said to inhabit a cave in the Dane Hills of Leicester. She preys on lone travellers or on children, even snatching infants from houses when times are lean. She could be kept at bay by herbs efficacious against **witches**.
▷ **cailleach bheure**

Blackbeard

ENGLISH PIRATE, real name Edward Teach (d.1718). After serving as a soldier in the War of the Spanish Succession (1701–13), Teach began a lucrative career as a pirate, terrorizing the Atlantic coast of America and the Caribbean waters. The governor of North Carolina, where Teach based his activities, traded a part in the booty for a policy of non-interference, and Blackbeard continued his outrages of sadistic brutality and piracy. Finally a British naval force was sent in from Virginia and Blackbeard was defeated. According to popular legend the head, with the luxuriant beard and braided whiskers which had gained the pirate his name, was impaled on a spar of his ship and later made into a drinking cup, while the headless corpse swam three times round the ship before sinking.

Black Bess

LEGENDARY HORSE, the mount of highwayman Dick **Turpin**. She was created by William Harrison Ainsworth in *Rookwood*, a romance of 1834, as the horse that bore Turpin on his notorious ride to York.

Black Dogs

OMINOUS SPECTRES, generally foreboding death to the one who sees them. Celtic travellers who found themselves accompanied by a large black dog, making none of the usual doggy noises such as panting or the clatter of claws, would generally be seized by a deep despair and despondency, which in itself might eventually bring about death. More usually, the dog is a sign of impending doom. The beast has several names; it is known as the barghest in the north of England (where it is occasionally reported as headless) and the Moddey Doo in the Isle of Man.

Elsewhere in England, and particularly in Somerset, there is a tradition of a benevolent Black Dog which accompanies lone travellers as a silent protector and guide.
▷ **gytrash**

black magic see **witchcraft**

Bladud

MYTHICAL ENGLISH KING, father of **Lear**. A would-be magician, he was killed in a failed attempt at flying when his artificial wings gave way and he fell into the Temple of Apollo. He built Bath and dedicated its springs to Minerva. Our information about him comes from the unreliable Geoffrey of Monmouth's *Historia regum Britanniae*.

Blánik

KEY SITE OF CZECH NATIONALISM, a hillside beneath which a troop of Hussites (followers of the Bohemian reformer John Hus, martyred in 1415) sleep awaiting the call of their country in its need.
▷ **sleepers**

Blarney stone

MAGICAL STONE OF IRELAND, with the power to bestow eloquence on anyone who kisses it. Set in the wall below the parapet of Blarney Castle near Cork, the stone can nowadays only be reached with some danger to life and limb, as the kisser must lower himself down from the very top. Legend has it that Cormac MacCarthy faced a difficult lawsuit in the 15th century, and was advised in a

Blarney stone

dream by **Clíodna**, one of the fairy queens of Munster, to kiss the first stone he came across in the morning. He pleaded his case with such eloquence that he feared all the country would want to kiss his marvellous stone, and therefore caused it to be set where it remains today. Another, more historically plausible, version of the legend tells how MacCarthy made a laughing-stock of Elizabeth I's official Lord Carew by his smooth talking, continually promising the surrender of his castle while never actually delivering it up.

Blemmyes

FABULOUS RACE OF ETHIOPIA, said to inhabit Nubia and parts of Upper Egypt. According to Roman writers they had no head; features such as the eyes and mouth were located in their chests.

blood

THE ESSENCE OF LIFE, a substance bound up in folk belief around the world with the continued life, health, courage and soul of all life. Primitive peoples have interpreted blood flowing from the body as a sign of life itself draining away, which of course it effectively is, and hence identified it with that life. Since it contains the life of the individual, then, it must be carefully guarded since if spilled blood were to come into the hands of an enemy skilled in **magic** it would put the victim in that enemy's power. Blood that soaks into the ground has the power of making that ground at worst barren or dangerous, at best holy. Blood is frequently portrayed like sperm, as a life-giving fluid that engenders life when it falls to (impregnates) the ground (the **Furies** sprang from the blood of Uranus, for example).

The dietary laws of many religions are based on the avoidance of unclean animal blood, and in general folk belief the blood of certain animals is said to impart certain qualities, according to the principles of **sympathetic magic**. Warriors going into battle will often drink the blood of fierce creatures such as **lions**, while they would avoid that of an animal such as the **hare**. In folk medicine a sickly child is given the blood of a healthy playmate to drink, and a newborn boy might be given a little of his father's blood to impart bravery and the qualities of manhood.

Blood can function as a **life token** even after death; a common European belief is that a corpse will begin to bleed afresh in the presence of the murderer. Murderers may also find it difficult to remove the accusatory bloodstains from their hands, clothes or weapons (as Lady Macbeth discovered). Ineradicable blood as a sign of guilt appears too in the **Bluebeard** tale. A popular American urban legend tells of the 'death car', an expensive sporty make that is being sold for a song because a man committed suicide in it and the blood stains on the back seat, along with the stench of death, cannot be removed.

Because of its immense significance, blood is widely used in contracts and covenants to signify an unbreakable pledge. Two individuals swearing mutual protection and eternal amity seal their promise by making ritual cuts and mingling the blood in the vein—they become blood brothers. A Roman pledge of immense solemnity was taken by mingling the blood of the parties in a cup, from which each would drink. Many warrior groups, such as the **Red Branch** and the Knights of the **Round Table**, pledged their loyalty in a blood covenant. The Christian rite of the Eucharist or Mass, in which believers partake of the body and blood of Christ, echoes this ancient significance of both life-giving essence and solemn pledge.

Since members of the same family are bound by blood ties, the blood feud is a common phenomenon; a member of the family must satisfy the blood of a murdered relative by spilling the blood of the murderer or one of his relatives.
▷ **menstruation**

Bluebeard

EPONYMOUS VILLAIN OF A EUROPEAN FOLKTALE, archetype of the murderous husband. The brothers Grimm included the tale in the first edition of their *Nursery and Household Tales* only; in the revised edition of 1819 *Blaubart* was omitted, ostensibly because it was too obviously French rather than German in origin, relying too heavily upon Perrault's literary version, and also because the gory subject matter was considered unsuitable for children.

Bluebeard is generally a wealthy merchant or tailor who takes several brides (usually seven sisters) in sequence but all mysteriously die. Finally he marries the youngest sister. Some time later he leaves on a journey, entrusting the keys of his castle to his bride. One room only does he forbid her to enter or even approach. His wife is of course consumed by curiosity, and leaving her friends who are busy exclaiming over the riches of the castle she slips upstairs and unlocks the forbidden door. Behind it she finds a scene of horrific carnage— the corpses of her sisters, Bluebeard's previous wives.

Her disobedience is revealed to Bluebeard on his return by a magic token— either an **egg** that he charged her to keep safe is broken, or the key itself becomes indelibly bloody—and he begins to menace her. She saves herself by prevarication, begging time in which to prepare herself for death, or pray for her sisters. In some versions she is saved by the approach of her brothers, in others by a page whom she then marries, in others she herself kills Bluebeard with a sabre. In some late forms of the tale she resuscitates her sisters and tricks Bluebeard into carrying them home where he is killed by her brothers, while she, disguised as a bird, flies above him.

This seems to be an ancient and traditional folktale; it was included in Perrault's *Contes de ma Mère l'Oye* in the 17th century and in its various versions is widespread throughout Europe. In Italy the villain figure is the **Devil**, in Scandinavia a **troll**, but in the version immortalised in literary tradition he is a man, sometimes a magician, whose chief peculiarity is the vivid blue of his beard. Both Perrault and the Grimm brothers emphasize the moral point of the story as a warning against curiosity on the part of the woman, and many commentators have seen in the tale a double warning; for children to obey their father's authority, and for wives to obey their husband lest they incite his wrath. This is an interesting example of the changes and cultural weight invested in a tale, which was originally a grisly adventure story telling of an **ogre** and the rescue of his victim.

The motif of the murderous husband is found in many tales worldwide, and the key motifs of the forbidden door and chamber are among the basic building blocks of folktales. In later editions of *Nursery and Household Tales*, the tale of Mary's Child replaces the story of Bluebeard. Here the figure of authority is the Blessed Virgin herself, and the moral imperative against disobedience is therefore made unambiguous.

The tale has been a favourite with folklorists applying a psychoanalytical reading to folk narrative. Bluebeard's chamber is said to contain the corpses of previous wives or others on which Bluebeard fed, or an enormous basin of blood, and in the symbolism of flesh, blood and guilt psychoanalytic readings have seen the suggestion of **adultery**, and suggested that the tale was a warning against unfaithfulness.

blues

TYPE OF LYRIC FOLK MUSIC, a secular form developed by American blacks in the South soon after the Civil War which has proved an enormous influence on many forms of popular music since. The characteristics of blues music are an eight- or more commonly twelve-bar structure; syncopation and the complex rhythmic qualities typical of African music; a wide range of vocal tone making use of falsetto breaks, the flattened third and seventh intervals and non-verbal vocalizations (humming or 'scat', nonsense syllables); and a pervasive downbeat, melancholy mood and subject-matter.

Blues music grew out of the spirituals, call-and-response gospel songs, field hollers and **work songs** of the slaves, and its characteristic keynote is that of an oppressed, deprived but nonetheless poetic sensibility. The subject-matter ranges from the ever-present theme of lost love to the slave topics of hard work with no thanks to more sophisticated urban themes as the genre spread north along the Mississippi to Chicago. The earliest commercial blues singers were women vocalists backed by jazz bands, such as Ma Rainey and Bessie Smith, whose success followed on from the popular reception in 1912 of W C Handy's *Memphis Blues*, but with the diffusion of blacks during the Depression in the 1930s, a more specifically blues ensemble emerged.

Three different blues schools can be distinguished: the rhythmically regular blues of Georgia and North and South Carolina; the high-pitched singing and rippling arpeggios of Texas; and the moody, half-spoken lyricism of the Mississippi delta. This last style has been the most influential, employing features now firmly associated with blues music such as a slide or bottleneck to give the guitar strings a plaintive, whining, almost human tone. The strength of the blues lies in its soulful lyricism rather than the flow of narrative; as a means of creating a mood of emotional intensity it is unsurpassed. Although the original folk character of blues music has been largely lost in commercialization, its roots in folk culture are still considered a vital part of its compelling attraction.
▷ **jazz**

Blunderbore

GIANT OF ENGLISH FOLKLORE, a gull of the **Jack tales**. Hearing of Jack's exploits as a **giant**-killer, Blunderbore gives him a bed for the night intending to club him to death while he sleeps. The wary Jack however places a log in his bed and curls himself up on the floor beneath it, and the giant cudgels the senseless wood while Jack sleeps soundly. Next morning the giant, much surprised to see his guest still breathing, enquires how he slept, whereupon Jack replies that he fancied he had been tickled by a mouse's tail during the night.

By now much surprised, Blunderbore attempts to keep up with his guest in putting away vast quantities of hasty pudding for breakfast, unaware that Jack is in fact surreptitiously stashing the food in a bag under his clothes. When Jack plunges a knife into the bag to allow the porridge to escape Blunderbore, eager to relieve his fullness in the same way, sinks a knife into his belly and kills himself.

Bóann

OLD IRISH FAIRY QUEEN, ruler of the **Tuatha de Danann**, sister of **Béfind** and mother of **Angus Og**. In her arrogance, she boasted that the well of Nechtan, which none but Nechtan himself could look into for fear of losing his eyes, had no power over her, and proceeded not only to look into it but to walk three times anticlockwise around it. Three waves arose from the well, one taking out an eye, another a hand and the third a thigh, and Bóann fled in shame towards the sea. She was overtaken and drowned by the water in the river that now bears her name, the Boyne. In another version of the tale, Bóann is the wife of Nechtan who has an affair with the god **Dagda** and attempts to prove her innocence by walking round the well, with the same disastrous consequences.

boar

ANIMAL OF THE HUNT. Several heroes have been killed by boars while out hunting, including Adonis in Greek legend and Diarmuid in Celtic, and in Japan the beast is a symbol of the ideal qualities of a brave warrior. It has been a popular choice for sacrifice in Northern Europe, and it is from this custom that the tradition of serving a boar's head for Christmas dinner stems; a boar was sacrificed in Norse mythology at the feast of Freyr at Yuletide. A *Boar's Head Carol*, which would have been sung as the head was brought in ceremoniously, survives from the 15th century in the Bodleian Library, Oxford.

boats

boats

SMALL SAILING VESSELS, the construction and maintenance of which require much care. All the spiritual influences converging in a boat—timber, water, craftsman and deities—must harmonize if the boat is to be a trustworthy, secure craft which will find its way easily across the water. Ceremonies of blessing are common at nearly every stage of construction, including prayers, sacrifices and libations poured into the boat. A relic of this is the modern custom of smashing a bottle against the side of a boat while speaking a blessing over it immediately before launching.

A boat whose captain has died is unlikely to cooperate with a new master, and it is probably wiser to send boat and captain off together as a floating pyre, with the body lying in state and the boat set ablaze before being pushed off and left to drift.

▷ **figureheads**; **sailors' lore**

bodach

MALICIOUS SPIRIT, a Celtic **bogey** found chiefly in the Scottish Highlands. He appears as a shrivelled, wrinkled old man, who lives in the chimney keeping warm in the smoke of the fire. By night, when the fire is extinguished, he slides down the chimney and enters the room of a naughty child. He terrorizes the child by tweaking and pinching, pulling his or her eyes open and thus inducing the most frightful nightmares. He will not trouble good children, but a child who feels himself at risk can protect himself by sprinkling **salt** in the hearth, which the bodach will not cross.

The bodach glas is said to be a spectre foretelling death to those who see it.

Bodb

OLD IRISH HERO, son of **Dagda**, chosen king of the fairy folk, the **Tuatha de Danann** after the battle of Tailtiu. He features widely in the Irish **Mythological cycle**; he was the one who discovered for **Angus Og** the identity of his beloved Caer.

bogey

ENGLISH MONSTER, also known as the bogeyman, particularly used to terrify children into obedience. His appearance, beyond the fact that he is black, is a matter of mysterious conjecture, although it is generally accepted that he is masculine. As a shadowy figure of fear, the bogey has accumulated a reputation for all manner of wickedness and mischief. He is credited with many characteristics traditionally associated with evil: in one legend he is unable to seize a young donkey because of the protective cross on its back; in the legend of the Green Lady of Herefordshire the witch is revealed dancing with a bogey; and of course he is often credited with the power of **shape-shifting**. This last characteristic is one of the most enduring and fruitful of all folkloric themes so it is unsurprising that it has been linked with the figure of the bogey, but it is particularly appropriate as a warning for children to be wary of the unfamiliar, however innocent-seeming.

The natural habitat of the bogey is the night, and children often fear darkness because it may contain such monsters. The bogeyman is said to lurk in the dark to punish naughty children or, especially in the south west, to take away souls. Powerless in the daytime, like demons and ghosts across the world, the bogey is a relic of ancient fairy-lore, more closely linked to demons than flowers.

The derivation of the word bogey, also spelt bogie or bogy, is unclear. It seems likely that, along with other similar-sounding words such as **bogle** and **boggart**, it may be derived from the Middle English word *bugge*, meaning terror, as

73

in **bugbear**. In Old Welsh the form developed in a similar way, *bwg*. There are many dialectal variations, eg bogle in Scotland and boggle or boggart in Yorkshire, and bogie is probably a southern variation of the late 19th century. Claims that the word is connected to the Slavonic form *bog*, meaning 'god', are tempting but unlikely. In the 19th century, 'Old Bogey' was a common **euphemism** for the **Devil**. More recently, the 'bogey' has been adopted into the language of golf, denoting the number of strokes a good player might be expected to take for a course and therefore a standard target, from an anecdote that in 1890 one Major Wellman, playing by this new system, declared himself matched against a bogeyman. In modern use, after the introduction of more sophisticated equipment and therefore lower averages, it refers to a hole played one shot over par. Bogey, or bugbear, is still used to mean something which is feared, usually needlessly.

▷ **puck**

boggart

HOBGOBLIN FIGURE OF NORTHERN ENGLAND. Although closely related to the **bogey**, the boggart is more closely linked to a specific house. He is also said to perform helpful tasks in the house on occasion, although like many such **household spirits** he becomes mischievous when angered, and he is easily enraged. He generally displays a tendency towards poltergeist activities, mischievously rearranging furniture or rapping on windows, tormenting the family with mischievous pranks such as snatching food from their mouths, slamming doors and throwing crockery.

The boggart is as tenacious as he is troublesome; one famous Yorkshire tale tells how a farmer tormented by a boggart decided to leave his farm. As the final bits and pieces were loaded onto the cart, the farmer was explaining to a neighbour that the boggart was making life in the house intolerable when a voice from the top of the pile in the cart chimed in, 'So you see, Johnny, we're flitting'. So back went the family, since they might as well be tormented in the

old house as in a new one. Some folk traditions hold that the boggart is a troublesome ghost rather than a spirit.

▷ **hobgoblin**; **mischievous spirits**

bogle

MISCHIEVOUS SPIRIT, a **hobgoblin** found mainly in the Scottish borders (although sightings have been recorded in Lincolnshire), close kin to the Northern English **boggart** and the southern **puck**. Some tales do indicate that, while capable of general mischief, the bogle is especially quick to attack those guilty of petty crimes, such as thieving, on behalf of their victims.

A famous folktale of Scandinavia, found in various forms throughout northern Europe, is *The Bogle in the Mill*; a bogle plagues his host the miller with his annoying pranks, allowing the grain to spill and making holes in new sacks etc, until a travelling bear-trainer leaves his bear temporarily in the miller's barn. The bear frightens the bogle so much that it quits the mill, and returns each year to ask the miller whether the 'big brown cat' is still there. Each year the miller assures him that it is, and finally says that it has had kittens, at which the bogle disappears in despair to trouble the miller no more. A variation of the tale tells how an **ogre** is chased from the room by a 'big white cat' (a bear), and is made to stay away by the claim that the cat has now had many kittens.

bokwus

FOREST SPIRIT OF NORTH-WEST AMERICA, who moves stealthily through the dense foliage and is seldom seen. His face is said to resemble that of a man's, covered with mysterious warpaint. He is particularly a menace to fishermen, using the sound of the river to conceal his approach and then pushing his victims from their rocky seats to death in the quickly-moving waters below. He is said to command the spirits of the drowned, and anyone whom he kills in this way is doomed to serve him in the forest as a spirit attendant.

bolero

SPANISH FOLK DANCE, a lively rhythmic dance for couples in 3/4 time (occasionally 2/4) originating from Castile. In its original form, the dancers performed intricate steps to the accompaniment of hand-held **castanets**, tambourines and the strumming guitar, characterized by gliding steps with legs extended to the side, beginning with the *paseo* (walk) and ending with the *bien parado*, or sudden stop.

bones

POWERFUL RELIC OF THE PHYSICAL SOUL, the most enduring constituent of the person. Many precautions are taken to prevent the animal (as opposed to the spiritual) soul of the dead person returning to animate the skeleton, including sacrifices, spells and practical measures such as a scythe placed over the neck or a slab of stone set over the grave (see **death** and **vampires**), but the rattle of bones is still considered a clear sign of the presence of a restless **ghost**. Since the bones are so vitally connected with the soul, many groups believe that the preservation of the skeleton is necessary for continued existence in the **afterlife**.

Bones of **saints** are venerated by the Catholic Church because they contain a vestige of the holiness once present in the living body (according to doctrine set out by Cardinal Newman), and they are therefore thought to have amuletic powers of healing and protection.

Bones have been used in **divination** since ancient times; small bones, especially from the vertebrae, would be scattered and the resulting pattern studied closely. From this practice popular games such as jacks developed, and dice are thought to be a development of those throwing bones. A rather more robust form of bone-throwing was practised in Scandinavia; once the meat had been gnawed off in the feast, the bones would then be thrown into the air, to be caught by fellow-revellers and tossed back. This sport also functioned as a means of social control; weaker members of the group or those who had committed a crime would find themselves the target for a large number of well-aimed missiles. In the Icelandic sagas, **trolls** and **giants** are particularly fond of this sport.

Bones appear in a common folktale, collected by Grimm as *The Singing*

The Tor Abbey Jewel (c.1546), a memento mori made of gold and enamel, hung around a corpse's neck

Bone, in which a shepherd takes a bone from the skeleton of a man (or woman) murdered by his brother. He makes of it a flute, which when played pipes the secret of the murderer's identity. This is closely related to the motif of the reeds that whispered **Midas**'s secret (the barber had confided in them that the king had grown ass's ears).
▷ **singing bone**

bonga

EVIL SPIRIT OF THE SANTALS OF BENGAL, India, bongas are the ghosts of the dead (although women killed by childbirth become **churels** and uninitiated children become **bhuta**), but they are generally represented in folktales as female. In one Santal tale, a prince is imprisoned by his father because he refuses to marry and gains his release when he agrees to wed the bonga woman who spent the night with him. Although generally feared, bongas do not appear to be particularly evilly intentioned towards humans.

Book of Leinster

MIDDLE IRISH TEXT, a manuscript probably begun in c.1160 with additions in the early 13th century, containing verse and prose drawn from ancient oral tradition and contemporary sources. It is generally attributed to one Áed Hún Crimthaind, abbot of Terryglass, Tipperary. Along with the genealogies and historical poems of Leinster kings and heroes and the battles in which they triumphed and fell, it contains a great deal of folk narrative. Two of its best-known tales are the great **Táin Bó Cuailnge** and the oldest extant version of *The Fate of the Sons of Usnech* (see **Deirdre**). Nearly 200 place-names are treated in the extensive *Dinnshencas*, which gives the legends behind folk etymology and is thought to date from the sixth century.

Book of the Dead

ANCIENT EGYPTIAN TEXTS, a guide for the dead. The 'book' is in fact a collection of different texts, thought to have been written by many different hands over the period from c.2400BC to the 16th century BC; copies of the whole book or sections of it were placed in the grave to protect the soul of the deceased and offer advice for the **afterlife** (this included tips for the journey to the underworld, Amenti, and suitable answers to be given to the judges in the court of Osiris). These hymns, incantations and magical formulae were said to have been originally transcribed by the god Thoth, hence the alternative title, *The Book of Thoth*.

The collection gained its common name from the German Egyptologist Richard Lepsius, who in 1842 published the first edition of modern times. The Egyptian name in fact translates as *The Chapters of Coming Forth by Day*.

Book of the Dun Cow

OLD IRISH MANUSCRIPT, the oldest of its kind surviving, called in Gaelic *Leabhar na h-Uidhre*. A collection of legendary and historical tales dating from the eighth and ninth centuries, with interspersed religious texts, it is thought to have been written in c.1100 by monks at Clonmacroise monastery, drawing on oral tradition and older written sources. It contains tales of both the **Mythological** and **Ulster cycles**, including an incomplete version of the **Táin Bó Cuailnge** (The Cattle Raid of Cooley), a poem to

winter ascribed to **Finn Mac Cumhal**, and the tale of **Bricriu's Feast**.

Its name derives from the legend that the Táin Bó Cuailnge was dictated by the ghost of **Fergus Mac Roich** to the monk Ciarán, who transcribed it upon the hide of his famous dun cow.

Boone, Daniel (1734–1830)

AMERICAN FOLK HERO, a pioneer of the Kentucky frontier. He is credited with discovering the Cumberland Gap, a natural pass in the Appalachian Mountains. He led the group that in 1775 built the Wilderness Road from east Virginia into the wildernesses of Kentucky and on to the unexplored West. He had gained fame in folk legends even before his death, having twice survived capture by hostile native groups (he was briefly adopted as a son by the Shawnee chief, Blackfish). His legend spread with the publication of John Filson's *Discovery, Settlement and Present State of Kentucky*, and was enhanced by a mention in Byron's *Don Juan* (1823). Among the legends associated with him is the tale that he used to keep a coffin, which he would try for size at intervals, under his bed.

Borak

FABULOUS CREATURE, also known as Al Borak, with the face of a man but the cheeks of a horse, the wings of an eagle and the voice of a man. It shone with a dazzlingly bright radiance, and had eyes blue as sapphires and bright as the stars. According to Muslim legend, the archangel Gabriel brought it to Muhammad as his transport to the seventh heaven, and it is one of the few animals to be admitted into Paradise.

bottle imp

SPIRIT CONTAINED WITHIN A BOTTLE, capable of performing magical services when temporarily liberated by its owner. The bottle imp is a common motif in Arabian folktales, and appears too in Hebrew and Philippines tales and less commonly those of northern and central Europe; the most famous example is the jinni contained within **Aladdin's** marvellous lamp. Although possession of a bottle imp may bring a mortal great

wealth and power, in some versions of the belief its one great drawback is that anyone who dies the keeper of a bottle imp will infallibly go to hell. The bottle cannot be destroyed, and if purposely lost will return to its owner; the only certain method of disposing of it is to sell it to another for less than was originally paid for it.
▷ **bakru**; **jinn**

bracken

LARGE-LEAVED COARSE FERN, genus *Pteridium*, found throughout the world's temperate and tropical regions. Christian legend tells how the infant Christ was laid on a bed of bedstraw (cleavers) and bracken; the bedstraw blossomed with pride at the honour and was thenceforth rewarded with golden flowers, but the bracken paid no homage to Christ and has been without blossom ever since.

Its ubiquity has given bracken synonymity with fertility, particularly in Ireland. In folk medicine an infusion of bracken is thought to be efficacious against intestinal worms when drunk, or a salve for burns and scalds when applied as a cool poultice. Practical peasants have long known that the roots of the bracken will give a lather in water, hence its common appellation, 'poor man's soap'.

brag

MISCHIEVOUS SPIRIT of the north of England, a **shape-shifting** goblin who appears particularly as a horse. The brag delights in luring humans to mount its back, whereupon it will take them on a bone-bruising ride of terrifying speed and finally deposit them in the middle of a pond.

Bran, son of Febal

OLD IRISH VOYAGING HERO, a traveller to **fairyland**. Bran fell asleep one day to the sound of sweet fairy music, and on awakening found himself clutching a silvery branch of apple-blossom. He carried it back into his dun, or fortified mound, and was confronted by a mysterious and beautiful woman who told him in song of the Isle of Women, Emhain, where tiredness and want were unknown

Bran, son of Febal

under the kingship of Manannan, son of the sea-god Lir. She disappeared, taking Bran's wonderful branch with her, and Bran set off the next day with a fleet of curraghs in search of this marvellous island. On the way they met Manannan himself, driving his chariot across the waves, and bypassed the Island of Delight whose inhabitants did nothing but laugh all day long.

Eventually they arrived at Emhain, where the women welcomed them onto the island and they enjoyed every luxury and pleasure they could imagine. After some time however Bran's companions became homesick for Ireland, and wished to return. The women warned them that this would bring only sadness, but the men were insistent and finally they were allowed to go, with the stern warning that they must not touch the ground itself but only shout to the inhabitants on the shore. They arrived to find the country changed beyond recognition and nobody who knew them, although some remembered ancient tales of Bran who had sailed in search of the Island of Women; the year they had spent away had been centuries of mortal time. Nechtan, one of the sailors, flung himself out of the boat and made for the shore, but as soon as he stood on Irish soil the weight of mortal years caught up with him and he crumbled into dust.

Seeing this, Bran and his fellows told the incredulous folk their story and sailed off, never to be seen again.

This is a famous version of a very widespread tale-type, including motifs such as the voyage to the island **otherworld** inhabited by attentive women, the **taboo** against touching the ground (elsewhere this takes the form of a taboo against eating something or opening a certain box) and the home changed by the magical passage of time.

▷ **Herla, King**; **Oisín**; **Rip Van Winkle**; **Thomas the Rhymer**

Bran and Sceolan

HUNTING DOGS OF THE IRISH WARRIOR HERO FINN MAC CUMHAL. They were the whelps of Tuiren, wife of Iollan (one of the **Fianna**) who had been changed into a bitch by the jealous Uchtdealb, a **sidhe** woman and a former lover of Iollan's. She gave birth to Bran and Sceolan while in her changed state in the care of Fergus Fionnliath, to whose care Uchtdealb had entrusted her because she knew of his dislike of dogs. Finally Iollan persuaded Uchtdealb to restore Tuiren to her human shape; Finn took charge of the two puppies and they became his favourite hounds. A Highland version of the tale tells how Finn won the two dogs from a monster he had defeated.

Bran was the swiftest and best-loved of the two; she was said to run faster than the flight of wild geese. The two recognized Sadb, the wife of Finn, in her deer form and brought her back unharmed to Finn's dun, where she was restored to human form, and it was they who recognized **Oisín**, the child of Finn and Sadb, and brought him back naked from the forest.

Finn himself eventually killed Bran, saving a fawn from her jaws, and he mourned her the rest of his life.

Bran the Blessed

ANCIENT IRISH HERO, also known as Bendigeidfran, originally a deity of bards and poetry, son of Llyr and brother of Manawyddan and Branwen. In later lore his mythological aspect decreased, and he became a legendary giant-king of Britain, whose tale is told in the **Mabinogion**. Because of his enor-

mous stature, Bran was obliged to live and hold court in a tent; no palace was big enough to contain him.

Matholwch, king of Ireland, sailed to Britain to ask from Bran the hand of his sister Branwen, a marriage which he said would cement forever the band between Britain and Ireland. During the festivities however Evnissyen, Bran's envious and malcontented half-brother, mutilated the horses of the Irish king by slicing off their lips, eyelids and tails. Bran pacified the furious Matholwch with unstinting apologies and gifts, making up the loss and adding many more treasures, most importantly the magic **Cauldron** of Healing, powerful enough to restore a man from death, which had itself first come from Ireland. Eventually Matholwch consented to forgive the insult, and Branwen was taken back to Ireland amid great rejoicing. She lived there happily for a year and bore her husband a son, Gwern, but soon the Irish people grew angry at the memory of the insult they had sustained at her half-brother's hands. She was banished from the king's presence and treated with abominable cruelty, and any Briton who visited Ireland was prevented from returning lest he carry news of this indignity to Bran. Branwen however trained a starling to recognize her brother and sent it off to Bran with a letter telling of her plight. In fury, Bran

Bran the Blessed

gathered a huge fleet and set off for Ireland, wading through the sea since no boat could hold him.

Matholwch tried to pacify this terrifying giant; he proposed to build a palace to house him, and to this Bran agreed, but Matholwch treacherously placed two men in sacks at each of the 100 pillars, to surprise Bran and his men at the supposed peace meeting. Evnissyen, touring the new house, crushed the skulls of each with one hand. When peace was finally concluded, the new king Gwern, young son of Branwen and Matholwch, was brought out to general affection and acclaim, until Evnissyen threw him into the fire, at which a bloody battle broke out. The Irish were gaining the advantage as they threw all their dead into the Cauldron of Healing, and when Evnissyen saw this he too hurled himself into it and cracked it from within, thereby killing himself in a final act of heroism.

Bran was wounded in the rout, and he told his seven remaining companions to cut off his head, which he said would give them merry companionship, and take it back with them to Britain. For more than 80 years Bran's head, known as the *Uther Ben* ('Noble Head'), presided over the feasting and merriment at his court, but it was finally buried under the White Tower in London, looking towards France in accordance with Bran's instructions, where it would protect the country from invasion forever. **Arthur** however later dug the head up, preferring his warriors to trust in their own valour rather than a supernatural guardian. Some versions of the legend add that the only humans left alive in Ireland were five pregnant women who had sought refuge in a cave; their offspring repopulated the country.

In later lore, Bran became Christianized as St Bran the Blessed, a Prydein king who brought Christianity to the Cymric people of Britain. He appears in medieval legends as Brandegore and Sir Brandel, among other names.

This legend is an interesting example of mythology translated into popular lore, and it incorporates several familiar features, such as the protective buried head and the thwarted concealing of warriors in sacks.

Branwen

HEROINE OF THE MABINOGION, the wronged queen of King Matholwch of Ireland, who is avenged by her brothers **Bran the Blessed** and Manawyddan.

breakstone see saxifrage

Brendan the Navigator, St
(c.486–c.577)

THE TRAVELLING ABBOT OF CLONFERT, who set about founding monasteries throughout Ireland, including Clonfert (in 559) which became an important missionary centre with about 3000 monks and survived until the 16th century. He also travelled extensively in Scotland, befriending Columba at Argyll according to Adomnan, and very probably in Wales and beyond, but it is impossible to detail the events of his life with any real certainty. He probably died while on a visit to his sister Brig in Annaghdown.

Brendan's great influence in southern Ireland is attested by the significant number of place names which are named after him, most famously Mount Brendan on the Dingle Peninsula. From the ninth century onwards there is evidence of a strong cult of St Brendan in Ireland, and he was popular too in Wales, Scotland and Brittany.

The stories of Brendan's wide travelling gave rise to the *Navigation of Brendan*, a 10th- or 11th-century visionary romance written in Latin which describes Brendan's seven-year voyage to a 'Land of Promise' in the west, identified by some as the Hebrides and Northern Isles, by others as Iceland, and by some as the Canary Islands or even North America. An expedition by Tim Severin in 1976–7, aimed at duplicating the voyage in a hide-covered curragh, succeeded in reaching Newfoundland via Iceland and Greenland, which would seem to agree with the journey described in the epic. Most scholars however accept the work as a charming and romantic fiction in a well-attested genre (see **echtrai** and **imrama**) whilst recognizing its popularity and influence in the Middle Ages. Matthew Arnold's poem *St Brandan* retells the story, and the saint is a popular figure in art, standing aboard ship giving mass while the fish crowd round to listen. His feast-day is 16 May, and he is a patron saint of sailors and travellers.

Brer Fox

CREATURE OF FOLKTALES, immortalized in Joel Chandler Harris's **Uncle Remus** tales. Brer Fox is the wily adversary of **Brer Rabbit**, usually outwitted by the quick-thinking trickster but occasionally coming out on top, as in the **tar baby** tale (he even lets this advantage go, however). This characterization corresponds to a long tradition in European folklore of the cunning **fox**, and grafts on to it African traditions and tale-types.

Brer Rabbit

TRICKSTER, HERO OF THE UNCLE REMUS CHILDREN'S TALES. In the trickster-tale traditions of Africa and Native America, Rabbit is the **trickster** par excellence, who despite his diminutive size outwits his more powerful opponents by quick thinking, and many of the most characteristic of these tales are collected in the Brer Rabbit stories. Joel Chandler Harris's first collection of Negro tales, *Uncle Remus, his songs and his sayings; the folklore of the old plantation* was published in New York in late 1880. In the introduction, Harris claimed that his intention was to preserve the legends in their original form and dialect, choosing the version of each which seemed to him most characteristic. The Southern American Negro dialect is conveyed in the spelling; 'Brer' for example is the representation of the Negro pronunciation of 'Brother'. This device is regarded by some as overly difficult, and many more accessible translations have been made, but others consider the idiosyncratic language an essential and inseparable feature of the tales.

The book takes the form of a series of tales related by a Negro slave (Uncle Remus) to his master's young son. Most of the tales centre around the exploits of the hero, Brer Rabbit ('Bred en bawn in a brier patch!'), and the unsuccessful attempts of **Brer Fox** to catch him. Other characters, such as Brer Tarrypin (Terrapin) and Brer Wolf, are included; the race between Brer Fox and Brer Tarrypin, in which the slower creature defeats the swifter by deception, is a trickster version of the famous **Hare** and **Tortoise** fable. In 1883 the sequel *Nights with Uncle Remus* was published, also aimed at serious folklorists, but later volumes such as *Uncle Remus and his Friends* (1892) were written mainly for children. In the West, the tales have traditionally been regarded as diverting children's stories.

▷ **tar baby**; **rabbit**

Bres

OLD IRISH HERO, known as Bres the Beautiful, son of the king of the **Fomorians** and a **sidhe** woman and the husband of the ancient goddess Brigit. His beauty and his astonishing growth (by the age of seven he appeared as a boy of fourteen) persuaded the **Tuatha de Danann** to entrust him with the kingship of all Ireland (their king Nuada had sustained injury in the Battle of Mag Tured, fought by the invading Tuatha de Danann for control of Ireland when they first arrived). Bres proved himself unworthy of the honour, treating the leaders of the Tuatha de Danann as menials and taxing his new realm heavily. Finally the Tuatha de Danann requested the kingdom back from Bres's control, and he raised an army to meet their challenge. At the second Battle of Mag Tured many warriors were lost, including **Balor**, killed by his grandson and the champion of the Tuatha de Danann, **Lugh**. At the end of all the slaughter the Tuatha de Danann proclaimed their victory over all of Ireland.

Bricriu's Feast

OLD IRISH LEGEND, one of the oldest and longest tales of the **Ulster cycle**, known in Gaelic as *Fled Bricrenn*. It is a rumbustious, humorous tale telling of the rivalry between the Ulster heroes.

Bricriu, a **trickster**, prepares a great feast for **Conchobar** and his warriors who are unwilling to accept the invitation—they all know of Bricriu's reputation for trouble-making. Finally Conchobar is persuaded to accept, but he and his chiefs ensure that Bricriu himself is not allowed into the hall. The damage has already been done however; Bricriu has secretly promised the champion's portion to three different chiefs, Lóegaire, Conall and **Cuchulainn**, and the position of honour to each of their wives. The resulting confusion, with no champion prepared to concede his place, leads to a series of contests to demonstrate the strength, valour and skill of each man, but at the end of it all no unanimous decision can be reached as to which is worthy of precedence. Bricriu is brought in but professes himself unworthy to judge, and **Medb** and **Ailill Mac Matach** are equally indecisive, so the matter is taken to the great magician **Cú Roi** who declares Cuchulainn the winner. Cuchulainn in fact waives the honour, preferring the goodwill of his companions.

On a later occasion however an axe-wielding giant terrorizes the court of Conchobar at Emain Macha, proposing a beheading bargain, and Lóegaire and Conall, among others, both accept the challenge; they behead the giant, but when he returns whole the next day they fail to offer themselves for beheading as agreed. Cuchulainn however keeps his part of the bargain, at which the giant brings down his axe beside the hero's unscathed head and reveals himself to be Cú Roi, vindicating his choice of champion by proving Cuchulainn not only brave but true to his word.

▷ **Gawain, Sir**

bride

A WOMAN ABOUT TO BE MARRIED, OR NEWLY MARRIED. A plethora of customs and superstitions have grown up surrounding the bride on her all-important wedding day, mainly as a result of the ancient belief that at this time the bride is particularly vulnerable to envious, malicious spirits. The veil is used to ward off the **evil eye** and to confuse evil spirits, and the bridesmaids surround their friend and make her less easy for such evil influences to distinguish. The colour of the wedding dress is vital; white is 'right' in Europe and the New World but black and green are considered especially unlucky. In Britain the bride should conform to the old recipe for happiness

by wearing 'Something old, something new, Something borrowed and something blue'. **Pearls** are frowned upon, because of their ominous resemblance to tears.

It is considered unlucky for the bride to allow the groom to see her before the ceremony on her wedding day; he should also not see the dress before then and ideally the bride should refrain from trying on both ring and dress until the hour of the ceremony. As with any important journey, the bride should be careful to step first with her right foot on leaving her house for the church.

Bride cakes were baked by the Vestal Virgins in ancient Rome, to be carried before the bride to her new home and broken over her head before being shared among the guests as a sacrifice to Jupiter. This custom survived in varying forms in Europe, often with the addition of a coin or coins given by the guests to draw the evil eye from the couple, and the cake is a feature of weddings around the world.

▷ **marriage**; **virginity**

Brigid, St or Bride (c.453–c.523)

THE MARY OF THE GAEL, second only to St **Patrick** in the love of the Irish and credited with countless miracles and blessings, foundress of the first convent in Ireland. Difficult though it is to disentangle the factual information about Brigid's life from the rich tapestry of folklore spun around it, it seems probable that she was born into a peasant family near Dundalk in Ireland, of parents baptized by St Patrick himself. She became a nun at an early age, probably professed by St Mel of Armagh, and after spending some time near Croghan Hill with seven companions she followed Mel to Meath in c.468. The central achievement of her life came in c.470, when she founded the first convent in Ireland at Kildare. The foundation was a double monastery, with Brigid as abbess of the convent, and in time it became a centre for Irish spirituality and learning around which the cathedral town of Kildare grew up. Brigid is credited also with the founding of a school of art there.

Although the miracles attributed to

her are sometimes fantastic, it seems likely that the compassion, charity and strength which characterize them all were real attributes of the historical Brigid. She is known as the Mary of the Gael from a vision of Bishop Ibor, who supposedly saw a vision of the Virgin the day before seeing Brigid and pronounced them identical. Brigid died at Kildare and was buried there, but her relics were reburied at Downpatrick, along with those of Patrick, during invasions by the Danes. Place names and churches throughout Britain testify to the extent of her cult, most notably St Bride's Bay in Dyfed, Wales, and the church on Fleet Street in London. In art she is shown as an abbess, usually holding a lamp or candle and often with a **cow** nearby recalling the legend that the cows she kept as a nun once produced milk three times in one day for the benefit of her visitors.

A poetic passage in the *Book of Lismore* testifies to her special position in the Irish religious tradition: 'It is she that helpeth everyone who is in danger: it is she that abateth the pestilences: it is she that quelleth the rage and the storm of the sea. She is the prophetess of Christ: she is the Queen of the South: she is the Mary of the Gael.' Her importance during her own day, however, has been exaggerated; one popular tradition holds that she was consecrated as a bishop by Ibor, which is almost certainly untrue, and it is sometimes claimed that the abbots and abbesses of Kildare enjoyed supremacy over the whole of Ireland, another fiction which has given much credibility to the expansion of Brigid's cult and the proliferation of her *Lives*. According to one popular Celtic tradition she was midwife to the Virgin **Mary** at the birth of Jesus.

She is the patron saint of Ireland (after St Patrick), poets, blacksmiths, healers, cattle, dairymaids, midwives, newborn babies and fugitives, and her feast-day is 1 February. Her cult was assimilated into native Celtic worship of the pagan goddess of poetry and prophecy Brigit (or Brigantia in the north of England), the equivalent of Roman Minerva. Brigit's feast-day was 1 February, the great festival of **Imbolc**, when ewes came into milk.

Brisingamen

MAGICAL NECKLACE OF SCANDINAVIAN LORE, crafted by **dwarfs** in Svartalfheim. The goddess Freya coveted it, but the dwarfs Dvalin, Alfrigga, Berling and Grerr would not part with it until she agreed to sleep with them all in turn. She wore the necklace, emblem of the stars and of fecundity, constantly, but lent it to Thor to enable him to pose as her and deceive the giants. Loki stole the necklace but was spotted by Heimdall, who pursued him. There followed a classic contest of **shape-shifting**; Loki turned from a fly into a flame, Heimdall became a cloud of rain, Loki became a polar bear, Heimdall a bear also. Loki then transformed himself into a seal, quickly followed by Heimdall, and was finally defeated and forced to give back the necklace.

Although strictly a mythological tale, this is a significant instance of the shape-shifting contests found in many folktales.

Brother Jonathan

EARLY PERSONIFICATION OF THE UNITED STATES, later supplanted by **Uncle Sam**. The name seems to have been derived from Puritan New England settlers, and particularly one Jonathan Trumbull (1710–85), governor of Connecticut, whose advice was habitually sought by George Washington.

Brown, John (1800–59)

AMERICAN ABOLITIONIST, renowned among other things for fathering 20 children. He fought for the anti-slavery cause in Kansas and Iowa, but his most famous exploit was at Harper's Ferry in Virginia, where he seized and occupied the federal arsenal on 16 October 1859. His followers were killed and he himself was tried for insurrection, treason and murder and hanged. He became a symbol of the abolitionist cause, regarded as a folk hero, and the rousing ballad *John Brown's Body*, which claims that 'his soul goes marching on', was an anthem for the North.

brownie

BRITISH MISCHIEVOUS SPIRIT. The true brownie is found in Scotland, occa-

brownie

sionally in the Highlands and Islands but especially in the lowlands, and in the north and east of England and areas of the Midlands, but the pwca of Wales and the Manx **fenoderee** are very similar beings. Typically, they are small, man-like beings, about three feet in height, dressed in a ragged brown cloak and hood, and although occasionally reported in groups, particularly in the Highlands, they are usually treated as solitary fairies. The brownie attaches himself to a particular house and emerges at night to perform any task that needs doing, such as reaping and threshing, herding the livestock or sweeping the floors. He often favours one member of the family in particular, whom he will take especial care to please.

It is vital never to repay a brownie directly for his services; he will instantly vanish, never to be seen again, either offended or released from his bond to serve. One grateful old woman made a new set of clothes for the brownie who had so faithfully served her; he put them on and disappeared, chanting in delight; 'Gie brownie coat, gie brownie sark, Ye'll get nae mair o' brownie's work'. Correct etiquette is to leave the choicest cake and a bowl of cream where he might come upon them as if by accident. Another sure way to drive the brownie from a house is to offend him by taking his work for granted; a farm hand remarked one day that since the corn

was not stacked as well as usual the resident brownie was becoming lazy, and the furious sprite revenged himself by throwing the entire harvest over a nearby crag before disappearing forever. A brownie offended in such a way (and brownies are easily offended) will often not leave, but become instead a **boggart**, remaining to plague the unfortunate householder.
▷ **Aiken Drum; mischievous spirits; nisse**

Brunhild see **Brynhild**

Brut

LEGENDARY KING OF BRITAIN, a descendant of Aeneas of Troy. Having mistakenly slain his father, Silvius, while hunting, he fled to Greece with the remnant of the Trojans, where he secured the hand of Imogen, daughter of the Greek king. He sailed on to Britain and established a kingdom there, calling his centre of government Trinovantum (New Troy), now London. The word Britain is said to derive from his name.

Brut's tale is told in the ninth-century *Historia Britonum* of Nennius; it is mentioned by Geoffrey of Monmouth in the 12th century and is the starting-point of Layamon's early-Middle English *Brut*. His descendants include **Camber**, **Bladud**, **Llud**, **Cymbeline** and **Arthur**. He is also known as Brute or Brutus.

Brythonic folklore see **Celtic folklore**

Brynhild

GERMANIC HEROINE, an **Amazon**-like princess. In the Norse *Volsungasaga* and the poems of the **Eddas**, where she is sometimes referred to as a leader of the **Valkyries**, Odin punishes her for her rebellion against him by laying on her a magical spell of sleep and surrounding her with impenetrable fire. Only **Sigurd** (called Siegfried in the *Nibelungenlied*) is able to ride through the flames and claim her, sealing the union with his magic ring, **Andvaranaut**, but later in the land of the Nibelungs he drinks a magic potion that causes him to forget his love for Brynhild and is persuaded to marry **Gudrun**. Sigurd takes the place of Gunnar, Gudrun's brother, to win Bryn hild for him by his bravery and strength and disarms her by taking her magic girdle and the ring he himself had given her. Brynhild is tricked into marriage with Gunnar, thinking that he has truly won her, but when she discovers the deception she plots Sigurd's death. Afterwards, overcome with love and remorse, she kills herself and is laid with him atop his funeral pyre.

In the Germanic *Nibelungenlied* she is known as Brunhild, and her supernatural qualities are down-played. Wagner based his Ring cycle on her story.

bucca

CORNISH SPIRIT, a **hobgoblin** nebulously connected with both sea-faring and mining. Like his Germanic cousin the **kobold** he was said to dwell in tin mines, but he was also thought to travel on the sea-winds, foretelling shipwrecks. Although volatile, he could be propitiated by the courteous offering of some crumbs at harvest, a fish after the catch had been landed, or a few drops of ale spilled deliberately for the purpose.

▷ **coblynau**; **knockers**; **mischievous spirits**

buffalo

IMPOSING ANIMAL, found in Asia and Africa. The North American bison, a closely-related species of Bovidae mammal, is commonly known as the plains buffalo. The plains buffalo was central to the way of life, food supply and economy of the Native Americans before the advent of the Europeans who massively depleted the herds until protection was enforced in the early 20th century. Many tales among native American groups tell of **beast marriage** of humans with buffalo and the exploits of their offspring, and of an underworld populated by buffalo. The creature is closely associated with rain; a Shawnee shaman may summon rain by sprinkling water onto the earth with a buffalo's tail, and many Plains groups performed buffalo ceremonies in a drought. Mimetic buffalo dances were also performed to attract the buffalo and ensure success in the hunt, and involved much stamping and snorting.

Buffalo Bill (1846–1917)

AMERICAN SHOWMAN, real name William Frederick Cody. An army scout and pony express rider, he earned his nickname after killing nearly 5000 buffalo in 18 months in pursuance of a contract to supply the workers on the Kansas Pacific Railway with meat. He served as a scout in the Sioux wars, but from 1883 toured with his Wild West Show. The town of Cody in Wyoming stands on part of his former ranch.

bugbear

ORIGINALLY, AN ENGLISH HOBGOBLIN APPEARING AS A BEAR, a nursery monster invoked to frighten children into obedience. Like so many similar words, **bogey**, **boggart**, **bucca**, **puck** and so on, it is closely linked in etymology to Welsh *bwg*, meaning ghost, and perhaps the ancient Slavic *bug* or *bog*, meaning god. The degeneration of myth into folklore is strikingly illustrated here. The word has come to refer in common usage to anything feared without reason.

buggane

MISCHIEVOUS MANX SPIRIT, a particularly dangerous breed of shape-shifting **goblin**. He seems to be a water-spirit, found mainly by waterfalls, who appears most frequently as a horse or calf, or alternatively in semi-human form with an enormous head, long teeth and predatory nails.

▷ **kelpie**; **shape-shifting**

bull see **cattle**

bull-roarer

PRIMITIVE INSTRUMENT, of obscure origins, found virtually everywhere in the world. It comprises a flat piece of material, usually bone, stone or wood, tapered at both ends. A cord is threaded through a hole at one end and the whole thing is swung above the head, producing a loud, harsh roar. The noise, which may be used to terrify enemies or spirits, to summon rain or to ensure fertility, is almost exclusively associated with male dominance. In Australia particularly it is a key feature in the puberty and initiation rites of the young men, and women are forbidden to see or touch it for fear of death. In Brazil too, where the bull-roarer is often used in death rites, attended only by males, its noise is a signal for women to hide their eyes. Its size and shape are thought to be associated with male sexual potency.

▷ **cattle**; **initiation**

bundling

COURTING CUSTOM OF EUROPE, particularly common in Britain, Ireland, Holland and later in New England. A young couple, unmarried but often engaged, were encouraged to lie together, clothed, in the same bed. As well as the practical reason of keeping warm during a private meeting (bedrooms were not generally heated), an inverse logic operated whereby it was thought that meeting temptation head on in this way would reduce the risk of the young people succumbing to immoral desires. Naturally enough, this seldom proved the case and the custom eventually died out as late as the early 19th century in some areas, having achieved notoriety as a target for 18th-century moralists.

This comfortable custom was in some cases extended to late-night visitors too, and in modern urban lore travelling salesmen report apocryphal tales of colleagues invited to spend the night in the bed of the householder's daughter. This seemingly extreme hospitality is a relic of the days of the common bed, when the entire household slept packed in the same bed for warmth and to be excluded was at best an insult, at worst fatal.

bunyip

MONSTER OF AUSTRALIAN ABORIGINE FOLKLORE, a large, black amphibious creature said to inhabit inland water and swampland especially in south-east Australia. It is described as a bulky creature, often compared to a **hippopotamus** or giant seal, with a loud harsh cry and a taste for human flesh, and particularly that of women and children. It is possible that the bunyip originated with occasional distant inland sightings of seals. It functions in many Aboriginal groups as a means of social control, a **bogey** to stop children wandering too far from the settlement and to deter women from approaching **initiation** sites. The word

appears in popular modern Australian usage to refer to any mythical object or fanciful chimera, 'chasing the bunyip'.

bush soul

FOUND PARTICULARLY IN WEST AFRICA, the bush soul belief is closely related to **totemism**. The soul of each individual dwells in a wild animal, and their two fates are inextricably linked. It is considered very serious therefore to attempt to harm another person's bush soul. Bush souls are usually inherited, but may be purchased. In some societies the soul-animal is thought to be one born at the same moment as the child. This concept of a dual soul, or even a multiple soul, since a chief especially may have more than one bush soul, is distinct from the concept of reincarnation of the soul in animal form, another popular belief.

▷ **separable soul**

bushido

'WAY OF THE WARRIOR', the Samurai code of conduct which became in the 19th century the ideal pattern for morals and behaviour for all Japanese society. It emphasized the traditional Japanese virtues of military skills, bravery, self-discipline, integrity and filial respect. The ideals of bushido developed from the Kamakura period (1192–1333) on, absorbing elements of Confucianism and Buddhism but remaining fundamentally the same, and its principles infuse the folk tales of Japan.

▷ **hero**

Butch Cassidy (1866–?1909)

AMERICAN OUTLAW AND FOLK HERO, real name Robert Leroy Parker. He was the leader of the Wild Bunch, a gang of criminals who terrorized trains and banks throughout the American West at the end of the 19th century. His first close confederate was Elzy Lay, and after Elzy's capture he made a profitable association with Harry Longbaugh, the Sundance Kid. In 1901, with increased pressure from the law closing in on the Wild Bunch, Butch Cassidy and the Sundance Kid flitted to New York and then spent several lucrative years ranching in Argentina, but they returned to train robbing and were finally apprehended near San Vicente, Bolivia. According to some versions of the legend, the Sundance Kid was killed here and Butch Cassidy shot himself, but in other versions they died during a bank robbery in Uruguay in 1911, or Butch Cassidy died alone and in obscurity in Alaska or Nevada in 1937.

Butch Cassidy's anarchic lifestyle suited him perfectly for the role of daring romantic outlaw, the epitome of the swashbuckling impudence of the pioneer, and his legend spread quickly throughout the West and beyond. In the 20th century he was immortalized in the popular Hollywood film, *Butch Cassidy and the Sundance Kid*.

butterfly

FLYING INSECT. Much folklore has accrued around this dainty, often brightly coloured creature. In Christian iconography the life-cycle of the insect, from **caterpillar** to shrivelled chrysalis to winged butterfly, has been adopted as a symbol of resurrection, specifically Christ's own resurrection. Gnostic Christians however view the fragile butterfly as a symbol of the flesh, corrupt and perishable.

In very many societies across the world the butterfly, like the **bird**, is seen as the **separable soul** of a human. To catch or kill a butterfly or to wake someone while the butterfly soul was absent could be fatal. The Maori and others believe that after death the soul returns to the earth in the form of a butterfly. Slavic peasants believed that a butterfly was the visible soul of a witch, which if it entered the body of a sleeping human, whose own soul was thereby absent, would allow her to possess him. However, if the witch could be moved or her mouth closed while her butterfly soul was absent it would be unable to find its way back in and the witch would die. Moths are sometimes regarded as **witches** in Europe, especially in Scotland and Bosnia, or as troublesome, thieving fairies.

buzzard

CARRION-EATING BIRD, properly a bird of prey of the genus *Buteo* and in North America the common name for **vultures** such as the turkey vulture. Among many Native Americans these buzzards, closely associated with death because of their diet, are considered powerful in healing and cleansing. A charm of buzzard feathers will soothe a fretful teething child, a feather burned beneath the nose of an epileptic or one who has fainted will dispel the evil influence afflicting them. The Pueblo use buzzard feathers extensively in exorcism.

Hopi tales tell how Buzzard gained his bald head from pushing up the sun to make it a comfortable distance from the earth.

bwbachod

WELSH HOUSEHOLD SPIRIT, a local variety of **brownie**. As well as exhibiting characteristic brownie behaviour, performing tasks around the house when unmolested and playing destructive pranks if offended, the bwbachod's distinguishing feature is his antipathy towards teetotallers and dissenting ministers of religion, especially Baptist ministers, who unluckily fulfil both these conditions and are thus particularly prone to finding themselves plagued by the spirit. In other versions the Welsh brownie is known as *bwca*.
▷ **mischievous spirits**; **puck**

byliny

RUSSIAN BALLAD FORM. Like ballads found elsewhere in Europe, the bylina is generally short, narrative and dramatic, but the metre and rhyme are less structured than is usual in ballad form, and there is no division into stanzas. In fact byliny have been considered by some scholars as a form of heroic or epic literature, since the subject is usually the exploits of a hero, and several byliny dealing with the same character may be loosely linked together into a cycle. The heroes include the giant Svyatogor, Volga (who can converse with the animals and birds and has the power to change his shape) and **Mikula**, a bluff peasant of enormous strength.

cabbage

COMMON VEGETABLE, *Brassica oleracea* of the family Cruciferae, a traditional staple of the peasant diet in much of northern Europe. Babies are said to be found under cabbage leaves in many areas, and in Ireland cabbage stalks are said to serve as magical mounts for fairy horsemen.

cactus

FLOWERING PLANT, any member of the family Cactaceae, typically leafless with spines and green fleshy stems, found in arid areas particularly in the Americas. Some contain the powerful hallucinogen mescaline and are widely used in Native American religious rituals. Several groups use the cactus as an **initiation** ordeal or a proof of courage; the initiate

cactus

may be required to rub himself against a cactus or allow himself to be flogged. Such flogging, which is believed to impart strength and good fortune as well as demonstrating manly fortitude, is used also in the induction of chiefs in groups such as the Zuñi. One reason for this close association of cacti with masculinity is the characteristically phallic shape of many plants; several Native American tales deal with obscene uses of cactus made by culture heroes.
▷ **peyote**

Câd Goddeu see **Battle of the Trees**

Cader Idris

'THE SEAT OF THE GIANT', a rough, stone-hewed seat on the summit of the mountain to which it has given its name in Gwynedd, Wales. Idris was an ancient Welsh giant, prince and astronomer, and it is said that anyone who passes a night in his seat will be found in the morning either dead, mad or a poet of genius. Few have considered the risk a worthwhile one.

Cadmus

ANCIENT GREEK KING, the founder of Thebes and brother of the ill-fated Europa, who was abducted by Zeus in his disguise as a bull. While searching for his lost sister, Cadmus was instructed by the Delphic oracle to found a city in Boeotia. In doing so, he slew the **dragon** that guarded the nearby fountain of Dirce, and on Athene's advice sowed the dragon's teeth in the ground. An army of warriors sprang up, and Cadmus diverted their march on him by flinging a precious stone in among them. The soldiers immediately set upon each other until only five were left standing, and with these five Spartoi ('sown men') Cadmus built his city. He and his wife Harmonia were later transformed into serpents by their own request to the gods.

Cadmus is popularly credited with inventing the Greek alphabet, importing the principle from Phonoecia.

Caer see Angus Og

cailleach bheure

HAG OF THE SCOTTISH HIGHLANDS, known also in Ireland, where she is called cailleach bera. She seems to have once been a Celtic deity, a personification of winter and the restoration of life in the spring. In some tales the cailleach is said to transform herself into a grey standing stone at the beginning of May, to be reborn with the next winter, but other versions have her as a **loathly lady** who rewards kind-hearted young men by revealing herself as a beautiful, accommodating young woman. She is said to have been a lover of at least one of the **Fianna**. In many tales and especially in later literature in which her terrifying aspect is largely lost, she is an emblem of great wisdom and the elegiac loss of beauty with age. She is, more primitively, the guardian of wild creatures such as deer and wolves.

Along with many supernatural or superhuman figures (for example **giants** or **Paul Bunyan**), the cailleach has been credited with any number of land formations. Island groups such as the Hebrides were formed from the rocks that fell when the strings of her apron broke, and there are several huge rocks purporting to be her seat or bed. Loch Awe is said to be the result of her negligence; one night atop Ben Cruachan she fell asleep before placing a stone over her well there, and awoke the next morning in horror to find the plain beneath flooded and humans and animals drowned in the torrent.

Another aspect of the cailleach is her function as corn-spirit, embodied in the last sheaf to be garnered from the field. In some areas this is an enviable possession, and seeds taken from it will ensure a good harvest for the one who feeds them to his ploughing team or scatters it in the furrows at the start of the next sowing season. In other areas the cailleach is a booby prize for the last farmer

cailleach bheure

to finish his reaping, in contrast to the corn maiden awarded to the first.
▷ **Black Annis**

cairn

PILE OF STONES, usually placed as a marker especially on mountain routes or over graves. In mountainous areas such as the Scottish Highlands or the Himalayas cairns mark the summits, or the tops of passes, and each traveller to have survived thus far adds another stone. Sometimes offerings of food were left on mountain cairns, half as an oblation, half as a courtesy to the next passer-by. It is likely that this recalls an earlier sacrificial function of the cairn, which may explain the link between such way-markers and the cairns used to mark graves. Here too the mourner or passer-by is expected to add another stone. These cairns function to protect the body from desecration (the unwelcome attentions of scavenging wolves, for example) and to guard the living against the uprising of the deceased's body or spirit.

cakes

CELEBRATION CAKES, often with highly specific recipes, shapes and decoration, have been used in an enormous variety of ceremonial occasions throughout history. The origin of such customs was almost certainly as offerings to propitiate gods or spirits at such critical times, for example the dough thrown to Demeter and Persephone at harvest time in ancient Greece, and the Japanese cake offerings to sun and moon at New Year. In later lore, the communal eating of cakes at times such as harvest and New Year was regarded as a way of securing luck and prosperity for the coming year, as well as expressing the natural impulse towards feasting.

Cakes were often included among the possessions laid out for the dead, as nourishment for the journey to the afterworld, and 'soul cakes' persisted for many years in Europe, to be eaten with a prayer for the souls of the dead.

In Christian lore pancakes are widely eaten on Shrove Tuesday, the day before the 40 days of Lenten austerity commemorating Christ's fast in the desert, and on Good Friday it was considered lucky to eat a 'hot cross bun', marked with the form of the cross.

Cakes have been widely used in **divination**. **Beltane** cakes are thought to have originated as a means of selecting the honoured sacrificial victim, a tradition analogous to the shilling or **bean** hidden in many European celebration cakes which brings good luck to the one who finds it. Young Scottish women would bake a 'dumb bannock' in the

hour before midnight on **Hallowe'en** and each carve their initials in the dough; the group mutely watched the bannock bake and turned it once only, and if they kept complete silence a shadowy male figure would appear at midnight and indicate the initials of the one who was soon to be a bride. Once married many European women, especially in Italy, kept a fragment of wedding cake under the pillow of the marriage bed to ensure conjugal happiness and fidelity in the years ahead.

▷ **birthdays**; **Christmas**; **New Year**

cakewalk

POPULAR COUPLE DANCE, in which the man and woman promenade in a square with a high, mincing step. It originated with black American slaves, as a mute satire on the affectations of their white masters and the elegant dances fashionable in the late 19th century. In early contests, around the turn of the century, a decorated cake was awarded to the couple judged to have performed in the most grotesquely elegant fashion, or in some cases to have carried, in the most stylish fashion, a bucket of water on the head without spilling a drop. The dance was adopted by fashionable American whites, few of whom appreciated its satirical origins, as an entertaining social diversion, and became a significant element in the developing American musical forms of **jazz** and ragtime.

Calamity Jane (c.1852–1903)

AMERICAN FRONTIERSWOMAN, real name Martha Jane Burke, née Cannary, born in Princeton, Missouri. She became a living legend for her skill at riding and shooting, particularly in the Gold Rush days in the Black Hills of Dakota. She teamed up with the renowned US marshal, Wild Bill Hickok (1847–76), at Deadwood, Dakota, before he was murdered. She is said to have threatened 'calamity' for any man who tried to court her, but was married in 1885.

calinda

BATTLE DANCE, performed by dancers (originally men only) armed with sticks. It is thought to have spread into the southern states of North America from the Antilles and its popularity with black slaves led to a fashion on the white dance-floors of the South in the early 19th century. In early forms of the dance, each mock-combatant would fight with a bowl of water balanced on his head, and victory went to the one who succeeded in not slopping any of the water. The dances became so lewd as their popularity grew that in 1843 they were made illegal under Louisiana law.

Calinda songs were popular in Africa and the West Indies, composed of loose, improvised refrains dealing with topical and often highly satirical or scurrilous material, often sung as a **work song**.

▷ **cakewalk; folk dance**

calumet

SACRED PIPE OF NATIVE NORTH AMERI-CANS, a key element in all ceremonies of peace and welcome. To smoke together is a symbol of kinship amongst most groups, but for many of the Plains peoples especially the purpose of the calumet went far beyond the expression of friendship. Ascending smoke, which disperses into the sky, is a medium peculiarly associated with the Great Spirit and to inhale and expel this smoke was to invoke the presence and blessing of the god, and any pacts or promises make in such conditions would be sacred and binding. Hence pipe-smoking cere-monies were hedged round with ritual, often involving elaborate dances with members of the group specially ap-pointed as pipe-bearers. In such cere-monies smoke functioned like incense, as a burnt offering.

The calumet itself, differing from everyday pipes in its sacred function, tended to be highly decorated as befitted such an important artefact. The Pawnee developed a particularly intricate cere-mony known as *hako*, in which the calumet stems sported eagle feathers, perforations and tokens symbolic of earth, water, trees and the air. The bowl of the calumet was generally carved from catlinite, the soft red stone of Dakota, and the stems from ashwood. As com-mercially minded whites spotted their market and began to manufacture mass-produced pipes in Europe to be exported and sold to Native Americans, the calumet fell into decline.

calusar

ROMANIAN DANCE, performed in mid-winter and on **All Souls' Day** by a male troupe incorporating a **hobby-horse,** a fool, a goat and a hermaphroditic figure sporting both male and female char-acteristics. The ritualistic dance they perform represents the battle for succes-sion of the seasons, and was formerly so realistic as to prove fatal to the parti-cipants. Its pagan roots are similar to those of the English **Morris dance**, and the participants are required to take similar oaths.

calypso

CARRIBEAN SONG FORM, originating in Trinidad, which features highly imagina-tive and topical lyrics in simple verse forms. Words are improvised to fit a scheme of eight-line stanzas followed by a four-line refrain, a typical **ballad** form, with a simple rhyme pattern. This formal simplicity belies the sophistication of the lyrics, which are traditionally topical, allusive, satirical and very witty. Words are given characteristically distorted stress patterns to fit the syncopated rhythms of the music, local dialect is often exaggerated and colloquialisms are widely incorporated. Traditional instruments accompanying the calypso include **guitar**, maracas, tamboo-bamboo (varying lengths of bamboo struck against the ground) and more recently steel **drums**. Calypso songs match perfectly with the **carnival** mood, and the form's development has been clearly linked to carnival dances.

In calypso contests, singers exchange improvised allusive insults and are judged by the delighted audience. In the modern carnival season at the beginning of each year a new calypso 'king' is chosen and new songs added to the calypso repertoire.

Camber

PRINCE OF BRITAIN, the second son of **Brut**. He is said in legend to have received Wales as a portion from his father, and to have given his name to the area, Cambria.

camel

DOMESTIC ANIMAL, found mainly in Asia and North Africa (although the wild descendants of domestic camels also inhabit the Australian outback). They have traditionally been utilized by caravans of Arabian nomads, as their astonishing capacity to forgo water and food during long tramps across the desert makes them ideal travelling companions. Less accommodating however is their notorious temperament; they are given to bad-tempered spitting and stubbornness, and can kick and bite very nastily Because of their value in the Middle East they are highly prized as offerings, and a camel producing ten young is considered sacred. In India camel bones buried under the doorway are thought to protect from **ghosts**. Hebrews consider camels unclean, Aristotle regarded it as an animal of unbridled libidinousness, and elsewhere, in Germany for example, the word camel is an insult to denote a clumsy, offensive person.

In Christian lore, the camel's capacity for abstinence made it a symbol of self-restraint and because of its lowly duties as a beast of burden it was closely associated with humility and penitence (John the Baptist for example wore rough clothes of camel's hair). Mohammed's camel Al Adha was said to have borne his master from Jerusalem to Mecca with just four steps, earning by his swiftness a place in heaven.

In most animal fables of Asia and Africa however the camel is the butt of the other animals' jokes, characterized as slow and dull.

Camelot

LEGENDARY CITY, where **Arthur** held court among the Knights of the **Round Table**. Controversy rages as to its actual site; Malory locates it at Winchester in his *Morte d'Arthur*, but more ancient legends make the claim for Caerleon in Monmouthshire, Cadbury in Somerset, or Camelford, near Tintagel, in Cornwall.

Camilla

VIRGIN QUEEN OF THE VOLSCIANS, a devotee of the chaste goddess Diana and like her an accomplished archer. According to Roman legend her father, Metabus, arrived a the river Amazenus pursued by his enemies. He lashed his baby daughter to a javelin, committed her to the protection of Diana, and threw her safely across the river before himself swimming over to join her. She aided Turnus in his fight against Aeneas. She is best remembered perhaps for her swiftness of foot; according to Virgil she could run across a field of corn without making a single blade bend, and skim across the sea without getting her feet at all wet.

Camlan, Battle of

BRITISH BATTLE, at which **Arthur** was mortally wounded. It signified the end of the Arthurian age and the dispersal of the Knights of the **Round Table**.

camomile

PUNGENT HERB, genus *Anthemis* (family Compositae), widely used in Europe particularly in medical preparations. Ancient Egyptians considered camomile sacred, so effective was it as a remedy, and in ancient Rome it was used as an antidote to snake bites. An infusion of camomile leaves and/or flowers was widely drunk in Europe; in Ireland it was believed to cure pleurisy, Culpeper recommends it for stitches and other sharp pains, and in many areas camomile tea is drunk to ward off colds, aches and nausea. In Germany it is considered particularly useful as a treatment for toothache, and the flowers, known as *Heermännchen*, are said to be the souls of damned soldiers. In genteel Elizabethan England camomile lawns were much in vogue, as they produced a sweet smell when crushed underfoot.

campus lore

COMMON BREEDING GROUND FOR MODERN AMERICAN FOLKLORE. Various time-honoured stories, usually of a macabre character, have accumulated in college campuses throughout the country to form a student lore of anecdotes. One of the most famous is the 'Hook' story, reported to have occurred in innumerable locations. A co-ed and her boyfriend have stopped the car in a secluded lane, but as they kiss the news comes over the radio that a dangerous prisoner, with a hook for a hand, has escaped from a nearby prison. Terrified, the girl insists that the boy drive her home and he does so, although in his irritation he pulls away very sharply. When they reach campus, they discover a hook hanging from the passenger's door-handle. Such tales are usually recounted to new students late at night in a suitably hushed and erie atmosphere, using the techniques of pleasurably terrifying tales told around the world.

Another branch of campus lore deals with more light-hearted aspects of college life, such as exam papers. One popular anecdote in circulation in numerous colleges tells of the student who, faced with a question about which he knows nothing, writes a variation on the following formula: 'Many of the greatest minds of our time have considered the question of x, and who am I to criticize their life's work? I would prefer today to address the important issue of y . . .', going on to write about a more familiar topic. Invariably the student passes.

▷ **urban legends**

Candaules

KING OF LYDIA, the last ruler of the second dynasty. He was overthrown by **Gyges**, in some accounts because he boastfully exposed his wife to him; the outraged queen then plotted with Gyges the destruction of her husband. She later married the usurper to remove her shame. Plato's version of the legend records how he was overcome by the use of a magic ring of **invisibility**.

candle

ANCIENT SOURCE OF LIGHT AND HEAT, known to the ancient Egyptians and Myceneans. Candles most commonly consist of wax, tallow or some similar slow-burning material surrounding a fibre wick. Because of the medieval Christian tradition that **bees** came from heaven, it became *de rigeur* to use only beeswax for church candles. As a portable and convenient miniature fire, that most numinous of elements, candles have been utilized in sacred ceremonies and rituals in many civilizations. The tradition of placing candles around a corpse laid out before burial, still observed especially in many Catholic countries, derives from the ancient belief that evil spirits may not pass through a circle of fire.

Many superstitions exist concerning the significance of the candle flame's behaviour; if the flame has a blue cast it indicates the presence of a ghost in the room, or perhaps the onset of a frost. Should a spark fly from it it presages a letter to the one it falls by, although in Austria this is signalled by the wick separating into two distinct flames. In nearby Germany this phenomenon is regarded as an omen of coming death.

▷ **hand of glory; nursery rhymes**

Candlemas

CHRISTIAN FEAST, also known as the Presentation of Christ in the Temple, the Feast of the Purification of the Virgin **Mary** (until the calendar reforms of 1969) or, in the Greek church, Hypapante. Celebrated on 2 February, it commemorates **Mary**'s journey to the Temple to present the infant Jesus 40 days after his birth, as Jewish law demanded (Luke 2: 22-38). Its name may derive from the custom, dating at least form the fifth century, of celebrating the day with candle-lit processions, although some scholars say it was not used until the eleventh century when candles were blessed at the altar on this day. These customs recall ancient pre-spring festivals, in which torches were carried to purify the fields and prepare for new life.

The weather on Candlemas day was watched closely in Britain, since it was a forecast for the year ahead:

> If Candlemas Day be fair and bright
> Winter will have another flight;
> If Candlemas Day be shower and rain,
> Winter is gone and will not come again.

This has been translated in the US into **Groundhog Day,** a secular celebration on the same day.

cante fable

FORM OF NARRATIVE TALE, found in many different cultures, combining prose narration and song. The parts to be sung are generally the key elements in the tale: dialogue, magical spells or repeated incantations, riddles, or proverbial sayings. The cante fable form is found in the tales of Grimm, the *Panchatantra*, Celtic hero tales, Teutonic sagas, the *Arabian Nights*, and particularly in oral tales of Africa and the Caribbean. Ancient, seemingly disconnected snatches of rhyme that survive in many folk cultures, for example in **children's lore** in the West, may derive from cante fables now all but lost, the prose narrative forgotten and the kernel of verse alone surviving.

Canute

DANISH KING, ruler of England, Denmark and Norway. He was widely respected, renowned in his day and celebrated in subsequent lore as a wise, courageous and enlightened ruler. He is chiefly remembered for the legend recorded in Holinshed's *Chronicles*, as the king who sat in his throne on the shore and commanded the tide to desist from coming in. Naturally enough, the waves paid no attention and Canute was soon waist-deep in brine. Although this is frequently taken as a warning against false pride, it seems that Canute may have had the rather nobler motive of proving to certain over-flattering elements in his court that there were limits even to his influence.

Canute

cap of invisibility

MAGIC OBJECT, a staple **motif** of many European folktales. The wearer of such a cap may observe his enemies without himself being seen. In Greek mythology it was the work of the **Cyclops**, possessed by Hades and borrowed by Hermes and **Perseus**. In **fairy tales** the young, enterprising hero often comes by it clandestinely, stealing it from a giant or from other mortals who are occupied with a quarrel. Occasionally, as in the **Jack tales**, it may be given as a gift from a supernatural. Such a cap is also a feature of several Native American tales, particularly among the Plains groups and peoples of the south-west.
▷ **invisibility; yeck**

Cap o' Rushes

ENGLISH FOLKTALE, known throughout Europe. It shares many of the features of the **Cinderella** tale type, such as the **recognition token** and the motif of menial disguise feature. A father asks his daughters how much they love him, and when the youngest tells him her love is like that of bread (or meat) for **salt** he banishes her in rage, not realizing that she in fact loves him best. The heroine goes through many hardships and finally becomes a minion, disguised in a hooded cape made of rushes. Her father comes to the castle at which she works; she prepares a meal without any salt and only then does he appreciate the true value of her love, at which point she reveals herself. In some versions the three-fold visit to a ball as a mysterious princess who wins the heart of the prince is also included, and the unsalted meal is the wedding feast at which the father is present.
▷ **King Lear judgement**

Captain Kidd (c.1645–1701)

HISTORICAL PIRATE, immortalized in British and American balladry and popular lore. Scottish-born William Kidd started a lucrative ship company in New York City. He originally aided the British colonial government in its fight against pirates, but decided in 1697 that a career in piracy offered better prospects. After many buccaneering adventures, all now celebrated in song, he was eventually apprehended by the British authorities and hung. The songs telling of his deeds are generally **come-all-ye** types, sung by sailors who generally call him Robert for reasons which are unclear. As well as moralistic tales urging the listeners to avoid such evil exploits by pointing to Kidd's ultimate fate, there are many legends relating to the pirate's alleged treasure, supposed to have been buried in a variety of different sites and still guarded from discovery by his spirit.

carnation

FRAGRANT HERBACEOUS FLOWER, genus *Dianthus* of the family Caryophyllaceae, a native of the Mediterranean and widely cultivated for its decorative frilled petals.

In Christian lore the carnation is said to have sprung from the tears of **Mary** on her way to the Cross; in some versions it appeared when Jesus was born. Partly because of this association, and partly because in Victorian flower language the carnation represented 'admiration', the pink carnation was named in 1907 by Anna Jarvis of Philadelphia as the symbol of Mothers' Day in the USA.

In Elizabethan times it was used as a frugal alternative to cloves to spice wine and ale, hence its traditional name, sop-in-wine, and its early name gilli-flower derives from the Latin for clove, *caryophyllum*. This association also linked with the carnation many of the virtues traditionally ascribed to cloves, particularly efficacy in curing fevers and toothache.

Native Mexicans regard the carnation as a flower sacred to the dead, and pile blooms around a body as preparation for burial. It is used in Korea for **divination**; a stem bearing these flowers is placed in the hair and the order in which the blooms fade indicates the future of the wearer—if the first to dry is the top bloom, old age will be the hardest stage of life, if the middle, the middle years, and if the bottom, the youth of the wearer will be hard. It is considered extremely unlucky for all three to wither together.

carnival

FOLK CELEBRATION, a riotous festival which freely mixes pagan and religious tradition. Carnival itself originated in Europe in the Middle Ages as an exuberant, colourful and usually licentious celebration to celebrate the return of Spring. It was later established in the period before Lent, the last few days before abstinence was required by the Church. It has survived most fully in those countries with a strong Roman Catholic tradition, and hence also in Spanish colonies such as Mexico. The word itself is popularly supposed to be derived into Italian from the Latin *carne vale*, farewell to meat, but it is more likely to be a contraction of Latin *carnem levare*, the putting aside of meat. The Mardi Gras of France corresponds to Shrove Tuesday, the day before Lent and therefore the height of the celebrations.

In the most primitive societies there are to be found traditional festivals, celebrating the arrival of spring and new life with much noise and activity to drive

carnival

away winter and its harmful demons. Many carnival practices, such as the fool's stick, the obscenities, disguise and the throwing of fire, originate from such fertility rites. More formalized festivals in Roman times, such as the Lupercalia or **Saturnalia**, had an enormous influence on European tradition. By the Middle Ages, carnival was an established part of the Church's year, with elaborate costumes and processions of floats throughout the cities.

Bands of players grew up to perform the traditional dances and drama of carnival, the **mummers** and Morris groups of England (from which the morality plays would later develop), the Basque *Masacaradas*, the *Scheller* in Germany. As European influence spread to the New World with colonization, carnival developed different characteristics as the native traditions incorporated the new festival. Hence in the famous Mexican carnivals native dances survive alongside those imported from Spain and the religious rituals take place together with native rites. Carnival in America is mainly confined to Central South America, but here it is celebrated on an astonishing scale, with ornate costumes and **masks** and magnificent floats.

In recent times the great carnivals of Rio de Janeiro and the Mardi Gras of New Orleans, while retaining their opulence, have lost much of their original symbolism and meaning and have become little more than magnificent entertainment. The word itself has come to be applied more generally, referring to any large festival or celebration without reference to its place in the Church's calendar.
▷ **Fastnacht**

carol

TRADITIONAL ENGLISH SONG, more specifically a late medieval form in which verses alternate with a repeated refrain which begins and ends the piece. The earliest carols were probably sung to accompany dances and may have covered a wide range of subjects, but by the early 14th century the carol was seen as primarily a religious song, particularly one appropriate to **Christmas** festivities. Popular subjects included the Virgin

Mary, the Christ-child and the Passion. During the 15th century carols became more complex, with polyphonic voices and elaborate rhythms transforming the early vernacular form into a musical and literary art, but many carols survive from the more purely folk tradition. A common type is the call to neighbours to worship the Christ-child, with a list of humble presents appropriate to the lives of the peasants who sang the song. So for example, a child might bring a ball or toy for the new baby, a shepherd warm sheep's milk, and so on. The situation of the folk themselves is revealed as clearly as the plight of the Holy Family; a carol from Burgundy describes the pains taken by an old man with crippling gout to make his pilgrimage to the stable. Many carols preserve pre-Christian traditions, for example nature carols such as *The Holly and the Ivy* and the wassails, ancient songs of drinking to ensure healthy crops for the new year. The medieval courtly tradition is evident in a few carols, for example *I Sing of a Maiden*.

With the Reformation and especially with the austerities of Puritan rule in the 17th century the carol tradition died out, to be revived by churchmen such as Wesley in the late 18th century. Along with new carols such as *O Little Town of Bethlehem*, with their unambiguously Christian message, more ancient folk wisdom was resurrected in carols such as *I Saw Three Ships Go Sailing By* and the perennial concerns of the folk during the winter feast resurfaced in songs such as *Deck the Halls with Boughs of Holly*.
▷ **ballad**; **Christmas**

Carson, Kit (1809–68)

AMERICAN TRAPPER AND HUNTER, real name Christopher Carson. He was renowned for his extensive knowledge and understanding of Native Americans, and served as guide for the explorations of John Charles Frémont. He entered American pioneer lore as the archetypal backwoodsman, with marvellous skill and empathy for nature, around whom many **tall tales** accumulated.

Casanova (1725–98)

ITALIAN ADVENTURER, full name Giacomo Girolamo Casanova de Seingalt.

His name has passed into popular folklore as a byword for an amorous philanderer. After expulsion from a seminary in 1741 for scandalous behaviour, he took on several more or less disreputable positions and escaped from prison in 1756 to spend the next 20 years wandering throughout the aristocratic centres of Europe, indulging in fraud, satire and romantic liaisons and always moving on briskly from the last scandal. His colourful life was preserved in his salacious autobiography, *Mémoires écrites par lui-même* (first published in 12 volumes, 1828–38).

Casey Jones (1864–1900)

BALLAD HERO OF AMERICAN LORE, real name John Luther Jones. He was a railroad engineer in Illinois, noted for his speed and resourcefulness. One day however his daring went a stroke too far, and he died in a train collision after warning the stoker to jump. He was found with one hand still on the whistle and the other on the brake. The original ballad celebrating his skill and his death was composed by his friend Wallace Saunders, and another version published by Lawrence Siebert and Eddie Newton in 1909 became a vaudeville hit and brought his legend into popular lore.

castanets

FOLK INSTRUMENT, especially characteristic of Spanish and Balearic music, formed from two hollowed-out ovals of wood (or occasionally another substance such as ivory), held between thumb and forefinger and clicked rhythmically, usually while dancing. The instrument is thought to have been imported into Spain by Phoenicians; similar instruments were known among ancient Greeks, Romans, Egyptians and Moors. The name is derived from Latin *castaño*, chestnut, which aptly suggests its rounded, polished appearance.

Castanets are used particularly in exciting, rhythmic dances such as the **tarantella**, **flamenco**, **fandango** and sarabande. This reflects an ancient tradition; castanets were once employed by the worshippers of Dionysus in their orgiastic rituals.

Caswallan

KING OF BRITAIN, brother of Llud, whose story is told in the *Mabinogion*. While **Bran the Blessed** was absent in Ireland, Caswallan cast a spell of illusion over his enemy's son, Caradawc, so that the youth could see only Caswallan's sword as it flashed in battle and not the man himself. In some versions this was achieved by a cloak of **invisibility**. He is supposed to have held power when Caesar invaded in Britain in 54BC.

cat

ANIMAL OF SUPERSTITION AND FOLKLORE. Since the days when it was sacred in Egyptian and other ancient religions, the cat has enjoyed a significant degree of respect in folklore. In much European, Native American and African tradition it is considered very bad luck to harm a cat, for fear of retribution from the **Devil** or the cat itself, and this is probably the remnant of a more ancient taboo.

The cat is frequently said to portend either good or evil fortune; a black cat crossing one's path, for example, can be thought to signify either. The black cat is often regarded as a supernatural being usually associated with the Devil or **witchcraft**; many old women who enjoyed the company of a pet cat were executed in the witch-hunt fever which swept Europe and America in the 16th and 17th centuries.

Some European traditions claim that if a cat jumps over the coffin at a burial, the corpse will become a **vampire** unless the cat is caught and killed. Among some South American groups, the *Ccoa* is feared as an evil and terrifying cat-spirit.

The sight of a cat washing its face is said to indicate the approach of rain; when the cat performs its toilet in the parlour, it is a sign that guests will soon be arriving. Many ships traditionally carried a cat as a lucky **mascot**, and the sailors would look to it for weather predictions. If the cat were especially frisky, they would expect strong winds. It was also thought that if the ship's cat were to be caught and caged, the ship would run into unfavourable winds. The 'catseye', a gemstone showing a line of light across its cut surface like that of a cat's pupil, is often used as a protective charm in Asia.

cat

The antipathy between cat and **mouse** has passed into the folk consciousness of nearly every nation, along with the parallel relationship between **dog** and cat. Numerous proverbs have been recorded on the theme; an old English jingle observes that 'When the cat's away, the mice will play'. A Serbian proverb, 'Who doesn't feed the cat feeds the mice', neatly shows the need for prudence in economy. Another popular belief which has passed into proverb-lore is that the cat has nine lives, presumably because it seems to escape danger so agilely. Allied to this is the observation that a cat will always land on its feet, and this has been used as an illustration of a person who seems miraculously to avoid trouble.

Although generally domesticated, the cat of course belongs to a family of rather more ferocious beasts, and this latent wildness is the subject of several proverbs: in Italy, 'A trapped cat becomes a lion', in Spain 'The cat always leaves its friends scratched'.

The cat features in several popular folk narratives, most famously as **Dick Whittington**'s cat, who made his master's fortune by his prowess as a mouser, and **Puss in Boots**. It plays a less heroic part in a common urban legend, as a corpse being transported in a cardboard box or plastic bag from its adoring owner's high-rise flat to a friend's garden for burial. In the course of the journey, the package is stolen and

the interest of the tale lies with the shock occasioned to the thief, usually an old lady, on discovering her prize. Sometimes the package is lost by accident, when the owner mistakenly picks up an old lady's shopping instead of the cat at the butcher's, and the listener is left to imagine the reaction of the other party.
▷ **belling the cat**; **King o' the Cats**

Cat Maiden

ANIMAL FABLE, found in the collection of **Aesop** and elsewhere world-wide. A female cat, enamoured of a comely young man, begs Venus for help. Venus takes compassion on her plight and duly transforms her into a beautiful woman, and the two quickly declare their love and marry. Venus however begins to doubt whether the transformation from animal to human has been entirely successful, and to test the woman sends a **mouse** scuttling before her. Cat-like, the woman pounces upon it while her young husband watches in revulsion and dismay. Her true nature thus revealed, the girl is returned to her cat shape by Venus. Aesop's moral is that 'what is bred in the bone will never be absent in the flesh.' In the *Panchatantra* a similar tale is told of a mouse transformed into a woman who is unhappy with all the various suitors proposed for her and finally asks to be transformed into a mouse again so that she can marry the mouse king.
▷ **beast marriage**; **shape-shifting**

cat's cradle

STRING FIGURE GAME, widely played in Europe and North America by children particularly. Two players exchange a loop of string between both hands in set movements to produce a limited series of patterns all of which have loosely appropriate names such as fish-on-a-dish, tram lines and so on. This is a poor remnant of a much more ancient and varied custom, still alive in parts of Africa, the Americas and the Pacific. String figures may be used to illustrate folktales (often requiring an effort of imagination on the part of the listeners) or as a test of skill, but there are deeper, more mythical purposes too. Inuits and others use such figures in rituals to hold back the sun descending from the summer **solstice**. Often the figures themselves form a miniature narrative sequence; a house might be constructed, attacked and destroyed or a trap is built to catch a trouble-maker and sprung.

catch tale

TYPE OF STORY, a tale told not primarily for narrative or imaginative content but to trick the listener into making an inappropriate or foolish response. Such tales are a feature of **children's lore** in Europe and North America, and exist in limited forms in African folklore. An example is the widespread type in which the victim is enjoined to repeat the words 'just like me' after each phrase. This he dutifully does without consequence until the last phrase, 'I saw a little monkey', at which he may unthinkingly make himself the butt of the teller's joke. A similar concept underpins the old rhyme 'Adam and Eve and Pinchme':

Adam and Eve and Pinchme
Went down to the river to bathe.
Adam and Eve were drowned,
And who do you think was saved?

The unwary response, 'pinch me', is then mischievously interpreted as an invitation. In a particularly disorientating Canadian catch tale-type, the teller is 'killed off' in his own narrative.

▷ **jokes**; **riddles**

caterpillar

LARVA OF A BUTTERFLY OR MOTH, a sectioned, cylindrical creature having multiple legs and six eyes, with jaws well adapted to munching through leaves. They have traditionally been regarded with suspicion in Europe, as companions of **witches** (in Germany), as the fruit of the **Devil**'s tears (in Romania), and among the Bantu they are said to embody the souls of the dead.

They have their uses in folk medicine however, as a salve applied to the skin after a poisonous snake bite, or, when chewed, to relive toothache. In England a caterpillar was used as a charm against fevers.

Catherine, St (c.290–c.310)

'THE BRIDE OF CHRIST', who gave her name to the 'Catherine wheel'. Born of a wealthy, possibly even a royal, family in Alexandria, she was converted by a vision at the age of about 18 and denounced the emperor Maxentius for his persecution of the Christians. Thinking to silence this upstart girl, the emperor confronted her with 50 pagan philosophers; instead of exposing the fallacies of her faith through reason, however, they were unable to answer her arguments (some accounts say they were all converted) and the furious Maxentius had them executed. He then tried to bribe Catherine into silence with the offer of a royal marriage, and was further enraged when she refused, calmly declaring herself 'the bride of Christ'.

Catherine was imprisoned, but not silenced. On returning home from a camp inspection one day Maxentius found that his wife, his chief soldier Porphyrius and 200 of his imperial guard had been converted to Christianity. By now almost insane with anger, Maxentius executed them and prepared a spiked wheel on which Catherine was to be broken, but he was thwarted again when the wheel burst leaving Catherine unharmed, although several spectators were killed by flying splinters. Finally he had the troublesome saint beheaded, at which it is said milk rather than blood ran from her veins.

The various traditions are unanimous that the saint's body was miraculously translated to Mount Sinai by angels, where Emperor Justinian built a monastery for hermits in 527. The monastery has born the name of St Catherine since the eighth or ninth century, and her shrine is displayed there. It is thought that monks returning from pilgrimage may have brought these precious relics back to their monastery in the eighth century.

From this spectacular legend, and flourishing especially in the devout and credulous Middle Ages, the cult of Catherine swept the Christian world. There are countless church dedications, many cycles of her life in murals and stained glass survive in Britain, and she is frequently depicted in paintings, tapestries and manuscripts, identified by the wheel of her martyrdom or shown confounding the pagan philosophers.

The obvious association of her legend with learning and Christian apologetics has led to Catherine's patronage of various related groups; the link with libraries may also be due to the famous ancient library at Alexandria. Her feast-day is 25 November, and she is the patron saint of philosophers, preachers, librarians, young girls and craftsmen working with a wheel (eg potters, spinners etc).

Catskin

EUROPEAN TALE CYCLE, which shares significant elements of the Cinderella type. The eponymous heroine flees cruelty at home and disguises herself in animal furs or skins (sometimes in rags or even a wooden cloak). She takes a menial position at court and appears periodically and mysteriously in her original fine clothes or magically robed. When the prince pines with love for this unknown beauty she reveals herself, usually by some token of recognition such as a ring given to her by the prince.
▷ **Cinderella; recognition token**

cattle

ANIMALS OF MYTH AND FOLKLORE, symbols of fertility and health. Many ancient religions emphasized the sacred nature of cattle; the **cow** is still regarded as a sacred animal in India today. In Africa too, and wherever pastoral society survives, cattle are revered and carefully protected with charms and rituals.

In ancient Egyptian times, the priestess and royal princesses were closely associated with bulls. A bull stood in the temple of Osiris, to which the princesses were reported to ritually expose their sexual parts, and Egyptian princesses were sometimes buried in sarcophagi shaped like cows, accompanied by a sacred bull. Since the rate at which cattle bred and produced milk determined the livelihood of their owners, fertility naturally became an issue of burning importance, and was quickly linked with the human sexual act. Classical myth supports this connection; Zeus appears as a bull to seduce Europa, and Pasiphae, inflamed with lust for a bull, disguises herself as a cow and subsequently gives birth to the hybrid **Minotaur**.

Bulls have long been regarded as an emblem of divinity in the East, especially in ancient Persia and Egypt; even the God of the Israelites was worshipped as a bull (Exodus 32). As an extension of its divine attributes, parts of the bull were frequently used by Greek priests, who would drink bulls' blood before making their prophecies. The great strength of the bull has led to its frequent use, especially in Africa, as a ritual meal for warriors to impart strength and courage. In pastoral Europe, removed from the strong Eastern tradition of the sacredness of cattle, various customs grew up to ensure the fertility of this most valuable of possessions. Cows would be driven through fire or beaten to ensure their well-being, and protective charms of leaves and plants hung over their sheds. Folktales such as **Jack and the Beanstalk**, in which the foolish Jack exasperates his mother by parting with their cow for a handful of beans, illustrate the centrality of cattle in the folk economy and consciousness.

In Europe, cattle were widely believed to receive the gift of speech annually on **Christmas** Eve, commemorating the time when they stood around the manger in Bethlehem to worship the Christ-child, and it was said that they discussed the names of those fated to die before the next Christmas.
▷ **bull-roarer; Speewah, The**

cauldron

MAGIC OBJECT OF FOLKLORE, a characteristically Celtic motif which appears occasionally in African, Native American and Asian folktales.

Probably the most famous example is **Bran the Blessed**'s marvellous fairy-wrought cauldron of regeneration, which according to the *Mabinogion* had the virtue of restoring to health even a fatally wounded body placed in it. In a parallel ancient Greek myth, Demeter places the son of Celeus (Demophon) in a cauldron above a fire in an attempt to make him immortal.

In Norse mythology the magic cauldron Odhrerir contained the draught of poets, concocted by the **dwarfs** Fjalar and Galar from the blood of the wise

Kvasir. Odin coveted this potion, which could impart ancient wisdom and occult knowledge, and transformed himself into a **snake** to drink the cauldron dry. He thus carried the mead back to **Asgard**, home of the gods, where he spat it into a vessel. The concept of potions in cauldrons has traditionally been associated with **witchcraft** in Western folklore, and such potions were said to be noxious and evilly purposed, containing such unwholesome ingredients as aborted foetuses or toads' eyes.

In European folktales the motif of the inexhaustible cauldron is common; **Dagda** of the **Tuatha de Danann** possessed one such pot, and the old woman in the tale collected by Grimm finds it impossible to stop the pot that is endlessly spewing porridge. The cauldron of **Annwn** is variously reported as inexhaustible or blessed with peculiar discrimination, such that it refuses to prepare food for a coward.

ceasg

FABULOUS CREATURE OF THE SCOTTISH HIGHLANDS, a type of **mermaid**. Her upper body is that of a beautiful woman, but her lower half resembles the tail of the salmon. Like her distant relative, the **selkie**, she may agree to grant three wishes to the mortal who captures her and has even been known to marry human men, producing sons remarkable for their skills at sea and their powers of navigation. However she may use her beauty to lure young men into the sea, from whence they may never return.

Celtic folklore

THE TERM CELTIC is generally applied to cultures in Ireland, Wales, the Highlands and Western Isles of Scotland, Cornwall, the Isle of Man and Brittany. In Ireland and Scotland especially, situated on the westernmost fringes of European civilization and still largely rural even today, the Celtic traditions have been astonishingly well preserved over the centuries. Two distinct linguistic and cultural traditions can be identified; Goidelic (Ireland, Scotland and the Gaelic-speaking Isle of Man), and Brythonic, from which developed the Welsh, Cornish and Breton varieties of language.

In all the Celtic areas, but especially in Ireland and Brittany where it has endured the longest, the influence of Catholicism has been enormous. Many ancient myth tales have been transferred on to **saints**, so for example the Celtic goddess of fire, fertility and crafts, Brigid, became identified with the sixth-century saint **Brigid**, or Bride, 'the Mary of the Gael'. In Ireland and Cornwall there are many holy springs, ancient cults made Christian by naming the springs after saints, and the peasants would leave tokens such as pins or buttons in the water, or tie rags on nearby trees, to secure their request for healing.

Brythonic folklore

Welsh and Cornish folklore is characterized by a wealth of fairy-lore rather than the epic cycles of the Gaelic tradition, although it may well be that these once existed but are now lost. Eleven of the most popular tales are collected in the *Mabinogion*, preserved in 14th-century texts, in which the traditional form of telling is made more consciously literary, and the inclusion of French romances demonstrate the strong Norman influence already felt in Wales, at least among the literate classes. In Cornwall the main areas of folklore which survive are anecdotal tales of travellers who encounter fairy bands, or **changelings**. In Brittany these fairy tales and anecdotes are equally prevalent, but there is also an older, more complex surviving lore, including belief in Ankou, a personification of death as a skeletal figure destroying his victims with a scythe or a sword. The creaking of his cart would strike fear into the heart of the Breton peasant.

Goidelic folklore

Much of the Goidelic pre-history and mythology has been preserved in Ireland's early epics, most notably the **Ulster cycle**, which chronicles the king of the Uliad people, **Conchobar**, and the great warrior **Cuchulainn**. The stories circulated in oral tradition from early times, and were probably first written down in the eighth century. A later prose work, the **Fenian cycle** of the 12th century, deals with the adventures of the warrior hero **Finn MacCumhal**, and it too was probably drawn largely from oral tradition.

A characteristic form of Old Irish legend is the voyage-story, or **imrama**. The earliest surviving manuscript is the eighth-century *Voyage of Bran*, and many more were written over the next eight centuries. The hero is usually driven by a desire to revenge himself, or to find the 'Happy Isles'. This **otherworld**, an island of amazing beauty, is a pagan paradise in the earlier works, with debauchery and feasting for the successful travellers, but in later works it becomes a metaphor for the Christian Heaven, most fully realised in the legend of St **Brendan the Navigator**, *The Voyage of Brandon*.

By medieval times the professional priests and bards had lost their monopoly on myth and the lore became the province of the peasants. Removed from the economic and scholarly influences of the Renaissance in the rest of Europe, the Irish continued to transmit through the generations their centuries-old lore of tales, farming and seasonal festivals. Although widely Christianized by St **Patrick** and others after him, the strong pagan traditions of Ireland had held

their own and the new religion was practised alongside the old for many centuries.

The shanachie, or professional story-teller, preserved the rich store of Irish folktales well into the 20th century, when bodies such as the Irish Folklore Commission began to collect and preserve them in a scholarly manner. Scottish and Manx Gaelic began to differ from the Irish only in the 16th century: the three areas shared a common body of tradition but nowhere else is the lore preserved as well as in Ireland.

▷ **Glas Ghaibhneach**; **Christianity and folklore**

centaur

MONSTERS OF ANCIENT THESSALY, half-human, half-horse. They were said to be the offspring of Ixion and Nephele (who appeared as a cloud), or of their child Centaurus who lusted after the mare Magnesian. In other versions, they arose from the semen of Zeus, the result of his lust for Aphrodite. In reality, their myth may simply have originated with the wild tribes of Thessaly, known as extraordinarily skilled horsemen.

Although some centaurs, such as

centaur

Chiron (son of Cronos) and Pholus, were stately creatures whose wisdom was sought by ancient Greek heroes such as **Jason**, Achilles and **Heracles**, most of the breed appear to have been licentious, violent creatures, best known for their debauched behaviour at the wedding feast of Hippodameia and Pirithous of the Lapiths, at which they attempted to rape the female guests and slaughter the men. Because of this reputation, they became an emblem for base, bestial nature in medieval Christian thought, and by extension man's integral animal nature.

The archer of the **zodiac**, Sagittarius, is said to be the centaur Chiron, who was accidentally struck by a poisoned arrow from his friend Heracles during a battle with other centaurs. Being immortal, he appealed to Zeus for release from the poisonous wound and was set in the sky as a constellation. This constellation was represented by a centaur in Babylonian civilization, around the 11th century BC.

▷ **sky people**; **stars**

Central Asian folklore

CENTRAL ASIAN GROUPS have tended to be pastoral/nomadic. One of the largest racial groups in the continent is the Mongoloid type, who are found in Siberia and Central Asia. In Siberia, less developed and more sparsely-populated than the rest of the continent, aboriginal groups still survive, occupied mainly in reindeer herding, hunting and fishing.

The Islamic peoples of the Middle East are traditionally strongly patriarchal, and many customs relate directly to this. For example, if there have been several infant deaths in a family, a baby boy might be dressed as a girl and referred to in the feminine to protect him from evil spirits by making him less desirable. There is no reward for the messenger who brings news of a baby girl, and no celebration for the birth. A menstruating woman is considered dangerous, likely to transmit evil spirits, and must remain secluded and isolated. Many cultures share this fear of **menstruation**.

Another feature of the lore is the belief in the **evil eye**, which causes illness and death, and is attracted particularly by good luck and happiness. To delude the evil eye, parents may keep their children unkempt in public and may constantly complain about them, and will often make gloomy predictions about their affairs. Ancient Hebrew writings such as the Old Testament reveal a fund of stories showing fairytale motifs, such as the speaking animal (Balaam's ass), the **taboo** (Lot's wife who looks back as she flees the city and is turned into a pillar of salt) and the hero exposed as a child (Moses in the bulrushes), and a vast fund of popular Hebrew wisdom is collected in the Proverbs attributed to Solomon. The epic of **Gilgamesh** is composed of several originally distinct tales with folkloric motifs such as the fight against the Ogre of the Mountain.

chameleon

TREE-DWELLING LIZARD, whose chief characteristic is a capacity for changing colour in response to environmental factors. Chameleons (belonging to the reptile family Chamaeleontidae) are found mainly in southern Africa, especially Madagascar, although certain species inhabit southern Europe, India and Sri Lanka. Chameleon features as a character in many African **animal tales**; in a Duruma tale of East Africa Chameleon loses a race with Lizard and thereby forfeits eternal life for humans, and this is why he now goes so slowly and sadly on his way.

changeling

FAIRY LEFT IN PLACE OF A HUMAN BABY, often a deformed or ill-favoured supernatural child. The healthy human child is kidnapped and brought up by the fairies. The ancient belief that children are particularly vulnerable to attacks by evil spirits seems to be relevant to this common belief, since those susceptible were babies who had not yet received the protective rite of baptism. The original child can sometimes be restored, if the changeling can be made to laugh, or treated so badly that its fairy parents would be persuaded to take it back. This belief was undoubtedly the cause of much suffering for many deformed babies.

▷ **fairies**

chansons de geste

'SONGS OF DEEDS', Old French epic poems telling of heroic battles and demonstrations of manly courage. The most famous, and probably the earliest, is the 11th-century *La chanson de Roland*, which sets the tone for what was to become an enormously influential genre. Most of the surviving *chansons de geste* are concerned with the doings of **Charlemagne**; the events they chronicle occurred in the 8th and 9th centuries yet they seem not to have been written until the 12th century at the earliest. It remains a matter of controversy whether the poems survived in oral form in the intervening centuries, and therefore truly folkloric, or whether they are the literary creation of later generations. Their form, kernels of historical truth overlain and distorted by legendary accretions, suggests that at least some of the material may have been transmitted as oral narrative.

Later *chansons* are more literary, dealing with courtly love.

▷ **ballad**; **Guillaume d'Orange**; **Roland**

chant

FREE, RHYTHMIC FORM, part-way between song and speech. The chant is known in many forms across the world and can be used for purposes as diverse as sacred ceremony and children's counting games. It is characteristically associated with religion or magic however. Certain members of Native North American groups are credited with the power to attract game by reciting charms, and shamans chant their formulae to heal, summon supernatural spirits or bring disaster on their enemies.

▷ **charms**; **ritual**

chantey see shanty

charivari

MEDIEVAL FRENCH CUSTOM, especially associated with **marriages** that did not meet with general approval. The newly-weds were subjected to teasing and torment ranging from a noisy serenade on tin pots, horns, and any domestic object that could be appropriated to produce a din to the bed-clothes of the bridal chamber being tied together or soiled.

Such pranks became so troublesome, and eventually so licentious, that the Church finally banned the practice and the charivari survived only in rural districts and in an attenuated form elsewhere. The French imported their custom into French Canada and Louisiana, and it found a new lease of life among the rough frontierfolk. Modern survivals include the pranks played upon bridegrooms especially, such as being handcuffed naked to a bridge, and in boisterous processions of cars with tin mugs and boots rattling from the back. Some scholars have speculated that the custom derived from ancient practices to protect the newly-weds, such as making a noise to scare away evil spirits.

Charlemagne (747–814)

CAROLUS MAGNUS, Charles the Great, king of the Franks and Christian emperor of the west, grandson of Charles Martel and the eldest son of Pepin III the Short. On Pepin's death in 768 the Frankish kingdom was divided between Charlemagne and his younger brother Carloman; three years later, on Carloman's death, he became sole ruler. The first years of his reign were spent in strenuous campaigns to subdue and Christianize neighbouring kingdoms. In 778 he led an expedition against the Moors in Spain, but withdrew the same year when his presence was required elsewhere; the celebrated rearguard action at Roncesvalles in which **Roland**, his chief paladin, is said to have been overwhelmed, gave rise to the heroic literature of the *Chanson de Roland*. In 800, after numerous other campaigns, he swept into Italy to support Pope Leo III against the rebellious Romans, and on Christmas Day, 800, in St Peter's Church, was crowned by the pope Emperor of the Romans as 'Carolus Augustus'. The remaining years of his reign were spent in consolidating his vast empire which reached from the Ebro in northern Spain to the Elbe.

He and his twelve followers or paladins are the central figures of most of the surviving *chansons de geste*. In Christian iconography he appears in his armour beside the emperor Constantine

charms

the Great, crowned, with the orb and sceptre of kingship or a miniature model of the cathedral at Aix-la-Chapelle, where his body is supposed to lie.

Many legends are associated with Charlemagne. One of the most famous records how the king was woken by an angel one night and commanded to go out and steal something. On his way, Charlemagne unhorsed a knight who had challenged him, a well-known highwayman named Elbegast. With Elbegast's help, Charlemagne stealthily entered the bedroom of one of his ministers and overheard a plot to assassinate him the following day. Silently stealing a trinket from the room as evidence of his visit, Charlemagne slipped back to his own castle and the following day was able to foil the conspiracy. Elbegast was so impressed at the magnanimity of his Emperor, who had let him go free and had forgiven the contrite conspirators, that he entered Charlemagne's service as an honest man.

In the legend of St Giles, the holy man is Charlemagne's confessor. While celebrating Mass one day, Giles saw before him a tablet let down from heaven bearing details of an unconfessed sin of Charlemagne's; the emperor broke down and confessed his sin (which has been speculatively identified as incest with his sister) and received absolution from Giles.

Charlemagne is said to have ordered the building of Aix-la-Chapelle after a magic ring with the power of great attraction over him was thrown into a pool there. Like **Arthur** and several others, Charlemagne is said to be sleeping in Olenburg, Hesse, awaiting the call of his country in its greatest need.

▷ **sleepers**

charms

PROTECTIVE MAGIC ARTEFACTS, bringers of luck, used to protect the bearer from the **evil eye** and other malevolent forces. In every society, at every level of sophistication, people have recognized the existence of danger and attributed it to some kind of external evil force, from which they have sought to defend themselves. A charm may take one of many different

charms

forms—it may be a physical object, such as an **amulet**, or a **chant** or **ritual**—but its basic purpose is to defend the one using it against danger, 'bad magic', by more powerful magic. Sometimes this magic may be used not simply in defence, but for example to lure prey or to ensure the affections of a loved one, or even to cause harm to an enemy.

▷ **amulet**; **hex**; **ritual**; **spell**; **talisman**

chastity test

FOLKTALE MOTIF, a type of **act of truth** in which the fidelity or virginity of a woman (most usually) is put to the test. One of the most common methods of administering this test is by **ordeal**; the woman may be required to place her arm in fire, or, in the famous case of Queen Matilda, to walk across red-hot ploughshares. Another form of the test is a **magic object** that changes appearance when the owner's virtue is compromised—a ring that contracts to pinch the wearer and cannot then be removed, for example, or a sword that rusts if its owner is untrue. Such tokens recall the key given by **Bluebeard** to his last wife, which becomes blood-stained as she disobeys him. **Sita**, the wife of **Rama**, demonstrates her faithfulness by calling the earth to open up and receive her.

In a development of this motif, English Jacobean playwrights made much of elaborate chastity tests, such as the chemical concoction to test Beatrice Joanna administered by Alsemero in *The Changeling* by Middleton and Rowley, and the allied and equally

ancient theme of substitution of a virgin on the wedding night.
▷ **sword of chastity**; **virginity**

chenoo

ENORMOUS STONE GIANTS, neighbours of the Iroquois of North America. They fight amongst themselves frequently, using uprooted trees as clubs and tossing boulders around until the mountains reverberate with their noise. They are shy of humans however, and if approached will freeze and become indistinguishable against the rocky landscape.

cherry

TREE AND ITS FRUIT, genus *Prunus* (family Rosaceae). The fruit may be sweet or tart. In folklore throughout the world, and especially in China, the cherry functions as a symbol of female sexuality: Marjatta in the **Kalevala** becomes pregnant with Ilmori, the Air, after consuming a cherry. In Switzerland it was customary among the folk for a new mother to eat the first cherries of the year, to ensure a good crop for the rest of the season.

The uses of the cherry in folk medicine world-wide reflect this association. Black slaves in the southern states used to give a cold infusion of cherry bark to stem excessive menstrual or post-natal blood flow, and among several Native American groups cherry roots were used to treat syphilis.

To dream of a cherry-tree in England and parts of America signifies impending disaster, although in Japan it represents prosperity.

An apocryphal Christian legend which became an English ballad **carol** tells how **Mary** and **Joseph** visited a cherry-orchard before Jesus's birth. Mary asked Joseph to pluck her a cherry, he refused, and the unborn Christ bade the tree bend down to offer its fruit to his mother. The blending of ancient and pious traditions here is especially interesting.

In modern lore, children are warned against swallowing cherry stones which, they are told, will grow into a tree inside them.
▷ **twins**

chestnut

TREE AND FRUIT, genus *Castanea*, of the beech family (Fagaceae), found in temperate northern regions. The nuts themselves are regarded as highly efficacious against aches, including rheumatism, throughout Europe and are frequently carried as medicinal **charms**. In England such a charm had to be begged or borrowed from another to be effective. In Italy chestnuts are placed on the household table for the benefit of the souls of the dead.

The horse chestnut *Aesculus hippocastanum*, a native of the Balkans, is not in fact a true chestnut but belongs to the Hippocastanaceae family. Its glossy brown nuts known as conkers, usually encased in pairs in spiky green capsules, are beloved of school children especially in Britain, where conker-smashing competitions are a feature of playground culture. A nut that has proved its worth by remaining whole while smashing a number of others is a treasured possession, sometimes attributed with amuletic properties, and various ruses such as soaking in vinegar are used to produce a conker of the desired durability.

Chichevache see Bicorn

childbirth

FIRST RITE OF PASSAGE, surrounded by mystery and danger. It is in birth that so many of mankind's most fundamental preoccupations meet: blood, new life, pain, and always the possibility of death. In many primitive societies birth is regarded as both sacred and dangerous. Blood is thought to contain or symbolize the mysterious forces of life, which might contaminate any unwary on-looker, and might also infect the objects in the house. In Brazil, bows and arrows are taken from the place of birth lest they become unlucky.

The new or expectant mother is often removed from the community which she might otherwise contaminate; this is an extension of the blood **taboo** which operates during **menstruation**. Even in highly sophisticated societies a ritual of purification must often be undergone after birth; the fear of female bleeding is strong and widespread. Often the woman returns to her mother's home for the birth. In general the usual attendants at a birth are women (hence modern mid-wives), and the father is not expected to be present, although there are occasional exceptions. Some groups expect the father to act as midwife, and both male and female relatives to be present.

In various parts of the world, different practices are common to ensure safe delivery. Often **amulets** may be used to make the birth easier, such as the snail-shells worn by pregnant women in ancient Mexico in the hope that the child might come out of the womb as gently as the snail emerging from its shell. Other charms might be present to ensure the health and success of the new child, such as miniature weapons to make of him a good hunter. In Europe, the day of the week on which a child was born was said to foretell its fate; this belief survives today in the popular rhyme 'Monday's child is fair of face, Tuesday's child is full of grace'. Although there is some disagreement over the significance of days later in the week, all versions of the rhyme agree that to be born on a Sunday is especially blest, since on this holy day the baby would be protected from the influence of evil spirits.

Once safely delivered, the child was believed to be especially vulnerable to evil influences, and so would often be protected by some means, often the all-over application of oil, **eggs** or other substances. This may be the origin of the holy water sprinkled over babies in Christian countries. After the birth the mother often undergoes a time of ritual purification, usually involving bathing, to restore her to the society cleansed of the evil spirits and dangerous life force that clung to her during the birth.

The vulnerability of the newborn child does not, however, end after purification. In many societies, especially in the Middle East and southern Asia, relatives are careful not to praise the child too enthusiastically lest they attract the **evil eye**, and parents in patriarchal societies will often disguise a baby boy as a girl in order to make him less an object of envy. It is possible that the long christening robes still common in the West today originated in attempts to

disguise the baby as an adult in order to deter any evil spirits.

Protective charms are often placed in the baby's cradle, and in some societies where belief in the **bush soul** is strong, **ashes** may be placed around the cradle so that the tracks of the twinned animal, who will come to see his human double, can be identified and the taboo against killing that animal established.
▷ **birthdays**; **couvade**

Childermas

DAY OF THE HOLY INNOCENTS, an English feast-day commemorating the slaughter of children by Herod (Matthew 2:16) celebrated on 28 December. The day is believed to be particularly unlucky; any new ventures or journeys should be avoided. It was traditional for parents to beat their children before they arose, to impress on them the significance of the day, and in later folk custom this became an opportunity to punish late risers.

children's lore

A UNIQUE BODY OF RITUAL AND SUPERSTITION, inherited and preserved in the folklore of the playground. Even in fully literate and urbanized societies, the lore of school children remains an area of untameable oral transmission. The tenacity of the verses and rituals they perform is remarkable (many verses current today are known to date from at least the 16th century) and the speed with which a new rhyme travels the national network of playgrounds is astonishing. When Edward VIII abdicated in 1936, a variation upon a popular Christmas **carol** was reported across England from London to Liverpool in the space of a month: 'Hark the Herald Angels sing, Mrs Simpson's pinched our king'. This rate of dissemination is all the more remarkable because children's lore is rarely if ever sanctioned by adult authority. It differs radically from the stuff of **nursery rhymes** and children's literature, which is usually propagated by the family and school and is invariably of adult origin. The chants of school children endure through oral transmission between succeeding generations of playmates, in a culture as unselfconscious as it is removed from that of the adult world alongside it. Recently the field of children's lore has been recognized as one of great value for the folklorist; the transmission and adaptation of popular chants is a pattern of the development of folklore throughout history and across the world.

Means of transmission

Adults, especially school teachers, often marvel at the spread and tenacity of children's chants. What is especially interesting to the folklorist is the variation shown over time and distance and the reasons why it comes about. Since the chants and rhymes are transmitted without ever being transcribed, words are often changed if they are unfamiliar to the children (maybe foreign, dialect or archaic) and may be replaced by more familiar equivalents. So for example in *Mother Goose's Melody* of 1795 we find:

Who comes here?
A Grenadier.
What do you want?
A Pot of Beer.
Where's your Money?
I've forgot.
Get you gone
You drunken Sot.

A **counting-out rhyme** recorded in Attica in 1950 by Iona and Peter Opie (*The Lore and Language of Schoolchildren*, 1959) is both strikingly similar and significantly different:

Mickey Mouse
In a public house
Drinking pints of beer.
Where's your money?
In my pocket.
Where's your pocket?
I forgot it.
Please walk out.

Often words will be misheard, and nonsense verses especially vary considerably from region to region as the syllables become confused in transmission. One popular clapping rhyme for example, 'My name is . . .', occurs in a myriad of forms; 'Ella Bella, Cinderella, Chinese chopsticks, Indian feather, Woo woo woo woo, How!', 'Alli alli, Chickerlye chickerlye, Om pom poodle, Walla walla whiskers, Chinese chopsticks, Indian chief says 'How!' and, from my schooldays, 'Kalai pickalai,

Pickalai kalai, Humbug charlie, Big Chief How!'

Rituals

Children's lore is full of **ritual,** from the choosing of teams for games by traditional counting-out rhymes to the enforced isolation of a misbehaving or unpopular playmate ('sending to **Coventry**'), to the declaration of truthfulness in countless solemn oaths. Like the chants and rhymes, these rituals pass through generations of children across the world with surprisingly few fundamental changes, but much variation. The formula 'Cross my heart and hope to die, Never, never tell a lie' for example is earnestly repeated by schoolchildren throughout Britain. In one development, linked to the tradition that lies may freely be told if the **fingers** are kept crossed, a child may allow another to pull his crossed fingers apart, thereby binding the speaker to the truth. The practice of wishing upon oneself death or disaster (usually a lightning strike or a slit throat) is also widespread. The primitive belief in the potency of saliva is startlingly attested in such cases; a child in Britain or North America will often show his wet finger, wipe it dry, then use it to describe a cut across his throat.

To gain possession of an article that he or she has found, a child may chant a variation of the old rhyme 'Finders keepers', which was recorded by J T Brockett in a survey of Northern England in 1829. The usual corollary, especially if the item is claimed by another, is 'Losers weepers', or in Scotland, 'Finder keeps, Loser greets'. The dictum that possession is nine tenths of the law seems to be generally accepted in the playground.

Another interesting and widespread ritual is the use of a specific word to claim a respite or truce, maybe to catch breath or examine an injury. The word varies according to region but is always understood by all children present; 'kings' is used in eastern England, 'barley' or 'barrels' in Scotland, and 'faynights' in London. In public schools and in school literature the term is often given as the Latin *pax*. This truce term is particularly interesting since it appears to have no direct correspondent in the adult world.

Omens and beliefs

Playground culture, like that of many primal societies, is incurably superstitious, and many rituals and beliefs are accepted as a part of everyday life. It is common for children to protect themselves from the evil omen of seeing an ambulance by holding their collar and not releasing it (or alternatively not swallowing) until they see a four-footed animal. Beetles on the other hand are generally considered lucky, and it is taboo to kill them. One of the most widespread superstitions involves walking along a pavement: if one steps on a crack or upon the line between flags, bad luck will inevitably follow, although there is much regional variation as to what form the evil will take. The institution of school examinations has also bred a lore of its own; many children bring **mascots**, favourite toys, lucky stones or **talismans**, and some utilise the magic of finger or leg crossing throughout the examination to ensure success.

The folklore of schoolchildren is a vast and varied field. In addition to its intrinsic value, the study of children's lore is also helpful as a means of examining at first hand the mechanisms of oral transmission and the development of ritual, superstition and folksong.

Chimera

MYTHICAL GREEK MONSTER with the head of a lion, the body of a goat and the tail of a serpent. She was said to be the child of Typhon and Echidna, along with Cerberus, the hound of hell, and the **hydra**. Homer, Virgil and Ovid all make reference to her, and in Spenser's *Faerie Queen* she is the mother by Cerberus of the Blatant Beast.

The Chimera terrorized the country around Lycia and Caria until she was killed by an arrow from Bellerophon, mounted on Pegasus. The word is now frequently used to refer to any fabulous beast or fanciful idea.

Chinese folklore

IN CHINA the ancient symbol of yin-yang, universal balance, became the principle of conflict, while the keystone of Southern Asian lore is the opposition of good and evil, light and dark. In ancient Chinese tradition, the desire to maintain the balance between the universal opposites such as male/female, dark/light, has given rise to an enormous number of folk beliefs and customs. The fullest expression of this theory is of course in Taoism, the Tao being the way of harmony in uniting the oppositions, but the common folklore of the Chinese, more flexible and inclusive than the constructed theory of Taoism, utilises the principle too. In folk medicine, for example, the parts of the body are considered variously male and female. The practice of **geomancy** (Feng Shui) is also related to this principle: houses are planned carefully to absorb only the yang (male/strong) influences from their environment, so for example they generally face south and may be protected by a screen of trees from northern yin influences.

Belief in spirits is a feature of Chinese folklore; each man has two souls, the animal one (p'o), which enters him at conception, and hun, the spirit soul, which enters at the moment of birth. Usually the p'o disintegrates with the body, fed for a time by the sacrifices of relatives. Should it escape the body, it will become a troublesome ghost (**k'uei**). The hun will hopefully overcome all the obstacles to reach T'ien, heaven, but if the sacrifices are not correctly performed it, along with the p'o, will become discontented and malicious. Apart from these human souls, there exists in Chinese lore a plethora of demons and spirits, some of whom can take on human form and mingle unnoticed with the living. Shamanism, the belief in the invisible spirits of ancestors, demons etc who can be reached by and communicate only through the shaman, is widespread in East Asia.

Chinese **astrology** is a complex system by which favourable or unfavourable influences can be calculated exactly for any action, from the 12 year cycle (with each year named after a different animal) to a two-hour division of the day. These influences are consulted before all major and some minor decisions, so for example the marriage arranger will consult the horoscopes of a couple carefully before advising the families whether or not the marriage should go ahead. The field of Chinese folklore, much of which has survived undiminished well into the present century, is a vast and complex one much complicated by the integration of outside influence over centuries of foreign contact, but its relative isolation from the West until comparatively recent times has ensured the sense of a culture fundamentally different from that of Europe.

chlevnik

RUSSIAN SPIRIT OF THE CATTLE-SHED, a troublesome and exacting presence. He may express a partiality for colour and breed of cattle, for their arrangement within the shed or for the location of the shed itself; if his whims are not humoured, he may revenge himself by harming the cattle. An offering is made to pacify him with every new arrival to the shed, and he is sometimes driven out with noisy shouting and banging on the walls by long-suffering farmers.
▷ domovik; **household spirits**

Christianity and folklore

THE INTRODUCTION OF CHRISTIANITY in pagan societies has resulted in a fascinating blend of traditions. Many Märchen were adapted to include **saints** and the **Devil** in place of the old heroes and demons, and in fact many of the old tales that survive seem to indicate medieval cultural patterns, although these almost certainly overlay older, pagan structures. The older elements tend to surface most clearly in the demonology of tales, for example the **troll** which features in Scandinavian or Icelandic lore, the witch in Germany and Scotland and the nereid in Greece.

The meeting of pagan and Christian traditions is beautifully portrayed in the Irish tale of **St Patrick** and **Oísin** arguing over the relative merits of the Christian heaven and the ancient heroes. More recently, the efforts of Christian missionaries around the world have resulted in many traditional tales being adapted to feature **Mary** or a saint alongside the original animal or spirit characters.

saint's shrine at Sakopane, Poland

Aid is sought, especially in countries with an unbroken tradition of Catholicism such as France, Spain and Italy, from supernatural agencies in the form of saints, and the offerings left at saints' wells recall pagan votive sacrifices. The ancient rituals to ensure the success of the crop have developed into the practice of the local priest blessing the seed, or, in pastoral communities, the animals, on certain feast-days, and the old practice of protecting oneself by means of charms has given way to the patron saint cults.
▷ **Celtic folklore**

Christmas

WINTER FESTIVAL, central festive season of the Christian church but including an inextricable mix of pagan and Christian elements. The traditional date on which Christmas is observed, 25 December, became fixed only by Pope Julius I in the fourth century; before then the Mass of Christ was celebrated on a variety of different days. Old Christmas Day, before the calendar changes of 1752, was celebrated on 6 January, modern **Epiphany**, and this is still observed as Christmas Day in Armenia and a few other areas. The dating of the festival by the early Church probably had less to do with the date of Christ's actual birth than with a desire to incorporate into the Church a season immemorially given over to festivities. The wild celebrations of the **Saturnalia** in Rome began on the 17 December and were observed throughout the Empire; usual conventions of rank and decorum were overturned, houses were decorated with greenery and the city was hung with lights. Saturnalia ended with the great celebration of the birth of the sun, *natalis invicti solis*, dedicated to the god Mithras, on 25 December, and this correspondence led to charges of idolatry (the Puritans in England and America forbade observance of the day in the 17th century on these grounds). One especially interesting survival from the Saturnalia in the medieval Church was the selection of a boy bishop, who was invested on St Nicholas's day (6 December) and who preached and performed all other episcopal duties except Mass until Holy Innocents' Day (28 December). This seems to have been derived from the role-reversals of master and slave so characteristic of the Saturnalia, but it has also been linked to St **Nicholas**, said to have become bishop in Myra at an early age.

Further north in Europe the festival of Yule was celebrated at the winter solstice of 21 December, when the sun began once again the long climb back to summer. Fires were lit to Odin and Thor, the houses were filled with evergreens and lamps, and mistletoe branches were ceremonially cut. This was however a more serious festival than that of Saturnalia: the Northerners were in the grip of winter, they dedicated their celebrations to ancestral spirits, and one of the chief beliefs of the season was that of the **Wild Hunt** of the gods, *Asgardsreid*, raging outside. The practice of decorating the house with greenery such as **holly** seems to have developed from these festivals, but the Christmas tree appears to have been a later addition from Germany over the last two centuries. The exchanging of Christmas cards was an even later innovation, begun in Victorian Britain.

Since the Church had little chance of stopping the traditional festivals of her new converts, it was a prudent move on

her part to focus the celebrations into suitably Christianized channels. The result has been a rich intermingling of Christian, pagan and local customs, together with family traditions developed over generations, which has made Christmas one of the richest fields of research for folklorists.

From its earliest, pre-Christian days, the Christmas period has been a time for unrestrained social and family intercourse, when the demands of work were set aside and the usual social codes forgotten or reversed. Children were allowed to join in the festivities, and in Cornwall they stayed up until midnight on Christmas Eve, toasting the Yule log with their families. Villagers were accosted by wassailers singing, demanding fruit or money, performing practical jokes and wishing blessings for the new season on the houses they visited. It was traditional also to wassail the apple trees in south-west England, with ceremonial libations of ale and cider, to ensure a good crop for the coming year.

The Yule log is a relic of these ceremonies, which were probably brought to Britain by Scandinavian invaders. A log was selected, brought back to the house and decorated with ribbons to be ceremonially lit on Christmas Eve. It blazed throughout the Twelve Days of celebration, and its charred remains were kept as a charm to protect the house through the year, and were used to kindle the next year's log. The log was considered a potent bringer of luck, and its burning also symbolized the end of past feuds. Often some of its **ashes** would be mixed with the corn sown the next spring to ensure a healthy crop.

In such a time of celebration and feasting, it is inevitable that some of the most popular customs centre around food and drink. Each country has its own characteristic Christmas delicacies; one of the most ancient is the boar's head or roast pig complete with apple or orange in the mouth, served mainly in Northern Europe, a custom which seems to be derived from the Teutonic ritual of sacrificing a pig to Frey to ensure fertility in the coming year. In the privation of winter, Christmas was not only an excuse to indulge, it was a means by which the New Year might begin as it

Christmas

was hoped it would continue; to refuse any festive food was considered unlucky, since one was thereby rejecting prosperity and plenty for the coming year.

It was commonly believed in Europe that certain animals were specially blessed at Christmas; **cattle** in particular were said to receive the gift of speech on Christmas Eve, the night they watched over the Christ-child, but anyone who overheard them was said to hear ill omens for himself. Bees too were said to hum the Hundredth Psalm among themselves on Christmas Eve, and **cocks** crow throughout since it was a cock who first announced the news of Christ's birth, 'Christus natus est'. Many legends have grown up around the Christian element of the festival, most famously the Glastonbury thorn, said to have been brought to England by **Joseph of Arimathea** and to flower every Christmas.

Christmas was supposed to be a popular time of year for the return of ancestral spirits, and before leaving for church it was usual to prepare and clean the house for their arrival. If the spirits were pleased and took a meal in the house, a successful year was assured. This was also believed to be a particularly favourable time for **divination**, to discover what the New Year held in store; in England a single girl would bake a cake, mark it with her initials, and leave it on the hearth over Christmas Eve night. In the morning the initials of her future husband would be added under hers. A child born on Christmas Day was thought to be marked for blessings and success, and may be credited with the ability to see spirits.

Although many look to the Magi bringing gifts to the baby Jesus as the origin of gift-giving, the practice in fact extends back to the Saturnalian festivals, where *strenae*, gifts, were commonly exchanged. In some European countries, especially in the South, gifts are given at **New Year** rather than at Christmas. In England, the season of gift-giving and the levelling spirit of the Saturnalia extended to Boxing Day, when it was customary for employers to give presents to their workers.

Western Christmas celebrations today demonstrate the mix of Christian sentiment and blatant paganism that has characterized the festival in various ways since its inception. The festival seems set to continue, as it has for centuries, with the preservation of many old customs, many less than half understood, and the development of new ones, although many have expressed fears that its original spirit of good-will may be lost in the unprecedented commercialism that now surrounds the season.

▷ **Befana**; **cakes**; **hodening**; **Knecht Ruprecht**; **Kriss Kringle**; **New Year**; **Santa Claus**; **wassailling**

Christopher, St ONE OF THE MOST POPULAR OF SAINTS, traditionally invoked by the pious and the doubter alike for protection when travelling. His martyrdom, traditionally held to have taken place at Lycia in Asia Minor during the persecutions of Decius, is the only fact known about him. The early classical legends associated with his name developed through the Middle Ages into the story popularized by the *Golden Legend* of Jacques de Voragine, based on the saint's name, which means 'Christbearer'. According to this, Christopher was a fearsome-looking giant who, being so powerful himself, vowed only to serve the most powerful of masters. At first he believed this to be Satan, but on realizing that the Devil was afraid of Christ, he pledged his allegiance to the latter.

Searching how best to serve his new master, he met a hermit who instructed him to perform Christian service by living alone by a ford and carrying travellers across the river on his massive back. One of his passengers, a small child, grew so heavy that half way across the river Christopher feared they would both be drowned, despite his great strength. The child then revealed himself as Christ, and explained to the exhausted giant that he had just carried the creator of the world and all the weight of its sin on his back. To verify his words, he told Christopher to plant his staff in the ground where the next day it would sprout leaves and flowers. This is a common motif of world folklore (see **act of truth**).

Christopher is said to have preached in Lycia with enormous success until his imprisonment. While in prison, two women were sent to seduce him but rather than weakening he is supposed to have converted his temptresses. He underwent various tortures, including being shot by arrows, but according to legend the arrows turned on his captors, one of whom was wounded in the eye and later healed by Christopher's blood. Finally he was beheaded, and his enormous body dragged through the city's streets.

Because of his protective role, Christopher has become the patron of all travellers, and motorists especially in modern times. It was believed that anyone who saw a picture of St Christopher would not die that day; hence the popularity of his representation on particularly conspicuous church walls, and the custom of carrying a medallion bearing his image when on a journey. He is most frequently shown carrying the Christ-child across the river.

Although the cult has always been immensely popular, it has been widely condemned as superstition from the time of Erasmus's *Praise of Folly*. With the advent of motorized transport and air travel, with their new dangers, however, his cult has widely revived. There was much popular opposition in 1969 when his feast, 25 July, was reduced to the status of a local cult.

chrysanthemum

'GOLDEN FLOWER', of the family Asteraceae, the national flower of Japan from the 14th century. It is regarded throughout Asia as a symbol of purity and longevity. A legend of Nai Myang, China, tells of a spring rising in a bed of chrysanthemums that has the virtue of conferring new life (see **water of life**). Feverfew (*C. parthenium*) and tansy (*C. vulgare*) are traditional ingredients of many folk medicines.

Chu'ang Kung and Chu'ang Mu

CHINESE GODS OF THE BED, the immortals who watch over all activities of the bed including sleep, love-making, **childbirth** and **death**. Their chief interest is in bringing about successful fertilization and pregnancy, and in preventing quarrels between husband and wife. Chu'ang Kung is fond of tea, his wife Chu'ang Mu (or P'o) prefers wine, and tea, wine and sweetmeats are left as offerings to ensure the goodwill of the two, and thereby secure a comfortable and companionable night's rest.

Chuang Tzu (c.369–c.286BC)

TAOIST PHILOSOPHER, born in Meng in the Sung state of China, author of the key Taoist work *Chuang Tzu*. So many legends and anecdotes have attached to him that he can be regarded as a folk as well as a religious figure; his unkempt appearance and eccentric habits endeared him to the common folk. One of the most famous of the many tales associated with him tells how a friend finds him singing and beating time on a basin after his wife's death. In reply to his friend's astonished questions, Chuang Tzu sets out the Taoist belief in the cycles of birth, being and dying, concluding that 'For me to go about weeping and wailing would be to show my ignorance of destiny. Therefore I desist.'

churching

BRITISH CUSTOM, known in Scotland as kirking—the purification of a mother after childbirth. It consists of a special service held on her first attendance at church after the delivery to give thanks to God for the safety of mother and child and to pray for her recovery from confinement. Until this has been done, the woman is considered unlucky and vulnerable. Similar customs exist elsewhere in Europe, and also among African and Native American groups. The Mosaic law demands similar rituals for the purification of mothers. Clearly the fear and sense of mystery associated with new birth led not only to concerns for the woman but to a suspicion of the power made immanent in her and her possible harmful effect on others with whom she came into contact; this power had to be neutralized by invoking a stronger beneficent power to make her safe.

▷ **childbirth**; **blood**

churel

INDIAN SPIRIT, the **ghost** of a woman who has died in childbirth or while otherwise ceremonially unclean. She preys on young men, keeping them captive until they are withered and old and she has sucked their life-essence. She is easily recognized: her feet are back to front, and she has no mouth.

▷ **revenant**; **vampire**

churning

DAIRY PROCESS, by which butter is produced by agitating milk. This is sometimes a long drawn-out task, and malignant spirits were frequently blamed if the end result was particularly slow in coming or otherwise unsatisfactory. **Witches** or **fairies** were generally said to be the culprits throughout Europe, and woods such as rowan, thought to be effective against such mischievous charms, were often incorporated into churns or tied on top of them. An English remedy was to drop a hot **horseshoe** in the milk to remove the charm; sometimes the horseshoe would be nailed on the base of the churn as a preventative measure. Irish dairymaids burned turf beside the churn to ward off the fairies.

Cid, El (c.1043–99)

'THE LORD', Spanish warrior hero, properly Rodrigo Díaz de Vivar. A patriot in the service of Alfonso VI of Castile, he fought constantly from 1065. In 1081 he was banished for an unauthorized raid, and began a long career as a soldier of fortune, serving both Spaniards and Moors. He besieged and captured Valencia (1093–4) and became its ruler.

In addition to the great epic *El cantar de mío Cid* (The Song of the Cid) there are nearly 200 ballads connected with his exploits. He quickly became a national hero, and the folk figure created in a growing body of lore soon obscured the historical man. In addition to embellished accounts of his strength and feats of daring, supernatural elements characteristic of folktales became attached to his legends. It is said that an insolent Spaniard once attempted to touch the **beard** of El Cid as he sat embalmed for 10 years after his death in the church of San Pedro de Cordena. As he reached up to do what none had ever dared even to think while the Cid was alive, the corpse's hand flew to the hilt of his sword and began to draw the weapon from its scabbard. The man, needless to say, fled.

cigouaves

HAITIAN DEMON, a night spirit who stealthily castrates men as they sleep. To avoid his unwelcome attentions, it is advisable to sacrifice the genitals of animals as an offering to satisfy the demon.

Cincinnatus, Lucius Quinctius

ROMAN HERO, about whose story much legendary material has accrued. He is said to have been a farmer who was prevailed upon to assume the dictatorship during a crisis; the consular army was trapped by Aequi forces in the Apennines. Cincinnatus relieved the army in only one day, and relinquished power immediately after celebrating his triumph in Rome and restoring order to the Empire. He went back to a life of obscure contentment on his farm.

Cinderella

EUROPEAN FOLKTALE, an example of a cardinal tale type found in some form in virtually every society of the world. The

Cinderella

form of the tale best known to English speakers is that borrowed from Perrault, who included 'Cendrillon' in his *Recueil des pièces curieuses et nobles* in 1697. This tells of a beautiful and good-natured girl who is forced to act as a drudge in the household of her step-mother and treated cruelly by her two step-sisters. When the sisters and step-mother are invited to a grand royal ball (other late European versions substitute a visit to church), Cinderella is obliged to help them prepare but is herself left behind by the **ashes** of the kitchen fire. There she is found by her **fairy godmother**, who transforms a pumpkin, mice and lizards into a magnificent coach and horses, and magically dresses her in great finery. Cinderella leaves for the ball with the injunction to return home before the stroke of midnight, when her riches will revert to rags, and she does so. The prince, captivated by her beauty, organizes another ball for the following night in the hope that she will return. Once again they dance together, and once again Cinderella is forced to flee as the clock begins to strike 12; this time, in

her haste, she leaves one of her glass slippers behind her. The prince sends servants throughout the land to search for the woman whom the slipper fits: Cinderella's two sisters cannot make the slipper fit and despite their protests the prince's servant insists that Cinderella try. She slips the shoe on easily, produces its partner, and is taken amid much rejoicing to marry the prince having forgiven her step-mother and sisters.

Perrault's version, although the one most widely known in the West today, includes many details fundamentally different from more authentic oral versions. The glass slipper and the fairy godmother, for example, appear only in his narrative. The more usual beginning to the story is the death of Cinderella's mother, who continues to help her faithful daughter from the grave. In many other versions Cinderella is helped by birds and animals.

Although Cinderella is now so widely diffused that it is impossible to return to any one 'original' version of the tale, certain elements are clearly more

Cinderella

common and ancient than those added by Perrault. The earliest version surviving can be traced back to China and the 9th century AD; it seems probable that the tale was originally Oriental and spread to Europe and thence on to the New World. The fundamental theme of the tale in all its forms is the unexpected elevation of the despised younger daughter, who captivates a prince-figure while disguised and is then identified by means of a test, usually the fit of a slipper or ring.

Most versions, particularly in Europe, emphasize the fact that Cinderella is helped by her dead or transformed mother. The mother may have been transformed into a domestic animal (usually a **cow**), died naturally or, in some bizarre versions, have been killed and eaten by her two elder daughters. Before her death she advises Cinderella how to call upon her for help; sometimes the mother herself responds to Cinderella's plight, for example the girl finds her fine clothes in the grave, but often it is an animal who fulfils the mother's promise to help. In the German version given by Grimm the helpful creature is a white bird which lives in the tree that Cinderella planted over her mother's grave. The motif of the loving mother continuing to care and provide for her child even after death is a common one in folklore, found in several Central European and Indian tales.

The motif of the **helpful beast** is found all over the world, and it seems likely that it was included in the earliest versions of Cinderella. Several countries relate impossible tasks set by the cruel stepmother, which are performed by helpful birds and animals, most commonly the picking up of seeds or the sorting of grain. The Slavonic forms of the tale tend to concentrate more on the helpful animal than on the ball itself, sometimes omitting the latter altogether.

The **recognition token** is a widely used plot device (compare the **salt** in the **Cap o' Rushes** tale-type) but the loss of the shoe is characteristic of the Cinderella cycle. Only in Perrault's version is it made of glass. It has been suggested that *verre* (glass) was a misreading of *vair*, an obsolete word for fur, a neat solution

which would appear to tie in with the **Catskin** theme. In many other versions it is said to be of gold, and this seems probable as the older form, possibly associated with ancient solar myths. In the *Rig Veda*, dawn is portrayed fleeing the sun (Prince Mitra) with a marvellous lightness of step, leaving behind her a tiny shoe, and it is possible that this myth rests on extant folklore. One old Indian tale tells how a king discovered a dainty shoe and fell in love with its unknown owner, and a similar fable from Egypt about the courtesan Rhodope was recorded by Strabo in the 1st century BC. In general in Oriental tradition the shoe appears to be symbolic in some way of female sexuality (see **shoes**).

The treatment of the cruel stepmother and sisters, although less central, varies in different versions of the story. Perrault has them reconciled and forgiven by Cinderella, but Grimm's German version, together with Slavonic and Scottish types, has the sisters in particular treated much more harshly. The birds that have helped Cinderella expose the sisters, who have cut off part of their feet in order to make the shoe fit, and peck out their eyes as they return from the wedding at the end. It seems clear that the original forms of the tale included the meting out of such simple, primitive justice, while later sentimentalized versions attempted to make the ending more palatable for delicate sensibilities.

Drawing as it does on the most basic themes of folklore—the victory of the oppressed hero, the aid of anthropomorphized animals, the love interest and the satisfaction of revenge—the Cinderella tale has been absorbed by virtually every culture to a remarkable degree. Its development as a tale for children in the West has lost much of the force of the original by sentimentalizing the heroine (even in Perrault's version Cinderella was a girl of wit and character) but its popularity testifies to its great imaginative power.

Circe

GREEK WITCH, daughter of Helios the sun god and Perse, a sea-nymph. With the aid of her potions and chants, she transformed human beings into beast form, generally wolves, lions or swine. Her most famous exploit was the transformation of Odysseus's crew into pigs. She was compelled to restore them by Odysseus, however, who was protected from her spells by the sprig of moly given to him by Hermes (see **herbs**). Odysseus remained with the enchantress for a year on her island, said to be off the coast of Italy, before continuing on his voyage. She prefigures the evil witches of European Märchen, who are given to transforming princes into frogs and the like.

Cirein Crôin

SEA MONSTER OF THE SCOTTISH HIGH-LANDS, an enormous **sea-serpent** who could devour seven whales at a sitting.
▷ **Leviathan**

ciuateteo

AZTEC SPIRITS, also known as ciuapipil-tin, the ghosts of women who died during childbirth. They live in an after-world in the west, Tamoanchan, under the rule of the serpent woman Cihuacoatl, and were entrusted with the safe delivery of the setting sun to the **underworld** every night. On certain days they returned to earth to revenge themselves, bringing diseases such as epilepsy upon children and inciting men to troubled lust. They could appear in the form of women with skin a ghastly hue of white, or as an **eagle**, swooping in from the west. To avoid their attentions mothers keep their children indoors on such days, and offer bread sacrifices at special temples built beside crossroads.

Clíodna

OLD IRISH HEROINE, daughter of the chief druid of Manannan, lord of the sea. When the irresistible Ciaban was exiled by **Finn Mac Cumhal** because the **Fianna** were envious of his way with women, he was brought by supernatural aid to Tir Tairngaire (the Land of Promise) and the city of Manannan. There he impressed Clíodna by his prowess at juggling, and the two eloped together in a small curragh. Ciaban left the slumbering Clíodna in the curragh while he went inland to hunt a deer, but an enormous

wave crashed upon the shore, overturning the curragh and sweeping Clíodna out to her death.

She is notorious for appearing as a seductress to tempt young men. Certain Munster families claim her as their **banshee**.
▷ **blarney stone**

clootie

SCOTTISH TERM FOR THE DEVIL, deriving from Scots *cloot* meaning a cloven hoof. He is frequently referred to as Auld Clootie or Auld Cloots, and it was customary to leave a patch of ground untilled (often one that was untillable in any case) for Clootie's own use. This demonstrates the simultaneously familiar and fearful attitude of many folk to the Devil.

clover

FRAGRANT, SMALL-FLOWERED PLANT, any of the 300 or so species of the genus *Trifolium*. Its most distinctive characteristic is the three-toothed leaf. It is said that St **Patrick** used a clover leaf as a visual aid to explain the mystery of the Holy Trinity to King Leoghaire of Ireland: three leaves, yet one leaf; three persons, yet one God. Hence in Christian lore the clover has traditionally been regarded as a powerful protection against evil and **witchcraft**. The plant was sacred for the Druids, as a symbol of both good and evil, and used by them too as a protective **charm**.

The uncommon four-leafed clover is considered a powerful charm for luck in much of Europe and North America, especially if it is held close to the body secretly, although it is sometimes said to lose its potency if given away to another. A five-leafed clover, should one ever find one, is considered less fortunate; it will bring bad luck unless given away and may foretell sickness.

To dream of clover is a sign of a happy and prosperous marriage in England, and in Victorian flower language the clover represented fertility. This may be because of its associations with luck and marriage, but it may also derive in part from the peasant observation that the presence of clover indicates good soil; it is in fact a soil-improver, imparting high levels of nitrogen to the ground.

clowns

FIGURES OF CARNIVAL AND DANCE, bearers of supernatural authority. Although now considered entertainment for children, clowns and fools have traditionally fulfilled a far deeper purpose, and the similarity of many of the features they share suggests that their role of licensed buffoonery is one fundamental to human society.

Some of the more highly organized clown systems are found among Native North Americans, most famously among the Pueblo tribes. Here clowns show the traditional characteristics—ludicrous appearance, backwards or nonsense speech, and abnormal (often obscene) actions—and they are often organized into highly complex social groups. Dressed in ceremonial **masks**, and often in tattered rags or animal skins, they carry **rattles** and sometimes a whip to frighten evil spirits. They are regarded as powerful beings, capable of curing illness, but because they are free from social restraint this power can also be used punitively; clowns are often the only members of a tribe licensed to criticize the chief by ridicule, and they fulfil a useful social function, controlling individuals' behaviour. They are often thought to practise **witchcraft**. The origin of the clown's power, and of his grotesque appearance and backward behaviour, lies with the spirits of the dead and the forces of nature. They are thus able to control health, death, fertility, weather and so on, and cannot be made subject to the usual tribal authorities. Their chaotic behaviour is a reminder of the powerful pre-creation world acknowledged by many societies.

Alongside the frightening aspect of course the clowns fulfil a broadly comic role too, with their unrestrained gluttony, often eating excrement and soaking each other with urine, and their wild antics of burlesque and game-playing. Sometimes too they distribute food and gifts to the people, more often they themselves beg. One of the clowns' most common comic function, rooted in fertility magic, is the obscene mime accompanied by a phallus, which often involves female impersonation. Masks are used in all kinds of impersonation, depending on the magic or comedy being

clowns

performed, from supernatural spirits, to diseases, to animals, to the female essence of fertility. It has been suggested too that one of the functions of the sacred clown was to distract the attention of evil spirits from the religious rituals.

In the theatres of Greece and Rome, clowns appeared alongside more serious actors and parodied their rhetoric to the delight of the audience. They also frequently interacted with the crowd, usually in an abusive way, or (especially in Roman mime) served as the gull for the sport of other actors. The characteristic clown humour, an expansive and physical routine, survived as a comic interlude into the Middle Ages, when it began to emerge as a form of entertainment in its own right. In the late 16th century the travelling companies of the Italian Commedia dell'Arte developed from their range of stock comic figures the clown Arlecchino (Harlequin), an acrobatic and immensely popular trickster figure. The medieval morality plays in England produced the Vice character, which developed into another type of clown figure, the clever buffoon, whose immorality was freely enjoyed by the crowd since it was always suitably punished at the end. Circus clowns, a development of the 19th century, retain many of the ancient properties of clown figures, including their masks (as make-up), ludicrous costumes and coarse, physical comedy. Although their sacred role has now been lost, the clown and comedian still retain the social privilege of ridiculing the stupidity of their fellows.

cluricaun

IRISH MISCHIEVOUS SPIRIT, identified by some traditions with the **leprechaun**. Like the leprechaun he is portrayed as a wizened old man, and like him too he is said to know of hidden treasure, but the cluricaun (or cluracan) is unique in that

cluricaun

he lives in wine-cellars, where his presence is something of a mixed blessing. He may tend and guard the barrels, scaring off thieving servants if rewarded with his supper, but his love of mischief and inveterate untrustworthiness mean that he may also steal the wine himself.
▷ **biersal**; **mischievous spirits**

Clym of the Clough

ARCHER AND OUTLAW, a friend of **Adam Bell** and **William of Cloudesly**, who also appears alongside them in the ballad collected in Percy's *Reliques*. Like them, he is said to have inhabited Englewood Forest, near Carlisle. His name, which is also rendered Clim of the Clough, means 'Clement of the Cliff'.

coachman legends

TALE TYPE OF HUNGARIAN FOLKLORE, a cycle of tales featuring a supernatural coachman blessed with immortality and magical powers. He is typically able to perform all the tasks required by his master without appearing to exert himself. Often he passes his knowledge on to a younger coachman, or his secret is discovered, since he cannot enjoy the release of death until he has communicated his magical secret.

coblynau

WELSH SPIRIT OF THE MINES, close relative of the **knockers** of Cornwall. They are ugly, good-natured little people, who guide miners to rich seams of ore by their knocking. If angered by human impudence they may throw stones at the offender, but otherwise they are harmless.

cobra

HIGHLY POISONOUS SNAKE, a member of the family Elapidae. When angered or defensive it rears up to strike and expands the ribs of the neck to form an imposing hood. In India the marking on its hood are said to be the imprint of the god Krishna's foot. In northern India particularly the cobra is sacred, a symbol of life force, and if accidentally killed it is cremated in a ceremony like that of a dead human. Childless Indian women supplicate the snake with regular offerings to ensure fertility.

The cobra plays a leading role in many Hindu legends and Indian folktales. Its traditional sparring partner is the mongoose, who generally defeats the cobra by means of his quick wits and agility.
▷ **basilisk**; **nagas**

cobra

cock

MALE BIRD, in general usage a rooster. Its early morning call is associated with sunrise in folklore throughout the world; ancient Greeks identified it with the sun god Apollo, and in many folktales the cock's crow puts evil creatures of the night to flight and turns **trolls** into stone.

Because of its aggressiveness towards other cocks it was sacred to Mars, god of war, among the Romans, and this is one of the features that led to its adoption as a symbol of male virility. Bridegrooms of eastern Europe would traditionally bear a live cock in the marriage procession and it was widely regarded as a symbol of fertility. In Mexico particularly cock's blood was an efficacious sacrifice. Roman augurs consulted the entrails of the sacrificed cock, and in much of later Europe the cock has been renowned as a prophet of weather, hence its traditional use as the symbol on a weather vane. Later Christian lore attempted to explain the use of cocks atop church spires by recalling the salutary tale of Peter's denial of Jesus ('Before the cock crows you will deny me three times.' Matthew 26:75), or by claiming it as a symbol of resurrection, associated with the new day.

The medicinal uses of the cock are many and varied. In Scotland, anyone swallowing a stone from within a cock's stomach would by **sympathetic magic** obtain strength and courage. In Morocco it is used against tuberculosis and in many cases as an antidote to the bite of a poisonous snake.

▷ **alectryomancy**

Cockaigne, Land of

OTHERWORLD OF MEDIEVAL EUROPEAN LORE, also spelled Cockayne, a land of unbridled pleasure and gluttony, where the houses are made of cakes and the streets of pastry, where jolly shopkeepers press the visitor with free confections while buttered larks fall from the sky, and there is nothing to be done but to enjoy this lavishness. It is described in detail in a 13th-century Middle English poem, *The Land of Cockaygne*, a satire on the duties of the monasteries, but an earlier Irish version of the tradition is *The Vision of Mac-Conglinne*, in which a gluttonous king sees a vision not of heavenly delights but of the marvellous land of Cockaigne. In Germanic tradition it is known as Schlaraffenland.

In some traditions this marvellous land is identified with London, due to folk etymology from 'Cockney'. Such lands are a feature of **lying tales**, told especially by travellers and **Münchausen** figures.

cockatrice see **basilisk**

cockroach

WINGED INSECT, any one of over 3 500 species of the family Blattidae. The cockroach has remained virtually unchanged for hundreds of millions of years; its ancestors are among the oldest fossil insects we possess, found in Silurian sandstone. It is a native of all but the very coldest areas of the world, although it prefers hot, humid climates.

Cockroaches are generally regarded as nuisances, due to their voracious appetite for all animal and vegetable materials (including clothes and paper), and various methods of disposing of them have been propounded in folklore: in many areas of Europe a roach is caught and displayed impaled on a small spike as a warning to his fellows, or a cockroach trapped in a box is presented to a corpse to remove the pest from the living. In Ireland the cockroach is said to have revealed the hiding place of the Holy Family (cf **spider**), and so it is legitimate to kill one if it is encountered. Many Russian and French peasants, however, looked on the cockroach as a beneficent, protective spirit, and to lose

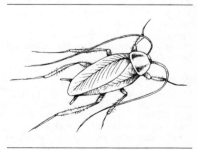

cockroach

ones roach population was considered very unlucky.

There appears to be an association with witchlore; in Ireland **witches** are said to appear as cockroaches to plague innocent farmers, and in Mississippi black slaves used to place jars as traps for cockroaches, believing that by killing a roach they were killing a witch.

coffee

TROPICAL SHRUB AND ITS BEANS, genus *Coffea* of the Rubiaceae family. The drink produced by these beans, usually roasted, ground and brewed with water, is a stimulant containing caffeine. An Ethiopian folktale tells how Kaldi, a goat-herd, tried chewing the beans after noticing that his goats seemed particularly frisky when they had been browsing on a certain bush. Discovering this stimulation for himself, Kaldi took the beans in some excitement to his Islamic leader, who recognized in them the perfect solution to the problem of keeping the faithful alert during their long night-time prayers. Similar tales are told in Europe (in the context of a Christian monastery), with novices working as shepherds and taking the beans back to their brothers.

Cole, King

NURSERY-RHYME KING, a 'merry old soul' who 'called for his pipe, And he called for his bowl, And he called for his fiddlers three'. This cheerful character is traditionally said to have been a third century prince, later king of Britain, after whom Colchester was named. Another theory is that the song refers to a wealthy merchant of Reading known as Cole-brook, although Sir Walter Scott subscribed to the more romantic view that Cole was the corrupted form of the mythical father of **Finn Mac Cumhal**, 'son of Cumhal'.

colour

SYMBOLIC CODE, an important part of folklore around the world. The pervasive effect of colour upon popular culture can be heard in everyday conversation; common phrases in the West include 'to feel blue', 'green with envy', 'to see red' and so on. Various colours

have become associated with various qualities in various cultures, such as yellow for cowardice, purple for royalty, white for purity and so on. The origins of these associations are sometimes obvious—the appearance of blood, for example, almost certainly explains the use of red as a colour of danger—but often the same colours vary widely in their interpretation from culture group to culture group, suggesting that each society creates its own system of meaning. In folk literature such as tales and **ballads** these symbolic patterns form a system of clichés, by which for example a lady's lips are likened to rubies and her skin to snow. This is an especially useful convention, since it enables the narrator to introduce a character type and demonstrate its properties very economically: consider Snow White, for example. The natural opposition of black and white provides a useful symbolic framework for the moral polarity of many European **fairy tales**.

This language of colour feeds into a system of folk belief, in which red-haired people are thought to be fiery-tempered, the **Devil** to be associated with black, and the blood of royalty to run blue in their veins. Some cultures have astonishingly complex systems of colour beliefs, particularly the North American Pueblo groups. They ascribe a colour to each direction (north, south, east, west, up and down) and to each colour a particular bird, animal and god. The Cherokee tribe also include qualities such as success, linked to red and the east, and cultures in Europe and Asia have also been observed to possess a similar system linking colour and direction.

The most basic cultural rites are often linked closely with specific colours in the traditions of a society. In Europe white is associated with birth (for example the christening robes) and **marriage**, while black is the colour of mourning. In ancient Rome however orange was the colour of marriage and (as in modern China) white the colour of mourning. The expensive Tyrian dye of the ancient world has led to the tradition of dressing royalty in purple. The precious blue pigment extracted from lapis lazuli was used by Renaissance painters in the portrayal of their most revered subjects, particularly the Virgin **Mary**, and this artistic convention became part of religious folk consciousness.

In modern times, colour has become a trigger for nationalism, with the development of national flags and even the characteristic strip of each country's sports teams. In such ways, colour remains an intrinsic part of the folklore of a people, influencing their customs, beliefs and communication.

come-all-ye

SONG TYPE, a popular **ballad** form found particularly in Ireland and North America. Its name comes from the characteristic opening phrase, 'Come all ye jolly sailor-boys' and so on, and it differs from more traditional ballads in that the interest is more closely linked to the everyday concerns of working men and occasionally women—lumberjacks, miners, navvies, maids. The rhythmic structure is distinctive, with syllables crowded into a line, and unlike other ballad forms dialogue and drama are relatively insignificant, replaced by a detailed, first-person narrative of day-to-day life.

This type of ballad gained popularity in English streets in the 17th century. Irish peasants made it their own and developed the style in the succeeding centuries, and with massive Irish working-class immigration across the Atlantic it took a firm hold in the new world of America.
▷ **shanty**; **work song**

Common Ridings

SCOTTISH SUMMER FESTIVALS, celebrations traditionally held in the Border towns to mark the annual claiming of the town's common ground for the people. Typically, a group of horsemen will ride around the limits of the town's boundaries, cheered on their way by the townsfolk, and the day is marked by general roistering and good humour.
▷ **beating the bounds**

comparative method

METHOD OF FOLKLORE STUDY, used particularly by supporters of the **anthropological theory**. It is based on the tenet that all cultures evolve through roughly the same stages of development, although all at different times and at different rates, and therefore a seemingly inexplicable tradition or superstition among a relatively developed people can be illuminated by referring to another culture at a more primitive stage of development.

complaint

TYPE OF FOLK SONG, a lyrical dirge commonly sung at funerals to pacify the spirit of the deceased with mourning and eulogy. It survives mainly in Scotland (where it is known as a coronach) and in Ireland, as a **keen**.
▷ **death**; **funeral customs**

Conchobar

OLD IRISH HERO, king of Ulster at the dawn of the Christian era, said in later legends to have died of impotent rage on the day that Christ was crucified. He succeeded Fergus (Fergus's wife and Conchobar's mother, Nessa, secured the succession for her son). In some legends his father was the druid Cathbad. Conchobar adopted and brought up his nephew, the great **Cuchulainn**.

Conchobar held court at Emain Macha near Armagh. When Cathbad prophesied the doom that the new-born **Deirdre** would bring about, it was Conchobar who spoke out to save her and had her brought up under his protection to be his wife. In this episode he appears in a less than favourable light, as the treacherous killer of the sons of Usnech, and he is punished for his deceit; before his own death he sees the deaths of all his sons.

Conla

OLD IRISH FIGURE, the ill-fated son of **Cuchulainn** and Aoife. His mother sent him to Ireland to his father when he was grown, but placed on him a **geis** that he should not reveal his identity to a lone warrior. When he arrives Cuchulainn sends out a succession of warriors to ask his name, all of whom the boy rejects, but since it is against the Ulster code of honour for more than one warrior to meet a single stranger his appeals to meet with two are rejected. So each of Cuchulainn's men challenge this taciturn stranger, and all are defeated by Conla. Finally Cuchulainn himself approaches, and in fury at this seeming insult fights the son he does not recognize; as Conla lies dying he breathes his mother's name and Cuchulainn, too late, understands all.

contradance

TYPE OF FOLK DANCE, a basic and widespread pattern in which couples stand face to face, usually in a line. Popular in Europe in the late 17th century and throughout the 1700s, it gave way to couples dances such as the waltz in the 19th century. The form itself, however, is more ancient than its ballroom vogue, serving as a model for the universal principles of mating—attraction, advance, flirtation and union—enacted in the context of the wider community. The patterns of the dance can be immensely complex, involving much circling, interweaving and progression of couples. Three of the best-known forms are the Italian *cuntradanza*, the Spanish *contradanza* and the French *contredanse*. Formal dances such as the quadrille developed from such patterns, and more informal versions remain popular in Scottish ceilidhs and American barn dances today.

conundrums A TYPE OF RIDDLE, usually shorter and less sophisticated. Conundrums often depend on a pun rather than on a series of similarities, and are hence characteristic of illiterate cultures or verbal transmission among the literate. A modern example of this type of **riddle** drawn from the large number on a biblical theme:

Who was the largest woman in the Bible?
The woman of Samaria [some area].

Cophetua

FIGURE OF ENGLISH BALLAD LORE, an imaginary king of Africa. Despite his rants against women, he chances to see a beautiful beggar named Penelophon, falls passionately in love and, in the best fairy-tale tradition, marries her. The two live happily and enjoy enormous popularity among the people. The ballad *Cophetua and the Beggar-Maid* is

included in Percy's *Reliques* and has proved attractive to literary minds throughout the ages; Shakespeare refers to the legend in *Romeo and Juliet*, *Love's Labour Lost* and *Richard II*, and it is the subject of Tennyson's poem *The Beggar Maid*.

coral

BRANCHING STRUCTURE, usually stonelike, formed from the skeletons of invertebrate marine creatures, class Anthozoa (phylum Cnidaria). It is usually pinky-red, but many occur as brown, blue, white, yellow or even black. It is widely prized as a potent **amulet** against evil spirits and sickness, although its precise properties vary from place to place. In ancient Rome it was placed around babies' necks as a general charm, effective against disasters such as storm and shipwreck as well as sickness. It was said to defend the wearer against **witchcraft**, magic and deception, and this belief has survived in many areas of Europe. In medieval Europe it was ground by apothecaries and used to cure every conceivable ill. It was thought to be particularly effective in dental care (appropriately enough, since it like teeth is a structure of calcium), and teething infants often wore a necklace of coral. Brown coral is the exception to this litany of benefits; in Italy especially it was said that evil spirits were attracted by this colour.

Cormac Mac Airt

OLD IRISH KING, ruler in Tara at the time of **Finn Mac Cumhal** and the **Fianna** (c.227–66). Probably a historical figure, he is renowned in legend as a just and generous ruler whose wisdom was comparable with that of Solomon.

Cormac's cup

MAGIC OBJECT, a wonderful golden vessel given to **Cormac Mac Airt** by Manannan Mac Lir, god of the sea. It had the property of divining truth; if three lies were told over it it would shatter in pieces, but three truths would make it whole again. The cup aided Cormac to dispense his legendary justice, but it disappeared upon his death, as Manannan had prophesied.

Cormoran

CORNISH GIANT, one of the many tricked and slain by **Jack the Giant-killer**. Cormoran terrorized the Cornish coast until King **Arthur** appealed for a brave hero to put an end to him; Jack captured the giant by luring him into a deep pit, and on presenting the severed head to Arthur was rewarded with a marvellous belt inscribed:

This is the valiant Cornish man
That slew the giant Cormoran

This is a later addition to the **Jack tales**, an attempt to dignify the indolent Jack by linking his name with Arthurian legend.

corn dance see harvest celebrations

corn dolly see harvest doll

cornflower

COMMON GRAINFIELD FLOWER, most usually *Centaurea cyanus* (family Asteraceae), the bachelor's button. Its Latin name derives from classical myth; the **centaur** Chiron healed a wound poisoned by the **hydra**'s blood by covering it with petals from the flower. This legend reflects the importance traditionally given to the plant in folk medicine.

cornflower

Cyanus was a Greek youth sick with love for Chloris (Flora), who occupied his time gathering blooms to pile on her altars, and after his death she transformed him into the flower.

In a Russian folktale, a young man named Basilek was transformed into a cornflower after succumbing to the siren call of the nymph Russalka. Lucian claimed the cornflower could be burned to repel snakes, and in Jamaica it is an ingredient in cures for headache.

Corpus Christi

'BODY OF CHRIST', a Roman Catholic feast-day to honour the presence of Christ's actual body in the Host. It dates from 1246, and was instituted after Juliana, a nun near Liège, claimed to have seen a vision denouncing the Church for failing to honour the Eucharist. She claimed to have seen a full, bright moon with one single dark spot, which, Christ informed her, represented the lack of a feast for this purpose. The feast was extended to the whole church in 1264, and by the 15th century it had become the chief festival of the Western Church.

The feast was suppressed by Protestant movements at the Reformation, when the doctrine of transubstantiation was rejected. It is celebrated on the Thursday after Trinity Sunday, and involves spectacular processions especially in Spain, Portugal and the south of France. These processions incorporate many pre-Christian elements; figures representing **dwarfs**, **dragons** and **giants** dance behind the priests carrying the Host. Miracle plays were performed by trade guilds in the Middle Ages, and symbolic battle dances were widely performed, especially in Spain and Latin America, representing the battles between Moors and Christians.

corrigan

CELTIC FAIRY, a native of Brittany. She is an ancient pagan survival, said to be a druidess, and is therefore set upon making mischief for Christian folk. One of her favourite pranks is to snatch healthy human infants, replacing them with withered fairy **changelings**.

corroboree

AUSTRALIAN ABORIGINAL FESTIVAL, a term used by east-coast groups to refer to all ceremonial gatherings.

coulin

IRISH 'FAIRY TUNES', the ancient folk melodies of Ireland which are said to have been overheard by musicians from the invisible harps of the **sidhe**.

counting-out rhymes

SORTING DEVICE OF CHILDREN'S LORE, a nonsense incantation by which a candidate may be selected for the undesirable role of 'It' or 'He' (the one, for example, who must find all the others in a game of Hide and Seek). Such rhymes are strongly rhythmic; at each stressed syllable a child is indicated, and the one on whom the final stress lands is the one selected. The authority this selection procedure commands is often remarked on by wondering adults—the chosen child invariably accepts the decision with fatalistic resignation.

Repetition and the oral nature of such rhymes has meant that ancient phrases are preserved in a distorted, gibberish form; 'eeny, meeny, miny, mo', for example, one of the commonest beginnings of such rhymes, is thought to be a relic of early peasant numerals. Another line, appearing in several forms, for example 'otcha, potcha, dominotcha', 'hocus, pocus, deminocus' or 'hotchy, potchy, cotchy, notchy', while apparently pure nonsense syllables, derives from a fragment of one of the most solemn lines in the Catholic Mass: *Hoc es enim corpus meim* (This is my body). Such fossil-phrases can be traced to a wide variety of mainly oral lore, especially that invested with mystic significance; masonic passwords and rituals, druidic chants and eastern mantras, spells of the Romany folk, Latin liturgy and saints' names, to name but a few.

Counting-out rhymes extend over vast geographical areas, with surprisingly few alterations. 'Eena, meena, mona, my' in parts of Britain is clearly paralleled by 'ene, tene, mone, mei' in Germany. Variations occur frequently however when children substitute topical allusions or familiar words to fit the jingling rhythm and rhyme, for example in the USA children may chant 'icha bacha, soda cracker, out goes you!'. The incantatory nature of such rhymes has suggested to some folklorists that they are connected with more sinister ancient purposes, such as the selection of victims for druidic sacrifice.

With their strongly rhythmic structure, speed of delivery and emphasis on alliteration and assonance, counting-out rhymes superficially resemble another staple of children's lore, **tongue twisters**, but there is a crucial difference. Whereas tongue twisters are deliberately contrived to present a problem to the speaker at speed, counting-out-rhymes tend to evolve as chants so smooth that once begun they almost say themselves.
▷ **children's lore**

couvade

RITUAL OF CHILDBIRTH, the confinement or restriction of the father for a period after the birth of his child. Sometimes the father takes to his bed as the mother approaches labour, and simulates the painful act of birth as a symbol of his involvement with the child; more usually he retires after the birth.

The origins of the couvade appear to be a belief that the activities of the father intimately influence the safety of the new child; everyday occupations such as hunting, wielding sharp implements and even travelling could be injurious to the vulnerable life of the newborn. Eating certain foods is also forbidden, lest the undesirable properties of the animal are transmitted to the child by **sympathetic magic**. Some scholars have suggested that the custom arose at the transition from matrilineal to patrilineal society, with the father asserting his mystical link with the child over the more obvious connection of the mother, and also the child's dependence upon him. In some cases the mother would be expected to get up immediately, on the day of the birth, to wait on the father, who was resting in bed.

The custom has been recorded worldwide, and as recently as the early 1900s in Brazil and some Basque areas.
▷ **childbirth**

Coventry, to be sent to

TO BE CUT OFF FROM SOCIAL INTERCOURSE, a punishment in which an individual is by common consent cut out of all social activities and discourse. It is a highly effective social sanction, used particularly by schoolchildren (see **children's lore**) although not generally for sustained periods. The term is said to have originated among the citizens of Coventry, England, who, having a strong antipathy towards soldiers during the Civil War, punished in this way any woman who was seen talking to one.

cow

FEMALE RUMINANT, a sacred animal of Hindu religion and many earlier mythologies. It has been associated since ancient times with the cosmic feminine principle, simultaneously symbolizing the lunar goddess and the Earth mother (its horns represent the crescent moon, yet it is a source of life and energy for humans). In Norse mythology the cosmic cow Audhumla created the first man by licking **salt** from the earth, and the Indian **culture hero** Prithu pursued the earth, in cow-form, through the heavens until she agreed to provide him with milk, the liquid of fertility and life.

Cows rarely take an active role in folktales, although they occasionally appear as advisors or **helpful beasts**; in a Polish folktale a girl disenchants a transformed prince by following the advice of a cow who directs her to keep vigil in an enchanted castle. More usually it features as a prized possession, and is the object of more or less successful plots. Jack exchanges the family's only cow for a handful of magic beans in **Jack and the Beanstalk**, a simpleton hoists the cow onto the thatched roof to graze in a popular European folktale, and in an Indian tale two brothers left a cow by their father agree to share it—the elder brother chooses the rear end and hence gains all the milk, while his younger, duller sibling has the front end and is therefore obliged to feed the beast.
▷ **cattle; Dun Cow; Glas Ghaibhneach**

coyote

NEW WORLD CREATURE, *Canis latrans*, a member of the dog family (Canidae). In Native American lore, particularly of the Great Basin, Plains and Californian groups, Coyote is the chief **trickster** figure and **culture hero**. In the latter role he is revered as the bringer of fire and teacher of crafts, but as a trickster he is a lustful, bullying, sharp-witted and often brutal figure—in several Coyote tales children are instructed that they must take care never to act like Coyote in this situation, despite his entertaining escapades.

Some groups have a ritual coyote dance, in which dancers wearing coyote heads imitate the movements of the creature to a rhythmic drumbeat. It is generally performed to mark the death of a warrior, and may indicate a role for Coyote as guardian of the warrior dead.

crab

CRUSTACEAN, any short-tailed member of the order Decapod. In a Japanese folktale the Heike, a proud 12th-century family, took on a rival family, the Genji, in battle. They lost, and in humiliation threw themselves into the sea where they were transformed into crabs leaving their features only as the imprint on their shells.

In Tahitian lore the crab is the shadow and symbol of the god of fugitives, since a hero escaped from his enemies on the back of a fresh-water crab.
▷ **Doctor Knowall**

crane

LONG-LEGGED WADING BIRD, any member of the family Grudiae. The species is an ancient one, and is found throughout the world, though absent in South America. In China the crane is regarded as a symbol of longevity, and in Chinese as well as Japanese and Greek mythologies it is a messenger of the gods to humans.

In many European tales the crane is a crafty **trickster**. A famous example tells how the crane (in some versions a heron) offers to transport fish to a 'safe' pond, away from the perils of fishermen, and having persuaded them to climb inside his beak feasts on them. He is eventually discovered by a crab, who seizes his throat and kills him. In Native North American tales Old Grandfather Crane is wily but generally benevolent; he stretches out his long leg to allow the hero to cross a river but when his enemies attempt to follow the crane drops them into the water. In tales of eastern Europe and India the crane is often the animal guide who leads the hero, usually the youngest brother, into adventure and success.

Aesop gives a version of a widespread tale-type in which the crane and the fox, both traditionally crafty animals, are pitted against each other. The crane invites the fox to dine with him, but serves the food in a deep narrow dish which suits his beak admirably but does not permit the fox even to taste his share. In revenge, the fox politely invites the crane to sup with him, and provides his food on a shallow dish. The crane injures his beak trying to eat. In another tale, again collected by Aesop but of more ancient origin, the crane offers to teach the fox how to fly but drops him once airborne.

In one widespread European tale, demonstrating the folly of expecting gratitude from the ungracious, the crane removes a troublesome bone from the throat of a **wolf** with his long beak. When he asks for the promised payment, he is told that he is lucky to have retrieved his beak intact.

cricket

INSECT, any member of the family Gryllidae (order *Orthoptera*), found widely in Europe, America, Africa and Asia. It is generally considered lucky to have a cricket in the house, and to kill it is not only unlucky but inhospitable. It is also considered bad manners to attempt to imitate the chirp of a cricket. In England and in North America particularly it is seen as an embodiment of the spirit of the house.

In one Hungarian tale included in **Aesop**'s collection, an ass tries to emulate the cricket's musical chirrup by feeding on dew, which the crickets inform him is their diet. Naturally enough, he does not lose his bray but instead starves himself to death. The Cherokee prescribe a tea made from crickets to impart a good singing voice. Ancient Greeks used a concoction of the insects as a cure for asthma. The sound of a cricket is said to indicate the approach of rain or the return of an absent loved one, depending on locality

▷ **grasshopper**

Crockett, Davy (1786–1836)

AMERICAN FOLK HERO, a frontiersman from Tennessee who distinguished himself battling under Andrew Jackson against the Creek in 1814 and was later elected to the Tennessee state legislature. He was killed by Mexican troops at the Alamo, itself a potent battle of American folklore.

His carefully cultivated persona, of a plain honest frontiersman and rustic eccentric, secured his popularity as a politician and made him a figure of popular legend even in his lifetime. It was said that he would climb a mountain on the night Halley's Comet was due to pass overhead and tear off its fiery tail with his bare hands. He encouraged the accumulation of folklore, telling **tall tales** about and against himself (such as his claim that his grin was so ugly it would stun a racoon from the tree) and playing up the image of rustic buffoon in his *Autobiography* (1834). A series of Crockett almanacs, published between 1835 and 1856, extended and developed the legend, and many humorous or outrageous tales in the characteristic pioneer mould became attached to him

crocodile

CARNIVOROUS REPTILE, any member of the family Crocodilidae. In ancient Egypt the crocodile was considered a symbol of godhead, since by virtue of the membrane covering its eyes it enjoyed the god-like attribute of seeing while not being seen. Because of its sinister aspect it was also regarded as an embodiment of evil, and this parallel representation is shown in the crocodile as representation of Set, Sebet and Horus.

Linked too to the popular association of crocodile and deity is the common motif of ordeal by crocodile, a form of the **act of truth**. An Arabian test of innocence was to throw the accused into a pit of crocodiles; if he emerged unharmed, his innocence was proven. In West Africa, to be attacked by a crocodile is also an indication of guilt, since crocodiles are thought to be the souls of murdered men who are seeking revenge. More commonly in Africa crocodiles are said to be incarnations of the ancestors, and therefore simultaneously fearful and beneficent. Some scholars have suggested that the ritual feeding of crocodiles in parts of Africa, recalling the religious ceremonies of ancient Egypt when a tame crocodile was kept in the temple pool and ritually fed honey, meat and wine, have similar religious significance, in addition to the understandable desire to avoid having hungry crocodiles nearby.

European travellers reported back to the Old World that the crocodile moaned and sighed as though in pain to lure its victims and even wept over their carcasses as it devoured them; hence the phrase 'crocodile tears', denoting insincere grief. Another popular belief was that the crocodile had no tongue.

In Pacific lore, there is a large body of tales of **beast marriage** between women and crocodiles.

▷ **alligator**

crónán

DRONE OR HUM, a feature of Irish folk songs. Often appearing as a chorus, crónán demands great breath control and stamina from a singer, and an Irish tale tells how Senchan the poet and his company nearly killed themselves before a demanding audience; not until all 27 had fallen to the ground and Senchan himself had had an eye burst out of his head with the effort were they allowed to stop for breath. The form is most commonly sung as a **lullaby** or to soothe cattle during milking.

croquemitaine

FRENCH HOBGOBLIN, an ugly sprite used as a **bugbear** to frighten children into obedience.

cross

CHIEF CHRISTIAN RELIGIOUS SYMBOL, emblem of the crucifixion of Christ, although its use is not confined solely to the Christian church. There is an enormous variety of cross forms. The simplest is the Greek cross, a vertical line bisecting a horizontal line of equal length, but the one most commonly found in Christian usage is the Latin cross, or *crux immissa*, in which the lower vertical stroke is longer the other three. Other, more elaborate variations include the Egyptian **ankh** (a T-shaped St Anthony's cross surmounted by a loop in place of the upper stroke), the **swastika** or *crux gammata*, the Celtic cross, and the chi-rho monogram used as shorthand for the name of Christ.

The basic cross shape is found in many cultures world-wide, often invested with religious or magical significance, although the precise meanings associated with it have been hotly contested by scholars. The function of location and direction however seems ubiquitous; just as weathervanes appear in the form of crosses today, and on maps 'X marks the spot' while the compass rose indicates orientation, so the cross carried by the Aztec weather goddess symbolized control over the different winds and Native Americans marked the limits of their group's territory by crosses carved on trees.

In Christian lore, the cross only gained its significance gradually. Although the death (and resurrection) of Christ was central to the early church, the cross as symbol only gained currency in the 4th and 5th centuries, and not until the 13th century was the cult of the cross firmly established in the Western church particularly. The legend of the True Cross is told in Jacques de Voragine's *Golden Legend*: at Adam's death his son Seth placed three seeds from the **Tree of Life** into his mouth, cypress, cedar and pine. These grew twined together as a single trunk. The legend traces this tree through various biblical episodes (it appears as the tree under which David sat and wept for his sins, for example) to its role as the wood for Christ's cross and then to AD328, when St Helena, the 80-year-old mother of the Emperor Constantine, uncovered it at Calvary. Pieces of this cross were said to perform great miracles of healing, and so many fragments of the cross were attested that another miracle was asserted—that the wood of the cross could reproduce itself for the faithful. The cross features in all Christian art and architecture (churches

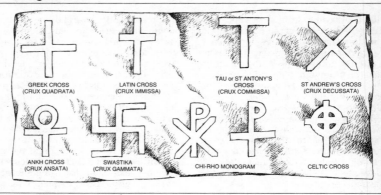

GREEK CROSS (CRUX QUADRATA)
LATIN CROSS (CRUX IMMISSA)
TAU or ST ANTONY'S CROSS (CRUX COMMISSA)
ST ANDREW'S CROSS (CRUX DECUSSATA)
ANKH CROSS (CRUX ANSATA)
SWASTIKA (CRUX GAMMATA)
CHI-RHO MONOGRAM
CELTIC CROSS

types of cross

were commonly built to cruciform plans) and in popular lore it is regarded as a **charm**, the most potent protection against evil in existence. **Vampires** and other ghostly monsters fall back before a cross; the **Devil** cannot stand the sight of it; a dying sinner, no matter how degenerate, is said to be saved at the last by only grasping a cross. Many European tales tell of peasants outwitting the Devil in Faustian contracts by slyly inserting a cross into the document, or by making the sign of the cross against him.

crossing the line

CROSSING THE EQUATOR, a significant event aboard ship which is celebrated by a number of jocular **initiation** practices. The uninitiated, who have not crossed the line before, are tried in a mock court in front of a pantomime 'Neptune', often ducked in tubs of brine, lathered (occasionally with pitch) and shaved or made to eat soap. Testimony such as the account written in a letter of Charles Darwin to his father suggests that even quite recently such ceremonies, now generally good-natured buffoonery, were extremely rough. The tradition may have its origins in sacrificial rites, an observance to pacify the deities of the ocean in these perilous waters where the danger of becalming is ever-present.

crow

BLACK BIRD, a member of the family Corvidae, found in North America, Europe and Asia. Because of its black plumage, the crow was commonly identified with the **Devil** in European lore, and its midsummer migration and moulting was interpreted as a journey to the **underworld** where the crow gave its black feathers as homage to its master. Crow appears as a **trickster** figure in some Native American tales, especially among south-western and Plains groups.

Several moralistic animal fables exploit the folk perception of the crow as a shabby, deceitful bird. In a Latvian tale the envious crow spatters a **swan** with mud, in an attempt to make them look alike, but while the swan can wash itself clean, the crow can never make itself white. In a similar tale, the crow decks herself out in borrowed feathers on her wedding day; she looks ridiculous but believes that she has made herself beautiful. In a Russian tale, the crow is so aggrieved at being punished for his crimes by the **eagle**, the judge of the birds' assembly, that he slanders other birds to see them punished too.
▷ **Badb**

Cú Roi

OLD IRISH SAGE, a wizard of the South, to whom **Cuchulainn**, Conall and Loegaine repaired to discover which of them deserved the champion's portion. Cú Roi chose Cuchulainn, and vindicated his judgement by appearing disguised as an unslayable bachlach in **Conchobar**'s court and testing the integrity of the three (see **Bricriu's Feast**).

Cuchulainn

OLD IRISH HERO, central figure of the **Ulster cycle**. The son of the sun god **Lugh** and Dechtire (sister of **Conchobar**), he was the greatest of Conchobar's warriors, the knights of the **Red Branch**, and beloved of the gods. His given name was Sétante but he won his name ('hound of Culann') for killing the ferocious guard dog of the smith Culann and, in some versions, serving as his hound until he could find another. He gained renown for his feats of courage and strength as a child, and his extraordinary qualities were compounded by his unusual physiology; in addition to his phenomenal size and beauty he possessed seven fingers on each hand and seven toes on each foot, and seven pupils in each eye. In the heat of battle he became **berserk**, deformed and unstoppable in his blood-rage.

Cuchulainn's most famous battle was his stand against **Medb** and her forces in the **Táin Bó Cuailnge**, when he was 17 years old. Medb's satirists later brought about his death however, when they tricked him into throwing away the **gae bulg**.

cuckoo

SMALL BIRD, any member of the Cuculidae family but most commonly the common (or European) cuckoo, *Cuculus canorus*. The distinctive cry of the cuckoo is considered a herald of spring, and is heard joyfully throughout much of Europe. German peasants turn over the coins in their pockets to ensure prosperity for the new cycle of seasons when they hear the first call. Along with many other birds, the cuckoo is regarded as oracular and its calls are interpreted to divine length of life, marital status and even the time of day. Perhaps because of its associations with spring and new life, the cuckoo is widely regarded as a bird of love, especially illicit love. The Indian god Indra and Greek Zeus both assumed the form of a cuckoo during their amorous adventures.

The most famous characteristic of the cuckoo in popular lore, and one which reinforces its association with illicit sexual appetite and hence **adultery**, is its parasitical habit of laying an egg in the nest of another bird. Often the cuckoo mother will push other eggs from the nest, both to allay the host's suspicions that an egg has been added and to reduce competition for her own young once hatched. The young cuckoo is also known to push its adoptive siblings from the nest. The word 'cuckold' referring to a man whose wife has been deceitfully unfaithful, derives from *cuculus*.

A popular English numbskull tale recounts how the Wise Men of **Gotham** built a tall hedge to confine the cuckoo so that they could always enjoy its spring-time call. When the bird flew away after all their labour, they castigated themselves for not building the hedge high enough.

cueca

FOLK DANCE OF SOUTH AMERICA, particularly Chile, Argentina and Peru. Its full name is zamacueca, also known as marinera, and in Mexico the dance is called chilena. It is a courtship dance for couples, characterized by rapid advancing and retreating steps and the twirling of handkerchiefs held aloft. The dance is accompanied by the rhythmic strumming of **guitars**.

culture hero

KEY LEGENDARY FIGURE OF A GROUP, the founder of its cultural values. The culture hero may be human, animal or supernatural, he (or, very rarely, she) may be thought to be still living, or transformed into a rock or star, or to have died in pre-history. What is common to all culture heroes, however, is that they are credited with bringing the benefits of their culture to a people, such as fire, sun, the seasons and cultural practices such as farming or hunting techniques, the making of weapons, traditional crafts and songs. Having taught all these things to the people, they are often said to have disappeared to a world above or to the west of this one, to wait until their people should have need of them.

The culture hero is frequently identical to the group's trickster figure, who features in many folktales as either cunning and successful or over-confident and gulled. This composite figure often also includes the creative role, functioning as the creator of the entire world, of the tribe's local area, or of the tribe itself. This kind of culture hero is especially typical of Native American groups, where the hero is usually an animal or bird; he is **Coyote** for central Californian tribes and those of the Plains, and **Rabbit** elsewhere in the south east. Occasionally the culture hero is human, or at least appears to be so: Apache tribes of the south west revere Killer-of-Enemies, for example. In Native South American folklore, the culture hero is frequently human, and he is often regarded as the powerful Ancestor who created the world and performed many transformations which account for natural features of the landscape. He is benefactor of the tribe in the usual way, teaching skills and giving social and religious laws, and then generally retires west. Most famous of these figures is Bochica, worshipped in ancient Colombia. In most cases, however, the culture hero is an animal who exhibits human characteristics and behaviour.

The many tales told of the culture hero are usually set in a mythical time before the world became as it now is, sometimes before the arrival of human beings, when animals and supernatural beings would converse. The existing order is explained by reference to the culture hero's adventures; often, Prometheus-like, he steals the secret of fire from the upper world, or sets the sun in its course, or fights and destroys a terrible monster, or produces rivers and game for the tribe, and on the Gold Coast of Africa they tell how Anansi (**Spider**), originally spoken of in mythology as the creator of the world, stole the sun and set it in the sky. African culture heroes such as Anansi tend to have become purely trickster figures, leaving behind their mythological aspect to a greater degree than is common in America. The ancient civilizations of South America, on the other hand, appear to have regarded their culture heroes with more reverence than did the tribes of the North. It may be that many of the trickster figures, **clowns** and fools that are found established by ancient tradition around the world once bore a deeper mythological significance, although their role has degenerated to that of mere entertainment in much of the world.

cumulative stories and songs

PLAYFUL STRUCTURE OF FOLK NARRATIVE, in which a song or tale adds successive elements, found all over the world. Repetition is generally acknowledged as a characteristic of all folklore, since it is so fundamental as a memory aid, and for public performance as a means of structuring a narrative. In cumulative forms however, repetition becomes the central feature of the narrative. A new element is added to the original simple statement at each verse or during the course of the narration and the growing list may be recited backwards at the chorus or reversed in the resolution of the tale.

One of the most famous of all cumulative songs is the Christmas **carol** *The Twelve Days of Christmas*, which lists each of the presents sent throughout the 12 days, the number of items corresponding to the day, and after each new item reiterates the previous presents back to the original 'partridge in a pear tree'. Another famous example, now a **nursery rhyme**, is *The House that Jack Built*, which builds on the simple sentence 'This is the house that Jack built' to produce a whole gallery of animal and human characters, each verse ending with the original line. The final, longest verse runs:

> This is the farmer sowing his corn
> That kept the cock that crowed in the morn,
> That waked the priest all shaven and shorn,
> That married the man all tattered and torn,
> That kissed the maiden all forlorn,
> That milked the cow with the crumpled horn,
> That tossed the dog
> That worried the cat
> That killed the rat
> That ate the malt
> That lay in the house that Jack built.

More ancient examples of cumulative songs include a song listing the Twelve Apostles (in some versions these are replaced by the ten commandments), which is found in many different languages including Hebrew.

The tale of the Old Woman and the Pig, included in *Mother Goose Tales*, is a good example of a cumulative tale that retraces the plot to finish. An old woman buys a pig which refuses to jump over a stile; she appeals to a dog to bite it, and when the dog refuses appeals to a stick to beat the dog, and then to a fire to burn the stick, and so on until she obtains milk from a cow and is thus able to feed the cat and set in motion the whole mechanism and the pig finally jumps the stile. A very similar plot structure is found in a Mexican song about a frog who refuses to stop singing, and one of the earlier forms may be the Hebrew *Had Gadyo* chant, known from the mid-16th century at least.

Narratives in which the form is a more significant element than the plot are known as formula tales, and they are usually performed playfully. The patterns around which such tales are constructed are traditional and widespread, although the details of plot may vary. Circular tales are common, in which the speaker comes back to the beginning of his narrative in the course of a tale and begins it over again. Also popular are catch tales, in which the speaker tricks his listeners into answering inappropriately by a sequence of questions, for example:

You remind me of a man.
What man?
A man with power.
What power?
Power to hoodoo.
Hoodoo?
You do.
Do what?
Remind me of a man etc
▷ **Gingerbread Man**

Cupid and Psyche

BEAST MARRIAGE TALE, one of the earliest forms of the **Beauty and the Beast** type. The extant version by the Roman poet Apuleius is probably taken from a Greek source. As in Beauty and the Beast, the heroine is the youngest of three sisters, and is so beautiful that Venus's temples are emptied and her wrath awakened. Venus orders Cupid (her son) to cause Psyche to fall in love with a monster. Psyche is left to her fate on a mountain; she falls asleep and awakens in a glorious palace where she is lavishly attended, but she never sees the being who visits her bed. Her trouble-making sisters persuade her that she is sleeping with a serpent, and Psyche breaks the **looking taboo** by lighting a lamp. Her husband disappears, and in her search to find him Psyche faces a series of impossible tasks and various taboos, the last of which she fails to fulfil, and she is struck down. Cupid saves her, Psyche completes her mission to take a jar of ointment to Venus, and Zeus allows Cupid to marry Psyche and make her immortal.

The **taboo** motif which features so prominently here appears widely in beast marriage tales.

curse

MAGICAL IMPRECATION, the bringing down of evil. Although the word curse is used quite loosely today, to refer to any persistent bad luck, in folk terminology it generally means the voluntary invocation of evil upon a person and the outworking of that malediction.

The person casting the curse will generally invoke a supernatural power, often by magical formulae or spells in archaic language handed down through generations. The power invoked may be divine or, more usually, demonic, or neither, but in all cases the only ways in which the cursed person can avoid the threatened ill-fortune is to invoke a stronger power for his protection or to propitiate the evil force by sacrifice or some such placatory measure.

Once spoken, the curse is often considered to be so powerful that it must be fulfilled; in Hebrew folklore a curse once placed cannot be withdrawn, although it may take effect several generations later. There is also the danger of the curse being too strong for the one invoking it, in which case it will either come down upon him instead of his intended victim or affect both curser and cursed, along with anyone who inadvertently overhears it. Other types of curses are less severe, directed only at an individual's possessions and not his life, perhaps, and by effective counter-magic the cursed one may be able to limit or reverse the effects of the curse. Curses may be directed by one individual or group towards another for a specific reason, often in revenge, or take the more general cultural form of the **taboo**.

Clearly, curses and taboos remain most vitally alive in societies with a strong belief in the supernatural as an active element in the human world. In ancient Rome for example many curses were inscribed on tablets to be left along with sacrifices at the shrines of gods, half prayer and half spell. In secularized societies curses are rarer, yet it is interesting to note the power of folk tradition: curses are still a matter for much speculation and interest in popular culture and the mass media and many who have little or no belief in the supernatural world would nevertheless feel uneasy under a curse. Along with ghosts, curses have survived in the Western world as a half-belief of the folk.

Cyclops

GIANTS OF GREEK MYTHOLOGY, terrifying beings with one eye in the centre of their forehead. According to Homer they

Cyclops

were pastoral cannibals, traditionally said to live in Sicily, and Odysseus escapes their chief, Polyphemus, by first blinding him and then concealing himself and his men beneath the giant's sheep. Hesiod says the three Cyclops were the sons of Uranus and Gaea, and that they forged Zeus's thunderbolts. In later tradition they served as the assistants of Hephaestus in his forge below Etna. Several ancient walls were attributed to them. The one-eyed giant is found elsewhere in folklore, for example the Celtic king **Balor**.

cymbals

METAL PERCUSSION INSTRUMENT, consisting of two circular plates (flat or, more usually, concave) struck together to produce a ringing crash or in more recent times hit singly by a stick. Cymbals were used in religious rituals by several ancient cultures including Assyrians, Egyptians and Israelites, and spread into Greece, Rome, India and, by the Middle Ages, northern Europe. Smaller cymbals, held in one hand after the manner of **castanets**, are common particularly in indoor ceremonies and their tinkling sound has led to a tradition of such cymbals being played by and associated with women. The larger cymbals that produce a loud clashing sound are more usually played by men, and have become associated particularly with military music and dramatic climaxes of more lyrical works. In primitive music cymbals often played a part in inducing frenzied ecstatic states, and in Crete they were used in the celebration of the anarchic god Dionysus.

Cymbeline

LEGENDARY ROMAN KING OF BRITAIN, a descendant of **Brut**, recorded in Holinshed's *Chronicles* as having two sons, Guiderius and Arviragus. He is held by some traditions to be identical to King Cunobeline, after whom Colchester (Roman Camulodunum) is said to be named. Shakespeare's play *Cymbeline* is based largely on the tale of Imogen from Boccaccio's *Decameron*.

daddy-long-legs

COMMON INSECT, any member of the arachnid order Opiliones (or Phalangida), differing from the **spider** in having extremely long, slender legs, up to 20 times the length of its rounded body. In England especially its folk name is harvestman, from the scythe-like appearance of its curved legs, and its prevalence in the fields in late summer. It is considered very unlucky to kill one while bringing in the harvest. Other names include straddlebug in parts of America and grand-daddy in the US and Britain.

daffodil

FLOWER ASSOCIATED WITH SPRING, genus *Narcissus* (family Amaryllidaceae), also known as the Lent lily. Its name derives from Greek *asphodelus*; Pliny and Theophilus speak of the asphodels that grow beside the Acheron, the 'woeful river' of the **underworld**, bringing a little pleasure into the land of the dead, and it was said that daffodils carpeted the fields of Elysium. This association, and the fact that the daffodil heralds spring and new life, may explain the widespread tradition of planting daffodils on graves. Asphodel became affodil in English, and eventually daffodil.

The daffodil's use as an emblem of Wales is of relatively recent origin, coming into favour in the early 20th century among those who considered the traditional **leek** too vulgar to represent a nation. It is however an old Welsh belief that whoever finds the first daffodil of spring can be sure that they will gain gold in the coming months.

Dagda

OLD IRISH FAIRY KING, literally 'good god', the chief of the **Tuatha de Danann** and father of **Aedh**, **Angus Og** and Brigit (originally a goddess of poetry, craft and divination). Dagda possessed many marvellous objects, including an inexhausti-

ble **cauldron**, orchards that bore fruit perpetually, two pigs, one of which was always roasting while the other lived and fatted itself for the next feast, a club that could both take and restore life, and a magical **harp** which played itself and summoned the seasons.

He fought at the battle of Mag Tured, killing many **Fomorians**, and afterwards divided up the hills and mounds (from which the **sidhe** get their name) of Ireland among his people. For himself he kept the Brugh na Boinne, which was later won from him by cunning by his son Angus Og. Dagda was almost certainly an early agricultural deity, and his cauldron, swine and fruit trees recall his ancient role as provider.

Dagonet, Sir

THE FOOL OF KING ARTHUR and his beloved companion, according to the *Morte d'Arthur* of Sir Thomas Malory. He is a later, literary addition to the **Arthur**ian cycle.
▷ **clowns**

Daire Mac Fiachna

OLD IRISH CHIEF OF ULSTER, best known as the owner of the fateful Brown Bull of Cuailgne coveted by **Medb** of Connacht. Having agreed to lend the bull to Medb for a year, Daire changes his mind when he overhears one of his servants, in an indiscreet and drunken moment, comment that Medb would have taken the bull by force had Daire refused it. When Medb sent her messengers to collect the bull he treated them insultingly, and so Medb led her forces into Ulster to seize her prize. Thus began the **Táin Bó Cuailnge**.

daisy

GARDEN FLOWER of the family Asteraceae, most commonly the oxeye daisy (*Chrysanthemum leucanthemum*) or the English (or true) daisy (*Bellis perennis*).

Both forms are natives of Europe but have become widespread in North America. Its name derives from Old English *dæges ege*, meaning day's eye, from its characteristic closing at night.

The English daisy in Christian lore is sacred to St Margaret of Antioch (from its French name, *marguerite*) and has many medicinal uses, particularly against gout, aching bones and migraines. The oxeye daisy is the sacred flower of both St John and **Mary Magdalene** (said in some legends to have sprung from the penitent tears of the latter). In Europe it was widely used to cure ulcers, calm madness and treat wounds to the chest.

As a symbol of innocence and faithfulness, the daisy plays a prominent role in love **divination**. The popular ritual of pulling off a daisy's petals to the chant 'He loves me, he loves me not' survives today, as does a similar chant to indicate the date of one's marriage—'This year, next year, sometime, never'.

Damon and Pythias

CLASSICAL LEGEND, an example of the common **Two Brothers** tale-type. The two friends lived in Syracuse in the fourth century BC under the tyrant Dionysius I, who condemned Pythias to death. Damon offered to stand as hostage so that his friend could go home and put straight his affairs, on the understanding that should Pythias not return he would die in his place. Pythias returned just before the allotted time expired and Dionysius, touched by this faithful friendship, pardoned him.

dance

ONE OF THE CENTRAL IDENTIFYING FEATURES OF EVERY CULTURAL GROUP, involved vitally in the life of the community. Idiosyncratic forms of traditional dance have been recorded in every cultural group; it seems that the impulse to move rhythmically both individually and as a community, whether purposefully at specific times of crisis or celebration or as a pleasurable diversion, is one of the most fundamental known to humanity. It is likely that meaning was expressed in movement even before the development of speech. Folk dance differs from more sophisticated forms

(such as ballet), and even from ethnological dances, in being the result not of one choreographer or a single creative process but a spontaneous development from the way of life and preoccupations of a given group.

Although it is inevitably speculative to comment on prehistoric forms of dance, it seems clear from evidence such as cave paintings and from the elements that have survived in dances of widely different cultures that there were certain motives and patterns behind the earliest forms of dance. They would generally be performed by men only, unless the dance was intended as a fertility rite; the dancers would enact the basic movements of their lives, imitate the movements of animals around them, and perhaps prove to each other and to the watching women their skill, strength and endurance.

Ritual and religion
Throughout America and Africa and in some areas of Northern Europe, hunting dances developed to enable the hunter to gain power over the animal being mimicked, and to propitiate its spirit, and where animal spirits are revered as totemic ancestors these mimetic dances also had religious significance, in worship, healing or intercession.

As civilizations developed, dance became a vital element in religion. In Indian mythology for example the god Shiva brought the world into being and sustains it with his dancing. In primitive societies, worship of a deity, typically the sun, was accompanied by ritual dancing, and this is thought to be the origin of one of the most basic forms, the circle dance. The Incas had a famous **sun dance**, and some small-scale societies of North America and Canada developed dances to be performed in an **eclipse** to frighten away the monster attacking the sun and to restore its light. Many groups world-wide, especially in northern areas, celebrated the **solstices**, the height of summer or the point at which the sun began its return.

Ritual dance was an important part of classical Greek culture, in the dramatic festivals which began as gatherings for sacrifice, and in the worship of Dionysius the Orgia or ecstatic dance was encouraged. In ancient Rome this became the riotous, debauched dancing of the Bacchanalia, in honour of the god of wine, Bacchus. Many other cultures perform ecstatic dances in which the participants whirl and leap to a driving drumbeat, often in a trance in which they may inflict self-mutilation. Most famous of all these are the Islamic Whirling Dervishes, but many Native American dances of north and south display similar features, with the dancers thought to be possessed by an animal or ancestral spirit. **Clowns**, regarded by many early peoples as powerful figures closely associated with the supernatural forces of healing, fertility and destruction, often performed their own ceremonial dances, usually involving grotesque costume and actions, with the aid of **bells**, **rattles**, sticks or whips.

Male and female dances

Many forms of dance involve sticks or other implements, such as the **Morris dance** in England, with its characteristic rhythmic striking of the ground. It is probable that such dances originated from early fertility rituals, with men belabouring the ground into wakefulness and driving off the evil spirits that would harm the crops. In **war dances** and battle mimes weapons are often carried; these dances were performed to raise the group's morale before battle and to celebrate victory (the **Highland Fling** is thought to have developed from the customary victory dance performed on the shield of the vanquished enemy) but they were used too as vehicles for the display of masculine prowess. **Stick dances**, mock duels, performed throughout Europe, were also a means of developing fighting skills. Dances for men tend to involve elements drawn from hunting, riding or other such 'male' pursuits; they are generally strenuous and exciting, both strengthening the bonds within the group and displaying virility to the females. One of the most famous examples is the Cossack style from Russia and the Ukraine. Female dances on the other hand, especially in Europe, tend to be more lyrical, and often involve actions of domestic life such as spinning (as in La Filado from Spain).

One of the most common of the mixed-sex forms is the courtship dance, which appears in various forms in virtually every society. Dances act out attraction, pursuit, rejection, flirtation, eroticism and (usually) eventual acceptance, from the most obscene to the sophisticated demureness of set dances. Latin countries in Europe incline towards dances in couples with much passion but little physical contact, for example in the Spanish **flamenco**; most northerly European countries tend to have sets of couples dancing together, the men and women linked by the close peasant hold. The most common forms of social dancing in the West today originate from these courtship dances. Although much African dance is obscene, particularly that which imitates animal life, there are no known native erotic couples' dances, in fact women and men seldom dance together socially.

Social functions of dance

In addition to the obvious area of courtship, dance has traditionally been regarded by many cultures as an integral part of social interaction. Many groups, particularly in Polynesia and South America, perform special dances to welcome guests. Others have dances of friendship to be performed within the tribe. At social gatherings such as weddings it is an almost universal practice to celebrate with dances, such as the Lauterbach of Switzerland.

Where **initiation** rites mark the progress of a child to puberty or adulthood, the ceremonies are generally accompanied by ritual or celebratory dances. Here the dancing is partly magical, to drive away evil spirits from the vulnerable initiate, but it is also an expression of group identity and traditions.

The last rite of passage, death, is also widely marked by dancing throughout the world. This may be solemn and mournful, but is more commonly a means of making merry, to restore the morale of the group and to protect the living by pleasing the spirits of the dead. Dance is essentially life-asserting and this is its primary quality in the various dances of death around the world, for example in the reels and jigs danced at funeral wakes in Scotland and Ireland.

Traditional dance forms

While certain patterns and steps recur around the world without apparent connection, and there has been an enormous amount of cross-cultural exchange over the centuries of immigration and trade, it remains true that most cultural groups retain a characteristic style of dance. African dance tends to be exuberant and acrobatic, whereas Oriental dance forms, particularly among the higher castes, are more stylized, characterized by precision in intricate hand and arm gestures. The peasant dances of North Europe concentrate on group formations such as squares, long sets and chains, ranging from the simple to the highly ingenious, with couples turning and passing one another to produce new patterns, although in Russia the traditional forms are more individualistic. Native American dances are often based on animal characteristics, but later settlers in America brought with them quadrilles and reels from Europe and developed from them a healthy folk dance tradition of their own. Although many steps are common to the choreography of different cultures, for example the basic two-step is found throughout Europe and America, no step is universally used and no one pattern, of rhythm or partnering for example, is to be found in every culture. Dance may be a universal element of society, but its endless variety testifies to the breadth of human imagination and experience. Folk dance continues today, spontaneously in many cultures and as a tradition, enthusiastically revived, among others. Even in industrialized societies, popular dance of the folk continues to change and develop not only as recreation, but as a means of expressing cultural identity.

Folktales often warn of the dangers of dancing too much: several Native American myths tell how a group of disobedient children who refused to stop dancing were caught up to the sky where they dance forever as the **Pleiades** constellation. To join the dance in a fairy circle is also thought to be dangerous; a human may be trapped for many years or perhaps forever.
▷ **death dance**

dandelion

dandelion

PERENNIAL HERB, genus *Taraxacum*, family Asteracaea, most commonly *Taraxacum officinale*. It is a native of Europe and Asia, now found throughout much of North America. One of the best-known aspects of dandelion lore is its function as a timepiece; once in seed, the downy tufts are blown upon and the number of puffs required to remove them all is the hour of the day.

The dandelion is also useful in folk medicine; dandelion wine is said to be a tonic and, in Ireland particularly, a guard against heart disease. In England the roots give an infusion that purifies the blood and elsewhere sap from the stalks is rubbed onto warts to remove them.
▷ **ragwort**

danse macabre see death dance

daoine maite

'THE GOOD PEOPLE', the diminutive **fairy** race of recent Irish folklore.
▷ **sidhe**

daoine sidhe see sidhe

date palm

FRUIT-BEARING TREE, *Phoenix dactylifera* (family Arecaceae, or Palmae). Its name stems from the ancient belief that the tree will renew itself if destroyed, like the mythical bird. It is found mainly in the Middle East, northern Africa, India, Pakistan and, more recently, in California. It has enjoyed a high reputation in the plant lore of many peoples, chiefly owing to its versatility in meeting the various needs of a community: its root is medicinal, used for stomach upsets and swellings; the wood is used for building; the juice in wine; the seeds can be ground into oil; the leaves are woven into furniture and baskets and the fibre into rope; and, of course, the fruit is good for eating.

In ancient Egypt and China the date palm was the **tree** of life, and in Christian lore **Mary** gave birth to Jesus under this tree, and any new mother wishing blessings on her baby should eat three dates.

Davy Jones

THE EVIL SPIRIT OF THE SEA. The phrase appears to have originated among sailors in the 18th century but its origins are obscure. Some scholars suggest that Davy is a corruption of **duppy**, the West Indian term for devil, and that Jones may perhaps recall Jonah who was swallowed alive by a **whale** in the biblical story. Alternatively, it may be the name of a notorious pirate. Davy Jones's Locker, the depths of the sea, is the repository for all drowned sailors.

dead man's hand

POKER HAND CONSISTING OF EIGHTS AND ACES, a pair of each, so called because it was that held by Wild Bill Hickok when he was shot in the back by Jack McCall at Deadwood in Dakota's Black Hills on 2 August 1876. His fingers could not be loosened from the cards.

dead rider

A MOTIF OF EUROPEAN BALLADRY. A recently deceased man appears on a horse and attempts to carry someone away, usually his wife, sweetheart, sibling or older child. Often these living persons are unaware that the beloved is dead and will accompany the riders willingly. In many cases the abduction proves fatal, or the living person is saved only by a fateful chance, such as the crowing of a **cock**. The motif is found mainly in northern and central Europe.
▷ **erlking**

dead rider

death

FINAL RITE OF PASSAGE, and the greatest human mystery. Death is one of the few events common to all cultural groups and because of its mysterious finality it is always invested with ritual significance. It is often possible to discern from the behaviour of the group at the death of one of its members the most fundamental principles by which that group lives, since in the light of death the most basic beliefs of life are revealed. The most consistent principle governing the lore of death is that the dead are envious of the living and may wish to harm them, especially if they are given cause for dissatisfaction. Those thought to be most vulnerable are those closest to the deceased, especially spouse, children or siblings.

Despite the pervasive fear of the dead, there is much evidence in folklore to suggest a parallel belief in the power of the deceased for good. In the **Cinderella** tale-type, for example, the dead mother acts from beyond the grave to provide for her distressed daughter. Most primitive societies practised ancestor worship, and called upon the spirits of the dead for help and healing as well as placating them with reverence and sacrifice. The general feeling seems to be that the dead are immensely powerful, and that, although this power is usually directed against the living in much the same way that the **evil eye** operates upon an incautiously lucky person, it may be used for good if the living please the dead.

After a certain length of time also, when the body has decomposed and the strong ties with the living have weakened or been forgotten, the spirit is considered less apt to do harm.

Funerals are raucous affairs in many cultures, with much singing, dancing and feasting. Hired mourners are often paid to raise the **keen**; the noise is at once a protection for the living against the powers of the dead, a mark of respect for the passing of the deceased, and perhaps most fundamentally an assertion of life in the face of the mystery of death.

death dance

A WIDESPREAD RITUAL that can take many forms, most usually performed as a funeral rite or in **carnival**. Among Native Americans particularly the chief function of such dances is to exorcise the spirit of the deceased or to speed the spirit's ascent to the Great Spirit. Like most **funeral customs**, its primary motivation is a belief that a recently dead spirit is envious of the living and may cause them harm unless placated, misled or otherwise diverted from its purpose. In such dances images of the dead may be burned and sacrifice made, amid much noise-making. Characteristically, directions and signs used in such dances are reversed from the normal patterns, a precaution intended to confuse, and therefore render impotent, the spirits.

In medieval Europe the *danse macabre* developed to reflect the contemporary obsession with death in the wake of the Black Death. It is an allegorical representation of the all-pervading power of death, in which Death personified features as a skeleton leading all ranks of humankind, from emperors to lowly clerks, to the grave. This dance, which was depicted in literature, art and drama of western Europe, was also performed in carnivals, especially in Germany, Spain and Spanish America. In areas of Spain and Mexico the cavorting figure of Death, a skeleton or a ghastly **clown**, remains a key figure in such processions.

deer

LONG-LEGGED HOOFED MAMMAL, any member of the family Cervidae (order Artiodactyla), species of which are native to Europe, Asia, North Africa and North and South America. Among many Native North American groups the deer is a sacred totemic animal, but it is widely hunted for food and several groups have deer dances with steps mimicking the movements of the deer to bring success in the hunt. Such dances are often also considered valuable for curing. The deer is a chief character in many Native American folktales, but unlike most other animals it is not usually portrayed as a **trickster** figure. In **beast marriage** tales a deer wife proves a valuable companion to her human husband until she is offended by a careless remark or act, when she returns to her deer form and departs forever. The wife of **Finn Mac Cumhal**, Sadb, took the form of a deer.

defects

CHARACTERISTICS OF FAIRY FOLK, an imperfection or deformity that cannot be entirely concealed by **glamour** and by which dazzled humans might know them. This is a common motif of European fairy-lore, which appears to be closely related to the concept of the **Devil**, with his cloven hoof, and the medieval identification of fairies as fallen angels. So in Aberdeenshire **brownies** were said to have mitten-like hands, with no separate fingers but only a thumb, and Scandinavian **elves** were careful never to turn their backs on humans lest they reveal their hollowness. The **henkies** limped as they danced throughout Shetland, and the **banshee** was variously reported as wanting a nostril or having unnaturally pendulous breasts or a single, ugly tooth.

Deirdre

OLD IRISH HEROINE, 'Deirdre of the Sorrows'. Her legend is part of the **Red Branch** cycle of Irish folklore, also known as the Heroic cycle, which deals with an epic period just beyond the reach of history, with the texture of legend rather than primitive myth. The main figure of the cycle is **Cuchulainn**, but the legend of Deirdre, *The Fate of the Children of Usnech*, is an eloquent story (an *Aithid*) in which he does not feature. The oldest surviving version of this famous tragic tale is found in the 12th-century *Book of Leinster*.

Conchobar, High King of Ulster, is being feasted at the house of his chief story-teller, Fedlimid, when his host's wife gives birth to a baby girl. The Druid Cathbad prophecies that this child will bring ruin to Ireland and to the Red Branch, the king's warriors, who immediately call for her death. The king however refuses to defy fate; he orders that Deirdre be brought up in one of his houses in the forest, one day to become his wife.

So Deirdre grows up, seeing only her nurse, her tutor and Levarcham, a trusted servant of Conchobar's. One winter's day her tutor kills a calf and a **raven** comes down to feed: Deirdre is filled with desire for one with skin as white as snow, cheeks as red as blood, and hair as black as the raven. Levarcham tells her of Naoise (in some versions she herself has already seen him at play with his fellows), Deirdre persuades Levarcham to bring him to the house, and the two fall in love. They elope to Scotland with Naoise's two brothers, Ainle and Arden, the other sons of Usnech, and live there happily for several years until Conchobar finally sends Fergus to promise them safe conduct home. Deirdre suspects treachery, but the sons of Usnech are persuaded by the king's message and they return to Erin. Conchobar tricks Fergus by imposing a **geis**, or taboo, to separate him from his charges, and the brothers and Deirdre are received in the quarters of the Red Branch. There, despite the attempt of Levarcham to warn them, the sons of Usnech are attacked and finally overcome by the spells of Cathbad. The Druid had made the king swear not to harm his prisoners once taken but Conchobar immediately kills all three in jealous rage; Deirdre laments by their bodies then kills herself. In some versions she is taken as wife by Conchobar for a year and then given to one of his warriors, whereupon she leaps from his chariot and dashes her head open on the stones. Conchobar is said to have planted **yew** staffs to mark the graves, and these grew into intertwined trees.

Because of Conchobar's treachery in breaking his oath, he is deserted by many warriors (including Fergus) and the next story of the cycle, the **Táin Bó Cuailnge** (Cattle Raid of Cooley) tells of his war against them and the rulers of Connaught, **Ailill Mac Matach** and **Medb**.

Deirdre has been compared with Helen of Troy, doomed by her beauty to be a pawn of kings, but in fact Deirdre's great eloquence and self-determination make her one of the most commanding of the ancient heroines. The tale developed greatly from its earliest, starker forms to display an astonishing range of psychological insight and lyricism, and its subject inspired many later writers such as John Millington Synge, A C Russel and W B Yeats. It is a good example of an ancient folk narrative which has passed into the literature and consciousness of a nation.

delphinium see larkspur

dendan

FABULOUS SEA MONSTER OF ARABIAN LEGEND, an enormous black fish whose peculiarity is that it must die if it touches human flesh or even hears a human voice. In the *Arabian Nights*, Abdallah the Fisherman covers himself with the fat from a dendan to enable him to visit his friend, Abdallah the Merman, underwater. During his visit a dendan approaches menacingly, but the shout of the fisherman kills it instantly.

Devil

PERSONIFICATION OF EVIL, the opponent of God and good. Satan, from an Arabic word meaning adversary, is in Semitic and Christian belief the archfiend who was created an angel but whose pride and rebellion brought about his fall. He is now the source of all evil, constantly attempting to thwart the good purposes of God by winning the souls of humans for himself. In some monotheisms, and heresies such as Manicheism, the Devil is one aspect of the single god, good and evil in one person. In popular belief he differs from other princes of darkness such as Hades by his malicious intent, and the folk of Europe in particular lived in perpetual fear of his evil machinations; churches contained pictures to

Devil

instruct illiterate folk, graphically illustrating the horrors of Hell being inflicted on the condemned by legions of devils.

The custom of never referring to him by his name developed from this fear; he is generally known by a variety of **euphemisms** such as Old Nick, the Old Gentleman, Clootie or the Dark One. Despite the fear he inspired, however, he was often treated with good-natured mockery in the peasant tales of England and Germany, and portrayed as mischievous rather than wholly evil. Since this image of the Devil is so far from accepted theology, it may suggest that Satan's origins or at least the model upon which his portrayal is based is that of an ancient deity of crops, both beneficent and malicious, much in the way that Native American **culture heroes** inspire both reverence and ridicule.

Satan is usually conceived of as red, the colour of fire and blood, a man with horns, a pointed tail, and cloven hoofs for feet, but in older representations more emphasis is laid upon his bestial qualities. He is often shown as a **goat**, **snake**, **bird** or grotesquely fanciful monster. This corresponds to the traditional

portrayal of demons in ancient art from Mesopotamia and Egypt, and with the African and Native American beliefs in animal spirits as deities and demons. The goat especially is closely associated with lechery and sexual appetite, a common theme in the folk concept of Satan.

Although Satan is considered the chief adversary of God, many cultures have beliefs in devils or demons which cause mischief to mankind. Often good and evil are not so polarized as in Christian tradition, and demons proliferate even in monotheistic Jewish lore, with examples such as Behemoth, demon of animal strength, and Asmadeus, demon of lust and rage. Many cultures in Asia, Africa and America perform 'devil dances', a frenzied dance in which the performer impersonates a demon. These are generally intended to propitiate the spiritual forces and thus ensure good crops, or for **exorcism**, to draw out the demons from a sick person. They are often linked to puberty or initiation ceremonies, at which the participants are thought to be particularly vulnerable to demonic influence.

As popular legends grew up around

the **saints** in Europe, so too did folk culture appropriate the lore of the Devil. He was popularly supposed to be the master of **witches** and warlocks, who were thought to converse intimately or even copulate with him, and hence their activities centred around reversals of godly themes such as the reading of the Lord's Prayer backwards or demonic baptisms and sabbaths (see **witchcraft**). It was thought that one who was greatly accomplished, especially in music for which the Devil had a particular fondness, might well have sold his soul in return for skill and worldly success. Such a contract was traditionally supposed to be signed in blood and usually sealed at a crossroads, and after a certain number of years had elapsed the Devil would return to claim his price, the human soul. This is the basis of the **Faust** legend, but in other folk tales the hero tricks the Devil by finding a loophole in the contract, and thus secures for himself wealth, skill and an intact soul.

Devil's bedstead

THE FOUR OF CLUBS, said to represent the **Devil**'s four-poster bed. It is therefore an unlucky card, and any wager made on a hand containing it is doomed.

devolutionary theory

ONE OF THE EARLIEST THEORIES OF FOLK-LORE AND LEGEND, proposed by the brothers Jacob and Wilhelm Grimm when they produced the first volume of their *Kinder und Hausmärchen* (known as *Grimms' Fairy Tales*) in 1812–14, is a 'devolutionary' view of folklore as the remains of a complex mythology, suppressed when organized religion was imposed on the world and now surviving only in fragmentary form in the motifs of tales and legends. A later development of this idea, occurring when the ancient Indian language Sanskrit was discovered in the mid 19th century and hailed as the origin of all European languages, was that the tales derived from ancient Indian mythology which broke down in its diffusion to be remembered only as a general animistic principle by which the deity's attributes were transferred to animals, sky, water and so on. This in its turn developed into the tales which are documented today.

diamond

PRECIOUS GEM, a mineral composed of carbon molecules, that is the hardest known naturally occurring substance. Its durability and its extraordinary brilliance, due to its high refractive capacity, have lent the diamond prestige and significance throughout human history. Some cultures however were suspicious of its hard brilliance; Persian folklore held that it brought bad luck to the wearer, and that it was created by evil forces, and it was a common belief that a diamond was poisonous if swallowed. In India however diamonds brought luck, friends, long life and wealth, depending on the 'caste' of the gem, and in medieval Europe the diamond was worn as an **amulet** to ward off poison, disease, insomnia and nightmares. It was also said to protect against incubi, and, along the same lines, its clarity was invoked as proof of a woman's fidelity. It is the **birthstone** of April.

Diarmuid

OLD IRISH WARRIOR, a member of the **Fianna** and kinsman and friend of **Finn Mac Cumhal**. He attracted the attentions of **Gráinne**, who was pledged in marriage to Finn, and despite his misgivings she persuaded him to elope with her. Finn gave chase, and the two were overtaken. Diarmuid finally died because Finn would not bring water to him as he lay in the forest.

Dick Whittington (c.1358–1423)

LORD MAYOR OF LONDON, previously a merchant, and later a renowned philanthropist. The historical details of his life have been overshadowed in folk history by the story of his quest for his fortune on the streets of London, aided by his faithful **cat**, a typical example of the **helpful beast** motif attached to a historical personage, dating from the 17th century. Equally famous is the tale of the **bells** that summoned the dispirited Dick back to the city, pealing out 'Turn again Whittington, thrice Lord Mayor of London'.

diffusion theory

SCHOOL OF FOLKLORE SCHOLARSHIP, the hypothesis that similar **motifs** and tale-types around the world had a common origin and then spread (diffused) across cultural boundaries. This theory contrasts with that of **polygenesis**, in which different cultures are said to have originated similar structures independently. For example, one of the classic tenets of the school is that European **fairy tales** originated in Asia and spread west through trade, migration and the influence of travellers. The strongest evidence for such a theory is the duplication of extraneous detail in a tale. The motif of the persecuted heroine in the **Cinderella** tale may or may not have originated in a variety of cultures, but the widespread retention of details such as the magic tree that grows up over the grave of the mother of the **helpful beast** indicates that the story has been diffused from a common source. It seems probable that neither polygenesis nor diffusion theory alone can account for the development of folktales, but that each has played a part. The debate continues to rage amongst scholars as to the extent of these respective roles.

directional spirits

SPIRITS OR DEITIES IDENTIFIED WITH DIRECTIONS: up, down, north, south, east, west and sometimes more, depending on the group's orientation system. The Pueblos lay particular emphasis on such systems, ascribing to each direction a **colour** and a cohort of spirits.

disease

THE FOLKLORE OF SICKNESS. The wisdom of the folk has grappled for centuries with the problems of the causes of illness and the nature of disease. For societies with a strong belief in the supernatural, illness is most usually seen as a sign of demonic activity. Specific diseases might be caused by a specific type of spirit, for example spirits of the dead are blamed for nervous illnesses and rheumatism is thought by some Native Americans to be caused by the buffalo spirit. **Epilepsy** in particular was explained by demon possession, and in many cultures was thought to indicate great oracular powers, and was thus regarded with reverence. Other cultures took measures to exorcise the demons, with sacrifice or special prayers. For many Native Americans and others all illness originated with the spirits of the dead, and the only way to remain healthy was to correctly perform certain rites in their honour and to observe a myriad of taboos. To heal someone who is sick the demon must be induced to leave his body. This may be achieved by the power of the shaman or tribal healer, or it may be done by cunning; in Borneo for example the people use effigies of wood or dough in an attempt to fool the demons into abandoning their human victim for them.

In Hebraic and Christian folklore sickness is often considered a punishment from God, and repentance the only cure, as witness the advice of Job's neighbours. It was more usually regarded as a sign of satanic or demonic activity however, and a priest would often be called in as a healer where the doctor had failed.

▷ **medicine**; **separable soul**; **transferance healing**

divination

THE MAGICAL ART OF VIEWING THE UNKNOWN. Since the desire to know what life holds in store and the limitations of human knowledge are frustrations common to every civilization, it is natural that many should attempt to invoke supernatural means to see into the future. The astonishing variety of systems and codes developed to this end is nevertheless remarkable; virtually every object, sacred or everyday, and every type of natural phenomenon or event, has been utilized at some point by some group as an oracle. Divination depends upon a sympathetic correspondence between the object or event being observed and some future event which is said to be revealed, or with some other unknown such as the location of an object or the state of mind of a lover. The necessary interpretation is generally thought to require special powers or skill, and a specific group is usually credited with divinatory abilities—shamans, augurs, astrologers or fortune-tellers. A distinction can be drawn between the organized and systematic forms of divination, which are usually designed to give very specific answers and are often taught to initiates, and the popular lore of the folk, which may borrow heavily from such systems but is in general more fluid, less specific and transferred as oral superstition rather than as occult science.

In its original sense, 'divination' means the discovery of divine will, and in many societies it is a practice closely connected to religion. Roman augurs consulted the entrails of sacrifices offered to the gods and the citizens consulted oracles dedicated to gods like the famous shrine of Apollo at Delphi. In shamanism the god is said to speak through the human medium in a similar way to the seances or channelling more familiar in the West. These systems all presuppose the existence of supernatural agencies, usually divinities or spirits of the dead, with power to influence events in the everyday world and this is the central tenet of all divination; a message from an **otherworld** is communicated by a sign which must be interpreted.

When confronted by an unresolvable dilemma, whether a villager was a witch or merely a harmless old woman, for example, many peoples have resorted to divination as a means of discovering the truth. Trials by **ordeal** or the casting of lots are common means of discovering the will of the gods in such situations, as were practices such as placing a key in a Bible which would then fall out when the name of the guilty party was mentioned. In primitive societies where legal procedures are undeveloped and the existence of the community depends on events out of its control, such as weather and the health of the leader, collective divination has traditionally been extensively used. In the West at least such communal use of divination has generally been replaced by materialism or by individual divinatory practices such as **astrology** or **numerology**.

Various ancient religions and some modern parasciences such as graphology have complex, highly developed systems of divination which, although they may have developed from popular traditions, are no longer strictly in the domain of folklore. Of the folkloric methods of divination, that is, those handed down orally, many are concerned with love and marriage. Plucking the petals from a

daisy to the chant of 'he loves me, he loves me not' is one of the most common, but more complex practices were common especially in Europe; an invocation to the new moon would ensure that one dreamed of one's future partner, and when peeling an **apple**, a girl would throw the unbroken peel over her left shoulder with the right hand, and look at the shape to discover the initial of her future husband's name. To discover their compatibility, a couple would each place a nut into the fire's embers. If the nuts burst or crackled instead of merely smouldering, the couple would face a quarrelsome future together.

Almost every conceivable object has been used as a means of divination by some culture. Dice and playing cards are obvious examples of commonly used objects since they allow for systematization and refinement, but there are less sophisticated means of prediction. A female guest is foretold by a dropped fork, a male guest by a dropped **knife**, whereas two forks crossed accidentally portends slanderous rumours, and two knives bad luck. A **mirror** breaking is said to be followed by seven years' bad luck, and a picture which falls off the wall foretells the death of a relative, especially if the glass is broken. The direction in which a fowl points after its death is thought by some Mexican tribes to signify whether or not a person will recover from his illness. Even the humble axe has been used as a tool for divination, revealing the future by the way in which it falls when balanced on its head (**axiomancy**).

divji moz

WILD MEN OF SLOVENIA, a race of powerful forest-dwellers. They are usually helpful to humans, and will often pass on their enormous knowledge of forest arts, but they can be mischievous; they will sometimes try to confuse or even attack lone travellers.

divorce

RITUAL OF SEPARATION, the annulment of **marriage**. Divorce does exist in some form in many societies, but it is almost always regarded as a private legal arrangement and is not invested with the wealth of folk custom and community participation as marriage. It is not considered a *rite de passage* since it does not celebrate the acceptance of the individual into the wider society.

Dobrýnja Kikitich

RUSSIAN HERO, a **dragonslayer** who features in several **byliny**. In one bylina he leaves his wife the morning after their wedding to do battle with the **dragon**, charging her to wait seven years for him. He is delayed, however, and she is reluctantly forced to marry his blood brother, Aljoša Popovič. Dobrýnja returns disguised to the wedding feast where he reveals himself by a token of his ring and claims his wife. This is very similar to the classical Odysseus tale (see *Odyssey*), in which Penelope stalls suitors and Odysseus finally comes back to claim her and defeat his rivals.

Dobrýnja was said to have been transformed into a bull by Marina, a witch whose **dove** he had mistakenly killed, and to have finally met his end at the hands of a giantess. In reality he was a soldier with a reputation for outstanding courtesy, who fought against the Tatars and was killed at the battle of Kalka in 1224.

Doctor Knowall

FOLKTALE TYPE, the peasant who succeeds despite his stupidity. This widespread form illustrates the central principles of comic folktales; misunderstanding, disguise and the triumph of the peasant. The title comes from the most famous version of the tale, told by Grimm—**Doktor Allwissend**—but various forms of the tale are to be found across Europe, Asia, Africa and America.

In Grimm's version, a peasant named Crab (Krebs) decides to pose as a learned doctor. He is approached for help by a nobleman who has been robbed, and he and his wife go along to the nobleman's castle for a sumptuous meal. Here the comedy of misunderstanding begins: as the servants bring in the courses Crab nudges his wife and whispers knowingly 'There's the first', 'There's the second' and so on, meaning the dishes. The servants however, who

Doctor Knowall

are in fact guilty of stealing their master's money, assume that he is referring to them and become more and more terrified. Finally a covered dish is set before him and he is asked to demonstrate his wisdom by telling what it contains. Certain that he will now be discovered for a fraud, the peasant cries out 'Alas, poor Crab!' and thus saves himself. The dish does indeed contain crabs, and the servants rush to confess to this all-knowing savant. Crab tells the lord where his treasure can be found without revealing the culprits, and thus gains favour and reward from both parties.

Although it is difficult to pinpoint the origins of such a widely-diffused tale, it seems likely that it may have developed in central Asia and spread out to the Far East, Africa and Europe, from whence it was carried to the New World. Many versions include an episode in which the hero steals and conceals an object, often a horse or other animal, and then demonstrates his remarkable knowledge by 'finding' it. Sometimes a whole sequence of animals is used in this way to increase the fake doctor's reputation. The constant motif in all variations is that of fortuitous misunderstanding, involving a play on two meanings of the same word. The crucial word may be the hero's name, as in the Grimm tale, or another; in one version the doctor expresses his despair and helplessness when confronted by the covered dish with an expletive meaning excrement, and this is of course precisely what is hidden beneath the lid.

The hero is a blunderer who succeeds through luck rather than skill, unlike many fairy-tale heroes who overcome obstacles by cleverness or virtue.

dodder

PARASITIC CLIMBING PLANT, also called strangleweed, of the genus *Cuscuta* (family Convolvulaceae). It roots in the ground and sends out exploratory shoots, but as soon as it has made contact with a host plant it twines round and penetrates its stem, drawing nutrients and water from it, and its own root rots away. It can cause enormous harm to the host plant, but was frequently used in folk medicine on the principle that it absorbs the vital essence and healthful power of the host. It is sometimes used in love divination; if a piece of dodder thrown backwards over the shoulder towards a loved one thrives, so will the affair.

dog

ANIMAL OF FOLKLORE, one of the earliest of domesticated animals and therefore prominent in the tales and lore of many cultures. Its roles range from sacred animal to comic character of folktales. Dogs often function as the familiars of shamans, sometimes as invisible spirits, who attend them at seances and assist them with **divination** or healing. In some Native American lore the dog was originally supposed to have been a human, who was transformed into an animal because of his misdeeds (usually of a sexual nature) and still retains some human understanding and sympathies. Along with **pigs** and **cattle**, the dog was one of the earliest creatures to be kept domestically by primitive societies across the globe; unlike these animals, however, the dog tended to function as a companion rather than as livestock, helping with the hunt and protecting the house. This perceived affiliation with humans is still remarked upon in the West today, where a dog is 'man's best

friend', and although the dog has in many cases become a pet, it retains its function as a co-worker in many others, for example as sheep-dog, hunter or guard.

In many folktales the dog is the helpful creature who enables his master to win the prize. In a tale from West Africa, the dog tells his master the names of two beautiful sisters and the master is thus able to claim them as his wives.

Alongside the tradition of the dog as faithful companion is another portraying it as a despised or dangerous creature. This is a view particularly prevalent in the Middle East, and much European lore combines the two uncomfortably. Much European proverbial lore is drawn from Eastern sources, especially from the Hebrew Scriptures, and portrays the dog as an outcast, a dangerous scavenger. The worst insult to be given to a fellow-human was to call him a dog, and a familiar Biblical curse, which fell upon Jezebel for one, was for one's remains to be eaten by dogs instead of being ceremonially buried. In coarse Western slang today dog is still used as a term of abuse, although interestingly mainly for women.

The famous injunction to 'let sleeping dogs lie', and the warning to 'beware of a silent dog and still water' teach the need for caution by using the dog as an image of danger, and a warrior or hero is often confronted by a fierce dog which he must defeat. Cerberus, the hound guarding hell who was overcome by **Heracles**, is an example from classical mythology, and in some versions of the Old Irish legend **Cuchulainn** gets his name by killing the fierce guard-dog of the smith, Culann. One of **Aesop**'s most famous fables tells of the dog who churlishly prevented the horse and ox from enjoying their hay by growling and snapping; 'dog in the manger' is still a byword today for a selfish person who begrudges others even what he himself has no need for.

In a popular **urban legend**, an elderly lady and her cossetted poodle are caught in the rain. Anxious to prevent her pet catching a chill, the lady places him into her new microwave oven to dry off quickly and goes to dry her own hair. The dog, of course, cooks through or in some versions explodes. Another such legend, drawing on the tradition of the dog as faithful companion, tells of a guard-dog (usually a rottweiler) who appears to be choking when his female owner enters the house. The woman takes him straight to the vet's and leaves him there to be examined, but the moment she reenters her house, the telephone rings. It is the vet telling her to leave the house immediately; the obstruction in the dog's throat was two (or three) human fingers, and he suspects that the intruder may still be in the house. Sure enough, the police later find the terrified would-be assailant, hidden in a wardrobe, usually unconscious, and bleeding to death.

The **Black Dog** is a commonly reported ghostly apparition, whose appearance generally portends death.
▷ **Gelert**

Dog Husband

WIDESPREAD FOLKTALE, a **beast marriage** form common world-wide but especially in North America. A woman of the tribe takes a mysterious lover who is **dog** by day and human by night; in one popular version of the tale she subsequently gives birth to puppies and is abandoned by the tribe, but her sons grow up to become great hunters after she destroys their dog-skins and thus makes them fully human, and they are eventually welcomed back as saviours and heroes by the famished tribe.
▷ **Bear's Son cycle**

dogwood

SMALL TREE, genus *Cornus*, of the family Cornaceae, native to Europe, North America and East Asia. Red dogwood (*Cornus sanguinea*) is said to have gained its name from the widespread practice of washing dogs in liquid from its berries or bark to cure mange. Flowering dogwood, found particularly in North America, was widely used by Native Americans to treat fever and by colonists suffering from malaria; it contains the active principle of quinine. It is considered unlucky in Tennessee to chew dogwood, for fear of losing one's lover, but elsewhere in the South a liquid distilled from dogwood bark is added to whisky as a tonic.

One North American tale tells how a chief with four beautiful daughters demanded gifts from the many suitors importuning him, and for his greed was turned into the gnarled dogwood, along with all his gifts which became flowers. The plant's four white bracts are his daughters.

doll

SMALL HUMAN FIGURE, an ancient plaything once invested with great significance. For over 4000 years at least, among Babylonians, Egyptians, Aztecs, Greeks and Romans, the doll has been a child companion, made from a vast variety of materials—dough, wood, leather, wax, clay or shells. Dolls were often placed in graves, presumably to guard the occupants and provide companionship, and a doll might also be placed in the cradle to draw into itself the sickness of a child, or in European lore to guard against the introduction of a fairy **changeling**. Chinese women who desired children would carry a doll on their backs as a fertility charm, a form of **sympathetic magic**. This may be the origin of the traditional bride and groom dolls atop the wedding cake. In ancient Greece girls who had reached marriageable age were expected to offer their dolls at the shrine of Aphrodite, goddess of erotic love. Many Indian brides were presented with elaborate dolls at their wedding, and some South African groups give post-pubescent girls a doll to keep for her first child, and another after the first has been born, for the second.

During harvest in Britain and other parts of Europe it was traditional to make a **harvest doll** from the last sheaf, an embodiment of the spirit of the harvest, which would often be elaborately decorated or dressed. Here the doll functions as a vegetative spirit of fertility.

dolphin

AQUATIC MAMMAL OF THE WHALE FAMILY, renowned for its intelligence, playfulness and friendliness. Pliny claimed that it was the swiftest of all sea creatures. In classical lore the dolphin was credited with bringing shipwrecked humans to shore, notably the poet Arian

dolphin, wall painting in the palace of Knossos

and Telemachus, son of Odysseus. This role of carrying humans was extended and the dolphin was represented in Roman and Christian art bearing the souls of the dead across the waters to the Blessed Isles. In early Christian iconography the dolphin, as the King of Fishes, was a symbol of Christ. Among Native Americans dolphins were commonly considered messengers of the gods. It is considered very unlucky to kill a dolphin.

domovik

RUSSIAN HOUSEHOLD SPIRIT, also known as domovoi. He is an ancestral guardian who lives behind the stove (or occasionally under the doorstep) and keeps a sharp eye on the day-to-day running of the domicile; he is never referred to directly, but obliquely and respectfully as 'grandfather' or 'himself' (see **euphemism**). His wife, domovikha, inhabits the cellar. Should the family disgrace or displease him, he will burn down the house. If the family moves house, brands from the old stove should be carried to light the new and an invocation spoken over it, to ensure a welcome for the domovik. The spirit becomes busy at night, when his guarding duties really begin, and some supper is always left on the table for him. A human may feel the domovik brush against him; if the spirit feels hairy, it is a sign of good fortune, if smooth, it bodes ill. There are many specific breeds of domovik in every house, with responsibility for different areas of the domestic sphere.

▷ **bannik**; **chlevnik**; **ovinnik**

door

SYMBOL OF TRANSITION AND DEFENCE, not only functional furniture but deeply significant in folklore. Since the door defines the limit of a building, the point at which one either enters its influence or passes into the world beyond, it has become a potent symbol in many cultures and has attracted to itself a great deal of folkloric tradition. In mythology, doors and gates are features of many otherworlds—Heaven, Hell, Valhalla and Tartarus are all examples—and with these doors come door-keepers, admitting or refusing entry. Here the door is a sign of limited access, or, in the case of Hell, of no retreat once admitted, and the culture's religion will often be directed towards the qualifications for entering the desired door. The idea of a door as a gateway into the spiritual world is common too, and in northern Britain all the doors in the house were opened when an inhabitant lay dying, to aid the soul's journey. This may also be a sign of **sympathetic magic**; a similar practice is observed among women in Indonesia when a difficult labour is being undergone, to encourage the emergence of the child. In Negro belief a steady gaze at a door will often reveal a ghost.

Since it is the means of entry to a house, many societies protect their homes by placing charms or signs upon their doors. These are generally thought to guard the inhabitants and the property from the unwanted attentions of **witches** or evil spirits, and to bring good luck. The range of such signs is vast; in the Passover story of Exodus the Israelites protected their homes from the Angel of Death by sprinkling the blood of the sacrificial lamb on their lintels, and Jews still attach the mezuzah to their door-frames, a box containing seminal verses of Scripture. One of the commonest symbols is that of the red hand, believed to repel the **evil eye**, which is particularly common in North Africa and the Near East. A **horseshoe** hung over a door in Europe or America is considered a bringer of luck; it is always hung with the opening at the top, so that none of the luck it catches will be spilt.

Another kind of mark on the door is that spotted by **Ali Baba**'s servant, **Morgiana**; a code for the robbers to identify the householder they wished to kill. This is an interesting reversal of the usual protective functions of door signs.

The first person to cross the threshold at **New Year** is vitally important; he should be male, dark and preferably a stranger, carrying coal, money and food as tokens of a prosperous year. The groom traditionally carries his new bride into their house, and it is considered extremely bad luck to stumble over it when leaving the house at the start of a journey. These superstitions are the remnants of a time when ritual focused on the threshold; it was a favourite place for sacrifice, and in some cultures it was believed to be the home of ancestral spirits. In Asia many social customs such as the removal of shoes as a mark of respect before entering a house acknowledge the significance of the threshold.

In ancient Rome, the god Janus, from whose name January is derived, was the guardian of the door, and his image was often placed at the doorway. He is shown with two heads, guarding both entrance and exit simultaneously.

doppelgänger

LITERALLY 'DOUBLE-GOER', the shadow-self of a living person in German folklore. This is an extension of the **separable soul** belief, in which the other self, which usually functions identically with one's true self, can assume volition and a form of its own. To see one's doppelgänger is an omen of imminent death or disaster. Occasionally this double may appear to friends or family, either through mischief, to cause confusion, or as a warning or appeal for help.

▷ **fetch**; **shadow soul**; **wraith**

dove

BIRD OF THE PIGEON FAMILY, Columbidae. In many mythologies it is closely linked to divinity; the doves that drew Aphrodite's chariot were said to be transformed nymphs, and in Christian and Muslim traditions the dove is used to represent the Holy Spirit. A Muslim legend tells how a dove fed from Mohammad's ear, convincing his followers that he was receiving direct guidance from the Holy Spirit. The Holy Spirit is said to have descended on Jesus in the gospel account of his baptism, and the dove descending on **Mary**, with all its connotations of divinity, gentleness and femininity, is a key image in Christian iconography. The dove is said to be so holy that the **Devil**, the ultimate **shapeshifter**, cannot assume its form.

In contrast to this imagery, the dove also has a long tradition as a symbol of erotic love. From its early associations with Aphrodite and Ishtar, the Babylonian goddess of love and war, the dove has been linked with sexual attraction and black slaves in the American South used to swallow a raw dove's heart to ensure reciprocation of their love. This aspect of belief survives in the common phrase 'billing and cooing', describing the behaviour of lovers.

A dove's cooing can signal death in the house, and in Wales miners regard a dove flying over the mine as a portent of danger. However a wish made on hearing the first dove of the year will infallibly come true, and it is a good omen to dream of a dove. In much Native American lore, the dove is the embodiment of the souls of the dead.

dowry

A GIFT OF PROPERTY OR MONEY, presented in many areas of the world to a husband by the bride, or more usually her parents. This may originally have been a security for the bride, since the gift was

conditional upon the husband treating her well, in cultures where women had few civil rights, and might serve also to insure against her husband's death. It also emphasized the fundamentally economic nature of marriage, a transaction in which the woman passed from father to husband as an economic liability or property. In some societies the husband is expected to pay a bride-price to his wife's father, but this is less common. Through traditional use, the dowry came to signify the worth of the family and the bride, and great pains were taken that each daughter was married with a suitably impressive dowry. It may be made up of land, money, even livestock; it enables the young couple to establish an independent household in some societies, although in others the newly-weds live as part of either side's extended family.
▷ **marriage**

dowsing

DIVINATION APPLIED TO THE SEARCH FOR HIDDEN OBJECTS, most usually underground water. It is usually performed with a rod or pendulum which indicates by its movement the presence of the desired object; **hazel** is the preferred material for the rod although different practitioners claim virtue for different materials. This is one of the simplest forms of divination in that it gives a binary reading requiring little interpretation beyond positive or negative.

drac

FRENCH SPIRIT IN HUMAN FORM, mischievous beings who inhabit river caverns. They entice humans into the water by appearing as golden treasure just beneath the surface, then pull their victims down to their death.

Dracula

LITERARY ARCHETYPE OF THE VAMPIRE. The enduring popularity of the **vampire** legend is due largely to this gothic novel of Bram Stoker, simply entitled *Dracula* (1897), which led to a series of vampire films in the early 20th century. Count Dracula of Transylvania, based on the historical 15th-century tyrant of Wallachia, Vlad the Impaler, became the archetypal vampire villain, preying on innocent and beautiful young girls in their sleep. A vast body of popular lore grew up based partly on ancient folk belief and partly on a literary creation.

dragon

MYTHICAL BEAST, featuring in the folklore of many cultures of Europe and Asia. The Latin bestiaries of the early Middle Ages spoke of the dragon as the largest of all creatures, an enormous snake or lizard which ensnared even **elephants** in its coils and suffocated its prey to death. This observation comes from the classical authority Pliny, who was probably referring to pythons. In Roman times Herodotus wrote of flying serpents, winged snakes who flew from Arabia towards Egypt and were killed by the revered ibises. Still the exact physical attributes of the dragon vary with time and place. The term is broad enough to encompass various forms; dragons with or without wings, with any number of heads, or with bodies made up from almost any combination of animals (for example the elephant-dragon of India). It was only in medieval Europe that the dragon acquired his now famous characteristics; the head of a lion breathing forth fire, the enormous body coiled round a pile of treasure, the whole beast identified with Satan himself.

Although even in classical times the dragon was associated with evil, it has also traditionally been regarded as a symbol of war, presumably as a means of terrifying the enemy. Viking ships had prows carved into the shape of dragon-heads; **Uther Pendragon**, father of **Arthur**, was said to have favoured the dragon as an ensign in battle and it still remains central to the Welsh arms.

The earliest dragons were closely associated with water, presumably because of their reptilian origins, for example the dragon slain by **Perseus**. In early legends of the **saints**, especially Celtic saints of Ireland, such water-serpents figure prominently. It was said that when St **Patrick** drove the snakes out of Ireland he did not banish the dragons (known as 'peists') completely, but instead ordered them to remain imprisoned in the waters they inhabited. Later saints distinguished themselves by

dragon

subduing those monsters who defied Patrick's prohibition.

In later medieval tales, dragons gradually lost their close association with water and became largely land-dwelling; they usually retained the ability to fly, however. Their greed became their chief characteristic; dragons were generally supposed to hoard great wealth, and often to demand human victims to satisfy their enormous appetites.

In the East the dragon, although still regarded as a dangerous being who must be propitiated, has retained close connections with divinity and ancestor worship. It remains a potent symbol of positive force, epitome of the 'yang' principle, and was used as a royal ensign until the formation of the Republic in 1911. The Chinese dragon typically has no wings, but is nevertheless regarded as an air being, one of the divine natural forms of Taoism. In the great processions of the Chinese **New Year** the dragon is a key figure, with **mummers** costumed as an enormous dragon parading the streets, and intricate dragon kites too are very popular, recalling the belief in the dragon as an air being.

Draco, a northern constellation known as the Dragon, is portrayed in ancient **astrology** as a serpent whose tail coils between the two Bear constellations.

dragonslayers and dragon-slaying

HEROES OF MYTH, LEGEND AND FOLKLORE.

The combination of hoarded wealth and human victim associated with the **dragon** lent especial dramatic charm to the many stories about such figures. **Perseus** and St **George** both acted to save a beautiful maiden from being sacrificed to the dragon, and they received the grateful maiden as their reward. **Beowulf** fought **Grendel**, the monster who was devouring the warriors of Hrothgar, and his final battle is with a dragon who is enraged because a cup has been stolen from his treasure pile (before he dies Beowulf sees the wealth distributed among his people).

The cruelty of the dragon legitimated the hero's attack, and the **saints** who defeated dragons were symbolically overcoming Satan himself. In later folktales however the hero's adventure was enlivened by the great prize that was to be won. The slaying of a dragon is a legend that tended to attach itself to any hero figure of local lore. Other dragonslayers include **Heracles**, the prophet Daniel (in the apocryphal *Bel and the Dragon*), King **Arthur**, and St Michael.

dreams

THE ADVENTURES OF THE FREED SOUL. Because dreams are so mysterious, in their very nature and often also in their content, virtually every society has developed beliefs to explain dreaming and its significance. One of the most common explanations for dreaming is that the soul leaves the body and wanders, meeting with other souls, of the dead and of other sleeping humans. Dreams therefore may often contain messages from the powerful spirits of the dead, especially omens of the future, and should be interpreted skilfully by the spiritual leader of the group, the shaman or seer. It is interesting that after the days of Freud and the discovery of the subconscious, this role has been taken over by psychoanalysts. In West African folklore, the dream soul is one of a hierarchy of souls in man (and to a lesser extent in woman), which sleeps during the day and leaves the body to mix with other dream souls at night.

One of the chief roles attributed to dreams is that of prophecy; the dreamer is said to receive messages either from powerful spirits (usually the dead) or from gods. The Egyptians catalogued dreams and their interpretations (an early form of the dream books still popular today) and the Bible, in both Old and New Testaments, records several examples of divine revelation in dreams. One of the most famous is Pharaoh's vision of the seven fat and seven lean cows, interpreted by Joseph to mean seven years of plenty followed by seven of famine. For many people the phenomenon of *déjà vu*, when a new experience is accompanied by a strong but inexplicable feeling of familiarity, is explained as the memory of a prophetic dream.

Freud suggested (in *The Interpretation of Dreams*, 1900) that the origin of many myths and folktales might be common dreams expressing deep-seated fears and wishes. Hence the classical myth of **Oedipus** arose from wish-fulfilment dreams of the male and provided a means of externalizing the impulse and setting the story within an acceptable moral context, in which the transgressor is punished. In a Freudian theory, myth and dream are closely related as outlets for the most fundamental subconscious urges of all humans.

Dreamtime

THE MYTHICAL CREATION TIME OF THE AUSTRALIAN ABORIGINES, also known as 'The Dreaming'. During this never-ending time period the totemic Ancestors emerged from the ground and travelled the continent, bringing it into being by shaping and naming as they travelled. The soul comes from the Dreaming at the moment of conception, and on the death of the individual it passes back into the Dreaming, so all human life is caught up in this mythic framework, and linked to the creative force of the Dreaming.
▷ **Australian Aborigine folklore**

droit de seigneur

FEUDAL PRACTICE OF MEDIEVAL EUROPE, also known as *jus prima noctis*, the right of the feudal lord to take the **virginity** of every woman within his territory on her wedding night. If the practice did indeed exist, it may reflect the widespread belief that defloration, the breaking of the hymen, was not only a significant life event for the woman but, being bound up in the dangerous and mysterious powers of blood and female sexuality, was an operation that should ideally be performed by one with special power or immunity; a priest, healer, noble or stranger. However the evidence for the practice in Europe consists mainly of records of moneys paid to have this right waived. It seems likely that, although the *droit de seigneur* might have been extracted for a time in some parts, in the main it was an extra source of revenue for the lord, a form of taxation. The Old Irish *Book of Leinster* however says that **Conchobar** was pressed by fathers to take the virginity of their daughters, that some of his nobility might be transferred to their offspring, and this gave rise to the legend that Conchobar enjoyed the virginity of every maid in Ulster.

drowned civilizations

MANY EXAMPLES EXIST in folklore of drowned cities and villages, for example that of Ker-ys in Brittany, a city drowned by the treachery of the king's daughter who subsequently died in the flood. The most famous example is of course **Atlantis**, the lost continent. In most cases the flood is brought about as punishment for the crimes of the citizens collectively or an individual.

drum

MUSICAL INSTRUMENT, probably the most basic, widespread and ritually significant of all instruments. There are endless variations and refinements, but the basic drum consists of a hollow vessel over which is stretched a taut membrane, which is beaten to produce a resonant sound. The main exceptions to this basic construction are the primitive slit drum, in which a length of wood is hollowed out by means of a long slit then struck to produce the sound, and the friction drum, in which the membrane is rubbed (often by a stick piercing it) rather than beaten to produce a rasping noise amplified in the drum's body.

Drums, also known as membranophones, may be tubular, vessel or frame. The most diverse form is tubular, encompassing waisted, cylindrical, barrel, conical, footed and long variations. Vessel drums, such as the kettle drum, have only one potential playing head and typically a rounded body. In frame drums such as the tambourine, the body does not provide resonance. Membranes may be made from fish or reptile skins (as in the earliest Neolithic examples), animal skins (the most common material) or even parchment. The membrane may be glued over the drum, pegged or nailed, or laced. Lacing offers the advantage of allowing tuning, by adjusting the tension of the strings. Whatever method is used, construction is often regarded as a sacred task in many societies and only shamans or highly skilled individuals are permitted to make ritual drums.

The rounded, hollow form of the drum and the shape of the stick often used to beat it led in many societies to an identification of drum-playing with the act of intercourse, and hence the drum itself was associated with ancient female principles such as water, moon and fertility. Women were frequently forbidden to use beaters (although they often played drums with their hands, hence the traditional association of the frame drum with women in the Near East), and the all-important ceremonies for fertility were often accompanied by the vigorous playing of drums, particularly friction drums, mimetic of the act of fertilization.

Drums have also been used from ancient times as a means of communication, particularly over distance, by agreed signals or by mimicking the actual patterns, intervals and inflections of human speech. As the voices of the gods or spirits they are widely used in **initiation** ceremonies, and to drive out sickness. They accompany most social occasions, as a protective measure during funerals and weddings (since they keep away evil spirits), and on a functional level to set the pace for communal dancing or folk songs. Many dances depend on the rhythms dictated by accompanying drums, such as the fevered Egyptian dervishes or the Italian **tarantella**. In Asia the tuned drum allowed a melodic as well as purely rhythmic function, not adopted by the West until relatively recently. **Work songs** are often accompanied by a simple drumbeat, to emphasize and coordinate the work stroke for maximum efficiency. A development of this, closely linked to the traditional virile associations of the beaten drum, is its military use, as an aid to marching but also to inspire battle-lust and bravery.

Dubricius, St (Dyfrig, Devereux) (d.c.612)

'CHIEF OF THE CHURCH IN BRITAIN', one of the most important of the early saints of South Wales, around whose name innumerable and improbable legends grew up. It seems clear that he was particularly influential in south-east Wales and Herefordshire, where he worked mainly from his many monastic foundations. The town of Saint Devereux in Herefordshire takes its name from a corruption of St Dyfrig. As an old man Dubricius retired to Bardsey Island, where he died peacefully.

Many unreliable details have become attached to his legend: he was believed to be the first bishop of Llandaff and archbishop of Caerlon-on-Usk, who handed over his metropolitan status to David at the Synod of Brevi, clearly an anachronism, although it is likely that he and St Deniol were the ones who persuaded David to attend the Council. The translation of his relics to Llandaff in 1120 did much to popularize his cult. Geoffrey of Monmouth, who is not renowned for his accuracy, reports that it was Dubricius who crowned **Arthur** King of Britain and Tennyson takes up the legend in his *Idylls of the King*; Dyfrig is the High King in *The Coming of Arthur*. In art he is represented holding two croziers and the archbishop's cross. His feast-day is 14 November.

dugong

LARGE MARINE MAMMAL, the only surviving member of the Dugongidae family, also known as a sea cow. Its habit of feeding its calves on two pectoral teats, observed by early sailors, is thought to have given rise to much **mermaid** lore. In the folklore of Malaysia it is said to be formed from the remains of a pig eaten by Muhammad, before he declared pork unclean. When the carcass was cast into the sea, it became the first dugong. Its tears are said to be a potent aphrodisiac.

dumi

TYPE OF UKRANIAN FOLKSONG, a **ballad**-form characterized by rhyming couplet lines of variable length and a prosaic style. The subjects of dumi are usually historical, dealing with relatively recent events, and there is little use of the supernatural or traditional folk motifs.

Dun Cow

MAGICAL BEAST OF ENGLISH FOLKLORE. It is said to have been an enormous and savage beast owned by a giant, who kept her on Mitchell Fold in Shropshire. She would daily give an inexhaustible supply of milk until one day an old woman, having filled her pail, attempted to fill her sieve too. The cow was so incensed at this greed that she broke loose and ranged across to Dunsmore Heath, where she was fought and slain by **Guy of Warwick**. The tale is preserved in *The Legend of Sir Guy* collected in Percy's *Reliques*.

Dunmow bacon

MEASURE OF CONJUGAL HAPPINESS, from a custom said to have been established by a noblewoman named Juga in 1111. She promised to award a flitch, or a side of cured pork, to anyone who would kneel on two stones before the church door at Dunmow, Essex, and solemnly swear that over the past year and a day he and his wife had never argued, and that he had never once wished himself

unmarried. The custom was revived by Robert de Fitzwaller in 1244, and then periodically until the late 19th century, but few couples were able in conscience to claim the prize. The phrase became proverbial; 'Few married folks peck Dunmow bacon'.

duppy

GHOST OF THE WEST INDIES. A duppy may be summoned to perform a service to the living, usually to attack an enemy. It can be kept at bay by a protective circle of **tobacco** seed.
▷ **Davy Jones**; **jumby**

Durden, Dame

FIGURE OF ENGLISH FOLKLORE, the mistress of five milking maids and five serving men who inevitably courted the maids. Her name became a generic term for a busy, cheerful housewife.

dvergar

DWARFS OF SCANDINAVIAN LORE, created by the gods from maggots in the flesh of Ymir the **giant**. Their home was underground, where they mined and fashioned beautiful jewellery, weaponry and magic objects. They avoided going above ground lest they be caught in sunlight, which would turn them to stone, but if caught by a mortal would pay vast sums of dwarfish money in ransom.

dwarf

GERMANIC FAIRY TYPE, hot-tempered and quick to take offence, but nevertheless generous and loyal to those they befriend. In Teutonic folklore, and especially in Scandinavia, they are a homely, diminutive species of fairy living inside mountains or down mines. In Scandinavian mythology, dwarfs (the **dvergar**) were created by the gods from the giant Ymir and although less powerful than their creators were wiser than humans. In their underground kingdom they build splendid palaces and enjoy great feasts and dances; they work long and hard in their mines too and are said to produce magnificent, magical weaponry and armour. There are several different types of dwarf, for example the Black Dwarfs, who like all dwarfs are highly skilled in metalwork but are bad-tempered and live morose and solitary, without the usual dwarfish music and revelry. These dwarfs are unfriendly to humans, and their wonderful weaponry can only be bought dear. Brown Dwarfs on the other hand are more gregarious and good-natured, though still much given to mischief in their doings with humans. They are said also to abduct children as human slaves to work their mines. Like most dwarfs they enjoy the power of **invisibility** when they choose by wearing their small, belled brown caps. A human can gain great wealth and power over a dwarf if he manages to capture this cap. The White Dwarfs are the most beneficent of all dwarf types; they too live in mountains and mines where they make their marvellous artefacts, but when spring arrives they venture above ground and spend their nights in festivity and dancing. Mortals may hear their music but will never see the revellers. White Dwarfs are also thought to reward humans for their good deeds.

Like their close relatives the **trolls**, all dwarfs avoid sunlight. Whereas trolls turn to stone at daybreak, most dwarfs are merely trapped above ground, and must wander miserably until night falls and they can escape back to their underground homes.

Dwarfs are always small, about the size of a human toddler when fully grown, and they are generally portrayed as wrinkled old men, stooped and bearded. Great longevity was often attributed to them, and with it a reputation for ancient knowledge and great wisdom. Advice from a dwarf is to be highly prized. In general they keep aloof from mortals, although the Swiss dwarfs are said to help farmers in their work and bring back strayed animals, and in Germany and Scandinavia they are occasionally spoken of as meddlesome mischief-makers. If a human were to render service to a dwarf, however, he would be richly rewarded from his secret underground trove. It is useless to try and gain such treasure illicitly, since any stolen gold will turn to dry leaves, or else some great misfortune will overcome the thief. Gifts given by dwarfs are superior to those of many fairies because they are real, and not the result of illusion (**glamour**). To the occasional, favoured mortal was extended an invitation to visit the home of the dwarfs underground and to participate in their revels; if the visitor behaved with proper decorum, he would undoubtedly return wealthy. Mountain dwarfs are said to be more kindly than their mine-dwelling brothers.

Many cultures world-wide have beliefs in supernatural beings which resemble dwarfs. They are commonplace among Native Americans, especially among the Inuits, as diminutive supernatural beings, mainly benevolent but also capable of mischief, often hunters who live on land or in water.

Dwarfs have an established place in folk literature, from ancient Norse myth in the Poetic Edda, the Prose Edda, the *Volsungasaga* and the *Nibelungenlied* to J R R Tolkein's great work of fantasy, *The Lord of the Rings*. They also appear in many literary fairy stories, such as Snow White and the Seven Dwarfs.

▷ **knockers**

dwarf

dybbuk

JEWISH GHOST, a restless spirit who cannot find peace because of some unforgiven sin and prowls in search of a human body to inhabit. A person displaying a nervous or mental disorder would often be taken to a rabbi to have the harmful dybbuk exorcised. The belief was especially prevalent in Eastern Europe during the 16th and 17th centuries.

Dyfrig see **Dubricius**

Dziwozony

WILD WOMEN OF POLISH FOLKLORE, a tall athletic race of forest-dwellers. The Dziwozony throw their breasts over their shoulders to enable them to run swiftly and comfortably. They often attack lone humans, but will occasionally force younger men to become their lovers. Like **fairies**, they are often credited with leaving **changelings** in place of human babies.
▷ **Amazons**

each uisge

CELTIC WATERHORSE, found in parts of Ireland and the Scottish Highlands. It is a close relative of the **kelpie**, although it prefers lochs and sea inlets rather than running water. Like the kelpie it is evilly disposed towards humans. It appears most commonly as a magnificent, sleek horse offering itself as a mount for a traveller, but anyone foolish enough to try to ride it is borne beneath the water and devoured.

eagle

BIRD OF PREY, traditionally associated with sky, power, war, sun and storms. In classical mythology the eagle was associated with Zeus/Jupiter, who abducted Ganymede in the form of an eagle. Since Zeus was the god of lightning, it was thought that the eagle could never be struck by lightning and hence the body of an eagle was frequently buried in fields to protect the crop from storm damage.

In many folklores the eagle has served as a symbol of longevity and even resurrection; a Hebrew belief that the bird could plunge into the sea and, **phoenix**-like, renew its youth and plumage every ten years is alluded to in Psalm 103:5—'my youth is ever new like an eagle's'.

Such properties made the eagle a natural choice as an emblem of kingship and power, and it appeared on many of the imperial arms of Eastern Europe, but when the bald eagle was chosen as the symbol of the new United States Benjamin Franklin pointed out that the scavenging bird in fact represented cowardice and immorality; he would have preferred to see an honest **turkey** chosen.

In Native American lore, Eagle is a prominent character in the tales of Californian, North Pacific and many other groups. Eagle feathers were highly prized, and widely used in ceremonial costumes, pipes and headdresses; such a headdress represents the Great Spirit or Thunderbird, and its eagle feathers carry the prayers of the group up to the sky. Many groups perform an annual eagle dance, in which dancers holding eagle-feather fans hop and crouch to mimic the movements of an eagle on the ground to obtain favourable winds and rain or to ensure success in war.

In much European folklore the eagle functions as a bird of warning, helping humans by knocking aside a cup of poison, luring them away from dangerous areas (such as a cliff edge about to crumble) by snatching a hat. In the *Kalevala* **Väinämöinen** is plucked from the sea to safety by an eagle, and this reflects an ancient Swedish tale in which a boy is carried off by an eagle and raised in an eyrie; he later woos and wins the princess with the foster-eagle's help.

eagle

ear

A BURNING SENSATION OF THE EAR is said in Northern Europe to indicate that one is being talked about; to have such a sensation in the right ear means that good things are being said, but slander is being spoken if the left ear burns. More generally in Europe, a tingling in the right ear is considered a good omen.

Ornaments for the ears, generally pendants inserted by piercing the lobe or plugs to distend the hole in the lobe, have been popular throughout the world since earliest time. They probably functioned first as **amulets** to guard the body's orifices but became vehicles to express concepts of physical beauty and, of course, wealth. In the Far East and among many Native American and African groups both sexes wear earrings, but in the classical world and the West they have been considered primarily a female ornament, despite periodic vogues for men's earrings, and everywhere they are generally worn as identical pairs.

Easter

CHRISTIAN FESTIVAL, celebrating the resurrection of Christ after the crucifixion. It was probably the earliest of the Church's annual festivals, coinciding with the Jewish **Passover** (Pesach), and in Europe it has fused with elements of pagan spring festivals, celebrating new life. The dating of Easter was a source of great controversy and division in the early Church, settled only in the eighth century; due to different methods of calculation, the Eastern and Western churches still usually celebrate the feast on different days, and until the Synod of Whitby in 664 Celtic and Roman methods of calculation coexisted in Britain.

Easter is central to the Christian calendar; it is preceded by the 490 days of Lenten abstinence climaxing with Holy Week and the solemnity of Good Friday, and its celebrations are followed by Eastertide, the fifty days until Pentecost (**Whitsunday**). Among the Orthodox churches a dramatic re-enactment illustrates the centrality of the festival to the religious community; there is a procession around the church symbolizing the search for Christ's body, the

crucifix from St Croce, France

call to the Eucharist, and then hundreds of **candles** are lit.

Many folk customs have become attached to the festival, many dating from pre-Christian times. **Eggs** are a feature of Easter in Europe and North America, symbols of new life that had traditionally been forbidden during Lent. The Easter **rabbit** recalls the more ancient **hare**, the Egyptian symbol of fertility, and some scholars have claimed that the word Ester derives from Ostora (German *Ostern*), a Germanic goddess traditionally accompanied by a rabbit. In some parts of Germany and Austria *Schmeckostern* are exchanged; the men beat their wives on Easter Monday and the women return the favour the next day. **Birch** branches in bud are most commonly used, to transfer their new life to the one being beaten. Several Slavic countries practise similar customs.

Although Easter is greeted throughout the Christian world with flowers, singing, torches and bells, these celebrations reach their peak in the **carnivals** of Spain and Mexico particularly.

echtrai

ADVENTURE TALES, old Irish tale-type

telling of a hero's journey to an **other-world**. In general the hero is entranced by descriptions of the world given by a beautiful woman or a splendid warrior, its endless pleasures, eternal youth and convivial company. His guide offers to take him or direct him, and the hero leaves his world for the magic land. He may never be heard of again, or he may return to the mortal world bearing great treasure, or he may crumble as he touches the ground of his old home and mortal years catch up with him. Although similar to **imrama**, voyage tales, the narrative interest is less on the journey itself. The oldest of such tales is that of Coule, a prince of Ireland who despite his father the king's attempts to save him was bewitched by a fairy woman who told him of the Land of the Living and sailed away with her in a coracle of glass, never to be seen again. **Cormac Mac Airt** obtained his marvellous cup of truth, which broke over three lies and was restored by three truths, from Manannan in the Land of the Living; the *Echtrae Cormaic* tells how an otherworldly warrior exchanged a magical golden bough with the king for three boons, which he claimed as Ailbe and Cairpre, Cormac's daughter and son, and Eithne, his wife. Cormac pursued them and after becoming lost in a magic mist found himself in the Land of the living, where he regained his family and received the wonderful cup, and brought them all safely back to Tara.

Eckhardt

FIGURE OF GERMAN FOLKLORE, who appears on Maundy Thursday to warn unwary humans of the dangers of being outside on that night, when ghostly horses and deformed riders are said to throng the streets. He was said to have been swept up from the mortal world by the train of Old Mother **Holle**. Meister Eckhardt was a Dominican Friar and mystic theologian of the late 13th century, but the name more probably derives from Eckherdt the Faithful, the companion of **Tannhäuser**.

eclipse

ASTROLOGICAL PHENOMENON, the alignment of the **sun**, **moon** and earth so that either sun or moon is partially or fully obscured from an observer on earth. Many folktales developed to explain these awesome, terrifying spectacles; in many cultures the sun or moon was said to be under attack from some monster (a **dragon** in China) devouring it, and groups in North America shoot burning arrows into the sky, to scare away the beast and to rekindle the sun's light. Almost without exception eclipses were regarded as evil omens, requiring urgent sacrifices, noisy ritual dances and incantations to restore the natural order and deflect ill fortune, and many groups world-wide avoid business such as sowing, travelling or decision-making while an eclipse is in progress.

Another common theme of eclipse lore is that the sun and moon are engaged in a quarrel or in some nefarious activity, usually incest.

Eddas

LITERARY COLLECTION OF ICELANDIC LORE, two books composed in the 13th century known as the *Prose* (or *Younger*) *Edda* and the *Poetic* (or *Elder*) *Edda*. The *Prose Edda* was written by Snorri Sturluson, an Icelandic chieftain, as a handbook for poets, giving instruction in the complexities of traditional Icelandic metre and in the ancient sagas, often unclear to a Christian generation. The first of its three sections, *Gylfaginning*, ('the beguiling of Gylfi') is of prime folkloric interest; it tells how Gylfi, king of the Swedes, visits **Asgard**, home of the gods, and is regaled with tales about the origins of the world, the doings of the gods, and the coming end, Ragnarok. The second part, *Skaldskaparmal*, lists the elaborate kennings (riddles and metaphors) of ancient Scandinavian poetry, and the third part, *Hattatal*, details 102 variations of metre in a poem by Snorri.

The *Poetic Edda*, although a slightly later work, comprising much ancient material by unknown writers from the 8th to the 12th centuries AD. Less elaborate than the poetic skalds of the *Prose Edda*, the tales are written as dramatic dialogues in a simple style that suggests a closer relationship to oral lore. The first half is mainly mythological, concerned with creation and cosmic powers, including the Sibyl's prophecy (*Völuspá*); *Hávamál*, the amoral precepts of Odin; and the *Thrymskvida* (Lay of Thrym), telling how Thor's hammer is stolen by the giant Thrym who demands Freya as ransom. Thor disguises himself as the goddess, and the humorous poem tells of Thrym's consternation as his 'bride' consumes improbable amounts of food at the wedding feast. The second half deals with Germanic heroes, chiefly **Sigurd** (Siegfried), although **Wayland the Smith** also appears. These lays constitute the oldest surviving forms of the legends that make up the *Nibelungenlied*, tales of violence and deceit concerning Sigurd's marriage to **Gudrun**, his subsequent death and the fate of the Nibelungs.

eel

LONG, SLENDER FISH, any of a large number of species from the order Anguilliformes, found in fresh and salt water worldwide. In some areas of the United States there are tales of fishermen landing huge catches of eels by baiting their hooks with human flesh, supposedly irresistible to eels. In one Japanese legend eels are disguised **dragons** who attack horses in the water and suck the blood from their legs. This recalls the ancient association of dragons and water serpents. Eels are taboo food in many areas of the world, believed to be the souls of the dead or simply poisonous.

Eels can however be used in medicine; eelskin wound round a joint is believed in many areas to cure an ache, and the skin of a live eel (or the skinned eel itself) placed in a drunkard's glass will cure his drunkenness forever. (This seems very plausible.) The fat of eels can be applied to make a player in a ball game as slippery and as hard to hold as an eel, and in some parts of Europe such an ointment is said to enable a mortal to see **fairy** beings.
▷ **Gotham, Wise Men of**

eeny meeny miny mo see counting-out rhymes

Egil

A PEASANT OF TEUTONIC MYTHOLOGY, who on occasion stabled Thor's goats and chariot. When his family were starving, Thor offered to let them eat his goats, on condition that they preserve the **bones** and skin. But the trickster Loki persuaded one of Egil's sons to break one of the leg bones to get at the marrow, and when Thor restored his goats to life one was lame. Egil was obliged to give his son and daughter as servants in atonement.

Egil

FIGURE OF ICELANDIC LORE, who with his brothers Slagfin and Volund stumbled upon three **Valkyries** bathing. The brothers stole their swan feathers, thus trapping the bathers as women, and married them, but after nine years the Valkyries discovered their stolen feathers and flew off as swans.
▷ **swan maiden**

eggs

SYMBOLS OF LIFE. Since out of it comes new birth, and because it is eaten to sustain life, the egg has featured prominently in the folklore of many cultures, in rituals, tales and customs. A surprising number of ancient cultures shared a belief in a mythological egg from which the human race, and sometimes its creator, emerged. This cosmic egg is found in the mythologies of ancient Greece, India and Egypt and is paralleled in the mythologies of many small-scale societies in America and Africa.

In Slavonic and Germanic fertility rites eggs were smeared onto the plough at Easter to ensure a good harvest at the end of the summer. In France a bride was traditionally expected to break an egg as she entered her new home, to ensure that she would not be barren. They were also considered effective in healing, and one widespread treatment among European and Native American groups was to rub the body of a patient with an unbroken raw egg. The egg would then be broken and examined; its appearance revealed the exact nature of the illness and the healer could then proceed with the appropriate cures. If the sufferer had a fever, the egg might be placed whole in a stream so that the heat it had drawn out of the patient's body might be cooled.

Because of the identification of the

egg with the mysterious forces of life and creation, it was widely used in dealings with gods or supernatural beings as a means of placating them or discovering their will. An egg was considered an appropriate sacrifice to the spirits of the dead, always desirous of life; it was a common custom in parts of Asia and Europe to bury an egg along with the corpse as a symbol of new life in the face of death. Care had to be taken however lest evil forces use the eggs for powerful magic; the Romans destroyed the shells of their eggs after eating the flesh, and a tradition survives in Europe and North America that **witches** will use egg-shells that are left whole as vessels to set out to sea in order to wreck ships.

Telling the future with the aid of an egg is known as oomancy: common especially in Europe, it usually involved dropping the raw white of the egg into water and basing the predictions on the shapes which resulted. In **dream** divination, eggs are generally associated with good luck, often a wedding (probably owing to the link with fecundity), but broken eggs often signify a quarrel. Many eggs portend coming riches, which may be connected to the proverb about not putting all one's eggs in one basket, meaning that one should invest one's resources carefully.

In Europe and North America eggs are now most frequently associated with **Easter**, because of the symbolism of new life in the Christian Resurrection and more anciently with the return of spring itself. The custom of decorating and painting eggs was common throughout Europe, and in Russia especially grew to be a highly sophisticated art-form. The rolling of eggs down hills, adopted also in the United States, is another common European custom associated with Easter. More recently, decorated eggs have given way to chocolate Easter eggs, brought to good children by the **Santa Claus**-like figure of the Easter Bunny.

eingsaung nat

BURMESE GUARDIAN OF THE HOUSE, a benevolent nat believed to reside in the southern or south-east part of the house.

El Dorado

'THE GILDED ONE', originally the king of the legendary city of Manoa (or Omagua) on the Amazon, who was said to be annually covered with oil and dusted with gold before plunging into the river to offer the gold to the gods. His subjects were said to throw gold and jewels into the water after him. The native groups of Central and South America told such tales to the new settlers, perhaps hoping that their own settlements would be left in peace while their greedy conquerors travelled on in search of this fabulous place. Many expeditions were dispatched to find the city, which itself became known as El Dorado, led by Philip von Hutten and Sir Walter Raleigh among others, all doomed to disappointment. The name has come to represent any unrealistic 'promised land' where riches can quickly be amassed.

Elaine

FIGURE OF LATE ARTHURIAN ROMANCE, the daughter of the **Fisher King**, who died for love of **Lancelot of the Lake**. She is variously known as the Maid of Astolat and the Lady of Shalott. Her love was unrequited, since Lancelot's passion was centred on **Guinevere**, although Lancelot lay with her once (believing her to be Guinevere in his bewitchment) and **Galahad** was born. She requested that after her death her body be placed on a barge and taken to **Camelot**. She held in one hand a **lily** and in the other a letter revealing her tragic tale. **Arthur** provided a queen's burial for her.

elder

SHRUB OR SMALL TREE, genus *Sambucus* of the family Caprifoliaceae, with white flowers and purple or red berries. In popular European belief elder was the wood of the cross and the tree from which **Judas Iscariot** hanged himself, hence its unpleasant smell. In many areas elder wood is avoided in the making of ships or cradles, since it is susceptible to evil influences. In Germany and England an elder branch is said to bring **witches** or the **Devil** into the house with it, but in Scotland it can be used as an **amulet** to keep evil spirits at bay.

Among Native Americans elder bark or elderflower tea is widely used, as an emetic, laxative, tonic or a cure for colic or headache. In Europe green elder twigs were rubbed on warts and then buried; the warts would disappear as the wood rotted. Elder has been used in innumerable ways around the world to treat almost every ill, including epilepsy, strangulation, depression, rheumatism, toothache, insect and snake bites, and dropsy.

elephant

LARGE MAMMAL, only surviving member of the order Proboscidea, found as the Indian elephant in south-east Asia and the African elephant, with larger ears, native to sub-Saharan Africa. In Hindu lore particularly, the elephant is a sacred beast; it is a manifestation of the benevolent god Ganesha. Especially sacred in India is the white elephant, whose presence calls up rain-clouds, and in a Buddhist folktale Queen Maya's dream of a white elephant revealed the coming birth of the Buddha. Unlike other elephants, white elephants were con-

Ganesha, the elephant-headed Hindu god

sidered too sacred to use as draft animals yet their owners were obliged to keep them well. A legendary king of Siam is said to have ruined those courtiers who incurred his displeasure by making them a gift of a white elephant, hence today the phrase refers to anything that costs more than its value.

In early classical lore, and persisting into medieval belief, the elephant was said to lack knees. It was said to sleep standing up, and if it fell over it was thought that it could never right itself. Aristotle rejected this myth; he considered it the most intelligent and gentle of all creatures.

In China the elephant symbolizes kingship, strength and prudence.

Elfhame see Alfheim

elves

GERMANIC FAIRY TYPE, the little people of Scotland, England and Scandinavia. Elf was a name used in ancient Germanic lore to mean any kind of supernatural spirit, and in Anglo-Saxon to refer to fairies in general, but as fairy lore developed, and more complex divisions were recognized, it came to be applied more specifically to small fairies in England, and in Scotland to those of human stature. In the other great home of the elves, Scandinavia, the folk recognized both light elves and dark elves; the Anglo-Saxon concept of the elf probably derived from Scandinavian mythology and later merged in varying degrees with the Celtic **sidhe** to produce the typically English fairy.

The ancient Scandinavian division between the light and dark elves roughly corresponds to the **seelie court** (kindly fairies) and the **unseelie court** (malignant spirits) of Scottish lore. Light elves were fair while the dark elves were pitch-black. These elves were similar to the fairies envisaged by Shakespeare in *A Midsummer Night's Dream*; small creatures dancing among the flowers, playing tricks on humans, with a clear hierarchy and court. Scandinavian elves were originally led by Freyr, god of vegetation, and they lived in the mythological realm of **Alfheim**; some scholars have suggested that they may have developed from primitive beliefs in the beneficent spirits of the dead. The elves, also known as the huldre folk, are generally portrayed as dainty, beautiful creatures, but in some traditions male elves are squat and ugly while the females are, from the front at least, lovely, and dance to seduce human men without ever turning their back. In Danish lore huldre folk can be recognized by this **defect**; from the back they are hollow like a blasted tree. In other areas of Scandinavia the tell-tale sign is their long tail like that of a cow.

The elf is generally portrayed as a volatile, laughing spirit of human shape, usually diminutive. Its pranks include bringing disease upon livestock and (less commonly) humans and substituting deformed **changelings** with unbaptized human children. Elves were also widely credited with inducing bad dreams by sitting on their victim's chest; the German word for **nightmare** is *Alpdrücken*, meaning 'elf-pressure'.

elfhame see **Alfheim**

elixir vitae

ALSO KNOWN AS THE ELIXIR OF LIFE, a magical potion or powder sought by the alchemists, with the virtue of restoring and prolonging life. The term is often applied to the **philosopher's stone** with which the potion was closely linked.
▷ **alchemy**

ellyllon

WELSH FAIRIES, a beneficent race of **elves**, smaller and airier than the **tylwyth teg**. An ellyl will often enter a needy household as a **brownie**, helping invisibly with tasks until offended by a thoughtless act or invasion of privacy.
▷ **Gwynn**

elm

FOREST TREE, genus *Ulmus* in the family Ulmaceae, of temperate northern areas. In Teutonic mythology the first woman, Embla, was created by the gods from an elm tree. In England the tree is closely associated with **elves**. The red or slippery elm, *Ulmus rubra*, contains within the inner bark a gluey substance used to treat sore throats or chewed to quench thirst by many Native Americans. It was also used to treat syphilis. The leaves of the elm are widely used as a poultice.

Elmo's fire, St see **Erasmus, St**

emerald

BRIGHT GREEN GEMSTONE, a variety of beryl. It was said in classical legend to be obtained from the nests of **griffins**. Its intense colour was said to improve failing eyesight, and emeralds were often worn as **amulets** to guard against evil spirits, epilepsy, leprosy and dysentery. An emerald in a ring would burn to warn of the approach of poison.

The catalogue of benefit ascribed to the emerald is impressive; it was said to confer eloquence and quicken the mind, calm storms at sea, protect against snake-bites, test the truth of a man, and impart riches, happiness and long life. Powdered and added to water an emerald made a valuable medicinal tonic, and it was said to be particularly useful for women, as a guard for chastity and as an aid in **childbirth**. As symbols of longevity and eternal life emeralds were often placed in graves.

empyromancy

METHOD OF DIVINATION, the observation of objects when placed upon a sacred fire and the art of drawing prophetic conclusions from their behaviour. Common objects used in this way include incense, eggs, nuts and flour.
▷ **divination**

Eochaid

KING OF THE FIRBOLGS, the race defeated by the **Tuatha de Danann** when they invaded Ireland.
▷ **Etain**

epilepsy

RECURRENT CEREBRAL SEIZURE, a disorder affecting an estimated 0.5% of the population, characterized by fits of muscular convulsions and lapses of consciousness which exhibit varying degrees of intensity. Its common folk name is falling sickness, since the victim of an attack often (though not invariably) falls down. In many ancient and primitive cultures a 'grand mal' epileptic seizure was thought to indicate possession by a god or oracular spirit, and epileptics were venerated. Shamans, priests and priest kings were often those whose epilepsy proved their affinity with the supernatural. In Hindu and Hebrew lore however, and elsewhere, seizures were said to betoken possession by evil spirits, not gods, and such cultures developed rituals of **exorcism** for epileptics.

Many folk cures have been proposed for epilepsy. In medieval Europe apothecaries swore by rhinoceros horn shavings mixed with a little blood, but a distillation of **coral** (or **pearl**) was also considered effective. **Mistletoe** was widely used in Celtic, German, Swedish and Dutch lore, since mistletoe grows high above the earth and is therefore able to keep one from falling down. In Ireland a necklace of nine **elder** twigs was considered an effective **amulet**.

Epiphany

CHRISTIAN FESTIVAL, from Greek *epiphaneia* (manifestation), celebrated on 6 January. It was first observed in the Eastern church to mark the birth of Christ, but when **Christmas** became fixed at 25 December by about 354 in Rome, the Eastern church celebrated the feast as Christ's baptism, at which his deity was revealed, while for the Western church it commemorated the visit of the Magi to the infant Christ, the revelation of the saviour to the Gentiles. Outside the Church calendar it is known more widely as Twelfth Night, in relation to Christmas. It is marked in Europe by festivities dating from pagan times; noisy pageants to expel evil spirits and the beginning of the **carnival** season to welcome the new year. The **Abbot's Bromley horn dance** was traditionally performed on this date. It is also the night on which all Christmas decorations should be taken down, if they are not to bring bad luck.

Erasmus, St (Elmo) (d.c.303)

THE SAILOR'S FRIEND. He was a bishop of Formiae in the Campagna in Italy and was probably martyred during the persecutions of Diocletian. By confusion with another martyr, one Erasmus of Antioch, his legend claims that he was a Syrian who fled to Mount Lebanon during the persecutions to live as a solitary. His hiding place was discovered and he was brought before the Emperor, beaten, covered in pitch and set ablaze.

Miraculously he survived unhurt, and was imprisoned only to be released by an angel and taken to preach in Illyricum. Here he carried on with his work of preaching and teaching. The number of his converts was so great that he was soon discovered anew and underwent more torture. Once again he was delivered by an angel, this time to Formiae, where he died of his wounds.

As Erasmus had proved immune to the various tortures to which he had been subjected in the past, a popular legend developed which claimed that a new and particularly grisly death had been devised for him. The saint was cut open at the stomach and his entrails were wound out while he was still alive. This torture legend is the source of his patronage of those suffering from stomach pains. His relics were supposedly translated to Gaetea when Formiae was attacked by Saracens in 842, and he is invoked as patron there.

His emblem in art is a windlass; this has been variously explained as a symbol of his patronage of sailors, which grew from a legend that he was unafraid of a violent storm, refusing to stop preaching even when a thunderbolt landed beside him, or as the instrument of torture with which his entrails were wound out which was then mistaken for a nautical capstan, whence his patronage of sailors began. The phenomenon of lights which sometimes appear at the mastheads of ships after a storm, caused by electrical discharge, was known as St Elmo's fire by Neapolitan sailors, since it was believed to be a sign of the saint's protection through the time of danger. In some parts of Europe the light is thought to be a human soul; German sailors interpreted it as a dead fellow-sailor indicating the coming weather—good if the light rises, bad if it falls.

Erasmus's cult was widespread throughout Europe, with hagiographers embellishing the legend throughout the Middle Ages, and he was named as one of the Fourteen Holy Helpers in the 15th century. His feast-day is 2 June, and he is patron saint of sailors, invoked against birth-pains, colic and danger at sea.

Erh-shih-ssu Hsiao

CHINESE COLLECTION OF TALES, 24 individuals whose stories demonstrate the key Chinese and Japanese virtues of filial respect and devotion. The stories range from Wu Meng, who refrained from brushing away the mosquitoes that were keeping him awake for fear of sending them to trouble his parents, to Kuo Chu, who offered to kill his sons to feed his mother, but was forestalled by finding a bar of gold given as a gift by the gods.

Ériu

OLD IRISH HEROINE, queen of the **Tuatha De Danann**, the last of the three queens to be met by the invading **Milesians**, who promised that her name would be given to the country for ever. Erin, the common name for Ireland, is derived from her name. The coronation of early Irish kings was conceived as a symbolic marriage to Ériu.

erlking

GERMANIC GOBLIN, a malevolent being often portrayed as the king of the **dwarfs** who lured mortals, especially children, to their deaths in the forest. In Goethe's ballad *Der Erlkönig*, translated by Sir Walter Scott, a father is riding through the forest with his son when the child sees the Erlking calling to him. Despite his father's attempts to hold him back, the Erlking succeeds in winning the boy's soul away and the father is left alone with his dead son in his arms.

ermine

A NORTHERN WEASEL, genus *Mustela*, characterized by a coat that becomes white in winter. This white fur was highly prized, and used for royal robes in many European countries. In popular legend the ermine valued its beautiful fur so much that if surrounded by mud it would allow itself to be captured rather than bespatter itself. White being traditionally associated with purity and innocence in Western lore, the ermine was often used as a symbol of chastity, and **Mary Magdalene** is frequently portrayed in medieval art with an ermine cloak to make it clear that her former way of life had been reformed.
▷ **weasel**

Etain

OLD IRISH HEROINE, the fairy bride of King Midhir. Midhir's first wife Fuamach was envious of her rival, and by enlisting Druid assistance contrived to turn her into a fly which she then blew away from **Tir Nan Og** into the mortal land of Ireland. Fuanach's crime was discovered and she was beheaded by **Angus Og**, but in the meantime Etain was blown around for seven years until she fell into the cup of Etar's wife and nine months later was born again and named Etain.

When grown she was courted by **Eochaid**, who took her to Tara. Eochaid's brother Ailell fell sick with love-longing, and at last Etain reluctantly agreed to his suit to save his life; Midhir instead met her at the tryst, but she refused to leave Eochaid. He was forced to play chess with Eochaid to win the right to kiss Etain, and then despite all Eochaid's precautions he snatched her away to Tir Nan Og. Eochaid hunted them down and waged war on the fairy land until Etain was finally restored to him.

Etain

This tale is a typical example of the heroic fairy tale in Irish lore, and includes many characteristic motifs such as the game of chess and magical reincarnation.

euhemerism

THEORY OF FOLKLORE SCHOLARSHIP, the contention that myths derive from historical events and personages, so for example that Zeus was in fact a Cretan king whose cult began after his death. The word derives from Euhemerus, a Greek writer who gave the theory its fullest expression about 300BC in his *Sacred History*. The concept predates him however, possibly originating with the Phoenecians. Some tribal gods and ancestor spirits can be traced back to early chiefs, and civilizations such as ancient Rome and Japan deified and mythologized emperors, but euhemerism is not by itself considered an adequate explanation for the origins of gods and world myths by most scholars.

euphemism

CIRCUMLOCUTION, a form of **taboo** in which the speaker avoids using a proper name. In European lore one of the most commonly euphemized beings is the **Devil** (Old Nick, Clootie or The Old Boy Himself), although other ill-omened words such as death (to kick the bucket, cash in one's chips or pass on) and coffin (casket or box) also attract alternative euphemisms. African and Native American groups generally refer to a feared or totemic animal by a respectful title such as Grandfather or Sir. The Old Man with the Fur Coat is the common phrase for a **bear** among the Lapps.

The purpose of such discretion is generally to avoid attracting to oneself dangerous attention by offending a spirit, or inadvertently summoning it.

In many areas the **name taboo** means that to speak another's name renders that person vulnerable to malign influence and therefore rulers were given titles to protect their name from becoming common currency. This was especially true in East Asia.

The Hebrew God, whose name is now rendered Yahweh, went under many different euphemisms, since his name was so holy that it could not be spoken, and in Christian lore, since it is considered blasphemous to use the names God or Jesus Christ lightly, mild euphemisms such as Gosh, Gee, Crumbs and Cripes have emerged.

European folklore

THE INFLUENCE OF EUROPEAN CULTURE ON THE REST OF THE WORLD has been immense. Although one of the smallest of continents, about a quarter the size of its neighbour, Asia, Europe has a climate and a geography that are both generally hospitable, and so became heavily populated in the spread of humankind. Since there was no shortage of water or of arable land, the settlers did not need to group themselves around water sources or fertile deltas as had many of their Asian ancestors. Many tended to settle in loose communities in small family units, with a limited amount of cooperative work. The typical European peasant worked to provide a subsistence crop and/or livestock level to feed his family.

The ancient civilization of Greece knew the lands to the north as backward and barbarian, and carried out most of its trade and cultural exchange with Asia to the East, but the expansion of the Roman Empire brought a political unity to the continent for the first and last time in its history. After the fall of Rome, Europe retained a surprisingly high degree of cultural uniformity. Despite the obvious differences between the various European countries, their linguistic origin can largely be traced back to Indo-European immigration, the basis of the three main language families; Romance (eg French, Spanish, Italian), Germanic (eg German, English, Dutch) and Slavonic (Russian, Polish, Czech etc). Non-Indo-European language families existing in the east of the continent include Finno-Ugrian, Turkic and Semitic. Many folktales can be found throughout the continent exhibiting slight variations but essentially demonstrating the same theme, structure and preoccupations.

The traditional home of the white man, Europe has sent out from its shores an enormous number of its inhabitants to explore and colonize new lands. The empire building of many European countries in the 16th to 19th centuries changed forever the cultures of the New Worlds, replacing Native American and African tribal lore with the belief systems and market economy of the whites, and although the transplanting of Old World lore to the colonies produced a rich and individual body of folk culture in each, much of the original folk wisdom was suppressed and lost forever. Some white settlers attempted to record the beliefs and customs of the natives in their new lands, but this was often done unsympathetically.

Compared with other continents, Europe has surprisingly few animal tales. These were presumably once common throughout the continent, but with increasing sophistication this basic folktale type gave way to more complex stories of humans or supernatural beings. Of the animal tales that have survived, most are concentrated in Russia and its surrounding countries. Many traditional folk melodies have survived however, usually linked with national dances or lyric sequences. From France in the 12th century came a new song form, based on a rhythmic, rhyming structure, which soon swept the continent and largely superseded the original non-rhyming forms. Along with this development, and sharing many features with it, came the **ballad** form, the narrative song. Ballads are often quite nationalistic in character, and it is often claimed that they represent the remains of the ancient epic form in Europe.

In other areas of folklore, cultural and economic differences in development have led to significant variations. The poetic **saga** of Norway and Iceland seems not to have existed elsewhere in Europe, where such historical material was usually dealt with by literate chroniclers in the Roman tradition. Likewise, since Spain and Russia were late in developing widespread literacy their store of proverbs tends to be significantly richer than those of their neighbours, since oral transmission of knowledge remained vital.

The industrialization of much of Europe in the 18th and 19th centuries destroyed much of the original folklore,

breaking up communities, facilitating travel and emphasising scientific knowledge. However, with intellectual development there came also a recognition of its value and significance, and the first attempts to devise a systematic study of folklore originated in Europe with scholars like the Grimms in Germany and Lönrat of the Finnish school. In fact, throughout its history the literature and art of Europe has been greatly influenced by its folklore: Chaucer and Boccaccio drew from tales of their day, the great Arthurian cycles developed from folklore, **Sleeping Beauty** became a ballet, La Fontaine wrote many French tales, and Wagner drew heavily on Scandinavian legend.

Although Europe has largely lost its naivety and the traditional wisdom of the folk been replaced by scientific investigation and the written word, it has also developed a sense of the importance of its folk legacy and a commitment to recording its tales, beliefs and customs before they become extinct.

evil eye

THE POWER TO INFLICT HARM BY LOOKING AT AN OBJECT. Belief of some form in the evil eye is found in many different parts of the world, primarily in Europe, North Africa, the Near East, South Asia and Central America. There are many variations on the superstition, as to who is able to cast the evil, what it is aimed at and who may be susceptible, for example, but the common foundation of all the superstitions is belief in power directed from the eye causing sudden injury to an object or person, which may be averted by the use of charms or rituals. In most cases envy is cited as the motivation for such an attack.

The vast geographical spread of the belief, coupled with the surprising similarity of practices associated with it (the use of a red ribbon to guard children against the evil eye is common in Scotland and India, for example), suggests that it is a very ancient one, predating the divisions of Indo-European and Semitic languages. It seems probable that the belief in Latin America, at least in its fullest form, was brought over with Columbus, although the eye seems even before then to be associated dimly with mystery. In the earliest forms of human contact, and even in primates, a sustained gaze usually precedes any decisive interaction between two of the species, particularly aggressive action. This may well have been the origin of the significance of the eye in folklore, but as the superstition developed it became a means of explaining otherwise random personal disasters, providing a focus of responsibility. In Christian societies the **Devil** was held responsible for the evil eye.

The evil eye was cast by a god or by a human who, knowingly or not, invoked superhuman powers; therefore it could be combated by invoking superhuman powers in defence, hence the close association of **charms** and **amulets** with belief in the evil eye. As more complex societies developed and possessions became attached to individuals, envy became a more significant factor, and **cattle**, wives, children or other possessions were regarded as the most likely targets for the evil eye.

Since the most common cause of the evil eye is envy, many cultures have adopted the protective habit of speaking disparagingly about their goods and their state of their own and their family's health; an Italian peasant will rarely claim to be more than 'not too bad', and in the Middle East children are often dressed in rags and seldom praised in public. In many South Asian cultures compliments tend to be regarded with suspicion, since they leave the one complimented vulnerable to envy and therefore the evil eye, and similarly many peasant communities are wary of expressing emotion, especially joy, too openly. The tradition that a bride should wear a veil on her wedding day may well have originated as a protective measure against the evil eye. Amulets may be worn to deflect the power of its gaze; certain creatures thought to be particularly repulsive, such as **toads**, were considered especially effective. Signs of luck, like the four-leafed **clover**, **rabbit**'s foot or the Irish **shamrock**, may be carried to counter-balance the cure. One of the most basic ways of avoiding the effect of the evil eye of course is to avoid altogether anyone suspected of possessing the power. In many cases this may be

anyone considered a stranger or different from the group (hence Gypsies have traditionally been credited with possessing the evil eye in Europe), or anyone possessing a peculiarity such as a squint or odd-coloured eyes.

A striking example of the evil eye motif in ancient legend is the Greek **Gorgon**, most famously Medusa, who turned whomever she looked upon into stone.

Excalibur

THE SWORD OF KING ARTHUR. The name is thought to derive from the **sword** of old Irish legend *Caladbolg* ('hard belly', therefore able to consume anything), which is rendered Caliburn by Geoffrey of Monmouth. Caladbolg was forged in **fairyland** and wielded by **Fergus Mac Roich**; Excalibur was said by Geoffrey of Monmouth to have come from **Avalon**, and by Malory to have been a gift of Vivien of Fairyland.

The famous legend of the young **Arthur** drawing the sword from the stone where all else have failed, thus establishing his right to rule, does not appear before the 12th century. The description of how the mortally wounded Arthur bids Sir Belvidere three times to throw the sword in the Lake, and how a hand rises to catch it when Sir Belvidere finally discharges his task, is almost certainly a literary invention of Malory's.
▷ **Lady of the Lake**

exorcism

RITUAL OF CLEANSING, for the removal of a troublesome **ghost** or poltergeist. The formula is usually religious, intended to drive out the spirit by appeal to a stronger power, or to finish the business the person left undone and thereby put his or her mind at rest. In Christian tradition the exorcism ritual involves the symbolic **bell**, book and **candle**; a bell is rung as a summons, a malediction read out and the Bible shut up, and a holy candle is extinguished.

eyes

A COMMON TALE-TYPE IN NATIVE AMERICAN LORE is that of the eye-juggler. The trickster is given the ability to throw his eyes into the air a limited number of times and retrieve them; inevitably he oversteps this limit and his eyes are lost. In most versions he goes on to find a replacement pair, often from an animal, but sometimes of pitch. The Crow have another version of the motif of substitute eyes: the trickster is challenged to a contest with the snakes to see who can stay awake longest during the telling of a long tale, and he wins by exchanging eyes with a jackrabbit, thus appearing wide awake even while he dozes. Such tales are common throughout North America.

fable see animal fable

Fables of Bidpai

COLLECTION OF ANIMAL TALES, the name given to the English translation of fables from the *Panchatantra*. Bidpa was said to be a wise courtier in the service of an evil Indian king, who wrote the tales as examples to his master.

fabulous creatures

STRANGE COMPOSITE ANIMALS, usually but not exclusively fearsome, are a feature of folklore and mythology around the world. Often such non-existent creatures originate with the reports of over-enthusiastic travellers, received with credulity and a propensity for exaggeration by those at home; the **mermaid** for example may have originated with sailors' sightings of the **dugong** feeding her young at sea.

The folk imagination is quick to endow such inventions with characteristics, feeding habits and moral character, along with means of catching, killing or avoiding hurt from the creature should one ever encounter it. In classical and later Christian **bestiaries** fabulous animals were catalogued earnestly, often with a moral lesson to be drawn from their observation, for example the **unicorn**'s close associations with chastity.

In the pioneer lore of North America particularly, this ancient habit found humorous expression in an entire zoo of fictitious animals, often invoked as **bogeys** to scare or dupe greenhorns; the guyascutus for example was said to have a pair of legs on one side longer than those of the other, to give it stability when feeding on a steep hill. The haggis too, the traditional Scottish dish, has enjoyed a career as a humorous animal invented to dupe tourists.

fado

PORTUGUESE FOLK SONG, an urban form reminiscent of the **blues** of the United States. It appears to have originated in the late 18th century, and while its roots are obscure it seems clear that there is much African influence (perhaps via South America). Two guitars are used, one providing the melody and the other rhythm, and the songs are typically narratives of personal love and tragedy, nostalgic or meditative, sung, like the blues, with loose rhythm and gravelly voice. Although the lyrics are often topical, the melodies are derived from ancient folksongs.

faet fiada

'THE LOOK OF AN ANIMAL', a magic power of **invisibility** of the Druids and the **Tuatha de Danann**. According to legend Manannan gave this gift to the Tuatha de Danann after the victory of the **Milesians**, to enable them to survive. The belief survived the passage into Christian lore; St **Patrick** was credited with turning himself and a fellow-traveller into **deer** to enable them to bypass enemies who would have prevented them reaching Tara to spread the new faith. Patrick's hymn, *The Deer's Cry*, is the equivalent of the spells of the Druids to effect the faet fiada.

Fafnir

DWARF OF TEUTONIC LORE, son of the **dwarf** king Hreidmor. After Otter's accidental death, Odin, Hoenir and Loki paid a ransom to Hreidmar, and the *Volsungasaga* records how Fafnir killed his father to secure this treasure for himself, refusing to share it with his brother Regin, and became a **dragon** brooding in solitude over his wealth. He is killed by **Sigurd** who hides in a pit and stabs the soft underbelly as the dragon passes above him, and secures the treasure for himself. In Wagner's *Ring* trilogy Fafner (Fafnir) kills his brother

Fasolt over the golden ring given by **Alberich**.

fairy

SUPERNATURAL BEING, most famous of the creatures of folklore. Since the term 'fairy' has come to be applied so widely to all diminutive sprites, mischievous or friendly, visible or not, it is difficult to define it with any precision. Generally, however, a fairy is a supernatural being with the ability to become visible or invisible at will, usually smaller than humans and sometimes very tiny, capable of enchantment and usually involving itself in human affairs. Fairies are usually thought to live underground, especially under hills, in a magical **fairyland** where they indulge their taste for dancing and dainty foods. In more recent folklore they have become romanticized and are rarely harmful; in more superstitious times however they were thought to be dangerous, spirits to be placated and avoided rather than actively sought.

Various theories have been suggested to account for the world-wide presence of fairy beliefs. According to some folklorists, fairies are the detritus of ancient animistic beliefs which attributed a spirit to all physical objects, personified in later lore. Certainly there is evidence that figures of old myth were transmuted into fairy personages in later belief, for example the great warrior queen **Medb** (or Maeve) of Connaught who fought **Conchobar** and **Cuchulainn** in the **Ulster cycle** is probably the origin of Queen Mab, queen of the fairies in English lore.

Another possibility is that fairies were originally spirits of the dead; hence their underground dwelling and their reputation for enticing away mortals who, having once eaten of fairy food, cannot return to the land of the living but will sicken and die (compare the myth of Persephone who ate six **pomegranate** seeds in the underworld). Like ghosts and **vampires** too, fairies must in most cases return to their underground homes at daybreak.

The word itself is a late derivation from *fays*, which in turn comes from Latin *fatum*. (Fairy lore may well contain elements from the three classical Fates who directed the lives of humans.) Originally 'fay-erie' meant enchantment, or the land where such enchantment took place; only later did it come to be applied to the inhabitants of that land. Fairies are known by different names around the world—**elves**, **sidhe** or **abatwa**, for example—and they are found as a rule in more sophisticated cultures. American and African groups have relatively little fairy lore, but it is well developed in Asia and Europe.

Literature in Europe has appropriated much fairy lore, and the medieval romances in particular developed the themes of chivalry and love interest, and the organization of the fairy world, ruled over by **Oberon** and his queen, **Titania**. They developed too the idea of fairy-

fairy

animals, from the primitive belief in supernatural creatures of myth like the dangerous wild horses of the Scottish Highlands, **each uisge**, and beasts such as the **Black Dogs** of England to the sophisticated mounts and hunting-dogs of the fairy court.

As well as kidnapping human babies and leaving **changelings** in their place, fairies would also attempt to lure older humans, especially girls, by their cheerful merrymaking and offers of delicious food and drink. Once trapped, the victims can never return but live as the fairies' slaves, often providing milk for their children. Midwives are luckier; although often abducted to help with fairy births they are as a rule released afterwards, often with a substantial reward. On a lesser scale, fairies are much given to the theft of food, often just taking away the goodness or substance while leaving the appearance behind. They may also steal objects such as farming implements or grain, but often they will be scrupulous in returning these in pristine condition. Some ethnologists have suggested that the figure of the fairy may have originated with conquered peoples forced off their land to a precarious existence in the wild, making occasional surreptitious raids on their conquerors to meet their needs and to wreak a small revenge where possible. These nightly, unseen visitations may have suggested the idea of a mischievous or dangerous fairy race to the conquerors.

Should the fairies set their favour on a mortal, however, he was lucky indeed. They might teach him the secret of their wonderful crafts, the making of cloth and artefacts of incredible strength and beauty, or bequeath the knowledge of their wonderful music. A family that welcomes and aids them might be rewarded with delicious fairy food, or by magical gifts of never-failing gold or grain.

In addition to the legends of folklore and literary traditions, there is an enormous body of superstitious belief associated with fairies. Since their enmity is greatly feared, a complex etiquette has developed to avoid angering the fairies, who are thus often referred to euphemistically as 'The little people', 'the good

neighbours' or, in Ireland, 'the gentry'. Many peasant homes leave food spread out for them in the kitchen overnight to win their friendship, being careful to avoid adding any **salt**. Since they are so fond of milk, and are sometimes said to weaken cows by milking them themselves, some farmers leave one cow unmilked for their use, or let the first few drops of milk fall when milking, as the fairies' portion. Milk spilled outside should always be left to please the fairies. It is considered a breach of fairy etiquette to thank them for a gift of food; the recipient must however be careful to express his thanks by praising the food. Although they are given to abducting mortals or enticing them into their circles, fairies are notoriously fierce about their privacy, and it is highly dangerous to be caught spying on them. Most peasant folk will be careful to avoid spots likely to be populated by fairies, especially at night.

▷ **changeling**; **fairyland**

fairy godmother

SUPERNATURAL PATRONS OF DESERVING HUMANS. The figure of the fairy godmother is derived from the three personified Fates (the origin of the word **fairy** itself) who visited a child at birth and bestowed upon it good or ill fortune. From this tradition comes the wholly benevolent fairy godmother, imported by Perrault into his influential version of **Cinderella**. This unambiguous morality is characteristic of later, romantic and literary visions of fairies, and is markedly different from the ambiguous figures of authentic folklore, who are capable of both good and evil and must be propitiated.

▷ **guardian spirits**

fairyland

OTHERWORLD OF POPULAR BELIEF. Many Celtic folktales in particular tell of humans stumbling upon the land of the fairies (the **sidhe**), ruled over by a fairy king and queen, where time is out of joint with the natural world and the inhabitants sing, dance and feast all day long. The theme of the supernatural passage of time is one common to nearly all **fairy** beliefs, and it may work either

way; the mortal visiting fairyland may discover that many human years have passed in what seemed but a short time, or he may return to find that his long sojourn in fairyland has taken only a few minutes of human time. The most common stories tell of humans who join a fairy dance or feast to find that a year or a century has gone by, and that they have been mourned as dead (a similar theme is found in medieval legends of **saints** who stand entranced by heavenly singing or in meditation while many years pass their less spiritual brethren by). Those who return from fairyland, and especially those who have tasted fairy food, are almost without exception doomed to pine and die, losing all interest in the everyday world, and in many cases they, like the mortals who return having married fairy lovers, simply crumble into dust on their return. One example of this prolific tale type will serve: **Oisín** (or Ossian), a warrior and poet of the **Fianna** and son of **Finn Mac Cumhal** himself and his fairy wife Sadb. Oisín travelled across the sea with the fairy princess Niamh to **Tir Nan Og**, the Celtic otherworld of perpetual youth. He rode back after many years expecting to meet his old companions; instead he found all changed, and on breaking the **geis** laid upon him by Niam and touching the ground with his feet he withered into an ancient man, his horse fled back to Tir Nan Og, and he lived the rest of his life as a relic from the heroic age, arguing with St **Patrick** about the inadequacies of the Christian heaven (what is an afterlife without hunting or the ancient pagan heroes?).
▷ **food taboo**

fairy marriage

THE UNION OF HUMAN AND FAIRY BEINGS. There are several tales, especially in the medieval romances, of **fairy** brides married to mortal men, following the ancient traditions of gods and animal spirits having intercourse with humans. As in the best of these traditions, the result is nearly always tragic, and the fairy bride is often lost back to **fairyland** by the violation of a **taboo**, for example against striking her in anger. In other tales the hero descends to fairyland to marry one of its inhabitants, but after some time expresses the desire to see his home again. He is allowed to do so, but many years of real time have passed unbeknown to him, and often he crumbles into dust.
▷ **beast marriage**

fairy tales

TYPE OF FOLK NARRATIVE. The English phrase 'fairy tale' is somewhat misleading; many of the narratives encompassed by it make no mention of fairies. In fact stories about fairies are usually not fairy stories at all, since they usually involve some kind of belief in fairies' existence and a description of their habits to instruct or warn unwary humans. Most folklorists prefer to use the German word used by Grimm, Märchen, although this too is less than fully satisfactory since it can be applied quite loosely to other tale-types. Fairy tales in the narrowest sense are mainly a phenomenon of Asian and European culture; set in some indefinite land and time, where supernatural events are accepted along with the everyday and the outcome of events is always happy, they are tales told as fictions for entertainment and sometimes for moral instruction rather than legends, myth or customs which involve at least an element of belief. This definition, although valuable, is not without its problems, since a fairy tale such as **Cinderella** may appear world-wide, regarded with varying measures of fantasy and belief.

To an even greater extent than in most oral lore, fairy tales are distinguished by the use of formulaic phrases and recurrent motifs. Form is vitally important: the repetition of events, usually in threes, the sequence of departure, journey and achievement, of task and fulfilment, of loss and restoration, are all made rigid and stylized. The result is a satisfyingly familiar order that is all the more convincing since it carries with it an accepted set of codes, no matter how marvellous the action. Realistic understatement despite the supernatural events is especially characteristic of European fairy tales, in which the most astonishing events are received with stolid acceptance.

There is an instantly recognizable cast of stock characters: youngest brothers, abandoned children, kings, swineherds and **witches**, few of whom are actually named. They are types rather than individuals, whose character and function in the plot can be deduced from their first appearance and thus the tales developed and were transmitted and recalled down the generations. The clearly-delineated moral structure of the fairy tale is another essential feature; the good (who are equated with beauty) are rewarded and the evil punished, often remorselessly. Events and characters tend to follow this neat polarization, so the good–evil opposition is reflected in light–dark, elder–younger structures and in simple patterning of male and female.

While the educated classes of the Middle Ages in Europe developed romances and chivalric adventures, the peasants went on telling their fairy stories around the hearth. In Victorian Britain, and earlier on the Continent with Perrault and his like in the late 17th century, the literary fairy tale developed in which plot and character were refined and the moral lessons clearly set out for children. Until then however, the fairy tale was almost exclusively the preserve of the folk. In it their imagination, sense of humour and uncomplicated moral code can all be clearly discerned.

Because of its popularity in Asia and Europe (the most famous examples include **Aladdin** and Cinderella), it has been suggested that the ancient beginnings of the fairy tale lie in the Indo-European cultural tradition. Since tales showing similar plot and motifs are common throughout the world, however, and not solely where borrowing can be established, it seems safer to suggest that the building blocks of fairy tales are part of the most primitive human heritage, although its distinctive narrative style may have developed within the narrower traditions of Indo-Europe. The fairy tale in Europe took on a distinctive flavour, more romantic and less fantastic, as it grew, and famous examples such as Cinderella and **Sleeping Beauty** exhibit surprisingly few variations across Europe.

Faithful Henry

TYPE OF THE FAITHFUL SERVANT, an ancient folkloric motif. He appears in Grimm's *The Frog Prince* as the transformed prince's old servant, who has had three bands of iron laid round his heart to stop it breaking with grief. These bands burst apart with joy when the prince is restored to human form and marries the princess.

Faithful John

MOTIF OF FOLKLORE, the most famous incarnation of the trusty servant figure found in many folktales of Europe and Asia. In one of Grimm's Hausmärchen a dying king calls his old and trusted servant to his side and commends the young prince to his care. He especially warns the servant not to let him enter a certain locked room, since the portrait within it would undoubtedly bring disaster upon him. Of course the prince does discover the portrait and despite the dissuasion of the servant falls in love with its subject and vows to find her.

Faithful John, despite his misgivings, helps his young master to arrange the journey. They discover the princess in a far-off country, and once she is lured on board by the magnificent treasures with which the prince's ship is loaded, he sets sail and carries her away. After he has thrown off the disguise of a merchant with which he tricked her, the princess consents to be his bride, but Faithful John is horrified when he hears three **ravens** discussing the couple's future. The prince faces three dangers: a beautiful horse which will fly away with him; a bridal robe which will be fatal to the princess; and a snake which will kill the princess in the nuptial bed (in some versions she is fated to swoon, never to recover unless three drops of blood are taken from her breast). The ravens add that if anyone were to repeat these perils, he would be turned to stone.

So when the horse is presented to the prince, Faithful John kills it without explanation. The prince is puzzled but trusts his servant, and he does not demur either when John takes and burns the beautiful robe offered to the bride. But when he sees the old servant stooped over his bride on their wedding night (as he kills the snake or removes three drops of blood) he is enraged and condemns him to death. At the moment of execution Faithful John pours out the whole story and is immediately turned to a statue, which the remorseful couple keep in their palace for years. One day they are told that the blood of their two children will restore life to the statue; they cheerfully sacrifice their offspring and, touched by the blood, the statue comes to life and Faithful John proceeds to restore the two children.

The figure of the faithful servant is thought to have originated in Asia, probably in India, from whence it spread westwards over 2000 years ago. A similar motif is that of the **helpful beast**, in which a beast helps the hero perform his tasks or attain his prize, and this is found world-wide. Devotion and loyalty feature in folklore in general as a means of overcoming evil. Although European versions of such tales emphasize sentimentality and the moral aspect, they have not entirely lost sight of the original mystical element, the belief in the efficacy and life-giving powers of blood. The tales have inherited from ancient mythology the identification of blood with life and hence the Faithful John tale (along with many others) show blood reanimating and regenerating the dead.
▷ **Faithful Henry**

fandango

SPANISH COUPLE DANCE, an intoxicating and passionate representation of courtship performed in 3/8 or 3/4 time to the accompaniment of strummed guitars, **castanets** and the clicking of the dancers' heels. The tempo quickens as the dance progresses through flirtation, attraction and pursuit, with sinuous gestures and moments of immobility as the music suddenly pauses. The dance is especially popular in Castile and Andalusia, and it is thought to have developed from Moorish and gypsy origins. The fandanguillo, 'little fandango', is generally performed by a solo woman who scarcely moves from the spot. It consists of an elaborate drumming of the heels and manipulation of castanets, and although dramatic it lacks the extrovert enthusiasm of the full fandango.

Songs also known as fandangos may be performed solo or to accompany the dancing. These songs reveal Moorish influences in their tonality, but are traditionally improvised by the singer (c **calypso**).

fantine

SWISS LITTLE PEOPLE, a benevolent fairy race of the Vaud valleys who are responsible for providing good growing weather for the farmers. They thoughtfully supply the cattle of favoured humans with tiny **bells**, to prevent them becoming lost.

Fastnacht

GERMAN CARNIVAL, meaning the eve of fasting, a development of the ancient Teutonic ship-cart pageants in honour of the Germanic goddess of fertility Hertha. The pagan festival was Christianized, and statues of **Mary** replaced images of Hertha, but the traditional license and the antics of the masqueraders persisted and developed into the riotous Fastnacht plays. Popular etymology claims that the term actually derives from the word for speaking nonsense, *fasen*, but there is no evidence for this.
▷ **Fastnachtsbär**

Fastnachtsbär

THE BEAR OF FASTNACHT, a man covered in straw and ropes who is led throughout the village at Fastnacht or Shrove Tuesday in Germany and other areas of Germanic central Europe. He sometimes wears a bear's mask or bearskin. He is led into each house, along with a procession of musicians, to dance with all the females, and receives gifts of food and money from each one. This revelry is widely considered to bring luck with the crops and straw taken from his costume and placed under the hens will encourage them to lay plentifully.

Fata Morgana

MOST FAMOUS OF THE ITALIAN FAIRIES, or *fata*, better known in English as **Morgan le Fay**. In the **Charlemagne** cycle of legends she was an underwater enchantress, lover of Ogier, whom Orlando defeated. She has given her name to the mirage sometimes seen in the Straits of Messina, said to arise from her magic.

Faust

Fatima (c.605–33)

THE SHINING ONE, daughter of Muhammad, considered in Islamic lore as one of the four 'perfect women' (along with her mother Khadija, **Mary** the mother of Jesus, and Asiyah, wife of the pharaoh who drowned while pursuing Moses and the Israelites). She is said to be virginal—her title is 'bright-blooming', meaning one who has never menstruated—yet she bore her husband Ali three sons, whom Shiite Muslims recognize as the true heirs of Mohammad's authority.

Fatima

FAIRY-TALE HEROINE, the last wife of **Bluebeard** who survives and brings about his downfall.

Fatima

CHARACTER OF THE ALADDIN TALE. In some versions of the tale she is the holy woman whom the necromancer kills, and in whose clothes he gains entrance to **Aladdin**'s palace. The jinni of the lamp reveals his identity to Aladdin and he is killed.

fauns

ROMAN WOODLAND SPIRITS, derived from the god Faunus. Although probably an ancient agriculture god, Faunus was mingled with the Greek Pan and portrayed as a merry, musical **satyr**, half human and half goat, who spoke oracles through the sounds of the forest. His biannual festivals, at which sacrifices of goats were made, were marked by revelry, games and debauchery. The mischievous spirits of the countryside associated with him and portrayed, like him, with goats' hoofs and horns, were known as fauns.

fauns

Faust

THE GRAND MAGICIAN, figure of legend and literature. The historical Dr Faustus was one George (or Johannes) Faust, a noted magician who died in c.1540. Medieval society was characterized by its preoccupation with the supernatural, particularly the activities of Satan, and many floating legends of miraculous deeds and diabolical pacts came to be associated with the historical figure of Faust. Stories told of other, earlier magicians such as Paracelsus and Simon Magus were attached to Faust by popular tradition; he became the representative type of a diabolical magician and his story developed into the locus classicus of a familiar motif of folklore, the pact with the **Devil**.

The basic Faustian story tells how an ambitious magician rejects legitimate forms of learning and turns instead to necromancy; summoning a demon, he signs an agreement with the Devil that in exchange for a period of unbounded power, knowledge, youth and licentiousness (usually 24 years) he will surrender his soul to Hell. For the agreed period, during which his exploits win him equal measures of renown and suspicion, he is accompanied by a demonic familiar, in some versions a shaggy dog with blood-red eyes, in others (notably that of Marlowe) by the devil **Mephistopheles**. At the expiring of the allotted time, Faust is claimed by the Devil and dragged down to Hell. The legend was received with much credibility in medieval and Renaissance Europe, where quacks and charlatans travelled every country with their pseudo-scientific sorcery and **alchemy**. Lutheran church leaders such as Martin

175

Luther himself denounced Faust in all earnestness, while magic pamphlets were published in Faust's name explaining how to go about tricking the Devil in such a pact. Meanwhile the popular lore surrounding the tale developed; Faust's exploits generally included a ride on an inanimate object such as a bale of hay or a barrel, a bunch of grapes fetched from across the world to be produced in the middle of winter, and the summoning of various spirits, most famously Helen of Troy.

In the earliest work on the subject, the *Historia von Dr Johnson* of 1587, Faust appears almost exclusively as a wonderworker, and popular interest centred for a long time on his exploits rather than the theological implications of his pact. A more literary, tragic approach was begun by Christopher Marlowe with *The Tragicall History of D. Faustus* (1604) and in 1784 Gotthold Lessing wrote an unfinished play in which Faust was reconciled with God. A fellow German writer, Goethe, developed this idea in the greatest of all works on the legend, his two-part poem *Faust* (1808 and 1833) in which the magician is almost eclipsed by the philosopher and the themes of good and evil are treated with complexity; ultimately Faust is redeemed. The folk figure is here made to stand as a symbol of Western culture and learning, demonstrating its great potentiality and equally great danger, and it is this literary Faust who has had the most impact in modern consciousness. Nevertheless, the basis of the legend is popular lore, and much of its appeal can be traced to its status as popular entertainment which confronts some of the most fundamental of human preoccupations: the search for knowledge and power, good and evil, the inevitability of old age and death and the desperate fight against them.

fay see **fairy**

féar gortac

'HUNGRY GRASS', a magical grass which causes insupportable hunger in anyone unfortunate enough to step on it. Eating cures this famishment immediately, but if the traveller has not taken the precaution of carrying food with him it may well prove fatal. In some versions, the féar gortac is a spirit of hunger, appearing as a shrivelled old man in times of famine.

Feast of Fools

A FESTIVAL OF THE MEDIEVAL CLERGY, celebrated especially in France (26–28 December), in which the Mass and other ecclesiastical rites were burlesqued, and a mock bishop or pope (often a boy) elected. The tradition died out with the Reformation.
▷ **Lord of Misrule**

Febold Feboldson

FOLK HERO OF THE GREAT PLAINS, hero of a series of **tall tales** run in US newspapers and comics in the early 20th century. Febold was a Swedish pioneer for whom no job was too big and no hardship insurmountable. Like **Paul Bunyan**, this fabricated figure attracted floating tall-tale motifs melded together with the flavour of the local environment to produce a familiar yet idiosyncratic body of lore. The hyperbolic tales include accounts of corpses being resurrected by the healthful prairie wind and of Febold inducing rain by persuading the frogs to croak during a drought.

Fenian cycle

OLD IRISH TALES OF THE FIANNA. Characteristically patriotic, the cycle tells of the rise and mourns the fall of heroic, virtuous Irishmen, celebrating the greatness of their deeds with enthusiasm and hyperbole. The **Fianna** were the embodiment of the heroic ideals of Gaelic culture, truthful, brave, strong and ultimately fated to tragedy, and their tales have always been particularly beloved of the common folk. A vast number of folktales developed around the cycle, and it appears that the literary cycle itself grew out of a thriving folk tradition, rather than being largely the work of bards as was that of the **Red Branch**. From the first reference to the cycle in the seventh century until as late as the 18th century new tales of Finn and his warriors were constantly being produced and incorporated into the saga, which suggests an unusually high level of involvement and continuity of oral tradition among the folk. The tales of the

Fianna tend to be more humorous, less lofty and removed than those of **Cuchulainn** and the Red Branch; they smack less of myth and more of the lore of the common folk.

One of the surviving sagas of the cycle is the *Dialogue of the Ancients*, in which the old poet Caoilte and **Oisín**, who has returned from the Land of Youth to Ireland, tell St **Patrick** of the heroic deeds of the Fianna. Although their virtue is pagan, St Patrick respects this vision of heroic Ireland and gains permission from the angels to write down their wonderful tales.

fenoderee

THE MANX BROWNIE, a helpful but touchy spirit. Unlike many other regional **brownie**s, he is as large as a human and has great supernatural strength. According to some legends, he was originally a **fairy** who was banished to the land of mortals for loving a human girl. He is generally described as an individual rather than a species of fairy, although from the number of farms laying claim to have him in residence he is also capable of multiple appearances. Like all brownies, he will desert anyone who makes him a present of clothes.

Fenrir

TERRIBLE WOLF OF NORSE MYTHOLOGY. Born of Loki and a giantess, he was bound by the gods to a rock until Ragnarok, when he will break free and devour Odin, king of the gods, and in some versions the sun, until he himself is killed by Odin's son Vidor. He is also known as Fenrisúlfer.

Ferdiad

OLD IRISH HERO, half-brother and sworn friend of **Cuchulainn**, who is compelled by **Medb** of Connacht to fight him during the **Táin Bó Cuailnge**. The two battled for three days, neither wishing to harm the other, and both exchanging food and restorative herbs each night, but eventually Cuchulainn kills Ferdiad. Cuchulainn's grief-stricken lament for his friend is one of the most moving episodes of Irish legend.

Fergus mac Roich

OLD IRISH HERO, a warrior of the Red Branch and tutor to **Cuchulainn**. He was sent by **Conchobar** to fetch back **Deirdre** and Naoise with promises of forgiveness, but after Conchobar treacherously killed the sons of Usnech he went into self-imposed exile, in disgust at Conchobar's behaviour and his own forced complicity.

fern

NON-FLOWERING PLANT, numbering many thousands of species in the class Filicopsida or Filicinae, that reproduces by means of spores. In many parts of Europe ferns are considered efficacious against toothache; in Cornwall to bite on the first fern of the year is a means of keeping toothache at bay all year. Another widespread use is in the treatment of burns and scalds and it is also brewed to make a medicinal drink.

Fern seeds, the tiny spore of the fern, have long been associated with witchcraft and magic. In some areas they conferred the power of **invisibility** on anyone who carried them, especially if the seeds had been gathered on **Midsummer** Eve. In Old Bohemia, fern seeds were said to blossom only once a year, on Midsummer Eve. Should anyone find and pluck this golden bloom, and climb a mountain with it, he would infallibly find treasure. Alternatively, in Russia, he might throw the precious flower in the air and dig for treasure where he sees it land. Among black slaves in Georgia, fern seeds sprinkled around the house were believed to keep away ghosts and evil spirits.

fetch

A SPIRIT-DOUBLE, A GHOST OR APPARITION, usually of a living person, in Irish and English lore. Although occasionally seen by those with second sight, its appearance is more generally seen at night by loved ones and relations at the moment before or after the individual's death. If it appears in the morning however, it can be a sign of long life.

A fetch candle or fetch-light is a small, ghostly flame moving through the night. It is generally interpreted as a warning of death to the one who sees it, or of the death of someone close to him or her.

▷ **doppelgänger**; **shadow soul**; **wraith**

fetish from Basonge, Zaire, age unknown, made from wood, shells, copper wire and nails

fetish

MAGIC CHARM, an artefact believed to embody spiritual powers. The word derives from Portuguese *feitiço*, 'something made'. The word is widely used more loosely to denote an idol or other representation of a deity.

Fianna

OLD IRISH HEROES, the men of **Finn Mac Cumhal**. A select band of warriors, they were a kind of Irish militia, famed for their prowess as fighters and hunters, their courage and strength, and their courtesy towards women. To enter the group a man had to accept four *geasa* (taboos): never to accept a **dowry** with a wife, but to take her only for her virtue; never to act violently towards a woman; never to refuse even the most precious thing that was demanded of them; and never to flee before fewer than ten warriors. They were all highly skilled poets. Many of the Fianna, such as Finn's son the poet **Oisín** and his son Oscar, and **Diarmuid** O Duibhne, have clearly defined adventures of their own within the cycle. The Fianna began to break up, however, as the feud with Aedh Mac Morna of Connacht

worsened, and Finn himself behaved treacherously to one of his own warriors, pursuing Diarmuid and his promised wife **Gráinne** and finally causing his death. The brotherhood was broken, the heroism compromised and Finn's authority weakened, and the band now faced opposition from many of their own countrymen and the new High King at Tara. The Fianna were finally defeated at the Battle of Gabhra.
▷ **geis**

fiddle

STRINGED INSTRUMENT, a European development of the 10th century that probably owed its roots to Arabic instruments played with a bow. The term is generally applied to any stringed instrument with a neck played with a bow rather than plucked or strummed, and such instruments are found worldwide, from the bamboo and snakeskin hu chin of the Far East and the kamanga of Islamic North Africa, made of a coconut shell and gourd, to the classical violin of post-Renaissance Europe.

In folktales the fiddle has a reputation as a magical instrument, closely associated with spiritual or fairy forces. The **Devil** is said to be a virtuoso fiddler in European lore, and anyone with such a gift might be regarded with suspicion since it was a favourite gift of his in exchange for a human soul. To dance to the music of a strange fiddler, no matter how compelling the music, may place one's soul or life in his power. In witchlore a girl who falls in with a merry dance may find she has unwittingly become a witch, in the power of the master fiddler himself. The fairy dances that so often entice mortals into protracted spells in **fairyland** are often performed to a fiddle. Even a mortal who is skilled in fiddling may find he has the power to enchant wild animals.

The relative ease with which a fiddle can be made and the variety of moods it can create, from foot-stamping cheeriness to plaintive solitude, have made it one of the most popular and enduring of folk instruments. It is especially useful for accompanying dances, as in the ceilidhs of Scotland and the barn dances or ho-downs of the United States.

field spirits

VEGETATIVE SPIRITS, the personification of the harvest.
▷ **harvest doll**

fig

FRUIT TREE, genus *Ficus* of the mulberry family (Moraceae), one of the earliest to be cultivated by humans. It has been a staple food of many cultures in Asia, parts of Africa and Mediterranean Europe since ancient times, and enjoys a reputation as an emblem of plenty and prosperity. In Islamic lore it is sacred, since Muhammad swore by it, and the Romans held the fig tree sacred to Dionysus. Buddha is said to have found enlightenment under the pipul tree, a form of fig, and in many cultures the fig is a **tree of life** or of knowledge. Adam and Eve clothed themselves with fig leaves when they apprehended their nakedness in Eden, and in some traditions the fig was the forbidden fruit. In Sicilian lore **Judas Iscariot** hanged himself on a fig tree, and it is therefore infested with evil spirits. Contrastingly, in Estonia it is said that a fig tree once sheltered Jesus from the rain and was rewarded by evergreen foliage.

Figs have been used to treat a vast litany of complaints, particularly tooth and gum disorders, coughs and skin sores. The milk of the tree is widely used for babies and as a general restorative.

To 'make a fig' by inserting the thumb between the middle and index fingers of the same hand, or by biting the thumb, is considered a highly offensive gesture in much of Europe. The first of these is thought to represent the vulva and penis, and interestingly it was originally offered as a good luck sign, to ward off the **evil eye**. An Italian legend to explain the significance of biting the thumb tells how Frederic **Barbarossa** revenged himself for a slight on the citizens of Milan by compelling each of them to remove a fig inserted in the rectum of a donkey with their teeth.

figureheads

ORNAMENTAL IMAGE, either carved or painted, placed on the bow or some other forward part of a boat or ship. In earliest times eyes were painted to

figurehead

enable the vessel to find its way across the waters, but by 1000BC heavy stemposts were being carved in more or less intricate forms. As well as the practical use of distinguishing ships, figureheads transferred the powers and virtue of the object represented by **sympathetic magic** to the boat. Jason's magical bough guided the Argonauts from the prow of the ship, and the **dragons** of the Viking longboats were an invocation for powers of ferocity and shrewdness, with the advantage of intimidating other tribes. The later tradition of using a barebreasted woman as a figurehead refers to the popular superstition among sailors that, while real women were unlucky aboard ship, the sea would calm its tumult at the sight of the uncovered female breast.

Findabair

A BEAUTIFUL PRINCESS, daughter of **Medb** and **Ailill Mac Matach** of Connacht, betrothed to and beloved of Fraech. Her father however, concerned for his political stability with so many rival kings suiting Findabair, opposed the marriage. Her unscrupulous parents used Findabair to gain support in their fight against **Cuchulainn** in the **Táin Bó Cuailnge**; they secretly promised her hand in marriage to every hero if he would fight and defeat Cuchulainn. She died soon after Fraech was killed by Cuchulainn, either of humiliation for the virtual prostitution imposed on her or of a broken heart.

Fingal

SCOTTISH NAME FOR FINN MAC CUMHAL, whose son **Oisín** was said by James McPherson to have provided the source for his epic poem *Fingal* (1762). There is no evidence to suggest this. Fingal's Cave is a basalt formation on Staffa, an island of the Scottish Hebrides, said to have housed the hero, and Mendelssohn's atmospheric *Hebridean Overture* (1830) is often known as *Fingal's Cave*.

fingers

POTENT MAGICAL SYMBOLS. The agility of the fingers is one of the primary features that sets humankind apart from the animals, and given their centrality in the majority of everyday activities it is not surprising that many folklore customs and rituals have developed around them.

Probably the most famous use of the fingers is in playground lore, when children cross their fingers while telling a lie. The origin of the belief is that a cross will cancel out the sin, and will drive away the **Devil** who might otherwise come to take the soul in its moment of wickedness. In Western society today it is still common for people to cross their fingers 'for luck', originally a means of keeping the **evil eye** or other malign influences at bay with the sign of the cross. A similar belief lies behind the common American superstition of crossing the fingers while crossing a graveyard, as protection against evil spirits and the jealous dead. While in the graveyard, it is considered highly dangerous to point at a grave, since this is an invitation for the ghost to chase you and you will soon meet death. On the other hand, were you to be so unlucky as

to hear the call of the whip-poor-will, you can avert the death omen by pointing a finger at him. The index finger is thought to be especially potent; it was widely believed in Europe that it was poisonous, and that if it were to touch an open wound that wound would never heal. This may be the source of the polite European convention, 'it's rude to point'.

In many cultures fingers are very closely associated with life-force. The Benga of West Africa keep the first finger joints and the fingernails of the dead to pass down the generations as relics linked to the ancestral spirits, and this kind of veneration is found too in the Solomon Islands. The living may often sacrifice a finger to propitiate the dead at funeral ceremonies, especially in the Pacific Islands, and among some African tribes the finger of a sickly new-born baby may be amputated as a sacrifice to the evil spirits in the hope that its life may be spared. This is particularly common when several children in the family have died. The practice of keeping the fingers of **saints** as relics was widespread in medieval Europe too. In the light of this widespread belief that the soul of the individual is connected in some way to the fingers, it is interesting to consider the modern use of finger prints to identify an individual; the system introduced in 1901 at Scotland Yard relies on the fact that the pattern of ridges on each person's hand is unique to them. Some ancient heroes were identified rather more obviously by their fingers; **Cuchulainn** for example was said to have seven fingers on each hand.

The decimal system is based on units of ten, the standard number of fingers and thumbs on both hands, and many societies use fingers as basic counting devices. Most Western children learn to count first upon their fingers and toes, accompanied by nursery counting songs. There is even a British rhyme for which day of the week is most propitious for cutting the fingernails, which ends 'Cut them on Sunday, your safety seek, The Devil will have you the rest of the week'. Signs made with the fingers are very common in most societies, for the example the V for victory popularized by Winston Churchill or the circle formed by the thumb and index finger to mean 'OK' in modern US usage.

▷ **children's lore**; **defects**; **hand of glory**; **nails**; **Sedna**

Finn Mac Cumhal

WARRIOR HERO OF THE OLD IRISH FENIAN CYCLE. Finn Mac Cumhal or Mac Cool (the name means son of Cumhal) was the leader of Ireland's most famous band of warriors, the **Fianna**. He is thought to have lived in the third century AD, about 200 years after **Cuchulainn**, and the many legends and romances recounting his deeds and those of his warriors are known as the Fenian cycle.

In common with those of most legendary heroes, Finn's early years are replete with prodigious feats, such as throwing a boulder over a house and running to catch it on the other side. He served the bard Finegas for a time, and gained enormous wisdom by tasting fish which had fed from the nine hazel trees of wisdom. His father Cumhal was slain by Aedh Mac Morna of Connaught at the battle of Castleknock; Finn took upon himself the reorganization of the Fianna and to avenge his family perpetuated in battle the rift with Connaught which eventually brought about the end of Fenian power.

Finn's first love was a deer-woman, Sadb; she gave birth to a son who was discovered and brought back from the forest by Finn's hunting dog **Bran**. The boy, **Oisín**, grew up to be one of the most famed of the Fianna. It was Finn's own treachery in pursuing **Diarmuid** and his bride that contributed to the downfall of the Fianna. Finn is now said to be sleeping in a cave deep beneath the hills of Ireland, together with his band of heroes, ready to rise when the Fenian chant is heard again (see **sleepers**).

Finnbearra

FAIRY KING OF ULSTER. He is the subject of many tales, demonstrating typical **fairy** qualities (when an old woman offers him food he refuses the **salt**, for example), and he is generally regarded as a benevolent force in the area, bringing good crops. In some tales he seems to function as lord of the dead, whose subjects are recognized by mortals who claim to have seen them as the dead of the parish, and this accords well with the link perceived by many scholars between the land of the dead and **fairyland**.

Fionnuala see **Lir, Children of**

Firbolgs

PRIMITIVE RACE OF IRELAND, defeated by the **Fomorians** and subsequently ejected from the country by the **Tuatha De Danann**. Although these 'people of the bogs' are a mythical race, it is likely that the legend arose from early pre-Celtic tribes that suffered defeat and extinction under succeeding waves of invasion.

firebird

MAGICAL BIRD OF RUSSIAN FOLKLORE, a magnificent beast with eyes of crystal and golden wings. One of the most famous of the many tales in which it appears tells of Prince Ivan and the grey wolf; the firebird purloins apples from the king's magic tree so Ivan is instructed to stand guard and catch the thief. He cannot hold the firebird however; all that is left is a marvellous incandescent

Finn Mac Cumhal

feather. So the king sends Ivan and his two brothers on a quest to capture the firebird. The brothers prove treacherous, killing Ivan and taking the firebird and the beautiful Yelena back to their father. Ivan is resurrected by the **helpful beast** he has befriended, the grey wolf, and returns to the palace to claim his bride and take credit for his prize.

first-footing

NEW YEAR RITUAL, founded on the belief that the fortunes of the coming year are intimately bound up with the identity and attributes of the first person to cross the threshold. In many parts of the world it is considered lucky for the first-footer to enter bearing gifts—usually money, coal to symbolize warmth, or food—thus ensuring that the household will not want for comforts in the coming year. In other areas it is usual to greet the first entrant into the house with a gift, a kiss, a coin or food. It would be highly unlucky to have an ill-favoured person bring in the new year. These strong beliefs, which take various forms around the world, are bound up with the idea of **New Year** as a period of transition, and therefore vulnerable to influence of good or bad, and the focus upon the **door** reflects this preoccupation.

Fisher King

THE KEEPER OF THE HOLY GRAIL, a late addition to the Arthurian cycle and a figure almost obscured by mystery and metaphor. He goes by many names, including Bron or Brons (probably deriving from the ancient Celtic god **Bran the Blessed**), Pelles (possibly from **Pwyll** or Cornish *peller*, 'the wise one'), or Amfortas. After a wound to his thighs he is unable to ride out as a knight and passes his time fishing. He meets **Perceval** and invites him to his castle—he can be healed only by the touch of the one questing for the **Grail**. Later versions have the pure **Galahad** as the one who asks the question by which the Fisher King is healed; 'Whom does the Grail serve?'.

In earlier French works he is referred to as the Rich Fisher, and it seem likely that his original title derived not from a literal occupation but from Christ's words, 'I will make ye fishers of men'. There is also a pun with French *pécheur*, 'sinner', which embraces two key concepts of folklore; the physical defect corresponding to inner evil or wrongdoing, and the health of the **king bound** up with the health of the land (by ancient Irish law no man with a physical defect could become High King). In some versions he is the father of **Elaine**.

flamenco

COUPLE OR SOLO DANCE OF THE ANDALUSIAN GYPSIES. It is a powerful, dramatic and erotic dance, characterized by complex rhythms, counterpointed by clicking fingers and stamping feet, sinuous arm and body movements and, especially for the men, elaborate footwork. *Cante jondo* or *grande*, 'deep song', is the most moving and intense form of flamenco, occasionally sung unaccompanied but usually sung to the characteristic strumming of the guitar. Both music and dance betray some Hindu influence, in tonality and sinuous gestures. Lighter forms of flamenco, *chico*, are more purely Spanish. The

flamenco

castanets so closely associated with flamenco in popular imagination were not in fact part of the original gypsy tradition.

The word *flamenco* is thought to refer to the flamingo bird and by extension to the Flemings, alluding to their high pinkish colour as perceived by darker-skinned Andalusians.

flea

SMALL, BLOOD-SUCKING INSECT of the order Sisphonaptera. Fleas have troubled humankind for centuries, and a large body of flea-lore has developed concerning their habits and the best way to rid oneself of them. In one European animal tale which has migrated to Texas a **fox** evicts his unwelcome guests by backing into a pool of water with a hay bundle or piece of moss in his mouth. As the water rises the fleas migrate to the hay, and finally the fox opens his mouth and submerges himself while the fleas float away. In ancient Egypt a slave of little value would be smeared with milk as a decoy so that every flea in the house would be attracted to him. According to Pliny, one has only to take the earth on which your right foot is standing at the very moment the first **cuckoo** of spring calls, and sprinkle it around the house (particularly in the bed) to be free of fleas all year. If still troubled, one should jump over the Midsummer bonfire according to English lore. In Britain fleas are thought to return each 1 March, and if the doors and windows are clean and barred to them on this date they will go elsewhere. A flea bite is not always bad news; in Austria and Germany a bite on the hand indicates that a kiss is imminent, and should you find yourself deserted by fleas it is recognized in many areas as a sign that you have not long to live.

Fleeing Pancake see Gingerbread Man

fleur-de-lis

HERALDIC EMBLEM, particularly associated with the French royal arms. It is a stylized representation of a **lily**, although similar designs occur in art around the world and do not always represent flowers. The lily is traditionally the

fleur-de-lis

emblem of purity, and a French legend tells how Clovis (King of the Franks, c.466–511) received a lily from heaven at his baptism. From the time of Louis VIII the golden lilies on a blue background were established as the royal arms, but in 1376 Charles V decreed that there should be only three fleurs-de-lis, in honour of the Trinity.

floating islands

MOTIF OF FOLKLORE, an **otherworld** of pleasure such as **Tir Nan Og** in Irish lore.

In classical mythology **Jason** succeeded in evading two rather different floating islands, the Symplegades, which crashed together to crush any ship that attempted to sail between them. Jason sent a pigeon between the rocks as the Argos was poised to pass; the islands rammed together, and as they withdrew the Argos sailed at top speed between them, emerging with only a grazed stern as the rocks belatedly realized the trick. After this defeat, the islands became fixed, and never troubled sea-farers again. A similar Inuit tale has a kayak evading two clashing ice-bergs, and comparable tales have been recorded throughout North America. Such floating islands are related to the clashing gateway or passage, for example the rocky gates of Teutonic lore that close so quickly upon the adventurer that he loses a heel. The gates to the **underworld** are equally perilous. Some scholars have seen in this common theme an echo of the *vagina dentata* preoccupation.

Floral Dance see Furry Dance

flute

WIND INSTRUMENT, one of the earliest and most widespread of all musical instruments. Sound is produced by blowing across a narrow hole at one end of a tube rather than by a vibrating reed, and as early as Neolithic times finger-holes had been added to give variety of pitch. Although in most cases flutes are played with the mouth, the nose flute is especially common in Oceania, and the Greek Aeolian flute was played on by the breeze. Flutes may be vertical or, as in the classic Western flute, transverse; some globular flutes are fashioned to resemble animals or birds.

Generally however the flute is tubular, and this shape has accorded it much significance in folklore around the world as an emblem of masculinity. Flutes are played throughout North and South America during courtship dances, and in fertility rituals and **harvest celebrations**. Partly because of its simple construction from reeds and also because of its close association with pastoral gods such as Pan, the pipe is traditionally thought of as the shepherd's instrument. The resemblance of the flute's note to animal calls has reinforced the common motif that a musician can captivate animals, and in a Kurdish folktale a humble shepherd wins his bride by playing so beautifully that his sheep forgo water for three days, thus fulfilling his impossible **task**.

Flying Dutchman, The

PHANTOM SHIP, said to haunt the seaways around the Cape of Good Hope bringing doom to all who see it. According to legend, the Dutchman himself was Hendrik Vanderdecken, who cursed God as he struggled to navigate the waters of the Cape in a storm, or alternatively made a pact with the **Devil** in return for a safe voyage, and now he and his men are doomed to sail eternally round the Southern Capes seeking forgiveness. George V of Britain, then a prince, recorded a sighting of the ghost ship in 1881, which was followed by the deaths of two crew members. The story inspired Wagner's opera *Der Fliegende Hollander* (1843).
▷ **phantom ships**

The Flying Dutchman

Fodla

OLD IRISH QUEEN, one of the three encountered by the invading **Milesians**, who gave her name to Ireland.
▷ **Banba**; Ériu

folk art

TRADITIONAL ART OF FOLK CULTURE, the non-elite, self-taught, visual art and craft of an ethnic group. Since 'folk' and 'art' are both terms whose precise definition remains elusive, folk art itself is notoriously difficult to pin down. Any art produced by a small, non-urban and non-industrialized group which perpetuates designs and methods traditionally used within that group is unarguably folk art. The artist works within a range of designs, techniques and materials prescribed by tradition, but the artistic traditions which draw inspiration from such designs are not truly of the folk, since such derivative art operates under artificially, not culturally, imposed restrictions.

Folk art generally produces functional, hand-made objects for a specific use within the community, or a work which utilizes imagery and symbols meaningful to the group specifically. Artefacts may range from pots to portraits, from christening robe to carpenter's bench, from children's toys to religious images. As in folk narrative, folk artists do not set a premium on originality but rather on conservatism, preserving the traditional representations of repetitive events in the life of the community (birth, death, marriage, harvest etc) and the functional designs taught by the previous generation. Art and craft become almost inseparable terms here, although many philosophers have treated them as mutually exclusive. It has been said that art is creative, expressive and, as Oscar Wilde said, entirely useless, whereas craft serves a definite function and is constructed to a preconceived plan. The artist, it is argued, cannot foreknow exactly the result of his labour; the craftsman can and indeed must. To view a work of art is primarily a contemplative, private experience; in this case, folk art itself becomes a problematic term since it refers to art for and by a community of people. Although folk art is generally produced by a single craftsman, it is a communal product in that it reflects the preoccupations, needs and aesthetic preferences of the community and only secondarily those of the individual, whereas a work of fine art is thought to express the artist's personal vision. The philosophical debate rages on, but it seems clear that the enormous aesthetic value of much folk art cannot be dismissed as merely utilitarian.

Primitive art
In its strict definition, folk art can only exist in apposition to academic or elitist art traditions of the society; where there is no such elitist art among the ruling or moneyed classes, the art of the people is more properly known as primitive art, where primitive means not elementary or inferior but belonging to an entirely unsophisticated culture, or the early period of a developed one. This art may be crude, but is often highly aesthetically developed. Primitive art is often concerned with religion, myth and magic; the amulets and icons of elementary cultures are examples, and in non-literate groups it can often function vitally as a means of communication. Egyptian hieroglyphs are a development of such primitive art. A feature of primitive art (and of folk art in general) is its disregard for the Western convention of naturalism. Animal features are often incorporated in anthropomorphic designs, and highly stylized abstract patterns may be used in the representation of the supernatural, which since it cannot be seen requires its own set of conventions in visual art. Among Native American tribes, for example, the **culture hero** will be so familiar that his form (a **coyote** or **rabbit** perhaps) can be distorted or abstracted into the design of a totem pole yet still retain its significance for the group. Items of art are themselves often invested with power: intricately carved totem **masks** or face painting which imparts the qualities of an animal to a warrior; the **talisman** which gives speed to the hunter or skill to the craftsman. In folk art the potency of such symbols is often lost, although the designs are retained and accepted as part of tradition; the sense of the object actually being imbued with supernatural power as in primitive art is extremely rare.

Materials and methods
Both primitive and folk artists share a tendency to use as their materials whatever is most readily to hand; where elitist art uses marble for sculpture the folk artist will reach for wood, shells or horn; where fine art is produced on canvas folk art appears on the side of **boats**, houses or cooking pots, on fur, leaves and bark. To a large extent the nature of these materials and the available tools dictate the methods used. The item is always hand-made without the aid of mechanical devices, and although it may occasionally be primarily decorative, such as the famous portraits of American folk art, it usually serves a useful function in the community. Typically there is no sub-division of skills; one craftsman works to produce the finished piece. A folk artist is an amateur in that he or she has no formal training and produces for his or her own use and pleasure, or for that of a small cultural group. However many artisans use their trade aesthetically; a blacksmith might turn his skill to producing an exquisite wrought-iron gate. The productive processes tend to be mechanically simple, but the manual skills required may be immensely complex, from intricate embroidery stitches to layering vegetable dyes onto hide.

Folk art and elite art

Although the two traditions of folk art and elite art are clearly distinct, they are seldom entirely separate. Elite art, usually developed around urban or courtly centres, tends to move to the dictates of fashion or with the influence of immigrants or travellers, whereas folk art, in more isolated areas, is more self-referential and conservative. Some influence from fashion inevitably percolates down however, and in time the cultural patterns of the elite may at least partly reshape those of the folk, often a century or so after their vogue. In the course of immigration from the Old to the New World many of the folk art traditions of Europe underwent gradual but radical change as the settlers adapted to their new environment and its demands, and the early colonial art of the Americas was born. The French in Canada for example used indigenous wood to make cathedrals in the style of the stone-built ones back home. Many of the cultural advances in Europe and Asia especially were linked to the development of religion, and these advances were taken up in different ways by the peasantry. So while magnificent cathedrals were being built in the cities and the Byzantine and Renaissance forms of religious painting developed the folk produced their own devotional art; roadside shrines to the Virgin or village Buddha sprang up, and the new religious symbolism was cheerfully grafted onto earlier pagan traditions (see **Christianity and folklore**).

With the rise of industrialization and increased communication in Western Europe in the 19th century, pure folk art began to die out since functional items were now made available more quickly, cheaply and to a much higher technical standard than the hand-worker could hope to match. Even as folk art decreased however there was a movement in the elite art world to recognize its aesthetic and, in the developing nationalism of the time, its cultural value. Artists began consciously to derive motifs and inspiration from folk designs, and the naive or folksy style became popular and has been periodically revived up to the present day. Henri Rousseau was a naive painter who successfully crossed into the world of academic art at the turn of the century.

The rise of Romanticism in Germany in the early 19th century brought with it a recognition of the importance of folk art to the national identity and also a sense of individual value, of the craftsman taking pride in his work and enjoying the act of creation. In most areas of Western Europe now, with industrialization long established, folk art in its pure form has virtually died out, but like **folk song** and **fairy tales** it has been reborn as a form of popular culture.

folk instruments

THE MOST BASIC INSTRUMENTS, and the most widely used in folk music, are those made simply out of materials to hand: **rattles**, grass whistles, long trumpet-like pieces of wood. These are all distributed throughout the world, and it seems likely that different cultures developed them

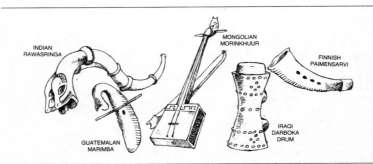

INDIAN RAWASRINGA

MONGOLIAN MORINKHUUR

FINNISH PAIMENSARVI

GUATEMALAN MARIMBA

IRAQI DARBOKA DRUM

folk instruments

independently. They are associated particularly with primitive religion and ritual, for example the **bull-roarer** whose harsh cry is thought to represent the voice of supernatural spirits, and in more developed societies they are often made and used by children. More sophisticated instruments such as simple **fiddles**, bagpipes and the xylophone probably spread from Asian civilizations, while others were adapted by European folk cultures in particular from classical or popular forms. The hurdy-gurdy, for example, is descended from the medieval organistrum, and the **guitar** and violin survive in both art and folk styles of music.

Instrumental melody exists to some extent in isolation from the folk song, where it functions as background to dancing, for example, and tunes may be matched to different words. It is rare in true folk culture however to have music unaccompanied by ritual, dance or lyric, played purely for entertainment, as is usual in the classical tradition. Music, like all other folk art forms, is founded on its function within the everyday life and ritual of the community.

folk music

ORAL TRADITION OF LYRIC AND MELODY, vital to the functioning and identity of a society. Like folk art, folk music can only truly be said to exist alongside an alternative urban, elite or popular tradition. These other forms tend to be disseminated by the media, to be subject to fluctuations of fashion and outside influence, and to reflect the relative economic prosperity and cultural diversity of the population. Folk music, on the other hand, is the property of a smaller, more homogeneous cultural group and deals with themes pertaining to the entire group; it is transferred orally rather than in writing or recording and is thus subject to change and development with each performance. In general folk songs are shared by the entire group, and specific training and formal techniques are rare, although talented performers are of course recognized. This contrasts with the popular and elite music traditions, in which performers are set apart from audience and much emphasis is laid on rehearsal and teaching.

Some folk songs are however intended for a specific small group or individual, such as the lyric songs of Yugoslavia usually sung by women, or special bridal songs. Occasionally gifted singers or bards may approach professional status, called upon by the community for their skill in entertaining or keening.

Development of the folk song

The impulse to sing seems to be universal in human society, like those of dancing and creative art. In pre-literate or primitive cultural groups songs often carry a magical significance, such as love spells or invocation of spirits, and their use may be carefully controlled. In many societies, primitive and otherwise, songs are used as preparation for wars, death, marriage etc, and during work such as harvesting, to lighten the communal spirit and originally perhaps to safeguard the crop. As the individual reaches the various turning-points of life, these are marked in specific songs in which other members of the group may participate, binding the life of the individual into the wider life of the community. Babies are sung the same lullabies, as children they sing game-songs together, and each stage of their growth is accompanied by songs teaching the moral code of the group and its shared heritage. The significant days of the group are marked by song too, for example the Christmas **carols** and wassails of Europe. Only in relatively highly-developed cultures does narrative folk song feature as a popular folk form.

It seems clear then that folk songs were originally primarily functional in form, created as a framework for communal activity and to mark the significance of certain times in the calendar or in the life of an individual. These functional songs tend to be the simplest in form, with much repetition, and they are generally found in societies which have had little historical contact with the progressive urban musical traditions. The highly-developed narrative forms such as the **ballad**, common in Western Europe, the Russian **byliny** or the long narrative poems sung in Asia, appear to be a later development.

Folk and urban music

In the Romantic view, folk songs were a

spontaneous outpouring of the simple peasant spirit, untroubled by artistic theory and utterly unselfconscious. There is some truth in this certainly, but in general the integrity of the folk tradition is not so absolute. Literary sources have often been found for popular songs, and the fashionable styles often filter through to the folk in a belated and attenuated form, to be incorporated into the existing tradition which although fundamentally conservative is constantly changing and developing in small ways if it is still alive. In its turn folk music has affected the songs of the urban traditions, and from the late 18th century onwards there have been many folk revivals in Europe and later in America too. Folk music is now considered by many as a brand of popular music, although since it is written down, performed by professionals with sophisticated electrical equipment and broadcast to an audience containing vastly different cultural traditions and lifestyles it is certainly not folk music in the technical sense. The Protestant Reformation claimed many traditional tunes for its new hymns and the folk songs of the settlers in New England in the 17th and 18th centuries are virtually inseparable from their hymns.

Form and structure
The forms of folk song vary across the world from 'nonsense' lyrics, often originally significant as incantations or a call to war or work, to epic narrative works such as those performed in Scandinavia, or lyric songs of tragic love in Eastern Europe. A common characteristic is a strong emphasis on rhythm, with the singers accompanied by **drums**, **rattles** or simply the beating of feet or hands. There may be no other musical accompaniment, or there may be instruments such as **fiddles**, **flutes** or pipes.

Repetition is an almost universal feature of folk song, as it is to a lesser extent of folk tales, since it aids memory and provides a strong structural framework. Refrains are frequently used at the end of each stanza for this purpose; often such a refrain may consist of a string of meaningless sounds, which may suggest that it has been imported from older,

forgotten forms. The organization of the song depends very much on the language pattern of the group; in Eastern European syllable-timed languages for example, where rhythm is determined by syllable count rather than the metric foot, the lyrics tend to be organized in lines of a given number of syllables. One common example is the Deseterac, the ten-syllable line of Slavic folk song. The stanza is widely used as a larger repetitive unit, as it accords well with the preference for short easily remembered forms in folk song in general. In much of Europe the four-line stanza, with a simple rhyme scheme such as abab or aabb is common, and in Yugoslavia the favoured form is the couplet. Melodic form ranges from the very simple, for example the single repeated musical line of many children's songs, to the choral songs of Russia and the Ukraine in which there may be four different parts. Polyphony is uncommon in Britain and much of Western Europe, although very complex monophonic melodies have developed, but it occurs more frequently in the South and East of Europe. Parallel singing, the melody sung by two voices a consistent musical interval apart, is a widespread form of polyphony in Asia and parts of Europe.

It has often been noted by folklorists that singers find it difficult if not impossible to give the text of a folksong without singing it. The words and melody are inseparable, although tunes may be interchangeable; the same or a similar melody line may serve for a number of songs. The performance aspect is vital to folk song as it is to narrative tales, and in addition to the text and basic melody, the style of performance is what brings a folksong to life and makes it truly authentic. Traditional details of style such as ornamental notes and intonation are an intrinsic part of the whole. There are two main schools of style in European folk song: *parlando rubato*, which is free in its interpretation of metrical and rhythmical structure, and *tempo giusto* which is more controlled and precise. It is especially difficult to accurately notate folk songs sung in *parlando rubato* style. The fact that folk singers have no formal training and that they seldom come into contact with perfectly tuned instruments means too that the pitch and intonation are more flexible than in urban traditions.

Fomorians

MYTHICAL RACE OF IRELAND, a savage people who appear to have been the country's original inhabitants, since no mention is made in the records of their arrival. Each of the invading groups had to battle with this demon-like race until they were finally defeated and evicted by the **Tuatha de Danann** at the battle of Mag Tured. Their name is sometimes used as an emblem for all the hostile forces against which humankind must battle—weather, storm, disease, sea and so on.
▷ **Firbolgs**

food taboo

MOTIF OF FOLKTALES, commonly found in tales of an **otherworld**, especially the underworld. To eat food while sojourning there makes one unable to return to the land of the living. Hence in Finnish lore **Väinämöinen** refused a drink of beer in Tuonela, twilight island of the dead, and the Greek grain goddess Persephone was fated to spend six months of the year in the underworld for eating that number of **pomegranate** seeds there. Those who eat food in fairyland become immortal, but can never return home.
▷ **fairyland**; **taboo**

footprint

THE IMPRESSION OF A HUMAN FOOT in the ground is thought by many groups to contain something of the life essence of its author. This property can be used for good; in the American South black slaves would take earth from their beloved's footprint and carry it with them as a love charm to make the object of their desire follow them, and the Zuñi of North America believe that a similar charm will keep a spouse faithful. Should the fairy host pass you on All Hallow's Eve (Samhain) in Ireland, you can compel them to release any humans they may have abducted by throwing after them the dust from your print. **Ashes** strewn around the cradle of a new-born baby in many parts of Africa will reveal the next morning the identity

of the **bush soul** which has visited in the night.

Usually however a footprint leaves one vulnerable to less amiable influences, and the common practice of obliterating one's prints is due to more than just the practical fear of being followed. In parts of Australia and Africa, an enemy can lame a man by placing sharp stones or glass in the imprint of his foot, and in Asia a sore on the foot is attributed to an evilly disposed person with access to a footprint.

Marks on rocks, mountains and fields throughout the world are identified as the indelible footprints of some god, hero or saint. The footprint appears in Icelandic folktales as a **life token**, filling with blood when the hero dies in battle, or water if he drowns. Other common motifs include the transformation into animal form brought about by drinking from that animal's tracks, and the magic footprint that imparts something of the author's virtue, as in the Good King **Wenceslas** story, where the page gains warmth from treading in his master's steps.

forso

GHOSTS OF NORTHERN AUSTRALASIA, troublesome spirits who must be placated with offerings or by frequent human company if they are not to become restless and vindictive. Ancestral bones are often kept on display in the village to reduce the risk of the forso becoming displeased.

Fortunate Islands see Islands of the Blest

Fortunatus

MEDIEVAL FOLKTALE HERO, probably from Asian sources, who possessed a variety of **magic objects** such as a wishing cap and an inexhaustible purse of money.

fox

ANIMAL OF FOLKLORE, of legendary cunning and swiftness. Western traditions of fox lore have developed largely from the shrewd, amoral creature of **Aesop**'s fables. In a typical tale a fox who has fallen down a well-shaft persuades a goat

fox

to leap in after him for a drink and makes his escape by climbing on the goat's back, leaving his more foolish companion to his fate. This shrewd instinct for self-preservation is shown in other Aesopic fables; a **lion** who captured his prey by pretending to be sick and then pouncing on those who ventured too close could not persuade a vixen to the same fate, since she noticed that of the many tracks going into the lion's cave none appeared to come out again.

Similarly, a hunting party of lion, ass and fox set about distributing their catch. The ass divided it into three equal portions and was promptly torn apart by the lion, who then invited the fox to make the division. Profiting from the fate of his friend, the fox gave the entire catch to the lion and professed himself happy with the scraps.

The second main source of Western fox-lore, which in turn springs at least partly from Aesopic tradition, is the medieval beast satire cycles of **Reynard the Fox**, in which the hero is amoral, sly and crafty yet still sympathetic, overcoming brute force and stupidity to survive by his cunning.

The fox is one of the chief characters in Oriental **shape-shifting** tales. Whereas in European lycanthropy belief a human is temporarily transformed into a **wolf**, Eastern shapeshifters are essentially animals who can take human shape. Usually the foxes are female, and in their sexual relationships with humans they feed on their lover's life-essence. The characteristics of foxes in much Asian lore are their eroticism and debauchery, and foxes who have transformed themselves into humans are often discovered when drunk, since they revert to their animal shape. Although foxes are occasionally faithful and affectionate to their human paramours, they are represented as malicious and mischievous in the majority of tales.

▷ **Abe no Yasuna**; **beast marriage**; **fox maiden**

fox maiden

CYCLE OF FOLKTALES, found widely throughout Eurasia and America but probably originating in China, closely related to the **swan maiden** type. A man is astonished to arrive home one night to find the dinner prepared and the house clean. After several days have passed in the same way, the puzzled man decides to keep watch, and discovers that a fox slips into his house and sheds its skin to become a beautiful woman who tends the house. He steals the discarded skin and hides it, then marries the woman and lives in contentment for several years. One day however his wife discovers her fox skin and runs off, or alternatively her husband comments on her musky smell and she disappears, offended.

Francis of Assisi, St (1181–1226)

'IL POVERELLO'. The young Francis followed his father into the silk business, spending his spare time in hedonistic extravagance until his capture as a prisoner of war in 1202, when fighting against the Perugians. He was held for a year, and soon after his release underwent a long period of serious illness: the experience was a sobering one. Back in Assisi after the wars, while praying in the run-down church of San Damiano, he saw a vision of Christ speaking to him, saying 'Repair my home, which is falling into disrepair.' Ever literally-minded, Francis began to raise the money to pay for the rebuilding of San Damiano by selling a bale of cloth from his father's warehouse. A fiery conflict ensued between father and son, which ended only when Francis dramatically renounced his inheritance, throwing down even the clothes he was wearing, and left empty-handed to espouse 'Lady Poverty' (cf **nudity**).

Begging around the town he raised enough money to complete the rebuilding of San Damiano, and lived otherwise as a homeless pilgrim, owning nothing, caring for the sick and always preaching. Within a few years he had attracted several followers; they settled at the Portincula chapel, near a leper colony in Assisi, forming a community dedicated to poverty, community life and inter-dependence. The brothers studied little as they did not even own books; simplicity rather than learning was the concern of the new community. After founding the Poor Clares with St Clare, a community of women living by his rules, Francis headed east for several abortive attempts to convert the Saracens. He returned after a time of pilgrimage in the Holy Land, disappointed by his failure and disillusioned by the Crusaders whom he had seen to be debauched adventurers rather than holy warriors.

Many of Francis's most famous doings belong to the last period of his life, after his official leadership of the Franciscans. He built the first Christmas crib at Grecchia in 1223, beginning a custom still celebrated across the Christian world. Even more famous perhaps was his experience of the stigmata while praying on Mount La Verna in 1224, wounds on his body corresponding to those inflicted on Christ in his Passion; these were said to be visible until his death, although Francis usually kept them covered. His last years were marked by blindness and intense pain, both from illness and from the attempts of doctors to cure him.

After Francis's death at the age of 45, the Franciscans became a unique force for reform and evangelism throughout Europe, although the developing movements of reform and scholarship within its ranks tended to compromise the original simplicity of Francis's ideals, especially his strictures on absolute poverty.

Francis himself has always been an enormously popular saint, loved for his austerely attractive poverty, his dramatic life story and his legendary affinity with nature. He is a favourite with artists, usually shown as a small Franciscan, bearded and bearing the stigmata, in any one of a number of scenes from his life: throwing off his clothes before his father and marrying Lady Poverty, surrounded by animals and birds, together with St Clare, St Dominic and the Virgin, or contemplating a skull. He has been popularly adopted as the patron of all animal lovers, which to some extent is a distortion of his concerns. His feast-day is 12 August, and he is patron saint of merchants, animals, animal welfare societies and (since 1980) ecology.

Frederick I see **Barbarossa**

Friar Rush

GERMAN HOUSEHOLD SPIRIT, Bruder Rausch. A mischievous **puck**-like spirit, who was responsible for getting people drunk, he later developed a more sinister aspect as a minion of the **Devil**, appearing to monks and others under religious vows and tempting them to fall away from their oaths.

Friar Tuck

THE JOVIAL MONK, companion of **Robin Hood** and a key figure in **May Day** celebrations in England. Despite his popularity, he was a relatively late addition to the legend.

Friday

THE DAY OF CHRIST'S CRUCIFIXION, therefore a particularly ill-omened day in general European lore. It is usual to avoid beginning ventures such as voyages, journeys, business schemes or marriage on a Friday, especially if the date coincides with that unluckiest of numbers, **thirteen**. Dying on a Friday, however, is considered fortunate by the Irish; one can be buried on the Saturday and have a Mass on the Sunday.

frog

TAILLESS AMPHIBIAN, usually having smooth, moist skin, long legs designed for leaping and swimming, and protruding eyes. Species of frog are found throughout the world, most usually as aquatic creatures but occasionally dwelling on land or in trees. In many cultures the frog is closely associated with rain because of its affinity with water; Plato considered the frog as a rain-bringer and in many Native American groups the frog is invoked as the power of water (the Great Frog Spirit) during rain-making ceremonies.

The connection with life-giving rain, and the contrast of the frog's moist skin with the dry dustiness of death, have led many peoples to view the frog as an emblem of resurrection, and frog **amulets** have been found in many ancient Egyptian tombs. The Egyptian goddess Hekt or Heket, a creator with responsibility for the new-born, was represented with a frog's face. In Christian lore too the frog is often linked with resurrection, but confusion with the **toad**, an attribute of the **Devil** and poison, has muddled the symbolism.

The cacophonous croaking of a frog community has given rise to much folklore, most notably the common Eurasian concept of the parliament of frogs, producing more noise than enlightenment. A fable of **Aesop**'s with many parallels in East European lore tells how the frogs assembled to petition Zeus to send them a king. Zeus acceded to their request and threw into their pond a log, which made such a splendid splash that the frogs were suitably awed and impressed with their new ruler. Soon however they grew bolder, and finally, tiring of a king who did nothing even when they climbed all over him, they reconvened and asked Zeus to send another, more animated king. Zeus obliged by sending a **stork**, which began devouring them. Again the frogs clamoured to Zeus, but he was weary of their pestering and refused to act. Aesop is said to have told the tale to Athenians pressing for the overthrow of Pisistratus, as a warning to let well alone.

In a West African tale, the frog brings death into the world by reaching the gods with his own message before the dog sent by humans to ask for their eternal life. In another tale, also told by **Aesop**, the frog tries to puff himself up to the size of an ox and bursts in the attempt. Probably the best known of all English folksongs is *Frog Went a-Courting* or *The Frog He Would a-Wooing Go* (first mentioned in 1580 as *A Moste Strange Weddinge of the Frogge and the Mowse*), detailing the wedding feast and the various guests. This is an elaborate example of the birds' wedding tale-type found widely in Europe, and the frogs'

council parallels the court of birds, although it lacks the presiding authority of the **eagle**.

Frog Prince, The

EUROPEAN FAIRY TALE, collected by the brothers Grimm. It has many features in common with **Beauty and the Beast** but is generally regarded as an independent tale-type since it lacks the important **taboo** motif. A young princess promises a frog that he can eat with her and share her bed if he retrieves the golden ball that she has lost down a well. The frog returns the ball and she thinks no more of her promise until he arrives at the palace gates to remind her. The king orders his daughter to keep her word, and the frog eats with her and is duly taken to her room that night. When he demands to be lifted onto her pillow the princess throws him against the wall in revolted temper; the spell is broken, his princely shape restored, and the two marry.

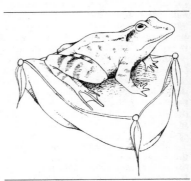

The Frog Prince

The figure of the trusted servant appears as **Faithful Henry**, the erstwhile companion of the prince before his translation, who had had three bands of iron laid round his heart to stop it bursting with grief. These bands spring asunder when the overjoyed servant witnesses the restoration of his master and his marriage to the princess.
▷ **beast marriage; Faithful John**

Frolka Stay-at-Home

RUSSIAN FOLK-TALE HERO, a **dragon-slayer** who rescues three princesses by slaying the many-headed dragons that guard them.

funeral customs

RITUALS TO APPEASE THE DEAD AND PROTECT THE LIVING. In archaeological and historical investigations, some of the most valuable evidence for the beliefs, customs and development of ancient civilizations is to be found in the tomb. The Egyptians buried great wealth with their kings, together with food and drink to equip them for the journey into the **afterlife** in the manner to which they had become accustomed. Often in Teutonic cultures shoes are provided, for comfort on the arduous journey.

In many areas of the world graves are constructed with huts or underground chambers in which the soul of the dead person may be made comfortable. Many burial customs derive from a desire to placate the spirit of the deceased and to prevent it from returning in jealous dissatisfaction to haunt the living, and this may be the origin of the common habit of taking flowers or, in non-Western countries, sacrifices and libations to the grave. The **cairn**, a pile of stones placed over the grave to which the passer-by is traditionally invited to add one as he passes, served not only to mark the grave and protect the body from predatory animals, but also to keep restrained the spirit of the dead. The custom of throwing soil or **ashes** into the grave may have had a similar origin, to 'lay the ghost', or it may have derived from the practice of throwing gifts to be buried with the body. The gravestone common in Europe probably developed from earlier shrines or from the cairns; it now serves mainly to mark the grave and to express hopes of immortality or praise for the deceased. Even the tradition of 'not speaking ill of the dead', and the graveside eulogy which often contains more flattery than sincerity, may derive from this primitive taboo against angering the dead.

Similarly, many rites traditionally practised at funerals have developed from the primitive desire to protect the living from the influence of the dead wishing to return or to take another with them. It has been suggested that the wearing of black, common as a mark of mourning in the West, was originally designed to make those near the corpse less conspicuous and therefore less likely to attract to themselves evil forces. Likewise, the mourners were careful to avoid direct sunlight, hence the custom of drawing the curtains in a house which has recently seen a death. The wearing of sackcloth and ashes was originally a precaution against the envy of the dead rather than a sign of grief; for this reason too, many peoples attend funerals barefoot, or at least in old clothes and shoes. Mourning clothes also serve to disguise the living and thus protect them from the unwelcome attentions of the deceased spirit. The dead person may wish to draw another member of the family with him, so he is usually carried from the house feet first so that he cannot beckon another to follow. Once the funeral procession is underway, it is considered unlucky to have to stop it; the restless spirit must be laid to rest as quickly as possible.

Furies

VENGEFUL SPIRITS OF CLASSICAL LORE, the Erinyes (the angry ones), also known euphemistically, and less accurately, as the Eumenides (the kind ones). In Graeco-Roman mythology they were said to be daughters of Gaea (the earth) who sprang from the blood of her consort, Uranus, although Sophocles has them as daughters of Gaea and Darkness. They became formalized in literature as a group of three and were even given suitable names: Alecto, Tisiphone and Megaera. Their function was to pursue and torment guilty men.

Their origins are obscure, but it is possible that they derive from the ancient tradition of the vengeful **ghost**, returning to revenge itself on the murderer. They may also be the personification of **curses**.

Furry Dance

CORNISH SPRING CELEBRATION, often known as the Floral Dance from a 19th-century mistranslation from Latin *feriae* (festival). It is traditionally performed on 8 May at Helston, part of the pre-Christian rites of Spring celebrated throughout the country, and has sur-

vived in modern times as a processional
dance by prominent townsfolk.

fylfot

ALTERNATIVE NAME FOR THE SWASTIKA, a
15th-century word possibly derived from
fill-foot, meaning a design to 'fill the
foot' of a stained-glass window.

fylgia

NORWEGIAN SHADOW SOUL, a guardian
spirit or occasionally a **doppelgänger**.
Although the fylgia frequently appears
in dreams, often in animal form, to see it
while awake is an omen of death.
▷ **fetch; wraith**

gae bulg

'NOTCHED SPEAR', the awesome spear of **Cuchulainn** in Old Irish legend. Formed from the bones of a sea monster, it was notched in such a way that it caused massive damage on being withdrawn from the body. Cuchulainn received it from Aoife, and it was this spear that he used in ignorance to kill their son **Conla** when he came seeking his father. In the **Táin Bó Cuailnge** Cuchulainn kills his friend **Ferdiad** with the gae bulg, and in his last battle he is tricked by one of **Medb**'s satirists into throwing the gae bulg and is soon afterwards slain.

Galahad, Sir

KNIGHT OF ARTHURIAN ROMANCE, the son of **Lancelot of the Lake** and Elaine, the pure knight able to succeed in the quest for the Holy **Grail** and to be blessed with a vision of God. His worth is proved when he sits with impunity on the Siege Perilous, left empty at the **Round Table** for the one who will succeed in the Grail quest.

In the earliest Arthurian tales the blundering **Perceval** is the hero of the Grail cycle, replaced in later versions by Lancelot, but in the mystical climate of the medieval Christianity of the 13th century a more chaste, austere and morally upright figure, whose lineage could be traced back to the House of David, developed. Galahad first appears in Walter Map's *Queste del Saint Graal*, part of the Vulgate cycle (or *Prose Lancelot*).

games

TRADITIONAL RECREATION. The games played by the children of a society reflect the everyday nature of adult life within it. True folk games are those handed down from each generation of children to the next, and played spontaneously, not organized or initiated by adults.

Most of these games have clearly defined, often very complex, rules, which are however rarely rigid, and are usually adapted by the children as they play. Many psychologists have seen in this universal tendency to play an essential social function; the games are a means of practising the skills of social intercourse or directly relevant skills to be used in adult life such as domestic work or hunting. As children become aware of the possibilities and uncertainties of the world, as well as observing the everyday routines of their elders they assert their growing control and imagination in 'pretending' games, in which they act out their responses to realistic or fantastic situations. Another social function of games is their emphasis on roles, the opportunity to command one's fellows, to initiate a new game, or to compete with each other. In virtually all cases games are characterized by a strict morality; the rules must be accepted by all the players and if they are broken by an individual that person is accused of cheating. This sets the game situation apart from normal life, in which achieving effectiveness is usually more important than accepting restrictions. No children's game is ever truly anarchic, since as soon as the rules break down the satisfaction of pursuing the game is lost. This morality however is self-imposed, and the rules and purposes of games often bear little reference to adult morality. Games may be used as illicit courtship rituals away from parental eyes, for example in the widespread 'kiss-chase' type in which the girl caught is kissed by her captor as a penalty or reward, depending on age and point of view. Many 'pretend' games such as 'doctors and nurses' serve too as opportunity for early sexual exploration.

The conservatism of children's games is astonishing; popular European and North American games such as hide-

and-seek, tug o' war and blindman's buff have survived virtually unchanged from classical times, and the convention of making a certain gesture while pronouncing an agreed word to gain respite was known in the Middle Ages. As in every field of folklore, along with this conservative tendency runs a living tradition which constantly varies the details of the game with time and distance. Iona and Peter Opie, in *Children's Games in Street and Playground*, give as an example the popular British game 'Off Ground He', in which a player avoids being caught by perching above ground level, which is known as Dobby off-ground in Nottingham, High Tig in Scotland, Off-ground Touch in the West Country and by many other variants. In some cases too the sanctuary is specified as, for example, a stone wall.

Scholars have long disputed the exact categories into which games should be placed for consideration, and the fluid nature of the material has complicated the issue. Broadly speaking, children's games fall into two categories: physical games requiring strength or dexterity and games of chance which require guesswork or luck. Alongside these exist the more loosely constructed imitative games, in which children assume roles mimicking those of the adult world, such as Mummies and Daddies. Into these categories can be fitted most of the truly traditional games. Some of the games requiring specialized equipment, whilst distinct from the more spontaneous games played with whatever came to hand, pebbles, chalk or sticks, are nevertheless so flexible that they too pass into the folklore of a culture, for example games played with marbles.

In Western society, increased sophistication has meant the loss of games traditionally played by adults; the games now in vogue require sophisticated equipment and inflexible rules with little scope left for spontaneity or variation. Even in many more primitive societies adult games are infrequent, since the serious business of survival and daily work takes precedence, and recreation is more likely to be expressed in activities such as communal singing or dancing. It may be, as some psychologists have it, that for adults the need to practise social and life-skills in play is no longer present.

Those games that do survive to adulthood, whether physical or mental, tend to be highly competitive, and regarded more seriously, for example chess, tennis or Adji (a backgammon-like game of counters moved between hollows on a board, widespread in Asia and Africa). The emphasis is on the social nature of the game and the skill of an individual participant who will often be fêted by the community. In some cases adult games themselves come from ancient popular traditions, although their history tends to have been more formalized than those of children, which are almost never committed to writing. Hence the many forms of games with playing cards derive from ancient Asian or Oriental cards used primarily (and still in some cases today) for **divination**.

In general however the games most interesting to the folklorist are those played unselfconsciously, and therefore usually by children, which are transmitted orally and undergo constant variation. Such games, while unlikely to require special equipment, are complex examples of group interaction which reflect the social structure and way of life of the group itself.

Gandreid

NORWEGIAN TERM FOR THE **Wild Hunt**.

Gargantua

GIANT OF MEDIEVAL EUROPE, renowned for his astonishing capacity for food. He may have originated in Celtic lore, but in the 16th century his literary fame was established by Rabelais's satire, in which Gargantua is the father of Pantagruel and leader of a group of buffoonish companions. He is said to have swallowed five pilgrims, staves and all, as a salad, and his name became proverbially applied to anyone with a large appetite (hence the adjective, gargantuan).

garlic

BULBOUS PLANT, *Allium sativum* of the family Liliaceae, with an onion-like smell and a pungent taste. Its powerful aroma has given it a reputation in

garlic

folklore around the world as a **charm** against a variety of unwholesome influences, most noticeably **vampires**, the **evil eye**, **witches**, the **Devil** and evil spirits, and it is frequently hung on the person or in the house for this purpose. By extension, it is used medicinally against any diseases, particularly those such as plague and malaria that were thought to be transmitted in the air. Modern science has confirmed the benefits of eating garlic, which has antibiotic and antiseptic properties and improves circulation.

In a Russian folktale, however, garlic is said to have sprung up from the print of the Devil's left foot (along with **onion** from that of his right foot). In areas of India too the colour of garlic can indicate the presence of evil spirits.

A belief common from Pliny's day until corrected by Sir Thomas Browne in the 17th century was that a magnetic compass becomes useless in the presence of garlic.

Gawain, Sir

ARTHURIAN KNIGHT, the nephew of **Arthur**, a hero of the earliest forms of the romances. It seems certain that Gawain is derived from a Celtic solar deity; Sir Thomas Malory and others record that his strength grew with the rising sun and failed towards evening, and several tales associated with him are drawn from Irish **Cuchulainn** lore, another hero descended from an ancient solar deity. He appears as Gwalchmei in the *Mabinogion* and Welsh lore. In the earliest tales he is a noble, heroic figure, probably the first hero of the **Grail** quest, but his best-known adventure is recorded in the 14th-century poem, *Sir Gawayne and the Grene Knight*, which records how a supernatural challenger approaches King Arthur's court and proposes a beheading bargain; he will allow a knight to strike off his head for the pledge of a return blow one year later. Gawain accepts the challenge but the Green Knight picks up his severed head and bids Gawain keep his appointment as he leaves. A year later, Gawain arrives at the Green Knight's castle but does not recognize his host. He is tested by the lady of the castle and despite her blandishments remains chaste. His only concession is to keep a magic girdle instead of giving it to his host, having vowed to give him anything he received during his stay.

When the Green Knight reveals himself Gawain prepares to receive his death-blow, but the knight only nicks his proffered neck. The bargain was a test of honour instigated by **Morgan le Fay**, and while Gawain has proved his honour his light wound is a reprimand for having kept the girdle. This is an ancient tale drawn from oral lore (cf **Bricriu's Feast**).

In later Arthurian romances, especially the Vulgate cycle, Gawain is portrayed as an unworthy knight who fails in the quest for the Grail because of his spiritual blindness and even, in later works, his cruelty and treachery, contrasting with the purity of **Galahad**.

geis

POWERFUL TABOO OR COMPULSION of Old Irish legend. To break one's geis (either by performing the forbidden action or by failing to perform the compulsory one) means death. Like **Oedipus**, most of the Old Irish heroes are fated or forced by circumstance to break their geasa and therefore die.

Gelert

DOG OF WELSH FOLKLORE, the companion of the 13th-century Prince

Llewelyn. Llewelyn returned to his castle from hunting one day to find the child he had entrusted to Gelert's care missing and the dog's teeth covered with blood. In anguish and horror the prince killed his dog on the spot, but then advancing further he discovered his son, safely sleeping beside the carcass of a wolf (in some versions a serpent) slain by Gelert.

This motif, the faithful animal rashly killed, is a common one in folktales of Asia and Europe. An Indian version of the same tale is entitled 'The Brahman and the Mongoose'. A related tale tells how a poor man leaves his beloved dog in payment for a debt at the home of a rich creditor. The dog aids the rich man by leading him to a cache of goods stolen from him and is gratefully dispatched back to his owner, with a note saying that the debt is cancelled. The poor man, thinking that the dog has run away, kills him before finding the explanatory letter.
▷ **hobyahs**

genius

ROMAN GUARDIAN SPIRIT, an attendant on the individual from birth to death determining that individual's fortune and character. In its earliest form, the genius was a masculine power paired with the iuno (juno), the house-father and house-mother who presided over the family's procreation and perpetuation. In later Roman belief however, influenced by the Greek concept of the *daemon* or *daimon*, the genius came to be regarded as a personification of the individual's nature, tastes and talents. Being divine, a genius might be worshipped by its human charge or by others, as in the case of an emperor.

A genius could also be assigned to a building or place, or even to an organization such as a trade-guild. Such genii were generally portrayed as serpents rather than humans.

geomancy

A FORM OF DIVINATION, an ancient technique of reading messages from the earth. In Arabia marks made at random in the sand were studied, elsewhere a handful of earth was thrown up and the

pattern in which it landed examined carefully. The most systematic form of geomancy is that practised in China, known as Feng Shui, in which landscape forms are studied so that tombs or houses may be positioned auspiciously, in such a way as to receive maximum benefit from the male (yang) and female (yin) influences.
▷ **Chinese folklore**

George, St

THE ARCHETYPE OF CHRISTIAN CHIVALRY. All that is known for certain is that he was martyred either at Lydda in Palestine or Nicomedia, and that he was probably a soldier in the Emperor's army. His cult is an ancient and popular one and much mythical material attached itself to his figure; the fullest and most popularized form of the legend is found in the 13th-century *Golden Legend* of Jacques de Voragine, translated into English by Caxton.

According to Voragine's story, George was a warrior from Cappadocia. Passing through Sylene in Libya, he found the town terrorized by a **dragon** which demanded human flesh to satisfy its appetite. The victims were chosen by lot, and on the day George arrived it was the turn of the king's own daughter. She had been chained to a rock outside the city, dressed as a bride to await her death. George seized his lance and marched forth to meet the beast; he conquered it and led it tamely back to the town, drawn by the princess's girdle. He then told the townsfolk that he would kill the dragon if they were to confess Christianity; naturally they were quick to comply and 15000 men were baptized. The legend also includes more historically based material chronicling George's suffering and death in the persecutions of Diocletian and Maximus. This is a Christianized form of the ubiquitous **dragonslayer** tale-type, bearing many similarities to the tale of **Perseus** and Andromeda particularly.

Although known in England from about the seventh century, George's popularity increased dramatically during the Crusades. It was said that the victory over the Saracens at Antioch was due to a vision of Saints George and Demetrius which heartened the men. Edward III named George patron of his newly-founded Order of the Garter in c.1344, and Henry's famous invocation at Agincourt, immortalized in Shakespeare's play *Henry V*, made his name a rallying-call for nationalistic pride. He gradually overtook even Edward the Confessor as the favourite saint of the English. His feast-day is celebrated on 23 April.

George appears as a popular figure in several early English mumming plays, some of which unashamedly proclaim English nationality for him. He was at one time regarded as patron of several European states, including Venice, Genoa, Catalonia and Portugal, but it was in England that devotion to him remained the highest. The 'St George's Arms', a red cross on a white background, formed the basis of every British soldier's and sailor's uniform, and it is included as the sign of England in the Union Jack.

Geraint

FIGURE OF ARTHURIAN ROMANCE, a Prince of Devon and knight of the **Round Table**. In Welsh lore he is the son of Erbin. His legend is drawn from the French *Erec et Enide*.

ghost

SPIRIT OF THE DEAD. Belief in ghosts is one of the most universal and enduring tenets of folklore. Virtually every society has or has had at one time a tradition of belief that the disembodied souls of the dead can return to the world of the living in some form. Ghosts may be visible, or apprehended by other senses such as hearing or even smell, the so-called 'perfume ghosts'. Even in the most sophisticated, materialistic modern cultures, **ghost stories** are circulated enthusiastically, with a half-belief and thrill of entertainment characteristic of so much folk tradition. In fact ghost stories of recent times have demonstrated the enormous vitality of folklore; cases such as the shadowy Spectre of the Brocken Mountain, although proved in 1818 to be a phenomenon of light and water particles, have persisted in popular legend as supernatural manifestations.

Although in the West ghosts are now largely a matter of superstition, para-scientific research and anecdotal evidence, in more primitive cultures they are greatly feared, and many rituals have developed to propitiate ghosts and thus neutralize their malevolence (see **funeral customs**) and there are also ceremonies performed by hunters after the kill for a similar purpose (see **hunting magic**).

Where ghosts are so greatly feared, humorous anecdotes tend to be lacking and the ghost lore takes the form of ritualistic measures for protection against ghostly evil rather than ghost tales. There are however some tales which echo European parallels, of infant ghosts which return to comfort their distraught parents or drowned mothers appearing in order to suckle their children. A young or unmarried person, a victim of violence or someone with close and unfinished ties with the living (the mother of a young child, for example, or a suitor) were thought to be especially likely to return as ghosts. Murderers in many societies take great precautions to protect themselves from the ghost of their victim which would infallibly return to seek vengeance if not bound by charms or made powerless by dismemberment or cremation. To see a ghost is often a sign of one's own imminent death; a familiar motif in European balladry is that of the **dead rider**, who returns to carry away on his spectral horse a loved one who may not even realize that he is dead.

The most common form attributed to ghosts is the likeness of the deceased, either nebulous or (especially in recent times) so clear that the onlooker may be unaware that what he or she is seeing is a spirit. In primitive ghost lore the spirit is often conceived of as being grotesque or monstrous, for example the *khu* of ancient Egypt, envisaged in animal form, the Irish *tash* which can be human or animal, or the demons of Aboriginal lore. There are reports too of ghostly dogs, horses and even swans, and the European tradition of the phantom coach, an omen of death to anyone who sees it. Mediums of more recent years have claimed to materialize ghosts from ectoplasm, a strange, plastic substance which can take a variety of forms; it has been shown in many cases to bear a startling resemblance to cheese-cloth or egg-white. In the spiritualist vogue of the 18th century, such demonstrations were common in Europe, as were photographs on which ghostly 'extras' could be seen along with those present or in the landscape. The majority of these were subsequently revealed to be double-exposed fakes or tricks of the light, but some remain unexplained.

Night is usually the most likely time to see a ghost, since darkness is the preferred medium of most spirits and demons, and the best sites for ghost-spotting are usually graveyards, since the separated spirit tends to linger around its old home. Scenes of violent death or treachery are also fruitful however, and many ghosts prefer to haunt the house in which they previously lived, for the sake of familiarity, the company of the family (and presumably other ghostly ancestors) or to warn future generations of coming danger.

ghost stories see urban legends

ghouls

DEMONIC BEING OF ARABIC LORE, known in Arabic as ghūl, a cannibalistic creature that haunts graveyards and will kill humans when it tires of corpses. They are a class of **jinn**, thought to be the children of Ibis, the Islamic Prince of Darkness. Although they are adept at **shape-shifting** to catch unwary humans, they can always be identified by their asses' hooves (see **defects**).

Ghouls were also said to inhabit the desert, preying on travellers, often in the form of a beautiful woman. If attacked by a ghoul one's only hope is to strike it dead with a single blow, as a further blow invests it with new life. Ghouls are frequently used as **bogeys** to frighten children into obedience, and the word is commonly employed today to refer to a morbid sadist, cannibal or grave-robber.

giant

MONSTERS OF MYTH AND FOLKLORE, strong but stupid enemies of mankind. According to Greek myth, giants were sons of the earth (hence their name, derived from *ge genis*) who sprang from

the blood of Uranus as it fell on the earth after Cronos had castrated him. They were implacable enemies of the gods, who fought Zeus for supremacy, and he could only defeat them with the help of a human, **Heracles**. Giants challenged the gods too in Norse mythology, to be defeated by Thor and the trickster god Loki. In Biblical lore, giants were created by the union of heavenly beings with mortal women and in Irish legend they were themselves gods who had fallen from heaven.

The striking elements in virtually all accounts of the origins of giants is the emphasis on their close links with the earth (in many cases they are said to live underground) and their opposition to the sky or heaven. This has led many scholars to suggest that giants were originally personifications of great

giant

natural forces of the earth, such as earthquakes or volcanoes, which seem to answer the thunder and storms of the skies.

From these elemental or semi-divine beginnings, giants became characterized in Western folklore at least as dull, bumbling, often cannibalistic monsters whose enormous strength and size could be overcome by the resourceful cunning of the hero. Unlike the **ogre**, who may appear in many forms, the giant is nearly always of human form. In Native American lore tales of giants in animal form are more common, for example the fabulous Tornit of Eskimo mythology or the widespread story of the giant bird who carries a boy onto a high ledge.

The giants of folklore are distinct from the giant races which inhabited the earth in creation time. These latter are more properly figures of mythology. In folktales giants tend to be solitary or in couples; they inhabit the faraway land of folklore which is not located in time or place, and they are usually only included as a foil to the courage or cunning of the hero. The **Jack tales** of British folklore, including such tales as Jack and the Beanstalk, are folkloric derivations from the ancient **dragon-slaying** myths, in which the hero cuts off the head of the monster.

Giants are generally held to be responsible for any unusual topographical feature. One of the most famous examples is the Giant's Causeway.

▷ **jötnar**

Giant's Causeway

PROMONTORY OF BASALTIC COLUMNS IN NORTHERN IRELAND, known in Irish as Clochán an Aifir. These astonishing regular hexagonal columns, up to 6m/20ft high, were formed by the rapid cooling of lava as it reached the sea. Since similar formations occur in Staffa, on the west coast of Scotland, the Giant's Causeway is said to have been constructed by a race of giants intending to build a road across the Irish Sea. The workers however fell to squabbling, as giants are prone to do, and the causeway was never completed.

Gilgamesh

ANCIENT MESOPOTAMIAN HERO, whose epic is one of the longest and most enduring of the Middle East. The historical Gilgamesh was probably a ruler of Uruk about 4500 years ago, but the cycle of tales that grew up around his name owes more to the folk imagination than historical accuracy. This great cycle is thought to have developed from early oral tales, loosely worked together in the manner of other great epic cycles such as the *Odyssey* and *Beowulf*, and displaying many motifs and themes in common with them. The best-preserved text is that on twelve Akkadian tablets from Nineveh, dating from the seventh century BC. This text is incomplete, but fragments found elsewhere in Assyria and Mesopotamia, together with five ancient Sumerian poems thought to date from the early second millennium BC, have been drawn together to fill the gaps.

According to legend, Gilgamesh was a semi-divine being endowed by the gods with superhuman strength and stature, yet they withheld immortality from him.

Giants' Causeway, Co. Antrim, Northern Ireland

He became a proud, lustful and despotic ruler, and the goddess Aruru, to curb his unchallenged pride, creates from clay a mortal of comparable strength, beauty and stature, Enkidu. Enkidu grows up among animals as an untaught savage, but he is initiated into human ways by a prostitute who then leads him to Uruk to meet King Gilgamesh. Enkidu challenges Gilgamesh to combat, and although he is defeated he wins the king's devotion—Gilgamesh had seen in his dreams a worthy companion such as this but had almost given up hope of meeting him. His rule softens, and Uruk enjoys peace and prosperity while their king is happy in his new friendship.

The two heroes venture into the forest beyond the city to seek out Humbaba (or Huwawa), a **Gorgon**-like creature, the guardian of the sacred **cedar** tree. Together they fight and defeat Humbaba, and Enkidu triumphantly beheads the monster with a blow from Gilgamesh's sword. They fell the sacred tree, and from henceforth events move swiftly forward towards the doom of Enkidu.

Ishtar, goddess of love, is so captivated by Gilgamesh's daring that she invites him to her luxurious bed; mindful of the fate of her previous lovers, however, Gilgamesh repulses her, and the offended goddess prevails upon her father Anu to create a mighty Bull of Heaven to revenge her. Gilgamesh, with the help of Enkidu, defeats this too, but while they exult the gods hold council and conclude that Enkidu must die for his offences to the gods. The sickness of Enkidu, his dream of the 'house of dust' for which he is bound, and his state funeral led by the grief-stricken Gilgamesh are all related in tablets VII and VIII.

Brought thus abruptly to face mortality, Gilgamesh embarks on a journey to visit the sage Utnapishtim, the hero of the Babylonian flood tales. His journey is perilous, and he encounters a variety of obstacles recounted in tablets IX and X, but eventually he reaches Utnapishtim, who relates to him the Flood story (which closely parallels the Hebrew version in Genesis). Utnapishtim also tells Gilgamesh of the plant of immortality, but after the king has plucked it the plant is stolen and eaten by a serpent while Gilgamesh refreshes himself with a swim on the way back. In despair, he returns to Uruk resigned to death. An addition to the epic has Enkidu's spirit returning to give a grim account of the underworld to his friend.

The Gilgamesh epic demonstrates several key motifs of hero tales in folklore around the world: the divine origins and attributes of the hero; the savage brought up by animals (see **animal nurse**; the battle with a guardian monster (see **dragonslayer**); the quest for the plant of life (see **tree**); the succession of supernatural helpers on the quest; and the **snake** cheating mankind of immortality.

ginger

AROMATIC SPICE, the underground stem of *Zingiber officinale* (family Zingiberaceae), a native of south-east Asia. Medicinally, it is traditionally chewed as a cure for flatulence and to aid digestion, and in Russia and other areas it is used as a cure for toothache. In the Philippines it is thought to keep evil spirits at bay.

Gingerbread Man

A EUROPEAN CHAIN TALE, also known as the Fleeing Pancake. The pancake or gingerbread figure springs up when cooked and runs away from the woman who baked him. He is accosted by various animals and avoids each one, adding each to the cumulative list of which he boasts; 'I ran away from the old woman, and the dog, and the cat, (etc) and I can run away from you!'. By the time he reaches the **fox** however this litany is too long, and the fox, without stopping to argue, swallows him whole. This tale is found throughout Northern Europe, and has became a favourite in the United States.
▷ **cumulative stories and songs**

ginseng

'ROOT OF HEAVEN', either *Panax pseudoginseng* or *P. quinquefolium*, herbs of the family Araliaceae native to North America and Asia. Its significance in folklore has come about partly because of the resemblance of the root to the human form (cf **mandrake**), and it has been highly prized in all areas. Although much ginseng is grown commercially, in Korea it is said that only wild ginseng has medicinal value; it can be found only by the pure, and it will impart strength and longevity.

Ginseng tends to be used as a general restorative and performance-enhancer, an elixir, rather than to treat specific ills, and this seems to be born out by scientific analysis, which indicates that ginseng has a normalizing and arousing effect on the system. The root is generally taken powdered as a tea, or in wine.

Girle Guairle

IRISH FAIRY OF FOLKTALE, a **Rumpelstiltskin** figure. Girle Guairle agrees to spin for a mortal woman, requesting only that she should remember her name. The woman forgets the name and is terrified of the consequences, but one day she overhears a fairy rhyme containing the name, and when the fairy presents her with the finished work she greets her with 'Welcome and good health, Girle Guairle'. The fairy disappears, enraged and disappointed.
▷ **Tom-Tit-Tot**

glamour

CHARACTERISTIC OF FAIRIES, a Scottish term to denote the enchantment and illusion associated with the **fairy** presence and fairy magic. A mortal might see the fairies as beautiful, richly attired ladies, until the glamour was dispersed by the touch of a four-leafed **clover** or by the ointment with which the fairies anointed the eyes of their own children, when he or she would perceive them as withered **imps**. Often glamour functions merely as a means of **invisibility**, and anyone who has touched the corner of his eye with fairy ointment is able to see them where other mortals cannot. Many seemingly rich fairy gifts and food are the products only of glamour, not substance.

Glas Ghaibhneach

A MAGICAL, BENEFICENT COW common to both Goidelic and Brythonic Celtic traditions, literally 'the grey cow with white loins'. She was said to belong to Goibniu, the divine smith, or to a master-smith of Ireland. She was remarkable for giving an inexhaustible supply of milk, and was popularly believed to reappear to the peasants in times of need. She was easily offended, however, and when a woman tried to collect more milk than she needed in order to sell the rest, she disappeared across the sea into Scotland. According to some versions of the tale, she still mysteriously appears to families in need, but will only stay until she is struck or someone milks her into a leaky bucket, and then she disappears again. In Welsh lore, she is known as Fuwch Frech, the brindled cow, who disappeared when she was milked dry by a greedy old woman.

glass mountain

MOTIF OF FOLKTALES, probably originally a land of the dead at the end of the earth, found especially in Teutonic, central and Eastern European and British lore. In later tales the glass mountain was a magical, sterile place to which despotic fathers removed their beautiful daughters, and which the hero must scale to win her (see **tasks and tests**). The ascent may be accomplished by a magical horse, or by using bones or borrowed animal claws to build a ladder up the mountain.

gnome

UNDERGROUND BEING, a dwarfish **goblin** inhabiting treasure mines. The gnome is closely linked to the neo-Platonic theories of elements and humours popular among the humanist Renaissance scientists; as the **salamander**'s element is fire, so the gnome's is earth, and according to the 16th-century Swiss alchemist Paracelsus, the gnome is able to move through earth in the same way that a fish moves through water or a human through air. The word is thought to be derived from the Greek *ge-nomos*, earth-dweller. In medieval art gnomes are represented as hunched, gnarled old men, often guarding treasure. In common usage the term is often confused with **dwarf** and **goblin**.

Gnome, The

GERMAN FOLKTALE, collected by Grimm. Three brothers set out to rescue the king's three daughters who are trapped underground. The youngest learns from a gnome where the princesses are being held, and he is lowered down a well by his two brothers. He finds the first princess guarded by a nine-headed **dragon**, the second by a five-headed dragon and the third by one with four heads, and kills each of the monsters in turn. Returning to the well bottom, he calls his brothers to haul the princesses up in the basket one by one, but when his turn arrives to be lifted he recalls the gnome's warning against his treacherous brothers, and instead of climbing in himself he weights the basket with a heavy stone. Sure enough, the brothers let the basket fall and, believing their sibling dead, race back with the princesses to claim their reward. The younger brother is magically rescued and returns to the palace just in time to forestall the weddings. He claims the youngest princess as his bride, and his thwarted brothers are duly punished.

The tale is a close folkloric relation of the ancient **Bear's Son cycle**, incorporating the key motifs of the subterranean battle against the monster and the betrayal by comrades, although it lacks the epic mood of its cousin, *Beowulf*.

goat

ONE OF THE EARLIEST DOMESTICATED ANIMALS, probably second only to the **dog**. Goats have served as sacrificial animals in many cultures; when the Greeks defeated the Persians at Marathon they are said to have sacrificed 500 goats in thanksgiving. The Sumerian god Marduk, often accompanied by a goat, was pleased to receive them in sacrifice, and Dionysus, whom Zeus had once transformed into a black goat to conceal him from Hera, was known by his followers as 'the Kid' or 'the one of the black goatskin'. Euripides records in *The Bacchae* how the god's frenzied worshippers would rip a live goat apart and devour its flesh. **Fauns** are said to be half-human, half-goat. The scapegoat was the Hebrew sacrificial goat that took upon itself the sins of the community.

In general European lore the goat is proverbially associated with lechery, and this is paralleled around the world where goats are used in fertility ceremonies. This reputation was compounded in Europe however by the goat's association with **witches** and the **Devil**, by virtue of his cloven feet (see **defects**). The parable of Jesus telling how God will one day separate the sheep from the goats (the good from the evil) has done little to enhance the goat's reputation.

▷ **gwyllion**

goblin

EUROPEAN MISCHIEVOUS SPIRIT. Derived from the Greek word for a roguish spirit, *kobálos*, the term goblin is generally applied to any wandering malicious spirit in Western folklore, particularly in England and France. Goblins are usually portrayed as small, grotesque figures, much given to wreaking havoc in the house by night, breaking dishes and banging on walls. The **hobgoblin**, although mischievous and fond of practical jokes, is a friendlier and more benevolent type of goblin. At their worst, goblins can be terrifying **bogeys** used to frighten children, for example the cannibalistic **hobyahs** who carry off an old woman in a Scottish and American folktale, or the evil spirits of Christina Rossetti's poem *Goblin Market*, but more usually they are mischievous

goblins

household spirits, who may help around the house, reward children when they are good and punish them for disobedience. They should be offered food and milk to keep them good-humoured, since an offended goblin, like most **fairies**, can be a troublesome enemy.
▷ **mischievous spirits**

Godiva, Lady (fl. c.1048–80)

ANGLO-SAXON GENTLEWOMAN, patroness of Coventry. A popular legend first recorded in the early 13th century tells how her husband Leofric, earl of Mercia, became exasperated by his wife's repeated pleas on behalf of the townsfolk to lower the heavy taxes he had imposed, and finally agreed, on condition that she ride naked though the streets. Godiva (Godgifu in Old English) let down her long hair and ordered all the citizens to remain shut in their homes while she did so. A 17th-century version of the tale tells of Peeping Tom, a tailor who opened his shutters to watch the lady go by and was struck blind for his ungentlemanly disobedience. Leofric is said to have revoked all taxes except those on horses, abashed by his wife's selflessness.

Other tales of **nudity** undertaken for social protest are known in folklore; St **Francis of Assisi** for example is said to have dramatically divested himself of his clothes in public to wed himself to Lady Poverty. This is the tradition to which Godiva's nude ride belongs rather than the sometimes orgiastic religious ceremonies in which priestesses danced naked to invoke rain, ensure fertility, or drive away evil spirits.

Gog and Magog

IN BIBLICAL LORE Gog is a prince under Satan's sway and in apocalyptic tales Gog and Magog will appear as aides of Satan before the end of the world. Elsewhere Magog appears to refer to the land of Gog, rather than a separate being.

In folk history, Gog and Magog were the last surviving members of the race of British **giants** defeated by **Brut**. They were the sons of demons and the husband-slaying daughters of Diocletian (see **Albion**). They are now represented by enormous wooden figures in London's Guildhall; such figures have been in residence since the time of Henry V at least. The original pair were destroyed in the Great Fire and their replacements, installed in 1708, suffered a similar fate during an air-raid in 1940. Today's Gog and Magog date from 1953.

In Geoffrey of Monmouth's account, Gogmagog was a Cornish giant slain by Corineus, a friend of Brut.

Goidelic folklore see Celtic lore

gold

PRECIOUS METAL, SYMBOL OF PURITY AND POWER, invested with spiritual and magical powers throughout history. Although it has not always been the scarcest or the most valuable of all metals, gold's beauty and its resistance to tarnishing have made it consistently the most highly prized. It has been linked to religion from the earliest days of civilization; gold icons and sacred objects of virtually every ancient culture have been found.

Many cultures have attempted to explain the existence of gold in their creation myths. Some ancient authorities held that it was engendered by the action of the sun, and medieval alchemists echoed them when they claimed that gold could be produced by mercury subjected to the sun. Even those cultures which accepted the fact that gold occurred underground and could be mined like other metals attributed supernatural qualities to it; in Central America many groups will only collect the ore after the proper fasts and rituals have been observed, to avoid offending the spirit of the gold. In many cultures it is considered presumptuous to mine it at all; in Borneo the gold spirit is believed to take revenge upon any who do so.

In addition to its religious significance, gold has traditionally been used as a potent magical force in everyday life. In China and Europe gold, either in leaf form, as a poultice or dissolved in acids, was a commonly prescribed medication along with others even more difficult to obtain such as powdered **unicorn** horn. It was thought to preserve and perfect life through **sympathetic** magic, since it itself was free from rust and tarnish.

This concept of gold as a perfect, enduring metal led to its traditional use in the West and elsewhere in the making of wedding rings, to symbolize perfect, unending unity. Gold jewellery of course was known and prized long before this tradition began. A gold medal is traditionally regarded as the most suitable prize for the winner of a sporting event, replacing the laurels of classical traditions, expressing supremacy. There is an interesting parallel between the relationship of sun and moon, greater and lesser lights, and the precious metals associated with them by colour and symbolism, gold and silver respectively. ▷ **alchemy**; **philosopher's stone**

Golden Legend, The

LEGENDA AUREA, a collection of saints' Lives and pious writings compiled by the Dominican archbishop of Genoa, Jacques de Voragine, in the 13th century. The book achieved astonishing success in the Middle Ages, with translations into almost every European language, and Caxton's English version of 1483 was one of the first books printed in English. The tales display many common folktale motifs, such as the **dragon-slaying** St **George** who rescues the princess and leads the tame dragon back with her girdle, and the legends display the typical medieval blending of folk traditions and pious credulity. After the Reformation and with the new theories of history and humanism generated by the Renaissance the genre lost favour and credibility.

Goldilocks see Three Bears

gong

PERCUSSION INSTRUMENT, found especially in south-east Asia, consisting of a metal plate (usually bronze) with a turned-down rim, struck by a beater (a stick often tipped with leather or felt). Unlike **bells**, which resound at the rims, the crash of a gong emanates from the centre. The centre may be bossed or not.

The gong has great religious significance, especially in China; the sound of a gong drives out demons and therefore cures the sick. Gongs were also thought to be able to summon winds. To own a gong was considered a symbol of status in China, because of their expense and their magical virtue, and to drink from a gong after swearing an oath was the symbol of an unbreakable pledge. They are widely used to accompany dances, drama and song, and here the male and female tones of pitched gongs are used to great effect. Like **bells** and **drums**, gongs have been used as a means of communicating in code across distances.

goose

LARGE MIGRATORY WATERBIRD, associated with divinity in the mythology of many early civilizations. In Egyptian mythology Seb, god of the earth, Isis, Osiris and Hora were all associated with geese, and a goose laid the cosmic **egg** from which Ra (the sun-god) came forth. In Hindu lore the goose represents Brahma and the principle of creation. The Ostyaks of Siberia have a goose god who inhabits a fur-lined nest in the mountains. Greeks and Romans kept tame geese in their temples, especially those dedicated to Hera/Juno in her domestic aspect, and Livy tells how in the fourth century AD the cackling of geese in the temple courtyard alerted the Romans to the Gauls who had sent scouts under cover of darkness to scale Capitol Hill and thereby saved the city. This is a version of the animal warning, combining neatly with the **bird** of truth, a common motif in folklore. In China the goose symbolizes fidelity, and a pair of geese is a traditional wedding present.

Possibly the most famous goose of folklore is that which laid the golden egg, and which was killed by its foolish owner, greedy for more riches. Jack found a similar goose on his visit to the world at the top of the beanstalk (see **Jack and the Beanstalk**). An Indian version tells of an avaricious woman who tears out all the goose's golden feathers and is left with a pile of worthless goose-down.

Another famous golden goose has the power to make anyone who attempts to steal one of its precious feathers stick fast. This occurs most famously in a widespread European tale often called 'All Stick Together', in which typically the youngest of three brothers shares his

food with a beggar and is given the golden goose as a reward. The daughter of the keeper at the inn the next night attempts to steal a feather; she becomes stuck fast, as does the parson who attempts to pull her off and a succession of others. Meanwhile the youngest brother continues on his way, and is seen by the princess who has never smiled. She laughs uproariously at this ludicrous procession, and the hero wins her hand (see **laughter**).
▷ **Little Goose Girl**; **Mother Goose**; **swan maiden**

Gorgon

MONSTER OF GREEK MYTHOLOGY, a hideous female creature with wings, a flat round face and protruding teeth and, most horribly, a head of live snakes in place of hair. All who look directly on her are turned to stone. Although Homer speaks of only one Gorgon, Hesiod has three—Stheno, Euryale and Medusa—offspring of the incestuous relationship between the sea-god Phorcys and his sister Ceto. Of these three only Medusa was mortal, and she was slain by **Perseus** who went on to use her head as a weapon against his enemies before giving it to Athene for her aegis (shield).
▷ **Yama-uba**

Gotham, Wise Men of

PROVERBIAL NUMBSKULLS, inhabitants of a Nottinghamshire village during the late Middle Ages. A variety of numbskull tales were attributed to them, although many of the tales derive from India and Continental Europe. A copy of the *Tales of the Mad Men of Gotam* survives from 1630, but Gotham was proverbial even before then. Some of the exploits referred to include the attempt to catch a **cuckoo** by building a hedge around its tree, to drown an **eel** in the village pond and so on. One of the best-known tales has 12 Gothamites out fishing; they conclude that one of their number must be drowned, as each forgets to include himself in the count.

It is likely that 'wise' here was intended ironically, but a legend offering a rather different interpretation tells how the townsfolk tricked King John, who was preparing to pass through the

Wise Men of Gotham

town and assess its merits as the site of a royal hunting lodge. Wishing to avoid the expense and inconvenience this would inevitably involve, the townsfolk engaged in ludicrous activities. The king's messengers reported that the locals were fools and idiots; King John moved on elsewhere.

Grail, Holy

A MYSTERIOUS TALISMAN, the object of quest for Arthurian knights. The grail is most commonly said to be the cup used by Jesus at the Last Supper, and in some versions it was used by **Joseph of Arimathea** to catch a few drops of blood from Jesus as he hung wounded on the cross. Joseph was said to have brought this sacred cup to Britain, but it had vanished because of the unworthiness of its guardians. It is a symbol of God's grace, and can only be achieved by the pure. Some versions claim that the Grail was fashioned from an **emerald** that dropped to earth from Lucifer's crown as he fell from heaven. After Christ's death the Grail was said to have provided nourishment for Joseph of Arimathea, and later the first knights of the **Round Table** in Britain.

The word originally denoted a wide, shallow vessel (French *graal*), and the roots of the legend may be traced back to magical Celtic **cauldrons**, horns of plenty and never-empty platters. These mythical antecedents illuminate many puzzling elements in the tales, such as the question that **Perceval** must ask— 'Whom does the Grail serve?'— which derives from Old Irish tales of the sun god **Lugh**.

The earliest written version of the Christian Grail legend is that of Chrétien de Troyes, *Perceval*, or *Le Conte du Graal*, written in the late 12th century. Here the questing knight is the innocent Perceval, who meets the **Fisher King**, Amfortas, and proves himself a worthy knight of the Grail. In *Diu Krône*, a German romance of the 13th century, the hero was the perfect knight **Gawain**, but Gawain's character deteriorated in later medieval versions such as the *Prose Lancelot* or Vulgate cycle, and the chaste Sir **Galahad** replaced him as the Grail hero in the *Queste del Saint Graal*. In these later versions the influence of medieval Christian mystics such as St Bernard of Clairvaux is very evident. It was this version that Malory's influential prose work *Le Morte d'Arthur*, on which Tennyson based his *Idylls*, followed.

The Grail theme is one of the most resonant in medieval spirituality, but it seems clear that elements of the tale were drawn from pagan Celtic mythology as well as the Christian and French romantic traditions.
▷ **Arthur**

Gráinne

TRAGIC OLD IRISH HEROINE, daughter of **Cormac Mac Airt**, betrothed to **Finn Mac Cumhal**. She eloped with **Diarmuid**, one of the **Fianna** and a kinsman of Finn's. After Finn pursued them and Diarmuid died, she reluctantly allowed herself to be wooed by Finn and eventually married him. This pragmatic faithlessness has often been contrasted with the implacability of **Deirdre**.

Gram see Balmung

grasshopper

LEAPING INSECT, often interchangeable in folklore with the **cricket**. In Egyptian mythology the grasshopper is a symbol of happiness, thronging the fields of the afterworld. In Chinese belief the grasshopper represents happiness, good fortune, longevity and prosperity. A fable collected by Aesop tells how the grasshopper is shamed by the industry of the **ant**; when harsh weather arrives, he is unprepared.

grateful dead

WIDESPREAD FOLKTALE TYPE, the dead man as helper. Most commonly the hero comes upon a group of creditors refusing to allow burial to the dead man. He ransoms the corpse with his last penny by paying off his debts, and continues on his way, but is joined soon afterwards by a strange companion—an old man, servant, or occasionally fox or horse. This is the grateful dead man, who aids the hero in his quest by performing various supernatural tasks, sometimes with the condition that he is entitled to half the prize. Usually the prize is the princess, and the companion demands his half, but just as the hero agrees to cut his bride in two the companion relents and reveals his identity. Occasionally the prize demanded is the couple's first child (cf **Rumpelstiltskin**).

This tale contains many common folkloric motifs, including the quest for the stolen princess, the supernatural helper, the bargain and subsequent recognition. It occurs throughout Europe, the West Indies, Spanish America and parts of Asia.

Green Man

SPIRIT OF VEGETATION. In European tradition, a leaf-clad figure taking various forms, associated with spring festivals, and sometimes found depicted on inn-signs. He is part of a world-wide family of such vegetative spirits, embodying the life-force renewing the world in spring.
▷ **Jack-in-the-Green; Robin Hood**

gremlin

MODERN MISCHIEVOUS SPIRITS OF MACHINERY, diminutive **imps** first identified by airforcemen in World War I but only widely recognized in World War II, tradition awards the discovery of 'gremlin effect' (GE) to Pilot Officer Prune of the RAF. Gremlins delight in plaguing

gremlins

humans by causing tools and machinery to malfunction, loosening a screw here and blocking a pipe there to cause maximum disruption at the most critical moments. Descriptions of gremlins vary widely; they are said to range from 6 to 21 inches in height, and despite their high level of aerial involvement they have no wings and must hitch rides with the airmen they plague. This explains why gremlins occasionally work to bring back bomb-damaged planes that would otherwise certainly fall.

Although the etymology of the term is uncertain, it may derive from a collapsing of **goblin** with Fremlin's, the name of a Kentish brewer; the goblin that emerges from the beer-bottle. Another suggested root is *gremian*, Old English meaning 'to vex'.

Grendel

HALF-HUMAN MONSTER, the scourge of Hrothgar's hall. On one of his nightly raids he loses an arm to **Beowulf**, and retreats to his underwater cavern to die. His mother journeys to Hrothgar's hall to avenge him, and she is also defeated by Beowulf, in an underwater battle.

griffin

MYTHICAL CREATURE, a composite animal with the head and usually the wings of an **eagle**, the body of a **lion**, and occasionally the tail of a **snake**. They were particularly common in the Mediterranean and Near East by the 14th century BC, usually represented drawing the chariot of the sun (especially in Roman lore) or guarding their hoard of gold. They were perpetually in conflict with the **Arimaspians** who coveted their treasure.

The synthesis of two particularly noble animals, lion and eagle, recommended the griffin to many as a symbol

griffin

of power, valour and nobility, and in medieval Christian lore it was used as a symbol of Christ, combining in himself both human and divine natures, with the attendant associations of kingship and resurrection.

Groundhog Day

DAY OF POPULAR AMERICAN SUPERSTITION, 2 February, on which the groundhog (woodchuck) is said to emerge from his winter hibernation. If he sees his shadow on the ground, he will return to his burrow for another six weeks, and winter will last six weeks more, but if he does not then spring is around the corner. This superstition is common also in Europe, involving the **badger** in Germany and the **bear** elsewhere in Europe.
▷ **Candlemas**

guallipen

FABULOUS ANIMAL OF THE ARAUCANIANS, a native group of Chile, having the head of a calf on a sheep's body. If a pregnant woman encounters or dreams of a guallipen on three successive nights, she can be sure that her baby will be born deformed.

guardian spirits

BENEVOLENT SPIRITUAL FORCES, protectors of person and possessions. In primitive lore every aspect of human experience is affected by the many different forces, often malevolent, which take a lively interest in human life. Prosperity and health are fragile commodities in societies dependent upon weather for food, with primitive medicine and high mortality rates, and they must be protected. It is unsurprising then that cultural groups throughout history have enlisted supernatural aid to protect the well-being both of themselves and their homes, livestock, harvest, children and possessions. Usually these spirits are ambivalent to some degree; their power can be dangerous, but if they are propitiated and wooed correctly it will be used for the benefit of the human invoking them.

In Native American lore guardian spirits were usually conceived of in animal or bird form, and they were responsible for an individual rather than a house. Part of the puberty rites of many tribes is the solitary quest to find a guardian spirit to teach the initiate sacred songs, the secrets of hunting and other skills. Girls sometimes undergo a similar quest during isolation at the onset of **menstruation**. Such spirits usually showed themselves in visions and dreams; their help and advice was considered vitally important. Shamans called on such spirits to help them in their healing, and the spirits thus called would often appear as animal familiars.
▷ **fairy godmother**; **lares**

Guillaume d'Orange

OLD FRENCH HERO. He is the central figure of *La Geste de Guillaume d'Orange*, a cycle of 24 *chansons de geste* dating from the 12th and 13th centuries, which tells of a French family's loyalty to the family name, their king and Christendom in fighting against the Spanish Muslims. The king, Louis the Pious, is shown to be little deserving of such loyal service. Guillaume is thought to be based upon the historical figure of Wilhelmus, cousin of **Charlemagne**, whose family was prominent in Franco-Spanish affairs of the ninth century. The anonymous poems have undergone substantial changes at the hands of medieval scribes.

Guinevere

ARTHUR'S QUEEN, lover of **Lancelot of the Lake**. Her name in Welsh is Gwenhwyfar, perhaps meaning white ghost, but Geoffrey of Monmouth calls her Guanhumara and claims Roman descent for her.

In early Welsh literature, for example the *Vita Gildae* of the late 11th/early 12th centuries, Guinevere appears as a Persephone figure, abducted by Melwas, King of the Summer Land (Aestiva Regio) and resurrected by **Arthur**. Chrétien de Troyes in his late-12th century romance *Le Chevalier de la Charette* tells how Guinevere is abducted by Meleagant and rescued from his clutches by Lancelot. Here and in the early tales of the Vulgate cycle the courtly love of Lancelot and Guinevere is celebrated; only in the more spiritual later versions such as the *Queste del Saint Graal* is their adultery condemned, becoming the sin that disqualifies Lancelot as a knight worthy of the **Grail**.

Geoffrey of Monmouth tells how the treacherous **Mordred**, Arthur's nephew, seduced his queen while the king was in Rome. Later accounts (including Tennyson's) make Guinevere an unwilling victim, stressing her love for Lancelot as her only downfall. However the revelation of Arthur's betrayal by his queen and favourite knight ultimately brings about the end of the fellowship of the **Round Table**. Guinevere was condemned to death but was rescued by Lancelot; she subsequently became a nun and was reconciled in some degree to Arthur. Some versions add that she was finally buried alongside him at Glastonbury.

guitar

STRING INSTRUMENT, plucked or strummed with the fingers (or more recently a plectrum), probably derived from early Oriental instruments via Spanish Moors and the lute. Like the related ukelele and balalaika, the guitar is used most commonly for accompanying songs and dances, especially in Spain, Italy, Latin America and areas of Europe and North America.

As with the **fiddle**, virtuosity on the guitar is popularly regarded with suspicion since it may indicate a pact with the **Devil**, the master musician, who exchanges such skill for a human soul.

Gudrun

WIFE OF SIGURD, the daughter of Guiku, king of the Nibelungs. In the *Volsungasaga* her mother Grimhild gives **Sigurd** a potion to make him forget his betrothed, **Brynhild**, and he is tricked into marrying Gudrun. He is killed by her avaricious brother Guttorm, on Brynhild's prompting. She later marries **Atli** (Attila), Brynhild's brother and King of the Huns, but after he treacherously slays her brothers she kills their two children, feeds their hearts to Atli, then kills him too.

Gudrun

GERMAN PRINCESS, heroine of a 13th-century epic romance, the *Gudrun Lied*.

She is wooed by three royal suitors, Siegfried of the Moorland, Hartmut of Norway and Herwig of Zealand. While her father Hettel is engaged in wars with Herwig and Siegfried, Gudrun is abducted by Hartmut who imprisons her for 13 years. Because of her refusal to agree to his demands, she is treated as a servant. Hettel, Herwig and Siegfried unite to find her and rescue her. At last Herwig, Gudrun's beloved, rescues her with the help of her brother Ortwin.

Gunnar see Gunther

Gunther (d.437)

HISTORICAL KING OF BURGUNDY, known in Norse legend as Gunnar, hero of many medieval legends. He is said to have been killed in battle by Atli (better known as Attila) but was revenged by his sister **Gudrun**. In the *Volsungasaga*, **Sigurd** aids Gunnar to win **Brynhild**, Grimhild's potion having made him forget that he was himself betrothed to her, by riding through the ring of fire. When Brynhild recognizes Sigurd after the marriage, Gunnar is suspicious of his sworn brother, but having learned the story after Sigurd's death he allows Brynhild to be burned on his funeral pyre. When Gudrun marries **Atli** Gunther is invited to their court with his brothers, but takes the precaution of hiding the Nibelung gold in the Rhine. He is treacherously killed by Atli, refusing to tell where the gold is hidden.

In the *Nibelungenlied*, Gunther is aided by Siegfried to woo Brunhild and his sister Kriemhild (Gudrun) marries Siegfried. He is aided by his friend on his wedding night when Brunhild challenges his authority, suspecting that she has been won by trickery, and Siegfried dons his cloak of **invisibility** to thrash her. Believing that it was Gunther, she remains an obedient wife until her death. When Gunther goes to visit his sister and her second husband Etzel (Atli or Attila) he is overcome by their treachery and beheaded on his sister's command.

Guy of Warwick

HERO OF ANGLO-FRENCH ROMANCE, a chivalric knight who adventures in search of the fame that will make him acceptable to the beautiful Felice, daughter of his erstwhile master the Earl of Warwick. His many exploits include the delivery of Constantinople from the Saracens and the slaying of a **dragon** in Northumbria. Finally he returns to Warwick and weds Felice, but is almost immediately overcome by remorse at a life dedicated to the pursuit of love rather than godliness, and in penitence vows to become a pilgrim. It is in this guise, many years later, that he faces the **giant** Colbrand, champion of the invading Danes. Guy slays his enemy after a mighty struggle near Winchester, thus saving the town from the Danes (in fact, Winchester was saved from the historical invasion by payment of ransom, not the valour of a champion).

Guy retires to spend his last days as a hermit, and on his death-bed sends a messenger to Felice with the ring she had given him on parting (see **life token**). Felice hurries to his side, and he dies in her arms. His body was said to give off a sweet, curative aroma after his death, and his body had to be buried finally in his anchorite's cell, as 30 knights could not remove it.

The earliest accounts of the legend date from the 12th century, and it enjoyed enormous popularity in England and France up to the 17th century, and even later as a broadside **ballad** in England. Its appeal lay not so much in stylistic grace as in its combination of adventure, love and religious propriety—the prominence of this last element is thought by many to indicate the influence of monastic clerks in disseminating the legend. It appealed especially to English patriotism.

Gwydion

CELTIC MAGICIAN, the son of Don and brother (and incestuous lover) of **Arianrhod**, brother also of **Amaethon**. He is said to have fathered Arianrhod's twin sons Dylan and **Lleu Llaw Gyffes** and took upon himself the charge of the latter, cursed by his mother. After Llew's treacherous 'death', his transformation into an **eagle**, Gwydion discovered him and healed the poisonous wound.

Gwydion is popularly credited with instituting the first **April fool**, as it was on

1 April that he conjured up a vision of armies to trick Arianrhod into bestowing arms upon Llew despite her curse.
▷ **Battle of the Trees**

gwyllion

WELSH MISCHIEVOUS SPIRITS, appearing as hideous female **fairies**, who lay in wait for travellers at night along the treacherous mountain roads to deceive them and make them lose their way. They can be thwarted however by a knife held towards them; like many evil spirits they are sensitive to **iron**. In inclement weather they might take to the valleys, where they are always cordially welcome in the house lest they become offended and destructive. The gwyllion are closely associated with **goats**, and may sometimes take goat form.

Gwynn

WELSH FAIRY KING, leader of the **ellyllon**. He is thought to have originally been a god of the underworld, and he is traditionally pictured with an **owl**, recalling his mythological role.

Gyges (d.c.648BC)

KING OF LYDIA, who seized power after slaying the king and marrying his queen. According to Plato, Gyges was a shepherd who ventured into a chasm and discovered a brazen horse; he opened the horse to discover inside the body of a man from whose finger he drew a magic ring of **invisibility**. Wearing this ring, he crept into the royal bedchamber, murdered the king **Candaules**, and seduced the queen.

Another version of the tale, recorded by Herodotus, tells how Candaules, inordinately proud of his wife's beauty, compelled Gyges to see her naked. Furious at this humiliation, his queen commanded Gyges on pain of death to kill her husband and marry her himself.

Gyges was renowned for his great wealth, and made many rich gifts to the oracle at Delphi. The name is also given in Roman mythology to one of the three Hecantoncheires, the hundred-headed **giants** born to Uranus and Gaea.

gyromancy

FORM OF DIVINATION, in which the

inquirer walks round in a circle until he or she falls from dizziness; the direction and nature of the fall are then examined for their significance.

gytrash

SPIRIT OF THE NORTH OF ENGLAND, appearing as a silent horse or occasionally a large dog, which haunts lonely roads by night to wait for travellers. Although feared, a benevolent gytrash will sometimes guide lost travellers on their way.

▷ **Black Dog**

haddock

NORTH ATLANTIC FISH, *Melanogrammus aeglefinus*, characterized by a distinctive dark spot above each gill on the shoulders. These marks are said to be the finger and thumb print of St Peter, who picked up the fish to take the coin from its mouth on Jesus's instructions (Matthew 17:27). Other versions of the tale attribute the prints to the hand of Christ, who held the fish to break it at the feeding of the Five Thousand (Matthew 14:13–21). In New England however the prints are said to belong to the Devil's hand, and the dark lateral line along the fish records how his fingers slipped as the fish escaped.

hag

SUPERNATURALLY UGLY, withered old woman, generally considered as an evil **witch** in European folklore, closely associated with the **Devil**. Hags occasionally appear as beautiful young women, and may take the role of a **succubus** to seduce and weaken young men. A more common experience however is to be 'hag-ridden'; a hag literally rides a sleeping victim like a horse, pressing on his chest or stomach to give discomfort and **nightmare**, and may travel on her unwilling mount so far and at such great speeds to do her nefarious business that in the morning the victim is drenched and exhausted, with shadowy memories of terrifying, ghostly dreams. If such activities continue, the victim is certain to die.

Despite their sere appearance, hags are thought by many scholars to be the remnants of ancient fertility goddesses. In Celtic lore a hag, *cailleach*, is often said to be a wise ancient spirit with keen supernatural powers, and many tales are told of rocks falling from the apron of a cailleach to make mountains or cairns. They are irascible however, and humans occasionally hear the unmistakable sound of two hags arguing, at which they prudently retire indoors to avoid the hail of rocks and trees that will inevitably follow. Irish hags may even come into the home to help with the spinning.

In the tale-type of the **loathly lady**, a hag is transformed into a beautiful maiden by the act of love of the hero.

▷ **Baba Yaga**; **Berchta**; **cailleach bheure**

Hagen

IN THE NIBELUNGENLIED, THE UNCLE OF GUNTHER who killed Siegfried (**Sigurd**) to revenge Brunhild and thus earns the undying hatred of Kriemhild (**Gudrun**),

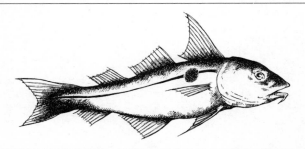

haddock

Siegfried's widow. He hides Siegfried's gold in the Rhine and, when he refuses to disclose its whereabouts to Etzel (**Atli** or Attila), is the last of the Nibelungen to be killed. Wagner's *Ring* opera has him as the son of Grimhild and **Alberich**, who is charged with restoring the ring to the **dwarfs**. He kills Siegfried and then attempts to remove the ring but takes fright when the lifeless arm moves to accuse him. He pursues the Rhine Maidens when they take the ring and is finally drowned.

Hagen

GERMANIC HERO. In the 11th-century *Gundrunlied*, Hagen is stolen by **griffins** as a child and grows up in a cave with three young girls. When a soldier's body is washed up Hagen uses the armour and weapons to kill his captors, and he and his three companions escape. He marries Hilde, one of the three, and they have a beautiful daughter also named Hilde. She is suited by Hettel, who abducts her in the face of her father's implacable opposition, but after a great fight Hagen agrees to the match, impressed by his new son-in-law's valour.

hair

HAIR HAS FEATURED LARGELY IN WORLD FOLKLORE, in tales, traditions and beliefs. Like **nails** and **footprints**, hair contains something of the individual's essence and it can be dangerous if fallen strands come into enemy hands to be used in **spells** and **curses**. To shave the head is a symbol of grief, repentance or humility, often undertaken as part of a religious commitment; when done by another it is not only a humiliation but

often an emasculation, as when Delilah shears Samson and his strength leaves him. A change in hairstyle is frequently a feature of **initiation**, the transition from childhood to sexual and social maturity. As well as being associated with a fiery temper because of the traditional language of **colour**, red hair means untrustworthiness in European lore, since Judas was said to have had red hair. In English lore especially any man with a red beard and a head of black hair was regarded with deep suspicion.

One of the most vivid uses of hair in the European **fairy tale** tradition is in the story of **Rapunzel**, who lets down her long braids to enable the witch, and later her lover, to reach her high window. This gentler, more seductive female aspect revealed in hair contrasts with the Medusa's snaky locks that had the power to turn men into stone. In a Spanish-American tale-type an innocent girl is buried alive by her step-mother; her hair grows into a bush or into ears of wheat that sing out her story as the wind passes through them and she is saved (cf **singing bone**). Irish fairy lore tells of a girl whose astonishingly beautiful golden hair, a gift from the fairies, is shorn off by an envious **hag**. The hair is here a **life token**; without it she pines and finally dies, but in her coffin the marvellous hair grows back. The belief that hair and fingernails continue to grow after death is widespread in Europe and America.

The 'hair of the dog' generally refers to a nip of whisky (or similar) taken to cure a hangover, but its origins are in ancient folk medicine. In many cultures a wound or illness, especially one involving magic, is thought to be curable only by the instrument that inflicted it; Telephus of Mysia was wounded by Achilles's spear and could only be restored by an ointment of its rust. Blacks in the southern American states used to apply patches of the offending dog's hair to a bite, and from this literal use the figurative expression developed.
▷ **beard**

Halfchick

ANIMAL HERO of a widespread European tale-type, found particularly in Spain, France, Russian and Estonia, but also known in India, Spanish America and

hag

215

the West Indies. Halfchick (Demi-coq in French and Mediopollo in Spanish) is either a runty chicken or a **cock** that has been bisected and magically restored to life. Halfchick sets out to ask the king for grain with some money he has found, and on the way befriends a river who decides to accompany him. Halfchick hides the river either in his anus or beneath his wings. He continues on his way, befriending and concealing a **wolf** (in some versions a group of robbers) and a **fox** in a similar way. When he arrives, the king, hoping to keep the money, accommodates him with the royal chickens, which he expects will peck him to death, but Halfchick releases the fox and the king wakes to find his poultry massacred. The next night he is placed with the royal horses, and he releases either the wolf to destroy them or the robbers who make off with the beasts. Lastly he is thrown in the oven; he quenches the fires and floods the palace with the release of the river. The defeated king sends him away with both grain and money.

Hallowe'en or All Hallow's Eve

HOLY EVENING, the festival observed on 31 October, the eve of **All Hallows' Day**. Although named as a Christian feast, Hallowe'en traditions owe more to the more ancient Celtic festival Samhain, marking the end of summer; Samhain eve was 31 October. It was a dangerous and magical time, when supernatural influences were at their peak, the pagan gods might walk among mortals, the spirits of the dead returned to earth to visit their homes, and spirits were at their most mischievous and destructive. Enormous bonfires were lit to drive away evil spirits, and elaborate sacrifices were offered to propitiate these fearful powers. However, those brave enough could use this unusual level of supernatural activity to their advantage, since even the **Devil** might be summoned on this day to aid in **divination**. Despite the Christianizing of the festival, the ancient beliefs persisted into modern times, and Hallowe'en is still more strongly associated with **witches**, **hobgoblins**, **ghosts** and so forth than the celebration of all the Christian saints. Popular customs surviving in Britain and particularly in

Hallowe'en jack-o'-lantern

North America include ducking for **apples** (biting apples floating in a tub of water, or suspended from a string, without the aid of hands); this, along with many games traditionally played at this festival, was originally a means of divination, to determine the marriages that would take place in the coming year or the fortunes of the family. Another popular tradition, especially in the United States, is 'trick-or-treat'—children go from house to house usually disguised in an appropriate costume such as a **witch**, **ghost** or black **cat**, and demand from the occupants a treat. If this is not forthcoming—usually in the form of a candy bar or a piece of fruit—a trick is threatened. Although such tricks were severe in the 19th century, with significant damage to property reported, they are seldom carried out in modern times. One of the most evocative symbols of Hallowe'en is the jack-o'-lantern, a hollowed-out **pumpkin** or squash (in Scotland a turnip) carved with a fearsome face through which the light of a candle inside shines. This may originally have been intended to frighten away demons and other ill-intentioned supernatural beings roaming the earth on this dangerous night.

haltia

FINNISH PROTECTIVE SPIRIT. There are various species of *haltia*, from the individual **genius** which develops three days after birth and remains with a human throughout his or her life, occasionally prompting its charge to mischief but generally serving as guide and protector, to the ancestral *talonhaltija*, the guardian of the home. Other minor haltia hold dominion over the bath-house, stable and so on, and the *metsänhaltia* is the ruler of the forest.

Hamlet see Amleth

handfasting

BETROTHAL CEREMONY, common especially in Denmark and Scotland, instigating a 'trial marriage' which may be dissolved after a year if it proves unsuccessful and no offspring is produced. The degree of commitment and intimacy varies with different cultures.
▷ **marriage**

hand of glory

MAGIC CHARM, the preserved hand of a corpse, preferably a hanged criminal (ideally a murderer). It is said in Western European lore to have the virtue of rendering the owner invisible, or of inducing an unconscious, trance-like state in those around him. Naturally such a charm was much in demand among burglars; holding a candle made from the fat of a corpse, or with its own fingers lit, the hand of glory ensured that no one in the house would wake while the thief pursued his activities.

The term almost certainly derives from *mandragore* (via French *main de gloire*) or mandragora, the **mandrake**, said to germinate from the spilled semen of hanged felons.

Similar beliefs have been recorded throughout the world; by the principles of **sympathetic magic** part of a corpse is widely thought to induce unconsciousness in the living.

handsel

A LUCKY GIFT, from Old English *hand-selen*, gift of the hand. It is associated with the beginning of a new phase of life or a new venture to bring luck to either the giver, the recipient or, as in the case of a new-struck bargain, both. A purse given as a gift should contain a coin to guard against emptiness. In some rural areas the first customer at the inn receives a free drink as a handsel.

hannya

JAPANESE DEMON, a terrifying cannibalistic ogress who is particularly fond of children. She is portrayed in masked No plays with fangs and horns.

Hansel and Gretel

GERMAN FOLKTALE, archetype of the abandoned children motif, with analogies all over the world. The father of Hansel and Gretel was a poor wood-cutter, who had difficulty finding food for his family at the best of times. When famine strikes the land and the family seem in danger of starving, the children's stepmother persuades her reluctant husband to take the children into the wood and abandon them there. Hansel and Gretel, unable to sleep for hunger, overhear their parents, and Hansel slips outside and collects a pocketful of small white pebbles. The next morning the family rise early and go off into the woods. As they walk, Hansel keeps dropping pebbles to mark their way. In the middle of the forest their father builds a fire and sets the brother and sister beside it, telling them he is going to chop wood, but he and his wife slip away as the children sleep. By the light of the full moon, however, Hansel is able to follow the trail of pebbles he has dropped and leads his sister back to the cottage, where their distressed father welcomes them joyfully.

Soon famine strikes again, and again the wood-cutter's wife insists that they abandon the children to save themselves. As before, Hansel overhears the conversation, but this time the door is locked and he cannot go out to collect pebbles. So the next day when they are each given a piece of bread for dinner, Hansel drops crumbs along the way to mark the path. Once again, the wood-cutter and his wife leave the children asleep beside the fire, saying that they are going to cut wood, but when the children wake alone in the late evening and try to find their path back home they discover that the crumbs have been eaten by birds.

They wander for three days without food, until they are led by a white bird into a clearing in which stands a house all made of bread, cake and sugar. They begin to eat in delight, until an old woman comes out of the house and kindly invites them in, to enjoy a meal and a good night's sleep. The next morning she seizes Hansel and throws him into a cage, and forces Gretel to cook and slave for her. Hansel she feeds abundantly, hoping to fatten him for her feast, but Gretel she starves. Each day she makes Hansel hold out his finger so she can feel if he has fattened, but Hansel holds out instead a piece of bone, and the short-sighted witch fumes with impatience. Finally she decides to eat him in any case. She commands Gretel to stoke the oven and to climb inside it to test the heat. Pretending not to understand, Gretel tricks the witch into climbing inside herself to demonstrate her meaning, whereupon she shuts the oven door upon her, frees Hansel, and the two return home with treasure from the witch's house. They cross a river on the back of a duck, and are welcomed joyfully by their father, the stepmother having died.

The story is an example of the children and **ogre** type, in which the ogre is typically burned to death in his own fire. It is well known throughout Europe (especially in the north), in India, Japan, Africa and among Native Americans and Pacific Islanders, but it is uncertain whether these versions all derive from a European original (although this seems most likely) or if they developed independently. The central motif is the tricking of the witch who preys on children; other key motifs are the wicked stepmother, the abandoned children, the trail of crumbs or peas which is eaten, and the stupid ogre who falls into his or her own trap. The edible house too is characteristic of the tale in all its versions.

Hanuman

MONKEY-GOD and benevolent spirit of Hindu lore, the chief of the monkey tribe. He plays a key role in the *Ramayana*, aiding Rama in his attempts to rescue Sita. One of his exploits was to enter Ravana's city as a spy; he was discovered and his tail set on fire, but he turned the tables by burning down the demon's city. He also carried the mountain of healing herbs to Rama's wounded army. He is an immensely popular deity, seen as an ideal of pious devotion, and is frequently portrayed in art. This is one of the most interesting developments of the helpful animal motif in religious lore.

Happy Hunting Ground

PARADISAL OTHERWORLD, the popular term among non-native Americans for the native concept of the **afterlife**. In most versions of this afterworld however hunting does not feature prominently: the dead are said to be invisible during the day but to emerge at night and partake of social activities such as singing, dancing, feasting and gaming. This otherworld is variously located in the vicinity of the group, across the ocean to the west or elsewhere. Many tales exist of mortals visiting the land of the dead, usually to seek a lost loved one, and returning to the world of the living to give an account of their adventures. No system of judgement after death is apparent in Native American lore, although several groups adopted the reward and punishment principles of Christian settlers and incorporated them into their traditional myths.

hare

LONG-EARED SMALL MAMMAL, of the family Leporidae, which differs from the **rabbit** in that the young are born fully haired and with open eyes. In Buddhist myth the hare is regarded as divine and in the East a hare is thought to be visible in the moon rather than a man. Perhaps the most famous example of the use of the hare in folklore is in **Aesop**'s animal fable, *The Hare and the Tortoise*; when the hare and tortoise decide to race against each other, the hare is confident of success. So complacent is he that after gaining a good lead with a smart run from the line, he lies down to take a snooze under a tree. While he sleeps the tortoise, who has been plodding patiently and determinedly along, passes him and snatches victory. The fable illustrates the value of perseverance over complacent self-confidence. It appears in African tradition too, as a trickster tale in which the tortoise, unusually, comes out on top.

▷ *Panchatantra*

harp

PLUCKED STRINGED INSTRUMENT, unique in that its strings, of varying lengths, are strung vertically. It has traditionally been highly regarded as a sacred instrument in Mediterranean and Middle Eastern cultures from the Egyptian and Mesopotamian eras at least; harps depicted in the tomb of Rameses III are played by priests. It contrasts with the more pastoral lyre, generally associated with common folk and entertainment.

Early forms included the horizontal harp, arched harps, where the neck forms a curve like that of a bow to enclose the strings, and angular harps, in which body and neck are set at an angle. The Western frame harp, with its supporting column, was a relatively late development (c.9th century AD) that allowed strings to be tauter and therefore higher in pitch.

Welsh and Irish bards plucked a harp to accompany their poems and songs, although since medieval chroniclers did not distinguish between lyres and harps it is difficult for modern scholars to ascertain which is meant in each circumstance. The reverence in which the harp was held in Wales especially, however, as a privilege of a free man and a necessity on a par with a virtuous wife according to the *Leges Wallicae*, suggests that harp is to be preferred over lyre.

The harp is the national symbol of Ireland, and popular Irish lore credits the origins of the instrument to an Irishman who, observing the soothing effect upon his wife of the wind playing through the sinews of a beached **whale**, created an instrument to reproduce the sound. Another Irish legend holds that the **Milesians** brought with them the first harper of Ireland. Irish (and Welsh) **fairies** are expert harpists, and their enchanting music may lure mortals to their doom.

A common motif of European folktales is the harp that reveals the truth, part of the **singing bone** tale-type (cf **flute**). Here the harp is constructed from the bones of a murdered innocent or, as in some versions of the Scottish ballad the *Twa Sisters*, strung with the hair of the drowned girl, and sings the tale when played.

harpies

FABULOUS CREATURES OF GREEK LORE, winged, usually ugly females. In early accounts harpies seem to be wind goddesses, and linked to this is their common association with death and ghostliness, the disembodied breath or spirit. Homer speaks of them as winds that snatched humans away, and in the *Iliad* he makes Podarge mother of Achilles's horse, sired by the west wind or by Zeus. Little is made of the Harpies' appearance in these early accounts, but in the later tales of **Jason** they are portrayed as repulsive, rapacious beings with talons, bringing pestilence in their wake. It is in this form that they appear as agents of justice sent to torment the Thracian king Phineus for his cruelty to his children; Phineus was saved from their fury by Calais and Zetes. This retributive aspect has caused some popular confusion between harpies and **Furies**, or Erinyes.

The harpies, although they properly belong to mythology, are part of a world-wide tradition of winged female spirits, with widely varying degrees of friendliness towards men, who generally serve as agents of the gods (cf **baginis**, **houries**, **Valkyries**).

harvest celebrations

RITUALS MARKING THE SUCCESSFUL GARNERING OF THE CROPS, performed in

harpist Hekenu playing arched harp, from Saqqara, Egypt, 5th dynasty (2563–2423 BC)

different forms throughout the world. Dances feature throughout the agricultural cycle, to ensure the soil's fertility before planting, to protect and bless the seed as it is sown, to request rain as necessary and to placate the powers upon whose pleasure the group's food supply depends.

At the end of this fraught period of waiting and hoping, then, the harvest dances naturally speak of relief, thanksgiving and celebration. They are generally danced by the entire community, emphasizing the interest and involvement of the whole group in the outcome of the harvest, and the celebrations often go on for days, throughout the collection and storage of the crop. A common pattern in such dances is the chain, formed by the participants linking hands to follow a leader who weaves among them. Native American corn dances are particularly intricate and significant. In them, as in most vegetative ceremonies world-wide, women play a prominent role (in contrast to hunting dances for example, which are performed almost exclusively by men). The power of female fertility is bound up in the mystery of growth and harvest for many peoples. Such dances are generally coupled with sacrifices of the harvest, followed by a feast, often orgiastic, on the abundance of the main food harvested, whether grain, vines, fruits or vegetables.

Pagan festivals in Europe were incorporated into the Christian Harvest Festival, in which the first-fruits of the harvest are traditionally brought in to deck out the churches as a form of sacrifice, and Thanksgiving Day in the United States preserves to some degree the celebratory and community aspects of the feast.
▷ **harvest doll**

harvest doll

SPIRIT OF THE HARVEST. The harvest doll has many names: in Scotland she is often known as the *cailleach*, the maiden or the **hag**; in the North of England she is the kern baby, corn dolly or harvest queen; in Poland the Baba, or Grandmother; in Germany the Old Woman or **kornwolf**. It is generally the last sheaf to be harvested or a doll made from it with varying degrees of realistic detail, and is carried home ceremoniously decked in ribbons and even sometimes in a dress, enthroned atop the load. It was originally thought to embody the spirit of the ripened grain, although in later belief it came to represent merely the abundance of harvest. To keep the harvest doll is generally considered lucky for the next year's crops, and it is often ritually soaked with water to ensure the continued productivity of the grain spirits.

Hasan

HERO OF THE ARABIAN NIGHTS. His tale seems to be a relatively late fabrication, drawing heavily from staple folkloric motifs. Like **Aladdin**, Hasan is an idler summoned by a sorcerer (here an alchemist) to seek out the treasure, the **philosopher's stone**, and is then abandoned. He is washed ashore at a palace where he befriends seven princesses and, then the alchemist returns, kills him. He enters a forbidden room from where he sees ten **swan maidens** and succeeds in stealing one of the feather garments, thus securing his bride. While he is away from the country however his wife discovers her bird-robe and flies off, calling to her mother-in-law that Hasan may find her in the islands of Wak. After many adventures, and aided by a band of helpers, a **cap of invisibility** and a magic staff that, like Aladdin's lamp, summons a jinni, Hasan eventually tracks his bride to the land of Wak Wak, populated by women, and brings her home.

Havelock the Dane

LEGENDARY DANISH HERO, the son of King Birkabegn who was abandoned after his father's death by his wicked protector, Earl Godard. In some versions Godard charges a fisherman, Grim, with his killing, but recognizing the boy's kingly destiny Grim flees to England with his charge. In other versions Havelock is set adrift on a raft and rescued by the kindly fisherman off the coast of Lincolnshire.

Havelock grows up as Grim's son and he eventually marries Goldborough, daughter of King Ethelwold of England. Havelock returns to Denmark with his bride and is eagerly received as monarch by the people, who recognize his 'king's mark' (in some versions a flame coming from his mouth). Godard is defeated, and after a few years Havelock returns to England to reward his guardian, Grim, who goes on to build the town of Grimsby with his new wealth.

hawk

BIRD OF PREY, particular species of the genus *Accipiter*, found throughout the world. Like the **eagle**, the hawk is widely associated with the sun, kingship and divinity. It was the ancient Egyptian symbol of royalty associated with the sun-god Ra, and in Greek myth it was said to be the messenger of the sun-god Apollo. In popular lore the hawk, again like the eagle, is said to be able to fly to the sun and to gaze upon it without blinking.

'The Hawk and the Nightingale', as told by Hesiod in his eighth-century BC *Works and Days*, is thought to be the earliest surviving Greek **animal fable**. The **nightingale** is captured by a hawk and begs for his freedom, pointing out that he is too tiny to satisfy such a great appetite, but the hawk remains unmoved, since even a small meal in hand is better than a large one not yet caught. The fable neatly demonstrates the pragmatic tone of many such fables, and has survived in English proverbial lore as 'A bird in the hand is worth two in the bush'.

hawthorn

THORNY SHRUB, genus *Crataegus* (family Rosaceae), usually bearing white or pink spring flowers and bright red berries. Its flowering is traditionally associated with spring celebrations, and in ancient Greece, because of this connection with fertility and new life, its flowers were used to make crowns and its wood to make the marriage torch at weddings; in Rome leaves of hawthorn were placed in the cradles of new babies as a protective **charm**. In Teutonic lore however it was more closely associated with death, often used for funeral pyres, as it was believed to have sprung from a lightning bolt.

In medieval Christian lore Christ's crown of thorns was said to have been formed from the bush, and it was therefore said to possess great virtue against evils such as shipwreck, storms,

ghosts and other malign influences. The flowering staff of **Joseph of Arimathea**, the Glastonbury thorn, is also said to have been a hawthorn branch.

In Ireland the hawthorn is a fairy bush, and to cut one down is not only unlucky but downright dangerous. Fallen boughs however may be nailed to the barn to protect the cattle and ensure a plentiful supply of milk.

Henry VII of England took the hawthorn as his symbol after the crown of Richard III was found on a hawthorn hedge at the Battle of Bosworth and later placed ceremoniously on his own head.

A tea of hawthorn blossoms or an infusion in wine is said to cure stomach pains and pleurisy, and a potion made from a distillation of the thorns is said to act as a poultice, drawing thorns and splinters from the skin.

Hayicanako

TLINGIT ATLAS FIGURE, 'The Old Woman Beneath Us', who guards the post supporting the earth or else holds it herself, making it shake whenever she feels hungry or restless. Whenever they feel the earth shift, the group rushes to pour on the fire grease or fat which will then melt and drip down to placate the old woman.
▷ **Atlas motif**

Hayk

ARMENIAN NATIONAL HERO, a comely **giant** who delivered his people from the tyrannical King Bel of Babylonia and led them to the mountains of Armenia, driving out the indigenous Urartians. When Bel sent his troops against the Armenians, Hayk defeated them by organizing his inferior army in an arrow formation. His emblems are a bow and triangular arrow. Armenians have traditionally called themselves the Hayk.

hazel

ALSO KNOWN AS FILBERT, a tree of the birch family (Betulaceae), genus *Corylus*. In Norse mythology it was closely associated with **lightning**, an attribute of the thunderer, Thor, and this was incorporated into medieval Christian belief when Germanic groups formed crosses from hazel twigs as **charms** against storms. A pious medieval German legend tells how Herod's wife Herodia attempted to kiss the severed head of John the Baptist when it was brought to her on a platter. The head, not permitting such lasciviousness even in death, opened its mouth and blew her to the top of a hazel tree, where she sits forever, unable to climb down.

In Celtic lore, and particularly in Ireland, hazel was the tree of knowledge; the salmon in Conla's well nibbled the nuts of the nine hazel trees of wisdom and became the wisest living being, and **Finn Mac Cumhal** gained his inspiration from sucking the thumb that he had burned while cooking the salmon for his druidic guardian. Hazel rods are used to drive cattle and to beat them with the **Beltane** fire as protection against the malignancy of the fairies.

Hazel is the preferred material for divining rods used in **dowsing**, especially if cut under specific conditions, most commonly on St John's night. Such rods were useful not only in the search for water but also for detecting criminals and treasure.

Another use of hazel in **divination** is the practice of placing two hazelnuts in the fire on **Hallowe'en** night, which reveal by their behaviour as they burn the fate of the lovers (cf **empyromancy**). An amuletic cross made from hazel is said to keep away evil spirits and to draw the poison from a snake bite. Ground hazelnuts mixed with pepper are taken to clear a stuffy head, while a double hazelnut was carried as a **charm** in England to protect the bearer from toothache.

healing see medicine

hedgehog

SMALL NOCTURNAL MAMMAL, family Erinaceidae, which defends itself by curling up to expose to predators nothing but its sharp spines. Plutarch popularized the belief that the creature collected food by rolling in fruit, particularly grapes and apples, and impaling them on its spines. These spines are popularly believed to give off a healthful odour when burnt.

The peculiar grunting of the hedgehog has in some cases associated it with demonic activity or **witchcraft**; in England and Ireland especially **witches** were said to take the form of hedgehogs to suck the milk from cattle by night.

Although hedgehog blood is said to be good for treating warts, warriors in Madagascar avoid eating hedgehog (tenrec) flesh lest they too roll up in a ball before their enemies (see **sympathetic magic**). The hedgehog features in folktales as a **helpful beast** and as a transformed prince restored to human form by the love of a princess.

Hedley kow

A TIRESOME SPECIES OF ENGLISH SPIRIT much given to practical jokes. Its favourite trick is to pose as a bale of hay which defies the attempts of labourers to carry or barn it by becoming impossibly heavy. When the exhausted worker stops for a rest, the 'bale' slopes off sniggering. Another of its tricks is to disguise itself as a domestic animal, a horse or cow, which slips out of the harness and prances around infuriatingly laughing its snickering laugh. Most everyday disasters, such as the spinning wool coming off the wheel, are attributed to his pranks.

Heldenbuch, Das

'BOOK OF HEROES', a collection of 13th-century German romances. The poems of the first cycle deal with lofty, heroic themes, focusing on the person of Dietrick von Bern, the archetypal medieval hero, while those of the second cycle featuring Hugdietrich, Ortnit and Wolfdietrich, are less lofty and more romantic.

helpful beast

MOTIF OF FOLKTALES, the animal companion who aids the human hero to fulfil the task, complete the quest or win the prize. The **mouse** is often a helpful figure in African and European folklore demonstrating the moral that size isn't everything. Other common creatures are the **dog** and **lion** (as in the archetypal tale **Androcles and the Lion**). The motif is one of the most fundamental building blocks of folktales around the world.

hen

FEMALE DOMESTIC FOWL. The hen is

traditionally associated with the female and fertility, because of her **egg**-laying. This identification has been extended further to link her clucking with a fussing woman, and hence the relationship between the **cock** and hen has in many areas become a metaphor for that between husband and wife, giving rise to the famous doggerel:

Whistling maid and crowing hen,
Neither fit for God or men.

'Hen-pecked' is a common term in English referring to a man who has allowed his wife to assume the dominant role in the household, thereby usurping the traditional order of patriarchy. On a more positive side, the hen is portrayed as a maternal protector; Jesus referred to this image when he spoke of gathering Jerusalem to himself as a hen gathers her chicks (Matthew 23:37).

Hens are frequently used in folk medicine; their blood is thought to be especially efficacious. They are also used, like cocks, in **alectryomancy**. *The Death of the Little Hen* is a popular European chain tale, in which a succession of animals and objects pay tribute to the hen in their own way.

henkies

TROWS OF ORKNEY AND SHETLAND. The most characteristic feature of these **troll**-like beings, much given to dancing, is their limp (see **defects**).

hepatoscopy

A FORM OF DIVINATION, much practised in ancient Greece and Rome, from the inspection of the **liver** of a sacrifice. The liver was thought to be the seat of the spirit and the vital principle.

Heracles

GREEK HERO, known in Roman mythology as Hercules, famed for his prodigious strength. The son of Zeus and Alcmena, his first feat, performed in his cradle, was the strangling of two serpents the jealous Hera had sent to kill him. Hera continued to torment him; after his marriage to Megara of Boeotia she sent a mad rage upon him in the course of which he slew his wife and their children and was obliged to spend 12 years as a vassal of Eurystheus, who assigned to him the 12 famous labours:

to kill the Nemean lion
to slay the **hydra** of Lerna
to catch the Arcadian stag
to destroy the wild Erymanthian boar
to clean the Augean stables in a day
to eliminate the cannibalistic birds of the Stymphalian marshes
to capture the Cretan bull
to catch the man-eating horses of King Diomedes
to obtain the girdle of the Amazonian queen **Hippolyta**
to steal the cattle of the giant Geryon
to pluck the apples of the Hesperides at the world's end
and to bring into mortal regions Cerberus, the three-headed hound of the underworld.

Heracles's mortal body was slain by the treachery of the **centaur** Nessus; Nessus had told Heracles's lover Deianeira as he lay dying that his blood was a powerful love charm, but when she presented Heracles with a cloak anointed with it the blood proved to be poisonous. By his life of toil and duty however Heracles had won immortality, and his immortal spirit joined the gods on Olympus where he married Hebe.

Heracles is central to European folk tradition as he proved the enduring archetype of the folk hero for centuries, marked by physical prowess, endurance, voracious physical and sexual appetites and good humour. The enormous body of tales concerning **tasks and tests** echoes his legend.

herbs

AROMATIC PLANTS, used for magic and medicine in every culture, often in widely different ways. A common characteristic of herb lore is the claim that their healing qualities, and the knowledge of how to use them correctly, are a gift from the gods. Native American groups often tell of how the **culture hero** revealed herbal secrets to the tribe, while in medieval Europe **saints** were thought to appear regularly to guide the faithful to plant wisdom. In one Hungarian legend, King Ladislaus discovers the herbal cure for a plague by shooting an **arrow** into the air with a prayer for divine aid. **Odysseus** was protected from the spells of Circe by the sprig of moly given to him by Hermes. The use of herbs in primitive society is closely connected to magical practices too, and many rituals involved specific herbs as incense, in the preparation of sacred food or as a hunting charm or amulet.

Every human complaint has been treated at some time by herbal medicine, whether by drinking an infusion, applying a poultice, wearing it as an amulet or smoking or inhaling it. In many cases different cultures have widely different remedies, so that the herb which is used as a poison by one group may be used in a different form as a remedy by another. In medieval Europe hagiography provided an acceptably authoritative link between diseases and herbs; since certain diseases were associated with the protection of a specific saint, the herbs sacred to that saint were necessarily the cure for the illness. By a similar system of primitive logic, the function of herbs was deduced from their appearance, so that red-coloured plants were used to treat the blood and heat, and the **mandrake** root, thought to be shaped like a human figure, was regarded as especially potent for all diseases. The names of herbs also suggested their use: **basil** was thought to be an antidote to the poison of the fabulous **basilisk**, probably through a process of folk etymology. It is also widely used against the poisons of scorpions, although in some cultures it is itself considered poisonous.

The distinction between remedies and charms is generally unclear in folk medicine; herbal remedies, especially in primitive societies, are generally administered along with ritual and magical incantation, and they were prepared in a similar way to love potions (often made from **mandrake** and **ginseng**) whose purpose was purely magical. The gathering of herbs demands the observance of ritual and taboo in many cultures: the ancient Greek quacks surrounded their trade with superstitious mystique, and in many folk societies the most highly skilled herbalists guard the secrets of their concoctions fiercely. Examples of some of the necessary observances include gathering the herb only by moonlight or only in conjunction with other herbs and the taboo against using an iron blade.

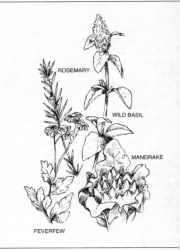

herbs

Much herbal lore, however, established with the experience and authority of centuries of tradition, has been found to be effective by scientific investigation. Herbals, which listed the properties and uses of various herbs, have been common in the West from classical times up to the present day, and provided the foundations on which the science of botany later developed.

Hercules see Heracles

Herla, King

LEGENDARY BRITISH KING, whose story is told by Walter Map in his 12th-century *De Nugis Curialium*. Herla one day met a diminutive king who invited himself and his retinue to Herla's forthcoming marriage, of which Herla himself had not known until that point. The dwarfish king and his followers appeared with great pomp and many presents to Herla's wedding feast, and a year later to fulfil his pledge, Herla travelled into the other's underground kingdom by means of an enormous cave. The king and his followers stayed beneath ground for what seemed to them three days, and as they prepared to return to their home the dwarf king pressed on Herla many rich presents and a tiny dog; none of the men were to dismount, he said, until this dog leapt down of its own free will. The men returned to find their land oddly changed, and Herla called out to an old labourer to ask after his queen. The old man, being a Saxon, scarcely comprehended the language of the Briton; more than 200 mortal years had passed during Herla's brief sojourn underground. Some of his followers dismounted in consternation and crumbled into dust; the rest still travel on their horses, endlessly waiting for the dog to jump down.

This typifies the common theme in **fairy** lore of the supernatural passage of time (see **fairyland**).

hero

CHIEF PROTAGONIST OF FOLKTALE OR LEGEND, commanding the listener's wonder and sympathies. Since it is the nature of folklore to be concerned with humankind rather than deities, and the common people rather than great historical figures, the true folk hero is usually portrayed as a human living in similar conditions to those hearing the tale. He or she is not bound to actual time or place however, and in almost all cases the hero encounters the supernatural as part of the everyday course of events.

Much has been written on the use of the hero-figure in fairy tales of Europe and Asia. Leaving aside the more fanciful psychoanalytic and sociological interpretations, it seems clear that the most basic pattern for the hero is one of dissociation from the known and the overcoming of difficulty to reach a position of secure, socially acceptable success. **Hansel and Gretel** in the woods, **Cap o' Rushes** serving in a strange house, the youngest son sent out to seek his fortune, all are examples of the hero triumphing in an unfamiliar and hostile environment. Another fundamental pattern is that of an inversion of reality; the lowly peasant girl becomes a princess or the princess disguises herself as a scullery-maid, and the hideous beast or **frog** is revealed as a handsome prince. The hero attaches to him or herself a sense of the potentialities of life, a positive vision of change and human success in a fundamentally benevolent universe. The hero may be virtuous, clever, lazy or foolish, but in the end he or she secures the prize.

The folk hero differs from the fairy tale hero in having at least some claim to historical existence, although the popular figure of folklore may bear little resemblance to the historical personage on which it is based. In general the hero's actual deeds will be exaggerated and he will attract to himself a body of floating lore, deeds worthy of the heroic stereotype such as the slaying of a **dragon** (hence the folk figure of St **George**). The folk hero is typically a warrior (and therefore almost exclusively male) on either a national level, such as **Charlemagne**, or more locally, for example **Robin Hood**. The folk hero often becomes a peg on which is hung a cycle of tales and anecdotes, whereas the hero of the fairy-tale tends not to feature in a series of tales. The progression is generally from anecdotes and **ballads** to folktale cycle and from thence to full epic form, such as that attained by **Beowulf**.

The selection of a folk hero and the tales spun around him often reveal much about the preoccupations and ideals of the folk themselves. American folk heroes such as Davy **Crockett** and **Paul Bunyan** (although the latter is largely a product of the mass media rather than the folk themselves) embody the virtues of the hard-working pioneer: brash, powerful, coarse-mannered and humorous. The outlaw heroes such as Jesse **James** and **Billy the Kid** are notable for their daring and violent deeds, their morality redeemed only because their deaths were brought about treacherously and hence folk tradition has rendered them loyal, brave and heroic. The English outlaw Robin Hood is celebrated most for his justice and championing of the poor, no matter what the facts of his life may have been.

Outside the humanistic traditions of the West, many folk heroes are altogether non-human or only ambiguously human. Native American and African groups generally tell their tales about animals, and their cycles develop around the **culture hero** or **trickster** figure, such as **Brer Rabbit**. These hero figures are rather more complex and ambivalent than those of Western tradition; they contain within themselves both good and evil, creative and destructive forces, and they may be as often gulled as they gull others. In many of these tales there is less use of external supernatural apparatus such as magic lamps and **fairy godmothers** and more emphasis on the resourcefulness and cunning of the hero himself.

hex

A WORKER OF SPELLS, a **witch** or **wizard**. This Germanic word gained currency particularly among the Dutch and German settlers in Pennsylvania. Individuals with particular skills as hexes are in great demand to lay protective spells on animals, to cure sickness or to bring about any desired result—occasionally this result may be ill-fortune to another. Hex spells generally involve incantation of magical formulae, rituals or specially constructed **charms**. The prevalence of hex signs over Pennsylvanian barns, colourful round motifs depicting simple floral or geometrical shapes, intended to combat the malign influences of **witchcraft** and the **evil eye** on the livestock, attests to the strength of the belief. Cases of alleged hexes were coming to the courts well into the 20th century in parts of Pennsylvania.

Hiawatha

LEGENDARY NATIVE AMERICAN, chief of the Onondaga group during the 15th or 16th centuries. He is revered as a powerful magician and **culture hero** in Native American tradition, teaching the skills of navigation, agriculture and medicine to mankind. He is credited with the formation of the great Iroquois League, or League of Five (subsequently six) Nations, a confederacy which eschewed tribal rivalries and did much to halt white settlement of the upper New York State area by their cohesion and highly organized resistance. His tale is recounted in Henry Wadsworth Longfellow's famous epic poem, *The Song of Hiawatha* (1855), written in the metre of the *Kalevala*, which tells of his education at the knee of his grandmother Nokomis and his marriage to the lovely Minnehaha. He is commemmorated by an imposing 15m/50ft-high statue in Ironwood, Michigan.

Highland Fling

Highland Fling

SCOTTISH DANCE, traditionally performed by a male soloist, involving very precise footwork. The characteristic step is a hop on one foot while the other beats rapidly in front of and behind the calf, with one or both arms raised above the head. It is thought to have originated as a victory dance among Highland clans, and some experts suggest that it was originally performed on the round shield of the slain enemy, hence its static tendency. Still performed widely today as a national dance, the fling demands great precision of execution and balance.

Hildebrand

HERO OF GERMAN ROMANCE, whose tale is told in the Old High German *Hildebrandslied* (Song of Hildebrand, c.800AD). The old man is a sage and magician, adviser to Dietrich von Bern (the Ostrogothic king Theodoric). After many years fighting the Huns he returns home and is challenged by his aggressive son, Hadubrand, who is ignorant of their kinship. The surviving fragment does not record the outcome of the duel, but it is clear that, like **Cuchulainn**, Hildebrand eventually slays his son.

hippogriff

FABULOUS CREATURE, the offspring of a **griffin** father and a mare, with the wings, head, plumage and front talons of the griffin and the lower half of a horse. Although this type of fantastical crossbreeding is a well-established folkloric tradition, the hippogriff was the literary creation of Ariosto in his *Orlando Furioso* where it functioned as a symbol of love.

Hippolyta

QUEEN OF THE AMAZONS, the warrior daughter of the war-god Mars. The ninth labour of **Heracles** was to obtain her girdle, which fearsome task he accomplished with relative ease in some versions since Hippolyta fell in love with him. Her subjects, however, fearing that Heracles was abducting her, attacked his ship and Hippolyta was slain in the battle. In other versions Heracles battled the Amazonian forces, slew Hippolyta and took the girdle from her dead body, and still other versions tell how he captured Hippolyta's general Melanippa and used her as a hostage to gain the girdle. He went on to give Hippolyta as a wife to Theseus, and they produced a son, **Hippolytus**.

Hippolytus

GREEK TRAGIC HERO, the son of Theseus and **Hippolyta**, a chaste devotee of Artemis. He was beloved of Phaedra, his father's second wife, but when he repulsed her advances she killed herself, leaving a note accusing her step-son of rape. Theseus, distraught, cursed his son and called on Poseidon to mete out his revenge, and Hippolytus was killed when a bull emerged from the sea and his horses took fright, dragging their master behind them over miles of rough countryside. Theseus then learned the truth. The theme of the slighted woman taking such revenge is a popular one, famously found in the biblical tale of Joseph and Potiphar's wife. The tale is best known through Euripides's tragedy *Hippolytus*.

hippopotamus

'RIVER HORSE', A LARGE AMPHIBIOUS MAMMAL native to Africa (*Hippopotamus amphibius*). Although it can be roused to attack, the hippopotamus is generally a placid creature, and its appearance is generally viewed in Africa as a sign of fertility; in ancient Egypt it was sacred to the goddess Taueret who aided women in childbirth. It was also associated with the malign influence of Set however, who took the form of a hippopotamus and was overcome by the spear of Horus. It has been suggested that the Hebrew monster **Behemoth** (Job 40:15–24), king of the land animals, was the hippopotamus.

historic–geographic theory

SCHOOL OF FOLKLORE STUDY. The **devo-**

Hippolytus

lutionary theory was generally super-seded by the historic–geographic school of the Finns in the late 19th century, an evolutionary approach proposed especially by Julius and Kaarle Krohn. Its guiding principle was the individual treatment of every folktale: after collating a series of tale-types sharing a common series of motifs, the scholar would be able to postulate one original underlying form, which he would then attempt to locate geographically and historically, before going on to trace a likely route of diffusion and hence account for the variants. This systematic approach proved invaluable in establishing a body of material, but the assumption that all similar tales derive from one source and the refusal to consider **motifs** individually has severely limited its usefulness. Some motifs are the fundamental building-blocks of myth and tale, not merely their components, deriving from the deepest preoccupations of humans universally.

hobby-horse

REPRESENTATION OF A HORSE, now usually a children's toy. The term, thought by some to be a diminutive form of Robin, was originally used for a small horse. It was later applied to the wickerwork frame worn by **Morris dancers**, supported around the waist with straps and usually having long trappings to hide the dancer's legs and fake 'legs' draped over its sides, to give the comical impression that the dancer is mounted on a horse. The use of the mounted mummer may be a relic of the legend of St **George**. By extension, the term is now used to refer to the stick topped with a wooden horse's head which is straddled and 'ridden' like a horse by children.

hobgoblin

MISCHIEVOUS SPIRITS, a generic term for friendly yet volatile beings such as the **puck** and **brownie**. Hobgoblins are not members of the **fairy** band proper with its underground dances and **glamour**, yet neither are they **bogeys**, demons or **goblins**, although they can be destructive if offended. They are characteristically good-humoured and irrepressible; in later usage and particularly among the

Puritans the word gained ill-omened connotations to refer to a satanic force.

hobyahs

CANNIBALISTIC GOBLINS, featured in a tale found in Scotland and New England. The hobyahs come run run running, skip skip skipping on the ends of their toes from the deep dark woods towards the old couple's house but are kept at bay by the barking of little dog Turpy. When the old man tires of his dog's nocturnal barking however he dismembers him night by night until, with the dog finally silenced, the hobyahs attack the house and carry off the old lady in a sack. The old man restores his faithful dog and they journey to the woods during the day; while the hobyahs sleep he releases his wife and replaces her with the dog. The hobyahs wake and begin to taunt their victim, preparing to feast, but Turpy leaps out of the sack at the terrified hobyahs and devours them all.

This is the only tale concerning the hobyahs, and it is almost certain that, unlike most **goblins** and mischievous spirits, they were nursery **bogeys** rather than objects of real folk belief. The settlers' fear of the unknown woods and the unfamiliar environment is evident in the tale.

hodening

CHRISTMAS RITUAL, celebrated in Kent in England. A man dressed as a horse is led from house to house with his companions, receiving money and gifts in return for singing carols.

Hogmanay

SCOTTISH FESTIVAL, deriving from a feast of the ancient Celtic calendar, celebrated on 31 December. It is traditionally observed as a riotous and sociable occasion, having much in common with **New Year** celebrations throughout the world. One characteristic feature is the ritual of **first-footing**—visiting the homes of friends and neighbours after 'the bells' to welcome the new year into their houses, preferably carrying **salt**, bread, whisky and other gifts to ensure that the coming year will be prosperous. Children may travel round the houses, soliciting oatcakes, wearing **masks** or singing. In old folk belief it was said that farm animals received the gift of speech on this night, during the striking of the bells at midnight, and would give advice to anyone who asked it of them during this interval.

Holle, Mother

GERMANIC FOLKTALE, collected by Grimm. The younger sister is forced by her step-mother to go down a well to retrieve the shuttle she has dropped. There she comes upon a batch of bread about to burn in an oven, which she swiftly takes out, and she obliges the apple-trees by shaking the ripe fruit down. She enters the service of Mother Holle, a benevolent **witch** figure, and rises early to shake the bedclothes until the feathers fly like snow. Finally, homesick, she takes her leave of the land at the bottom of the well and is showered with gold as she returns home. Seeing this, her step-sister hastens down the well, but she ignores the pleas of the bread and apples, and lies in all morning instead of shaking out the beds. She is dismissed by Mother Holle and hurries back home, only to be greeted by a shower of ineradicable pitch instead of gold.

The tale belongs to the world-wide type contrasting kind and unkind behaviour and their respective rewards. Holle (also known as Holde, Hulda or Hulle) was originally a Germanic sky goddess, who rode through the sky accompanied by **witches** on wild nights. Snow was said to be the feathers shaken from her bedclothes. The spirits of her realm who accompany her on her **Wild Hunt**-like progress are the souls of unbaptized infants. **Eckhardt**, an old mortal man, is said to have been swept up in their train and will remain at Holle's court until Judgement Day. The *holle kneish* was a custom observed by German Jews to protect their unbaptized children (particularly girls, who will not benefit from the protective rites of the barmitzvah) from Holde's malevolence. Holde is invoked to name the child after the mother's confinement by a group of children surrounding the baby.

She is associated with water and lakes, and the descent to the well's bottom was said to be a means of reaching her realm. Grimm's tale illustrates the degeneration of her mythological aspects; in later lore Holle became a nursery **bogey**, an ugly **hag**, whose beneficent aspects as goddess of hearth and spinning mellowed her into a kindly witch.

Holi

HINDU SPRING FESTIVAL, a riotous celebration taking place on or just before the full moon day Phālguna (February/March), when the spring crops are almost ripe. Ceremonial fires are lit and Saturnalian street processions take place; with the usual distinctions of caste, sex and rank suspended, the revellers cover each other in powders and coloured water and licentious frivolity is tolerated. The frolicking recalls Krishna's adventures with the cowgirls (*gopīs*). Images of the gods placed on special platforms are ritually swung during the festivities; this is the *Dolayātra*.

For all its popularity, the festival has

Krishna, venerated at Holi

229

little to do with the principles of ortho-dox Hinduism, and it seems clear that its origins are more ancient, lying in the primitive celebrations of new life and the need to restore fertility to the earth.

holly

EVERGREEN SHRUB OR TREE, genus *Ilex* (family Aquifoliaceae), characterized by glossy, prickly leaves, white flowers and red berries. In Roman times it served to decorate houses during the **Saturnalia** and this may be the root of its traditional use at **Christmas** in the West. Much Christian lore has grown up around the holly; it is said (along with many other trees) to have provided the wood for the cross of Christ, in punishment for which it is now fated to bear thorny leaves and berries like drops of blood, and be forever stunted. In many areas, particularly Wales, it is believed to be unlucky to allow holly into the house before Christmas Eve, since it will bring about family conflicts, and holly left in the house after Twelfth Night will bring a trouble for every leaf. During the Christmas season however holly is a powerful **charm**, with the power to keep demons and **witches** at bay and to make animals healthy and productive.

Holly berries are used medicinally in many areas to treat rheumatism, stomach pains, fever, gout and asthma. A tea made from the leaves of a South American holly (*Ilex paraguariensis*) is used by many Native Americans as a stimulant and to treat measles.

hoopoe

CRESTED BIRD, *Upupa epops*, found in Africa, Asia and southern Europe. It has a reputation, popularized by medieval bestiaries, as a filthy bird which feeds from dunghills and nests in its own excrement; a Rumanian tale tells how the hoopoe demanded such luxuries from God that its creator finally condemned it to a life in the dunghills as punishment. In Hebrew lore it was considered unclean, but Solomon is said to have honoured the bird with its crest because of its kindness in providing shade in the desert, or alternatively to have recognized its wisdom in refusing to honour females. It is also honoured among many as an example of filial devotion, said to bring food to its ageing parents.

A common Arab belief is that the hoopoe, known as 'Doctor Bird', can divine water, and will lead humans to it. This probably arose from the bird's habit of opening and closing its crest as it searches the ground for insects.

According to a tale collected by Grimm, the hoopoe is a transformed cattle-herd whose cry is 'Up! Up! Up!'—his erstwhile shout to his starved cattle.

hopscotch

CHILDREN'S GAME, popular in Europe and North America, in which the aim is to complete a figure drawn on the ground (scotch = a scored line) by hopping to designated, often numbered, segments without falling, touching a line or dropping the raised foot. There are many versions of the game, from lateral courses in which players must alternately

hopscotch patterns

hop and land with each foot in a segment to spirals with a 'rest' segment in the middle. Generally the aim is to complete the course successfully in order to initial a segment of one's choice, which can then be used as a rest stop for that player but must not be landed on by any other. The game continues until all but one have failed to complete the increasingly difficult course.

The widespread popularity of the game may stem from ancient super-stitions about the danger of treading on cracks, which has survived in many areas in **children's lore**.
▷ **games**

hora

FOLK DANCE OF ROMANIA AND ISRAEL, performed in a circle by the whole community; with joined hands, the dan-cers move forwards, backwards and sideways in simple steps. The dance's significance in Romania is in its state-ment of community—it is often per-formed at weddings, and while adoles-cents and those ending mourning are drawn into the circle, offenders are excluded. In Israel, where the dance is performed with a more stamping, grape-vine step, it functions primarily as a celebratory dance.

horn

WIND INSTRUMENT, originally formed from the horn of an animal. It is widely used as a signal, to warn or to summon aid, and to drive away evil influences. In Teutonic lore the horn is particularly associated with warriors and hunters, and the Giallarhorn features as the means by which Heimdall, watchman of the Norse gods, warns of attack.

Since the qualities of the animal pass into its horn, horns from **elephant** tusks are highly prized in Africa. Because of its crescent shape, the horn is widely used in **moon** rites; it is blown to drive away the monster eating the moon during an **eclipse**, for example, and at sunset to ensure that the moon will rise to replace the departing sun (see **alphorn**). In **amulets** and **charms**, horns are believed to bring good luck and to avert the **evil eye**.

horse

HOOFED MAMMAL, *Equus caballus*, a companion of humans for transport, labour and sport since ancient times (at least the second millennium BC). It is held in high regard for its swiftness, strength, intelligence and beauty, and many mythologies incorporate horses into the pantheon. Kwan-yin in China and Kuannan in Japan appear as white horses, as will Vishnu in his last appear-ance, and the Celtic goddess Epona and occasionally the Greek fertility goddess Ceres are horse-headed. White or golden horses were associated with the solar force—they drew the chariot of Apollo in Greek legend—while black horses are linked with rain gods, **witchcraft**, the **Wild Hunt**, the **Devil** and apocalypse. The horse is also portrayed as a wind-spirit, skimming the top of growing corn and imparting fertility. The winged Pegasus in his early forms carried the thunder and lightning of Zeus in the winds. These divine connec-tions, along with their economic value, made the horse a favourite animal for sacrifice in many cultures.

Horses in folklore are generally lucky; to dream of a horse or to see a white horse is particularly fortunate. Folktales tell of marvellous flying horses such as the brazen horse of Arabia, presented to Cambuscan by the king, which was controlled by a pin in its ear, and the horse often appears as a supernatural helper, sometimes as an enchanted prince trapped as a horse until freed by the hero he has helped. St Dunstan is said to have effortlessly shoed a horse by removing its legs, and then replacing them, shod, without harm to the animal. One of the most common themes in horse tales is the speaking horse, which can almost always be relied upon to tell the truth.

Like other animals such as **cats**, horses are widely credited with the ability to see **ghosts**, and when a horse inexplicably takes fright he may have just encountered such a spirit. In the case of **dead riders** or ghost carriages, a horse may itself appear as part of a ghostly entourage. The **Devil** and his servants, the **witches**, are known to take the form of horses to do nefarious deeds by night, and a Scottish tale tells how a farmer shod such a horse one night to find the next day a woman of the village suspected of witchcraft lying in agony with **horseshoes** nailed to her hands and feet (see **shape-shifting**). In an Aesopic fable, a horse allows itself to be saddled and harnessed by a human in order to gain revenge on a troublesome stag, but the man betrays his trust and the horse has been under his dominion ever since.

horse dances

DANCE TYPE FOUND AROUND THE WORLD, involving ritual simulation of riding. Occasionally, for example among the Comanche and Blackfoot, such dances are performed with live horses, but more usually a **hobby-horse** is used. Such dances are a display of wealth, virility and mastery, and may date back to ancient sacrificial practices.

horseshoe

U-SHAPED METAL FRAME, usually of iron, nailed to a **horse**'s hoof to give protection against wearing, which has become a symbol of good fortune in many areas of the world, especially Europe and North America. Its power may stem from the virtues of **iron**, which is believed to repel all malignant influences, but many scholars have suggested further reasons for its astonishing popularity. The connection with ancient Aztec symbols for fertility, shaped like a horseshoe and paralleled in other Native American cultures, provides an important clue, as may its resemblance to the two horns of the new moon.

The horseshoe should be placed above the door, outside not within the house, for maximum benefit, and its horns should point upwards so the luck cannot 'run out'. In Pennsylvania it is sometimes positioned with the ends pointing into the house, to allow the luck to spill in. The **Devil** cannot enter a house, church, barn or stable thus protected. One hagiographic legend tells how St Dunstan shod the Devil so painfully that he wrung from him a promise never to enter a dwelling where a horseshoe was displayed.

It is customary in many parts of North America and Europe to present the bride with an ornament in the shape of a horseshoe, as a token to bring good luck.

hotots

DEMONIC SPIRITS OF ARMENIA, who dwell in swamps and rivers. They appear to mortals, especially children, and also to cattle and horses, as cheerful, dancing spirits to lure their victims into the swamps, where they drown them. They can be recognized by the mire that always clings to them.

houries

BEAUTIFUL, BLACK-EYED VIRGINS OF ISLAMIC LORE, who welcome the blessed into Paradise. The Islamic word, *hawrā'*, signifies the beauty of the black iris contrasting with the pure white of the eye. Some parts of the Koran speak of these 'spotless virgins', who will satisfy the faithful Muslims sensual appetites in

houri

proportion to the strictness of his religious observance on earth, but in later writings the female attendants of the faithful are their 'purified wives'.

The sensual attractions of the houri became a subject of many folkloric elaborations. The houri belong to a world-wide tradition of nubile attendants in the **afterlife**.

household spirits

SUPERNATURAL BEINGS, A general term for a wide variety of mainly European spirits who inhabit human homes. They may act as guardians, but are more usually mischievous helpers, who perform household tasks but are easily provoked to malicious trouble-making ▷ **aitvaras**; **bannik**; **Billy Blind**; **boggart**; **brownie**; **bwbachod**; **domovik**; **goblins**; **nisse**; **penates**; **pixies**; **puck**; **puk**

Houssain

CHARACTER OF THE ARABIAN NIGHTS, brother of Prince **Ahmed**, and possessor of a marvellous flying **magic carpet**.

Hrolf Kraki

LEGENDARY DANISH KING, hero of the *Hrolfssaga*. He was renowned for his superhuman strength and his generosity; he gave away armoury, estates and precious rings among the people and threw gold on the ground as he travelled. He was accompanied by 12 loyal **berserkers**, a warrior-like hawk named Habrok and a dog, Garm, who defeated a magic boar set upon his master by an enemy. Like many other folk-hero kings (cf **Arthur**) Hrolf possessed a marvellous **sword**, Skofnung. He died tragically at Leire Castle in Zealand, the traditional seat of the ancient kings.

Huathicuri

FOLK HERO OF PERU, famous for his ability to speak with animals. He won his bride by learning from a **fox** the source of the chief's baffling illness, and so married his daughter, and was helped in his further adventures by other animals.

hula

SACRED DANCE OF HAWAII AND THE EASTER ISLANDS, originally performed in honour of the gods and said to have been handed down to humans from them. The characteristic hip-swaying, the result of shifting weight between the feet in a mainly static stance, and the sinuous arm movements are not primarily erotic but rather mimetic, like the Hindu dances from which the hula is descended. The highest order of hula communicates the divine principle, the next deals with the natural world, and the lowest order of hula, and that most famous today, is overtly erotic. The swaying of the dancers is emphasized by the traditional grass skirts of the women and ornaments

hula dancers

of whales' or dogs' teeth and flower garlands worn by both sexes. Singers accompanied by **drums**, gourd **rattles**, whistles and bamboo sticks perform with the dancers.

hummingbird

BRIGHTLY COLOURED BIRD, of the family Trochilidae, found mainly in South America. Because of their unusual wing formation, humming birds are able to fly not only forwards but backwards, sideways and vertically, and to hover motionless before flowers to feed. These abilities won the hummingbird a reputation for magical powers, and its feathers, or even a whole bird, were used throughout the continent in **charms**. It is especially efficacious in attracting admiration from the opposite sex, and is sometimes dried and crumbled into a drink to make a love potion.

hunting magic

RITUALS TO SECURE SUCCESS IN THE HUNT. Before hunting many Native American and African groups ask the permission of the spirit masters, whose animals their prey may be, and may draw the desired prey in the process of being killed to secure dominance over it. If the hunter is to be gone for some time, he often prepares by abstention from sexual intercourse, and the waiting family should avoid eating the flesh of male animals lest this bring about the death of the hunter.

Once the kill has been made, it is customary in many societies around the world to ask the forgiveness of the prey, explaining that its death is necessary to sustain the people and praising the animal's qualities of courage and nobility. This courtesy placates the animal's spirit. In some cases the hunters may ask the dead animal's spirit to bring to them other members of its species to partake in such honours (see **bear**). It is considered discourteous and even dangerous to kill animals not required for food, as this angers the spirits. In some groups a new hunter is forbidden to eat the first of each species he kills, as to do so would mean he would never kill that species again.

Husayn (al-Husayn) (624–80)

THE SECOND SON OF ALI AND FATIMAH (daughter of Muhammad), born in Medina in Arabia. Husayn's story is a central element in the Shiite Muslim tradition. He lived in Medina during the rule of the first Umayyad caliph Muawiya, but on his death he retired to Mecca without swearing allegiance to Muawiya's son Yazid. As Muhammad's grandson he had claims to leadership of the Muslim community and he was persuaded to go to Kufah in Iraq in 680, having received promises of support. However, he and about 600 men were surrounded by an army of about 4000 at Karbala near Kufah, and having refused to surrender they were finally massacred. Husayn's death took place on the 10th Muharram (10th October), and this remains an anniversary of mourning for Shiite Muslims. His death is viewed as a sacrificial martyrdom by Shiites and the drama of Karbala is remembered in art, folklore, spirituality and writing—and annually by frenzied and grief-stricken commemorative rituals in which devotees beat themselves in the streets. Karbala remains the most important shrine of the Shiite Twelvers.

hydra

FABULOUS GREEK MONSTER, a water-serpent with multiple heads (usually nine) inhabiting the marshes of Lena, near Argos. It was the offspring of Typhon and Echidna. The slaying of the hydra was one of the twelve labours of **Heracles**, who discovered that two heads grew for every one that he severed. He finally defeated the monster with the aid of Iolaus, who applied burning torches to the necks as Heracles cut off the heads, thus allowing Heracles finally to sever the last, immortal head. The blood of the monster, used by Heracles to tip his arrows, was a deadly poison. The hydra is closely related to the many heroic tales of **dragonslayers** found throughout the world, demonstrating such motifs as the link with water, the many heads, the

hydra

cunning required to kill the beast and the assistance of the loyal companion.

hyena

DOG-LIKE SCAVENGER, family Hyaenidae. Pliny claims that the *hyaenia*, a magical stone that imparts the gift of prophecy when placed under the tongue, is found in the creature's eye (see **jewel in serpent's head**). An ancient tradition claims that the hyena changes its sex each year. Hyenas are popularly said to be able to imitate the human voice, luring men and dogs to their death, and in many areas of Africa it is regarded as a popular vehicle for the souls of the dead to inhabit to take revenge on their enemies. It is a favourite form too of sorcerers and shamans. In Christian bestiaries the hyena represents treachery, hypocrisy, uncleanliness and vice.

Icarius

IN GREEK LEGEND, THE FIRST WINE-MAKER, pupil of Dionysus. He was slain by a group of peasants, who thought they had been poisoned when they began to feel the effects of the wine he had given them.

Icarus

TRAGIC FIGURE OF GREEK LORE, the son of the inventor Daedalus, who attempted to fly with his father from Crete on wings of wax and feathers. Disregarding his father's advice to 'take the middle way', the boy flew too close to the sun in his exultation; the heat melted the wax and Icarus tumbled into the sea.

Idris

LEGENDARY PRINCE OF WALES, a giant, whose enormous rocky seat is still visible on the summit of **Cader Idris**.

Iliad

GREEK EPIC POEM, attributed to Homer, dated c.900BC. It tells of the final stage of the great Trojan war and the victory of the Greeks secured when Achilles, who has been nursing a grievance against King Agammemnon in his tent, is finally roused to fight. Although it is thought to have been orally transmitted by some, the epic is of more interest to classical and mythological scholars than folklorists. Its portrayal of the hero figure in Achilles however is seminal in Western lore, and the episode of the hollow wooden horse (concealing a great number of armed men) left as a present which the unsuspected Trojans take into their city and thereby ensure their destruction, has also been influential.

Ilya Muromets

RUSSIAN FOLK HERO. Until the age of 3 Ilya was a helpless, sickly peasant who

Ilya Muromets

could not move from his cradle and then his bed. One day however two pilgrims stopped at his parents' cottage and repaid the generous couple with a magical draught of honey that imparted great supernatural strength. Ilya became a great hero, defending Christian Russia from the infidels. His attributes include a wonderful bow with which he could shatter oaks and a flying **horse**, and it is possible that aspects of his legend are drawn from the pre-Christian deity Pyerun. Having defeated a 'monstrous pagan idol' in Kiev, he set about single-handedly building the great cathedral there, but he became proud and boastful and was transformed into a stone statue, which was placed inside the cathedral.

Ilya Muromets is the central figure of a large cycle of **byliny** and features in numerous folktales.

Imbolc

CELTIC FESTIVAL, the spring quarter-day when debts were settled and new servants taken on, celebrated on 1 February. It was originally a lambing festival, associated with the pagan Celtic goddess Brigit, but was translated into **Candlemas** and held as the feast of St **Brigid** with the advent of the Christian calendar.

imp

A DEMONIC SPIRIT. The name comes from Old English *impa* or *impe*, meaning young shoot, sapling, and the word developed to mean off-shoot of the **Devil**. In later lore however the distinctions between these minions of Hell and secular malicious spirits such as **goblins** became blurred, and Puritans especially regarded all fairies as manifestations of Satan.

imrama

VOYAGING TALES', a type of Old Irish adventure story, in which the journey itself, rather than the destination, is the main theme (cf **echtrai**). Extant tales include 'The Voyage of Bran', 'The Voyage of the Coracle of Maelduin' and The Voyage of Brandon (**Brendan**)'— pagan heroes and saints were incorporated into the form without discrimination. In Brendan's imram however the

destination is a Christian **otherworld**, contrasting with the sensual delights encountered by **Bran, son of Febal**. The voyagers, who may be journeying for revenge, on a quest for the Happy Isles or out of sheer restlessness, visit many islands on their journey, populated by a variety of marvellous beings, and hear magical tales and otherworldly wisdom.

incubus

A DEMON IN THE FORM OF A MAN, who visits the beds of sleeping women to have intercourse, often thereby fathering a child. Offspring of such liaisons were usually deformed or demonic, sometimes **witches or magicians (Merlin** for example was said to have been sired by an incubus). Occasionally **twins** were said to indicate an incubus's activity.

Lecherous witches would welcome the handsome incubus, despite his cloven feet and sulphurous smell, but virtuous maids could protect themselves with herbs such as St-John's-wort, vervain and dill, or by amuletic rings.
▷ **succubus**

industrial lore

FORM OF MODERN FOLKLORE, the customs, tales and idioms of groups involved in a common occupation. With the development of industry and the growth of various sub-cultures of skilled workers, such groups developed a body of lore comparable to that of earlier self-contained ethnic and geographical groups. Hero figures like **Joe Magarac** of the steel mills, with his amazing strength, grew up, and the new worker still has to face **initiation** rites as gruelling as those of more primitive societies; he may be sent for some impossible object such as a jar of elbow grease or a left-handed hammer, for example.

initiation

RITE OF PASSAGE, marking the transition from an old life to a new standing in the community. Initiation rites exist in virtually all societies, marking the onset of puberty or adulthood, or entry into a select society. Such rituals are most frequently practised among men, and they invariably involve humiliation, isolation or even physical mutilation to be undergone willingly and without complaint by the initiate. The reward of the ordeal is acceptance into the ranks of the privileged, those accounted men or shamans or goldsmiths, for example.

The most common form of initiation in primitive societies is that from boyhood to manhood, the age at which the individual is deemed ready to be admitted to the fellowship of men. Such rituals vary from the casual to the harrowing, but most share certain features: isolation for a preparatory period, during which the initiate may have to fend for himself or fast; tests of skill, strength or endurance, often involving tortures and humiliation, which are supposed to be undergone without complaint; a ritual of initiation in which the initiate may be given a new name, take an oath, and sever links with his former companions, especially mother and younger siblings. After initiation, the new entrant is taught the secrets and allowed the freedoms of the privileged group; he is reinstated into the society at a new level. The whole ceremony is a symbolic death and rebirth, signifying the beginning of an entirely new way of life. This is made explicit in some cultures, in which the initiate is led into the mouth of a specially constructed 'monster', from which he later emerges, reborn. The Christian practice of baptism by immersion is based upon a similar principle. Sometimes the symbolic death comes close to actual death; the rites of some Native American tribes involve horrific mutilation such as threading a strip of hide through a cut in the initiate's skin and hanging him up by it. This is extreme, but many of the tortures of initiation are designed to leave scars which then serve as a proof of manhood. One of the most popular of such signs is circumcision, a practice known everywhere in the world except in Europe and in some areas of Asia. Circumcision is sometimes performed on infants, but more often upon adolescents before sexual activity, and upon non-members who wish to enter a religious group, as in Judaism.

Humiliation appears to be an important part of initiation, in both primitive and modern forms. The initiates may be smeared with excrement, or jeered at by the women and children of the tribe if they show pain in the initiation trials, but this temporary humiliation must be endured if the individual is not to suffer the contemptuous treatment meted out to those who, through illness or frailty perhaps, are not able to undergo initiation. Once the humiliation of initiation has been endured, the new entrant is entitled to treat non-initiates with the same contempt, and to exercise the rights of the select which may include for example the best food and women of the group. He is taught the secrets which had terrified him in his youth; the identity of the masked dancers in religious ceremonies, the nature of the **bull-roarer** which he had believed in childhood to be the voice of the spirits. He then perpetuates these secrets and exercises his power over the rest of the group.

Since women are seldom admitted to positions of privilege or authority in primitive societies, their initiation is less common. Such ceremonies do exist, however, usually centred around the start of **menstruation**, marking the onset of sexual activity and childbearing. These ceremonies may be similar to those of boys entering manhood, involving pain and isolation, but they are usually less extreme and there is less participation on the part of the community. The image of rebirth is often present, and it is common for the girl to be given new clothes, signifying a new identity, on emerging from the menstrual hut.

Throughout the modern world forms of initiation are practised which bear striking resemblances to more primitive ceremonies. As a rule such rituals take place among members of a trade, such as joiners or sailors, or a society such as a trade guild, or among students or school children. The main feature of such rituals is humiliation, sometimes torture, to be endured by the initiate either willingly or unwillingly. Apprentices may be sent on errands to fetch fictitious substances, for example, and new pupils made to run a gauntlet of kicks from their fellows. There are many accounts of European sailors performing 'baptism' of new crew members on such occasions as their first crossing of the equator, which may be performed directly into the sea or with a succession of buckets of salt water (see **sailors' lore**). Such ceremonies are less formal than those of primitive societies and are generally not sanctioned by the entire society, but they serve the same purpose in giving status and identity to the cultural group and preserving its secrets from non-participants. The successful initiate, proud of his acceptance, will usually be keen to perpetuate the rites of initiation for other entrants. The symbolism of death and rebirth and the magical and spiritual elements are largely lost however, and apart from this social function the main purpose of such ceremonies is to provide entertainment for other members of the group.

Sometimes respite or immunity can be gained by paying off one's tormentors, usually with an offer of liquid refreshment. The act of drinking together is an ancient symbol of fellowship, and once the initiate has paid for a round of drinks he is usually considered to have gained acceptance among the group. It is interesting that even where initiation rites as such are not practised, communal drinking sponsored by the new entrant is still considered a sign of integration.

More formal initiation rituals are practised by virtually all religions, the Bar Mitzvah for Jewish boys, baptism and confirmation for Christians, the *Upanayana* ('sacred thread') ceremony for Hindu boys. These may be marked by an attenuated form of mutilation such as shaving of the head (when Buddhists become monks, for example), but in general the emphasis is on learning the mysteries or teachings of the faith rather than on humiliation and ritual death. After the *Upanayana* ceremony, however, the initiate leaves his mother to make a symbolic journey of rebirth (traditionally he left to study for 12 years with a guru, a more literal new life).

The ritual of initiation is a central element of human society, practised in different forms amongst practically all peoples at all times. Although its deeper spiritual significance has been lost in secular society, the rituals are still preserved for their social value, as a means of integrating the individual within the group.

insects

INSECT LORE IS BEWILDERINGLY DIVERSE, since the insect world is so varied, and the distribution of various insect forms around the world so complete. Because swarms of insects often brought destruction to crops, they were closely associated with contagion and blight, and various charms were used against them in agricultural societies. One of the most complex was the staging of a funeral ceremony, complete with the corpses of a few locusts or **caterpillars** and a train of human mourners. By **sympathetic magic**, such a ritual was supposed to bring about the deaths of all the insects.

The concept of the giant insect is a popular and enduring one despite the physiological impossibilities entailed. In Sardinia the *musca macedda* is a mythical giant fly, a malevolent and destructive demon, and such folk creations are common. Insects are often used in threats to children, as a way or regulating behaviour, in the same way that larger animals such as **bears** and **rats** are used. 'The bugs will bite' if the child will not sleep; a child who refuses to wash is threatened with the prospect of lice; and spiders and beetles are frequently invoked to deter children from exploring dangerous or undesirable places. Often the insect is unspecified, and therefore even more mysterious and frightening. Such practices are most common in Westernized cultures, where revulsion towards 'creepy-crawlies' is surprisingly widespread, considering their relative harmlessness.

One particularly nasty tale, which reappears in various forms as an urban legend today, was that associated with Ann Liddel of Carlisle, England, in the 18th century; it was said that she hatched a 'frightful insect' in her cheekbone. Modern versions include details such as the victim scratching the sore spot on her face and thousands of tiny creatures breaking out, or the sore bursting in the bath (the victim is generally a woman recently returned from travel in foreign parts). Individuals whose personal hygiene is less than impeccable might be warned of 'true' cases of insect hordes hatching in unwashed human hair.

▷ **ants**; **bees**; **beetles**; **spiders**; **wasps**

invisibility

COMMON MOTIF OF FOLKTALES, found throughout the world. The state of invisibility allows the hero (or villain) to overhear confidences, to procure treasure, to win battles or to plague enemies. The most common means for a mortal to attain this convenient state is by a **magic object**. Among the most frequently used of these are the **cap of invisibility**, as worn by **Sigurd**, closely linked to the helmet of **Perseus** forged by the **Cyclops**; **Jack the Giant-killer**'s cloak; or rings such as that worn by **Gyges** in Plato's version of the tale to enable him to slip into the queen's bedchamber. In an Apache tale Lizard gives the **culture hero** a cloak of invisibility to enable him to tackle Buffalo. In Oriental tales ointment is commonly applied to the eyes to make oneself invisible; in European fairy lore a similar ointment disperses fairy **glamour** and reveals the invisible spirits to mortals. Other **talismans** believed to impart invisibility are the **hand of glory** and **fernseed**.

Several **fairy tales** utilize the motif of invisibility. In a Norwegian tale with many parallels a young man goes to work in a palace where he sees noone but obeys orders given by a disembodied voice. At the end of the year the spell is broken, the princess becomes visible and they marry. In the widespread European tale of the danced-out shoes, the hero discovers the secret of the princesses whose dancing shoes keep wearing out despite their confinement by donning a cloak of invisibility and following them to their nocturnal revels.

Many **mischievous spirits**, **ghosts**, **witches** and other supernatural beings have the power to become invisible at will, without any of the apparatus required by mortals. In modern lore the theme of a chemical solution that will cause invisibility has proved fertile ground for writers and filmmakers since H G Wells's *The Invisible Man* (1897).

iron

SERVICEABLE METAL, whose great useful-ness in folk industries is matched by its virtues in folk belief as an **amulet** to drive away evil influences. Although it is generally not considered suitable for sacred purposes (cf **gold**), iron is regarded as powerful against evil in most parts of the world. In Europe it is said to drive away **witches**, **fairies** and the **evil eye**, although **dwarfs**, being master smiths, have no such fear of iron. Iron implements are often placed over corpses to prevent animation by evil spirits, and Hindu brides wear iron wedding bands to keep evil spirits at bay. The **horseshoe** gains much of its potency as a bringer of luck from being crafted of iron, and only an iron blade will slay a **ghoul**.

Since iron was often derived from meteorites, early civilizations sometimes considered it a gift from the gods, and this may be the source of the astonishingly consistent belief in its virtue.

Islands of the Blest

GENERAL NAME FOR A COMMON TYPE OF OTHERWORLD, a paradise usually situated to the west in the path of the setting sun. These elusive islands may only be found easily by the souls of the blessed after death, but occasionally a heroic mortal may reach them. In early Greek mythology the islands were ruled by Cronus, the father of Zeus, but they were later conflated with the fields of Elysium. In pagan Celtic lore such islands were discovered by heroes such as **Bran, son of Febal**, inhabited by beautiful and accommodating females where the adventurers had nothing to do but feast and be merry all day. Later Celtic lore absorbed elements of Christianity to produce a hybrid Island of the Blest such as that discovered by St **Brendan the Navigator**, owing as much to the Christian heaven as Celtic tradition.

Many travellers reported tales of magical, extraordinary islands that could never be found again, such as Hy Brasil, originally said to have been one of the Aran group of Ireland, the Arthurian **Avalon**, and many others.

▷ **floating islands**

ivy

EVERGREEN PLANT of the Araliaceae family, genus *Hedera*. In Greek lore ivy was sacred to Dionysus; it was said that the god was so moved by a worshipper who danced herself to death before him that he transformed her body into ivy, which embraces its support. Dionysus wears a crown of ivy, and the plant was by association considered a **charm** against inebriation. In ancient Egypt it was held sacred to the god Osiris.

In Christian lore the evergreen ivy symbolizes immortality, and several superstitions relate it to graveyards. A grave on which ivy will not grow is thought to house a restless and discontented soul, but if the grave of a young girl sports ivy in profusion it is clear that she died for love, ivy being the symbol of constancy because it is not only evergreen but grows by clinging. According to **ballad** lore, ivy from the graves of star-crossed lovers will often intertwine to demonstrate their constancy and togetherness in the next world. Should a Welsh house lose the ivy that climbs its walls, it is an indication that ruin or disgrace is on the way. A gift of ivy to a friend however is widely considered unlucky, as it will break up the friendship. In some areas of the world ivy is regarded as male because of its tripartite leaves, conceived as the phallic trinity, but in other areas, particularly England, it is thought of as female and therefore, in contrast to its usual reputation for constancy, an emblem of fickleness.

In many places ivy leaves are applied to wounds, burns and corns to soothe pain, and its berries are ground to provide a medicine used for a variety of ills including plague, gangrene, toothache and jaundice.

Jack and the Beanstalk

ENGLISH FAIRY STORY, classic tale of the triumph of the simple fellow, widely known in the English-speaking world with many European variations. In the now famous version of the story, known in Britain since the early 18th century, Jack is the foolish, lazy son of a poor widow. His mother sends him to market one day to sell their last possession of any value, the **cow**, but Jack parts with the beast for a handful of prettily coloured beans. When he returns home, his mother throws them out of the window in despair. The next morning, however, they wake to find that an enormous plant stretching into the sky has grown up overnight. Despite his mother's warnings, Jack immediately climbs the beanstalk and finds himself in a marvellous land, with the enormous castle of a giant before him. On entering the castle, Jack meets the giant's kind-hearted wife, who hides him when her husband returns and pacifies the suspicious giant with a meal. After his meal, the giant calls to his magic hen (or goose) to lay him a golden **egg**, then falls asleep. Jack emerges from hiding and escapes back down the beanstalk, clutching the golden hen. He and his mother live happily for some time, then Jack ventures up the beanstalk a second time. On this occasion he manages to steal the giant's money-bags, but on his third attempt the golden **harp** he is making off with calls out to its master, and the giant wakes and gives chase. Jack scrambles down the beanstalk and reaches the bottom with the giant in pursuit; calling for an axe, he sets about chopping the beanstalk down, and the giant is killed by the fall. Jack and his mother live the rest of their lives in comfort.

The story is remarkable for the number of universal folktale motifs which it contains, including the foolish bargain, the upper world reached by a tall plant, the concealment of the hero by the giant's wife, the series of three thefts and the speaking **magic object**. In the 19th century there was an attempt to give Jack's actions a sounder moral base by including a fairy character, who tells Jack that the giant had long ago killed Jack's father, and so he must now take his revenge. This detail seems to have proceeded not from genuine folk tradition but from the scruples of writers for children.

One of the most famous elements of the story, the giant's 'fee, fi, fo, fum' chant, is a motif commonly associated with the cannibal **ogre** who smells human flesh; it occurs in various forms throughout Europe, Asia, America and Africa.

Jack-in-the-Green

MEDIEVAL ENGLISH MUMMER, participant in the **May Day** revels of the chimney sweeps in particular. The costume consisted of a tall wooden frame encasing the **mummer**, completely covered with greenery, usually **holly**, **ivy** and flowers, and fluttering ribbons. The Jack-in-the-Green, usually a young man or boy, danced at the head of the procession of sweeps as they paraded through the village singing and collecting money. The custom persisted into the 19th century.

It is likely that, as J G Frazer suggests, the figure is a relic of ancient European tree-worship. The custom is echoed throughout northern Europe with the Green George of the Slavs, the Swiss Whitsuntide Basket and other similar forms testifying to the widespread popularity of the custom.
▷ **Green Man**

jack-in-the-pulpit

NORTH AMERICAN PLANT, *Arisaema triphyllum*, distinguished by an unusual green and purple hooded spathe enclosing a spike of tiny flowers. It is known by several other names, including bog onion, brown dragon and, among the Penobscot who regard it as highly poisonous, Jug Woman's baby. If consumed the root induces agonizing cramps, and this property was utilized by Native Americans such as the Meskwaki in inter-tribal feuds. In minute quantities however the plant can be useful in the treatment of respiratory disorders, stomach pains or rheumatism.

Jack o'lantern see **will o' the wisp** and **pumpkin**

Jack o'lent

STUFFED FIGURE, pulled through the streets in areas of Europe at the beginning of Lent to be mocked and eventually burned. Although Christian tradition associates this figure with **Judas Iscariot**, the betrayer of Jesus, it is more probably a survival of ancient pagan spring festivals with the orgiastic associations of fire and revelry.

Jack tales

FOLKTALE CYCLE found in Britain and America with many European parallels (eg Jean, Hans etc). The hero is generally unpromising at the start of the tale, young, poor or foolish, but through a combination of luck and craftiness he triumphs against the odds. The morality of such tales is often dubious; they spring from the folk tradition which celebrates the wiles and audacity of the trickster figure, not the more lofty tone of the fairy tale. Various attempts have been made by later writers, especially those writing for children, to render the hero more worthy.
▷ **Jack and the Beanstalk**; **Jack the Giant-killer**

Jack the Giant-killer

CENTRAL TALE OF THE ENGLISH TALE CYCLE, the **Jack tales**, in which the traditional **dragonslayer** has become a comical giant-killer. Jack is a typical folktale hero, a peasant lad who outwits his stronger enemies against all the odds by the use of cunning. Since his enemies are all evil giants, the classic trickster form is given a place within the moralistic framework of European fairy tales, but although Jack is later credited with courage and chivalry, he shows no particular virtues or worthiness in the earliest forms of the tales.

The tale is based on a number of loosely related episodes, suggesting that a number of tales may have become attached to the hero figure in much the same way that ancient epic or the heroic cycles were formed. Jack is the only son of a Cornish farmer, who wins for himself great rewards and a reputation as a giant killer by luring the giant

Jack the Giant-killer

Cormoran from his cave on St Michael's Mount into a deep pit and presenting his head to the king. He leaves in search of more adventure, is captured by the giant **Blunderbore** and imprisoned in a tower. The resourceful Jack manages to strangle his captor by dropping a noose over his neck as he stands below the window of Jack's cell, and makes his escape with the reward. In later versions he hands the giant's riches over to three widows, also imprisoned by Blunderbore. He slays another giant in a battle of wits; while visiting the giant in Wales he avoids being clubbed to death in his sleep by leaving a log in his place in bed, and in the morning complains airily of some gnat bites in the night. He then challenges the giant to an eating contest and half way through cuts open a bag of porridge secreted under his coat. The giant, attempting to relieve his full belly in the same way, kills himself. In other episodes he causes two giants to kill each other by throwing stones each believes is from the other, and he demonstrates his remarkable 'strength' to a giant by squeezing water from a stone (a piece of cheese).

In one Arthurian development of the cycle, Jack meets **Arthur**'s son who is on chivalric quest but impecunious, since he has gallantly given all his money to pay off the debts of a dead man (cf **grateful dead**). Jack secures his lodging and entertainment by going ahead to a giant's castle to warn him of the thousand-strong force marching upon him. While the giant hides in his cellar from the imaginary threat, Jack and the prince feast and plunder in his castle, and the giant is so grateful for his safety that he gives Jack his most famous attributes— the cloak of **invisibility**, the **Seven League Boots**, the cap of wisdom and a **sword** that cannot be resisted. These are then used to free the lady sought by Arthur's son from enchantment, and Jack is rewarded by a seat at the **Round Table**. As a fairy tale hero, Jack frees the daughter of a Duke from the castle of the giant Galigantus, marries her and lives happily ever after.

jackal

CARNIVOROUS WOLF-LIKE CREATURE, genus *Canis*, native to Asia and areas of Europe and Africa. In ancient Egyptian mythology the jackal was the emblem of Anubis, god of the souls of the dead, entrusted with the task of accompanying souls to be judged by Osiris and then on their journey to the **otherworld** of pain or reward. In Hebrew lore the jackal is a symbol of destruction and desolation, and in India the howling of a jackal, especially if heard on the listener's left side, is regarded as an omen of great misfortune.

In many Indian tales the jackal is associated with the **lion** as his servile helper, frightening animals which the lion will then kill and eating what remains after his master has feasted. He is widely regarded as a scavenger and coward, and in many areas of Asia a jackal's heart is thought to induce cowardice in even the bravest warrior who consumes it. However in many parts of Africa the jackal is a favourite and affectionately regarded **trickster** figure, often wise if seldom particularly courageous, and in the North especially jackal's gall is prized as an ingredient in aphrodisiac potions and ointments of both sexes.

jackdaw

CROW-LIKE BIRD, widely regarded in folklore as a thieving, mischievous and talkative nuisance. The Jackdaw of Rheims is said to have stolen a cardinal's holy ring, and the curse pronounced upon him explains his bedraggled, ragged appearance.

jaguar

PREDATOR OF THE CAT FAMILY, *Leo onca*, found in decreasing numbers in Central and South America. It was regarded as the king of the animals and was represented in Mayan lore as a god, and as the emblem of Tezcatlipoca in Aztec mythology.

The jaguar is closely associated with shamans, as a familiar or inspirational spirit, and it is widely believed that shamans can transform themselves into jaguar form by night or after death, prowling the forest to attack their enemies. This were-jaguar belief is akin to the widespread **werewolf** beliefs of Europe.

A cosmic jaguar is held responsible for

eclipses among many groups, including Incas and Mojos, but in eastern Brazil Jaguar is a benevolent **culture hero** who rescued an abandoned boy and taught him the secret of fire. Tales of **beast marriage** between jaguars and humans are also common.

▷ **animal nurse**; **shape-shifting**

jalparī

WATER-SPIRIT OF THE PUNJAB, a predatory female who lures mortal men into her watery realm to keep her company or to provide food when she is hungry. An offering of flowers or an animal made at the side of the river may buy her favour.

James, Jesse (1847–82)

BALLAD HERO OF THE AMERICAN WEST, an outlaw from Missouri who with his brother Frank and a band of like-minded villains pursued a life of crime with such panache, daring and effrontery that they became celebrated as romantic heroes, typifying the devil-may-care spirit of the frontier. The band's train hold-ups and bank robberies were mythologized into **Robin Hood**-like tales of generosity to the poor, and Jesse's allegiance to the South and his subsequent persecution by the authorities after the Civil War was

Jesse James

advanced by sympathizers as an explanation of his life of crime. His treacherous death, shot in the head by a fellow gang-member greedy for bounty, while unarmed and adjusting a picture on his wall, lent tragic resonance to his legend.

The *Ballad of Jesse James* purports to have been written by one Billy Gashade, who is otherwise unknown. The popularity of the legend established Jesse as a folk hero among late-19th-century pioneers and in the 20th century as a romantic hero of the Hollywood screen.

Japanese folklore

JAPAN IS AN ISLAND STATE more self-contained than its neighbour China, which despite its close cultural relations with other countries such as China and Korea has never been successfully invaded, and so its own characteristic folklore is highly developed. The traditional religion is Shinto, which later cheerfully absorbed Buddhism, to the extent that all Shinto gods were declared reincarnations of those of Buddhism.

Among the most beautiful of Japan's rich store of folktales is the story of **Momotaro**, the hero who was found sitting in a big **peach** as a baby by an elderly couple who adopted him: he went on to defeat the demons on Onigashima ('Devil's Island') and returned with their wealth leading his three companions, a dog, a monkey and a pheasant. There are several tales with animal protagonists, but two animals repeatedly appear; the **fox** and the **badger**. Both are thought to be dangerous, powerful creatures, capable of changing their shape. The fox stories probably originated in China and were expanded within the culture.

One of the characteristic superstitions of Japan is the use of objects and **astrology** to secure good fortune, and the ekisha, professional fortune-teller and astrologer, is a popular figure. Even the scrupulous cleanliness characteristic of the Japanese is connected to superstition; in Shinto, impurity is said to be unlucky.

Jason

GREEK HERO, leader of the Argonauts and quester for the Golden Fleece, son of King Æson of Iolcos. When his father's half-brother Pelias usurped the throne, the young Jason was entrusted to the **centaur** Chiron. As a man he aided an old woman (the goddess Hera in disguise) across a ford, losing a sandal in the process; Pelias recognized him by this token when he entered Iolcos, having been warned to beware of a man with a single sandal, and to remove this threat he sent Jason on a quest to find the Golden Fleece of Colchis.

Jason and his followers (known as Argonauts from their ship, the *Argo*) reached Colchis after many adventures on the voyage, and with the aid of the smitten **Medea** he overcame the **dragon** that guarded the fleece. They returned to Pelias with the trophy, and Medea used her witchcraft to bring about Pelias's death, convincing his daughters that their father could be restored to youth and vigour by the simple expedient of dismembering him and boiling his body in a cauldron (an interesting perversion of the **cauldron** of regeneration motif).

Jason and Medea settled in Corinth, but Jason soon deserted her for the daughter of King Creon; Medea revenged herself by presenting his bride with a fatal robe and slaying her children by Jason. The hero was killed by a piece of the rotting *Argo* that fell on him as he sat in its shadow; in some accounts he committed suicide.

Several features of this myth resound in hero tales throughout world folklore: the quest for the magical treasure; the impossible **task** accomplished with the aid of supernatural helpers; the fatal bridal robe (cf **Faithful John**); the guardian dragon, and the wicked usurping uncle.

Jātaka

TALES OF THE BUDDHA, a large number of popular fables and folktales in which the Buddha appears in his former lives, as an **elephant**, outcast, king and so on. Over 500 are collected in a fifth-century Pali work, which has a structure reminiscent of the *Arabian Nights*; a frame story gives the context and reason behind the Buddha's telling of each tale, and this prose commentary is thought to be the work of a single author. The enormous variety of tales embedded in this framework however is drawn from ancient oral traditions of animal fables, Märchen and hero tales. Many are didactic, with the Buddha in his various forms demonstrating a particular virtue, but the collection is characterized by humour and imagination. Several of the tales appear in other collections, such as the *Panchatantra* or the collections of Aesop. Although Jātaka are popular and integral parts of all branches of Buddhism, for orthodox believers they constitute the autobiographical writings of Gautama Buddha himself and are sacred texts as well as entertaining and didactic folktales.

jay

WOODLAND BIRD, of the family Corvidae (order Passeriformes), found in North America particularly and in parts of Europe and Asia. They are noisy, gregarious birds, and in folklore have a reputation for boastful chattering (cf **jackdaw** and **magpie**). Jay is a **trickster** figure and **culture hero** among several Native American groups, and its shape is a favourite one for **shape-shifting** shamans to assume.

A well-known fable of **Aesop**, found in many areas throughout the world, tells how the jay comes upon some feathers shed by a **peacock**. Decking himself out in this borrowed finery, he begins to strut among his fellows, regarding his old associates contemptuously. Seeing a group of peacocks he saunters over to join them, but the proud birds set upon this thinly disguised impostor and strip him of his stolen feathers and some of his own. Sore and saddened, the jay returns to his kind, but the others have not forgotten his obnoxious vanity and they too drive him away. The moral is that one should be content with one's proper estate.

jazz

MUSICAL FORM, developed by African-Americans in New Orleans particularly at the end of the 19th century. Its roots are complex, but main influences include the rhythms and free form of West African folk music, urban and rural **work songs** of black slaves in the American South, and European har-

Jerome, St

monic structure and subject matter. In its early days and still to some extent today jazz was almost exclusively a spontaneous, informal and exuberant style, played by self-taught musicians and owing little to text books and theories of music. It relates closely to the traditional tones of African singing, the cornets and saxophones imitating human wails, growls and shouts, and the ecstatic, almost trance-like mood of the performers (frequently brought about by narcotic as well as emotional influences) recalls ritualistic folk music of possession by spirits.

From these raw, impassioned beginnings developed a finely honed style that in later times was taken over to the classical concert hall. Its history has been marked by virtuoso individuals—instrumentalists such as Louis Armstrong, Bix Beiderbecke and Jelly Roll Morton, band leaders such as Count Basie and Duke Ellington, and the singer Billie Holliday—and variations such as the frenzied bebop (chief exponents Dizzy Gillespie and Charlie Parker), the more sophisticated cool jazz of Gerry Mulligan, and concert pieces such as those by George Gershwin. Despite the richness and intensity of much of this later music, some of the unselfconscious spontaneity of the form's folk roots has inevitably been lost.

Jazz dancing developed to complement the music, a highly individualistic and usually energetic style of dancing to match the rhythms of the music. Much jazz dancing, for example post-war forms such as the jitterbug and boogie-woogie, incorporate African traditions of acrobatic abandon. An enormous variety of dances fall under the jazz umbrella, many given intriguingly evocative names—black bottom, shag, shimmy, duck-walk, mashed potato, Detroit jump and so on.

Essentially the music of black America, jazz has been adopted by American whites and in Europe, and its influence has pervaded many other forms. Despite, or perhaps because of, its association with a sleazy underworld, jazz has won aficionados across the world and enjoys popularity as both esoteric art form and spontaneous untutored 'jamming'.

Jephthah's vow

MOTIF OF FOLKTALE, named from its appearance in the Biblical tale of Jephthah (Judges 11:29–40). Jephthah rashly vows to sacrifice the first thing that comes to meet him on his return home to gain success against the Ammonites; his is met by his daughter, his only child. She spends two months in the mountains mourning the fact that she will die a virgin, and is then sacrificed.

The child unwittingly promised is a prominent theme of folktales in Europe and Asia particularly, although the consequence is rarely actual sacrifice. More commonly the bargain is made with an animal, a monster or the **Devil**, the bargainer expecting to be met by his faithful dog. The motif appears famously in **Beauty and the Beast**, and there are many similar child bargains such as that made with **Rumpelstiltskin**.
▷ **Angang**; **promised child**

Jerome, St (c.341–420)

TRANSLATOR OF THE VULGATE BIBLE, unmatched for his learning, his scholarship and his fiery temper. In 382 Jerome went to Rome and as secretary to Pope Damasus began the major task of revising the Latin version of the Bible to create a standard text. Beginning with the Gospels and Psalms, Jerome revised virtually the whole Bible to produce what became known by the 13th century as the Vulgate version, a Latin translation of clarity and great readability based on the text of existing translations.

Despite his achievements Jerome found it easy to make enemies; he could be sarcastic, impatient and even, it seems, arrogant and aggressive. It is said that Pope Sixtus V, contemplating a picture of Jerome in which the saint holds a stone with which to perform penance, commented that without this sign of voluntary penance Jerome would never have been numbered among the saints.

In art he is often represented as a cardinal, an anachronism prompted by his service to Pope Damasus. His emblem, appropriately enough, is a **lion**, which appears throughout the various representations of him as cardinal, scholar, Doctor and founder. This was

247

because of a popular tradition that Jerome had once plucked out a thorn from a lion's foot, and that afterwards the grateful beast followed him everywhere as a tame pet (see also **Androcles and the Lion**).

His feast-day is 30 September, and he is the patron saint of librarians.

Jersey devil

GHOST TALE OF MODERN AMERICA, a phantom said to terrorize the southern Jersey shore. A witch at Leeds Point, Atlantic County, with 12 children said that the next child, the 13th, should be born a devil, and her curse was fulfilled. It has been suggested that such a woman may have given birth to a deformed child whom she kept hidden, and this mystery together with the tale of the curse spawned a supernatural monster in the collective local imagination.

The devil's exploits up and down the shore were avidly reported by newspapers, and tales of its mischief-making and prying were rife. The Devil still appears in such tales today, taking the part often filled by escaped psychopaths in standard urban legends. In 1909 a so-called Jersey Devil (actually a kangaroo painted green with false wings attached) was exhibited by a Philadelphia showman. Now part of Jersey popular culture, and a profitable tourist theme, the Jersey Devil demonstrates the vitality of folk belief and ghost lore even in modern urban civilizations.

jewel in serpent's head

MAGIC TALISMAN, variously said to reside in the head of the **snake**, **toad**, **dragon**, **swallow** and so on. Its virtues vary with locality; it may be a love charm or protective **amulet**, an antidote to poison or a means of working magic spells, a source of light or simply a gem of priceless value. Early Greek writers popularized the belief, and Pliny added that the serpent must be alive when its head is cut off, or the stone will lose its potency. The concept of a precious jewel hidden beneath an unpromising exterior reflects the perennial themes of folktales: disguise, inversion and concealment.
▷ **hyena**

jinn

SUPERNATURAL BEINGS OF ARABIC LORE, a spirit below the level of angels and devils yet more powerful and non-corporeal than humans, often rendered in English as genie. The jinni probably began as a nature demon, found in all animate and inanimate forms, blamed for all troublesome occurrences and feared for their ability to punish mortals who have offended them, like **mischievous spirits** across the world. This folk belief was incorporated into Islam; Muhammad himself recognized the existence of jinn and agonized whether his inspirations should be attributed to Allah or to their demonic promptings.

In Arabian folktales, and especially in the *Arabian Nights*, jinn appear as supernatural helpers; they can be controlled by those possessing knowledge of sorcery or a **talisman** such as **Aladdin's** lamp. There are many different classes of jinn, from evil **ghouls** to **guardian spirits** of the house who often appear as serpents. A common form attributed to them is that of an enormous, well-muscled man, but they are cunning and may appear frail and aged, as for example the **Old Man of the Sea**. Like humans, jinn are said in Islamic belief to be subject to final divine judgement.
▷ **shaitans**

Joan of Arc, St (1412–31)

THE MAID OF ORLÉANS, one of the most inspiring women in history and a powerful national symbol of France. Youngest of the five children of Jacques d'Arc, a peasant farmer, Joan was only 13 when she first heard her famous 'voices' accompanied by brilliant light, which instructed her to serve the Dauphin and save France. She identified them as messages from Saints Michael, **Catherine** of Alexandria and Margaret of Antioch, but despite her conviction her attempts to join the French army were met with scepticism and derision. She persisted, and after her prophecies of defeat were fulfilled at the Battle of Herrings in 1429, Robert de Baudricot commander at Vaucouleurs, sent her to the Dauphin, to whom she proved herself by seeing through his disguise. A group of theologians at Poitiers cross-examined her for three weeks and finally gave their approval to this remarkable girl and her mission.

Joan's first expedition was to relieve besieged Orléans; in April 1429, clad in a suit of white armour, she led her troops and saved the city, capturing several English forts, her men inspired by her visionary courage. In June of that year she secured another important victory over the English troops, capturing Troyes. When the Dauphin was crowned Charles VII at Rheims on 17 July 1429 Joan stood at his side, but even at the pinnacle of her achievement she suffered mockery and suspicion among courtiers, clergy and soldiers.

Joan continued to lead the army. A mission to recapture Paris in August failed and the winter months enforced idleness, but in the following spring she set out to relieve Compiègne, besieged by Burgundy, the ally of the English. She was captured there in May and handed over to the English, as Charles made no effort to save her. In Rouen Joan was charged with witchcraft and heresy; she was convicted and persuaded to recant but when she defiantly resumed the male attire she had promised to abandon she was declared a heretic and burnt at the stake in the market-place of Rouens on 30 May. Her ashes were thrown into the Seine.

Twenty years later the case was reopened by a commission of Callistus III. They reached a verdict of innocent, but it was not until 1920 that Joan was canonized by Benedict XV. She is venerated as a virgin rather than a martyr. Joan has appealed to secular and literary minds as well as the pious, and many attempts have been made to explain her 'voices' and her significance as a patriot and as a woman in a male-dominated world. Her romantic life has inspired many artists, who usually portray her as a maiden in armour. Her feast-day is 30 May and she is the second patron saint of France, and patron saint of soldiers.

Joe Magarac

HERO OF THE STEEL MILL, American literary character created by Owen Francis in the 1930s. His name means 'jackass' in Slovak; Joe says 'Dat's me. All I do is eatit and workit same lak jackass donkey.' He was born in a mountain of steel ore and was made of steel, all seven foot of him. He worked day and night at the steel mill, stopping only to eat five enormous meals, making rails by squeezing molten lead through his fingers. He finally melted himself down in the mill, proving that he made better steel than the ore, to provide the best-quality metal for a new mill.

The popularity of Joe Magarac's legend recalls other marvellous labouring heroes such as **John Henry** and **Paul Bunyan**, and it also suggests the human lives sacrificed to the steel industry—workers fallen into melting vats and thus incorporated bodily into the 20th-century frenzy of industry.

John Barleycorn

PERSONIFICATION OF BARLEY MALT, a figure of English and Scottish lore, affectionate term for alcohol and its effects. He may be derived from the ancient spirits of vegetation.

John Henry

BLACK AMERICAN BALLAD HERO, a herculean rail-road worker who pits himself

John Henry

against a steam drill and succeeds in crushing more rock than the machine, but dies from the effort, his hammer still in his hand. Ballad lore tells of his super-human strength; he weighed 44 pounds at birth and set out to seek work after eating his first meal, and his sexual prowess and stamina were the subject of many legends. His tale gathered such accretions as it spread through the southern work-camps. Writers such as Roark Bradford (*John Henry*, 1931) popularized his tale, and in some areas he became a white man.

It is possible that John Henry's tale has some basis in fact; it is likely that when the steam drill was introduced in the 1870s to aid in the construction of the Big Bend Tunnel in West Virginia a comparative test of efficiency between human and machine might well have been carried out. Later writers saw in the tale a symbol both of the blacks' oppression by whites and the subjugation of human dignity by the machine.

John o'Groat

LEGENDARY BRITISH FIGURE, a Dutch settler originally called Jan de Groot, who came to Scotland with his two brothers in the reign of James IV. He is said to have built an octagonal house in his village near Dunnet Head, at the north-east tip of mainland Britain, containing an octagonal table, to ensure that the eight families of the o'Groats would cease squabbling over precedence at family celebrations (cf **Round Table**). A mound surviving in the modern village of John o'Groats is said to be the site of the house.

Johnny Appleseed

AMERICAN FOLK HERO. John Chapman (1774–1845) was an itinerant nurseryman and missionary who travelled from his native Massachusetts to the Ohio–Indiana frontier with appleseeds salvaged from the Pittsburgh cider presses, planting trees as he went. This eccentric figure fired the folk imagination, and Johnny Appleseed became a fictionalized 'natural man', around whom legends more or less based on his actual life accrued. He was reputed to have such a love for animals that he would extinguish his campfire to save mosquitoes from

Johnny Appleseed

incinerating themselves in it, and his extensive knowledge of herb lore and his affinity with all natural things made him a much-loved healer among settlers and Native Americans alike. His appearance was highly individual; he wore a mush pan hat over his long hair, an old coffee sack for a shirt, and ragged trousers. He was a kindly, bearded, barefoot tramp who existed on the few essentials he could trade for with his seedlings, and who preached an altogether more pure and pious simple life. He finally died of exposure, with 1 200 acres of land to his name. Folk tradition has made of him a saint, but the tangible reminders of his work survived in extensive orchards across the mid-West.

Johnny Armstrong

SCOTTISH BALLAD HERO, who died at the perfidious hands of James V of Scotland. Called before the king in peace and proud of the honour, Johnny courteously offers the traditional request for pardon in the king's presence—it is refused and he is condemned to death. Outraged at such treachery, Johnny and his men take on the court and are slain. Only a young messenger escapes to recount the woeful tale.

jokes

INVALUABLE INDICES OF THE VALUES AND IDENTITY OF A SOCIAL GROUP. Like music, art and dance, humour is one of the most basic social impulses in humans. Unlike these other activities, humour has traditionally received little in the way of serious study by folklorists. This may be because humour itself is such a slippery concept; what is uproariously funny to one group may be offensive, childish or just plain incomprehensible to another. Yet jokes, particularly dirty jokes, are probably the most prevalent folkloric item to be found in urbanized society. They circulate orally over vast geographical areas with an amazing speed and are seldom written down. They frequently undergo variation, depending on the memory or skill of the joke-teller, and may be adapted to become more topical. They may even form cycles in a similar way to folktales when a series of jokes develops round a single theme, such as the **elephant** (Why do elephants paint their toe-nails red? *So they can hide in cherry trees.* Why do elephants paint their toe-nails yellow? *So they can hide upside down in custard*).

The racist joke is one of the clearest examples of this, common in all societies since social groups first encountered each other in trade or warfare. The distinctive characteristics of the other group are seized upon and exaggerated; physical appearance, dialect or language, customs or characteristics. The image of one group held and mocked by another may bear little or no resemblance to fact, but this is not essential for humour. What is essential is that everyone in the second group recognizes and shares the same image of the first. So the blacked-up minstrels of the 19th-century music hall, with their shambling gait and exaggerated light circle around the mouth, were based on a caricature of popular conception rather than reality. Similarly, the caricatures of women in recent Western cartoons such as those on sea-side post-cards or in cheap magazines define their subject by a series of caricatured features; pouting mouth, enormous chest, curvaceous hips and empty head. These two examples also indicate one of the less attractive features of such jokes; humour is often used to reinforce the repression of ethnic or social groups.

A feature of joke lore in the industrialized world, closely linked to the impulse for social identity and value at the cost of another group, is the 'stupid minority'. This may be an ethnic or social group, usually living on the fringes of the main society either geographically or socially. The form seems to have developed from the earliest 'numbskull' stories, where the focus of the joke is on the stupidity of the act itself and the identity of the perpetrator is irrelevant, and early jokes told against neighbouring villages. Now virtually every Western country has developed its own repertoire of jokes about a 'stupid' group: the British about the Irish; the Americans about the Poles (or the Swedes, or the Portuguese); the Swedes about Norwegians and Finns; the Finns about Gypsies; Northern Italians about Southern Italians; and the French and Dutch about Belgians. The form of the joke is such that any nationality can be substituted at will; 'How do you confuse a—man?' 'Give him two shovels and tell him to take his pick!'
▷ **laughter**

joking relationships

Etiquette of family relationships, common among primitive societies. Two family members, often brother and sister-in-law, are encouraged to joke with and tease one another, often even obscenely. This may be because of the conventions for remarriage within the family following the death of a spouse.

Jormungandr

Sea monster. The **sea-serpent** figures largely in Teutonic mythology; Jormungandr, born of the trickster god Loki, was flung into the sea by Odin and grew until he could encircle Midgard (the earth) by biting his own tail. His thrashings were said to produce storms.
▷ **Kraken; sailors' lore**

Joseph, St

The foster-father of Christ, a poor man (despite his descent from King David) who earned his living as a carpenter: 'an upright man' as he is called in the Gospels. The tradition that he was elderly at Jesus's birth, originating with the apocryphal *Protevangelium* of James, is unfounded; he was probably no more than a few years older than the Virgin **Mary**.

When he learned that his fiancée was pregnant Joseph was understandably concerned, but was reassured of her virtue by an angel in a dream, and their marriage went ahead. He witnessed the visit of the Magi in Bethlehem. According to Matthew, it was to Joseph that the angel appeared with first a warning to flee to Egypt and then the command to return when the massacre of the Innocents took place. Matthew's Gospel largely presents the nativity story from the point of view of Joseph, while Luke concentrates more on the experiences of the Virgin Mary.

Joseph was alive when the 12-year-old Jesus was left behind in the temple at Jerusalem after Passover, but this is the last mention of him in the Gospels.

Joseph's cult began in the East with the popular apocryphal *History of Joseph* in the fifth century and only gained widespread popularity in the West in the 15th century: his name was added to the Roman calendar in 1479. In medieval mystery plays, Joseph is portrayed as a human character who provides light relief from the more venerable and sacred figures of Christ and the Virgin. As a human father-figure and tradesman he is widely loved and respected, with many churches and hospitals being dedicated to him. In art he nearly always appears in groups of the Holy Family, usually as an old man carrying a flowering rod and sometimes surrounded by his carpentry tools. He was declared patron of the universal Church by Pius IX in 1870, and Pope Leo XIII proclaimed him as a model for fathers in 1889. His feast-day is 19 March. He is patron saint of carpenters, fathers, workers, social justice and travellers, invoked in doubt and when house-hunting

Joseph of Arimathea

WEALTHY JEW OF BIBLICAL LORE, possibly a member of the Sanhedrin, who had Jesus's body taken from the cross and lain in his own tomb. This is virtually all the information given in the gospels, but Christian tradition has invested his legend with great detail. Most char-

acteristically he is the keeper of the Holy **Grail**. In some versions the Grail sustains him during 12 years in a Roman prison for his connection with Christ, and after his release he journeys with it and the spear that pierced Jesus's side to England, where he founds the abbey at Glastonbury and begins converting the Britons. He is said to have brought his staff, made of **hawthorn**, to England, and to have planted it in the ground at Glastonbury, where for years it flowered every old Christmas Eve (5 January) without fail. Much of the legendary material surrounding Joseph is found in Robert de Baron's epic romance, *Joseph d'Arimathie* (c.1200).

jötnar

TEUTONIC GIANTS, personification of the elemental force of nature. Much Norse mythology deals with the prickly relationships and intermarriages between gods and jötnar.

Joyeuse

THE SWORD OF CHARLEMAGNE, which was buried alongside him according to some versions of the legend, and a popular name for swords in the romance genre as a whole. **Arthur** is said to have rewarded Sir **Lancelot of the Lake** for defending **Guinevere**'s honour by endowing him with a beautiful estate, Garde-Joyeuse.

Juan, Don

LEGENDARY ITALIAN PROFLIGATE. He was said to be an incorrigible libertine and womanizer, who one day seduced the daughter of the commander of Ulloa and afterwards killed her father. The commander's statue was erected in a Franciscan convent, and the impious Don Juan invited to dine with him, whereupon the stone figure descended from its plinth and accepted the invitation. After the feast, it delivered Don Juan over to the **Devil**. The figure of the swaggering suave rake has inspired dramatists, writers and musicians such as Molière, Byron, Mozart and George Bernard Shaw.

Judas Iscariot

THE BETRAYER OF CHRIST, one of the 12 disciples, who accepted 30 pieces of silver to lead his master's enemies to him in Gethsemane. Biblical accounts give conflicting stories of his death, suggesting that he became a villain of popular lore very quickly; according to Matthew he attempted to give back his bribe and finally threw it down in the Temple before hanging himself—the priests subsequently bought a burial field with the money. In the Acts of the Apostles, however, Luke claims that Judas himself bought the potter's field, Aceldama, and that he fell to a gory death there.

Judas is the arch-villain of Christian lore, portrayed by Dante in the very heart of his Inferno, eternally gnawed in the maw of Satan. There is an ancient legend however that because of his compassion towards a leper in Joppa, Judas is loosed from his torment for an hour annually.

Legends grew up purporting to tell the tale of Judas's infancy; his mother dreamed that her unborn son would slay his father and commit incest and deicide, and the child was abandoned at birth (see **abandonment**). As with **Oedipus** and other abandoned babies, however, the prophecy will not be thwarted; Judas is brought up by a kindly king, whom he kills, before going on to commit the foretold crimes.

In folk art Judas is generally represented with red hair, often wearing yellow. Effigies of him were commonly burned on bonfires of Central Europe at **Easter**. In Islamic lore Judas is portrayed as a defender of Jesus rather than a betrayer, and one 14th-century theologian suggested that Judas assumed his master's form and was crucified in his place.

Judas tree

TREE WITH PINK FLOWERS AND HEART-SHAPED LEAVES, *Cercis siliquastrum* (family Leguminosae), also known as the redbud. It is said to be the tree from which **Judas Iscariot** hung himself. This legend is also associated with many dwarf trees, as is the parallel belief that such wood was used for Christ's cross.

jujube

SPINY TREE, genus *Ziziphus* (family Rhamnaceae), most commonly the native Chinese common jujube (*Z.*

jujuba) with its characteristic zig-zag stem. The black, olive-like fruit is a popular delicacy. The jujube is the Koran's Tree of Paradise, growing in the highest heaven, whose leaves bear the names of all living humans. Each Ramadan the tree is shaken, and those whose names are inscribed on the leaves that fall are fated to die in the coming year.

Some scholars suggest that it was the jujube's fruit that caused the indolent forgetfulness of Odysseus's companions, known as the lotus-eaters.

Julian the Hospitaller, St

HERO OF A PIOUS, ROMANTIC FICTION. His popularity stems from the story first found in the 13th century, written by Vincent de Beauvais, and immortalized in Jacques de Voragine's *Golden Legend* and more recently by Flaubert in his *Trois Contes*.

According to this tradition Julian was a nobleman who, while hunting a stag in his youth, was reproached by his prey and warned that he would one day kill his own parents. In an attempt to avoid such a terrible destiny, **Oedipus**-like, Julian fled the country and arrived at a foreign court where he performed such outstanding service that he was knighted by the king, and married a rich widow with whom he received a magnificent castle as dowry. Ever since he had run away from home, however, his mother and father had sought him unceasingly and one day, while Julian was absent from his castle, they finally arrived at their son's door and his wife gave them her own room to sleep in. When Julian returned his wife was out at church; he however, on entering her room and discovering the body of a man and woman in the bed, instantly assumed that she had taken a lover and killed the couple in fury. As he left the castle he met his wife returning from church and discovered his dreadful mistake.

Driven by anguished remorse, Julian left his castle vowing to perform a suitable penance. He and his wife eventually came to a ford across a wide river, and there they built a hospice for travellers and the poor. Julian would also, like **Christopher**, guide travellers across the river. One night, responding to cries for help, he found a traveller sick and almost dead from cold outside. He brought the man, a leper, into his house and gave him his own bed to sleep in but could not save his life. As the man died, Julian saw a vision of his departing soul which reassured him that God had accepted his penance, and soon afterwards he and his wife died.

The story caught the imagination and devotion of many: numerous hospitals have been dedicated to Julian, particularly in the Netherlands, and he is considered to be the protector of ferrymen, innkeepers and travellers. This patronage was extended in an interesting direction to include wandering musicians and circus folk. Various scenes from the legend are depicted in art, most commonly the killing of his parents in bed. Two famous cycles of his life from the 13th century survive in the stained glass at Chartres and Rouen. His feast-day is 12 February, and he is the patron saint of ferrymen, innkeepers, travellers, wandering musicians and circus people

jumby

SPIRIT OF THE DEAD, a general Caribbean term equivalent to the **duppy** of the West Indies. It may be connected with the more familiar Haitian term, **zombi**.

juniper

EVERGREEN TREE OR SHRUB OF THE CYPRESS FAMILY (Cupressaceae), genus *Juniperus*, the aromatic berries of which are widely used in the manufacture of gin and as a flavouring. In European lore it is generally recognized as a life-giving plant (see **Juniper Tree**); in Wales it is said that to cut down a juniper tree will bring death within the year.

Juniper oil is widely used as a cure for toothache and gum disease, and in North America it is popular as a treatment for snake bites, rheumatism and stomach pains.

Juniper Tree, The

TALE COLLECTED BY GRIMM. A wicked step-mother who serves her unwitting husband with his son. The father innocently throws the boy's bones under the table after his meal, but they are retrieved by the boy's sister who has witnessed his fate and buries them in a white handkerchief in the juniper tree in the garden. A bird rises from the bones and sings its doleful tale first to the goldsmith, who rewards him with a beautiful chain, next a shoemaker, who gives him a dainty pair of red shoes, and finally to a miller, from whom he receives a millstone. He returns home and begins his song again. His father rushes out to hear, and his son-bird drops the gold chain around his neck. The sister too comes running out, and is presented with the shoes, but when the greedy step-mother emerges the bird drops the millstone on her head and kills her; he is then restored to human form. The story appears in German, British, French, Magyar and Scandinavian lore: it is a version of the **singing bone** tale-type closely connected to the concept of the **act of truth**.

Juno and the Peacock

AESOPIC FABLE, deriving from the mythological association of the **peacock** as the emblem of Juno (Hera). Trusting to its high standing in the eyes of Juno, the peacock asks the goddess for a singing voice as lovely as the nightingale's, but the goddess refuses, saying that no one can be best at everything. The moral is that one should be content with one's lot.

kachina

NATIVE AMERICAN ANCESTRAL SPIRIT, or spirit representing all the powers of the natural world (wind, sun, animals etc), found especially among the Pueblo of the south-west. Kachinas return to earth during the winter but spend the summer months in the land of the dead. They are welcomed and sent off by ceremonial celebrations, typically involving masked dancers impersonating the spirits; a kachina dancer through his **mask** is invested with an individual spirit and is thus able to communicate with the spirit world. Although revered, kachina are not generally feared as they are beneficent spirits who bring gifts to the group, ensuring new growth and an abundance of animals for the hunt, and inspiring individuals to live correctly and endowing them with health and happiness.

The word also applies to the small dolls given to children while the kachinas are present on the earth, usually carved and painted to represent an individual spirit. Such dolls are thought to contain a fragment of the spiritual power they represent, and therefore serve as **talismans**, connecting the earthly with the spiritual.

kakamora

MELANESIAN SPIRITS, usually diminutive beings with long sharp nails and enormous strength, who inhabit caves and trees in the forest. Although generally harmless, they have been known to prey on unaccompanied children and even lone men. They can be kept at bay by displaying anything white, since they are terrified of this colour.

kalau

EVIL SPIRITS, a generic term in the lore of the peoples of Siberia. They are responsible for all disease and death, sometimes to punish wrong-doing but more usually simply to torment humans. The **culture hero**, Big Raven, is constantly at war with them.

Kalevala

FINNISH NATIONAL EPIC, compiled in the early 19th century by Elias Lönnrot from songs of oral tradition collected from across the land. Lönnrot added a short prologue and some linking material to draw the diverse traditions into a coherent whole. Kalevala, a poetic word for Finland, derives from the name of an ancient mythical character whose descendants feature in the epic or from a word meaning hero, hence 'land of heroes'. The three sons of Kalevala are **Väinämöinen**, Ilmarinen and **Lemminkäinen**.

Väinämöinen is an old seer, who works magic through his songs, and the early part of the epic traces his birth and his quest for a wife. Challenged by Louhi to build a magic sampo (a mill that will provide inexhaustible grain and money) to win the hand of her daughter, the

kachina

Maiden of Pohjola, Väinämöinen calls on the smith Ilmarinen for help. It is Ilmarinen himself however who wins the prize, and Lemminkäinen disrupts the wedding.

The three heroes later march on Pohjola to regain the magic sampo; the mill itself is lost in the lake but Väinämöinen gains victory over Louhi's troops. Finally, the virginal Marjatta gives birth to a child destined to become king of Karelia, and Väinämöinen departs the land forever.

▷ **Kullervo**

Kalevipoeg

HERO OF ESTONIAN FOLKLORE, a benevolent **giant**.

kantele

TRADITIONAL FINNISH FOLK INSTRUMENT, similar to a psaltery. It was used to accompany heroic songs such as those that make up the *Kalevala*, and was said to have been first invented by Väinämöinen, who used the jaws of a pike and delighted all of creation.

kappa

WATER DEMONS OF JAPAN, with the body and shell of a tortoise (or occasionally fish-scales), the legs of a frog, and a monkey's head, who devour humans and animals underwater from the inside out. The most striking feature of the kappa is the depression on the top of its head which is constantly filled with water. This liquid gives the creature its strength, and the way to defeat a kappa is to give a polite bow as soon as it approaches. Obliged to return the bow, the kappa will lose the water from this depression and must retreat beneath the surface to refill it and regain its strength, giving its 'victim' ample time in which to run away. Since kappa are extremely fond of cucumbers, another means of avoiding their unwanted attentions is to throw a cucumber inscribed with one's name into the water; this should mean that you will be spared in the future by the grateful demon. If tricked by or indebted to a human, kappa are commendably faithful to any promises they can be persuaded to make.

karawatoniga

MELANESIAN SPIRITS OF THE SEA-SHORE, harmless sky beings who resemble humans, with distinctive long ringlets.

kasha

CANNIBALISTIC SPIRIT OF JAPAN, a **ghoul** who feeds off human bodies left unguarded before cremation. Some groups keep a noisy watch over bodies before cremation to frighten away the kashas.

Kay, Sir

ARTHURIAN KNIGHT, the seneschal (steward) of **Arthur** himself. In early works such as *Kulhwch* he has mythological traits; he could make himself as tall as the tallest tree at will, and go for nine days underwater without breathing or nine nights without sleeping. He generated heat, as did **Cuchulainn** in early tales, and could start fire from his fingers to warm his frozen companions. In the later romance traditions he is reduced to a surly knight habitually defeated in combat, the aggrieved foster-brother of Arthur, who has eclipsed him.

keen

LAMENT FOR THE DEAD, a traditional Irish folk song form always sung by women and often by professional hired mourners. The good qualities of the dead person are expanded upon in long mournful phrases. It is a more sophisticated form than the raw wail of grief, the wordless *ullagone*.

▷ **funeral customs**

kelpie

SCOTTISH WATER-SPIRIT, usually appearing in the form of a magnificent horse.

kappa

He lures unwary travellers to mount, then plunges with them into the river, drowns his victims and devours them. Naturally, to see a kelpie is considered an omen of great misfortune, usually death. If a resourceful mortal could put a bridle on a kelpie however, according to some tales, he could compel the supernatural horse to do his will and bear him properly.

Kentigern, St or St Mungo (c.518–c.603)

THE FIRST BISHOP OF STRATHCLYDE, a potent figure in Scottish folklore. The earliest extant sources are from the 11th and 12th centuries, such as Jocelin of Furness's *Vita Kentigerni*, but they contain elements which are considerably older.

According to these legends, Kentigern was the illegitimate grandson of a British prince, possibly Uriel. His pregnant mother, a princess named Thenew (or Theneva) was thrown from a cliff when her shame was discovered, and being found alive at the bottom was placed in a coracle and left to drift on the Firth of Forth. She ran aground at Culross and was taken in by St Serf, who gave her child the petname Mungo ('dear friend') in addition to his more

St Kentigern, or St Mungo

formal name Kentigern, 'chief lord', when it was born.

Serf raised Mungo, who grew up to become a hermit in Glasghu (modern Glasgow) and was consecrated first bishop of Strathclyde in c.543. One legend claims that he exchanged pastoral staffs with the elderly St Columba, who was believed to have paid him a visit in c.584. He died an old man in Glasgow, and his relics are claimed by the cathedral of St Mungo there.

One of the most famous anecdotes associated with Kentigern tells how he came to the aid of an unfaithful queen, who had given the king's ring to a lover. The outraged king had thrown the ring into the sea and challenged her to find it within three days or face dire consequences. Kentigern comforted her, and one of his monks miraculously caught a salmon which had swallowed the ring, found unharmed inside it. The legend of the ring and the salmon forms the basis of the heraldic arms of Glasgow, and it is the most popular artistic depiction of the saint. He is also shown meeting St Columba in the presence of a column of fire. His feast-day is 14 January, and he is the patron saint of Glasgow.

keys and keyholes

SYMBOLS OF POWER AND ENABLING. Since **doors** are commonly represented as means of access to the **otherworld**, it is natural that keys and keyholes should also feature in mythology, the means of access to these supernatural realms. Those given charge of the keys were typically powerful deities or specially commissioned supernatural keepers; in Greek mythology Athene, patron of Athens, carried its keys, and the Roman god Janus, who stood at the cross-over from the old year to the new, bore a key in each hand. The heaven of Babylonian mythology was guarded by locked gates, and the Assyrian god Ninib possessed the keys of both heaven and earth. The Christian Hell was locked, to keep the inhabitants in rather than deterring would-be entrants, one presumes, and Christ is portrayed as smashing its locks and gates when he descended into Hell. St Peter is shown as the gate-keeper of Heaven from Jesus's words to him in Matthew—'I will give you the keys of the kingdom of Heaven'. In general the one to whom the keys are entrusted has the power to admit or refuse access to the otherworld to whomever they choose.

The association of keys with access to the otherworld has led to many folk customs involving the key; in some areas of the Mediterranean an **iron** key is placed on a corpse as a magical token whose two-fold purpose is to repulse evil spirits (a property of iron) and to allow the deceased access to the next world. Sick babies in Italy are protected with miniature key **amulets**, and similar amulets are used in Europe to ward off the **evil eye**. A bunch of iron keys is carried in many parts by a sick person, who would otherwise be especially vulnerable to evil spirits. In China the key is a **life token**, given to an only son that he may be safely locked into life.

As a symbol of access, the key features in childbirth customs of several cultures. Often all doors will be unlocked and opened and a key given to the mother to aid a difficult delivery. It is usual after the birth to keep the key in the lock so that fairies cannot enter through the keyhole and leave a **changeling** in place of the child. Evil spirits and the **Devil** himself are also said to use the keyhole to slip into rooms, and a plug of specially consecrated wax was often used to deter them. Should one wish to summon the Devil however, one sure way is to walk three times around a church and then blow through the keyhole of its door.

The sexual symbolism of the key and lock is often clear in customs and folktales; one way for a Serbian woman to protect herself against pregnancy was to close a lock and lay it and the key apart on the floor. A Moroccan male treats impotence with the aid of a key. Some folklorists have seen sexual symbolism too in the **Bluebeard** tale, in which the bloodstained key signifies the disobedience of the wife to her husband's command in his absence.

The giving or withholding of keys is particularly significant in Western culture. One of the last vestiges of our **initiation** rites is the symbolic 'key of the door', formerly presented to a young person at 21 but now more usually given at the age of 18 to mark his or her transition into adulthood. Another tenacious folk custom is the awarding of the keys of the city to a specially honoured guest, thus symbolically allowing the visitor free access to the city. Similarly, a besieged castle would signal its surrender by presenting the keys to the enemy.

In ancient Roman and Teutonic lore, **marriages** and **divorces** were often carried out by the ritual handing over and taking back of the keys to the marital home.

To identify a villain, a Bible is balanced on a key and the names of the suspects recited. The Bible will fall as the name of the guilty one is spoken. Alternatively, a key placed in an open Bible will turn at the appropriate name.

Khidre, El

SUPERNATURAL BEING OF ARABIAN LORE, the Green One, an immortal and saint. Many of the tales attached to Elijah in Hebrew lore are associated with El Khidr in Islam. In the Koran Moses becomes his follower and El Khidr demonstrates his wisdom in a series of seemingly nonsensical actions; he sinks a boat for example, and when questioned reveals that he has done so to delay the owners who would otherwise have been attacked by pirates. In oral lore, El Khidr appears in a variety of historical contexts (he is after all an immortal) and in Syrian lore he has been identified with the **dragon-slaying** St **George**. Elsewhere he is a water spirit who guards travellers undertaking perilous crossings.

kikimora

HOUSEHOLD SPIRIT OF RUSSIA, a female being who aids an industrious housewife in her tasks but plagues a lazy one. She is a rare example of a female **mischievous spirit**. In some areas she is the wife of **domovik**.

k'ilin

FABULOUS CREATURE OF CHINESE MYTHOLOGY, a composite animal with the body of a deer, the legs and head of a horse, the tail of a **lion** and a horn like that of a **unicorn**. It is a dainty, virtuous creature, symbolizing filial piety and self-restraint, and its appearance was said to have marked the birth of Confucius.

Kilkenny cats

FABLED CATS OF IRELAND, who fought until nothing was left of them but tails and claws. They represent the feuding cities of Englishtown (later Kilkenny), settled by the Earl of Pembroke and his English followers in the 12th century, and Irishtown, inhabited by their resentful native neighbours.

A late legend attributes the phrase to Hessian soldiers stationed in Kilkenny in the 1798 rebellion, who would tie two cats together by their tails and hang them over a rope to watch them fight to the death. When an officer passed by and cut the two animals free with a blow of his sword, the legend began that the two cats had eaten each other and hence only the tails were left hanging from the line.

kilyakai

FOREST SPIRITS OF PAPUA NEW GUINEA, diminutive wizened huntsmen with malicious propensities. They will steal human babies and pigs if they have the chance, and cause sickness among mortals. Malaria is said to be transmitted by their tiny poisoned arrows.

kingfisher

LARGE-BILLED BIRD, A member of the family *Alcedinidae*, typically having a crest and bright plumage. Many dive for fish. According to Pliny, the halcyon (kingfisher) lays its eggs on the sea or at its edge during the winter solstice. According to this popular tradition, the waves are calm for seven days before and following the solstice to allow the nestlings to hatch; these are the Halcyon days of modern proverb lore.

The bird is revered as sacred in many areas, as a messenger of the gods. Its colourful feathers are widely prized for talismans and especially in charms to protect the bearer from death by water or thunderbolts.

King Lear judgement

FOLKTALE MOTIF, central to the story of Lear, who disinherits the younger daughter who loves him most because of his lack of discernment but is finally convinced of her true worth. The motif is an ancient one in European fairy tales, for example in the widespread Cap o'

Rushes type in which the daughter is banished for comparing her love to that of meat (or bread) for salt, but is later able to demonstrate her point and reveal her identity to her father. Closely-related motifs include 'love like salt' and more general elements of the tale such as banishment for disobedience and the restoration of the vindicated younger daughter.

King o' the Cats

ENGLISH FOLKTALE. The grave-digger is confronted by a cortège of black cats, whose leader instructs him to take the message to Tom Tildrum that Tim Toldrum is dead (different versions display a variety of similar name pairs). Unsettled by this, the sexton rushes home to his wife who is dozing beside the fire with the cat at her feet, and tells the whole tale. His cat, Old Tom, becomes progressively more excited as his narration continues, and when he hears the news of Tim Toldrum's death shrieks out loud 'Then I'm the king o' the cats!' and rushes up the chimney, never to be seen again.

kings

SPIRITUAL AND SECULAR RULERS, inextricably linked with the divine. Much scholarship has been directed towards investigating the origins of kingship, the world-wide system whereby one individual assumes supreme power over a territory or group. Although in Europe in recent years (from the 17th century in Britain) the king's power has been held to be constitutional, deriving from the people, in its earlier forms kingship was intertwined with divinity, with the king representing the will of the gods or even himself deified. In primitive culture he is often chief priest of the group, regarded as a powerful magician, and it seems likely that his temporal authority derived from such supernatural powers, since his word and will, reflecting that of the god's, were so potent.

Kingship is usually conferred by heredity, divine election presiding over the birth, but alternative systems do exist. In medieval Germany kings were popularly elected, for example, and although in many societies power is sometimes usurped by force there are some cultures in which it is customary for the new king to ascend by defeating and killing the old. Early systems such as this may have meant an impracticably swift turnover of successive monarchs; another custom was the ritual killing of the king-god in fertility rites to ensure the cycle of birth and rebirth continued without diminution of age or feebleness. This was often replaced by a ritual involving substitutes, human or symbolic. Survivals of such traditions are to be found in the 'temporary kingships' of later cultures, in the Roman **Saturnalia** or the medieval **Lord of Misrule** who held sway over Christmas-tide. Many other local customs exist in which a temporary ruler is chosen, in the May Day celebrations of Europe for example, and these too may derive from a time when because of sacrificial rites kingship was a rather more precarious situation.

The enduring features of the king which emerged from such beliefs were absolute authority and immunity from judgement, and he was viewed as a symbol rather than as an individual. This archetypal nature lent itself well to inclusion in folktales, especially the **fairy tales** of Europe and Asia, in which the king is seldom named or placed in historical context but rather serves as a symbol of unquestioned authority whose decrees shape the action but who seldom takes an active part in it. Thus in the **Jack tales** the hero gains favour with the king by slaying giants and thereby secures his prosperity, and hence also the king commands his daughter to honour her promise to the **Frog Prince**.

Since folktales are often concerned with the triumph of the oppressed, however, kings often serve as foils to the wit and ingenuity of the folk hero. In **Cap o' Rushes** and other stories with the **King Lear judgement** motif, the king's authority is misused and the heroine succeeds in correcting his judgement. In many tales the king sets a riddle which baffles all but the wily folk hero, who wins the hand of the princess as his prize. Alternatively, the hero may be set a series of impossible tasks by the king which he accomplishes to win his bride. Marriage to the present or future king is

the ultimate destiny of many fairy tale heroines.

Although the king as symbol of authority (and occasionally of national identity) is always part of the consciousness of the folk, their lore is more vitally concerned with their everyday situation and immediate environment. In general the stories concerned exclusively or mainly with kings and courtly life properly belong to other traditions, literary and chivalric romance, epic or legend.

Knecht Ruprecht

SERVANT RUPERT, the knight of Christ in German folklore. He features in **Christmas** celebrations of the 18th and 19th centuries particularly, dressed in white robes, wig and mask, as the bringer of gifts to good children. If the parents reported that the child had been naughty he handed the father a switch instead, with instructions to discipline the child, and went on to the next house.

▷ **Kriss Kringle; Nicholas, St; Santa Claus**

knife

CUTTING IMPLEMENT, which has accumulated a large body of superstition associated primarily with its sharpness and the fact that it is generally made of **iron**. Ritual knives, used for sacrifices, are often carefully prepared and reserved for sacred purposes, and in some cases are made from special materials, such as the flint knives used by many groups for circumcision.

Much varied folklore surrounds the domestic knife; it is unlucky to give a knife to a friend as a present, as it will inevitably cut the thread of friendship if a token payment is not made. Knives crossed at the table will bring bad luck, as does a knife dropped to the floor, although this is generally lucky for the one who retrieves it. If the knife sticks upright in the floor, however, bad luck is averted; in this case the direction in which the handle is leaning predicts the direction from which visitors will shortly arrive. In some areas stirring a drink with a knife is said to induce stomach cramps, and anyone foolhardy enough to eat while knife is being sharpened will have his throat slit by the next morning.

Spirits of the dead are very susceptible to knives, since these are both sharp and made of iron. Those suffering from hag-ridden nightmares should surround their beds with knives, but in houses where a member of the family has recently died or been born the use of knives should be avoided as they may harm the vulnerable spirit.

The knife appears frequently in folktales around the world; it features as a **life token** in the tale of Bahman in the *Arabian Nights*, which told of his death by its blood spots. In an Estonian tale a resourceful beggar hands a charitable housewife a knife with which to cut him a slice of her bread. As she cuts he mentions that he has recently cut up a dog with the same knife; the woman loses her appetite and he receives the whole loaf. The magic knife which alone can slay the giant or monster is a common theme of folklore. In many mythologies, the afterworld of reward can be reached only by traversing a bridge; this is wide and easy for the good, but becomes as thin and sharp as a knife edge to send the evil tumbling to punishment.

knockers

CORNISH FAIRIES dwelling in tin-mines, a species of **bucca**. Although they are generally regarded as spirits of the dead they share many dwarfish characteristics. Their activities are restricted to mining; they do not practise the metal-working of their cousins, but they often warn miners of danger, or knock to lead them to the best tin.
▷ **coblynau**; **dwarfs**

knots

SYMBOLS OF BINDING AND RELEASE, invested with magical significance throughout the world. In religious ceremonies such as the **initiation** of high-caste Brahmin or a Zoroastrian, sacred knots are tied to represent the fast eternal principle.

One of the most popular occasions marked by ceremonial knots is **marriage**; in India particularly knots are employed liberally in wedding ceremonies to secure the love of the bride and groom for each other. This belief is

knots used in a marriage ceremony

echoed in the popular love knots, tied by lovers as a pledge of love or by a spurned admirer to bind the object of love to him or herself. In medieval Europe however a knot tied during the wedding would prevent the couple from ever having children or even from consummating their marriage, and shoes and clothes were worn untied. It was illegal for any ill-wisher to work a spell on a couple by tying knots, punishable by excommunication. The untying of the bride's girdle in the bridal chamber, often performed ritually or with solemn significance, symbolizes the preparations for conception.

In many areas women use knots to prevent conception; a preventative contraceptive based on the principle of **sympathetic magic**. Should she become pregnant however, perhaps because she has loosened these knots after deciding she wants a child, it is vital that all knots are untied in the birthing room and throughout the house to ensure a speedy delivery (see **childbirth**); this precaution is often reinforced by opening doors and windows and releasing captive animals to facilitate the baby's emergence.

Fishing communities since ancient times have believed that favourable winds can be caught and knotted, to be released at the fisherman's or sailor's pleasure, and many **witches** carried on a profitable trade in knotted handkerchiefs purporting to contain such winds. In the *Odyssey* Odysseus receives such a bag, carefully tied with a knot, from Aeolus.

kobold

MISCHIEVOUS SPIRIT OF GERMAN LORE, a **brownie**-like being who helps with household chores but loves to play pranks (such as pushing a crouching human off balance) and is easily offended. He will often hide objects, but when something is truly lost he is quick to aid the farmer to find it. He must be well fed if he is not to become discontented, and when content he will soothe the children of the house to sleep with sweet singing. A common variety of kobold dwells in underground caves and mines, and it is after these that the element cobalt is named.

Certain individual kobolds have gained special notoriety; Hödeken was renowned for plaguing unfaithful wives, and Goldemar was greatly feared by the clergy, since he made it his business to expose their secret sins.

kornwolf

CORN-WOLF, A TYPE OF HARVEST DOLL of French, German and Slav belief. He is a field spirit inhabiting the last sheaf to be cut, and the one who cuts that sheaf may take on the fearsome aspect of a wolf to terrify the children. As in other countries, this sheaf is shaped into a figure and becomes a focus for **harvest celebrations**, sometimes destroyed to allow for new growth next year and sometimes preserved respectfully through the winter to ensure fertility in the next season.

Kraken

SEA MONSTER, feared particularly in Norway. A round, flat beast, it is said to measure over a mile in circumference and creates devastation by submerging itself to create a whirlpool which can suck down even the sturdiest ships. The Kraken is a monstrous development of the octopus, and many tales around the world tell of attacks by similar beasts.
▷ **Jormungandr**; **sailors' lore**; **sea serpent**

kravyad

CANNIBALISTIC GOBLIN OF HINDU LORE, a terrifying **bogey**, whose name derives from *kravyad*, the flames of the funeral pyre that consume the body.

Kriss Kringle

FIGURE OF GERMAN CHRISTMAS CELEBRATIONS, derived from *Christkindl*, Christchild. In early celebrations of Germany and Austria the Christ-child himself was said to bring presents to good children on **Christmas** Eve, although he was not impersonated by an adult as was St **Nicholas** on his earlier tour of the village to ask the children what they wanted. In later tradition however Kriss Kringle became identified with **Santa Claus** or St Nicholas, as the judge of children and bringer of gifts, and was impersonated by a member of the village.
▷ **Knecht Ruprecht**

k'uei

EVIL GHOSTS OF CHINA, spirits of the dead who have not progressed to the **afterlife** but remain in the world to torment humans. In some accounts they can move only in straight lines, and so a screen placed inside a door will keep them out of the room.

K'uei Hsing

LEGENDARY DWARF, said to have been a star pupil in the literature examinations conducted by the Emperor. Because he was so ugly however he was refused the prize of the golden rose, and in bitterness threw himself into the sea. He was rescued by a **sea-serpent** or **dragon** and lifted to the sky, where he now resides as a star in the constellation of the Great Bear, Ursa Major.

Kulhwch

CELTIC HERO, also known as Culhwch, whose tale in the *__Mabinogion__* ('Kulhwch and Olwen') is one of the earliest of the Arthurian romances. Kulhwch refuses to marry his stepmother's daughter, and is then placed under a curse; he can never marry until he wins the hand of Olwen, daughter of the fearsome giant Yspadadden Penkawr. The giant however, who has been warned that he will die when his daughter takes a husband, attempts to thwart the suitor by requiring him to perform a series of impossible **tasks**. Kulhwch begins to find the 13 treasures of his quest with the aid of his marvellous companions, who number among their ranks **Arthur**, Kei (Sir **Kay**)and Gwalchmei (**Gawain**), but eventually kills Yspadadden and weds his daughter without troubling for his consent.

The earliest existing form of the tale is found in the 14th-century manuscript *The White Book of Rhydderch*.

Kullervo

TRAGIC HERO OF FINNISH LORE, whose story is told in the *Kalevala*. He is the last remaining male member of his family, his father Kalervo having been slain by his brother, Kullervo's uncle, Untamo. Kullervo was sent as a slave to the house of Ilmarinen, but he brought about the death of the greedy Maiden of Pohjola and fled to join his mother. He raped his sister, not realizing who she was, and when their relationship was discovered she threw herself into the river. Swearing revenge on his enemies, Kullervo set out to wreak destruction on Unatamo's land, but he returned to find the rest of his family dead and finally committed suicide at the spot where he had raped his sister.

Although the tale has some affinities with Russian **byliny** and Eastern European sagas, it is generally considered to be a relatively late invention.

ladder

FOCUS OF MUCH SUPERSTITIOUS BELIEF. A dream of ascending a ladder signifies good luck, while to climb down a ladder in a dream presages ill fortune. The common superstition about walking under ladders may derive from ancient fears about female menstrual blood and the lengths to which many cultures go to avoid contact with it, often involving a **taboo** about walking under objects. The commonly held belief that modern citizens avoid walking under ladders so that they will not have paint drip on them seems to echo this preoccupation. In Christian lore the practice has been rationalized as a respectful observance of the Trinity, symbolized here by ladder, ground and wall, but this does seem fanciful.

Ladders feature in folktales around the world, as paths to the upperworld; one of the most striking and common motifs is the ladder formed by **arrows** shot swiftly by the hero. Other forms of ascent include the beanstalk and the **rainbow**.

▷ **Mululu**; **Rapunzel**

Lady of the Lake

FIGURE OF ARTHURIAN LEGEND, an enchantress who inhabits a castle set in the middle of a lake. She is also known as Vivien, the lover of **Merlin**, who imprisoned him in a tree. She stole the infant Lancelot, submerged him in her lake (from whence he gained his common cognomen, Lancelot du Lac, **Lancelot of the Lake**), and presented him to **Arthur** once he was grown. It was she who gave Arthur his wonderful sword, **Excalibur**, in some versions of the tale.

ladybird

BRIGHTLY-COLOURED INSECT, known in North America as ladybug, of the family Coccinellidae (order Coleoptera). Lady-birds are most commonly red with black spots. Other names include God's cows or in French *poulettes à Dieu* ('God's chickens'), and together with the dedication to 'our Lady', the Virgin **Mary**, preserved in the common name, these demonstrate the widespread belief that the ladybird is of divine, or at least supernatural, origins.

In German lore the ladybird fulfils the role of the **stork** in bringing babies. In general European and North American belief the insect is a good omen, and it is considered discourteous and unlucky to kill one. This may be connected with the ladybird's usefulness to farmers; it is a carnivore that feeds on pests such as aphids, mites and scales. If a ladybird lands on one's hand, its behaviour can indicate one's future happiness; it is especially lucky if the beetle crawls up and down each finger before flying away.

A popular children's chant on seeing a ladybird is 'Ladybird, ladybird, Fly away home; Your house is on fire, Your children are gone [or Your children do roam].' This is thought to derive from the agricultural practice of burning hop vines after the harvest to clear the fields, which destroyed many ladybirds. In folk medicine, the insect has been used to treat colic, measles and toothache.

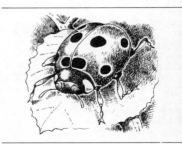

ladybird

Laestrygones

CANNIBALISTIC GIANTS OF GREEK MYTHOLOGY. They were responsible for sinking 11 of Odysseus's fleet of 12 ships and eating their crew while their companions in the remaining ship looked on in horror. Their king was Antiphates, and his court was in the city of Telepylus.

lamia

FABULOUS MONSTER OF GREEK AND ROMAN LORE, a nursery **bogey**. It was a composite being, having the head and breasts of a woman and the scaly body of a serpent. In Greek myth Lamia, the daughter of Belus and Libya, attracted the amorous attentions of Zeus and bore his children. Zeus's jealous consort Hera stole her children, and to revenge herself the distraught Lamia vowed to kill any human child she could entice into her power, since she could not harm the goddess. She turned from a beautiful woman into a cannibalistic monster, and Zeus granted her the gift of being able to remove her eyes at will. Philostratus recorded the tale of Lycius who marries an enchanting and seductive woman, but Apollonius recognizes the bride as a lamia and she vanishes in disappointed rage. Lycius had a lucky escape; lamiae, like **succubi** and **vampires**, suck the blood or vital essence from their lovers.

In later belief a Lamiae race was said to inhabit Africa, and in medieval Europe **witches** were often known as lamiae.

Lammas

CHRISTIAN FESTIVAL OF ENGLAND AND SCOTLAND, celebrated on 1 August. The feast was originally a first-fruits consecration, in which bread from the first grains of the harvest was brought for blessing, derived from Old English *hlaf*, loaf, -mass. Popular etymology however later construed it as lamb-mass, since the feast coincided with the feast of St Peter in chains when lambs were brought to church for blessing.

In parts of the Highlands of Scotland menstrual blood was sprinkled on the floor and on livestock on Lammas Day, when it was thought to be especially powerful as a charm to keep away evil. In many areas the day marked rent dues, hence 'at latter Lammas', the last day of reckoning, was in common use, meaning roughly never in a million years.

Lancelot of the Lake, Sir

ARTHURIAN KNIGHT, one of the greatest of the company of the **Round Table**, whose reputation in legend and literature is mixed. The son of Ban, King of Benoic, he was taken into the care of Vivien, the **Lady of the Lake**, who submerged him in the lake as an infant. She presented him to **Arthur** as a knight when he was grown, and he became the king's greatest champion and favourite knight. According to early sources, such as the 12th-century *Le Chevalier de la Charette* by Chrétien de Troyes, he rescued the kidnapped **Guinevere** and became her chivalric protector and lover. This is the first mention of the famous adulterous amour. In later version however this love becomes his downfall, and he is displaced as the **Grail** hero by his pure son **Galahad**, born to Elaine after Lancelot had lain with her, believing her to be Guinevere. Malory in his *Morte d'Arthur* tells how Lancelot and Guinevere are betrayed, how Lancelot returns to save his lover from the flames and how he finally becomes a hermit after the tragic death of his king.

Lancelot is probably descended from ancient deities of Irish mythology, possibly the sun god **Lugh**, whose name has been corrupted by transmission through Welsh lore with French influences. His battle with Meleagant to restore Guinevere has been seen by many scholars as a relic of ancient myth, portraying the annual battle between summer and winter for the goddess of flowers and fertility, the Persephone tale of classical myth, and if this is so it strengthens the argument that Lancelot is an ancient solar deity.

langsuir

FEMALE DEMON OF MALAYAN MYTHOLOGY, also known as langsuyar or langhui, the spirit of a woman who has died in childbirth. It is said that the first langsuir was a beautiful young woman who died of shock and grief when her baby was still-born. Langsuir can be identified by their long, tapering nails,

langsuir

green robes, and the black hair that falls to their ankles. This hair hides their tell-tale **defect**, a hole in the back of the neck through which they suck the blood of children. A langsuir can be rendered harmless if her hair and nails are cut off and stuffed into this hole; once disarmed in this way she can marry mortal men and even have her own children.

To prevent the corpse of a woman from becoming a langsuir after death in childbirth, glass beads are placed in her mouth, needles in her hands and eggs in her armpits; these precautions prevent her raising her arms to fly or shrieking.

Lanterns, Feast of

CHINESE NEW YEAR FESTIVAL, celebrated during the first full moon of the year. It is observed by hanging colourful and highly decorated lanterns from houses and graves, with street celebrations, fireworks and feasting. According to one legend, the feast originated when a mandarin's daughter, lost in the lake one dark evening, was saved by a party bearing lanterns, but it probably owes more to the traditional beliefs that fire and light keep evil spirits at bay, and their close association with festivity and revelry.

lapwing

BIRD OF THE PLOVER FAMILY, Charadrii-
dae, so-named for the lazy beating of its wings in flight. In common use the name usually refers to the crested Eurasian lapwing, *Vanellus vanellus*. One of its most notable features is its method of defending its nest, which it makes in an open field; the adult screams piteously and will feign a broken wing to distract predators away from the nest, then fly off unharmed before the jaws of the hunter.

The lapwing is said to pluck its food fearlessly from the open maws of the **crocodile**. In Islamic lore it is listed among the prophetic birds trusted by Solomon with his secrets, and it was as a lapwing that Zeus seduced the mother of Herophile, the Delphic priestess. In a common European superstition, old maids were said to be transformed into lapwings after death.
▷ **Battle of the Trees**

lares

SPIRITS OF THE HEARTH, worshipped by the ancient Romans. Their powers were also thought to extend over the city and state. Most important of the various *lares* was the domestic *lar familiaris*, the spirit of the founding ancestor of the family, which would receive worship and offerings of food and wine from the family in return for its protective ser-

Lanterns, Feast of

vices. The *lares* were sometimes said to be a division of the **penates**, the gods of private protection for whom **salt** and the first portion of food were provided at every meal and in whose honour the fire burned. The penates were worshipped along with the domestic goddess Vesta, and they were held responsible for the house's food supply and the success of the harvests.

▷ **guardian spirits**

lark

SMALL SONGBIRD, family Alaudidae (order Passeriformes). The lark most commonly referred to is the Old World skylark, *Alauda arvensis*, which sings its beautiful, sustained song even in flight. To gain a sweet singing voice British folk would drink three raw lark's eggs. In **Aesop**'s fable 'The Fowler and the Lark', however, the lark's sweet voice is of no avail when she pleads that she has stolen only one grain of corn; the fowler still breaks her neck.

larkspur

HERBACEOUS PLANT OF THE BUTTERCUP FAMILY (Ranunculaceae), genus *Delphinium*, with large, usually blue, flowers. Its common name derives from the resemblance of the flower to lark's claws, but the Greek name delphinium communicated the perceived likeness of the nectary to a **dolphin**. Because it was believed that the letters 'ai' could be seen in it, the larkspur was said to have sprung from the blood of the hero Ajax who fell at Troy. In a Roman tale it was a dolphin transformed into a flower by Neptune to save it from hunters. An Italian folktale claims that it sprang from **dragon**'s blood, hence both its blue colour and its toxic effects.

Native North Americans availed themselves of this toxic effect by giving a mild concoction of larkspur root to dull their opponents' senses when competing in games. It is considered very beneficial for the eyes, particularly the belladonna type, and was said in France to drive away ghosts.

laughter

FOLK TALE MOTIF AND CULTURAL INDEX. Many **jokes** and anecdotes rely on the obscene or violations of usual cultural taboos, and comic **clowns** provoke laughter by behaving in an irregular and licentious manner. Such violations of normal codes actually serve to reinforce them, defining the parameters of the social norm, and clowns are often a vital part of sacred or magical rituals since the laughter they provoke is a relief from their seriousness while simultaneously heightening it by contrast.

A favourite device of folktales is the impossible task motif of making a solemn princess laugh. In *The Golden Goose*, collected by Grimm, the simpleton hero succeeds where all others have failed by means of the trail of people stuck to his magic goose.

In the West laughter is primarily associated with fun and amusement, but this interpretation is by no means universal. Mocking laughter, although hurtful, is universally recognized and utilized; it serves to confirm normal and acceptable standards of behaviour, to punish those who transgress them, and to reassure the individuals who join in the laughter directed at another that they themselves are an accepted member of the social group. Another form of mocking laughter is that of the trickster tales, in which the humour is excited by the folly and subsequent humiliation of the gulls. In fact in the majority of cultures across the world it has been customary to laugh at anyone outside the social norm, the stranger, cripple or simpleton. Sometimes, especially in fairy tales, this pattern is reversed and the despised hero triumphs, while a lofty personage like the Emperor with his New Clothes becomes the laughing stock of the town.

In many cultures laughter is also associated with enjoyment and the spontaneity of festivals, and the laughter at the antics of the trickster unites the group in their shared identity and sense of humour.

Since human happiness is so precarious, much lore exists on the duality of laughter and tears. A traditional British proverb runs 'Laugh in the morning, cry in the evening' and there is a widespread **riddle** tale in the form of question and answer: 'What is your sister doing?' 'She's mourning last year's laughter' (She is nursing the child born of last year's affair).

laurel see bay tree

lavender

SWEET-SMELLING HERB, genus *Lavandula* (family Labiatae). **Mary** is said to have dried the clothes of the infant Jesus with the herb, imparting a heavenly scent to it. Lavender has been used as a perfume and bath preparation since classical times, and its scent is widely used in folk medicine to clear stuffy or aching heads, clean wounds, soothe upset stomachs and promote long life. Sachets of the healthful dried flowers are still widely used to scent clothes in chests and wardrobes.

lead

DULL GREY, HEAVY METAL, renowned in folklore for its impervious qualities. It was widely used for caskets containing precious or sacred objects from ancient times, since no evil influence could pass through it and no sacred essence could escape. It was generally agreed however that lead bullets could have no effect on **vampires** and **witches**, who must be slain with **silver**.

Lead was the favourite base metal of the alchemists seeking to convert it into gold by means of the **philosopher's stone**, and hence its chemical properties and compounds became well researched in medieval times. It was used to treat venereal diseases and in contraceptive preparations. Charms and spells involving lead tend to be destructive, since this dull heavy metal was considered unsuitable for business involving love or good luck.

▷ **alchemy**

Leanan-Sidhe

'THE FAIRY SWEET-HEART', a female fairy-being who seeks the love of a mortal man. If he can resist her she will become his slave, but since she can make herself appear so lovely to him he is unlikely to be able to do so, and she will take possession of his body and soul. She is not a malignant spirit, and will in fact impart poetic inspiration to her mortal lover, but the one under her spell is unlikely to live long. The Manx Lhiannan-Shee is more like a **vampire**, sucking the life-force from the man who falls under her spell.

Lear

LEGENDARY KING. Whether or not a King Lear ever actually existed has been hotly debated by scholars, but Shakespeare's famous tale draws on several ancient persons, themes and motifs. The tale of 'King Leir' occurs primarily in Geoffrey of Monmouth's 12th-century *Historia regnum Britanniae* (History of the Kings of Britain), which is not overly concerned with historical accuracy, and many have contended that the story it contains is pure invention and that the king himself never existed. Geoffrey often gave his fictions weight by attaching them to a historical figure, however, so others have argued that Lear and Cordelia may well have existed. Whether they are characters of history or myth, it is clear that Geoffrey Latinized their names from the Celtic originals Llyr (or Llud) and Creiddylad. Llyr was the father of **Bran the Blessed** and Manawyddan in the *Mabinogion*, which appears to be a fragment of myth, 'born of the sea' (lir = of the sea). Llud, which is often corrupted to Llyr, was the name of an ancient Celtic sea-god, and as myth broke down the name may have become legendary. Creiddylad is mentioned in *Kulhwch* (c.1100) as the daughter of Llud Llaw Ereint. Shakespeare's source was more probably Raphael Holinshed's *Chronicles* (1577), and it is thought that an anonymous play based on the Lear story appeared shortly before Shakespeare's own.

In the tale as it appears in Shakespeare's play Lear asks his three daughters which of them loves him most, and the elder two try to outdo each other in their protestations. Cordelia however claims that she loves him 'according to [her] bond', and Lear is so enraged that he banishes her. Time proves the hollowness of the promises of his two elder daughters and Lear finally recognizes the true quality of Cordelia's love. An older form of the tale (to which Geoffrey may well have had access) is a Buddhist parable of a man with three friends, who finds support in the one he had previously rejected.

▷ **King Lear judgement**

Leda

CONSORT OF ZEUS, who seduced her in the form of a **swan** as she was swimming in the river. She was the daughter of king Thestius of Aetolia, and wife of King Tyndareus of Lacedaemon. According to one form of the legend, Leda bore Clytemnestra and Castor by Tyndareus and the beautiful Helen and Pollux, Castor's heavenly twin, by Zeus, but other versions ascribe all four children to Zeus.

The image of the seduction in swan form has been very influential in Western art and thought, and it echoes familiar folkloric themes such as the **swan maiden**, reversed here, **shape-shifting** and **beast marriage**.

leek

ONION-LIKE VEGETABLE (*Allium porrum* of the family Liliaceae), the national emblem of Wales. The source of this ascription is unclear, but it is said to derive from the custom introduced by St David whereby Welshmen in battle wore leeks as a symbol to distinguish them

leek

from their Saxon enemies. Shakespeare locates the beginning of this tradition at the Battle of Poitiers. It may have carried significance as an **amulet** to protect the bearer from harm in battle.

An entirely separate tradition ascribes to the leek a beneficial effect upon the voice; Nero is said to have consumed large quantities of leeks to maintain a clear voice for public speaking.
▷ **daffodil**

legend

ORIGINALLY, SOMETHING INSCRIBED, commonly used to refer to religious formulae or exempla and, by extension, to Lives of **saints**, as in Jacques de Voragine's *Golden Legend*. The word has come to be applied to tales somewhere between myth and folktale, distinguished by an attachment to a specific historical event, person or place and generally told as a true story, based, however tenuously, on historical fact. There is much blurring of these broad generic boundaries; tales of the gods incorporate legendary figures such as **Heracles** and supernatural beings such as **dwarfs**, while floating folklore motifs such as **dragon-slaying** and heroic exploits in the cradle attach themselves to historical figures.

leippya

THE EXTERNAL SOUL OF BURMESE LORE, appearing as a **butterfly** that can leave the body when it is sick, asleep or dead. If the leippya is captured by an evil spirit or ill-wisher, the person may die unless elaborate ceremonies are performed to secure the leippya's release.
▷ **separable soul**

Lemminkäinen

FINNISH HERO OF THE KALEVALA, whose amours and adventures form a central part of the epic. He visited the island of Saari where he seduced all the women and married Kyllikki, who proved unfaithful. He was killed by an old Lappman whom he had earlier insulted, but his mother collected the fragments of his body from the river of death and restored him to life. He burst uninvited into the wedding celebrations of the smith Ilmarinen and the Maiden of Pohjola, whose hand Lemminkäinen himself had tried to win, and killed the husband of her evil mother Louhi. Eventually he joined Ilmarinen and **Väinämöinen** in an attempt to secure the magic sampo (the inexhaustible mill made by Ilmarinen), which ended disastrously with the sampo lost in the lake.

Lemminkäinen has many other names, reflecting his cheerful and amorous disposition—Lieto, Kaukomieli and Ahto or Ahti, recalling an ancient sea-god.

lemon

SMALL TREE, *Citrus limoni* (family Rutaceae), and its acidic yellow fruit. The sharp taste and astringency of the fruit has commended it as a medical and beauty preparation for centuries. Lemon rind was chewed in lieu of toothpaste in many societies and slices of lemon were applied to cure toothache and to prevent sea-sickness. In Europe lemon juice was widely used as a contraceptive and laxative, and it is still today in wide use in treatments for colds and upset stomachs. European ladies of the 17th century used lemon on their skin and hair to achieve a fashionably pale look.

lemures

MALIGNANT GHOSTS OF ANCIENT ROME, appearing in grotesque and fearsome forms by night to terrify the living, especially the surviving members of their own families. They were placated by the Lemuria, held annually on the 9, 11 and 15 May, when the head of the house would purify his hands and scatter black **beans** to appease the lemures. According to tradition, this observance was instituted by Romulus after he killed his brother Remus. The period of the Lemuria was considered to be inauspicious for marriages or new ventures.

lentil

LEGUMINOUS PLANT, *Lens esculenta* (family Leguminosae), and its small edible seed, a protein-rich pulse known since ancient times in Asia, North Africa and the Mediterranean. A proverb of India sums up the attitude of many peoples to this staple food-stuff: 'Rice is good but lentils are life.' It was for a bowl of lentil soup (a 'mess of red pottage')

that the starving Esau sold his birthright to Jacob, in Genesis 25:29

Lentils appear in several folktales. **Cinderella** is set the task of sorting lentils from **ashes** in a common version of the tale. In an Arabian fable a **monkey**'s greedy stupidity is demonstrated when, having dropped one lentil, he lets the rest fall trying to pick it up.

leopard

FEROCIOUS BIG CAT, *Leo pardus*, whose name derives from a medieval conflation of *leo*, lion, and *pard*, the early name for a cheetah. In ancient Egyptian and Greek religions the leopard was an attribute of divinity, specifically Osiris and Dionysus, and in Chinese and Biblical lore it was a symbol of war and ferocity. Among African groups the leopard is commonly a totemic animal, often closely associated with the ancestor spirits of the dead and therefore greatly revered. In Christian lore generally the leopard represents lust, cruelty and, by extension, Satan, and is portrayed in medieval art consuming the souls of the damned. The black **panther** however was regarded as a symbol of Christ, from its supposed practice of sleeping in its cave for three days and then emerging with a roar—a picture of Christ's death and resurrection. It was also claimed by some medieval scholars that the panther's sweet breath attracted all animals but repulsed the **dragon** symbol of Satan.

The common saying about the leopard that cannot change its spots comes from Hebrew tradition (Jeremiah 13:23).
▷ **panther**

leprechaun

MISCHIEVOUS SPIRIT OF IRELAND. The fairy shoe-maker may have come by his trade through a linguistic confusion; his race was originally known as the *luchorpan* or *lupracan*, meaning 'little body') but may have undergone corruption to be understood as 'half-brogue'. This cheerful cobbler, usually dressed in green, or in a red cap with a leather apron, is the owner of at least one crock of buried treasure and if caught by a human can be forced to reveal its hiding place. The leprechaun is sly however

leprechaun

and will usually succeed in tricking his captor and making him look away by crying that his cattle are straying, for example. Once the human has taken his eyes off him, the leprechaun vanishes never to be seen again.

▷ **cluricaun**; **mischievous spirits**

leshy

DEMONIC FOREST SPIRIT OF SLAVIC LORE, who delights in misleading lone travellers. Leshies are shapeshifters, the offspring of human women and demon lovers, and they are well known for luring beautiful young women into the forest and raping them. In some areas, leshies are said to disappear over the winter, perhaps returning to an **underworld** to hibernate.

letters

MOTIF OF FOLKTALES THROUGHOUT THE WORLD. One of the most common uses of the device is the letter of death, which unknown to the bearer demands his execution. Frequently the ill intentions of the sender are thwarted; when the resourceful hero or his supernatural helper alters the wording he is instead rewarded, as in the tale of Hamlet (**Amleth**) and a folktale collected by Grimm, in which robbers take pity on their victim when they read the letter he is carrying and alter it to bring about his marriage to the princess. A common European and Asian tale tells of a king who sends a message to the kiln that the next person to arrive should be thrown into the fire, but the intended victim is delayed or stops to say Mass and his enemy, rushing to the kiln to enjoy his triumph, is himself destroyed. Another common device is the mislaid or intercepted letter, which usually brings tragedy.

Many superstitions relate to the receiving of letters; a spark from a candle, a **spider** dangling before one's eyes, an itch in the nose and indeed a myriad of local variations all confidently predict the coming of a letter. It is very unlucky to place a letter in the left hand of a friend, and if one burns a love-letter the love will be destroyed (this can be useful to quell the pains of old romances).

lettuce

GREEN SALAD PLANT, *Lactuca sativa* of the Compositae family. The lettuce has a reputation as a soporific in folklore, supported by modern scientific analysis; along with hemlock, **poppy**, **ivy** and **mandrake**, lettuce milk was used in a medieval preparation to cause unconsciousness. Lettuce milk is also useful for calming fretful babies, and it is said in many areas to be a sterile plant and therefore useful as a contraceptive.

Leviathan

HEBREW WATER MONSTER, an enormous marine creature roughly equating to its land counterpart, **Behemoth**. The term seems to be used in Hebrew scripture to refer to a variety of creatures, including the **crocodile** and **whale**, but its more general use is as a mighty serpent.

life token

CENTRAL MOTIF OF ASIAN AND EUROPEAN FOLKTALES, an object mysteriously bound up with the life of an individual which displays that person's fate. The object varies widely, and it may be consciously chosen by the individual or born with him or her. Typical examples include a **knife** that oozes blood or becomes rusty when the hero is dead or in danger, a ring that becomes dull, a shirt that turns black, or a **footprint** that fills with water to indicate death by drowning.

In Africa and North America similar beliefs exist, closely connected with the concept of the **separable soul**; the lifespan and fate of a plant or animal is said to be intimately and inextricably bound up with an individual.

A closely related motif in Asian and European tales is the **act of truth**, as used for example in the **Bluebeard** tale; the token (key) given by Bluebeard to his seventh wife becomes blood-stained when she disobeys him.

lightning

AN OFTEN SPECTACULAR PHENOMENON, the discharge of atmospheric electricity. It has been regarded almost universally with reverence and attributed to great divine or supernatural powers. Together with the thunderbolt, it is regarded by many peoples as a symbol of divine wrath and punishment; the Babylonian god Adad, Zeus/Jupiter, the Hebrew Jehovah and many other deities have been represented holding a lightning spear to cast down to earth. Because of this retributory aspect, lightning is considered an ignoble death among many peoples, for example in Dahomey, as a clear sign of guilt punished. Because of lightning's elemental power, however, a fragment of a blasted tree is regarded by many as an **amulet** imparting great strength.

It is also lucky to carry such a charm because of the ancient and enduring superstition, held mainly in Europe and North America, that lightning will never strike the same spot twice. Ceremonial burning of wood can accomplish the same purpose, and this is one of the functions of the Yule log in Scandinavia and of ceremonial bonfires in many parts of Europe.

To dream of lightning is generally a sign of coming disaster, visited on the dreamer by an angry deity, and for a heavily pregnant woman in some native Californian groups it foretells death in childbirth. If caught in lightning without shelter, one can seek shelter from a stump or a tree that has already been blasted, or alternatively try to reason with Lightning, who is often represented in Native American lore as a young girl

or mischievous boy, and request her or him to go elsewhere.
▷ **thunder**

likho

DEMON OF RUSSIAN FOLKLORE, the malignant aspect of Fate (Dolya) appearing as a ragged old woman. She appears in a Russian tale 'The One-Eyed Evil' as an ogress, who cooks and eats a tailor and offers a serving to his companion, the blacksmith. In an attempted ruse, the blacksmith convinces Likho that he can restore her missing eye but she must allow him to bind her with ropes. She easily breaks these bonds however, and the blacksmith eventually escapes by plucking out her remaining eye and then, Odysseus-like, disguising himself with a sheep-skin.

lilac

FRAGRANT, COLOURFUL SHRUB, genus *Syringa* (family Oleaceae). A native of China, Persia and parts of Eastern Europe, it gained widespread popularity in medieval times for its large clustering flowers and heady scent. A folk belief of the south-west of England recommends bathing in dew from lilacs on **May Day** morning for beauty, but on any other day they are a sign that the wearer will never marry. One British tale tells of a young girl who, dying on the eve of her wedding day, requested that lilacs be planted on her grave. To bring white lilacs especially into the house is to court death.

Lilith

NIGHT DEMON OF JEWISH, CHRISTIAN AND ISLAMIC LORE, an **utukku**. She is probably descended from the Babylonian demon Lilit, spirit of desolate places, but in rabbinic lore she was identified as the first wife of Adam, ejected from Eden for refusing to recognize her husband's preeminence—God was said to have sent three angels after her to make her repent and return, Sanvi, Sansanvi, and Semengelaf, but she refused and was finally replaced by Eve, who brought her own problems.

In some traditions she is said to have had intercourse with Adam after he and Eve argued over the forbidden fruit—

from this union resulted a race of demons, Shedim. She is also said in Islamic lore to have borne the children of Iblis (the **Devil**), the **jinn**. Because of her rebellion against God she was punished by having her human offspring destroyed, and she is now eternally envious of human children, destroying them whenever she has the chance. An **amulet** bearing the names of the three angels Sanvi, Sansanvi and Semengelaf, and sometimes those of Adam and Eve, can be used in the cradle to keep her at bay (see **lamia**). A superstitious cult of Lilith survived among Jews up to the seventh century AD, and she later became a figure of medieval folklore absorbing many qualities such as those of ogress and **vampire**.

Lilith is also known as a **succubus**, preying on men sleeping alone and conceiving by her nocturnal relations with them more demons, *lilin*. Any man who wakes to find himself sexually drained should immediately say a **charm** to prevent the supernatural child he may have conceived from becoming a demon.

lily

LARGE ORNAMENTAL FLOWER, genus *Lilium* of the family Liliaceae, often white. In classical mythology the lily was closely associated with erotic love (the bed of Hera and Zeus was constructed partly of lilies), and represents fertility in China, Japan, India and Egypt, but in Christian symbolism it generally represents innocence and purity, specifically the Virgin **Mary** and the Christchild. In Hebrew lore lilies are said to have sprung from the tears of Eve as she left the Garden of Eden.

A common Hungarian belief is that yellow lilies are engendered by the blood of an innocent man unjustly executed. In Japanese flower-lore the lily represents peace, whereas the tiger-lily is an emblem of war.

The roots and petals of lilies have traditionally been used to treat muscular aches, burns and poisonous bites.

In a common pious European tale the lily-of-the-valley (genus *Convallaria*) was engendered by the drops of St Leonard's blood that fell as he fought a **dragon** (Satan) in Louvain. Another

common explanation for these dainty bell-like clusters is that they are the cups of fairies, hung on stalks while their owners dance and forgotten in the rush as day breaks. In Ireland they serve as climbing frames for the agile fairies. A poetic Norwegian legend tells how the spring goddess, wishing to brighten the bleakness of early spring, took shreds from her green dress and snow from the ground to create the dainty flower. A Cherokee tale tells how the bird of dawn left a trail of white pebbles that were transformed into tiny bells to help her find her way back down the mountain.

A distillate made from lily-of-the-valley has traditionally been used to clear the head and the complexion, to soothe sore eyes and apoplexy. It has also been widely used to treat heart conditions, and this use has been confirmed by modern scientific investigations.
▷ **Elaine**

lime tree see linden

linden

SOFT-WOOD TREE, genus *Tilia* of the family Tiliaceae, with creamy flowers and small pendulous fruit, often called lime tree in Europe. It is a sacred tree in Sweden, home of many domestic spirits, and in Germany and Austria it was said to house **dwarfs** and **dragons**; the *Lindworm* of ballad fame translates as 'linden dragon'.

In the classical legend of Philemon and Baucis, the old couple who entertained Zeus and Hermes unknowingly, Baucis is transformed into a linden at death and entwines her branches with the **oak** that was her husband. In the *Nibelungenlied* Siegfried's vulnerable spot was caused by a linden leaf falling on his shoulder, which prevented the potent dragon's blood from touching that spot. In ancient Rome linden leaves were much used in garlands for feasts, since they were said to prevent inebriation (cf **ivy**). In later European lore linden tea was widely used as a cure for hangovers, headaches and insomnia. Wine can be made from its sap, and honey produced from bees in a linden tree is renowned for its delicate flavour. The Meskwaki of North America used the inner bark of the tree to make a poultice and made utensils and hunting implements from the tree's fibres.

lion

'KING OF THE BEASTS', the impressive roaring **cat** *Leo leo*. It is almost universally regarded as a symbol of power, courage and kingship, and has been associated with gods and sun deities in an enormous variety of mythologies—the Babylonian Nergal, the nature goddess, the Egyptian war goddess Sekhmet, Greek Phoebus and Artemis, Roman Juno, Hindu Narashinha and Christ. In Arabian and European lore particularly the lion is also renowned for its mercy in victory, its generosity to those victims who plead or fall prostrate and its special tender-heartedness towards virgins and royalty. Yet alongside this positive, almost revered aspect is a tradition possibly deriving from **trickster**-type tales, of the lion as a fierce, blood-thirsty brute often shamed or outwitted by a smaller, smarter creature. In such cases, the trickster is often the **fox**; he notices, for example, that although many footprints lead up to the cave of the supposedly sick lion, none appear to return. In African lore it may be Mongoose, **Jackal** or **Hare**, and in Asian lore (especially the *Panchatantra*) usually Hare. The dichotomy between these two views of the lion is neatly illustrated by two European folktales, both based on an apparently similar premise. In the first, the lion shares equally between himself, the thief and a traveller the booty they have won. The thief demands half and the angry lion drives him away; seeing this the traveller decides he will not claim his share at all, but the lion presses half upon him. In a fable collected by **Aesop** however, the ass divides the kill up equally between himself, the lion and the fox. The lion devours him, then waits for the fox to make the division, and the fox shrewdly decides to give the carcass to the lion and take only the bones that are left.

In another well-known fable the lion releases a **mouse** that has disturbed his sleep and is later released from his cords by the tiny grateful creature, the strong dependent upon the goodwill of the weak.

A popular floating legend that has attached itself to Androcles, St **Jerome** and St Gerasimus, among others, is that of the grateful lion; the lion's roars are correctly interpreted by the hero as distress rather than aggression and he withdraws the troublesome thorn from the beast's paw. He is thereafter followed with undying devotion and gratitude.

Superstitions concerning lions abound: they are said to be afraid of the **cock**; in medieval lore the cubs were said to be still-born then given life by the breath of the male after three days; it was thought to whip itself into a frenzy to attack with a barb on the end of its tail, and it was commonly said to erase its tracks with its tail as it walked.

In Africa the lion is regarded as a totem by many groups (see **totemism**)

lion

and those involved in hunting the lion must observe many politenesses and rituals (see **hunting magic**). Among some groups, the one who kills a lion must be symbolically pardoned by the group.

Lion meat is a potent food—the heart is said to transmit courage by **sympathetic magic** and is also thought to impart wisdom and nobility. More prosaically, a 13th-centry English writer recommended sitting on a lion's skin as a cure for haemorrhoids.

Lir, Children of

TRAGIC TALE OF OLD IRISH LEGEND. Lir's first wife, Aeb, bore him four children—Fionguala (or Fionnuala), Aed (or Hugh), and the twins Conn and Fiachra. When Lir married Aoife, she transformed her step-children into **swans**. The enchantment was to cease only when a woman of the south wed a man of the north. The four spent a total of 900 years as swans, beginning on Lake Derryvaragh then moving to the Straits of Moyle and finally the open seas off the coast of Mayo.

Christianity reached these westernmost islands with the hermit Mo Caemóc; the swans sang to him their haunting fairy song and he took them in and cared for them. At last a Munster princess, Deac, married the king of Connacht, Lairgrén, and the enchantment was broken. The four children of Lir regained their human form, but the weight of mortal years now pressed hard upon them and Mo Caemóc was able only to baptize them before they died and were buried together. This story is the source of the general Irish **taboo** against killing or harming swans.

literature and folklore

LITERARY TRADITION has absorbed the tales and themes of the folk throughout history, although before the 19th century little was done in the way of transcribing oral tradition accurately to preserve it. Literature such as the Old English *Beowulf*, the *Odyssey*, the Sanskrit *Panchatantra* (known in Britain as the *Fables of Bidpai*) and the Old Testament developed out of a strong folk tradition, and in Medieval times

Boccaccio and Chaucer both wrote works in which characters amuse and instruct each other by telling tales, at least some of which were drawn from folk tradition, in the *Decameron* and the *Canterbury Tales* respectively. The tales of the *Arabian Nights*, probably collected between the 14th and 15th centuries, reached Europe in the early 18th century with the translation into French by Antoine Galland and like the *Decameron* and the *Canterbury Tales* consisted of a collection of narrative tales linked by a fictional framework. An embittered king kills his bride after the wedding night, until the wily **Scheherazade** saves her life by captivating him with her tales.

In the 17th century writers like the French poet Perrault began to write versions of the folktales current in their societies. Perrault is best remembered for his *Contes de ma Mère l'Oye* (1697), known as *Mother Goose Tales*, written in a simple, dramatic style which suited the genre well but was seldom matched by his imitators. Not until the Brothers Grimm in the early 19th century did the concept of accurately transcribing the tale as told by a narrator appear, and the practise of editing and rewriting folktales continued well into that century.

With the Romantic movement in Europe in the late 18th century came a revival of interest in folk culture, as opposed to the neo-Classicism and rationalism which had characterised the early part of the century. Collections of **ballads** were especially popular over the next few decades, as were folk themes such as the Scholar Gypsy, a figure of legend who became disenchanted with worldly knowledge and advancement. He left Oxford university to join a Gypsy band, and is said to haunt the Oxford countryside still.

As science challenged faith in the 19th century, and as the cities drew in large sections of the rural communities during industrialization, many English poets harked back to a more enduring folk wisdom for their inspiration. Later Irish writers such as J M Synge and W B Yeats drew from Old Irish myth and legend in the construction of their plays, searching for an earthy, mystical dimension

275

instead of the pervading naturalism of the European stage. Many writers have used folklore as a means of speaking symbolically, drawing on the easy acceptance of the supernatural to convey a sense of mystery and meaning in life.

Much folklore, especially fairy tales and animal stories, have passed into children's literature, most famously the tales collected by the Grimms and Hans Christian Anderson, and the collection of black American folktales of Joel Chandler Harris, the **Brer Rabbit** stories, and as such they have formed the minds of generations in literate societies.

The oral tradition has thus interacted with the literary tradition of developed societies to give a depth and imaginative power where the writer has sought not rational or scientific effect but a form of entertainment and wisdom crystallized through generations of telling.

Little Goose Girl

SCANDINAVIAN FOLKTALE, found in ballad form in France and Scotland. A little goose-girl informs the prince, who is riding past, that she will be married to him. She attends his wedding to a princess, and is substituted for the unchaste bride in the wedding bed because the prince has a magic stone with the property of discerning **virginity** or its lack. The prince gives his supposed bride several tokens, usually jewellery, and when the princess attempts to regain her place she is discovered and the goose girl is reinstated, recognized by these tokens.

The tale displays several motifs common in European Märchen—the substitution in the marriage bed, the **chastity test**, the **recognition token**—and is related to a widespread tale-type in which a faithful princess takes a menial job at court, disguised, to be near to her sweetheart, the prince. She is forced to substitute for the prince's bride on the wedding day, but by her conversation on the way to church (which reminds the prince of his former love), and the necklace he gives her on their wedding night, she is recognized when the false bride attempts to take her place.

In a version collected by Grimm, a wicked servant tries to usurp the princess's place as bride but her imposture is revealed by a speaking horsehead hung on the wall (see **speaking head**), and she is condemned to the punishment she had advocated for the other, a nail-studded barrel.

Little John

A COMPANION OF ROBIN HOOD, famed for his enormous stature (the nickname is ironic), great strength and skill at archery. Robin is said to have defeated him in a battle on a log over a river, and hence proved himself worthy of leadership.

little people

DIMINUTIVE SPIRITS, found throughout the world, most commonly referred to in Britain and North America as **fairies**, although this is a less inclusive term. Such spirits are found in water, forests, houses, mountains and mines; they are generally mischievous and unreliable, but some are fairly consistently beneficent and others always malignant. It is generally considered wise to speak of them with respect and to avoid offending them; even the most cheerful little people may attempt to steal human babies (see **changeling**). Such beings are generally shy of humans and are seldom seen, although accounts of their appearance are often very detailed.
▷ **mischievous spirits**

Little Red Riding Hood

POPULAR NURSERY TALE OF WESTERN EUROPE, derived mainly from Perrault's *Petit Chaperon Rouge* (1697) and Grimm's *Rotkäppchen*. Although it incorporates elements of oral lore, then, it is essentially a literary tale in its common form today.

Little Red Riding Hood travels though the forest carrying a basket of food for her grandmother. The grandmother however is devoured by a wolf who dresses in her clothes and awaits the arrival of this young juicy morsel. In Perrault's version he succeeds in devouring her too, but Grimm and other later narrators supply a woodsman who comes to the girl's aid, slits the wolf's belly and brings out the grandmother unharmed. The central part of the tale is the formulaic question-and-answer dialogue of Red Riding Hood and the wolf; 'What big ears you have, grandmother!' 'All the better to hear you with, my dear.' 'What big teeth you have, grandmother!' etc. This style feature recalls oral traditions of story telling, and is particularly closely liked to the tale of the 'Three Little Pigs', in which the wolf repeats his chanted threat to 'huff and puff and blow your house down'. Both are **ogre** tales, sanitized for children by 19th-century sensibilities.

liver

THE SEAT OF LIFE AND LOVE, the largest organ in the human body. In the *Odyssey* and in medieval and European lore the liver was the seat of love and erotic desire; according to Plato it mirrored the thought of the mind. Perhaps the most common belief associated with the liver however is its role as the seat of courage. It was a common European belief that the liver of a coward was drained of blood (hence 'lily-livered' as a term of derisive contempt). Classical augurs would examine the liver of a sacrifice to learn if victory was to be expected in battle—a pale, bloodless liver boded ill. Primitive groups around the world have celebrated victory by dining off the liver of their vanquished foes, thereby absorbing all their valour and strength. Inuits eat the liver of a victim of a private dispute to remove the fear of vengeance from his ghost.

Since the qualities of an animal are so closely identified with its flesh, and this is most particularly true for the liver, the essence of the creature's soul, many groups exercise great care over eating liver. That of an **ox**, **lion** or **bear**, for example, is conducive to manly courage and strength (and women would usually be forbidden to eat of such meat) but the liver of a **jackal** would be regarded as unfit food by many.

Egyptians of the second millenium BC recognized the dietary importance of liver, and recommended it to improve night-vision and their wisdom has been confirmed by modern science; liver is a rich source of carotene and retinol, which is essential to normal function of the retina.

lizard

ANY OF A WIDE VARIETY OF REPTILES, suborder Sauria, found mainly in tropical areas but throughout the world. The lizard had been regarded as a deity or as a messenger of the gods in many cultures, especially in Pacific lore, and it is often thought to embody an ancestral or guardian spirit, and many mythologies tell of the creation of humans from or by lizards. For this reason, as well as its usefulness as a predator on insects and rodents, the lizard is regarded with affection and reverence by many societies. In Europe its reputation is less unequivocal; it is widely said to be poisonous and is therefore a favourite ingredient for witches' brews.

Because of the lizard's practice of sloughing off its old skin it is often seen as an emblem of regeneration, and dried lizard is used in magical preparations in many areas to rejuvenate the elderly.

Lleu Llaw Gyffes

WELSH WARRIOR HERO, the son of **Arianrhod**. He is born, together with his twin brother Dylan, as Arianrhod attempts to demonstrate her virginity by stepping over the wand of Math, Lord of Gwynedd. His disgruntled mother imposes on the child three taboos: he will not be named until she herself names him; he will not bear arms until she herself gives them to him; and he will never take a human wife. The magician **Gwydion**, Arianrhod's brother and Lleu's father, tricks her into bestowing both name and arms upon the boy (see **April Fool**), and he and Math construct for him a woman made from the flowers of the oak, broom and meadowsweet, Blodeuwedd.

Blodeuwedd's beauty, however, is not matched by her faithfulness; she takes a lover, Gronw, and together they conspire to kill Lleu, who is virtually immortal. He is persuaded to reveal to Blodeuwedd his one vulnerable position, and as he demonstrates it, placing one foot on the back of a goat and the other over a jar of water, Gronw attacks him. Lleu is not killed however, but transformed into an eagle. Gwydion restores him to human form, and punishes the lovers, killing Gronw and turning Blodeuwedd into an owl.

The hero tricked by a lover into revealing his weakness is a common theme in myth and legend, for example in the tale of Samson and Delilah and that of **Sigurd**. Lleu's association with the oak and his eagle form may suggest that he was an ancient Celtic sun god, perhaps derived from the same ultimate source as **Lugh**.

Llyn y Fan Fach, the Lady of

WELSH FOLKTALE, collected by Sir John Rhys. A poor cattle-herd sees a beautiful fairy woman sitting on the lake of Llyn y Fan Fach in Carmarthenshire and falls in love with her. He attempts to win her three times, first with baked bread, then with dough, and finally, and successfully, with soft-baked bread. He then faces a recognition test to secure his prize, which he passes by noting the detail of his love's shoe-tie. The bride's father enjoins the delighted young man not to strike his wife three causeless blows, to which he readily agrees, but over the course of several years he forgets himself so far as to strike her lightly three times—once in jest, once in surprise at her tears during a wedding, and finally in reprimand for her laughter during a funeral. She immediately disappears, taking with her the oxen given by her father as a dowry. Although the broken-hearted husband never sees his wife again, the legend tells how she meets their three sons and imparts great knowledge of medicine and healing to them, particularly to the eldest, Rhiwallon.

The tale is a good example of the **fairy marriage** and **swan maiden** tale-types, including the recognition test and **taboo** motifs common to these types. The helpful departed mother is another common motif, found in many versions of the **Cinderella** tale. There are also echoes of earlier, more primitive beliefs; the bride's father seems to be a relic of an ancient sea-god or lake deity, rising in majesty above the water to present the goatherd with a test of his wisdom, and the departed mother instructing her sons is reminiscent of the **culture hero**, bringing wisdom to the tribe and departing to an **otherworld** which is not completely divorced from this.

Llyr

WELSH GOD OF THE UNDERWORLD, the equivalent of the Irish **Lir**, father of Manawyddan and **Bran the Blessed**.
▷ **Lear**

loathly lady

TALE-TYPE OF EUROPEAN FOLKLORE, a reversal of the **Beauty and the Beast** transformation tales. Chaucer's Wife of Bath tells the tale of an Arthurian knight who, having raped a maid, is condemned to search the world until he finds what it is that women most desire. His allotted year is nearly over when he meets a **hag** who promises to tell him this secret, on condition that he gives her whatever she asks. He agrees, and returns to court with her answer to save his life; women most desire 'soveraintee over men'. The hag then demands that he marry her, and the miserable knight keeps his word reluctantly. Finally he consents to go to bed with his wife and is given a choice: he can have her as she is, ugly but faithful, or he can have her young and fair and risk the consequences. Wisely, he leaves the decision to his wife and is rewarded by a transformation securing the best of both worlds, fair and faithful. A version of this tale is also told in the English ballad, 'The Marriage of Sir Gawain', and the motif recurs in Icelandic and Irish legends.

Loch Ness monster

FABULOUS WATER-CREATURE, alleged to inhabit Scotland's deepest loch. Nessie, as the monster is commonly known, was first spotted by a motorist in April 1933, who described it as approximately 30 feet long with two humps, central flippers and a snake-like head. Since then many others have claimed to see the monster, photographs have been taken and studied, newspapers have reported the stories in depth, and much scientific exploration has been carried out in the loch, all with no decisive conclusion. The frenzy of monster-spotting continues today, and the Loch Ness monster is one of the clearest indicators that the power of the old lore of monsters, sea-creatures and mystery, particularly the deep mystery of the female principle, is as powerful today as ever.

lodestone

MAGNETITE, iron oxide mineral (Fe^2O^4 or Fe^3O^4) with magnetic properties. Its popular name comes from Old English *lād*, meaning journey or way. Its attraction to iron made it a central part of the experiments of magicians and early alchemists (see **alchemy**), particularly in early experiments on perpetual motion, and in the early Middle Ages it was utilized in navigation.

It was considered a protective **amulet** in classical times, imparting courage and steadfastness, and Alexander the Great equipped his troops with lodestone to keep up morale. Its attractive force was utilized in love charms; jewellery made from lodestone would serve to keep the souls of absent lovers together. It could also be used to test a woman's fidelity; if the lodestone caused her to leap out of bed rather than attracting her into the embrace of her husband she was clearly demonstrated to be false. Indian lore held that magnetite increased male virility, and it was widely recommended during **childbirth** to draw out the child. In medieval Europe it was also said to draw out insanity if passed over the head.

Several anecdotal tales tell of magnetic mountains of lodestones that drew the iron pegs out of ships and leave the sailors bobbing among planks of wood (see **magnetic land formations**), or ground so full of lodestone that horseshoes are pulled off. Lodestone was said to lose its powers in the presence of **garlic** or **diamond**, but its effectiveness could be restored by feeding it iron filings or rubbing it with linseed oil.

Lohengrin

KNIGHT OF THE SWAN, hero of medieval German legend. In some versions he was the son of **Perceval** and Condruiramour, brought up with the knights of the **Round Table**. He arrives, drawn by a swan, to intervene as Else of Brabant awaits a champion to defend her in the duel to decide her guilt or innocence in the charge of parricide brought against her. Lohengrin defends the innocent woman, defeats her accuser Frederick and they marry. Lohengrin has been told by Perceval however that he must not reveal his identity, and he charges Else never to ask his name; eventually of course her curiosity becomes too much and she asks him. He tells her, then leaves forever, carried away by the swan that had brought him.

This version of the tale appears in the 13th-century *Parzival* of Wolfram von Eschenbach, and the tale appeared in many works throughout the Middle Ages, proving enormously popular throughout Europe. Its roots in oral lore are suggested by the common motif of name or origin **taboo**, generally associated with **swan maidens**. It may be derived from a Northern European tale, 'The Seven Swans', in which seven brothers are ill-treated by their wicked grandmother and are finally transformed into swans. The tale inspired Wagner's epic opera *Lohengrin* (first performed 1850) and the swan was adopted as the emblem of Cleves (now Kleve), where the incident was claimed to have taken place.
▷ **name taboo**

London Bridge is Falling Down

NURSERY SONG AND CHILDREN'S GAME, popular in Britain and North America. The song tells how the bridge is falling down and must be mended; various materials are suggested and rejected, then a 'victim' is chosen at random as the two leaders bring their linked arms down around the one is passing beneath their arch as the song finishes. In early versions of the game the 'prisoner' had to pay a forfeit, and many scholars have proposed that the song recalls ancient sacrificial rituals of bridge-building—a bridge was not believed to be secure until a death had been offered to it. Falling bridge songs such as this are common in many areas of Europe and the United States, the subject varying with locality, for example *Charlestown Bridge* in New England, *Die Goldene Brücke* in Germany and *Le Pont-Levis* in France.
▷ **children's lore**

looking taboo

MOTIF OF FOLKTALES, one of the commonest devices employing the concept of **taboo**. Generally, the warning is against looking through curiosity (eg Psyche sneaks a look at her mysterious lover, **Bluebeard**'s seventh wife unlocks the forbidden room), looking too soon or at all at an object of desire (eg **Orpheus** glances back to see Eurydice in the underworld, Peeping Tom spies on Lady **Godiva**) or looking at something with magical or divine import (eg Tiresias sees two snakes copulating and is struck blind, Lot's wife looks back at the destruction of Sodom and Gomorrah and is turned into a pillar of salt).

The motif echoes superstitious beliefs in many areas of the world. Just as sexual abstinence is required among many cultures for men embarking on hunting expeditions or religious or ceremonial observance, so in some groups they are forbidden to see their wives for a period or to look back to them as they leave, lest their strength be lost. **Initiation** rites in many areas involve segregation, and it is forbidden for women and children especially to see the initiates or the rituals performed (cf **bull-roarer**). The strictures in European Märchen against looking out of curiosity carry remnants of such magical beliefs, but they are also intended to warn children of the dangers of disobeying authority.

Lord of Misrule

MEDIEVAL ENGLISH MUMMER, also known as the King of Misrule. He featured in **Christmas** celebrations as a Saturnalian dignitary, attended by a riotous retinue of officers mounted on hobby-horses. He reigned from Christmas to **Epiphany** (the Twelve Days of Christmas) and in some areas from **All Hallows' Day** (1 November) to **Candlemas** (2 February), as master of revels in the royal court, in nobles' houses, at the colleges and in the lawcourts, burlesquing everything that was revered throughout the rest of the year and holding absolute sway. In Scotland this figure was called the Abbot of Unreason or of Bon Accord, in France the Abbé de la Malgouverné.

It seems likely, as **Frazer** suggests, that the Lord of Misrule and his counterparts such as the Boy Bishop who presided over Innocents' Day (28 December) and the French Abbas Stultorum on the **Feast of Fools** (1 January)

are relics of the ancient Roman **Saturnalia**, a period of anarchic revelry around the winter solstice in which roles were reversed and usual rules of conduct set aside. Frazer suggests that those who ruled over such events enjoyed a very pleasant and powerful spell of festivities which they paid for with death at the end of the revels, once their function of imparting vitality had been fulfilled.

lotus

A MAGICAL, BEAUTIFUL FLOWER—the name has been given to several different species. In Hindu mythology the lotus is a symbol of female sexuality and the procreation of life, representing the womb and hence the earth goddess, source of all creation. Brahma is born of the lotus, and the emblem became a focus of Buddhist religious symbolism also, and serves as the support in most images of the bodhisattvas. In Buddhist folk belief the birth of Buddha was heralded by the appearance of the lotus, and lotus flowers sprang up in the Buddha's **footprints**.

In China, as in ancient Egypt, the lotus is the water-lily, and since it blooms pure white through water and does not sully itself with earth it is an emblem of purity. In Chinese Buddhist descriptions of paradise each soul becomes a lotus on the sacred lake after death, and when the lotus opens the soul is released into the presence of the god. In Egyptian lore the

lotus

lotus opens to release the sun in the morning and closes to cradle it at night.

The ancient Greek lotus was a tree with large fruits, *Ziziphus lotus*, and the wine and meal produced by these fruits were believed to cause drowsy forgetfulness and lethargy, as discovered by Odysseus's men. Pliny and some others identified this fruit as the sour plum, *Cardia myxa*, but did not dispute its effects.

▷ **jujube**

love magic

ONE OF THE MOST WIDESPREAD FORMS OF FOLK MAGIC, consisting of a bewildering variety of charms, spells, potions, practices, superstitions and taboos associated with winning and keeping the object of one's love. Love magic is found in almost every society, in more or less sophisticated forms. The basic principle of much love magic is the transference of an aspect of the lover to the beloved—nail parings, an item of clothing, hair, blood, etc—the object is charmed with an incantation and then, usually secretly, placed in the possession of the desired one. This mysterious contract will ensure that love is generated in return. Similarly, an item of the beloved's can be appropriated into one's own possession and charmed in a similar way.

Professional magic-makers and **witches** may produce more general love-charms, compounds of ingredients such as **mandrake**, **ginseng**, the heart of the **hummingbird** or any such exotic and evocative combination. The 'love-in-idleness' herb used by Puck in Shakespeare's *A Midsummer Night's Dream* is of this ilk, having the general effect of arousing love (here for the first object seen upon waking) rather than giving specific direction.

Once love has been reciprocated, lovers throughout the world exchange pledges or tokens to ensure the continuation of their love especially in absence; in folktales these may be a **life token** such as a sword, but in common folk practice necklaces of hair, the plaited friendship bracelets popular even today, blood or rings (cf **marriage**) may be exchanged.

ludki

SLAVIC LITTLE PEOPLE, a **dwarf**-like race much given to music and singing who, although friendly towards humans, were driven out of the mortal world by the sound of church **bells**, which they could not stand. Their fate was shared by many pagan remnants who did not or could not adapt to the new religion. Their Hungarian cousins were known as lutki.

Lugh

IRISH DEITY, one of the sons of **Dagda**, also known as Lug. He was incorporated as a character in many Old Irish legends, but his origins as a sun god are suggested by details such as the red glow from his face during the day and his radiant visage (cf **Cuchulainn**). He is said to have been fostered as a child by Queen Tailtiu and trained as a warrior by Manannan, god of the sea, who gave him a marvellous sword and horse. *The Book of Conquests* tells how he asked to be admitted to the ranks of the **Tuatha de Danann** as they faced the **Fomorians**. All the skills he claimed were met by rejection from King Nuada—the Tuatha already included a smith, carpenter, poet, warrior and so on—but Lugh pointed out that none among his subjects combined all these skills in one person, as did he, and thus he was accepted. He demonstrated his strength by hurling an immovable flagstone, and proved his worth to the Tuatha by slaying **Balor** and ending the war. He seems to represent a later breed of god than his more primitive father, Dagda.

In some versions of the **Ulster cycle**, Lugh is named as the father of the great warrior **Cuchulainn**.

Lugnasad

ANNUAL IRISH FESTIVAL, historically held on 1 August at Teltown on the River Boyne and later more widely observed as a festival of first-fruits. Teltown is said to be named after the mother of **Lugh**, Tailtiu, said to be buried there, and the festival was believed to have been instituted by Lugh to commemorate her. This seems to be quite a late explanation for an existing fact however; it seems likely that the festival began as a symbolic marriage between Lugh and Ériu, the personification of Ireland, exactly nine months before the great **Beltane** celebrations to mark the beginning of summer, which is then symbolically the fruit of their union.

lullaby

CRADLE SONG, a universal method of soothing restless babies by inarticulate crooning or more sophisticated and even didactic reassurance. Wordless humming is known in this context even in cultures with little musical development, and the lines of reasoning pursued by more elaborate lullabies show remarkable cross-cultural similarities. The singer reassures the baby that he or she can sleep because there is no cause for alarm; mother (or sister or nurse) is there, and the rest of the household is safe and going about its normal business (father is hunting, sister is spinning etc). Often the natural world is invoked to reinforce this image—the sun is going to bed, the wind blows gently, the birds are quieting for the night.

Should this fail, another argument of the lullaby is that of bribery; if the child will sleep, he or she will receive a rabbit-skin (in 'Bye Baby Bunting'), a drum, a cake, a fish or whatever reward is appropriate to the community. Alternatively, the baby's fine qualities are listed and in a lullaby promising great future reward—the child will grow to become the greatest hunter, ruler, lover or boat-builder (again, as appropriate) that has ever lived if he will only go to sleep now.

Should all these blandishments fail, however, lullabies also make provision for threats in the form of nursery **bogeys**, or the displeasure of figures such as **Santa Claus** or Hotei (the Japanese god of luck who brings presents to good children but has eyes in the back of his head) whose approval is to be sought.

A smaller group of lullabies tell plaintively of the hard lot of the house, generally focusing on a drunken father and the weariness of the over-worked mother. Narrative tales too are often stamped with lullaby characteristics—repetition, a lack of expression and simple melody. Although almost any kind of song can be suited to the purposes of soothing a baby, and man researches have discovered the mos spine-chilling narratives sung to quie babies in the knowledge that it is th tone and not the words to which the respond, the lullaby survives as a dis tinctive form expressing both the hope of the mother for the children an perhaps a residual belief in the efficac of the song as a charm to bring abou these hopes.
▷ **crónán**

Lusmore

HUNCHBACK OF IRISH FOLKTALE, col lected by Thomas Crofton Croker as *Th Legend of Knockgrafton*. The nam literally means 'the great herb', and wa generally applied to the foxglove or fair cap, a sprig of which Lusmore sports i his hat. The legend tells how Lusmore an outcast from the village because of hi deformity, hears one night the strains o fairy music. He listens entranced, but a the words are no more than 'Da Luan Da Mort' (Monday, Tuesday) repeated endlessly he begins to tire of them and i a pause of the music he lifts his voice t chime in 'augus Da Cadine' (Wednes day). So delighted are the fairies wit this addition that Lusmore is swept int their company, feasted and fêted, an the hump on his back is magically lifte from him. He swoons, and on wakin finds himself alone beside Knockgrafto moat.

News of this marvel spreads, an another hunchback, Jack Madden, hear ing of Lusmore's release, comes to th moat of Knockgrafton himself. When h hears the fairy music however he doe not chime in time as Lusmore had don but bawls out 'augus Da Cadine, augu Da Hena' (Wednesday, Thursday), or i some versions entirely completes th listing of the days of the week. Th fairies are so angered at his presumptio that they fix Lusmore's hump on top o Jack's own, kicking him from the castle The next morning he is found half-dead and dies soon afterwards, cursing th fairy music.

The tale illustrates the familiar them of fairy etiquette, and the resultan rewards and punishments meted out b the fairies to humans. The pattern o success followed by failure due to gree is also a common one in folktales dealing with supernatural agencies.

lycanthropy

MEDICAL TERMINOLOGY, a rare mental disorder characterized by a belief that one is a **wolf** or other ferocious animal. In folklore, lycanthropy is the supernatural power (or **curse**) of transforming oneself into a **werewolf**, a belief held in various forms throughout the world since ancient times.
▷ **shape-shifting**

lying tales

TYPE OF FOLKTALE, a species of pure entertainment in which the emphasis is on the imagination and proficiency of the storyteller rather than the content or message of his tale, found in various forms and with varying degrees of credit throughout the world. Many cultures have informal (or occasionally formal) lying contests, taking place around the nets to be mended or ale to be drunk in the village inn, but frequently such contests, and tall tales in general, are couched within folktales and attributed to fictional narrators. The lying tale is closely linked to the **tall tale**, but need not rely upon a core of truth or couch itself within disclaimers and attributions. A challenge to fill a sack with lies is a motif in Märchen of Northern Europe in particular. Many African tales tell of lying contests and characters such as Baron **Münchausen** are attributed with exuberant untruths.

lynx

MEMBER OF THE CAT FAMILY, *Felis lynx*, found in parts of Asia, Europe and North America. The lynx of ancient Greek lore, which was renowned for its remarkable eyesight (it was even said to be able to see through mountains) is thought to have been a fabulous composite creature, half dog and half panther. This belief passed into medieval European lore and the lynx was thought to represent the all-seeing aspect of Christ.

Mab

FAIRY QUEEN OF EUROPEAN FOLKLORE.
She is almost certainly derived from the
Celtic **Medb** (or Maeve), queen of
Connaght, who warred against
Cuchulainn, through her Welsh manifestation, Mabb (meaning 'baby' or
'child'). In literature of the 16th and 17th
centuries she was referred to as the fairy
queen or midwife (giving birth to **dreams**
in humans in much the same way as a
hag), described as a typical diminutive
spirit, much given to causing domestic
mischief and exchanging human children
for **changelings**. Drayton in his mock
epic *Nymphidia* (1627) has her as Oberon's queen, but Shakespeare, although
he calls her Queen Mab, replaces her in
A Midsummer Night's Dream with the
more ethereal **Titania**.

Mabinogion

WELSH FOLKTALE COLLECTION, eleven
tales collected from ancient Welsh sources, a fusion of myth and folklore. The
title *Mabinogion* was given by Lady
Charlotte Guest to her pioneering translation of Welsh tales published 1838–49.
She coined it as the plural of *mabinogi*,
which appeared at the end of the first
four tales only, 'thus ends this branch of
the mabinogi', but in fact this word is
already plural, probably meaning something like 'concerning children or
descendants'. Her title has gained widespread popularity however, and has
been widely used for subsequent translations of all eleven tales.

The tales are drawn from a 14th-cen-
tury manuscript, the Red Book of Her-
gest, and later translators have consulted
older works, but it is clear that the tales
themselves are much more ancient and
were transmitted orally from early Celtic
times. They deal with mythical characters in a recognizable human context,
incorporating clear personifications of

pre-Christian deities and spirits within
the framework of popular lore.

The first group of tales, the true
Mabinogi, are probably the oldest, and
appear to have been written down by
one scribe, possibly in the 11th century.
The first tale is of **Pwyll**, prince of Dyfed,
who exchanges places with **Arawn**, king
of the underworld, for one year, slays
Hafgan, Arawn's enemy, and marries
Rhiannon who is later falsely accused of
murdering their son. The annual conflict
of Arawn and Hafgar is generally interpreted as a survival of a personified
struggle between winter and summer.
The tale of Branwen also tells of an
unfortunate queen, whose unjust exile
from court was the cause of a war which
almost wiped out the inhabitants of
Ireland. Branwen's brother Manawyddan (who probably derives from an
ancient Irish sea god) by shrewd tenacity
defeats the enchanter Llwyd (probably
from the sun god **Lugh**) and frees
Branwen and her son. The last tale is of
Math, lord of Gwynedd, who avenges
himself on two libidinous nephews by
translating them into beasts.

The short *Dream of Maxen*, similar in
plot to the older Irish *Dream of Oengus*,
is probably a literary piece, telling how
the Roman emperor conquered Britain
and regained Rome. The *Story of Lludd
and Llevelys* is a **dragon-slaying** tale in
which Llud overcomes three plagues
visited on Britain. *Kulhwch and Olwen*
and *The Dream of Rhonabwy* are set in a
Celtic, Arthurian court which includes
Old Irish warriors and fairy tale heroes
among its number. Kulhwch succeeds in
performing the impossible tasks set by a
giant to win the hand of his daughter,
Olwen, with the aid of his marvellous
companions, and it is especially interesting since it incorporates so many
common folkloric motifs and appears to
be one of the earliest Arthurian tales,
pre-dating French influence. *The Dream*

of Rhonabwy is a consciously literary piece, detailing the doings of **Arthur** and his court.

The final three tales are also Arthurian, but although they incorporate native elements they are later, more romantic works, probably written in the early 13th century and strongly influenced by French sources. *The Lady of the Fountain*, *Geraint the Son of Erbin* and *Peredur the Son of Evrawc* all recount the quests and adventures of Arthur's knights, and *Peredur* contains an early version of the **Grail** legend, in which the Grail is replaced by a plate containing a human head.

Lady Guest also included a late text, *Taliesin*, not found in manuscript before the 16th century but containing some authentic Welsh material. It is based on the figure of a sixth-century bard, and may have been constructed around surviving fragments of oral lore.
▷ **Taliesin**

Madoc

WELSH PRINCE, alleged to have discovered America with a fleet of two ships, landing at Mobile Bay, Alabama in 1170. The Madon, a Native American people now extinct, were said to be his descendants. The legend first appears in a a 15th-century Welsh poem.

Maeve see Medb

magic

CONTROL OF THE SUPERNATURAL, the attempts of humankind to bend spiritual and natural forces to its own will. Belief in magic is one of the most fundamental similarities between all folk cultures of the world, from aboriginal groups in which magic exists as the primary religion to the materialistic world of 20th-century Western society, in which superstition remains widespread, seemingly beyond the reach of the scientists. J G Frazer in *The Golden Bough* argues that magic precedes religion as an attempt to control and influence the external environment, since the primitive association of ideas on which it depends is a less sophisticated system than that of invisible deities or supernatural creatures which must be propitiated.

The potent words of the **spell** are usually accompanied by activity, the **ritual**, which must be exactly observed to make the spell efficacious and to control it. In many cultures magic can only be practised by certain members of the group, and even they usually have to observe certain conditions, such as abstinence from sexual activity, before performing a magic rite. In all cultures in which it is used magic is imbued with a sense of the sacred, and magic ceremonies are hedged around with **taboo** and purification rites. These, together with the archaic or meaningless language of the spells and the complexity of the ritual itself, reflect the significance attached to such magic by the community. Much primitive magic serves a social purpose—to aid the tribe against its enemies, to cause rainfall, to increase the fertility of the crop or livestock—and such communal concerns usually involve participation in the ritual by the entire community, under the guidance of the magician or shaman. Another form of magic lore, which has survived to a greater degree in developed cultures, is the personal magic, love-potions and **curses**, the securing of luck, etc.

Even in some ancient civilizations, the most primitive form of magic had evolved into highly complex systems drawing on both mathematics and religion. Magic squares, in which number or letters were arranged in significant patterns, were devised by Roman and Chinese magicians, and many have survived and are used by occultists today. The magic of the folk generally lacks the elite mysticism of the practitioner.

In folktales, however, magic is usually treated familiarly, as an unquestioned means of securing the marvellous. Magic objects enable heroes to perform impossible feats, or humans are enchanted into animal form, to be released by a stronger, positive magic. Such an unquestioning use of magic is characteristic of all fairy tales and many other folktales which are told not to be believed but to entertain or illustrate a moral purpose.
▷ **hunting magic**; **love magic**; **sympathetic magic**

magic carpet

MAGIC OBJECT, a **motif** particularly

common in Asian folktales. It has the property of transporting the one seated on it anywhere he wishes to go. In the Koran, King Solomon had a wonderful green silk carpet, large enough to accommodate his entire court, which he used to move from place to place speedily and in comfort. Prince **Houssain** in the *Arabian Nights* possessed a similar, although smaller, carpet.

magic object

ONE OF THE MOST COMMON MOTIFS OF FOLKLORE, found throughout the world in a myriad of forms. Some of the commonest types of magical objects include inexhaustible items (pots that produce endless porridge or meal, or a never-empty purse), **talismans** (the cloak or ring of **invisibility**, or the shoes of swiftness or the lamp that contains a jinni), a supernatural aid (a **horn** that summons fairy legions or a cudgel that beats off enemies) or an object of truth (the golden **goose** to which the thief sticks fast or the pot that breaks when three lies are told over it and is restored by three truths). Such objects are often given as rewards to humans by supernatural agents; they may also however be stolen by the hero or discovered.

Magic objects may be misappropriated by envious enemies or used without proper authority; if the thief is not the hero, the theft usually brings dire consequences. The magic mill that grinds meal as requested cannot be persuaded to stop until its rightful owner gives the command, or the stolen cudgel turns upon the thief. Sometimes the magic object loses its power when it is given away.

magnetic land formations

OBJECTS OF TRAVELLER'S LORE, generally a mountain or island group possessing enormous magnetic attraction. Pliny tells of such a mountain near the Indus, and Ptolemy locates his magnetic island in the Indian Ocean. Sir John Mandeville in his *Travels* (1449), places the magnetic island near the mythical kingdom of **Prester John**.

The magnetic island or mountain is greatly feared by sailors as it has the power to pull ships irresistibly towards it or to pull the nails from their holes, leaving the ship a wreckage of planks. Travellers' tales of the Middle Ages report ships made entirely from wood, with wooden pegs and cord lashings instead of iron pins and nails, 'designed to resist such dangers. These mountains and islands were said to be made of **lodestone**, magnetite; the nature of magnetism and the means by which the compass needle indicated the north, but could be swayed by metal, were still mysterious in these early days of science, and gave rise to much speculation that passed into common lore.
▷ **floating islands**

magpie

LONG-TAILED BIRD, most commonly the black-billed magpie (*Pica pica*) with its iridescent tail and characteristic black-and-white plumage; the name comes from maggot (Margaret) -pie (pied). In China especially and in the Far East in general the bird is a symbol of happiness and good luck, and to hear its voluble chattering is an indication that visitors or good news are on the way. Among some groups of North America the magpie is a symbol of hardiness; it does not migrate and hence can stand both heat and cold. Magpie is a **culture hero** among a few Native American groups.

Elsewhere in the world, particularly in Europe, the magpie has a less favourable reputation. It features in folktales as an irresponsible, vain, chattering thief, much attracted to sparkling objects which it mischievously steals to hoard in its nest. *The Stolen Necklace*, a tale of the *Arabian Nights*, tells how a servant woman is beaten and imprisoned for stealing the queen's necklace. Some time later she is pardoned when the king notices the necklace half-hidden in a magpie's nest. The stealing of such objects, especially rings, and the subsequent search for them, is a central device of much Asian and European lore. The magpie was said to have been ejected from Noah's ark because of its incessant chattering, and was obliged to perch on the ridge-pole throughout the deluge.

To see a magpie, particularly a single bird, is generally an ill omen in Europe. It can be countered by raising one's hat or otherwise greeting the bird. A British

magpie

counting rhyme lists the superstitions associated with magpie sightings; a modern version is 'One for sorrow, Two for joy, Three for a girl and Four for a boy', and an older version runs 'One for sorrow, Two for mirth, Three for a wedding, Four for a death' (or in the north 'Four for a birth'), and in Scotland it continues 'Five's a christening, Six a death, Seven's heaven, Eight is hell, and Nine's the De'il his ane sel'. This recalls the medieval belief that the magpie was a representation of the **Devil**. To kill a magpie is widely regarded as a crime, however.

Mahabharata

SANSKRIT EPIC OF THE BHARATA DYNASTY, an immense tale of heroism, war, romance and codes of conduct. One of the two great epics of India (the other is the *Ramayana*), the *Mahabharata* is probably the longest work of its kind in history, eight times longer than the *Iliad* and *Odyssey* combined. It is written in couplets, nearly 100 000 of them, divided into 18 sections or *parvans*, with the addition of a section detailing the genealogy of Krishna–Vishnu. Tradition names the scribe Vyasa as author, who dictated the complete work to Ganesha, the elephant-headed god; it seems probable that Vyasa compiled material circulating in oral form. The epic is a central work of Hinduism, and contains key religious texts such as the *Bhagavadgita*,

the sacred song, but it also contains a wealth of folkloric material, legend and history, and didactic directives. Unlike the *Ramayana*, it is based around narrative tale rather than sacred song, and although its present form is dated at c. AD400, it is drawn from more ancient material.

The central plot, which probably dates in essence from c.1500BC, is the feud between two great warrior families, the Pandavas and the Kauravas, as they struggle for supremacy. An old king, Santanu, desiring to remarry, is prevented by the condition imposed by his prospective father-in-law, that the child of the union should succeed to the throne in preference to the king's existing sons. However Bhisma, Santanu's eldest son by a former marriage, renounces his succession and pledges celibacy so that the marriage can go ahead. Santanu and his bride Satyavati have two sons, both of whom die without producing further heirs, so Satyavati pleads with Vyasa, half-brother of Santanu and the alleged author of the epic, to fulfil the law by giving children to her sons' widows. Because of his ugliness, the first widow shut her eyes and the second turned pale as they lay with him, and so the sons, Dhartarastra and Pandu, were born blind and pale respectively. The younger, Pandu succeeded to the throne because of his brother's infirmity, but later handed power over to him and went to live as a hermit, enjoined to celibacy by a prophecy that he would die in intercourse. Pandu's five sons, who are hence actually fathered by gods, are brought up with their 100 Kauravas cousins, sons of Dhrtarastra, at court, but enmity develops and they are forced into exile. After several years of feuding, the two sides fight in battle and the Kauravas are destroyed. After the deaths of Dhrtarastra and their friend, the deity Krishna, however, the five brothers set out for Mont Meru and the heaven of Indra. All but one are lost on the pilgrimage, but when the eldest, Yudhisthira, finally reaches the afterworld alone he finds his brothers waiting there for him.

Within this plot are many individual stories, traditional folktales of heroism, romance and the supernatural linked loosely together in the manner of most heroic epics. These episodes circulated widely in oral tradition, for example the romance of **Nala and Damayanti**. One of the most interesting episodes is the marriage of all five Pandava to Draupadi, which is presented as a highly irregular arrangement but which some scholars have taken to be evidence of polyandry in early Asian culture.

malingee

AUSTRALIAN NIGHT DEMON, whose knees can be heard knocking together as he walks. He does not seek out humans, but if provoked may turn stone knives and his terrifying strength upon them. His eyes burn in the dark to warn of his approach.

Man in the Moon

THE FIGURE DISCERNED IN THE MOON'S MARKINGS, variously interpreted as a man, an old woman (usually cooking), a hare and even a frog. Many tales exist to account for the creature's presence there, for example the Scandinavians tell of Hjuki and Bil (thought by some scholars to be the original Jack and Jill) who were rescued by the moon, together with the pail they carried, from their cruel father.

mandragora see mandrake

mandrake

NARCOTIC PLANT (*Mandragora officinarum* of the family Solanaceae), featuring in folklore and mythology around the world. Its potency derives from the fact that the root of the plant, often divided into two, resembles a rough human figure, and in many areas it was held to be a supernatural underground being, either make or female, that gave a blood-curdling scream as it was uprooted. This scream would kill or drive insane anyone who heard it, and any human whose hands touched the plant during the process would infallibly die, so the uprooting of the precious mandrake was carried out with great ceremony and many precautions; it was done at night, to preserve the plant's power, and the agent was a **dog** (prefer-

ably black) tied to the plant's base. The dog died as the plant emerged, but the humans, if they had remembered to block their ears against its shriek, were spared.

The mandrake was chiefly used in fertility preparations, from its resemblance to the male form, and it is widely considered an aphrodisiac and an aid to virility. Dried roots are carried as **charms** to incite love in some areas of the Mediterranean. It has been used to promote conception since the time of Rachel and Leah at least (Genesis 30). According to medieval bestiaries, the **elephant** could only excite itself to perform sexual intercourse after partaking of mandrake. Classical and medieval races of Europe made extensive use of the plant's anaesthetic properties.

In folktales the plant can be a charm to make the bearer invulnerable or to lead him to treasure; occasionally the mandrake (or womandrake) prophesied future events.
▷ **hand of glory**

manes

'GOOD SPIRITS', a **euphemism** referring to the spirits of the dead, the ancestors and the gods of the underworld. They were worshipped and appeased at the Parentalia (13–21 February) and the Feralia (21 February) festivals, when offerings of food were made and sacrificial blood poured over their graves as a libation. In later lore a manes came to refer to an individual's spirit after death.
▷ **lemures**

manta

MONSTROUS CUTTLEFISH, found in Chilean lakes in Araucanian lore. It can make the water boil if hungry or displeased, and will prey on any human who stands in the water. It can be slain only with the branches of the spiny native quisco bush.

manticore

FABULOUS CREATURE, having the head of a man, the body of a lion, the tail of a scorpion and the quills of a porcupine. First mentioned by Ctesias in the early fourth century BC, it featured prominently in medieval bestiaries as a representation of the **Devil**.

mantid

COMMONLY CALLED THE PRAYING MANTID, or mantis, large insect of the family Mantidae (order Mantodea). Its lower front leg folds up against the femur of the upper leg and gives the insect its 'praying' aspect. The word means in Greek 'diviner', and the insect has traditionally been credited with supernatural powers of prophecy and **divination**. Its accustomed pose, front legs outstretched and head raised in a motionless or slightly swaying attitude, as if in prayer, has contributed to such beliefs. Its saliva is said to be highly poisonous, causing blindness in humans, and a mule or horse who eats a mantid will die.

maple

TREE, any of the large genus *Acer* (family Aceraceae), found throughout the northern temperate zone but especially in China. The syrup produced from its sap has been enjoyed by Native Americans and settlers alike; one native tale tells how the syrup was discovered by chance when a lazy woman tapped a tree for liquid rather than travelling to the river. The meat she cooked in it turned sticky and she fled, terrified of her husband's wrath, but he thoroughly enjoyed this delicious treat. Other groups attribute the knowledge of the syrup to Nanabozho, the **culture hero**.

The attractive maple leaf features in much Native North American art, and has been adopted as the symbol of Canada. In Japan the unfurling of the leaves was greeted with the celebration normally reserved for flowers, the blossom festival.

Märchen see fairy tales

Marian, Maid

COMPANION OF ROBIN HOOD, a later romantic addition to the legend. She plays an important role in **May Day** celebrations in England.

marigold

FLOWERING PLANT, genus *Tagetes* (family Compositae), or the pot-marigold, *Calendula officinalis*. Plants of the *Tagetes* genus are characterized by orange, yellow or red flowers and strongly scented leaves. A popular legend asserts that the marigold sprang from the native blood that flowed when Cortés invaded Mexico. The pot-marigold gained its name from the pious legend that the Blessed Virgin wore it pinned to her bosom. To gaze at the pot-marigold was said to strengthen the eyes, and it could reveal a vision of a robber to his victim. Marigold tea is drunk by Jamaican women to regulate menstrual flow and ease period pains, and in Europe such a brew has been widely used in the 20th century for bronchial complaints.

marriage

CENTRAL RITE OF PASSAGE AND CELEBRATION, vitally connected to the interests and continuation of the group. Because procreation is so vital to the life of any community, the couplings of men and women have been invested with significance and ritual in every recorded society. The marriage ceremony may be very simple, from a casual union established when there is a child to be cared for to prenatal pledges fulfilled by elaborate ceremonies in the course of time. Since marriage varies so greatly between cultures it is difficult to attempt a general definition. There are certain features however which appear to characterize such unions in the majority of cultural groups; it is defined by legal and social specifications; it is considered an occasion of celebration, with emphasis laid both on the sexual nature of the contract made and often also upon its religious implications; and one of its main purposes is widely held to be the production and nurturing of children. The marriage also establishes the line of descent and inheritance, and defines the kinship relationships and permitted future partners of the child.

The expectations of bride and groom vary enormously between cultures. In traditional European marriages, romantic love and mutual attraction have become key factors especially in more recent times, but economic and social factors have traditionally played a weighty part. Marriage within the same broad social class is still considered usual.

The marriage ceremony itself may take place at any age; child betrothal is common among some Native American groups and has been practised in India, Africa and Europe, whereas other groups delay marriage until the age of 30 or more for fear of reducing their **hunting magic**. The most common arrangement is one bride, one groom, but among certain groups, in Korea for example, mass marriages are practised with hundreds of couples and in many societies the male (especially the chief) is expected to take many wives. Symbolic marriages, for example conventual nuns who become 'brides of Christ', have no male participant.

Most of the customs associated with the wedding ceremony are intended to secure fertility and conjugal happiness for the couple, displaying the sanction of the wider community. An object, for example an **egg**, may be ritually broken, to ensure by **sympathetic magic** a painless defloration, and fruits and grains may be displayed as a symbol of fertility. The tradition of giving gifts, like the practice of **first-footing** at **New Year**, is meant to establish a pattern of prosperity for the new couple. To symbolize the physical and spiritual union, the bride and groom may be linked by a sacred thread as in Thailand, the knotting together of garments, or the linking of hands. Often **life tokens**, especially rings, may be exchanged. The words of marriage ceremonies often express their ancient magical and religious significance; in Brahmin weddings the groom says 'I am the sky, thou art the earth; come, let us marry', which clearly echoes ancient cosmological myths. In many primitive cultures sexual intercourse was seen in direct correlation to the acts of ploughing, sowing and harvesting, to the seasonal changes and to the relationship of earth and sky, moon and sun, day and night. These mythic signifiers pervade marriage ceremonies across the world.

In Japan, the central part of the wedding ceremony is the *sansan-kudo* rite, in which the couple exchange special cups of *sake* nine times. Underlining the fundamental nature of marriage as a passing into the wider community and an establishing of interfamilial bonds, the service concludes with the formal introduction of the bride

marriage

and groom to each other's parents. In reality, until relatively recently it was the parents themselves who arranged the match with the help of the professional matchmaker.

Other customs have developed to protect the bride, considered particularly vulnerable to evil spirits on her wedding day, for example the wearing of a veil to hide her face and the bridesmaids, young unmarried girls who surround her and thus disguise her from the jealous spirits. A whole host of local customs have also developed in Europe, all of which generally mix the pagan and the Christian, superstition and religion, in celebrating one of the most fundamental of social relationships.

▷ **charivari**; **divorce**; **dowry**; **Dunmow bacon**; **handfasting**; **virginity**; **wedding anniversary**

Martin of Tours, St (c.316–c.400)

ROMAN SOLDIER, probably a conscript, whose life changed in c.337, when he tore his cloak in two and gave half to a freezing beggar. That night Christ appeared to him in a dream, wearing the half of the cloak he had given away. Martin was converted to Christianity, refused to continue fighting, was imprisoned and eventually discharged. It is said that when accused of cowardice, Martin offered to stand unarmed between the warring lines. After several years of austerity and preaching Martin was popularly acclaimed bishop of Tours in 372, despite his strenuous objections. Even as bishop he lived in a cell close to his cathedral at Tours and then at Marmoutier, where a community of 80 monks soon grew up. Various miracles were attributed to him during his episcopate of 25 years, including the raising of a dead man.

After Martin's death near Tours on 8 November his cult spread quickly. Hundreds of villages and churches in France are dedicated to him and his shrine at Tours became the major centre for French pilgrimage. He is most frequently represented in art dividing his cloak with a beggar, a symbol of charity and hospitality which has associated him with innkeepers. His emblem is a ball of fire over his head. The popularity of his feast is demonstrated by a second, later emblem, a goose: his feast-day often coincides with the migration of geese (see also **Martinmas**). Similarly, the phrase 'St Martin's Summer' refers to the spell of good weather which frequently occurs around this time. His feast-day is 11 November, and he is the patron saint of France, soldiers, beggars and innkeepers.

Martinmas

FEAST-DAY OF ST MARTIN OF TOURS, celebrated on 11 November. Since he was said to have been troubled by a noisy goose when trying to hide from those who would make him bishop, the day is celebrated in France especially with roast goose (cf **Michaelmas**). The tradition of sacrificing an animal on this day is widespread—in Britain and Ireland it may be an ox, wild bird or domestic fowl—and is explained in Ireland by a tale; an old woman, having nothing else in the house, once sacrificed her child to feed St Martin. The next morning the holy beggar left, and the woman found her child alive and well. Gratitude for the miracle should always be shown by a sacrifice made on St Martin's day. Many scholars see beneath this Christian veneer a tradition of pagan rites, taking place as the fodder grows low and livestock is slaughtered. A rather more prosaic explanation for the tradition may be the fact that the feast-day coincides

with the presence of flocks of migrating geese.

The association of Martin with wine lent the festival an air of conviviality that accorded well with the season of new wine, when the crops were all safely stored. In France and Germany Martin was said to go through the streets on his feast night, changing into wine the cups of water left out that night by children. In some areas of England children visited houses in the village for treats.

English weather-lore holds that a fine Martinmas means a cold winter; an early frost presages a mild winter. A particularly mild start to November is known throughout Europe as St Martin's summer.

Mary, Blessed Virgin

SAINT CLOSEST TO THE HEART OF THE FOLK, the link between human and divine. The figure of Mary, even more so than that of other **saints**, became associated with a vast number of improbable pious legends, many of which fit into common patterns such as tricking the **Devil**. Nothing is known of her parentage or

Blessed Virgin Mary

place of birth, although tradition has her as the daughter of **Anne** and Joachim.

The Gospels record how Mary was visited by the archangel Gabriel, who announced the Incarnation, God as a baby born by the Holy Spirit and not human intercourse, which she accepted simply and obediently. Her fiancée **Joseph** was also visited and reassured by an angel and the marriage went ahead. Soon afterwards Mary visited Elizabeth, then pregnant with John the Baptist, and on hearing Elizabeth greet her as the mother of God Mary expressed her thanks by singing the *Magnificat*.

She and Joseph were visiting Bethlehem for the census when Jesus was born; afterwards they were forced to flee to Egypt to avoid the jealous anger of King Herod, who had been told of the recent birth of a king of the Jews. After their enemy's death they settled in Nazareth, and little more is known of Jesus's early life beyond a journey to Jerusalem for Passover, when he was left behind only to be found by his distraught parents in learned discussion with the Jewish teachers in the temple.

According to John's Gospel it was Mary who prompted Jesus to perform his first miracle, the changing of water into wine at the wedding of Cana. After this she is mentioned as the mother of Jesus several times but does not feature in the gospel accounts until the crucifixion, when Jesus entrusts her into the care of John the Evangelist as they stand at the foot of his cross.

Byzantine art characteristically presents Mary formally, as a crowned and sceptred queen, but in the Renaissance much emphasis was placed upon her humanity and compassion. The stylised medieval portraits gave way to more tender, realistic depictions of the Virgin with her child or, most poignantly, with her crucified Son. The most famous examples of these are the *Pietàs* of Michelangelo. The iconography of Mary is complex and laden with significance, embracing almost the entire history of the Christian church.

Many feast-days are devoted to Mary, several of which have recently been reduced, and she is patron saint of the entire human race.

Mary Magdalene

MARY PROBABLY CAME FROM MAGDALA, a town on the west coast of the Sea of Galilee, and when Jesus began his ministry in Galilee she was one of the women who followed and supported him. The Gospels record that Jesus cast seven demons out of her, and throughout the church's history she has stood as the archetypal repentant sinner. Mary was one of the group of women who stood at the foot of Jesus's Cross and it was she, together with Joanna and Mary the mother of James and Salome, who discovered the empty tomb and heard the angel proclaim Christ's Resurrection. Most memorably of all, however, she was the first to see the risen Lord who appeared to her in the garden of his burial later that day; blinded by her tears, she at first supposed him to be the gardener. Later Christian lore filled out these meagre facts: Mary was said to have accompanied Lazarus and Martha (she is frequently identified with their sister, Mary) to Marseilles in a ship powered only by the divine will, where they converted the people. She is also frequently confused with the woman 'who was a sinner' mentioned by Luke, who anointed Jesus's feet with expensive ointment, washed them with her tears and dried them with her hair (Luke 7:37–8). This identification was strongly propounded by Gregory the Great, and has greatly influenced the iconography and popular cult of Mary Magdalene in the West, but it is now widely accepted that these are three separate women. Another legend has her travelling to Ephesus with the Blessed Virgin Mary and John the Apostle, where she is believed to have died and been enshrined. A later addition to this legend claims that she was originally betrothed to John but that he broke the engagement off when he was called by Jesus.

The idea of the penitent, weeping woman has given rise to the now rather pejorative term 'maudlin', meaning excessively sentimental or mawkish, which derives from her name. Her feast-day is 22 July, and she is the patron saint of repentant sinners and the contemplative life.

maschalismos

GREEK FORM OF MUTILATION, a precaution taken by a murderer to prevent the ghost of his victim taking revenge. The hands, feet, nose and ears of the corpse were cut off and tied together under the armpits, thereby incapacitating the dead spirit. A similar principle underlies forms of mutilation of the dead throughout the world, or milder practices such as the tying together of the two big toes so that the dead person cannot walk. As well as protecting a murderer and the living in general, such mutilation can be used to prevent the soul reaching the afterworld.

mascot

BRINGER OF LUCK, a person, animal or object believed to bring good fortune to an individual or group. The word derives from Provençal *masco*, hence little magic-worker. The mascot is particularly common among sports teams and colleges in the United States; a young boy in the team strip is thought to represent the team's luck. An individual may choose an idiosyncratic mascot based on superstitious magic—if previous success has been won while in possession of a certain object or while wearing a certain item of clothing, people in even the most sophisticated of societies will employ the logic of magical causation and retain that item as a mascot.

masks

FORM OF DISGUISE, an object worn to cover the head (especially the face) either partially or completely for a variety of reasons. The use of masks dates back to prehistoric times and they are found in virtually all cultures in some form, from the simplest to the most elaborate designs. Generalizations are difficult; this diversity means that no one of the many arguments and theories advanced by scholars to explain the phenomenon can be fully adequate, although they may be true in specific cultural circumstances.

One of the most basic motives behind mask-wearing is imitation; a participant in a religious or magical ritual represents and may even take on the essence of the god, animal or supernatural being con-

SRI LANKAN DANCE MASK

MELANESIAN ANCESTOR CULT MASK

IROQUOIS 'FALSE FACE' MASK

masks

veyed by the mask. The masks (or **kachina**) worn to represent the ancestors among the Pueblo groups of North America actually transform the dancer into a kachina for the duration of the dance. During **initiation** rites in Africa and North America particularly masks are worn by adults to represent the demons and ancestors who are leading the initiates into adulthood, and women and children, forbidden to approach the terrifying masked performers, frequently believe that the dancers are in reality supernatural beings. Here the mask functions not to convey religious import but as a means of social control.

293

In many primitive societies mimetic dances, representing animals of the hunt or the totemic animal of the groups, involve the use of masks. The earliest such masks were actual animal heads, placed over that of the human, but many societies developed highly abstract representation from whatever materials came to hand—wood, hide, stone, leaves, shells, grass, feathers, and later silver, gold, ceramics and so on.

Another common form is the funerary mask, laid over the face of a corpse before burial. This is one of the few cases in which human features are emphasized rather than being distorted or replaced by animal features. Such masks may be humble, or, as in the case of the Egyptian pharaohs, rich and exquisitely elaborate. Death masks were sometimes kept, as in Roman times, as a portrait of the lost one.

Masks liberate the wearer from the conventions of everyday life, allowing him to assume another role or simply to abdicate normal societal responsibilities. Thus the **clowns** of North America are beyond reprisal because their masks lend them ceremonial immunity; even in the modern Western world circus clowns perform acts that would otherwise be considered unacceptable, protected by the greasepaint that signals a ritual step away from everyday reality.

Masks have long been used in highly developed societies for such liberation; the much more formal *bal masqués* of Europe permitted sexual intrigue and a relaxation of social inhibitions while simultaneously suggesting urbane sophistication. Yet the principles are the same—disguise and decoration.

Since ancient Greece at least masks have been an integral part of theatre in many areas. Greek masks generally emphasized a particular human expression, projecting the nature and feelings of a particular character, and Japanese Nō drama crystallized stock characters into highly abstracted and colourful masks. Medieval mystery plays used grotesque masks to represent supernatural demons. Thus the actor, like the primitive dancer, has traditionally used the mask to subsume his or her own character and assume another, particularly non-human.

master thief

WORLD-WIDE TALE-TYPE, characterized by the ingenuity with which the hero carries out his thefts. In the most famous form of the tale, the hero is a good-for-nothing or the youngest of three brothers who all set out to learn trades; his chosen trade is stealing, and he becomes a master. His prowess is challenged by the earl, who sets him various **tasks**. The first, to steal the earl's horse, he accomplishes easily by disguising himself as a old woman and getting the stablehands drunk, or persuading them to chase a rabbit, or simply by leading the horse away to demonstrate how easily a thief could steal it. The earl then challenges him to steal the sheets from his bed and the ring from his wife's hand; the master thief succeeds by tricking the earl into shooting a corpse then, when he has left the room, slips in. Pretending to be the earl, he persuades the countess to give him the sheets to wind the corpse and the ring to bury with him, as a mark of respect. No longer amused, the count orders his execution, but the master thief convinces a parson to take his place in the sack by persuading him that he is St Peter, come to take him to heaven, or some such imposture. This motif recurs in Chaucer's 'Miller's Tale', where the crafty Nicholas talks the miller into crouching in a barrel suspended from the rafters to await the judgement flood while the clerk romps with his young wife.

Variations on this theme are endless. The master thief steals an ox (or ram) by placing two shoes (or a sword and scabbard) some distance apart around a bend in the road. When the ox-driver comes to the second he dismounts and runs back to pick up the one he has already passed; while he is out of sight the thief walks off with the ox. A version recorded in the Second Shepherd's Play of the Middle English York mystery cycle tells how Mak the shepherd conceals a stolen sheep by wrapping it like a baby and placing it in the cradle. **Ali Baba** is an example of the master thief who enters the treasure chamber by discovering a secret passage and who is unsuccessfully imitated by an envious rival, but he is unusual in coming upon his wealth so innocently.

The master thief may himself be duped, often by a fellow thief. An Indian tale tells how two thieves agree to exchange their boxes of loot; each then discovers that the other has given him a boxful of stones. In a tale found in Greece and India the thief descends a well to retrieve treasure (a silver cup) lost by a boy who stands weeping beside it. He intends to keep the cup for himself, but eventually returns cold and disgruntled having found nothing but mud, to discover the boy has stolen his clothes.

This tale-type illustrates perfectly the amoral nature of much folklore; the interest of the tale is in the ingenuity of the hero, and any subsequent moralizing is superfluous. The master thief is a **trickster** and his opponents are frequently analogous to the fierce but stupid beasts found in many animal trickster tales: ogres, kings and giants.

▷ **Ali Baba**; **Autolycus**

May

FIFTH MONTH, generally associated in the northern hemisphere with the welcome return of summer with the attendant connotations of fertility and new life. In Rome however the month was considered unlucky for weddings because of its associations with the festivals for the spirits of the dead (see **lemures** and **manes**) and that of Bona Dea, celebrating chastity. Many northern European countries warned against premature lightening of winter restrictions in unpredictable May—'Cast not a clout till May be out' warns those in the north of England not to don summer garments too early. In the south-west of the country a proverb held that 'Wash a blanket in May, wash a dear one away'.

May Day

ANCIENT EUROPEAN FERTILITY RITUAL which has survived as a modern spring festival. The first of May is regarded as a holiday throughout Europe and North America, and it is traditionally celebrated with local celebrations.

It seems clear that the festival began in pre-Christian times, as part of the agricultural rituals celebrating the annual battle between winter and summer, and to ensure that summer would win and

May Day

the sun return. In ancient Scandinavia mock battles were staged to represent this fight. The spirit of vegetation was also believed to have been contained in the maypole, originally branches gathered on May morning and brought back to the village ceremonially, 'bringing home the May'. These budding branches were thought to contain or to symbolize new life force, and they were traditionally carried from door to door before being set up in the village square. The custom may be a survival of primitive tree worship. As the custom developed and complex dances were devised around the pole, it became a fixed feature and the tradition of 'bringing home the May' lost its symbolism.

A man or boy is chosen to take the part of the vegetative spirit, adorned with leaves and branches and paraded through the village (see **Green Man**). The procession originally symbolized the return of the god of growth, bestowing renewed life as he passed, and in many countries it became customary to secure the blessing by giving gifts or money as it passed. The figure gradually lost the sense of a real spiritual presence and became a **mummer**, but the symbolism of his leafy appearance remains clear. In England he is known as **Jack-in-the-Green**, among the Slavs as Green George.

Often a girl would lead the procession,

the Queen of the May, traditionally selected from the prettiest of the village girls and ceremonially crowned with flowers and leaves on May Day morning. She leads the procession and the singing, and receives the gifts from each house, and her rule often extends over the coming year, as the honoured one presiding over other local festivities, although her rule ended if she should marry within the year. Often both King and Queen are selected to lead the festivities, probably originally intended to represent both ruling spirits and supernatural union. In other areas the couple are known as the May bride and bridegroom, demonstrating again the original emphasis upon fertility and the symbolic marriage of spring and nature.

Many of the traditions associated with May Day are to do with marriage and youth. In one French custom a man who has been jilted by his lover feigns sleep in a field; if another girl wishes to marry him she 'wakes' him with a kiss and the two go on to lead the dancing at the inn and should be married within the year. Girls who wish to keep their complexions beautiful are advised to bathe their faces in May Day dew, and in some parts of Europe they perform the logical extension and roll naked in the grass.
▷ **Beltane**

meadowsweet

SWEET-SMELLING HERB, *Filipendula ulmaria* (family Rosaceae), much used in the Renaissance to strew on floors. It is traditionally used in England to make a herbal wine or beer to cure indigestion and revive the senses. It is used for similar purposes in North America, and in Ireland it is used to scour cooking vessels after use.

Medb

OLD IRISH QUEEN OF CONNACHT, also known as Maeve, wife of **Ailill Mac Matach** and mother of **Findabair**, who initiated the **Táin Bó Cuailnge** by her greed. She employs sorcery and trickery to bring about the death of **Cuchulainn**. As a figure of war and greed, a destroyer of heroes, she became in later lore a **succubus** fairy figure, Queen **Mab**.

Medea

CLASSICAL HEROINE, the daughter of King Æetes of Colchis and niece of the great witch **Circe**, a priestess of Hecate. Aphrodite causes her to fall in love with **Jason** and she aids him in his quest, making him invulnerable by her witchcraft, instructing him how to handle the army grown from dragons' teeth and steal the fleece. She slew her own brother, Apsyrtus, to distract her father as they escaped, and revenged Jason for his father's death by persuading Pelias's daughters to kill him. This she achieved by demonstrating to them a **cauldron** of regeneration; she cut up a live sheep and threw it in, then drew out instead a whole lamb. She did not, however, work her witchcraft to restore the unfortunate Pelias.

When they settled in Corinth, Jason abandoned her for Glauce, daughter of King Creon. In anger and despair Medea sent Glauce a deathly robe and then killed her own children by Jason before fleeing to Athens and wedding Aegeus. She alone recognized Theseus as Aegeus's son when he came to court, and attempted to have Aegeus send him to his death at the horns of the **Minotaur**; when this failed she tried to poison him but Aegeus recognized his son at the last moment and Medea was banished to Asia where her son, Medus, became the ancestor of the Medes. Because she resisted the advances of Zeus, Medea was rewarded by immortality for her and her children by the long-suffering Hera, and in Elysium she finally found happiness as the wife of Achilles.

Her tale displays several folkloric elements; she is the supernatural helper and the girl as helper in one, the dismembering of her brother recalling the **obstacle fight** of much European lore, and she is instrumental in the sending of Theseus on his impossible **task**.

medicine

TREATMENT OF DISEASE AMONG THE FOLK. Where the sciences of anatomy, physiology and pharmacology are unknown, that is, in a large proportion of the modern world and almost universally in the past, the folk have always devised systems by which to comprehend and cure their afflictions. Since much of this lore is based on keen observation and experience, a substantial body of it is still circulated even in highly-industrialized societies.

Where sickness is considered to be due to the influence of evil spirits, supernatural means are required to treat it. This is particularly the case in many aboriginal societies of early Asia, Africa, North America and Australia. When pain is felt, it is generally assumed to be derived from an external influence, frequently a spell from a shaman or sorcerer paid by one's enemy or from a spirit of the dead. The usual means of doing this was to magically introduce an object, such as a dart or insect, or an evil spirit into the person, or to remove the soul in the case of wasting-illness. Preventative medicine to guard against such evils consists primarily in propitiating the spirits of the dead and faithfully observing certain taboos, especially those concerning the treatment of corpses. **Charms** and **amulets** have protective powers to guard the bearer from evil influence, and these are carried in virtually all primitive societies. If illness should strike despite all these precautions, the shaman or his equivalent is usually called in to defeat the evil with a stronger spell. He may go after the soul with a 'soul-catcher', a carved wooden or bone tube, in Native America, inviting the soul to return, or he may attempt to frighten the evil spirits away with aggressive dancing and shouting, clad in spectacular and symbolic clothing of feathers and fur.

If the disease was thought to be an intrusive object, the shaman might set about sucking the disease from the body, having discovered its whereabouts from his animal spirit familiar. The trance induced by frantic dancing enables him to prophesy as to the nature and source of the illness. One of the most important and widespread means of healing is **exorcism**, in which the evil spirit is driven out by the correctly performed incantation of the shaman. These rituals are often very long and complex, and many involve the entire community. Sometimes **doll** figures are provided to attract the spirit out of the patient and into themselves.

Shamans are generally summoned only in serious cases, or when an important member of the tribe is ill. There is a wide and efficacious body of medical lore, from superstition to herbal remedies, which is known to the folk themselves and does not require the spiritual authority or knowledge of the shaman to administer. In between these two extremes of medical expertise, the common and the elite, lies the specialist healer, who does not practise magico-religious healing as such (although he or she may often accompany their treatment with invocations and ritual) but rather administers mixtures of plants and **herbs**, the recipes for which are closely guarded. These remedies are often combined with techniques such as massage or bleeding. Some of this type of medicine is extraordinarily sophisticated; 17th-century explorers to Africa discovered that the inhabitants practised the inoculation of the small-pox virus to protect themselves against the disease.

For the non-specialist also, a wide range of medical knowledge was an accepted part of life. The application of hot or cold poultices for example is widespread, and probably derives from instinctive reactions to specific forms of pain. Likewise the potions made of plant or animal parts are widely used, although in some areas animals are perceived as the bearers of disease and plants as healers. These concoctions may be drunk or given as enemas, the liquid poured into a tube or taken in the mouth and blown through a tube into the patient's rectum.

One of the key principles of folk-medicine is its emphasis on harmony; to be effective, medicine must restore the natural equilibrium which has been disturbed to produce the sickness. Something is in the body which ought not to be, or something has been lost. It is therefore unsurprising that surgery is rarely practised among the folk. The removal of an organ logically produces an imbalance, and when disease is considered in spiritual rather than anatomical terms surgery remains very much the final resort. Some primitive operations have been recorded, at least a few of which appear to have been successful, such as trepanation of the skull (the removal of a circular piece of the cranium), amputation and even Caesarian delivery.

One of the great strengths of traditional medicine, and one of the reasons for its increasing popularity today, is its emphasis on treating the whole patient, mentally, spiritually and physically, and there can be no doubt that the rhythms of dance and song, and the support of the community, must have played as great a part in the efficacy of the treatment as the actual techniques applied.

The misleading term medicine man has now been generally abandoned by ethnologists, to be replaced by the more specific shaman, sorcerer, herb doctor, prophet or magician as appropriate. Often the healer of the village, who may be male or female, will indeed combine many of these functions, but in many societies specialization is practised. Such healers usually attain their post after rigorous study and **initiation**, although in some cultures they are given their powers by divine election.

Medusa see **Gorgon**

Melanesian folklore

MELANESIA ('BLACK ISLANDS') includes New Guinea, the archipelagos northeast of Australia and south of the Equator (for example the Solomon Islands, Bismark Archipelago, Santa Cruz and New Hebrides) and the islands of Fiji. It is thought that Melanesian culture is the result of a fusion between those of the Papuans, who inhabited the equatorial zone around New Guinea before the sea-level rose, and an Austronesian sea-faring group who settled much later in the Bismark Archipelago. These two cultures, the agricultural and the maritime, intermixed to produce the modern Melanesian, but there remain enclaves of Papuan or Austronesian culture. The island of New Guinea is now politically divided, with the west belonging to Indonesia.

Folklore here is amazingly diverse, with significant variations even within one small island, but certain themes are constant. Most Melanesian societies assume the pre-existence of the world in their mythologies, and the myths tend to deal only with subsequent refinements,

such as the discovery of fire or the reason for a certain rock formation. Some groups distinguish between myth (sacred belief), legend (historical stories) and folktales in their vocabulary. One common motif in folktales is that of the hero hampered by his stupid or malevolent brother. Ritual separation of the sexes is traditionally common throughout Melanesia, and the islanders place much importance on the sexual characteristics of females, particularly **menstruation**, and upon reproductive substances such as semen or vaginal fluids, all though to be powerful and dangerous. With a few exceptions, such as the Massim or parts of the Bismark Archipelago, societies are patrilineal, but the social and political role of women is widely respected.

Meleager

GREEK HERO, the son of Oeneus of Calydon and Althaea. He was one of Jason's Argonauts, renowned for his skill as a javelin-thrower, and killed the Calydonian boar. His life however was bound up with the fate of a piece of wood that his mother had snatched from the fire at his birth; later, in revenge for the deaths of her brothers, slain by Meleager, she threw the brand back on the fire and Meleager died as it burned.

▷ **amber**; **life token**; **separable soul**

Melusina

FAIRY BEING OF FRENCH ROMANCE, also known as Mélisande. She punished her father, who had offended her mother, by shutting him in a tall mountain, and was thenceforth condemned to assume the shape of a serpent from the waist down every Saturday (cf **mermaid**). When she married Raymond de Poitiers, count of Lusignan, she made him promise never to visit her chamber on a Saturday. One week however curiosity overcame him and he concealed himself to watch what would happen. He discovered his wife's fishy transformation, and she vanished. It was said that she could be heard lamenting in subsequent years whenever one of her descendants was about to die. The two children she bore the count have been claimed as ancestors by the nobility of Luxembourg, Rohan, Sassenaye and, of course, Lusignan.

The tale belongs to the literary romance tradition of medieval France, but contains many elements drawn from oral lore, such as the **looking taboo**, **shape-shifting** and **beast marriage**.

menstruation

POWERFUL FEMALE MYSTERY, discharge of blood and broken-down womb lining that occurs approximately every month in a female during her reproductive years. If the body's preparation for pregnancy becomes unnecessary because the ovum is unfertilized, menstruation takes place.

Menstruation is invested with great significance by many cultures. In most societies menstrual blood is regarded with awe and fear; among the ill-effects allegedly caused by menstruating women are death, poisoning, weakness and failure in the hunt, divine wrath, poltergeist activity, discordant string instruments, sour milk and thin mayonnaise, and livestock aborting. Since then she is potentially harmful, a menstruating woman is often kept in seclusion. This may be literal, a separate and isolated hut or even a suspended cage away from the village, and in parts of Brazil and Bolivia pubescent girls are traditionally sewn into hammocks suspended from the roof, so that they cannot contaminate anything, and periodically beaten to subdue the evil inherent in them at this time. It may rather be social, so that she is forbidden from touching food, participating in religious ceremonies, or having intercourse with her husband. This last is true in the majority of societies, often justified by belief that the offspring of such intercourse will be harmed. There may also be an additional period of restriction after menstruation, for purification. In some societies however the magic of menstruation is positive; it is occasionally used in **love magic** to secure the devotion of the beloved, and among the East African Warundi a newly menstruating girl is led around the house by her grandmother to touch every object, thereby imparting the newly fertile life-essence which she now embodies.

The onset of menstruation is widely regarded as the transition from childhood to womanhood, and although it generally lacks the elaborate **initiation** ceremonies devised by men for boys it is recognized by the women of the family at least. There are exceptions; in matrilineal societies or those with a female mother goddess the onset of menstruation is marked by celebration involving the entire group, as among the Chiricahua and Mescalero Apaches of North America.

Mephistopheles

THE DEVIL'S FAMILIAR. His name, meaning 'he who loves not the light', appears to have been coined in the 16th century by a writer of the **Faust** legend, and this remained his central role in folklore and literature. He is the one who secures Faust's soul and remains with him as a familiar, servant and entertainer until the time comes for Faust's soul to be rendered up to his master, Satan. He is not truly a part of the oral demonic and magical lore in which the story is ultimately based, but rather of the scholarly occult traditions.

Merlin

ENCHANTER OF ARTHURIAN LEGEND, an enigmatic figure. It appears that the historical Merlin was Myrddin, a sixth-century bard. Having gone insane at the Battle of Ardderyd (574) he lived as a wild man in the woods of Caledon (southern Scotland), prophesying to whoever would listen and eating roots and berries. Although no writings attributed to him survive, the supposed records of his prophecies in medieval texts were very influential.

This historical seer became conflated in medieval lore, mainly because of Geoffrey of Monmouth's influential *History of the Kings of Britain*, with a prophetic youth found in the *History of the Britons* of the Welsh antiquary Nennius (fl. c.800), Ambrosius. According to Nennius, King Vortigen was troubled by a mysterious nocturnal visitation that destroyed the walls of his fortress as fast as his men could build them. He was told that he could only be helped by a child with no human father—Ambrosius was said to have been sired by a demon but redeemed by the alert ministrations of his mother's confessor, Blaise. This child told Vortigen that two **dragons**, one red, one white, fought beneath the walls and by exposing the dragons solved the problem. When the treacherous Vortigen was overthrown Merlin/Ambrosius became adviser to **Uther Pendragon**, father of **Arthur**.

As the Arthurian legend developed, and notably with Robert de Borron's 13th-century romance *Merlin*, the seer became identified as the prophet of the Holy **Grail**. He is attributed with advising Uther Pendragon to begin the fellowship of the **Round Table**, and with prophesying that only the one who could pull the sword from the stone would be fit to be king and Uther's heir. Some versions of the legend, such as the early Vulgate cycle, portray Merlin as a more demonic character. He is popularly believed to have met his end at the behest of the faithless Vivien (Nimuë or the **Lady of the Lake**); blinded by his love for her he allowed himself to be trapped in a **hawthorn** tree, where he dwells forever. Other accounts say that in his dotage he mistakenly sat on the Siège Perilous, and not being a sinless man was swallowed by the earth. The dalliance with Vivien may be a vestige of the ancient story of Myrddin, who claimed to have sported under an appletree with a fair maid.

Although his roots are so complex and his portrayal inconsistent, the figure of Merlin, seer, magician, wise adviser and flawed old man, has been enormously influential in European lore.

mermaid

FABULOUS SEA-CREATURES. Tales of seadwelling divinities, part fish and part human, are common in ancient mythologies, and the mermaid folklore of Europe is ancient and surprisingly consistent. Mermaids are generally portrayed as beautiful women from the waist up, with flowing golden hair, and the lower body of a fish. Although mortal they generally live much longer than humans. They inhabit a splendid undersea world together with their male counterparts, mermen, but will frequently come up to the surface to sit upon a rock and sing while they comb their beautiful hair. Their beauty and that of

mermaid

their singing lures sailors to their deaths, and to see one on a voyage was considered an omen of shipwreck or other misfortune. In some traditions they are eager to drag mortals, especially the young men who are most susceptible to their charms, under the sea with them, where they keep their souls trapped in cages. A popular Scottish tale, 'The Laird of Lorntie', tells how the nobleman was saved from the mermaid's clutches when his servant stopped him from going to save a woman apparently in danger of drowning. Early Celtic tales tell of monstrous mermaids, but in later lore they developed into kindlier creatures, even offering advice to humans. They are often credited with the ability to grant three wishes, and in many folktales mortals succeed in catching a mermaid and demanding these wishes. Like most fairies however, though bound to fulfil the wishes thus extracted the mermaid will often contrive to twist the original meaning. Since they cannot move on land they are powerless if trapped by the receding tide; the other means of catching one was to entangle her in a fishing net. Some traditions hold that a mermaid cannot survive very long on land; other tales tell of mermaids who came ashore in human shape or who marry human males and live on land for many years. Common to nearly all these stories however is the mermaid's great desire to return to the sea, and she often persuades her human lover to join her. *The Little Mermaid* of Hans Christian Andersen is unusual; she falls in love with a human prince and pays the price of her beautiful voice to become fully human in shape, whereupon she attends him mutely. He eventually marries a human princess, and the mermaid's heart is broken.

Various legends purport to give an account of the nature and origin of mermaids. In Ireland they are thought to be female pagans banished from the land by St **Patrick** along with snakes and sea-serpents. It seems probable that the mermaid of folklore developed from ancient mythology, from figures such as the Greek goddess of love Aphrodite, who emerged from the sea, or the Chaldean sea god Oannes. Belief in the existence of mermaids was certainly very widespread from medieval times even until the 18th century, and there are many recorded sightings. It has been suggested that glimpses of sea-dwelling mammals such as the **dugong** or manatee, which suckle their young above the water's surface, contributed to the credibility of the lore.

▷ **Ben-Varrey**; **sailors' lore**

merrow

IRISH WATER BEINGS, a type of **mermaid**. Female merrows are as irresistible as their cousins, with long floating hair, but they tend to be better disposed towards mortals and though they occasionally take a human husband, producing offspring covered with scales, they rarely destroy him. Male merrows on the other hand, although said to be affable towards mortals and good drinking partners, are ugly green-tinted creatures with arms like fins.

Michaelmas

FEAST OF ST MICHAEL, observed in the West on 29 September and in the Eastern church on 8 November, and a quarterly rent-day in England. It is customary in many areas to eat roast goose on Michaelmas day, perhaps because they are so plentiful at this time of year, and an English proverb

promises that he who dines on goose on St Michael's day will not go hungry for the next year. An anecdotal legend tells how Elizabeth I of England dined with a loyal subject on St Michael's day 1588, and after the goose raised a toast to the destruction of the Spanish Armada. She had scarcely spoken the words when the news of English victory reached her, and thenceforth instituted the goose as an annual celebration (the Armada was in fact destroyed in bad weather in July). In Ireland, the finder of the ring hidden in the Michaelmas pie will soon be wed.

Micronesian folklore

MICRONESIA, 'THE SMALL ISLANDS', is a collection of island groups in the North Pacific including the Marianas, Carolines, Marshalls, Kiribati (Gilbert) and Nauru islands. Cultural diversity among Micronesian peoples is substantial, and there is a surprisingly large number of different languages. Living on such small territories, early Micronesians quickly learnt diplomacy and maintained good relations with their neighbours and the culture is characterized by an emphasis on politeness and a strong belief in the stability of society. Since land was such a precious commodity, its distribution is tightly governed by rules of lineage (usually traced maternally) and ancestral right, and the attachment to territory is a strong feature of the culture. So too is the emphasis given to leisure and the importance of childhood, especially upon the larger, volcanic-based islands where the ground tends to be more fertile. Children are usually brought into adult society at a relatively late age simply by participation, with little in the way of formal **initiation**.

The polytheistic native religion of Micronesia has been largely lost in the face of European missionary activity. As in Melanesian mythology, there appears to have been little attempt to explain the creation of the world, but rather the origin of a specific island or island group. The Micronesian island of Guam was the first inhabited Pacific island to have European visitors; the Portuguese explorer Ferdinand Magellan landed there in 1521 on his expedition to circumnavigate the globe for Spain, and Micronesian territories have been held by a succession of foreign powers including Spain, Germany, Japan and the USA since 1668. The European influence can clearly be seen in the folklore; the fairy tale model is widespread, in which the poor hero wins through against all odds and social disadvantage, completes an impossible task with supernatural aid and then wins the favour of the ruler. He then typically commits honourable suicide at the peak of his success, in sharp contrast to the European 'happily ever after' formula. The native value structures seem to have been closer to those of Europe than many other areas, and this may explain why the European cultural influence was integrated so smoothly.

Midas

PHRYGIAN KING, who, granted a boon by Dionysus for his kindness to the satyr Silenus, foolishly asks that anything he touches might turn to gold. His wish is granted, and for a while Midas revels in his exotic power. His delight turns to dismay however when his food and even his daughter are transmuted by his touch into lifeless metal, and he is finally freed of the gift turned curse by bathing in a spring. The silt of the river Pactolus, which sprang from this source, was thereafter rich in gold. Another legend in the Dionysiac cycle concerning Midas tells how Apollo changed his ears into those of an **ass** after Midas judged the satyr Marsyas superior to the god in a musical contest. Although the king tried to conceal his shameful secret, he could not hide them from his barber, and the poor man, bursting with the weight of his knowledge but forbidden on pain of death to even hint at it, whispered his secret into a hole in the ground at the edge of the river. The rushes that grew on the spot, however, broadcast the news every time the wind blew through them.
▷ **gold**; **singing bone**

Midsummer

THE HEIGHT OF SUMMER IN EUROPE, 24 JUNE. It is one of the most ancient and significant of European festivals, translated by Christianity into the celebration of the feast of St John the Baptist but still retaining many of its pagan features. Midsummer Eve is considered the most magical of all days, and any spells or charms prepared on this night will be of exceptional strength. All manner of supernatural beings—**witches**, **fairies**, **ghosts** and **mischievous spirits**—are thought to be active, and the midsummer full moon, representing the apogee of both solar and lunar powers, is said to drive mortals mad. Midsummer is especially a festival for lovers, and all manner of love divination and magic is practised on this night. **Dreams** of love on Midsummer's Eve are sure to be fulfilled.

The most notable and constant feature of Midsummer celebrations across Europe is the bonfire (although equivalent celebrations in Ireland took place at **Beltane**). Humans and animals passed through the flames to receive protection in the coming year, and brands from the fire were carried through the houses and fields. The fire in the house was relit with new fire from the Midsummer bonfire, and figures representing winter or sickness were ritually burned. According to some scholars, notably **Frazer**, such rituals were intended as sun charms to aid the sun at this critical turning-point in its course, but others suggest purification and renewal as the chief motives.

Mikula

RUSSIAN PEASANT HERO, a man with superhuman strength whose adventures are recounted in many **byliny**. He was the lover of mother Earth, Maki-Syra-Zemlya, who imparted his great strength to him. His cart, which he could lift with one hand, could not be shifted by an army of ordinary men. A Paul **Bunyan** figure, he can chop more trees and till more land faster and better than any other peasant.

Milesians

RACE OF OLD IRISH MYTHOLOGY, the fifth wave of invaders to visit Ireland, said to be ancestors of the present inhabitants. Originally a Spanish race, they first turned to Ireland when Ith glimpsed the land from a high tower and yearned to see it. Ith was ungraciously killed by the three Irish kings, and his nephew Mil set out to avenge his death. His fleet was hampered by the magical mists raised by the **Tuatha de Danann**, and they were compelled to circumnavigate the island three times before finally landing. They set off for Tara and met **Banba**, **Fodla** and **Ériu** on the way, promising each that her name would be that of the island forever. They conferred with the three kings (MacCuill, MacCecht and Mac-Greine) and agreed to mount an invasion to decide the rulers of Ireland. Despite the storms raised by the Tuatha de Danann, the Milesians were victorious at Sliab Mis and Tailltiu, the Tuatha were routed, and the Milesians took possession of Ireland.

milfoil see **yarrow**

mime

ORIGINALLY, A FORM OF CLASSICAL ENTER-TAINMENT presenting scenes from life in an exaggerated manner with accompanying music, song and some dialogue. In later use, the word represented a form of theatre in which body movement and facial expression only are used to convey

mime in Japanese No theatre

action and emotion, without the aid of speech or props, but often with musical accompaniment. The masks of early Graeco-Roman pantomime performers, who relied solely on gesture and movement, are echoed in the traditional white make-up of the modern French-style mime artist.

The basis of mime, mimicry, is the basis of ritual around the world, and many societies incorporate mime elements into dances and forms of communication. Folk dances lacking any religious or magical significance often enact everyday tasks and events, with or without the props associated with them, or, as in Japanese dance, using an object such as a fan to represent a myriad of objects. Perhaps the most widespread form of mime encoded in dance is the courtship ritual; numerous couples dances across the world are based on a mimed portrayal of attraction, flirtation, rejection and consummation, with varying degrees of subtlety.

Mime then is central to the religion and art of many societies, and its distinctive development in the theatrical traditions of East and West is one of the clearest points of departure between the two. Although rooted in realism, mime is essentially stylized, and in the mainstream Western theatre found real acceptance only in classical ballet, a silent form; here too it has recently given way to less highly conventionalized movement.

Minos

MYTHICAL GREEK KING, son of Zeus and Europa. His queen Pasiphae produced the **Minotaur**. Minos died in Sicily at the hands of King Cocalus's daughters, who poured scalding water over him in the bath. He became the chief judge of the underworld, to whom all mortals must give an account of their lives.

Minotaur

HYBRID MONSTER, born of the union of a bull and Pasiphae, wife of King **Minos** of Crete. She became enamoured of the sacred bull of Poseidon that Minos had neglected to sacrifice to the god as promised; with the aid of Daedalus, who constructed a hollow cow in which she

mint

Minotaur

could crouch, she managed to seduce the bull and gave birth to the Minotaur, half human and half bull.

Minos imprisoned the creature in a labyrinth constructed by Daedalus. When his son Androgeos was slain by the Athenians, jealous of his success at the Panathenic games, he warred against the city and compelled it to send seven young men and seven maidens to Crete every nine years as terms of peace. These he fed to the Minotaur, until Theseus killed the monster. The Minotaur may be a relic of ancient Cretan cults of the bull and the sun, which once demanded human sacrifice. It is also a classical example of the folkloric preoccupation with human and animal relations.

mint

AROMATIC HERB, any of the *Mentha* genus (family Labiatae) and in common use particularly spearmint (*M. spicata*) and peppermint (*M. piperita*). In classical legend the nymph Minthe was beloved by Pluto and transformed into

the plant by the jealous Proserpina; Proserpina could not however remove her attractive fragrance.

It has been valued for its strong scent, taste and medicinal properties since ancient times: mint was eaten by ancient Hebrews with the paschal lamb, and was introduced into Britain by the Romans. With **meadowsweet**, it was a popular strewing herb for floors.

The medicinal uses of mint are extremely varied, ranging from colds to hydrophobia. Mint tea is drunk in Jamaica and parts of North America as a tonic and to treat colic, and in Ireland spearmint is scattered in beds to drive away fleas. Pennyroyal (*M. pulegium*) is particularly renowned for driving away fleas and mosquitoes, and was used by medieval sailors to purify water. Among Native North Americans it was venerated as a powerful medicine, used by the Navajo particularly to cure just about any illness. It is also widely said to induce abortion or menstruation, although it can also be drunk during childbirth to ease the pains of labour and speed the delivery. Mint is still widely used today as an essence in medicine, hygiene and cuisine.

min-yo

JAPANESE TERM FOR FOLK SONGS, particularly the **work songs** sung by many different groups of labourers in different communities.

mirror

OBJECT OF FOLKTALES AND SUPERSTITION. One of the most popular beliefs associated with the mirror is that seven years of bad luck will follow if it is broken. This indicates the importance given to the reflection, the **shadow soul**, in ancient lore. Another common belief is that demons and **vampires** have no reflection (similarly, they cast no shadow), presumably since they have no soul. In folktales the mirror may be used as a **life token** or **chastity test**; in the Tale of Zayn al-Asnam in the *Arabian Nights* the King of the Jann supplies a mirror with the power of reflecting the virtue of a woman rather than her appearance— should she be impure in any way the image would be dark. The truth-telling mirror features also in the tale of Snow White, informing the wicked queen that her beauty has been surpassed and later that Snow White has survived her assassination attempts. The clairvoyant speaking mirror is a **motif** of Asian and European tales; Chaucer's Squire tells of the marvellous mirror of King Cambuscon, which warned when ill luck was on the way and whether love was requited.

mischievous spirits

MISCHIEVOUS HOUSEHOLD SPIRITS figure richly in European fairy lore, helping and hindering their mortal neighbours in roughly equal proportions. Any householder who found himself visited by fairies would feel rather uneasy, even if his visitors had performed household tasks or left gifts. Fairies are notoriously volatile and quick to take offence, and even a small breach of etiquette might result in troublesome petty revenge, such as the crockery broken, the butter spoilt, or the furniture rearranged. There is an enormous number of such mischievous, domestic beings, with names and characteristics varying with local tradition.

▷ **boggart**; **brownie**; **cluricaun**; **goblin**; **leprechaun**; **nisse**; **puck**

mistletoe

SEMIPARASITIC PLANT, particularly the common European mistletoe *Viscum album* (family Loranthaceae). It has glutinous white berries that turn yellow as the plant withers, and grows in a variety of deciduous host trees. The North American counterpart, often known as dwarf mistletoe, is *Pharadendron serotinum*.

The attribution of magical, mysterious powers to mistletoe is ancient and has much exercised the minds of folklore and mythology scholars. It has been invested with life-giving powers of fertility and healing and sacred properties throughout Europe. The 'golden bough' plucked from the sacred **oak** by Aeneas as a token of safe conduct through the underworld is thought to have been mistletoe; oak mistletoe was especially revered by Druids also, who would ceremonially cut it with a golden sickle, and it is still ritually cut on **Midsummer**

mistletoe

Eve in many northern parts of Europe. It represented the life or soul of the oak, the female principle to its masculine essence. It was thought in some areas to quench fire; this may derive from the ancient belief that it was engendered by lightning striking the tree. Among societies who recognized its rather more prosaic means of dispersal (seeds are deposited on branches in birds' excretions or by the sticky berry mush wiped from their beaks) the life-force of dung was still a powerful reason for venerating the mistletoe as a principle of fertility (cf **scarab** beetle). Frazer's seminal work *The Golden Bough* links the ritual cutting of mistletoe, the life of the oak, with the slaying of the priest-king by his younger, more virile successor. This reading is supported by the widespread sexual symbolism attached to the mistletoe.

Echoes of this richly symbolic heritage are evident even today in the custom of kissing beneath the mistletoe, popular at Christmas in Europe and North America. This recalls the principles of sexuality and fertility, and once signified the betrothal of the couple. Frazer associates the practice, part of the general **Christmas** revelry, with the licentious classical **Saturnalia**.

In medicine, mistletoe is *allheal* among many cultures. It is used in potions, powders, poultices and pills as well as **charms** to treat every conceivable ailment, particularly infertility, epi-

mole

lepsy, hysteria, dementia, palsy, ulcers and tumours. Since it is poisonous in large quantities however it was regarded ambivalently by some cultures, as a powerful yet dangerous mystery, the 'baleful mistletoe' as Shakespeare called it (*Titus Andronicus* II, iii). Reflecting this ambiguity is the Christian tradition that mistletoe wood (like many others) was used for Christ's cross; it is therefore simultaneously cursed and potent to heal. Hung over houses and stables it would keep **witches** and demons at bay. A divining rod of mistletoe would lead to gold rather than water.

mole

BLIND, BURROWING MAMMAL, especially those of the Talpidae family. Moles make their presence felt among farmers by molehills—vents to their deep burrows—and the ridges that mark their surface burrows, which often damage plant roots, but they aerate the soil and keep pests down. The animal has been used in many societies as a symbol of blindness, and in medieval Christian lore it represented greed and the earth principle. However because of the ancient association of blindness with second sight or intuition, the heart of a mole if eaten was believed to impart the power of prophecy.

Momotaro

JAPANESE FOLKTALE HERO, 'Eldest son of

Momotaro

a peach', born from a **peach**. He was adopted by a kindly old peasant couple and left when fully grown to seek his fortune. With the aid of three **helpful beasts** (dog, monkey and pheasant) he reached the stronghold of the demon Akandoji and overthrew him. He returned home to a life of honour and ease with the treasure hoard of the demon.

monkey

PRIMATE MAMMAL, generally excluding manlike apes and man. Having large brains, divergent digits and social clans, their behaviour, often characterized by curiosity and playfulness, frequently parallels that of humans. In fact the similarity of the monkey family to men has led to the belief among some African tribes that they themselves are descendants of monkeys, and that apes are perfectly capable of speaking but keep quiet for fear of being forced to work. Many groups recognize a kinship with monkeys and hold the meat **taboo**, as that of ancestors.

Hanuman, the Hindu monkey-headed god, is noted for speed, agility and loyalty; he features in the *Ramayana* as a supernatural animal helper. In Japanese lore the three mystic monkeys represent the key to right living—'See no evil; Hear no evil; Speak no evil'. A Filipino tale with many similarities to **Beauty and the Beast** tells of the Monkey Prince, transformed into a monkey by his slighted lover the witch whom he had failed to acknowledge before his father the king. He can only be restored to human form by the love of a human woman, and though he frequently kidnaps girls from a nearby village they all die of fright. Finally he finds one who responds to his kindness and recognizes his sorrows—she too has been unhappy in love—the spell is broken and the two marry. Despite its Indo-European flavour, some scholars believe this tale to be indigenous.
▷ **ape**

monkshood see aconite

monster

FABULOUS CREATURE, either animal or semi-human, usually carnivorous and malignant and of a terrifying appearance. Monsters appear in some form in virtually every culture, as mythical beings of prehistory, creatures of ancient legend or the never-land of folktales, or enemies of humans living alongside them—often a combination of several of these. Generally the hero demonstrates his worth by overcoming a monster. They may be one-off individuals such as the **Minotaur** or a monstrous race (eg **Aigamuxo** and **Blemmyes**).

▷ **bogey**; **dragons**; **fabulous creatures**; **giants**; **ogres**

moon

THE LUNAR CYCLE IS CLOSELY BOUND UP WITH HUMAN EXPERIENCE, particularly female; the menstrual cycle corresponds to it as do tidal flows, and many civilizations including Islam have organized their years into lunar months. In fact the words month, menses and moon all derive from the same root, Latin *mensis*, a unit of measurement. Generations have held the moon sacred for its pure light and the mysterious cycle of wax and wane. In many civilizations, and almost exclusively in Indo-Europe, the moon is viewed as female, partly due to this link perhaps but also because she was seen as subordinate to the bigger and stronger sun, which was correspondingly venerated as a male spirit or deity. Some aboriginal groups in Australia, Africa and South America however regard the moon as male, and in Western folklore there is a widespread belief in 'the man in the moon'. A few groups hold that the waxing power of the moon is masculine, the waning feminine.

The waxing and waning of the moon has fascinated all peoples, and many different mythical explanation have been devised. Where it is considered female, the pattern of crescent to full moon and then back to crescent is often explained as pregnancy and delivery. Where it is considered male, other explanations are produced; the moon has been well fed by his wives and then starved (Guyana), or he has angered the sun, who now slices pieces off him until he pleads for mercy and is allowed to grow again (African Bushman). The new moon is frequently invested with potent **sympathetic magic**; if one shows

one's money to the new crescent one's fortune will increase with it.

The full moon is considered an auspicious period, often celebrated by a rest from work: in the Jewish calendar it marks **Passover** and the Christian **Easter** is calculated from the full moon after the vernal equinox. Celebrations are also common at the full moon at the autumn equinox, the 'harvest moon', and the following 'hunters' moon'. On the other hand, the days between the death of one

moon

moon and the birth of the next are considered dangerous and uncertain; among some peoples the moon is thought to have been overcome by supernatural monsters or other heavenly beings, and on its reappearance is said to have been regurgitated or revived. New enterprises are deferred until the moon is securely re-established. Similar beliefs are associated with periods of **eclipse**, when the moon appears to be 'eaten' as the shadow of the earth passes over it. At such times many societies, especially in Africa and Native North America, perform ritual dances to frighten away the sky-monsters, or shoot burning arrows to drive them away and rekindle the quenched moon. In Tahiti an eclipse is viewed as the coupling of the sun and moon, which produces the stars.

The moon is widely used in folk **divination**; for example a red moon presages evil, a crescent which points upwards is holding water and therefore foretells a drought, and 'the new moon with the old moon in her arms' (the outline of the full moon visible in the new) is commonly interpreted as a storm warning at sea. Because of its association with night, mystery and ghostly powers, moonlight is considered an essential condition for the gathering of many ingredients for **witchcraft**, and even herbs for **medicine**. Root crops should be planted at the dark moon, a bright moon is auspicious for crops growing above ground. And because of the moon's age-old association with insanity, faery and illusion, it is considered highly dangerous to sleep in direct moonlight.
▷ **Man in the Moon**

moonstone

CLOUDY WHITE GEMSTONE, named for its moon-like iridescent appearance. In Hindu lore it was said to be formed from crystallized moon-rays. Its virtues are those associated with the moon; it arouses love, cools and soothes. If placed in the mouth beneath a full moon it can assume oracular properties, and the stone in the ring of Pop Leo X was said to wax and wane with the phases of the moon itself. Like the moon though it can be fickle, and may prove unlucky to its wearer if it is not his or her **birthstone**.

mopaditis

AUSTRALIAN SPIRITS OF THE DEAD, who may attempt to steal the souls of lone travellers to keep them company. This echoes the worldwide conviction that the dead must be propitiated by attention lest they become restless and demand companionship.

Mordred

TRAITOR OF ARTHURIAN LEGEND, also known as Modred, the nephew (in some versions the son) of **Arthur** and a knight of the **Round Table**. Geoffrey of Monmouth in his *History of the Kings of Britain* says that Arthur left his kingdom in Mordred's hands when he left to fight Rome, but his nephew proved treacherous and abducted **Guinevere**. Arthur engaged him in battle by the river Camlan in Cornwall and defeated him, but was himself mortally wounded.

In the 13th-century French Vulgate cycle of legends Mordred is the son of Arthur, born of his unknowingly incestuous relationship with his sister, and in a later version Arthur is warned by **Merlin** that this offspring will bring about his end. He attempts to have the child killed, but in a form of the **abandonment** motif Mordred is shipwrecked on his way to Arthur's court and is found by a fisherman who recognizes the quality of his silk wraps and gives him into the keeping of a noble. This tale has many Celtic parallels.

Morgan le Fay

ENCHANTRESS OF ARTHURIAN LEGEND, a mysterious and contradictory figure drawn from Celtic mythology, fairy lore, Breton mermaid lore and romance tradition. She first appears in Geoffrey of Monmouth's *Vita Merlini* (1150) as the ruler of **Avalon**, a skilled healer and **shapeshifter**. Chrétien de Troyes identifies her as **Arthur**'s sister in *Erec* (c.1165). In later legends she became portrayed as a malignant sorceress, wife of King Urien and mother of Ivain, who continually plots the downfall of the fellowship of the **Round Table** and of her brother Arthur particularly. In many cases incestuous desire is suggested. Certainly she is renowned for her seductive powers; she makes attempts on the virtue of **Lancelot** and others.

The conflicting elements of her character are due to the confusion of traditions in her roots; she was almost certainly a pagan goddess, the Irish **Morrigan**, who in turn is derived from the ancient European Matrona. Her cousins are the **mermaids** of Welsh and Breton lore, seductive but deadly. The mirages in the Straits of Messina are known as 'la Fata Morgana'. The Christian chronicles, while recognizing the attractive power of such a figure, understandably regarded this pagan relic with hostility and suspicion. The ultimate appearance of Morgan le Fay in the Arthurian cycle, however, bearing the wounded king away to tend him in Avalon, testifies to her origins as a beneficent water-fairy/goddess.

Morgiana

QUICK-WITTED SLAVE GIRL OF ALI BABA, who thwarts the robbers' plans of revenge. She marks every door in the neighbourhood with the sign they have made on **Ali Baba**'s house, and when the robbers infiltrate the house hidden in jars she discovers their ruse, heats the oil in the last remaining jar and pours some over each man. Finally she kills the robber chief after transfixing him with her dancing and is married to her grateful master's son. She is a type of the wily servant popular in folklore, unusual in being female.

morisca

FOLK DANCE, danced in many European countries, Latin America and the Caribbean, often depicting the battles between Christians and Moors. It is sometimes called the mourisca.

Morrigan

OLD IRISH WAR GODDESS, also known as Morrigu, one of the aspects of **Badb**. Her counterparts are Neman and Macha. To her were dedicated the heads of those slain in battle; she was portrayed waiting on the battlefield with the head of a **crow**, to feed from the carnage. She is said to have aided the **Tuatha de Danann** to overcome the **Fomorians** at Mag Tured, along with Badb.

In some versions she was enamoured of **Cuchulainn** but, after being repulsed by him, she became his antagonist. Her

tender feelings had not died completely however; she fought alongside him in the **Táin Bó Cuailnge** and on the morning of his last fight broke his chariot pole to try and keep him from going to meet his fate.

Morris dance

ENGLISH FOLK DANCE, derived from the **morisca** of Europe, usually performed longways by groups of six or ten men. Characteristic elements include sticks used to strike the ground and the sticks of other dancers, the use of handkerchiefs and ankle bells and, originally, the blackening of the dancers' faces. The troupe traditionally includes animal impersonators (see especially **Abbot Bromley Horn dance**) and characters such as Maid **Marian** (formerly Mother Eve), a **Robin Hood**-figure astride a **hobby-horse**, and a capering fool, sometimes named Malkin.

The dance is still widely believed to bring luck wherever it is performed. Such dances are common throughout Eurasia; they were traditionally associated with **May Day** celebrations and their significance as fertility rites is still evident in 'dibbing'—the thumping of the floor with the ends of the sticks, representing both seed-planting and the magical impregnation of Mother Earth.

The name Morris dancers has also come to refer to **mummers** who act, rather than dance, in a similar manner.

Morris dancers

mosquito

BLOOD-SUCKING INSECT, family Culici-
dae. Although the male contents himself
with nectar and plant juices, the female
of the species requires blood to mature
her eggs, and in preying on humans some
species transmit diseases such as malaria
and yellow fever. They can be a fearsome pest, and early travellers' tales of
Europeans in America and Africa tell of
man-eating mosquitoes, not too extreme
an exaggeration in some areas. Several
tales purport to account for the mos-
quito; in Romania they are said to be
bred from the smoke of the **Devil**'s pipe,
and in several Native American tales
they arose from the burned remains of a
fearsome cannibalistic monster, and
continue to extract his revenge.

Mother Goose

FICTITIOUS CHARACTER TO WHOM NURSERY
RHYMES ARE WIDELY ATTRIBUTED. She is
the personification of all old, story-tel-
ling women. The name comes from
Perrault's collection of fairy tales,
Contes de ma Mère l'Oye ('Tales of
Mother Goose', 1697), which in French
is a peasant phrase for 'old wives' tales'.
She is herself now the object of folklore;
a persistent legend identifies her with a
historical Elizabeth Goose of Boston. In
the United States, Mother Goose
rhymes is the common name for **nursery
rhymes**, taken from *Mother Goose's
Melody*, an American rhyme-collection
of 1780 that also drew its title from
Perrault's work.

motif

BUILDING BLOCK OF FOLKLORE, a useful
definition on which most systems of
folklore scholarship agree. This wide-
ranging term refers to any one of the
parts into which an item of folklore can
be broken down for analysis, for
example a particular step in a dance, a
symbol in art, or a pattern in a tale. The
three-fold question and answer repetition of many folktales is an example, as
is the lifting of the female in a courtship
dance. To be a useful aid to research, a
motif must show two characteristics: it
must be out of the ordinary and therefore able to impress itself upon the
listener as a salient feature of the

narrative or activity (hence a wicked
step-mother is a motif, not just any
mother) and it must recur and therefore
be useful in comparative study with
other similar items of folklore.

mourning songs

SONGS OF GRIEF, sung at the deathbed or
by the grave-side. Common forms are
the eulogy, **keen**, dirge, wail and lyrical
ballads. Although they express a variety
of attitudes towards death there are
some common characteristics such as
their slow, chanting, mournful style.
Such songs are commonly addressed to
the deceased, expressing reproach and
regret that he or she chose to leave this
world, listing his or her good qualities
and describing in what ways the world
will be poorer without them. The most
primitive, and most enduring, of all
mourning songs is the wail, an inarticulate cry of grief, which may be ritually
obligatory as well as spontaneous, and
frequently even the more highly developed, controlled and lyrical songs will be
punctuated by refrains including such
wordless expressions of pain.

The reasoning behind mourning songs
is that of most **funeral customs**, the
desire to appease the departed spirit and
ward off evil influences, to protect the
living. A spirit who is not mourned
adequately will be restless and vengeful,
and more apt to return as a malignant
force to torment its erstwhile relations.
Frequently of course mourners are
expressing genuine and heartfelt grief in
mourning songs, but the participation of
the entire community, the stylized attitudes and conventions associated with
the songs, their exaggerated and unqual-
ified praise and, in many parts of the
world, the practice of hiring a band of
mourners to see the body off in proper
style, all suggest that the reasons for the
mourning song run much deeper than
unmediated personal emotion.

Mourning songs are most commonly
performed by women, whose license to
display emotion is traditionally greater
than that of men, although certain
groups (eg in China and Dahomey)
appoint men to lead the mourning. It is
customary among many Native North
Americans for a dying person to sing his
or her own mourning song as death

approaches, prepared during sickness or improvised if there has been little warning.

mouse

SMALL RODENT, any of a wide variety of scampering species found throughout the world. Since they often inhabit human houses and feed on food supplies and organic material they are generally regarded as pests; a tale of German origin ascribes mice to the whim of **witches**, who make them out of scraps of cloth, and in other areas they are said to have fallen from the sky in a storm or to be an invention of the **Devil** designed to plague the inhabitants of Noah's' ark. Another version of this motif tells how the Devil himself took the form of a mouse to try to gnaw through the ark. Mice feature in witchlore as familiars and popular ingredients in witches' brews. In a European legend found especially in Germany and Switzerland a miser hoards grain during a famine in his tower; it is invaded by hoards of starving rats and mice who eat not only the carefully stored grain but the miser himself. This tale is especially associated with a watchtower at Binsen on the Rhine, where Archbishop Hatto is said to have met such a death.

In some areas the mouse, like the **butterfly**, is the visible **separable soul** of a sleeper, and to trap it or kill it will cause the sleeper's eventual death. A white mouse is considered a good omen in Bohemia.

Mice have been widely used in medicine; in England and parts of New England cooked mouse was thought to be an effective cure for bed-wetting, and elsewhere for whooping cough, smallpox and measles. According to Pliny, the ashes of a mouse mixed with honey are an effective cure for earache.

The mouse frequently appears in folktales as a seemingly ineffectual creature contrasting with a seemingly powerful animal, as in the Aesopic fable of the mouse freed by the **lion** who later repays the debt by gnawing through the lion's bonds. In another tale the mouse sits impertinently in the lion's mane, while he rages impotently. Two resourceful mice succeed in stealing an egg in a Latvian tale; one holds it between all

mice

four legs while her fellow pulls her into the mousehole by her tail. The mouse is frequently overcome by its stronger foes, however, in fables preaching pragmatism. An Irish tale tells of a drunken mouse who challenges a **cat** to fight, reminding it of its promise, also made when drunk, not to kill the mouse. 'That was the promise of a drunkard' says the sober cat, and kills him. In a similar Scandinavian tale, the mouse entertains the cat with a tale but at its end the cat still eats his captive. A widespread tale tells of the town mouse and his cousin the country mouse; the latter visits the town, wooed by his cousin's tale of high living and plentiful food, but after experiencing the stress and danger of city life he returns to his rural home, declaring that poverty with safety is to be preferred.

The animosity between cat and mouse is proverbial in many cultures, and in the majority of cases the cat is the victor.
▷ **belling the cat**; **rat**

Much

FIGURE OF ROBIN HOOD LEGEND, the son of the miller and one of **Robin Hood**'s merry men. In the **Morris dance** he appears as the fool, bouncing his bladder-balloon full of peas on the heads of spectators.

mugwort

YELLOWISH-FLOWERED PLANT, *Artemisia vulgaris* (family Compositae). Its Latin name betrays its ancient mythological status; as a plant sacred to Artemis it was associated with healing and particularly with women, and therefore used to treat all manner of female malady from menstrual pains and backache to labour pains and nervous fatigue. Among

Native Americans it was widely used as a restorative tonic for the old, and to guard against evil magic, mice and fatigue. The stimulating properties of the plant, which features in medicine lore throughout the world, have been usefully exploited by modern pharmacists. Its traditional use as an eye bath has also been supported by scientific evidence. More controversial is the claim among peoples in Germany that a stone found at the root of the mugwort on **Midsummer**'s Day is a charm against all illnesses (or alternatively a coal that turns to gold if picked up with the proper observances).

mulberry

TREE AND ITS FRUIT, most commonly those of the genus *Morus* (family Moraceae) found especially in North America and temperate areas of Asia. It was a sacred tree in ancient Rome and Burma (Myanma). The classical legend of Pyramus and Thisbe, recorded by Ovid in his *Metamorphoses*, tells how the two thwarted lovers arranged a secret rendezvous. Thisbe arrived first but was scared away by a lion, who then mauled the cloak she had dropped with maws still wet from the blood of an ox. Pyramus came upon this disheartening scene and, assuming that Thisbe had been devoured, killed himself. Thisbe later returned to discover her dead lover and she too killed herself in grief—their mingled blood soaked into the nearby mulberry bush and turned its fruit from white to dark purple.

In China the mulberry is a symbol of industry; it is used in paper-making (*Broussonetia papyrifera*) and in feeding silkworms (*Morus alba*). However, a mulberry tree planted outside a Chinese home is said to betoken death. In North America the bark is widely used for medicinal purposes.

mullein

TALL, SINGLE-STEMMED HERB, genus *Verbascum* (family Scrophulariaceae), mostly commonly topped with a spike of pale yellow flowers. Roman soldiers coated the sturdy stem with tallow to make torches, and Swedish settlers in the New World found the leaves a satisfactory tobacco substitute. Several native groups traditionally smoked the plant as a cure for asthma and throat infections, and in many areas of Europe too it is used to treat bronchial complaints. As a poultice it is efficacious in treating toothache and swellings. A form of love divination practised among Ozarks was to bend down the stem to point towards the house of the beloved; if it sprang up when released, love was requited, but if it lay flat and died the beloved's heart was cold. Medieval monks hung mullein stems around the monastery to keep evil influences at bay.

Mululu

AUSTRALIA ABORIGINAL CULTURE HERO, an ancestor of the **Dreamtime**. He became a star after his death and made provision for his four daughters, who would otherwise have been unable to support themselves, to follow him; the healer plaited his long **beard** to make a ladder to the sky and the four girls ascended it. They can now be seen as the crux or Southern Cross constellation, with their father nearby as the star we know as Centaurus.

mummers

MASKED ENTERTAINERS, popular throughout Europe in the Middle Ages. The basic plot of the mummers' play,

mummers

usually performed at **Christmas**, was a version of the St **George** dragon-slaying tale, featuring St George and an infidel knight who opposes him, a **dragon** (hobby-horse), fool, a doctor who resurrects the defeated combatant, a man wearing female clothes and occasionally Father Christmas. The duel is thought to be a relic of ancient vegetation rights. The participants today sport costumes of shredded newspaper; their medieval counterparts most probably wore animal skins and resembled the shaggy anarchic figures of the **carnival**.

The word's origins are uncertain; it may derive, with 'mumbling', from the onomatopoeic Old French *momer*, meaning to act in dumb show, or from German *mummer* (mask) and Greek *mommo* (a frightening mask or a nursery **bogey**).

Münchausen, Baron

GERMAN NOBLEMAN AND STORY-TELLER, full name Karl Friedrich Hieronymous Baron von Münchausen (1720–97). He fought with the Russians against the Turks (1737–9), and later retired to his Hanover estates to build a reputation as a marvellous raconteur, telling stories based on his experiences as traveller, soldier and hunter. The text we have today, *The Adventures of Baron Münchausen*, is largely the work of Rudolf Erich Rospe, who used the Baron's tales as the basis of a collection published anonymously in London in 1785. Since

the **tall tale** is such a popular and accepted folkloric form, further tales became attached to the figure of the Baron and the final version has little to do with a historical personage and everything to do with the folktale genre.

Typical tales include the snow-storm so severe that the Baron woke next morning, after the thaw, to find that the post to which he had tethered his horse was in fact a church steeple, from which the poor animal now dangled. Other characteristic tales include the cold so severe that the notes of the horn froze, and emerged as the horn thawed beside the fire, or the wild beast that the resourceful Baron overcame by reaching into its open mouth and pulling on the tail, thereby neatly turning the creature inside-out, in which state it was naturally running in the opposite direction. A common feature of the genre also exhibited in these tales is the motif of the marvellous companions, having astonishing powers of sight or hearing or legs that could carry their owner at the speed of a bullet.

The Baron's tales are made individual by their matter-of-fact, soldierly tone, which has endeared them to generations of willing disbelievers.

Mungo, St see Kentigern, St

mustard

PLANT, genus *Brassica* of the family Cruciferae, the seeds of which can be used to make a pungent condiment. It

Baron Münchausen

was highly regarded for its medicinal uses in the ancient world; Hippocrates recommended it for internal consumption and external application as a poultice, Pythagoras believed it to be an antidote for scorpion bites, and it was widely held to have contraceptive powers. Because of its fire, however, it is also regarded as an aphrodisiac in many cultures. In Britain mustard is primarily used for treating colds, especially in the form of hot mustard baths for the feet, but it also clears the complexion, soothes muscular aches, forestalls hair loss and cures toothache, epilepsy, lethargy and melancholy. Native North Americans use mustard for remarkably similar purposes, as a snuff to clear a stuffy head, as a poultice for aches, and as an antidote to poison. In rabbinic lore the tiny mustard seed is an emblem of something infinitesimally small; hence the modest amount of faith necessary to work miracles, according to Jesus (Matthew 27:20). In Hindu tales the mustard seed often has magical properties, enabling its owner to fly or to find hidden treasure.

myrtle

EVERGREEN SHRUB, genus *Myrtus* of the family Myrtaceae, particularly the scented common myrtle (*M. communis*) found in Asia and Mediterranean Europe. It features in Hebrew lore as the tree that Adam was allowed to take with him when he left Eden, still bearing the scent of paradise, and it symbolized the promises of God for Israel from the prophecy of Isaiah—'instead of the brier shall come up the myrtle tree' (Isaiah 41:19 and 55:13). It was associated with the eye, and branches of myrtle featured in the Feast of Tabernacles to represent the atonement for sins of looking. In Greece its perpetually green leaves were an emblem of immortality and life after death, sacred to Aphrodite, goddess of procreation and love. Although it retained its positive significance in Rome, where it composed the victory crown for those who had spilt no blood in battle, it also came to represent incestuous and unlawful love.

In general European lore myrtle is a lucky plant, bringing happiness to the house it surrounds. It has been used as an antiseptic and tonic in folk medicine.

Mythological cycle

OLD IRISH CYCLE OF MYTHS AND LEGENDS, collected mainly in the 11th-century *Book of the Dun Cow* and the 12th-century *Book of Leinster*. The tales cover the five waves of invaders to enter Ireland; firstly Cessair, secondly Partholan, thirdly the Nemedians, fourthly the **Tuatha de Dannan** and lastly the **Milesians**.

Cessair was Noah's granddaughter; since there was no room for her and her family on the Ark they escaped to Ireland but the flood overtook them even there and only her husband, Finntain, survived to tell their story. Partholan fled to Ireland to escape punishment in his unknown native country after killing his father and mother; he and his followers lived only 30 years in the country before being wiped out by a plague, the only survivor being Tuan mac Cuaill, shapeshifter and chronicler. The Tuatha de Dannan, the fairy race of Ireland, defeated the pirate fleets of the **Fomorians** at the Battle of Mag Tured and won a period of lasting peace, but they were eventually overcome by the Milesians and retreated to the *sidhe*, mounds.

Nacimientos

'BIRTH FESTIVALS', Christmas celebrations of Spain and Spanish America. As with **carnival**, the festival blends pagan and Christian elements cheerfully; much food and drink is consumed in honour of the Christchild, offerings are made to his cradle and there is much dancing involving evergreen branches.
▷ **Christmas**

nagas

SEMI-DIVINE SUPERNATURAL BEINGS OF HINDU AND BUDDHIST LORE, half human and half serpent, a strong, proud and beautiful race dwelling underground. They are descended from Kadru and Kasyapa, and in some versions they once lived on earth until Brahma relegated them to the underworld when they became too numerous. Their underground kingdom is called Patala-Ioka or Naga-Ioka; it is filled with splendid palaces encrusted with jewels, in which the nagas feast, dance and hold learned discussions. Since the women, nagis, are beautiful and clever princesses, many noble families of India have been eager to claim a nagi as ancestor, and there are thus many stories of intermarriage with humans. Nagas are potentially poisonous, but they only attack humans who have offended against the gods.

The **snake** as life-force and water deity is a common concept in world folklore, and it has been suggested that the nagas were originally a Scythian race of snake-worshippers. Certainly the mythological nagas share many features common to serpent-lore throughout the world, particularly the close association with water. Naga images are worshipped in many areas during droughts in the belief that they control rainfall, and their presence is said to be concentrated around wells, lakes and rivers. A coiled naga supports Uishnu-Narayana, or the

nagas

cosmic ocean. As water beings, their enemy is Garuda, king of the birds and the solar principle. They are also said in some legends to possess a marvellous gem in their heads (see **jewel in serpent's head**).

Nagas are frequently represented as guardians of treasure (cf **dragon**), which may be either gold and jewels or the metaphysical treasure of wisdom. In art they can appear either as serpents with one or many heads or as half human, with a coiling serpentine lower body. They frequently appear alongside gods, sheltering them with their **cobra** hoods. Mucalinda, king of the nagas, was said to have sheltered the meditating Buddha for a week after his enlightenment.

Naglfar

THE NORSE SHIP OF THE GIANTS, constructed from the nail parings of the dead. It will one day carry the **giants** to battle against the gods at Ragnarok. Its size depends on the volume of nail clippings available to make it, hence it is considered very important to trim the nails of a corpse very short to delay the completion of the ship and hence the end of the world.

nagual

ANIMAL SPIRIT OF CENTRAL AMERICA. In Aztec lore the nagual was feared as a nocturnal prowler bringing sickness, and in some areas it refers to the animal form adopted by shamans in order to carry out their evil intentions (the word derives from Nahuatl *nahualli*, meaning disguise). In many areas, however, it is the form assumed by the individual's guardian spirit, and hence a powerful force for good. Young members of many groups traditionally spend a night in a solitary spot; the animal appearing in their **dreams** or the one beside them when they wake is their nagual. The practice of spreading **ashes** around a baby's cradle to detect the tracks of the nagual that has visited in the night is also common. Societies vary in the details of nagualism; some believe that only chiefs and shamans possess naguals, for example, whereas others ascribe a nagual to each individual.

▷ **bush soul**

nagumwasuck

FAIRY RACE OF THE PASSEMAQUADDY, a shy and ugly people anxious to avoid human contact. They are well-disposed towards the group, however, and will often help invisibly in the hunt. They are sometimes said to have now deserted the earth, paddling away in a stone canoe because of the lack of belief among humans.

nails

OBJECTS OF SUPERSTITION, both the horny protective keratinous growth on **fingers** and toes and the metal pins used in construction. Like **hair**, human nails contain something of the life-essence of the individual, and if appropriated by an enemy nail-clippings can be used to work evil magic against their erstwhile owner. Conversely, nail-clippings can be used in **love magic**. It is important, therefore, to destroy all nail clippings in case they fall into the wrong hands. In Britain a popular rhyme dictates the days suitable for the operation of nail cutting:

Cut them on Monday, cut them for health

Cut them on Tuesday, cut them for wealth

Cut them on Wednesday, cut them for news

Cut them on Thursday, a new pair of shoes

Cut them on Friday, cut them for sorrow

Cut them on Saturday, see your true love tomorrow

Cut them on Sunday, your safety seek The Devil will have you the rest of the week.

Although this rhyme appears to contain a stricture against working on a Sunday, it is probable that its significance extends beyond Christian times to such pagan ideas of the soul inherent in bodily matter.

Metal nails, traditionally made of **iron** before the development of steel, partake of that material's virtues and serve as a convenient **charm** to keep all manner of malign influences at bay. They are frequently hammered into door frames throughout Europe, and are especially effective when hammered in the form of a **cross**.

▷ **Naglfar**

nain rouge

'RED DWARF', A HOUSEHOLD SPIRIT OF NORMANDY, with special responsibility for fishermen. In US lore it refers to an evil ghost or demon said to have caused the conflagration in Detroit in 1805, and some Americans paint a **cross** upon their door to avert its power.

näkh

WATER DEMON OF ESTONIAN LORE, the spirits of the drowned. Näkhs are shapeshifters, but usually appear in at least semi-human form or as a horse (cf **kelpie**). Both males and females lure their victims into the water with a sweet singing or bewitch them into dancing until they drown, exhausted; females are often described as **mermaid** figures with long hair, bared breasts and the tail of a fish. They are sometimes known as Näkinein. To see a Näkh is always a bad omen, usually presaging death by drowning.

Nala and Damanti

TALE OF THE MAHABHARATA. King Bhima selected the young king Nala as the only suitable husband for his beautiful daughter Damayanti and Nala, having never seen his bride, had also come to the conclusion from the reports that he had heard that she was the only woman he desired. At their marriage by choice (*svayamvara*), however, when Damayantī came forward to present the garland to the man of her choice, she found Nala flanked by four of the gods who had assumed his form. She correctly identified her lover, and the two were married. The gods were dissatisfied, however, and after some years Kali, the demon of unlucky gambling, entered Nala and he began to gamble away his kingdom. He left the faithful Damayanti, who returned sadly to her father while Nala, among other adventures, received from a jewelled snake a disguise of deformity and a robe that would remove it. Eventually Damayanti heard of the skill of a cook and charioteer in the service of the king of Kosala and recognized by these characteristics her lost husband. She contrived to have the king attend another *svayamvara* (driven by his charioteer). The king of Kosala was so impressed by Nala's charioteering skills that he offered to exchange his own gift of lucky gambling for it, and Kali departed, defeated. Damayanti meanwhile compelled this strange-looking attendant to reveal his true identity, finally he donned the cloak that restored his true shape and the two were reunited. They returned to Nala's kingdom where, with his new-found gaming skill, he quickly restored his fortune.

The tale contains many familiar folklore motifs, including the love of one unseen, the recognition of the beloved among identical companions, and the **act of truth**; Damayanti disposes of an amorous hunter by invoking the gods to strike him dead if she loves only Nala. She does, and they do. The tale is one of the best-known and best-loved in the *Mahabharata*.

In the ***Ramayana***, Nala is the mythical monkey king who constructed a bridge of stones floating on water to allow **Rama** to take his army from India to Sri Lanka and rescue **Sita**.

name taboo

POWERFUL PROHIBITIVE MAGIC. This is one of the most common types of **taboo**; one may be forbidden to reveal one's own name, or to speak the name of a god, demon, the recently deceased, the chief or king, animals such as the **bear** or **snake**, or certain family members such as mother-in-law. This practice often produces a fund of **euphemism**—Old Nick for the **Devil**, Grandfather for the bear, 'the dear departed' for the dead—the prevalence of which in modern society demonstrates the enduring nature of taboos.

The name taboo derives from the ancient magic principle that the true name contains great power, so to name a supernatural being or spirit of the dead was to invoke it or challenge it in some way, and to tell one's own name was to put oneself in the power of others. Folktales such as **Rumpelstiltskin** use this ancient convention, as do superstitious practices of **exorcism** and **divination**.

The widespread taboo against killing or eating the totemic ancestor may be associated with identity and kinship relations; to defile the supernatural bond between the ancestor or second soul in the animal and the hunter would be to invite disaster and death. This too may have a parallel in folktales, in the many stories of animals who beg for mercy from the hero and in return help him with his quest.

▷ **taboo**

Naoise

OLD IRISH HERO OF THE RED BRANCH CYCLE, ill-fated lover of **Deirdre**. He is one of the Sons of Usnech treacherously killed by **Conchobar**.

narcissus

BULBOUS FLOWERING PLANT, genus *Narcissus* of the Amaryllis family. In Greek mythology Narcissus was the son of Cephisus and Lirope, whose beauty proved fatal to himself and others. He spurned the advances of the nymph Echo, who pined away for love until nothing was left but her voice, and when he caught sight of himself in a pool he fell so violently in love with his own reflection that he too died of frustrated desire, the punishment of the gods for his harsh treatment of Echo. The plant grew up from his body. The tale is thought by some scholars to illustrate the ancient **taboo** against looking at one's own reflection.

The poisonous bulbs have been used in folk medicine as an emetic and purgative, and a poultice made from the root is applied to wounds as an antiseptic and to draw out splinters.

Nasnas

AN ISLAMIC DEMON, who appears to humans in the form of a frail old man. He waits by the side of a river and begs to be carried across, but if a kind-hearted traveller should consent he twines his legs around his benefactor in mid-stream with demonic power and drowns him.

▷ **Old Man of the Sea**

Native American folklore

THREE MAIN AREAS OF INDIGENOUS NATIVE AMERICAN LORE CAN BE DISTINGUISHED: the North American and Canadian groups north of the Mexican border, those of Central America, and the South American groups, who have been relatively little documented. All three areas have been heavily influenced by white settlers, but details of their traditional folklore survive in the records of the early colonists whose reports nevertheless often tend to be inaccurate or unsympathetic. In rare cases, particularly among South American groups, small numbers survive in remote areas relatively untouched by the centuries of colonization, and valuable work still remains to be done in documenting them more fully.

The folklore of the Native North American is characterized by creation myths and trickster tales, in which the **culture hero** who creates the tribe or aids them is the same as the trickster figure who practises unscrupulous deception and is often duped and ridiculed. The difference corresponds to the distinguishing factor between myth and folktale; time. Origin myths are set in a pre-human world, whereas trickster tales generally acknowledge the presence of humans in a world similar to that known by the speaker and his listeners. The trickster tales also tend to include much obscenity and buffoonery. Throughout the area there is a strong recognition of the dual purposes of the folktale, to entertain and to instruct, and although some tribes emphasize one function over the other, in most the two are inalienably linked.

Native tales may well vary in length from one episode to a vast cycle. The North Pacific coast groups are especially given to constructing long episodic or narrative cycles concerning the doings of the trickster or **culture hero**. The value placed on originality or conservatism varies from region to region too: in the South West the speaker is usually encouraged to improvise upon the tale, in other areas he may be chastised for doing so.

A characteristic common to much North American native lore is the contest motif, reflecting the love of games and contests of skill among the tribes. In these stories, the contest is usually won by clever deception on the part of the trickster figure.

The intermingling of cultures in Central America is unusually complete, and little original native lore is left. The early mmigrants were mainly 16th century Spaniards, and it has been suggested that the superstitious Catholic faith of the settlers may have absorbed much of the native folklore, such as belief taboos and magical observances, while Catholicism replaced the original impulses for the festivals of the Native Americans, and **saints** supplanted many of their spirits, but interfered little with their actual observance. The Spanish missionaries who zealously destroyed the pagan temples also recorded the customs and beliefs of the lost souls they hoped to convert, thereby ironically preserving and destroying the indigenous culture simultaneously.

In areas such as Mexico and Guatemala, the remains of Aztec culture before the conquest has given rise to a distinctive and more highly organized brand of folklore and religion which resisted influence from South America. Being also the richest in natural resources however, these countries were most extensively colonized.

A common belief in Central American mythology is that this world is the latest in a sequence, the earlier worlds having been destroyed as a result of breaking a **taboo** or by an angry deity, by flood, fire, wind and supernatural beasts. At the end of each cycle of 52 years (a round figure like a century in the Central American calendar) priests wait anxiously for the sign that this world is not now to be destroyed in its turn. If the **Pleiades** do indeed pass the zenith as hoped, new fire is kindled in the breast of a sacrificed victim and used to kindle the altar fire and those in every home in a ritual 'New Fire' ceremony.

Another characteristic belief in Central American lore is that of the **nagual**, an animal spirit twinned with that of a human so closely that either will die if the other is killed. To discover what animal is the nagual of a new-born child, the father will often spread **ashes** around the baby at night and look to see which tracks have been left by the nagual coming to inspect its twin soul (see **separable soul**).

The folklore of Native South Americans is fragmentary and little documented, yet some continuity of theme can be discerned among the vast number of groups. The creation myths for example are largely unconcerned with the origin of the world itself, but rather with its features such as the sun, moon and animals. The hero figures in this area are frequently the **Twins**, usually representative of the Sun and Moon, who generally also appear as culture heroes, benefactors of the tribe.

In Peru, Bolivia and Ecuador the influence of Inca culture is still apparent, and imported Christianity was fused with traditional religion so that pagan gods existed alongside God and Christ in popular belief.

nats

SPIRITS OF BURMESE (MYANMA) LORE, a generic term encompassing the vengeful spirits of the dead beneficent guardians, supernatural beings and nature spirits. They belong to a pre-Buddhist indigenous religion, and have survived in folk belief and have been incorporated into the national religion. An equivalent spirit in Thailand is known as a *phi*.

Most important among the nats are the Thirty Seven, spirits of specific individuals—generally warriors and national heroes, both male and

Thagya Min

female—whose images are displayed in the Shwe Zigon pagoda, Pagān. their tales are collected in the *Maha Gita Medani*. These nats, like all others, must be propitiated by offerings and reverence; since weather, crops, animals, wealth, health, property and the life of the community are in their power, and they range across the earth, air and water, their goodwill is essential to life. Food and flowers are the most common offerings; many Buddhist pagodas provide a special *natsin* (house or shrine of the nats) to please the nats. Verses from the Maha Gita Medani are read aloud by the medium (said to be passed by nats) at festivals, both honouring the nats and impressing appropriate moral values upon the listeners.

Thagya Min is the most important of the nats. He is portrayed in art standing as a **lotus** supported by three **elephants**, and his return to each marks the beginning of the Burmese year.

nettle

STINGING PLANT, most commonly genus *Urtica* (family Urticaceae). Its tiny hairs release an irritant when broken or crushed. This painful effect was held by rugged Roman soldiers to be a useful stimulant; nettles rubbed on cold skin produced warmth, or something quite like it, and in Germany nettle seed, from its association with this stimulating stinging, was considered a potent aphrodisiac. It has also been widely used medicinally, often on the homeopathic principle that a small sting will remove a larger. Nettle tea is considered a revitalizing tonic in England and Scotland, and the Meskwaki use such an infusion to treat colds. In this they follow the Romans, who steeped nettles in oil for the same complaint. In Russia nettle tea is said to ease toothache.

As the plant of the Norse god Thor, the nettle was believed in Northern Europe to impart courage and to ward off **lightning**, hence it was often used as a **charm**. Elsewhere in Europe however it was held to be a plant of the **Devil**, along with the **thistle**. Hans Christian Andersen records the tale of 'The Eleven Swans', in which the princess must spin nettles into flax to make the magic shirts that will restore the brothers to human

form. Nettles were in fact commonly used in spinning before the widespread importation of cotton fibres into Europe. A popular superstition surviving in many areas is that the nettle will not sting if grasped firmly rather than hesitantly; this has given rise to the proverbial expression meaning to confront a difficult issue head on—'grasping the nettle'.

New Year

CELEBRATIONS IN HONOUR OF THE BEGINNING OF THE YEAR, found almost universally throughout the world. Such observances may be primarily religious or entirely social, but they consistently demonstrate the significance attached to the renewal and continuation of life expressed in the calenderical cycle. Most scholars agree that New Year celebrations at their most basic are a mimesis of death and rebirth or recreation, mirroring and giving power to the most significant of the seasonal cycles; hence they are a *rite de passage* for the entire community.

The year is for most societies computed on a lunar calendar; since this does not precisely match the movement of the earth around the sun many resort to irregular months, extra days every few

New Year

years, or a system whereby some days simply 'fall off' the calendar and are not reckoned as real time. Since the moon is usually the basis of the year, most societies celebrate the New Year at one of the equinoxes or solstices (eg autumn for Egyptians and Persians) or the new moon nearest an equinox (eg the mid-March new moon in Babylonia). Later societies allocated fixed calendar dates for the New Year; medieval Europe celebrated Annunciation Day 25 March as New Year until the Gregorian calendar's introduction in 1582 (England did not implement the change to 1 January until 1752).

The most characteristic features of New Year celebrations around the world, which in their details are as diverse as the peoples celebrating, are licence and feasting. Often special foods are prepared, as in Japan where cakes are offered to the sun and moon and a purifying rice gruel is eaten to mark the end of the seven days of festivities. To eat well at the beginning of the year, no matter how meagre the fare has been until then, is a **charm** to ensure that the coming year will bring food in plenty. The representation of the Old Year as a hoary wizened man, overtaken by the cherubic New Year in Western Lore is a reminder of the roots of the festival, the dichotomy of death and rebirth that recalls ancient ritual **king**-slaying as a means of restoring vigour to the cosmos and the society.

▷ **Hogmanay**; **Rosh Hashana**

nhangs

EVIL SPIRITS OF ARMENIAN LORE, sea-dwellers often assuming the form of **mermaids** to lure their victims to their deaths. They belong to the ancient and widespread tradition of predatory, seductive female spirits.

Nibelungenlied

A 13TH-CENTURY EPIC POEM, 'Song of the Nibelungs', written in Middle High German by an unknown Austrian writer. It consists of 39 'adventures' or chapters recounting tales drawn from ancient Teutonic legend (much of the material is paralleled in the earlier *Volsungasaga*). The Nibelungs are the possessors of the treasure forged by the **dwarfs** (see **Alberich**) although the term is later used to apply to the Burgundians under its curse.

Siegfried (**Sigurd**) gains possession of the Nibelung hoard and meets at Worms the Burgundian princess Kriemhild, sister of **Gunther**. They wish to marry, but Gunther will grant his permission only if Siegfried accompanies him to Isenland and helps him to win the hand of the amazonian queen Brunhild (**Brynhild**). Wearing his cloak of **invisibility**, Siegfried aids Gunther to defeat Brunhild in a contest to see who can throw a spear and stone the furthest, and Brunhild is reluctantly obliged to fulfil her oath and marry Gunther. On their wedding night Brunhild deposits Gunther on a peg in her room where he hangs in impotent rage until morning. The next night he is revenged by Siegfried, who in his cloak of invisibility wrestles with Brunhild and overcomes her; she believes she has been defeated by Gunther and thenceforth submits to him docilely. Siegfried and Kriemhild also marry, but the two queens are fractious and through Kriemhild's needling Brunhild learns of the deception practised on her. She enlists **Hagen**, the vassal of Gunther, in plotting her vengeance.

Hagen learns through Kriemhild that Siegfried has one vulnerable spot (Siegfried had bathed in **dragon**'s blood to make himself invulnerable but a linden leaf stuck on his back and left that spot untouched). He advises Kriemhild to sew a cross on Siegfried's cloak to protect this spot, then uses this as a guide to spear the hero as he drinks from a spring.

After Siegfried's death the distraught Kriemhild remains at Worms and after several years she receives the Nibelung treasure, hers by marriage. Fearing that wealth will make her too powerful, Hagen intercepts the hoard and hides most of it in the Rhine.

In the second part of the poem, Kriemhild marries the inoffensive king of the Huns, Etzel (Atli or Attila), seeing a means of gaining revenge for Siegfried's death. Seven years after their marriage, she persuades Etzel to invite her Burgundian kinsmen to visit, making sure that Hagen too will make the journey. The visit ends in carnage between Huns and Burgundians when Hagen refuses to tell Kriemhild where he has hidden the Nibelung gold. She beheads her brother Gunther and lastly Hagen; finally she is herself slain by Hildebrand, who has watched her insane rage with growing outrage.

The epic has been an enormous influence on German culture and literature up to the present day. It was uncharacteristic of its time, eschewing the contemporary courtly conventions and drawing its mood and inspiration from more heroic sources, where uncompromising vengeance and violent emotion were the hallmarks. This accords well with the historical setting of the poem, loosely based on the overthrow of the Burgundians by the Huns at Worms in AD437—a period when literature and lore was stamped with the heroic rather than the courtly stamp.

Nich Noch Nothing

CELTIC FOLKTALE. The hero, Nich Noch Nothing, is challenged by a giant, on pain of death, to clear out a stable seven miles wide and seven miles long which has not been cleaned for seven years. He accomplishes this feat when the giant's daughter summons all the birds and animals to help. He is then commanded to empty a loch seven miles cubed (the giant's daughter calls all the fish to drink it dry) and finally to climb a branchless tree seven miles high and retrieve unbroken the eggs from its top. The giant's daughter cuts off all her fingers and toes to act as steps, but Nich Noch Nothing breaks one of the eggs at the foot of the tree and is obliged to flee. In the first test the influence of **Heracles**'s labours, the locus classicus of the task motif, is apparent; one of the Greek hero's twelve labours was to clean the Augean stables, which he performed by diverting two rivers through them.
▷ **tasks and tests**

Nicholas, St

THE CHILDREN'S SAINT, associated with mysterious, generous giving and the protection of the defenceless. Despite his enormous popularity as patron and protector of countless different groups and his prominence in European folklore, the facts about Nicholas extend no further than that he was bishop of Myra in Lycia (south-western Turkey) at some point in the fourth century.

There is evidence of a cult in the East as early as the sixth century, which gained popularity in the West during the tenth century, but his fame was secured after his relics were translated to Bari in 1087 and the reported emission of some perfumed substance called 'mana' or 'myrrh' from his shrine, which attracted countless pilgrims.

Among the legends that have grown up surrounding his name perhaps the most famous is that of his intervention to save the honour of three poverty stricken sisters; their father could not afford their **dowries** and in desperation was about to give them over to prostitution. Hearing of this, Nicholas secretly came by the house at night and threw a bag of gold, sufficient for one sister's dowry, through the window on three different occasions. This is the source of the traditional sign for pawnbrokers, three golden balls.

Frequent representation of the story with the three rounded money bags, may have led to a different version of the legend in which the three balls became the severed heads of three murdered children, whom Nicholas found and restored to life. The mystical number **three** recurs in Nicholas's legends; he is also said to have saved three prisoners who had been falsely condemned from execution by warning Emperor Constantine of their innocence in a dream and to have miraculously rescued three sailors off the coast of Turkey.

As patron of children, Nicholas' feast-day became associated in the Low countries with the giving and receiving of presents. Dutch settlers in North America created the modern figure of **Santa Claus** by linking Saint Klaus with the Scandinavian god Thor, figure of reward and punishment, whose chariot was drawn by **goats**.

Nicholas is usually shown in art with the three balls of gold, or else worshipping God as a baby, from the legend that he abstained from his mother's milk on Wednesdays and Fridays. His feast-day, 6 December, has recently been reduced by the Catholic church. He is the patron saint of Russia, children, pawnbrokers, unmarried girls, perfumiers and sailors.

nightingale

SMALL THRUSH, usually *Erithacus megarhynchosh*, a native of Asia and Europe renowned for its sweet crescendoing song. In Greek legend King Tereus of Thrace, entrusted with the task of escorting Philomela to see her sister Procne (his wife), raped her on the way and cut out her tongue to prevent her telling her the story. Philomela however wove the outrage into a tapestry which she sent to Procne. The two sisters revenged themselves by killing Tereus' young son Itys and serving him to his father in a stew. When Procne produced her son's head triumphantly, Tereus leapt to take revenge, but the gods transformed all three into birds; Tereus became a **hawk**, Procne a **swallow** and Philomela a nightingale. In some versions of the tale Procne becomes the nightingale and the tongueless Philomela a thrush. This tale embodies the common folklore motif of the loathsome feast.

In medieval literary tradition, the nightingale is said to press her breast against a thorn to keep herself awake all night for fear of snakes; her song is one of pain. Another version of the legend holds that the bird is enamoured of the **rose**, and uses the pain of the thorn to quell the tortures of love.
▷ **hawk**

nightmare

OPPRESSIVE NIGHT SPIRIT. The word derives not from mare meaning female horse, the common derivation of folk etymology, but from Old English *mare*, **incubus**; the nightmare is a fiend that sits on sleepers' chests and leaves them feeling oppressed, short of breath and panicky when they awake.
▷ **hag**

nine

ONE OF THE MOST POTENT OF MYSTICAL NUMBERS, the trinity of trinities (see **three**). It is also significant that the ancient lunar week had nine nights in the Roman method of counting. It appears frequently in folklore both ancient and modern; the Norse cosmos was composed of nine worlds, the **hydra** was nine-headed, a charm to make the **fairies** visible involves placing nine grains of wheat on a four-leafed **clover**, a cat has nine lives, and so on.

nisse

SCANDANAVIAN HOUSEHOLD SPIRITS, an ancestral spirit who exhibits many **brownie** characteristics; he is helpful but volatile and easily offended, and must be placated by discreet gifts of food.

nix

FRESH-WATER BEINGS OF GERMAN LORE, **shape-shifting** spirits who are generally malevolent towards humans. Nixes inhabit splendid underwater palaces, but their love of music and dancing often draws them into the realm of humans and they may appear at village dances as beautiful maidens. They can often be identified by their skill at dancing, or by their prophetic powers. Amorous liaisons sometimes occur between nixes and humans, but these can be dangerous for both parties. In general nixes aim to drown their human victims; in many areas it is said to be unlucky to attempt to rescue a drowning person and thus deprive the nixes of the sacrifice they demand. Occasionally they steal human children and leave **changelings** in their place; here the true appearance of the nix is visible, and according to such reports they are wizened green beings.

nocnitsa

HAG OF EASTERN EUROPEAN LORE, who prowls through the village at night to torment children. Careful mothers may protect their infants by keeping a **knife** in the cradle or, since this brings its own dangers, drawing a circle around the child with a knife or hiding an **axe** beneath the cradle. These practices illustrate the significance of **iron** as protection against malignant spirits.

North American folklore

A NEW FOLKLORE SPRANG UP AMONG THE EARLY WHITE SETTLERS OF AMERICA, in this new land so full of opportunity and danger, at once a hostile wilderness and a promised land. The settlers from the Old World brought with them the traditional customs, crafts and values of their native lands, but were forced to adapt their habits in the face of a very different environment. Contact with unfamiliar climate and creatures, and of course the constant presence of the native peoples, meant that a new body of experience and wisdom grew up among those facing the challenges together, a lore characterized by a grim humour. As the colonists expanded west, frontier heroes began to emerge. Figures such as Davy **Crockett** became renowned for their blunt, backwoodsman humour and incredible exploits in the face of danger, and they quickly passed into legend. Pioneer lore is also characterized by a fierce pride in the doings of the individual and in the land for which they fought so hard.

One particular group of settlers developed a very distinctive type of folklore; this was the Pennsylvanian Dutch culture, drawn originally from Germany, Protestant France and Switzerland, who settled on the East Coast and formed a strong and distinct community. Funerals here were often attended by many hundreds, and many other gatherings were held by the farmers, such as 'snitzings', where fruit was cut to be dried. Here also the Amish communities developed, in which hymns were often folk poetry and the tunes handed down orally in **ballad** tradition. The group as a whole believed strongly in **witchcraft**, a concern shared by many of the colonists. The concepts of God and the **Devil** too were very real to them, and many anecdotes have been recorded of felons who appealed to God and were instantly struck down. Probably the most famous demonstration of this preoccupation is the Salem witch-hunt of 1682, in which many lost their lives in the spate of hysterical accusations of witchcraft and Devil-worship.

On the other hand, the settlers were quick to hail a saint among them in the shape of **Johnny Appleseed**.

With the introduction of African slaves, especially on the plantations of the South, the rich black American folklore developed, characterized by its concern with religion and slavery, particularly the figure of the wise servant

finally triumphing over the oppressive master, which was well suited to the traditional African trickster type. Probably the most famous stories from the Negro tradition are those collected and retold by Joel Chandler Harris in his **Brer Rabbit** books. The blacks adopted Christianity and transformed it into an expression of their own hopes for redemption, producing many haunting spirituals and a highly idiosyncratic style of preaching and energetic worship.

With massive immigration from diverse cultures in the 19th and early 20th centuries, urban America became a repository of cultural traditions which gave rise to a modern lore while retaining elements of separateness: many tales are characteristically Jewish, Italian or Irish, for example. For many of these immigrants, especially the early arrivals who often lived in appalling conditions, the cultural identity conferred by the sharing of a common folk tradition with others of the same group was an important anchor for their lives in this confusing and alien world.

nose

THE OLFACTORY ORGAN. An immensely sensitive and complex structure, it takes in and prepares air for the lungs. As one of the body's orifices, it is thought by many groups to be a point of access or departure of spirits, hence the widespread use of nose-rings as **amulets** to guard against evil spirits. Many peoples seal the nose of a corpse, with decorative stones such as jade (as in China) or functional means such as fish-hooks or pebbles, to guard against evil spirits entering and animating the body. In many cultures nose-rings have achieved great importance as indicators of social class and economic status, as in India.

In popular Western lore the size of an individual's nose is believed to be in proportion to his sexual organs, and to signify a generous personality. Folk cures for nose-bleeds include a cold key dropped down one's back, or a red ribbon tied around the neck.

nudity

A POWERFUL MAGICAL AND SOCIAL FORCE. In primitive ceremonies nudity, especially female nudity, is most commonly utilized to control storms and rain. This may indicate a connection between the principles of life-giving water and the female principle. Sailors often follow Pliny's belief that the uncovered female breast has power to still storms (see **figureheads**). In many cultures evil spirits are believed to be frightened away by an exhibition of nudity, and hence farmers may patrol their fields naked to guard the crops.

A distinct and probably later tradition of nudity has its roots in social protest, a symbol of throwing off oppression and restriction (see St **Francis** and Lady **Godiva**).

numbers

THE HISTORY OF MATHEMATICS IS A FASCINATING AREA OF SCHOLARSHIP, embracing philosophy and music as well as anthropology. The earliest number sequences were basic, depending on the environment and needs of the culture; some groups only distinguished one, two and many, others could count herds of over 100 cattle or sheep. Some aboriginal tribes developed number awareness that depended not on counting sequences but on spatial awareness, knowing instantly when a member of a large herd was missing without the facility of counting. In many cultures too the idea of number was expressed by inflexion, the addition of a suffix or the mutation of a vowel, rather than by the use of a separate entity. But in most cultures, and increasingly as trade and economics became more sophisticated, a sequence of numbers which could be applied to objects became the most common means of measurement. In illiterate folk societies, people often resorted to numerical systems of their own, from the knotted plaits of reeds used by Pacific Islanders as a record of wages to the notches and

marks made on tally sticks by European peasants. Because of their abstract nature, which means they can be associated with any object, numbers can be used to link different objects symbolically.

There exists across much of the world a preference for odd numbers over even ones, which may be explained by the Roman philosophy that a number which could be exactly divided represented destruction and impermanence. In some areas of Asia even numbers of stairs, windows and so on are avoided in house-building.

▷ **nine**; **seven**; **thirteen**; **three**; **two**

numerology

COMPLEX SYSTEM OF DIVINATION. As practised in the West today, based on the sum of numbers in a name, numerology was found in ancient Egypt and other civilizations. It has its roots in folk belief; in nearly all cultures certain numbers are considered lucky or unlucky, and babies born at certain times for example are considered fortunate or not accordingly. Dates and letter-values are broken down and added together exhaustively, until a number from 1 to 9 is obtained, and this number when used in conjunction with specific dates can be used to predict events and assess character.

▷ **numbers**

nure onna

EVIL SPIRIT OF JAPANESE LORE, portrayed with long hair and a long, flickering tongue.

nursery rhymes

THE POETRY OF CHILDREN, usually the individual's first and lasting impression of folk culture. Although most of the traditionally nursery rhymes now common in Western homes are of relatively recent origin, with the majority dating from literature of the 18th and 19th centuries, there are a few which appear to have more ancient origins. The **riddles** which are so vital a part of folk culture in many societies have largely passed into nursery lore in the West; Humpty Dumpty is the most famous example of a riddle-rhyme, and its probable antiquity is attested to by its countless European relations, the

numbers

Hümpelken-Pümpelken of Germany and the Thille Lille of Sweden, to name but two. Similarly, some proverbial phrases have passed from common currency into that of the nursery, for example 'Jack Sprat could eat no fat, His wife could eat no lean' in its original form was a proverb extolling the efficacy of cooperation.

Themes from folktales are also to be found in old nursery rhymes, such as that recently popularized as a folk song, 'Parsley, sage, rosemary and thyme'. Early forms of the rhyme tell of the various impossible tasks demanded of a maid by a reluctant lover, and the maid's response of equally impossible provisions, a common theme of folklore across the world. The rhyme appears in this form in a 17th-century collection, but its origins seem to be in the traditions of Oriental folklore, and particularly a medieval European tale in which a king tests his future wife in a similar way, and she replies that he must first fulfil several impossible conditions (see **tasks and tests**). The addition of the refrain 'Parsley, sage, rosemary and thyme' may well be a relic of an old invocation, since nursery rhymes often preserve the superstitions and rituals of earlier cultures. The common chant 'Rain, rain, go away, come again another day' seems to be a relic of ancient weather invocation. It occurs in many different forms, 'Come on Martha's wedding day' for example, being a snide reference to the popular superstition that rain at a wedding was unlucky, or 'Come again on washing day'.

'Jack be nimble, Jack be quick, Jack jump over the candlestick' is probably related to the early English custom of **candle**-leaping; if a leap could be made without extinguishing the candle, good luck was sure to follow for the coming year. The protective chant 'Matthew, Mark, Luke and John, Bless the bed that I lie on' is an ancient Christian spell, a charm against the dangers of darkness. Even more ancient origins have been claimed for the popular rhyme 'Jack and Jill went up the hill To fetch a pail of water', which does not appear in literature before the 18th century; it has been suggested that the names are derived from the Scandinavian deities Hjuki and Bil, captured by the moon god Mani as they went to draw water and still visible along with their pail in the moon's markings. However since the habit of using the names in a generic sense, meaning no more than lad and lass, became common in early times, such speculation may be fruitless.

The majority of nursery rhymes, particularly the older ones, were originally composed for adult consumption rather than the nursery, and are the products of literary rather than folk traditions. Their transmission however demonstrates the interconnectedness of popular and folk culture; the rhymes are generally transmitted orally and conservatively, sometimes surviving virtually unchanged over centuries without being recorded in print, and hence they have become the property of the folk by use although they did not originate with the folk. *A Moste Strange Weddinge of the Frogge and the Mowse*, a ballad published in 1580, becomes *The Frog He Would a-Wooing Go* in the nursery, and the lesser-known rhyme 'One misty, moisty morning' (in which the old man speaks the memorable greeting 'How d'ye do, and how d'ye do, and how d'ye do again') is actually the first stanza of 'The Wiltshire Wedding', a 17th-century broadside ballad.

Topical events were customarily transmitted in ballad form before the widespread introduction of news-sheets, and several rhymes are thought to preserve historical events. 'Little Jack Horner' for example is popularly supposed to refer to one Thomas Horner, steward to the Abbot of Glastonbury during Henry VIII's dissolution of the monasteries. Hoping to secure his living, the abbot sent Henry a Christmas present of a pie in which were contained the title deeds to 12 manors; legend has it that the enterprising Thomas removed those of the manor of Mells, and took possession of it shortly after the abbot's eviction. A rhyme popular in the 17th century seems to support the legend, and the likelihood of its inclusion in the nursery repertoire; 'Hopton, Horner, Smyth and Thynne, When abbots went out, they came in'.

Perhaps the most famous origin story is that 'Ring-a-ring-o'-roses' refers to the symptoms of the Great Plague (red rashes, the bunches of herbs carried as **amulets**, the frequent sneezing), but parallel European versions suggest that the 'falling down' was a form of curtesy rather than a parody of death, and the rhyme may not in fact have such grisly origins.

Nineteenth-century nursery rhymes tend to be more literary, often with a moral slant quite removed from the underlying anarchy of earlier rhymes. Compare for example the faintly bawdy 'There was a lady loved a swine', popular by the 17th century, with the saccharin 'I love little pussy, Her coat is so warm, And if I don't hurt her She'll do me no harm'.

Rhymes clearly intended for children but found world-wide and throughout history include counting rhymes, such as 'One, two, buckle my shoe' and the ubiquitous nonsense-number series 'Eenie, meenie, miny, mo', used as a **counting-out rhyme**, which probably dates back to early peasant numerals.

nutmeg

PUNGENT, SLIGHTLY SWEET SPICE, the kernel of the *Myristica fragrans* (family Myristicaceae) or, in common usage, a number of other tropical trees. (The aril surrounding the kernel is dried to produce mace.) A whole nutmeg was often used as a **charm** against rheumatic limbs and irritated skin. In Jamaica the powdered spice is taken to ease labour pains.

oak

MASSIVE AND ENDURING TREE, any of the genus *Quercus* (family Fagaceae), considered a sacred tree by an astonishing number of societies. In classical legend the oak was the first tree, from which came mankind; it is rooted in the **underworld**, and as the tree sacred to Zeus was believed to speak oracular truth by the movement of its leaves or the **divination** practised beneath it. It was later held sacred to Thor and various Celtic deities, and worshipped by Druids, and **Merlin** was said to perform his magic under its shelter. Odin thrust the marvellous sword **Balmung** into the Branstock tree, the great oak in the Volsung palace.

In Northern Europe the oak is widely associated with fire and especially with **lightning** (hence the association with the god of thunder, Thor) and farmers would often protect their property from a lightning strike by planting an oak nearby. In the Christmas celebrations of Northern Europe oak is the traditional material for the Yule log (see **Christmas**). To see a blasted oak is generally a bad omen. In folktales, much use has been made of the fact that the oak never sheds all of its leaves in winter. A common motif in Northern European tales is that of 'the last leaf'; the trickster promises to pay his debts to another (often the **Devil**) when the last leaf falls, ie never.

Oak is highly regarded too for its medicinal properties; since the tree is a symbol of strength and long life an **acorn** carried in the pocket was a catch-all charm to ensure good health and good fortune, but there were many more specific uses. Some Native Americans make a tea of oak bark as a decongestant; to walk around an oak tree in Europe meant that one's illness would pass into the tree; and if an invalid child is passed through a cleft in an oak (or sometimes an ash) tree, a strong sympathetic bond is formed between the two, and the child will be sound as long as the tree survives.

▷ **trees**

Oakley, Annie

REAL NAME Phoebe Anne Oakley Moses (1860–1926) American rodeo star and fast-shooter, born into an Ohio Quaker family. She married Frank Butler in 1880 after beating him in a shooting match. They formed a trick-shooting act, and from 1885 toured widely with the **Buffalo Bill** Wild West show. A tiny woman under five feet tall, she shot cigarettes from her husband's lips, and could shoot through the pips of a playing card tossed in the air (hence an 'Annie Oakley', a punched free ticket). She passed into American folklore as a heroine epitomizing the tall-talking, shoot-from-the-hip virtues of the pioneers, and was fictionalized in the Irving Berlin musical comedy of 1946, *Annie Get Your Gun.*

oaths

SOLEMN GUARANTEE OF VERACITY, usually involving an appeal to a deity or invoking a dire penalty for falsity. Oaths have existed in various forms around the world and throughout history. It seems probable that the earliest oaths were specifically religious imprecations, either directly involving a divinity or referring more obliquely to a symbol of deity such as a sword or, in India, water from the holy river, the Ganges. In Christian lore the sacred object is the Bible; implicit in this form is the concept of divine retribution should the speaker be lying, and this is the theme of the majority of oaths in later societies. The schoolchild today still says, miming the appropriate actions, 'Cross my heart and hope to die, Never, never tell a lie' (see **children's lore**). There is an enormous variety of imaginative variations on this basic premise. A major subset of such oaths is the large group directed not at oneself but another, usually a relation—one's children, sister, the soul of one's dear dead mother.

Inevitably, much folklore has developed around the motif of the perjured oath, in which the penalty invoked by the liar actually falls upon him (see **act of truth**).

Oberon

KING OF THE FAIRIES. He appears first in a medieval French romance, *Huan de Bordeaux*, as Alberon, a supernatural helper, a **dwarf**-king who aids the hero in his impossible **task**. Here he is represented as the son of Julius Caesar and **Morgan le Fay**. He is almost certainly derived from **Alberich**, king of the Teutonic dwarfs and the guard of the Nibelung hoard. His fame in England came through Shakespeare's *A Midsummer Night's Dream* in which he features as the estranged and later reconciled husband of **Titania**, with the power of **invisibility** and a lively avuncular concern in the affairs of the four lovers.

obstacle flight

COMMON TALE-TYPE, found in various forms throughout the world. In its most basic form the hero and his or her helpers escape from a monster (usually a **giant**, **ogre** or **witch**) by casting behind them certain objects that immediately become magical obstacles. This motif often follows from that of the impossible **task** successfully completed; the supernatural helper is often the giant's daughter or a fellow-prisoner. The magic objects left behind in the giant's house conceal their flight for a short time by speaking in answer to the giant's questions. Eventually however he discovers the deception and sets out in pursuit; the fugitives then delay him further by throwing down, for example, a comb which becomes an impenetrable forest, a pebble or **mirror** that metamorphoses into an enormous glassy-smooth mountain, or a flint which instantly begins a raging fire. Alternatively or in addition the fleeing couple may transform themselves into innocuous objects, such as a **rose** and its thornbush (this is known as the transformation flight).

One of the most famous examples of this tale-type is that collected by Grimm as *The Water-Nixie*; two children are abducted by a **nix** and eventually escape by throwing down behind them the girl's brush (a spiny hill), the boy's comb (a precipitous jagged edge) and finally a mirror that becomes an insurmountable **glass mountain**. In an Inuit tale the old woman draws her finger across the ice and it parts, bringing her pursuers up short.

A variation of the motif is the throwing down of distracting objects, found in classical legend as the golden **apples** used by Hippomenes to win Atalanta and **Medea**'s dismembering of her brother to slow the pursuit of her father Ætes. In a Jamaican tale the hero casts down seeds to distract the animal chasing him.

obstacle flight

odori

JAPANESE DANCE, a generic term referring particularly to those with quick
intricate steps as opposed to the more
solemn *mai*. *Odori* may be pure folk
dance or theatrical performance. Characteristic elements of the Japanese
dance form are the stylized, symbolic
hand gestures, the use of fans (especially
by geishas) to represent a multitude of
objects from moon to bird to sword, and
the conventions differentiating male and
female including gesture and posture.
One of the most significant of these
dances is the silent, gliding *bon-odori*,
the dance of the dead, in honour of the
spirits of the dead.

Odyssey

GREEK EPIC, traditionally ascribed (along
with the *Iliad*) to Homer. The *Odyssey*
follows the fortunes of the eponymous
hero, Odysseus, king of Ithaca, as he
travels home after the Trojan War (it
tells also how Odysseus finally secured
the capture of the city with his marvellous wooden horse, taken inside the city
walls by the Trojans who little knew that
it contained a division of Greek
soldiers). It is the *locus classicus* of the
voyage tale (cf **echtrai** and **imrama**) and
has resounded throughout Western culture. Its themes, preoccupations and
motifs indicate its folkloric origins,
although scholarly debate still rages as to
the manner of its composition.

The epic begins with Odysseus a
captive of the nymph Calypso, while in
Ithaca Odysseus's faithful wife Penelope
is becoming desperate. She has been
besieged by importunate suitors in her
husband's long absence, and has stalled
them all by weaving a tapestry that must
be finished before she will agree to
marry again—each night she stealthily
unravels what she has woven that day.
Now she can delay no longer, and the
gods decree that Odysseus must return
home. The *Odyssey* goes on to recount
the many adventures that have led up to
this point; Odysseus and his followers
leave Troy and are driven off-course to
the island of the **lotus**-eaters where many
of the men sink into forgetful torpor.
Odysseus succeeds in rousing them and
they continue the voyage, only to

encounter the **Cyclops** Polyphemus or
their next stop. Many of the men are
devoured but Odysseus finally puts ou
the monster's single eye and he and his
remaining followers escape strapped to
the undersides of Polyphemus's sheep to
evade his searching hand. Of the
remaining 12 ships, 11 are destroyed by
the **laestrygones** after the men, inflamed
by curiosity, open the bag of winds that
Aeolus presented to Odysseus. The
remnant escape to the island of the
enchantress **Circe**, who transforms the
men into pigs; Odysseus forces her to
restore them. With Circe's help he visit
the underworld and converses with
many of the Greek heroes lost in the
Trojan War. He speaks too with
Tiresias, who instructs him on how to
proceed towards Ithaca. Armed with
this advice, Odysseus successfully
evades the dangers of the **sirens**, lashing
himself to the mast that he might hea
their unbearably sweet singing withou
losing his life, and navigates between
Scylla and Charybdis, the whirlpool and
rock. The crew lands on the island of the
Cattle of the Sun, a herd sacred to
Apollo and, despite Odysseus's stric
tures, his men kill some of the animal
for food. The ship is storm-wrecked a
punishment and Odysseus alone sur
vives, washed ashore on the island o
Calypso where, after eight years o
idyllic luxury, the narrative begins.

After the decision of the gods i
announced, Calypso releases her captiv
lover and Odysseus returns to Ithaca
where he attends Penelope's wedding
feast in disguise. He reveals his identit
by stringing and drawing his own bow, a
feat no other could accomplish. With the
aid of his son Telemachus he slaughter
the suitors, and regains his place a
husband and king.

The tale displays many commor
motifs of folklore. The voyage of adven
ture is itself a tale type found in man
areas, and some scholars have suggested
that the epic is a form of the **Bear's Sor**
cycle. Other folkloric features includ
the supernatural lover and helper, Cal
ypso; the visit to the **underworld**; th
recognition after appearing in disguise a
the wedding feast, and the never-endin
task, the completion of the tapestry.

The central importance of the char

acter of Odysseus for Western culture is difficult to overstate. His qualities of resourcefulness, strength and daring are the bench-mark for the hero of folktale and legend. He has been interpreted in various ways by various cultures, as a shrewd statesman, a romantic wanderer, a resourceful and quick-witted adventurer (cf **master thief**) or a duplicitous and unscrupulous leader, but his ruses and adventures have been uncritically echoed in folktales of adventure throughout Europe especially.

Oedipus

FIGURE OF GREEK MYTHOLOGY, a king of Thebes. He was the son of King Laius of Thebes, but after an oracle predicted that his son would slay him and marry his mother (Laius's wife) Jocasta, Laius had the child abandoned on Mount Cithaeron with a spike driven through his ankles (hence the name Oedipus, which means swell-foot). This was a practical means of immobilizing the body, but is likely to have been motivated also by a desire to keep the ghost from seeking revenge. Oedipus is found by a compassionate shepherd, however, and grows up in the care of King Polybus of Corinth. After visiting Delphi and learning of the oracle's prediction he leaves Corinth, horrified lest he should kill Polybus, whom he believes to be his father. Oedipus journeys towards Thebes, killing almost casually on the way an arrogant old man who has provoked a quarrel with him (Laius). He frees Thebes from the tyranny of the **Sphinx** by answering its riddle, and as his reward is given the throne of Thebes and the hand of the widowed Jocasta, with whom he has four children. This incest enrages the gods, however, who set famine on the land until the truth is eventually revealed; Jocasta commits suicide and Oedipus either blinds himself or is blinded by the outraged servants of Laius. His fate is uncertain; in some versions he continues to rule until his death, in others he exiles himself and is swallowed by the earth at Colonus to become a protective deity, while his brother-in-law Creon rules in Thebes.

This classical legend has influenced Western folklore enormously, and pro-vided the plot for countless playwrights from ancient times to the present day. It has also been seized upon by psychologists, most famously Freud, who coined the term Oedipus complex to denote the attachment of the son to his mother and his unconscious rivalry with the father. The tale is central to the **psychological theory** of folklore scholarship.

Among the folkloric elements embedded in the tale are the battle with the monster (see **dragon-slaying**) that proves the hero's worth; the abandoned baby rescued; the prophecy unknowingly fulfilled; and the death of the monster when the hero has discovered its secret (apparent in an attenuated form in the **Rumpelstiltskin** tale type). It seems likely that the tale, which was known in Homer's time, is the result of floating folkloric motifs attaching to the historical personage of a Theban king, and it is impossible now even to guess to what extent the tale is historical and how much is folk invention.

▷ **abandonment**; **riddles**

ogre

MONSTER OF FOLKLORE, characterized by gullibility and cannibalism. The witch of the **Hansel and Gretel** tale is a type of ogre. Witch-ogres can be either male or female, and can appear in both human and animal forms (in some versions of the tale, the bird which leads the children to the gingerbread house is actually the witch in disguise). The various ruses used by the children to fool the witch are typical of such ogre tales, and typical too is the ogre's death, tricked by greed into stupidity and burned alive.

Oisín

OLD IRISH WARRIOR AND POET, the son of **Finn Mac Cumhal** and the deer-woman Sadb. He was discovered in the forest by Finn's dog **Bran**. After the defeat of the **Fianna** at the Battle of Gabra Oisín was taken to **Tir Nan Og** by the beautiful Niam of the golden hair. There he spent what seemed to him a short time in pleasure, but one day wished to return to Ireland and seek out his old companion Caoilte. Niam warned him not to dismount from his horse on the visit. He returned to find many mortal years had passed and his companion was long dead. He broke the **geis** laid on him by Niam by jumping down to help some men lift a stone (or in some versions when he recognized the great stone trough of the Fianna) and immediately the mortal years caught hold of him, and the horse returned without him to Tir Nan Og.

Oisín eventually met St **Patrick**, to whom he told the stories of the glories of pagan Ireland. He was unimpressed by the sober worship of the new Christian religion and its ungenerous judgemental God, and despite Patrick's best efforts to convert him he died still protesting loudly the glories and virtues of Finn and the ancient ways.

Oisín is often known as Ossian, from the writings of the 18th-century Scottish antiquary and poet James Macpherson, who claimed to have discovered and translated the Gaelic poems of the hero he called Ossian. In fact these so-called translations, although they gained enormous popularity and were very influential among Romantics such as Goethe, were later proved to be largely fabrications, mixing Fenian and Ulster material indiscriminately and incorporating motifs from biblical and Homeric lore. The Ossianic ballads, however, are genuine late Gaelic poems dated from the 11th century onwards, first collected by Sir James MacGregor as *The Book of the Dean of Lismore* (1512–26). They contain the tales recounted by Oisín to Patrick, telling of the mighty deeds and glorious life of Finn and his men, alongside whom Patrick appears as a colourless, small-minded cleric. This contrasts with earlier forms of the legend, in which Christianity and pagan Ireland are more comfortably married as Patrick gains permission from the angels to write down Oisín's wonderful tales.

The tale of Oisín himself is an example of the common motif, the visit to **fairyland** and the supernatural passage of time (cf especially **Herla**, who still obeys the command not to dismount).
▷ **Fenian cycle**

Old Man of the Sea

AN EVIL JINNI, appearing to **Sinbad** in the *Arabian Nights* as a frail old man. Out of compassion Sinbad lifts him on his back to reach some fruit, but once on his victim's back the demon almost strangles him, then forces his unwilling mount to carry him around by means of kicks, punches and his vice-like grip. Despite his best efforts, Sinbad cannot shake the old man off and is driven around the island almost to the point of exhaustion. Finally he rids himself of the jinni by giving him fermented grape juice, and when the old man's grip has relaxed drowsily he throws him off and beats out his brains with a stone.

The motif of the unshakeable rider is found elsewhere in folklore, particularly in the **nightmare**, **incubus** and **hags**. Among the Iroquois and several other Native North American groups an old woman (sometimes called Burr-woman) persuades the hero to take her on his back and then will not dismount.
▷ **jinn**; **Nasnas**

Old Man, Son and Donkey

FABLE OF AESOP'S. An old man is riding his donkey along the road while his son walks alongside. On hearing a passer-by criticize him for letting the boy walk, he exchanges places with him, and when another comments how silly it looks for the young to ride while the old walk he climbs up behind his son and they both travel along for a while astride the donkey. Another passer-by then accuses them of cruelty to the donkey, so they both dismount, and eventually the old man and his son pick up the donkey and carry it themselves, provoking gales of laughter from the townsfolk. Their ill-judged attempts to please others have brought down ridicule upon them.
▷ **Aesop's fables**; **laughter**

olive

EVERGREEN TREE, *Olea europaea* (family Oleaceae), and its oily fruit. It has been central to the lore, economy and cuisine of the Mediterranean region since prehistoric times. In one origin myth, Athena is said to have created it to give to the new Athens as a symbol of peace and prosperity, and the Greeks held it sacred to the goddess. Greek brides carried olive branches to ensure a serene and fertile marriage, and any outstanding Athenian was presented with a crown of olives in recognition of his achievements. In Rome the crown of olive leaves was presented to victorious soldiers and symbolized a peaceful reign.

In Hebrew lore, too, the olive represented peace and reconciliation; the **dove** sent out by Noah from the ark brought back an olive leaf, thus signifying that the waters were receding. Early Christian representations of the Annunciation show Gabriel appearing to **Mary** with an olive branch in his hand, symbol of fertility, peace with God and fulfilment of the divine promise, but in later art it is superseded by the **lily**, emblem of purity.

Olive was widely used as an **amulet** in Italy and elsewhere to keep influences, such as **witches** and **lightning** at bay. A common tradition held that the olive crop was sensitive to virtue; it was said to yield better if tended by young innocent children, and if the farmer was unfaithful to his wife his sin would be reflected in a poor olive crop.

oneiromancy

A FORM OF DIVINATION, the interpretation of **dreams**. The practice is found throughout the world, with varying degrees of complexity, ranging from direct instruction or warning to complex allegorical symbolism or psychoanalytic interpretation. The language of dream-divination is said by many scholars to draw heavily on folkloric motifs and themes; since folklore is perceived as a product of the collective unconscious, it therefore relates closely to dreams, the product of the individual unconscious.

oni

DEMONS OR OGRES OF JAPANESE FOLK-LORE. They are generally represented with large heads, horns and fearsome teeth, but they are adept at **shape-shifting** and may appear as frail old women or beggars. They are ceremonially ejected from the house during the **New Year** celebrations. A common theme of Japanese tales and art is the oni who becomes a devout Buddhist, submitting to the monks who saw off his horns.

onion

PUNGENT VEGETABLE, *Allium cepa* of the family Liliaceae. The onion is thought to be one of the first plants to be cultivated by humans, and it has been highly esteemed for culinary and medicinal purposes ever since. Its bulb was a symbol of the cosmos in ancient Egypt, and the English name onion probably derives from Latin *unionis*, union, a whole and perfect entity. The strong flavour of the onion and the potency of its sulphurous oil, which brings tears to the eyes and stings the skin, have recommended it as a powerful medicine, and it has been used against colds, bites, warts, earache and fever. It is widely credited with the power of drawing sickness and malodorous influences into itself; the cut edge may be applied to draw infection from a wound or a string of onions may be hung in the house to absorb any unhealthy influences (these, of course, should never be eaten). Even carrying an onion as a **charm** against disease is considered effective in many areas. To dream of onions is widely considered a lucky omen.
▷ **garlic**

onyx

A FORM OF MINERAL AGATE, characterized by irregular and attractive bands of colour, found mainly in India and South America. It has a mixed reputation in folklore; in India it is said to calm lust but elsewhere it is the symbol of love. Worn as a **charm** it was said to induce contentment and reduce pain.

Onyx frequently appears in descriptions of great wealth; **Prester John** claimed to have an onyx-paved courtyard, and the wealthy abbey of St Albans in England was said to possess an onyx larger than a human hand. Onyx was one of the twelve stones embedded in the breastplate of the ancient Hebrew high priest (Exodus 28:20, 39:13).

opal

SILICA MINERAL, a gemstone characterized by the delicate colours that appear within it as it is turned under light. It appears in a variety of colours, most commonly a milky, translucent white; the most precious form is the black opal found almost exclusively in Australia. It was especially esteemed by the Romans, who ranked it second only to the **emerald**. In medieval Europe the opal was generally considered lucky, and the Holy Roman Emperors wore an opal in their crown as a symbol of honour. It was believed to strengthen weak eyes but also had the power to render the wearer invisible, hence its popularity among thieves. Its translucency was believed to reveal danger; it was said to cloud in the presence of poison or impurity (because opals are porous, some do indeed appear to change appearance in the presence of water).

After Sir Walter Scott wrote of an ominous opal in his popular novel *Anne of Geierstein*, opals fell out of favour in Britain and were popularly regarded as unlucky.

Open Sesame

MAGIC FORMULA OF OPENING, used most famously in the tale of **Ali Baba** in the *Arabian Nights* to open the robbers' cave. This is the best-known form of a common folklore motif, the magic token that opens a treasure cave. In many European tales the object is a stick, in some a flower, and some scholars have speculated that these formulae sprang from a tradition investing plants with magic properties; here the name of the herb itself is sufficient.

opossum

NEW WORLD MARSUPIALS, of the family Didelphidae, an omnivorous and often fiercely carnivorous mammal. There is a common folk belief that the creature gives birth through its nose; this probably arose from the mother's habit of putting her head into her pouch to clean it in preparation for the babies. When caught the opossum will often feign death, watching for an opportunity to escape. This has given rise to the common expression 'to play possum', meaning to feign ignorance or incomprehension. Many Native American folktales purport to explain Opossum's bald tail. In one version he attempts to brown his white tail in the fire on the advice of Racoon and singes off the fur, and in another tale he evades a **ghost** but loses the fur from his tail as it slips through the ghostly hands. The craftiness of Opossum is legendary; one tale tells how Opossum was caught by an irate farmer after he had stolen the family's last chicken and was himself placed in the oven for dinner, but survived, ate the potatoes and gravy in the pan with him and slipped out of the oven door as soon as it was opened. Around the Amazon Opossum is a popular **trickster** figure.

oral-formulaic theory

A THEORY OF FOLKLORE STUDY, adopted by Albert Lord in *The Singer of Tales* (1960) from his studies in Slavonic epics. He postulated that epics and tales as far back as Homer's *Odyssey* and *Iliad* are created uniquely by the performing **bard**, drawing from a conventional stock of images, expressions and epithets— the 'wine-dark sea' or more recently 'Once upon a time . . .'. This approach was later applied more widely to folklore. It is characterised by an interest in the individual narrator and his belief and value systems, rather than those of the cultural group en masse.

orange

SMALL TREE AND ITS ROUND JUICY FRUIT, genus *Citrus* (family Rutaceae). It is native to south-east Asia but spread to the Mediterranean areas as trade-routes expanded. It is widely regarded as a symbol of chastity and faithfulness, hence the extensive use of orange blossom in marriage celebrations (it is important, however, to dispose of any blossom used for the wedding before a month has passed or it will bring barrenness). Because the orange tree is perpetually green and bears both blossom and fruit throughout the year, it is the epitome of constancy and fecundity.

The sweet, sharp aroma of the orange was much in favour as an air-freshener in early societies, especially when stuck with cloves.

ordeal

MEANS OF ESTABLISHING INNOCENCE OR GUILT, an appeal to divine or supernatural intervention to demonstrate judgement. Trial by ordeal has been a historical practice in many cultures. **Witches** in medieval Europe (and even later) were tried by ordeal by water; if they floated they were proved guilty and executed, if drowned they were lamentably innocent. Another popular form is ordeal by fire or heat, in which the suspect must walk over hot coals, carry a heated object a certain distance, or pluck an object out of boiling water. If the gods grant him the ability to endure such tasks, he is proved innocent. An allied form is the ordeal by poison, in which the accused, voluntarily or under compulsion, swallows a poisonous substance. If he survives, his innocence is established. In Calabar in Africa a certain poisonous **bean** (*Physostigma venenosum*) is taken. Where two people contest an issue, both may agree to trial by 'wager law'; both swallow half of the bean and the survivor wins the dispute. A widespread form of ordeal is trial by combat, in which the accused and the accuser, or two champions, battle to decide the judgement. This is based on the premise underlying much ancient heroic lore, that right will triumph even against the odds with the aid of the divine powers. Trial by combat was enshrined in English lore until the early 19th century.

▷ **crocodile**

Orion

THE GREAT HUNTER, constellation visible in both northern and southern hemispheres suggesting the shape of a man. In primitive Egyptian lore this was the cannibalistic hunter Sahu, later the god Osiris making his nightly boat trip back across the skies to where he would rise again as the sun next morning. In Greek mythology Orion was accompanied by his dogs, the constellations Sirius and Procyon, and the hare Lepus lay at his feet. In Hebrew lore he was the giant Gibbor, also known as Nimrod, whose ungodliness earned him perpetual imprisonment in the sky. Hindus saw in the constellation the shape of a stag, and in the famous three stars of Orion's belt an arrow which pinned it to the sky. Later Greek legends developed to explain Orion's position in the skies; he had been bitten by a **scorpion** sent by the gods to punish him for his bragging, and then in pity the gods had placed both him and the scorpion in the skies, but far apart, so that they would never meet again, or Orion is the lover endlessly

chasing one of the sisters of the **Pleiades**, who endlessly flees him.

▷ **astrology**; **stars**

Orlando see Roland

Orpheus

LEGENDARY GREEK BARD, the son of Apollo by the Muse Calliope. He played his father's lyre with such skill that he was able to entrance animals and even inanimate objects. As a companion of **Jason**, he charmed the beached *Argos* back into the sea, stilled the Clashing Rocks and overcame the sirens with his music. When his nymph bride Eurydice was killed by a snake bite, Orpheus, overcome with grief, descended to the underworld to seek her. His lyre playing charmed Charon, who ferried him across the Styx, and calmed the ferocious dog Cerberus, and so he came to Hades, who was so moved by his grief and the beauty of his music that he agreed to let Eurydice return with him. However Orpheus was charged not to look at his wife until they had both left Hades. As they approached the sunlight Orpheus, unable to contain his joy, turned back to look at Eurydice, only to see her ghost forlornly retreating from him.

According to some versions of the legend, Orpheus killed himself in grief after this. More commonly however he draws on himself the wrath of Dionysus and Aphrodite by denying wine and hetrosexual love, and is killed by a troop of incensed female Bacchic worshippers, who tear him apart, their howls drowning out his enchanting music.

▷ **ghost**; **looking taboo**

Ossian see Oisín

ostrich

LARGEST EXTANT BIRD, *Struthio camelus*, with powerful legs capable of carrying it at up to 65 km/40 mi per hour, but no power of flight. Much folklore has accrued around this odd-looking bird, most famously the popular belief that it buries its head in the sand when afraid; this probably developed from the observation of ostriches lying flat on the ground with necks outstretched to avoid detection and was enthusiastically promulgated by Pliny. Pliny also maintained that the ostrich is capable of digesting anything, and this belief is echoed in heraldry where the ostrich is frequently portrayed holding an inedible object such as a key or horseshoe in its beak.

Ostriches lay their eggs in a communal nest dug in sand or soft ground; Hebrew lore held that it was a careless parent (Job 39:14–16) but Greek writers such as Aelian considered the bird a dutiful model. Medieval bestiaries reported that the eggs were hatched by the warmth of the sun; in fact both males and females take turns in hatching out the chicks.

In many areas of Africa the ostrich is a totemic animal, celebrated and venerated by mimetic dances. Its swaying motion is said to represent the twin life-giving principles of light and water.

otherworld

REALMS BEYOND THIS NATURAL ONE, often accessible to the living by luck or dangerous quest. Religious and folkloric thought typically incorporates a concept of at least one otherworld, inhabited by spirits or supernatural beings, yet available to mortals either as a final destination after death or through hidden doorways in the everyday world.

In most European traditions three otherworlds are generally recognized; the upperworld for blessed souls, the **underworld** for the damned, and **fairyland**, a pagan world populated by supernatural beings. The Greeks had Elysium, the pleasant fields in the west (or later in the underworld), for which the souls of the blessed were destined, and Tartarus, a place of torment for the damned, although in general the realm of the dead was a neutral underworld governed by Hades, who is in no way equivalent to the **Devil**. The souls of the dead were ferried across the river Styx by the ghostly Charon, and were permitted to enter by the ferocious guard dog Cerberus. Mortals could not enter, unless like **Heracles** and **Orpheus** they could overcome the guardians by strength or skill. The motif of the ferryman is common in tales of the underworld, for example it occurs in Mesopotamian myth. Another neutral underworld for the spirits of those dead

of old age or disease was Hel, or Niflhel (the hollow place), the mine worlds of Scandinavian mythology situated below the roots of the world-tree **Yggdrasil**. It was ruled by the goddess Hel and, like Hades too, was guarded by the fierce dog Garm. The destination of the Norse warrior hero however was **Valhalla**.

The **Valkyries**, who accompanied these warriors and waited on them at table dressed in becoming white dresses, are paralleled in many mythologies around the world. In early Iranian mythology, the righteous soul is escorted upwards, through the realms of the stars, sun and moon to paradise by its *daēnā*, a spiritual force in the shape of a beautiful virgin. Indian lore has similar beautiful virgins who accompany the ascending soul, and **Jason** and the Argonauts stopped off in Lemnos and enjoyed the companionship of the husbandless women of the island.

In Celtic mythology the souls of the dead went to Tech Duinn, below Bull Island, under the lordship of Donn, god of the dead. The blessed few however would achieve the Irish equivalent of Elysium, the Land of the Young, or the Delightful Plain, more closely allied to fairyland than the Christian vision of Heaven. Those who successfully made the voyage to this land of heroes enjoyed perpetual feasting, licentiousness and youth, once again met by beautiful and solicitous maidens, and if they returned home they would find many years had passed in the space of what had seemed only a day. The great Irish voyage tales, dating from the eighth century, tell tales of these visionary heroes, and it is interesting to note how the sensual pagan havens of the early tales give way to the more spiritual Christian paradise as reached by St **Brendan the Navigator** in *The Voyage of Brandon*.

In addition to such mythical otherworlds, European folktales had frequent recourse to unspecified otherworlds in which supernatural beings were encountered and magical deeds performed. Such worlds were often reached by means of a magical opening; Jack ascended to a land of ogres and magical geese by means of his marvellous beanstalk, Grimm's young hero rescues beautiful princesses from many-headed dragons at the foot of a deep well, Beauty's father finds the enchanted castle of the Beast when he is caught up in a storm. A popular means of bridging the gap between this world and the other is the **rainbow**.

Some Native American groups believe in a dual afterworld, an abode for the blessed and a less salubrious one for the damned. As in European lore, the happy land is generally associated with an island or situated in the sky, and the world of sadness is beneath the sea. Central Inuits for example tell of a delightful upperworld, Qudlivun, and an underworld of pain, Adlivun. As Christianity developed a multiple system, including the realm of temporary discomfort, Purgatory, so other cultures have multiple otherworlds; one Polynesian tribe has a specific destination for the souls of women who die in childbirth, for example. The concept of reward and punishment is rare outwith Indo-European, and especially Christian, tradition, however. The destination of a soul is more usually dependent on the efforts of the living to provide adequate sacrifices and the success of the soul in overcoming the various obstacles which it faces on its journey. The ruler of the underworld in Native American mythology is usually the **culture hero** himself, and there are tales of mortals, Orpheus-like, visiting such regions to find the dead engaged in normal social activities.
▷ **Avalon**; **food taboo**; **Jack and the Beanstalk**; **sky people**

overhearing

DEVICE OF FOLKTALES, a common motif found in tales throughout the world. The unseen hero overhears a conversation that provides him with information vital for his safety or the fulfilment of his **task** or quest. In the accepted definition of the motif the conversation is between non-human beings, generally **giants**, **ogres**, or, most commonly, animals or birds. So **Faithful John** discovers the plot against the princess and the means of thwarting it from three ravens, and the servant of the queen discovers the name of **Rumpelstiltskin** from the dwarf's gloating monologue.

A closely related motif is the understanding of animal and bird languages, sometimes assumed in the tale but often explained by a further mechanism.

overlooking

MAGICAL PRACTICE, the act of casting the **evil eye**.

ovinnik

HOUSEHOLD SPIRIT OF RUSSIA, the spirit of the drying kiln. If displeased (for example, if the family fire the kiln on a feast-day or if they fail to offer suitable thanks for his continued help) he may burn down the kiln. To be sure of his goodwill, the family may offer the blood of a sacrificed **cock** around the kiln.
▷ **domovik**

owl

PREDATORY BIRD OF THE NIGHT, any

owl

member of the order Strigigormes. In classical Greece it was the emblem of Athena and hence a symbol of wisdom (Athens was renowned for its profusion of owls). In Rome, however, the hoot of an owl was known as an omen of death, appearing at the deathbeds of several emperors, and a prophetic bird. Among the Pimas of North America owls were thought to embody the spirits of the dead. In Celtic lore, too, the owl was a bird of the underworld, the 'corpse bird'. In Asia and the Middle East the nocturnal visits of the owl are feared as he can carry off souls, although in some areas of Japan the owl is regarded as beneficent. It association with darkness led inevitably in medieval Europe to identification with the **Devil**.

Because of its night vision, the owl is venerated by several Native American groups and in India owl's eyeballs are a delicacy with the power to make one see in the dark. Owl feathers are a **charm** to induce sleep, and in some cultures bring about an easy delivery in childbirth.

A pious legend tells how Christ visited a baker's shop and asked for a cake; the parsimonious baker's daughter reduced the size of the dough by half and was transformed into an owl as punishment for her meanness.
▷ **Big Owl**

OX

VALUABLE DRAFT ANIMAL, *Bostaurus*, traditionally used in sacrificial offerings in many cultures, especially ancient Greece and Rome. In Iran, Geush Urvan is the cosmic ox from whose blood emerged all living things. In folktales the ox often functions as a truth-telling or oracular beast, often a transformed human being who may be disenchanted; a Spanish tale tells of two sisters transformed into oxen by a jealous **witch**.

In Christian folklore the ox is especially blessed as Jesus was born in its stall; it was said to have knelt in adoration before the Christ-child, and to be blessed with the power of speech every Christmas Eve in memory of this event.

The ox horn is a valuable **charm** against the **evil eye** in Italy.
▷ **Babe**

Pacific folklore

MELANESIA, MICRONESIA AND POLYNESIA are considered to be Pacific islands, but not the continent of Australia, the archipelagos related to Indonesia or Japan, nor the Philippines. Although the area includes more than 10000 islands, and the Pacific itself covers nearly a third of the earth's surface, its land area is tiny. The largest island by far is New Guinea (second largest island in the world after Greenland), and New Zealand, a Polynesian island, is the next biggest: the vast majority are very small indeed but each has its own ecosystem and cultural variation. Although the Pacific islands have now been Westernized to a large extent, some rural or isolated communities still preserve the traditional ways of life.

▷ **Melanesian folklore**; **Micronesian folklore**; **Polynesian folklore**

pajanvaki

SPIRITS OF FINNISH LORE, the guardians and elemental forces of metals.

Palm Sunday

CHRISTIAN HOLY DAY, the Sunday before **Easter**, which marks the beginning of Holy Week. It commemorates Christ's triumphal entry into Jerusalem, riding on a donkey, when the citizens were said to have laid palm branches before him to carpet his way. The use of palm leaves is an ancient tradition in sacred processional ceremonies. In medieval Europe Palm Sunday was observed by a solemn rite of blessing the palm branches (often **yew** in northern areas) which were then distributed among the congregation. The blessed branches were considered potent as **charms** and were often hung in stables and houses to guard against evil influences or on graves to protect the spirits of the dead and negate any evil intent on their part. In other areas the palms would be burned and the **ashes** sown with the crops to ensure a good harvest.

Panchatantra

INDIAN FABLE COLLECTION, the 'Five Chapters' of wisdom, known in Britain as the *Fables of Bidpai*. The original *Panchatantra*, written in Sanskrit between 100BC and 500AD, has been lost, and later translations into Persian, Arabic, Greek and especially the Hebrew translation by Rabbi Joel have been the source for all European versions. The earliest surviving edition of the tales appears to be the Kashmiri version, the *Tantrakhyayika*. The 'five chapters' of the title are framework stories in each of which a series of animal fables is related. Each part has its own broad theme; the means of dividing allies, of gaining allies, war and peace, the loss of riches and the consequences of over-hasty behaviour.

The text was originally a mixture of prose and verse, with aphoristic morals much in the vein of **Aesop's fables**. The stories tend to emphasize the virtues of expediency and shrewdness rather than altruism, using the common motif of the trickster using his wiles to overcome the odds. One tale tells how a community of **hares** agreed to sacrifice one of its number each day to a **lion** to prevent the beast from massacring them all; one day the victim arrives late and tells the lion that he has been delayed by another lion, who also wanted to eat him. The lion is furious at the thought of a rival, and when he is shown his own reflection in a well he attacks his supposed enemy and leaps to his death. A **crow** revenges himself on the snake which habitually steals its eggs by stealing a precious necklace from the palace and concealing it in the snake's lair. When the king's men find it there they kill the snake. Here, as in many cases, intelligence rather than morality is the lesson. Other tales demonstrate the need for efficient and unified government; a flock of birds is trapped in a net, and at first each bird struggles to free itself, but succeeds only in entangling itself further. Their leader encourages them to pull together and fly up, net and all, and their cords are later cut by an obliging **mouse**.

The overall philosophy of the work is practical, giving a balanced, optimistic yet realistic approach to life. Death is inevitable, but the value of life is affirmed, and the comforts of the flesh acknowledged. Ideals are noble, but in practical life intelligence is more valuable. Fate is powerful, but the human will is strong. The style is lively and idiomatic, influenced more by the wisdom of the folk and the traditions of oral narrative than courtly classical modes.

pansy

SPECIES OF VIOLET, most commonly the wild pansy (*Viola tricolor*, of the family Violaceae) variously known as johnny-jump-up, heartsease, love-in-idleness and St **Valentine**'s flower. In Scottish and German folklore it is known as Stepmother; the largest central petal is the stepmother, flanked by her two richly coloured daughters, while the two paler petals above them are her step-daughters. In a Romanian transformation tale the pansy was once a beautiful servant in the royal court, transformed by the jealous queen when her son the prince fell in love with her. The queen had wanted to make her into something ugly such as a **toad**, but the girl's character was so lovely that the queen could do no worse than the pansy.

The pansy is widely used in **love magic**; Puck in *A Midsummer Night's Dream* squeezes the juice of the plant onto **Titania**'s eyes to make her fall in love with the first creature she sets eyes on, and it is widely believed that picking a pansy still wet with dew will bring about the death of the beloved.

Medicinally, the pansy is used especially for chest complaints, asthma and epilepsy.

panther

BIG CAT, either the **leopard** or the puma. In medieval bestiaries the panther was credited with giving off a sweet scent that attracted all animals but repulsed the **dragon** (symbol of the **Devil**); it was hence associated with Christ. In later lore the dangerous, seductive nature of this attraction was emphasized, and it became a symbol of fatal female beauty and hypocritical flattery.

Panther is an important character in the tales of many Native Americans; he is a sacred animal among the Cherokee and Shawnee.

pantomime

THEATRICAL FORM, derived from the traditions of the Italian Commedia dell' Arte with its stock characters (the dumb lovers Harlequin and Columbine, the clown Pantalone and the wily servant figure). Its popularity in Britain as a Christmas entertainment began in the 17th century, and it is now generally based on popular European folk or nursery tales such as Snow White, **Cinderella**, **Aladdin** or **Jack and the Beanstalk**. Its anarchic buffoonery echoes many ancient folk traditions of drama and clowning but the form now bears little resemblance to traditional folk entertainment.

Paradise

A BLESSED OTHERWORLD, a place of ease and delight. The word is thought to derive from a Persian root meaning walled gardens, and in Judaeo-Christian tradition it refers to the Garden of Eden, where Adam and Eve enjoyed closeness with God and a harmonious relationship with nature; Islam too portrays paradise as a lush garden of delights. Eden was said to be located somewhere on earth, 'in the east', and many paradises are reported in travellers' tales of far-off places. In later Christian lore especially, paradise is conceived of as a heavenly afterworld, free from suffering, where closeness with God will be restored, and in Buddhism paradise (Nirvana) is not a place at all but a spiritual state of merging with the absolute principle, the loss of self-identity. In Hindu lore paradise is a state of union with the divine.

parsley

GREEN HERB, *Petroselinum crispum* or *P. sativum* of the family Apiaceae, used particularly as a garnish and flavouring in cooking. It was sacred to the dead in ancient Greece and Rome and was used to deck graves, hence the saying 'to have need of nothing but a little parsley', meaning to be dead and past all human help. In medieval Europe anyone who saw the **Wild Hunt** might protect himself from insanity or death by requesting a sprig of parsley from the leader of the hunt.

A widespread European belief holds that babies are found in parsley beds; this may be connected with parsley as a symbol of sexual licence, the plant carpeting Calypso's luxurious island in the *Odyssey*.

Parsley has been used medicinally in a variety of ways—to purify the blood, treat kidney infections, remove excess hair and impart a sound mind and memory. It counters strong or harmful influences; in Rome it was said to preserve sobriety, thrown into a dirty fish-pond it cleansed the water, and it is widely said to remove the smell of garlic from one's breath.

Passover

MAJOR JEWISH FESTIVAL, celebrating the 'passing over' of the angel of death, who left the homes of the Israelites untouched while slaying the first-born son of all Egyptian families on the eve of the Exodus. The sign that marked them to be spared was the blood of the sacrificial lamb, smeared on the door-posts in the direction of God (this reflects the enduring folk belief in the efficacy of blood to restore life).

The central ceremony of the feast is the *seder*, a ritual family meal accompanied by readings from the scriptures. Special foods are prepared, eg *matzah* (unleavened bread) recalling the haste with which the Israelites left Egypt and *haroseth*, a sweet mixture of fruit and nuts symbolizing the mortar used in building by the enslaved Hebrews. A cup of wine is raised for Elijah, who it is believed will appear one Passover to herald Israel's final deliverance and the door is left open for him.

Patrick, St (c.389–c.461)

PATRON SAINT OF IRELAND, a potent figure of Irish folklore. His exact birth-place is unclear; it is thought to have been somewhere between the mouths of the Severn and the Clyde, but some claim that he was born in Boulogne-sur-Mer or at Kilpatrick, near Dumbarton. His father Calpurnius was a Romano-British official and deacon and his grandfather was a Christian priest. Patrick was carried off to slavery in Ireland by a raiding party when only 16. Sold to a chief of Antrim named Milchu, Patrick escaped after six years and persuaded the crew of a ship to take him with them to the Continent. He began his clerical training and was consecrated as a bishop, and in 432 (the date is disputed) was appointed successor to Palladius as missionary bishop of Ireland by Pope Celestine I.

On his return to Ireland Patrick travelled throughout the island, evangelizing tirelessly and organizing an established church and monasteries. He had much success in converting Irish chiefs, including his old master Milchu, and secured the attention of the Irish king Laoghaire at Tara, Co. Meath, by miraculously overcoming the Druids. In about 454 he established his episcopal seat at Armagh, which became the centre for Christianity in Ireland.

In folklore Patrick is famous for expelling snakes from Ireland; the occasional sea-serpents left in the loughs are said to be demonic beings who defied his command. He is said to have explained the doctrine of the Trinity by reference to a **shamrock**, and this has become his emblem and that of Ireland. In the Old Irish tales he listens to **Oisín**'s tales of heroic pagan Ireland and secures permission from the angels to write them down, although in later versions he is portrayed as a cranky, desiccated cleric in contrast to the soaring heroic vision of pagan Ireland evoked by Oisín. He is often credited with single-handedly converting Ireland, but while his contribution was outstanding, this work took many more years than these legends allow. Irish immigration to America propagated his cult there and New York's main cathedral is dedicated to him. His feast-day is 17 March.

Paul Bunyan

A LUMBERJACK OF SUPERHUMAN SIZE AND

STRENGTH, from American folklore. Not only could he break up log-jams with spectacular ease, he is also attributed with creating lakes, rivers and even the Black Hills of Dakota and the Grand Canyon. Everything about him typifies the pioneering hero of the **tall tale**, his enormous physical stature, matched by a capacity for manual labour, phenomenal strength and an appetite to match. His stove at the lumber camp takes up an acre, and his griddle is greased by men skating across it with sides of bacon strapped to their feet.

Although stories about Paul and his companions, **Babe** the Blue Ox and Johnny Inkslinger, began to circulate in print in the early 20th century, with the first stories by James MacGillivray in the Detroit News Tribune, July 1910, he seems to have been a legend among the lumberjack fraternity well before this. His increasing literary popularity brought about a shift from the specialist world of lumbering to a more general public, and he became a national hero.

pea

EDIBLE SEED, any of a huge number of varieties of the family Leguminosae, most commonly that of the common garden pea *Pisum sativum*. It is said in European lore to act in love divination in much the same way as the hazelnut; if two peas are placed together on the coals their behaviour foretells the future of the couple—if they burn together brightly and strongly a long and happy marriage is forecast, but if one springs away the one who placed it will be unfaithful.

To find nine peas in a pod is an omen of good fortune. Many cultures advise planting peas while the **moon** is waning, so that they will grow to fruition as the moon is on the wax.

In a tale collected by Grimm, the **Princess on the Pea**, a princess is recognized and acknowledged when she is unable to sleep on a pile of mattresses below which is hidden a pea; only a true princess demonstrates such sensitivity.

peach

TREE AND ITS FRUIT, *Prunus persica*, of the rose family (Rosaceae). The peach is especially significant in China, where it functions as a symbol of immortality, a long and happy life, fertility and female sexuality. Brides carry peach-blossom, and the hero **Momotaro** was said to be born from a giant peach. Because of this positive force, peach branches, blossoms and fruits are often used as **charms** to keep at bay demonic influences. The world **tree** of Chinese lore was a peach, and any soul who ate of its fruit won 3 000 years of renewed youth.

In many areas of the world peach wood is highly regarded as a divining rod for **dowsing**. An infusion of peach wood or leaves is said to be good for an upset stomach and heart or chest pains.
▷ **Momotaro**

peacock

MALE PEAFOWL, of the family Phasianidae (order Galliformes) known for its dazzling iridescent tail that lifts into a splendid display to attract females. It has been associated with royalty and divinity since ancient times; in Roman times especially it was associated with Juno, consort of Jupiter. In Greek mythology Hera was said to have taken the hundred

peacock

eyes of the giant Argos, slain by Hermes, and placed them in the tail of the peacock. In Christian lore these 'eyes' were said to represent all-seeing Mother Church. It was also held by Christians to be a symbol of immortality, following St Augustine's curious assertion that peacock flesh does not decay. In Islamic lore the peacock stood guard at the gates of **Paradise** but carried Satan into the garden with it after consuming him. In China the bird was a symbol of the great Ming dynasty, equated with divinity, rank, power and beauty.

Although the peacock's beauty is extraordinary, it is believed to be matched in many cultures, particularly in recent times, by its vanity and bad temper. Its screech is said to be an omen of evil in European lore, and in Hindu lore it is said to have the features of an angel but the voice of a devil and feet so ugly that the bird screams every time it catches sight of them.

Peacock feathers are occasionally used medicinally, as a fan to dispel harmful influences and the odour of sickness, or, in the Punjab, smoked to cure snakebites. According to the *Kama Sutra*, a man wishing to make himself irresistible to women has only to plate a peacock's bone with gold and strap it to his right hand.

pearl

GEM STONE, formed by the secretion of nacre (mother-of-pearl) by molluscs. Many fanciful stories have been ascribed to this lustrous concretion: it is often said to be a raindrop swallowed by an oyster, or the distillation of a teardrop. In Hindu folk belief it was said to be found in the internal organs of the **elephant**, and in ancient Chinese folk belief pearls were said to be spat out by **dragons**. It may be this association with the water-serpent that led to the widespread use in the Orient of the pearl as a **charm** against fire.

The lustre of the pearl is often said to dim if the gem is worn continually; in some tales it functions as a **life token**, dimming as the fortunes of its owner ebb, and becoming altogether clouded in death.

Powdered pearl was a much sought-after ingredient in love potions and medicines of many civilizations. It was said to be an antidote for poison and a cure for insanity, epilepsy and hysteria. A solution made from dissolving the pearl in lemon juice was a common means of administering the elixir.

Pearls should never be worn at a wedding because of their resemblance to tear drops; they will bring unhappiness by association.

Pecos Bill

AMERICAN COWBOY HERO, created by the 19th-century journalist Edward O'Reilly. He personified the larger-than-life heroism beloved of the Western pioneers in the tradition of the true folkloric heroes such as **John Henry**, although he himself has little if any foundation in oral lore. He was weaned on moonshine and brought up by coyotes (see **animal nurse**) after being lost by his parents near the Pecos River, Texas. He rode bareback on a mountain lion, and used his enormous lasso rope to pluck buzzards from the air and on one occasion to halt a train. He defeated every other cowboy who dared to take him on, and taught his oaths and songs, which still survive today, to those who would listen. He is said to have died after

Pecos Bill

consuming a meal of barbed wire washed down with nitro-glycerine. His legend was adapted by pioneers in Australia and the Argentine.

Peeping Tom see Godiva, Lady

pelican

WATER BIRD, species *Pelecanus*, characterized by its capacious elastic throat pouch. In classical lore it is stigmatized as a greedy and treacherous bird, and in Hebrew lore it is an emblem of desolation, but in medieval Europe it became known as a model of maternal devotion; the female pelican was said to kill her young, either by smothering them overmuch or by knocking them with her wings, but after mourning them for three days she restores them to life with blood drawn from her own breast. This was used as an emblem of resurrection, and Dante likened Christ to 'our pelican'.

penates

HOUSEHOLD SPIRITS OF ROMAN LORE, originally the gods of the storeroom (*di penates*). Their images, often made of wax or ivory, were worshipped at special shrines in the house, with offerings made at each meal and a fire kept burning in their honour. They are clearly connected with the **lares**, the spirits of the dead, and the two words are sometimes used interchangeably.

The *penates publici*, the protectors of the Roman state, said to have journeyed with Aeneas after the fall of Troy, were worshipped in a state cult that did much to foster national unity and pride.

pennyroyal see mint

peony

FLOWERING PLANT, genus *Paeonia* (family Paeoniaceae), bearing distinctively large and showy blooms. Its name is said to derive from Paeon, the divine physician who treated the gods for wounds sustained during the Trojan War. In Chinese lore it embodies the male yang principle (unusually among flowers) and is closely associated with imperial power, light, happiness and spring. Its seeds were used in some areas as a **charm** against all manner of night demons.

pepper

PLANT OF THE NIGHTSHADE FAMILY (Solanaceae), genus *Capsicum*, generally bearing pungent, often hot-tasting, fruits. To secure a successful crop, many societies believe that peppers should be planted either by a red-head or by anyone in a suitably fiery and irascible mood. Whole chilli peppers are widely said to be good for colds and aches. Because of their fiery taste, peppers are generally held to be powerful aphrodisiacs.

pepper

PUNGENT SPICE, made from the crushed berries of the pepper plant (genus *Piper*). The spice spread from India across the world by the early trade routes; Rome paid part of its ransom in the valuable spice. In medieval Europe it was considered a cure-all, applied to all manner of complaints from toothache to short-sightedness to the plague. Used in large quantities, it is said to have an aphrodisiac effect.

Perceval

ARTHURIAN KNIGHT, the guileless fool who plays the part of the **Grail** hero in early versions of the legend. He is introduced in Chrétien de Troyes's *Perceval*, or *Le Conte del Graal* (c.1175) as an innocent simpleton, raised in the forests of North Wales entirely ignorant of the chivalric code and courtly courtesies. He makes many gaffes on being introduced to the world of **Arthur**'s court, but is trained as a chivalric knight and goes on the quest for the Holy Grail. He reaches the castle of the **Fisher King** but, wary of asking questions after his recent lessons in courtesy, refrains from speaking the key question that would heal Amfortas and win him the Grail. Wolfram von Eschenbach developed the legend in his 13th-century epic poem *Parzival*, emphasizing Perceval's spiritual development and his qualities as a Christian knight, and establishing him as the Grail hero.

In later Arthurian cycles Perceval is displaced by the pure Sir **Galahad**, although he retains a key role in the quest.

Perceval appears to derive from the

Welsh hero Peredur (d.580) and the tales associated with Pryderi in the *Mabinogion*. He combines strands from ancient French, Irish and Welsh lore, and remains one of the most enigmatic yet charming figures of Arthurian lore.

peri

BEAUTIFUL SUPERNATURAL FEMALES OF ISLAMIC LORE, originally evil demons of Persian mythology who were responsible for **eclipses**, droughts and crop failures. They later metamorphosed into graceful, dainty beings entrusted with the divine task of directing human souls to **Paradise**, said to be fathered by fallen spirits or engendered by fire.

periwinkle

TRAILING PLANT, genus *Vinca*, of the dogbane family (Apocynaceae), generally having blue or white flowers. Its name may derive from Russian *pervi*, 'first', one of the first plants of spring. It was highly valued by medieval herbalists as a cure for demonic possession, poison, fear and envy. Its picking, however, was carefully prescribed; it should be picked on certain nights of the lunar cycle, and always by a pure-minded individual. This ensured the flower's peculiar potency against all manner of evil influence.

Carried as a **charm** the periwinkle ensured prosperity and happiness, and if concealed in the conjugal meal by the wife it ensured the continued affections of her husband. One of its most common uses, perhaps because of its associations with spring and innocence, is on the graves of young children, especially in Italy. To remove a periwinkle from a grave angers the dead spirit, and the offender may find himself haunted by the wronged spirit.

Perseus

GREEK DRAGONSLAYER, the son of Zeus and Danaë. His maternal grandfather, King Acrisius of Argos, warned by an oracle that his daughter's child would kill him, imprisoned Danaë in a tower but Zeus impregnated her in the form of a shower of gold; after Perseus was born Acrisius set both mother and child adrift in a wooden chest but they were taken in by Dictys after being washed up on the shore of Seriphos. His brother Polydectres later fell in love with Danaë, but was unable to pursue his suit as forcefully as he wished because of Perseus who was by now a formidable warrior. Seizing upon a rash boast by the youth he sent him off on the impossible **task** of securing the head of the **Gorgon**.

Perseus, however, took advice from the gods and succeeded in his quest with the aid of various **magic objects**—a cap of **invisibility**, (the helmet of Hades), shoes of swiftness and a special pouch in which to keep the severed head.

Returning to Seriphos on his winged shoes he asked shelter of **Atlas**, who refused, and was thereupon turned into stone by the Gorgon's head. He also saw Andromeda in chains, about to be sacrificed to a **sea-serpent**, rescued her by using the head once more to transfix the monster into stone, and won her hand. At their wedding feast he brought out the head a third time, turning to stone a disgruntled suitor and all the guests.

Back in Seriphos, Danaë was under increasing and unwelcome pressure from Polydectres. Perseus brought out the head for the last time, turning Polydectres and his court to stone, then established the kindly Dictys as king. He presented the Gorgon's head to Athene in gratitude for her help (she placed it on her shield, or *aegis*) and returned to Argos with his mother, accidentally killing his grandfather with a discus at the funeral games.

The tale of Perseus, although properly belonging to the realm of myth, is the *locus classicus* of many widespread folkloric myths. The imprisonment of the princess by the envious or fearful father (the princess is usually successfully seduced despite this precaution) and the **abandonment** of the child who is taken in by a compassionate guardian and grows up to become a hero are staple motifs of many folktales, particularly Märchen and hero tales (see **dragonslayers**). The impossible task fulfilled with supernatural aid and the use of magic objects is similarly widespread, as is the slaying of the monster by beheading. The evil influence of the Gorgon's gaze parallels the **evil eye** beliefs around the world. The

Perseus

slaying of the sea-serpent and the rescue of the distressed maiden are even more closely connected to **dragon-slaying** myths such as that attached to St **George**.
▷ **Andromeda motif**

persimmon

TREE AND ITS FRUIT, genus *Diospyros* (family Ebenaceae), native to China (*D. kaki*) and central to southern North America (*D. virginiana*). In southern states of America colds can be transferred to the persimmon tree by means of magical **knots** or a tea made from the bark is used to treat chills. In some areas it is said to have the power of changing the sex of a girl who eats copiously of the fruit.

Pesach see Passover

peyote

CACTUS, also called mescal button, found almost exclusively in Mexico (genus *Lophophora*). It is renowned for its hallucinogenic effects, and has been widely used by Native Americans of the area in religio-magical ceremonies. Many groups believe that the tutelary peyote spirit is present in the plant, and that it can sing or speak to the one who picks it (cf **mandrake**).

phantom ships

OF ALL PHANTOM SHIPS, the most famous is the *Flying Dutchman*, the sight of which foretells disaster. Ships of fire are also common, for example the *Palatine*, wrecked in flames in 1738, is said to reappear in a ghostly blaze on the anniversary of its destruction. The fre-

quency of reported sightings of such ships, and the many anecdotes confirming the doom they forecast, has led to a wide and enduring belief.
▷ **sailors' lore**

philospher's stone

MAGICAL TALISMAN, the object of the alchemists' quest, the mythical substance that would combine with base metals to produce **gold**. Although descriptions of the philosopher's stone vary, and it has never been found and demonstrated, many accounts agree that it is formed of a perfect composition of sulphur and mercury. Many legends collected around the philosopher's stone; it was said to have been hung in the ark by Noah to give light to the animals, and to impart immortality to the one who possessed it.

The early alchemists, while inevitably disappointed in their search for this remarkable compound, laid the foundations of modern chemistry, discovering among other things such marvels as gunpowder (Bacon), Dresden porcelain (Bötticher) and the nature of acids (Geber).
▷ **alchemy**

phoenix

FABULOUS BIRD, emblem of the sun and resurrection. Although classical writers such as Hesiod and Herodotus claim Egyptian origin for the bird (probably closely connected to the *bennu*, the sacred hero of Rā), it seems likely that the myth began in the Orient. The Egyptians held that the bird lived in Arabia (to the east) towards the rising sun and that towards the end of its life span (never less than 500 years) it would build a nest of spice branches and set it alight, dying in the flames. A new phoenix arose from the **ashes**, and flew to the city of the sun, Heliopolis, to deposit the ashes on the altar of the sun god's temple. In some versions the bird flew to Heliopolis to die in the flames of the altar, whence arose the new phoenix. Only one phoenix lived at any time, eternally renewing itself in fire.

A symbol of immortality, the phoenix was adopted as the emblem of the undying state of Rome and appeared, wings outspread, on late coins. In early Christian lore it was interpreted as a symbol of resurrection and therefore associated with Christ. Medieval bestiaries claimed that the bird was the only one to be free from the taint of sin after

phoenix

the disobedience of Adam and Eve in Eden, and that it fed only on dew and harmed no living thing, despite its enormous size.

In Chinese mythology the phoenix, the Feng-huang, was one of the four fabulous sacred creatures combining in themselves both yin and yang principles and made of elements representing the whole cosmos. The appearance of the bird both here and in Japan was said to herald the beginning of a new age or the birth of a great emperor.

Pied Piper of Hamelin

FIGURE OF MEDIEVAL GERMAN LEGEND. In 1284, the town of Hamelin in Westphalia (Lower Saxony) was suffering under a fearsome plague of **rats**, when a piper dressed in quaint, parti-coloured clothes arrived and offered to clear the town of rats for a certain fee, to which the elders readily agreed. He began to play his pipe, the rats followed his music as if bewitched, and he led them into the River Weser where they all drowned. When the Piper returned to Hamelin to collect his fee the elders refused to pay, and the stranger began to play his haunting pipes again. This time all the children of the village tumbled after him, spell-bound by the music, and he led them inside the Koppenberg Hill, never

Pied Piper of Hamelin

to be seen again. In some versions two children were left behind, one blind and the other lame.

The legend became popular in the 16th century; it may be derived from the tragic Children's Crusade of 1212 in which Nicholas of Cologne led many thousands of German children to their deaths. Another possible explanation is that the tale is based on the massive migration of young people during German expansions to the east in the Middle Ages. Modern Hamelin still boasts the Rattenfängerhaus (Rat-catcher's House).

pig

WILD OR DOMESTIC ANIMAL, member of the Suidae family, often known in the United States as the hog. The pig has a very mixed reputation in world mythology, as both sacred (eg in ancient Rome) and unclean (eg Hebrew and Islamic law). Distrust of the pig passed into Christian lore partly from the Judaic tradition and partly from the biblical episode in which Jesus drives a legion of unclean spirits into a herd of swine. In many societies the reasons for avoiding pig-meat are bound up with **sympathetic magic** rather than religious beliefs; Zulu women avoid eating pigs lest they produce ugly babies. The Celts had no such qualms, and among Manannan's greatest treasures were two self-perpetuating pigs, one forever roasting while the other forever fattened itself to take its place.

In popular proverb lore the pig represents low animal nature and specifically greed, ignorance and filth. It is seldom featured in **animal tales**, and even more rarely as a **trickster** or a figure with intelligence and wit. In a Walloon (southern Belgium) tale also found in Catalonia and among Native Americans however the pig is caught in an apple tree by the **wolf** and saves himself by dropping into his persecutor's mouth, not the ham that he has promised, but a thorny branch that splits the wolf's gullet. In the popular European nursery tale of the Three Little Pigs, the three build houses of varying strength—one of straw, one of wood (or sticks) and one of bricks (or iron). Finally all the pigs take shelter in the last house. In some versions the wolf is killed when he tries to enter through the chimney and either falls or is burned by the fire.

pimpernel

FLOWERING PLANT OF THE PRIMROSE FAMILY, genus *Anagallis*, having scarlet, or occasionally yellow, blooms. The scarlet pimpernel (*A. arvensis*) is known as poor man's weatherglass in many areas of England and North America from its habit of closing its petals before rain and opening fully in fine weather. In some areas it is also a timepiece, opening at 7am.

The pimpernel is said to move upstream against the current if dropped in a river, and to possess great powers of resistance to **witchcraft** and other evil magic. Medicinally, it is widely used in France to smooth and clear the complexion, and its juice treats toothache and wounds of the head. In England especially it was considered effective in the treatment of liver and kidney diseases.

pine

EVERGREEN CONIFER, any of approximately 90 species of the genus *Pinus* (family Pinaceae). As an evergreen, the pine is a symbol of long life and immortality in many mythologies, particularly Greek, Semitic, Chinese and Japanese. Pine sap is drunk in China as a tonic to prevent ageing. Connected with this concept is that of marital fidelity and constant love, and in areas of Europe, particularly the Tyrol, the pine is a marriage tree. Its kernels were believed to immunize against gunshot wounds, a development of the old Roman military tradition that the nuts brought strength and endurance.

Since pine was widely used for ship-building in Europe, it was considered sacred to the gods of the sea. The Navajo of North America use pine gum to anoint the dead at funerals, smearing some on themselves as a mark of respect and propitiation.

Medicinally, pine gum is used by Native Americans to keep wounds from becoming infected. Drunk in a hot solution it is believed to cure worms and the smoke it gives off when heated should be inhaled by anyone suffering

from a cold or cough, or from rheumatism.

piskies see pixies

pixie

DIMINUTIVE SPIRITS OF THE SOUTH-WEST OF ENGLAND, a mischievous elfin race, sometimes referred to as piskies. They are homely spirits dressed in green, often red-headed, much given to moon-lit dancing, who delight in plaguing humans. Their most common prank is to lead travellers astray; anyone who becomes lost and confused is said to be 'pixie-led', and the term was extended to apply to anyone in a state of bewilderment. It is possible to work off this confusion by turning one's coat inside-out or back-to-front, thus confusing the pixies in their turn, or by a **cross** amulet.

Pixies also indulge in poltergeist activities, knocking on walls, blowing out candles, kissing young women in the dark to make them scream, or pinching lazy servants. They love to splash in water, and bowls are often left out for them at night. Young girls are especially susceptible to pixies; if a maid becomes suddenly clumsy, and food, utensils and even furniture start inexplicably moving in her presence, she is said to be pixie-ridden. Horses too can be pixie-ridden, driven in fairy circles (gallitraps) and left exhausted and confused, but a **horseshoe** over the stable door will generally prevent this.

Pixies are believed by many to be the souls of unbaptized infants; certainly they are generally agreed to be a distinct race from the **fairies**. They share some **brownie** traits, being willing sometimes to help in household tasks, and disappearing when offered a gift of new clothes. The first and fullest exposition of pixies was that by Mrs Anna Eliza Bray in her three-volume work *The Borders of the Tamar and the Tary*, a series of letters addressed to Robert Southey.

plantain

TALL PLANT AND ITS FRUIT, *Musa paradisiasa*, a member of the banana family (Musaceae). It is also known as way-bread or, among aborigines of the

Antipodes and North America, white man's foot. The fruit, which is eaten when green, is starchier than the banana and rarely eaten raw. A German tale collected by Grimm and found in similar forms worldwide shows the plantain as a woman waiting despondently by the roadside for the return of her lover; every seven years she is transformed into a bird and flies in search of him, and this is how plantains become distributed throughout the world.

The plantain is widely attributed with medicinal properties, especially in the treatment of bee stings. It is the 'leaf of **Patrick**' in Ireland, having divine properties to heal and soothe when placed in a poultice over wounds. The Chippewa, Iroquois, Meskwaki and other Native North American groups use the leaves and roots in a similar way; the Chippewa also powder the root and carry it as a **charm** against snake bites. Saxons in Europe bound plantain leaves to the forehead to cure headaches; Bavarian groups preferred simply to hold a plantain stalk in the left hand to clear the head, or place a piece in the ear to treat earache. In old Arabia plantain was 'lamb's tongue', used for all manner of illness and injuries. Broad-leafed plantains are boiled to produce a soothing eye-wash in Jamaica, and a tea to calm fever in many parts of North America. The seeds can be taken as a laxative.

Pleiades

SMALL CLUSTER OF BRIGHT STARS IN TAURUS. In Greek legend they were known as the seven daughters of **Atlas** and Pleiane, eternally weeping for their father, who was forced to support the world, or for the fate of Troy, and endlessly pursued by **Orion**. In Native North American lore the stars are often the sisters of seven deceitful brothers, or children who would not stop dancing and were swept one day into the sky where their constant twinkling shows that they are still dancing.

▷ **sky people**; **stars**

plum

TREE AND ITS FLESHY FRUIT, any variety of the genus *Prunus* (Rosaceae family).

Like the **peach**, it is regarded as a symbol of long life and immortality in China, and closely associated with the **New Year** as its blossom appears so early. A popular origin tale tells how a **dragon**'s ear was cut off and the plum tree sprang from the blood that fell to the ground.

A Welsh superstition holds that if a plum tree blossoms in December (an unlikely enough event) there will inevitably be a death in the family. Certain Native North American groups use a tea brewed from the bark of the tree to treat an upset stomach. Previously in English slang 'plum' was used to refer to a sum of £100 000; it has since come to mean a choice part of anything, a lucky windfall or desirable situation.

Pocahontas (1595–1617)

NATIVE AMERICAN HEROINE, original name Matoaka. She was the daughter of the Powhatan chief, who successfully intervened on two occasions to save the life of the English explorer John Smith. She was abducted or persuaded away from her people by the settlers, converted to Christianity and was re-christened Rebecca. She was ransomed by her father but wished to marry an English settler John Rolfe; the Powhatan and the settlers reached an agreement and the marriage did much to further peaceful relations between the two. She died in England just before her return to Virginia, but several worthy Virginian families claim descent from her son.

polong

MALAYSIAN DEMON, a diminutive flying spirit. It can be bred by a sorcerer from the blood of a murder victim and then directed to attack its creator's enemies. The effect of possession by a polong is a dramatic fit and loss of consciousness; the victim can only be saved by observance of the correct rituals and the exorcism of the polong by a more powerful shaman.

polygenesis

A THEORETICAL POSITION OF FOLKLORE SCHOLARSHIP, advocated by the school of **anthropological theory** particularly, the belief that similar tales found in different areas of the world should be explained not by diffusion but by independent generation. The central principle of polygenesis is that all human societies undergo similar stages of development (although these may occur at widely differing times) and that universal preoccupations (eg death, sex, family relationships) combine with these cultural development stages to produce similar tales and practices without reference to other cultures.

In reality, this position is too extreme for folklorists, most of whom accept to at least some degree the role played by diffusion in trade, colonization, travel, migration and so on. A middle way accepted by many scholars consists of recognizing the common origins of certain **motifs**, while accepting the independent traditions into which individual cultures work these elements to form tales. The tale-type of the **beast marriage**, for example, may have developed independently among different societies; the motif of the rash promises found in the **Beauty and the Beast** tale may be traceable to a common origin.

Polynesian folklore

POLYNESIA REMAINS THE MOST HOMOGENEOUS OF ALL PACIFIC GROUPS, both culturally and linguistically, although varying degrees of intermixing have complicated the racial and cultural divisions. Polynesia ('many islands') refers to the eastern islands, from Hawaii in the north to New Zealand in the south, stretching to Easter Island in the east. It was the last of the Pacific areas to be settled, and it is thought that the original settlers from the west were ancestors of the Polynesians who then spread to other islands, and that they may have had close links with the Melanesian island of Fiji. These settlers had a complex, detailed social system which defined each individual's place within it, and an equally complex set of rituals and beliefs which overlaid the business of everyday living, designed to protect the 'mania', the supernatural power inherent in the world. Craftsmen dignified their trades by claiming the distinction of the gods' participation, chiefs were said to have descended from divine families, and therefore to be endowed with great mania, and this sense of the awesome in

the everyday and a profound respect for the past bred a society of deep-seated conservatism. Items of vocabulary, the technical structures of canoes and tools, tales, songs and proverbs passed from island to island and generation to generation with little change. Along with the Polynesian's acceptance of his place within his family and society came a sense of his place within the universe, and an unusually clear orientation within the beautiful but hostile environment of the eastern Pacific Islands.

Lineage among Polynesians is generally traced through both the male and female lines, and one of the characteristics of the culture is the degree of sexual license allowed. Within certain limits of incest taboos and social rank, sexual activity is encouraged from a very early age. Violence is another characteristic element of Polynesian society, and the folklore reflects this preoccupation. The population expanded quickly and there were many inter-tribal wars. The highly structured rituals that abounded in Polynesian society frequently involved human sacrifice or cannibalism, and one who made a mistake in the complex ritual procedures might well be put to death.

▷ **hula**

pomegranate

MANY-SEEDED FRUIT, *Punica granatum* (family Punicaceae), native to Asia and cultivated since ancient times in Mediterranean areas. It is widely regarded as a symbol of fertility because of its innumerable seeds, and in Mesopotamia and other areas was eaten to promote fertility and as an aphrodisiac. This connection with sexuality may explain its ancient connection in Judaeo-Christian lore with the fruit disobediently taken by Eve in Eden. The Phrygian god of death and resurrection, Altis, beloved by the mother goddess Cybele, was said to have been conceived when his virginal mother Nana laid a pomegranate on her breast (Altis was later transformed into the **pine**). In the classical tale of Hades and Persephone, which embodies the common folkloric theme of the **food taboo** in the otherworld, Persephone is compelled to spend half of each year in the **underworld** because she ate six pomegranate seeds. To dream of a pomegranate in Europe is regarded as a clear sign that love is ahead. A Turkish bride throws a pomegranate behind her and examines the scattered seeds to discover how many children she will have.

The pomegranate was recommended by Muhammad to purge the system of envy and hatred, and this belief in its beneficial effects is echoed in Christian lore, where it is a symbol of hope. Pomegranate branches formed a potent **charm** among the Zoroastrians in Persia, and in Sicily the shoots were prized for their use in **dowsing**. The fruit is the Spanish national emblem, and appears on the arms of Granada, thought to be named after the fruit, *la granada*.

pooka see púca

Pope Joan

LEGENDARY FEMALE PONTIFF, said to have reigned as John VIII from 855 to 858 until her male disguise was exploded by labour pains. In fact Benedict III succeeded Leo IV in 855 after a period of only a few weeks.

One of the earliest forms of the legend is found in the 13th-century *De septem donis Spiritu Sancti* ('The Seven Gifts of the Holy Spirit') by Stephen of Bourbon; according to him Joan was elected pope in Rome in c.1100 after showing extraordinary learning as a scribe and notary, but upon giving birth during a papal procession to the Lateran Church her imposture was discovered and she was taken out of the city and stoned to death. Later accounts claimed that she died in childbirth during the procession, and it was said that subsequent popes avoided that street in their own papal processions. She was often known as Agnes or Gilberta or simply remained anonymous until the name Joan became the standard form in the 14th century.

The most influential source for the legend was Martin of Troppan, a 13th-century Dominican, who named her as Johannes Angelicus, born of English parents in Mainz, and set the date of her election at 855. She disguised herself as a man to follow her beloved to Athens, where she trained. The legend was accepted as historical for many centuries, and seized upon by Protestant reformers in the 16th and 17th centuries, but after the 18th century the myth began to lose credibility. It has been suggested that the fable may have originated from satiric criticism of the influential female senator Marozia in 10th-century Rome.

poplar

SHRUB OR TREE, genus *Populus* (family Salicaceae). In Roman legend Hercules (see **Heracles**) wore a crown of poplar leaves on his visit to the underworld; the tops of the leaves were blackened by the heat while their undersides received a silvery radiance from the hero's sweat. Perhaps because of this connection with this successful return from the land of the dead, the poplar is regarded in many areas as a symbol of life after the grave. The white poplar signified old age and autumn in the Irish tree alphabet. In ancient Greece and Rome a white poplar stick was a **charm** against leprosy, and in Rome the black poplar signified hopelessness. In weather lore, the upturned leaves of the poplar are said to signify rain.
▷ **aspen**

poppy

FLOWERING PLANT (FAMILY PAPAVERACEAE), particularly of the *Papaver* genus, appearing with blooms of various shades but most characteristically bright orange or red. It is from the poppy that opium, and thence morphine and heroin, is derived, and this has linked the poppy in the popular imagination since ancient times with sleep and therefore death. Ceres is said to have been granted sleep by smelling a poppy sent by the gods when she roamed exhausted in her quest for Persephone, and it has traditionally been used medicinally to induce rest and relieve pain, and recreationally to induce a pleasurably trance-like state.

The poppy is strongly associated with death; it is said in all areas of the world to grow from blood and hence is especially prolific on battlefields. In Christian lore it was said to have sprung from the blood of the crucified Christ. A **wheat** field bearing poppies alongside grain is tradi-

poppy

tionally viewed as an emblem of life bound up with death. The poppy is now regarded in the West as a commemorative symbol of those slain in the World Wars.

potato

EDIBLE TUBER, from the plant *Solanum tuberosum*, native to South America. It was introduced to Europe by returning explorers of the late 16th century and quickly became one of the world's main food crops. It formed the basis of the diet in Ireland almost exclusively until the blight and subsequent famine of 1845–6 underlined the dangers of absolute dependency. Potatoes were widely considered an aphrodisiac in Europe, and in 1728 they were legally prohibited by a distrustful Scotland on the grounds that the potato belonged to the ill-favoured nightshade family and was not mentioned as suitable food in the Bible.

To obtain best results, potatoes should be planted on very dark nights (a general rule of all root crops) and never on Good Friday. A potato can be carried as a **charm** against rheumatism and warts, although in Ireland anybody washing in potato stock will find himself covered in warts. The liquid is said to be good, however, if rubbed directly onto sprains and broken limbs. Cooling raw potato is placed on burns in Texas, and Mississippi slaves used to apply a raw potato poultice to a black eye.

potlach

GIVING CEREMONY, a ritual distribution of property and objects among Native North Americans of the Northwest Pacific coast. The purpose of the extravagant and elaborate giving was to establish or confirm social status; the larger the gathering, the more lavish the hospitality, and the greater the value of the gift, the more prestige was awarded to the donor. The ceremony could be used for political events, to establish superiority over a neighbouring group or a defeated enemy by out-giving its chief.

An individual succeeding to a rank or title, particularly that of chief, would be expected to give a potlach to validate his succession, and social occasions such as weddings, initiations or funerals would often be opportunities for the ceremony.

pray

EVIL SPIRITS OF CAMBODIA, particularly the spirits of women who have died in childbirth and unborn children. They inhabit trees and mock passers-by, often throwing missiles at them and occasionally killing them.

Prester John

LEGENDARY CHRISTIAN KING, said to be descended from the Magi who visited Christ's cradle, believed by Western Christians to be ruling in the East during the Crusades (later 11th to 13th centuries) and promoted in Europe as a potential ally. He was said to be a Nestorian, one of the independent congregation that had rejected the authority of Constantinople, and a powerful enemy of the Muslim Turks.

In the 13th century Alberich de Trois-Fontaines noted in his chronicle that a letter had been sent by Prester John to several European leaders in 1165. The letter was a literary fiction; it describes Prester John's realm as a marvellous

otherworld filled with peace, great natural riches and marvels such as a spring that confers immortality. John claims in the letter to guard in this remarkable realm the tomb of St Thomas, believed in hagiography to have evangelized India. Travellers' tales and the folk imagination supplemented the legend. Prester John had magic stones that could control the weather, turn water into wine, cause wild animals to line up for slaughter, and his subjects flew through the air on tame **dragons**, while enormous ants mined gold from the earth. The authenticity of Prester John was widely accepted by the Church, longing to believe in this ally, and Pope Alexander III sent a letter to him in 1177, probably requesting aid in his disputes with **Barbarossa**.

The fruitless search for the mythical realm of Prester John did much to develop trade and intercourse between the Europeans and the Mongols. The legend may have orginated after the Islamic conquest of Egypt, which meant the isolation of Christian Ethiopia from the West.

Princess on the Pea

LITERARY FAIRY-TALE, written by Hans Christian Andersen, based on the ancient folktale motif of the identity through sensitivity, or bed test. A king wishes to marry a true princess; a young woman claiming to be a princess promptly arrives that night and is given shelter from the storm, but to test her claim the wise old queen secretly places a pea under 20 mattresses which are in turn topped by 20 eiderdowns (different versions give different, but equally improbable, figures). The next morning the princess complains that she could not sleep for something painfully hard under her mattress; her authenticity is thus vindicated and the two marry.

In an old Swedish version of the tale the girl sleeps well all night, despite the fact that a pea has been secreted between each of her seven mattresses— she passes the test, however, because a **helpful beast** warns her to complain. The version collected by Grimm is *Die Erbensprobe*. The motif draws on the ancient and widespread belief that true nobility is characterized by extreme sensitivity, especially among women. In an ancient tale of India three queens suffer from such excessive sensitivity that one faints from the pain of hearing a pestle and mortar grinding in the distance, another is burned by a moonbeam, and the third is bruised by a **lotus** petal falling on her skin.

promised child

MOTIF OF FOLKTALES, found throughout the world. In most cases the child is promised to a demon or supernatural being in exchange for help or in payment for a wrong. So the queen promises her child to **Rumpelstiltskin** in return for a roomful of spun gold, and Beauty's father rashly promises to send the Beast the first thing that comes to greet him after plucking the **rose**. The motif embraces that of **Jephthah's vow**. In a medieval European tale, 'Robert the Devil', a mother promises her child to the **Devil** and Robert therefore grows up a slave to evil. He journeys to Hell to try to free himself from this bond by destroying the contract; there he sees the punishment that awaits his friend and helper, the thief Madej, and after successfully releasing himself returns to warn him. Madej seeks forgiveness and is given penance to perform until a dry staff blossoms (cf **act of truth**), when he knows he is forgiven.

Proteus

'THE OLD MAN OF THE SEA', a Greek sea-deity and prophet in all knowledge of past, present and future. He disliked imparting this knowledge to humans, however; those seeking an answer would first have to surprise him by binding him during his siesta, then keep a firm hold as Proteus, a master **shapeshifter**, ran a gamut of bewildering forms. If the quester could retain his hold, however, the sea-god would be compelled to give him a truthful answer. In later thought Proteus came to symbolize the principle of creation and the original substance for which the universe was created.

proverbs

PITHY SAYINGS, the condensed wisdom of a community, revealing memorably its beliefs, values and accumulated experience. In Ethiopia they say that 'Speech without proverbs is like food without salt', and it seems true of most societies that proverbial phrases are widely used to season conversation. A proverb is a short sentence, whose concise form is fixed by a tradition of oral transmission, which encapsulates some warning, advice, empirical observation or philosophical comment on life. By its nature the proverb tends to vindicate existing moral structures. While a proverb expresses the common experience of the culture, it is usually the result of an anonymous individual's neat formulation, and in some cases may be taken directly from an authority such as the Bible or a classical writer. Proverbs depend for their continuation less upon the validity of their message than on the simplicity or neatness of their form, hence many such sayings use contrast or balance ('better late than never', 'Faint heart ne'er won fair lady') or stylistic features such as rhyme, rhythm and alliteration ('All's well that ends well', 'Forgive and forget'). In fact it has often been observed that proverbs may contradict each other; surely if 'he who hesitates is lost' one cannot take time to 'look before you leap'. There is necessarily an element of truth in every proverb, but proverb wisdom is certainly not infallible.

The simplest type of proverb is that which is to be taken literally, encapsulating in a neat way some advice or observation, for example the Arabic proverb urging discretion: 'Hide your principles, your money and your journey'. Into this category too comes much weather-lore; 'After a rainy summer, a plentiful winter', or 'When the wind is in the east, 'tis neither good for man nor beast'.

More sophisticated than these formulated observations are the many metaphorical proverbs, which use a more indirect and often ingenious means of commentary. In this category are such phrases as 'Too many cooks spoil the broth', the Chinese observation that 'A great bend requires a great straightening' (strenuous attempts must be made to right a great injustice) and the Swahili comment on an insignificant event; 'The squirrel is not heard in the forest'. In many languages, especially in the Middle East, the word for proverb actually derives from the word meaning 'comparison'. It is interesting that similar ideas are expressed in widely different cultures by different metaphors, so the caution of one who has been injured is expressed variously as 'Once bitten, twice shy', 'He who has been scalded fears cold water' and 'He who has been stung by a serpent fears a rope on the ground'. Conversely, the same metaphor often appears in widely different societies, demonstrating the propensity of the proverbial comparison to be absorbed in different cultural milieux. So for example in Japan folk say 'Fish and guests are wearisome on the third day'; in Spain 'A guest and a fish stink in three days'; and in France 'A guest and a fish after three days are poison'.

Since indirectness is valued as a politeness in many cultures, proverbs often function as an effective and elegant means of expressing an opinion or giving advice on a subject without commenting upon it directly. This is especially true in many Middle Eastern and Oriental cultures, where proverbs can often be so sophisticated as to appear quite impenetrable until heard in context; a caution to know one's limits, for example, runs 'The lame duck avoids the ploughed fields'. This indirectness can also serve to protect the speaker by affording him a cloak for his criticisms or mockery—a skilled proverb-speaker will communicate his meaning subtly but aptly.

Although some religious leaders and texts have entered proverb lore, the most common application of the form is to the everyday rather than the spiritual or abstract. Many are shrewd, recommending pragmatism; 'Better a live dog than a dead lion', 'A bird in the hand is worth two in the bush', and the Irish wisdom of 'If you have only a goat, be in the middle of the fair with it'. These are strategies developed and used by the folk to meet hardship; they reflect the sturdy, humorous view common to most peasant and primitive cultures. But a loftier morality is often also in evidence; an Indian proverb runs 'The good we do today becomes the happiness of tomorrow' and a folk piety is evident in the Swedish proverb, 'The greater the need, the nearer is God'. Such moral or religious proverbs are generally didactic but not doctrinal; they serve to reinforce the traditional values and beliefs of the group and by appealing to a common fund of moral wisdom can provide advice for individual dilemmas. In West Africa particularly, proverbial wisdom is a powerful social weapon, used to impose discipline and conformity on individuals acting outside the accepted behaviour patterns and also as a means of self-control. Proverbs are traditionally cited in the court-room as the repository of wisdom and common practice which must decide the case, and they feature much more frequently in everyday speech than is usual in Europe.

Another common function is educational; in Africa generally the monster tales and moral stories of childhood give way in adolescence to the wisdom of proverbs, used by the parents as suitable situations arise to initiate the child fully into the wisdom of the tribe.

Many proverbs deal with interpersonal relationships, between masters and servants, parents and children, neighbours and friends. By far the largest such area however is that of husband and wife specifically, or man and woman in general. Since marriage and procreation are the central preoccupations of any society, and since the distinctions between sex-roles is usually sharp especially in primitive societies, this is hardly surprising. Most proverbs about women are derogatory, which supports the common view that the main purveyors of proverbs in a folk culture are men; the Fulani of Senegal say 'Woman is fire. If you have to, take a little', the Chinese 'Though a woman has given you ten sons, do not trust her', and one of the many proverbs alluding to the woman's alleged inability to keep quiet is that of the Bulgarians, 'A woman keeps secret only her age and what she does not know'. The good wife and mother however is respected; 'her price is far above rubies' according to the biblical book of Proverbs, and in India 'A wife is the ornament of the house'. Many proverbs ruefully acknowledge the paradox, such as the Arabic 'Wedlock is like a besieged fortress; those who are outside wish to get in and those who

are inside wish to get out'. Occasionally a proverb expressing the woman's view of marriage can be found, such as the Portuguese 'What is marriage, mother?—Daughter, it is spinning, bearing children and weeping'.

psychological theory

AN APPROACH TO FOLKLORE SCHOLARSHIP, which has been successfully combined with other approaches, where folklore is seen in primarily behaviouristic terms. Freud drew heavily on folklore material in his work, demonstrating that it contained hidden preoccupations, fears and desires and interpreting it symbolically, especially in terms of sexual imagery. Thus in the **Jack and the Beanstalk** tale-type, the beanstalk becomes a phallic symbol and the tale is revealed as a masturbation fantasy. Jung, heavily influenced by Freud, saw in folklore the repository of the 'collective unconscious'. Although susceptible to distortion by the preoccupations of the scholar, the results of this method are useful in exploring the impulses behind the development of folklore and as an insight into the enduring quality of many of its themes.

puberty rites see initiation

púca

IRISH MISCHIEVOUS SPIRIT, also known as pooka. He is adept at **shape-shifting** and is said to reward humans who please him by imparting the gift of animal speech. Although generally harmless, the púca is quick to punish criminals, especially grave-robbers and horse-thieves, or those who show insufficient gratitude for his helpful tasks around the house and farm. He has been known, however, to intervene to protect innocent peasants from harm, and to help the farmer catch his roaming cattle.

Púca is a close cousin of the English **puck**.

puck

ENGLISH MISCHIEVOUS SPIRIT. Puck was originally known as a malicious **hobgoblin**; in medieval times he was described as a devil. In later lore however he became identified with the mischievous but good-hearted Robin

puck

Goodfellow, and sometimes even with the folk hero **Robin Hood**. One of his favourite pranks is to mislead travellers like **will o' the wisp**, and he delights in ridiculing human folly and gullibility. He has **shape-shifting** powers, and in the shape of a horse will often dupe a passer-by into mounting him, whereupon the unfortunate fool finds himself suddenly ducked half-way across a river with a saddle but no horse beneath him. He also performs household duties like a **brownie**, although he is never so closely linked to a specific house. Analogous figures with similar names abound in Germanic and Scandinavian folklore (the *pukje* in Norway, **pwca** in Wales, *Puge* in Old Danish and *pooka* or *púca* in Ireland). Shakespeare's Puck in *A Midsummer Night's Dream* reflects the view of the spirit common in later folklore, waggish rather than malicious.

▷ **mischievous spirits**

puk

HOUSEHOLD SPIRIT OF THE BALTIC STATES, known for bringing stolen treasure back to its master's house. The puk is generally portrayed as a small **dragon**. It is almost certainly a legacy from German influence (in one tale the puk actually enters Lithuania as a dragon bought from a German trader) and may originally derive from the same route as the English **puck**, Irish **púca** and the Scandinavian *pukje*.

pumpkin

LARGE YELLOW FRUIT, borne by certain varieties of the family Cucurbitaceae. In the United States pumpkin usually refers to large slow-growing fruits from trailing plants while squashes are smaller, faster-growing fruits, but the two words are often used interchangeably. Its best-known function in modern folklore, apart from the traditional pumpkin pie served at **Thanksgiving** and **Christmas** in North America, is its use as a **Hallowe'en** decoration; the pulp is scooped out and a more or less menacing face cut through the rind, then a candle placed inside the cavity gives it a ghostly aspect. This is the jack-o'-lantern, popular especially in the United States.

In Chinese lore the pumpkin is a regal fruit symbolizing fertility and wealth, and a traditional ritual observed annually at the great Parisian market involved dressing an enormous pumpkin as a king, complete with paper crown, and parading it around the town to general hilarity and mock obeisance. The pumpkin was then cut up and its pieces sold for soup. A popular Eurasian tale tells of a numbskull who throws a pumpkin away, believing it to be an ass's egg. The pumpkin lands in some bushes and explodes and the numbskull is convinced that the rabbit that bolts from the bushes is a young ass. Perhaps the most familiar use of the pumpkin in Western folklore is as **Cinderella**'s coach, transformed by the **fairy godmother** and drawn by a team of similarly transformed mice coachmen.

A tea made from pumpkin seeds is used by many Native North Americans as a diuretic and to treat tapeworm.

Punch

HOOK-NOSED, HUNCH-BACKED PUPPET, a brutal bullying character and hero of the traditional English entertainment, the Punch-and-Judy show. In the basic form of this drama, Punch throws the baby out of the window for crying, or strangles it, then when his wife Judy takes a bludgeon to him in remonstration beats her to death. He is arrested by the Policeman but manages to escape, and successively defeats a dog, the Doctor, **Death** and the **Devil**. In some versions he tricks the

357

Puss in Boots

Punch

hangman Jack Ketch into hanging himself.

Mr Punch (as he is often known) derives from Punchinello (Italian *pulcinello*, diminutive form of a young chicken). His ancestry can be traced to the grotesque, wily clown figures of Roman comedy and the tradition of the French hunch-back fool. The story that survives today may have been developed by one Silvio Fiorillo, a Commedia dell'Arte professional in Italy in the early 17th century. The anarchic humour of the puppet show and its wanton brutality have lost it favour in more recent years, as slapstick has gone out of fashion, and Punch and Judy survive today mainly as archaic English sea-side entertainment for children.

Punch has made his mark in the folk imagination, however; 'as pleased as Punch' is a common phrase referring to the puppet's self-satisfied crowing at the success of his plots, and he gave his name to the long running British satirical magazine, *Punch*. Judy is thought to have been Joan originally; there seems little substance to the popular misconception that the character derived from Pontius Pilate (Punch) and **Judas Iscariot** (Judy).

Puss in Boots

EUROPEAN FOLKTALE. The most famous version of the tale was recorded by Perrault in his *Contes de ma Mère l'Oye*, but the original folk narrative is part of the world-wide **helpful beast** cycle. The poor miller can bequeathe to his youngest son nothing but a **cat**, but the creature secures his master's fortune and the hand of the princess by tricking the king into believing he is the servant of a Marquis. In Eastern European versions the cat is a **fox**, and a **jackal** or a **monkey** in Asia.

pwca

WELSH MISCHIEVOUS SPIRIT, best known for his **will o' the wisp** activities, leading travellers astray. He is a close relative of the English **puck**.

Pwyll

LEGENDARY PRINCE OF DYFED. He exchanges places with **Arawn**, king of the underworld, for one year, slays Hafgan, Arawn's enemy, and marries **Rhiannon** who is later falsely accused of murdering their son.
▷ *Mabinogion*

quail

SMALL GAME BIRD OF THE FAMILY PHA-
SIANIDAE (order Galliformes). It is
renowned in folklore throughout the
world as a particularly amorous bird,
and hence in English a **euphemism** for
prostitute or courtesan. In Rome the
quail was a traditional gift between
lovers, although interestingly it was also
an emblem of war and victory.

Medieval bestiaries claimed that the
quail was the only other creature besides
humans to suffer from falling sickness
(**epilepsy**), and a quail's brain was
believed to be a useful medicine against
the illness.

In Chinese lore the quail is closely
linked with the **phoenix**, as a bird of fire
and summer. This solar connection
appears consistently in many mythologies (in Greek tales Leto, the mother of
the sun god Apollo by Zeus, was transformed into a quail by the jealous Hera).

quartz

A WIDESPREAD MINERAL, primarily sili-
con dioxide in crystal form, regarded as a
gemstone from classical times at least.
Among many native Australian groups,
quartz is associated with rain; it may be
ground and thrown into the air to bring
about rainfall through **sympathetic
magic**, or used as rain-stones in ritual
dances. In Britain quartz was formerly
named 'star-stone', and was attributed
with divinatory and curative powers.

quest

COMMON THEME OF FOLKTALES AROUND
THE WORLD, a search for a specific object,
person or answer, often imposed upon
the hero by another (eg a sovereign,
dead spirit or prospective father-in-law)
but occasionally undertaken voluntarily
(eg the famous quest for the Holy **Grail**).
The quest motif provides a structure into
which related motifs such as the supernatural or animal helpers or **magic
objects** fit neatly, and is especially characteristic of Märchen. Typical objects of
quest are treasure (often guarded by a
dragon), the spring of youth, the golden
bird, or the answer to a riddle. In one
variation of the theme, the quest
becomes a chain on which the finding of
each object is dependent upon the
finding of another.
▷ **tasks**

Questing Beast

FABULOUS CREATURE OF ARTHURIAN
LEGEND, also know as Glatisaunt, featuring in Malory's *Morte d'Arthur*. It was
compounded of the body of a leopard,
the head of a serpent, the rear end of a
lion and the legs of a deer, and made a
fearsome noise like a pack of hounds
baying. A symbol of incest and lawlessness, it was said to seek water constantly
to slake its insatiable thirst. It was the
object of quest for King Pellinore, who
was later killed by **Gawain**.

rabbit

TRICKSTER FIGURE OF FOLKLORE. The rabbit and **hare** have traditionally figured prominently in world folklore; in the Indian *Panchatantra* and in tales of Burma and Tibet the rabbit is shown overcoming the jungle beasts by its quick wits, but it is in Native American and African folktales that the rabbit is portrayed as trickster figure *par excellence*, who despite his diminutive size outwits his more powerful opponents by quick thinking. In the Great Basin and in the south east of North America, Rabbit (or Cottontail) is regarded also as a **culture hero**, who either steals the sun to give the tribe light or brings back fire from across the sea. In Africa Rabbit as trickster is even more widespread, seriously challenged only by **Spider** (Anansi) and **Tortoise** in some regions. This shared feature seems to indicate some borrowing between Native American and African cultures, and there has been much debate as to which direction this borrowing took. Joel Chandler Harris, famous as the author of the **Brer Rabbit** tales, believed that the tales originated in Africa and were adopted by Native Americans.

rabbit

ragweed see **ragwort**

ragwort

YELLOW-FLOWERED WEED, genus *Senecio* (family Asteraceae), also known as groundsel, stinking Willie or (in America) ragweed. In Cornish lore its stalks were said to provide mounts for **witches**, and in Ireland it was the fairies' horse. Like the **dandelion**, it has a 'clock' that is used to tell the time.

As a cooling plant, ragwort juice is applied to sore eyes and the whole plant as a cold poultice on inflamed joints.

rahu

DEMON OF HINDU LORE, believed to be responsible for **eclipses**. He stole some of the divine nectar that confers immortality, and the sun and moon informed Vishnu, who beheaded him. The head cannot die, however, and it still circles endlessly watching for a chance to devour either of its enemies.

Railroad Bill

BLACK AMERICAN FOLK HERO, the **Robin Hood** of Alabama. Originally named Morris Slater, he absconded when arrested for possession of a gun, shot the deputy and vanished on a freight train. From then on he made his living stowing away on trains and looting the freight which he gave to the poor or sold cheaply. In popular lore he was credited with the power of **shape-shifting**, turning into an animal, most commonly a black **dog**, to evade his pursuers.

rain

THE PURPOSE OF MUCH WEATHER LORE. Since rain is vital to life—as drinking water, for crops and for livestock—and since much of the world suffers from periodic drought or continual dryness, the means of summoning rain are preoccupations of many societies especially in

Africa and equatorial regions. By far the most common methods among primitive societies are those invoking **sympathetic magic**; the rain-maker, magician or shaman performs a ritual which imitates the effects of rainfall, in the hope that rain will thus be encouraged to fall. Examples of such methods include spraying a mouthful of water into the air as a fine mist; beating a victim until blood flows onto the ground; quenching a fiery torch with water; or drenching members of the tribe (often naked women) with water.

In primitive religion, an appeal is made to deities and supernaturals for rain to begin or, less commonly, end. Often magic and religious rituals are combined; an appeal and sacrifice is made to a god and a ritual of sympathetic magic such as sprinkling water is performed to make the point entirely clear. One particularly effective method is to arouse the compassion of the gods through the suffering of innocents; an animal may be tortured until it howls, or children buried to their necks in hot sand while their mothers mourn, in order to bring about the relief of rain. The spirits of the dead are widely called upon in such circumstances, sometimes accompanied by rituals performed over an exhumed body or the grave of a chief. In other cultures animals are called upon to end the drought, used as sacrifices or beaten until the blood flows like rain. In such cases the animal used is invariably black, since the hope is to summon down rainclouds. Animals such as **frogs**, which are closely associated with water, are frequently used in such rituals.

If all else fails, the folk may endeavour to force the divinity into sending rain by intimidation or abuse. When long prayers and sacrifice before a fetish or idol have come to nothing, the image may be torn down and exposed to the sun, so that the deity might feel for himself the agony of drought, or publicly ridiculed to shame him into performing his duty. This was common not only among primitive and ancient peoples; according to Frazer in *The Golden Bough*, statues of **saints** were subjected to similar treatment in Sicily at the end of the 19th century. If the drought is seen as a punishment for some individual or communal sin, however, the society may take penitential measures to placate the deity.

▷ **sun**; **weather**; **wind**

rainbow

SPECTACULAR OMEN, a series of brightly-coloured arcs in the sky forming a spectrum, caused by sunlight refracting in water particles. It has been widely regarded as a supernatural message, along with other celestial events such as **eclipses** or **lightning**, as in the biblical flood story, where it functions as the sign of God's covenant not to flood the earth again.

In several mythologies the rainbow is a bridge connecting earth to a supernatural **otherworld**; for example, the Norse Bifrost, which connects heaven and earth and is guarded by Heimdall, is identified in the Prose **Edda** with the rainbow. In Hawaii too the rainbow is a bridge, and in Greek mythology it was the path taken by the goddess Iris, bringing messages from the gods to humankind.

The other main interpretation given to the rainbow is that of a cosmic serpent, common throughout North and South America, Australia and Africa particularly and shared by the ancient Persians. Often this snake is an earth deity arching into the sky to drink, and the widespread nature of this interpretation is closely linked to the almost universal association of serpents and water (cf **snake**, **dragon**, **Leviathan**). The rainbow snake is regarded reverentially by many groups as healer, **culture hero**, creator or sustainer; in some areas **initiation** is represented as being consumed then vomited back up by the rainbow snake, or he controls the human flow of blood and particularly the menstrual cycle.

In Europe and Australia particularly the rainbow is a symbol of gender confusion; it is widely represented in Aboriginal art with both male and female organs, and in Europe there is a widespread belief that one who walks under the rainbow or drinks the water at its end will change sex (cf the Greek myth of Tiresias, the prophet who changed sex and lost his sight on seeing two serpents copulating). However, a more general and enduring belief in

Europe is that the end of the rainbow marks valuable buried treasure, generally a crock of gold.

The rainbow has been incorporated into much weather-lore; it is most commonly received as a sign that heavy rain is ending, and a double rainbow especially means that a long period of sunshine will follow. One common rhyme gives an indication of the types of predictions associated with the rainbow:

Rainbow in morning, sailors take warning;

Rainbow at night, sailors' delight.

Rainbow to windward, foul falls the day;

Rainbow to leeward, damp runs away.

rākshasas

SHAPE-SHIFTING DEMONS OF HINDU LORE, who generally appear as animals or monsters, although the females more commonly show themselves as beautiful women. They are most to be feared at night and before the new moon gains strength, but they lose their power in daylight. Pūtatnā attempted to kill Krishna by suckling him on her poisonous breast, but the infant god was stronger and sucked all the life out her. Their ten-headed king, Rāvana, abducts **Sita** in the *Ramayana*.

Although in mythology rākshasas are utterly evil, in common lore they sometimes share the characteristics of the **yakshas**, nature spirits. They are said however to frequent graveyards and feed on human flesh, and to suck cows dry.

ram

MALE SHEEP, associated throughout the world with masculine virility and strength, and hence with solar power. Several pantheons include ram-headed deities or gods whose emblem is a ram, for example, the Egyptian Rā and the Vedic Agni, god of fire. The ram's spiral horns connected it with fertility; with such symbolic associations it is hardly surprising that the ram has been one of the most popular of sacrificial animals. This role has been lent special significance in Jewish lore from the tale of Abraham and Isaac; directed by God to sacrifice his only son, Abraham is about to bring down the knife when he is stopped by an angel and, having proved his devotion to God, is shown a ram caught by its horns in a bush to offer in Isaac's place.

Rama

HERO OF THE RAMAYANA. Rama (fully Ramacandra) is the seventh incarnation of Vishnu, associated with chivalry and virtue. He has been worshipped as the supreme dèity by some groups from the 14th century on; his popularity was due in large part to the dissemination of various sacred epics in the vernacular, such as Tulsidas's *Ramcaritmanas*, 'The sacred lake of the acts of Rama'. He balances the equally popular Krishna, who is loved for his amorous adventures and mischief-making. He is most frequently represented holding his bow and arrow, often accompanied by **Sita** and **Hanuman**, and usually richly dressed as befits a prince.

It is possible that Rama was originally

Rama

an ancient tribal leader, later deified. The name is also given to two other figures of Hindu lore, Parasurama and Balarama.

ramara

FABULOUS FISH OF CLASSICAL LEGEND, said by Pliny to be able to hold still a ship in the most turbulent conditions by fastening its mouth onto the keel, despite its diminutive size. He adds that it was this fish that held back Antony at Actium in 31BC. This marvellous creature is also known as echeneis, delaya and, in the medieval bestiaries, errius.

Ramayana

SANSKRIT EPIC, 'THE ROMANCE OF RAMA'. Unlike the *Mahabharata*, the other great Indian epic, the *Ramayana* was written by a single author, the poet Valmiki, probably writing in the late fourth century BC, and with only 25 000 or so couplets in its present form it is a quarter of the length of the other. It was probably translated into poetic form in the second century BC.

The hero of the epic is **Rama**, the seventh incarnation of Vishnu and deity of chivalry, reason and virtue. The historical Rama may have been a son of Daśaratha, King of Ayodhyā (Oudh), who had four sons. According to ancient Hindu mythology, the sons were each impregnated with a measure of divine essence given as a potion by Vishnu to the king and distributed among his wives. Rama's mother had the largest measure, half of the pot, Bharata's had a quarter, and the twins Lakshmana and Satrughna each received an eighth. Many legends were attached to Rama; in his youth he was said to have slain the demon Taraka, and he wins his bride, **Sita**, by his success in bending the great bow of Shiva, one of the three great gods of Hinduism. But Rama is exiled from court by the machinations of one of Dasaratha's wives, whose son Bharata is then named successor to the throne. He retires with Sita and Lakshmana, his half-brother, to the forest where he is greatly troubled by **rākshasas**, shape-shifting demons. One falls in love with Rama, and when repulsed she incites her brother Rāvana to lust for Sita. Rāvana

seizes Sitá and, having lured Rama and Lakshmana with a golden **deer**, bears her away to his capital, Lankā. Rama and his brother set out to rescue her, and aided by Sugriva, king of the monkeys, and his general Hanumān, they storm the city, kill Rāvana and regain Sita. Although Sita vigorously repulsed Rāvana's attentions, Rama abandons her in the forest when her honour is called into question by his subjects. She meets Valmiki the hermit (traditionally the first poet, and a reformed thief) and bears Rama's twin sons at his retreat, and over the next 12 years Valmiki composes the Ramayana itself. Finally Sita and Rama are reunited and Sita calls upon the earth to vindicate her faithfulness by opening to receive her, which it does. Soon afterwards Rama himself is recalled to heaven.

Like most ancient epics, the Ramayana is drawn from a rich tradition of folklore circulating orally. Three different versions exist today—the Bengal, Bombay and West Indian—and there are many other vernacular traditions. Whereas the *Mahabharata* is written in narrative form and its tales continued to be widely developed in transmission, the Ramayana is a poetic work which is usually recited; its recitation in India is considered an act of great religious significance and virtue, able to cleanse a person from sin. Rama himself is honoured annually at a festival in Benares, and he is widely revered, particularly by the dying.

The events of the Ramayana are celebrated too in dance, theatre and art; the tale has been fundamental to Indian consciousness and identity for over 2 000 years.

Rapunzel

THE MAIDEN IN THE TOWER, heroine of a folk tale collected by Grimm. She is a **promised child**, given to a witch by her father who has offended the witch and would otherwise die himself. Rapunzel is kept in a tall tower with only one high window, which the witch enters by climbing the girl's long hair like a rope. One day a prince comes upon the tower; he is entranced by Rapunzel's singing and hides himself to watch the witch make her customary ascent. When she

Rapunzel

doning her in the desert. When the prince arrives again and calls for Rapunzel to let down her hair it is the witch and not his lover on the other end of the ladder, and the prince escapes by leaping from the tower; he is, however, blinded by the thorns in which he lands. Finally the lovers find each other, and Rapunzel's tears heal the prince's eyes.

The tale contains many common motifs: the girl in the service of a witch to whom she has been promised; the imprisonment in a tower to preserve **virginity**; the marriage to a prince; the **abandonment** in the desert; the mutilation (putting out of eyes) as punishment; and the healing power of tears. The tale is found in various forms throughout Europe and travelled to the New World, especially Spanish America and the West Indies.

raspberry

SOFT SUMMER FRUIT, from bushes of the genus *Rubus* (family Rosaceae). In many areas of the world it is a symbol of remorse, and in the Philippines raspberry brambles are often outside houses in mourning, to entangle the dead spirit should it try to re-enter. Raspberry-leaf tea has been used since ancient times, with proven efficacy, for easing childbirth, and raspberry vinegar is used as an astringent to treat colds, fevers and sore throats.

rat

AGGRESSIVE AND OMNIVOROUS RODENT, any one of the many species in the genus *Rattus*. The folklore of the rat closely mirrors that of the **mouse**, with which it has frequently been confused, although it is generally less well-regarded. It is often a symbol of death, perhaps because of early apprehension of its connection with the plague virus. In modern folklore the sailors' superstition that rats can sense when a ship is about to sink, and will leave it, has become proverbial for the desertion of adherents experienced by any individual or project whose popularity is waning.
▷ **mouse**; **Pied Piper of Hamelin**

rattle

PERCUSSION INSTRUMENT, in which objects are strung together or enclosed

has gone, the prince too calls for Rapunzel to throw down her ladder of hair, and thus ascends to her chamber.

The witch, however, discovers the deceit, and punishes Rapunzel by cutting off her marvellous hair and aban-

wicker rattle from Ubangi Shari, Congo

a resonant container so that they produce a rattling noise when agitated. The earliest rattles may have developed from ornamentation; bundles of bones, shells or similar objects tied to a dancer's clothes would be used to accompany the rhythms of dancing. Primitive gourd rattles are also known to have been common in prehistoric times, and in almost all cultures rattles have been used for ritual, sacred or magical purposes.

The variety of materials used for rattles is astonishing; Alaskan Inuits use puffin-beaks attached to mittens, hunting groups use deer-hoofs or those of antelope, goats or buffalo; island groups use small shells as rattles and bigger shells as containers; agricultural groups use gourds, fruit-pips, nuts, wheat grains; other materials include tortoise shells, sticks, bird talons, pebbles and butterfly cocoons, with basketry and claywork as containers among several groups.

The method of construction varies from the simple clusters described above to a variety of more sophisticated instruments. Gourds, for example, may have shells tied around the rim, which rattle as the gourd is gently tossed and caught; two gourd halves might contain completely the rattling objects, often with an added wooden handle; smaller gourds may be fastened loosely together on a stick which is then struck regularly on the ground or a gourd may be loosely covered with a beaded mesh. This diversity reflects and in some ways dictates the similarly diverse methods of sounding the rattle. The main division is between passive and active manipula-tion—whether the rattle is totally identified with the dancer's movements by being fastened to the clothes or is actively shaken or struck. Naturally active manipulation covers a diversity of techniques depending upon the construction of the rattle or upon the desired effect; it may be struck against the hand or against the floor, shaken horizontally or vertically, vibrated constantly or shaken with a distinct accent or sounded in any combination of these techniques. Frequently the nature of the dance will determine the sounds produced by the rattle, from a staccato stomp to sinuous, gliding steps matched by a whispering sustained shake. In many societies fine degrees of timbre are utilized, and rattle-making and -shaking is a highly respected art.

It has been suggested that rattles developed as **amulets** to keep evil spirits at bay with their noise. This is supported by the fact that rattles are most widely and consistently used during ceremonies of **exorcism** or celebrations for the dead. The widespread use of rattles at puberty or **initiation** ceremonies is almost certainly intended to protect the initiates at this vulnerable time, to summon and control the powerful ancestral spirits. Shamans interpret the voices of the spirits in the rattles.
▷ **scraper**; **sistrum**

raven

BEARER OF TRUTH. In ancient Greece the raven was a prophetic bird sacred to Apollo, and in Teutonic lore Odin depended on two ravens for news of what was happening in the world. The **Valkyries** in their more fearful aspect were said to take the form of ravens. In European and Asian folklore generally the bird is regarded as an omen of death or ill-fortune.
▷ **Faithful John**; **Three Ravens**

recognition token

PLOT DEVICE, widely used in folktales and particularly in the **Cinderella** tale type. An item or marking peculiar to the central character serves to identify him or her, usually to an object of love. In the **Cap o' Rushes** tale type **salt** is used, but the lost shoe is more characteristic of the

Cinderella cycle. In the tale of the Lady of **Llyn y Fan Fach** the hero succeeds in recognizing his bride among two identical companions by noting the detail of her shoe-tie.

Red Branch

OLD IRISH WARRIORS, the guard and companions of King **Conchobar** of Ulster in the first century AD. In his great stronghold at Emain Macha were stored the heads and weapons of their defeated enemies. They were renowned as the fiercest, most touchy warriors in the history of Ireland, so volatile that they could not be trusted to wear arms as they feasted, and they were obliged to lay their swords in the Speckled House, another hall at Emain Macha, when they ate. Twelve of their number were especially celebrated as heroes: this twelve included **Cuchulainn**, **Fergus Mac Roich** and the three sons of Usnech, Naoise, Ainle and Ardan (see **Deirdre**). The tales of their exploits form a central part of the great **Ulster cycle** of Irish legend.

Redcap

MALICIOUS GOBLIN, found in the Borders of Scotland. His name derives from his habit of dyeing his hat in human blood, and he inhabits ruined castles or any dreary place where atrocities have been committed. He can be overcome by a **cross**.

Redcap

Renauld

RENAULD DE MONTAUBAN, the hero of a Old French *chanson de geste*, *The Fou Sons of Aymon* (see **Aymon, Four Son of**) and Tasso's famous epic poer *Rinaldo* (early 16th century). Followin a heated argument over a game of ches Renauld slays the nephew of **Charle magne** and is then besieged, along wit his brothers, at the fortress of Mo tessor. Renauld escapes with the aid the marvellous horse **Bayard**, despit the massed forces against him whic number his father Aymon among the ranks, and turns to a devout life Westphalia. He aids unpaid in th construction of Cologne cathedral, b his resentful workmates murder him an throw his body into the Rhine. company of angels escorts the body Dortmund along the river and Renaul is buried in state.

revenants

ANY SPECIES OF BEING THAT COMES BAC FROM THE GRAVE TO TROUBLE THE LIVIN either as a spirit, in its own dead body, having possessed the body of anothe The most common form of revenant the **ghost**; other types include **vampir** and **langsuir**. Revenants may appear ordinary humans (so that those encou tering one do not suspect its nature un it vanishes before them), as human-lik wraiths, as terrifying monsters or disembodied spirits, manifest either in mysterious light or by their destructiv activities. One of the most terrifyi forms taken by a revenant is that of th rolling head, which follows and devou the one that severed it from its body; th motif is known in Europe, Africa ar Indonesia, and many Native America have a similar species of **ogre**.

In general, revenants return on because they have unfinished busine on earth or some score to settle; there fore they are most commonly victims murder or violent accidents. The remain as revenants until their busine or revenge is settled, or until their fu allotted time has expired. This is n true, however, of non-human revena monsters, whose aim is usually th indiscriminate securing of huma victims, and who must be killed disabled by the use of special weapons and rituals.

Revere, Paul (1735–1818)

AMERICAN PATRIOT, one of the participants in the Boston tea party of 1773. He entered folk legend for his feat on 18 April 1775, the eve of the battles of Lexington and Concord, when he rode from Boston to Lexington and Lincoln to warn the people of Massachusetts that the British were on the move. The ride was celebrated in Henry Wadsworth Longfellow's poem *The Midnight Ride of Paul Revere*.

Reynard the Fox

MEDIEVAL BEAST SATIRE CYCLES. The original literary source of the cycle was probably a French work of the late 12th century, but it seems clear that this drew heavily from popular folklore. The main popular branches of the cycle are the *Roman de Renard* in France, the Italian *Rainardo*, the *Reinhart* of Germany and the Flemish *Reinaert*, the source of most subsequent versions, including Caxton's. A Latin version was also written in the tradition of the medieval beast epics, *Ysengrimus*. So popular was the cycle in France particularly that the name 'renard' completely replaced the old word for fox, 'goupil'. One incident in the cycle, when the wolf is persuaded to stick his tail in freezing water and thereby loses it, is found in folklore across the world, including that of Native North American groups, usually applied to the **bear**.
> **fox**

Rhiannon

HEROINE OF THE MABINOGION. She is a beautiful woman dressed in white and gold who rides past King **Pwyll** of Dyfed so swiftly that none of the men he sent after her could keep her pace. Finally Pwyll himself pursues her, and persuades her to stop by his declarations of love. The two marry and a son is born, but the child is stolen and the terrified watching-maids, who fell asleep over their charge, conspire to put the blame on Rhiannon. They smear her hands and face with the blood of a young dog and hide its bones in her bed, and when she

Rhiannon

awakes they accuse her of devouring her child in the night. Their calumny is believed, and Rhiannon is compelled to sit at the castle gate and serve as horse to all visitors, carrying them to the door on her back.

The child, however, is discovered by a peasant named Teirnyon, who brings him up as his own and names him Gwri. When he hears of Rhiannon's plight and notices the young boy's resemblance to Pwyll he takes Gwri back to the castle at Narberth, where he is unanimously declared to be the missing prince and renamed Pryderi ('trouble'). After Pwyll's death, Rhiannon marries Pryderi's friend Manawyddan.

Rhiannon is almost certainly descended from the horse goddess of the Gauls, Epona, and the Celtic Macha, the war goddess who could outrun horses. Some scholars think that in original versions of the tale Rhiannon actually appears before Pwyll in the form of a swift white horse.

rice

CEREAL GRAIN, most commonly *Oryza sativa* (family Gramineae), the basis of the diet of the millions in Asia especially.

The significance of rice as a sustainer of life in such societies is demonstrated by the elaborate ceremonies associated with the planting and harvesting of the rice crop. In Indonesia Rice Mother is the guardian goddess of the crop and its soul, often incarnate in the last sheaf of the harvest which is tied and dressed in semi-human form (cf **harvest doll**). Many groups address the rice spirit by respectful kinship titles—Grandfather, Mother, Grandmother—in acknowledgement of its role as provider and sustainer. In China the traditional form of greeting, an enquiry after one's welfare, translates roughly as 'Have you eaten your rice?'. In Japan one of the most heinous of crimes, second only to defamation of the Emperor, was the waste or desecration of rice, and many folktales tell of the dreadful punishments for such offenders (most commonly blindness). Rice was the second level, after Buddha himself, in the Buddhist ten-fold value system of classification. Rice cakes and *sake*, rice wine, are essential parts of sacrificial and ceremonial feasts in Japan.

In some areas, for example in Java, husband and wife are encouraged to have sexual intercourse among the growing rice plants, to stimulate the crop, but in many areas the sacred crop demands purity—abstinence from intercourse or ritual cleanness—hence women are frequently barred at critical times such as harvest or drought because of the negative magic of **menstruation**. The connection of rice with fertility and the life principle, although weaker in the West where other cereal crops provide the staple foods, survives in the marriage custom of throwing the rice over the bride and groom.

riddles

TALE TYPE OF QUESTIONS AND TRICKERY. Riddles are among the most ancient types of folklore, found throughout the world alongside folktales, myths and proverbs. It is uncertain whether riddles were indigenous to Native Americans or they developed a tradition after European contact. Rather than the practical wisdom or the creation stories of a culture, riddles contain its thought associations, which can often be startling

or beautiful and are usually witty. Fun damentally the riddle is a form o metaphor, linking together by th rational and imaginative processes o thought two otherwise dissimila objects. As a society becomes mor sophisticated, these simple connection lose the delight of freshness which essential to the most familiar riddle an in the West now riddles are general either complex parlour games or give over to children, who still perpetuate th old forms.

The earliest surviving riddles are fro ancient Babylonian school writings, an the word itself in English, German an Greek (*aineo*, from which we deriv 'enigma') derives from native forms of verb which could also mean 'to counsel Like fables, which they resemble in the allegorical interpretation, riddles hav been used throughout the ages t instruct. Solving riddles engages th mind with the external, puzzling worl rationalizing patterns of similarity an peculiarity, and bringing the environ ment within the compass of tribal com prehension. As well as being a means o coming to terms with the surroundin world, the riddle develops the capaci for sustained, imaginative application i the individual intellect of both childre and adults, a function which Wester adults have attempted to replac recently, with varying degrees of su cess, with the question-and-answe series known as a 'quiz'. In less sophi ticated societies, the groups will ofte gather for riddle contests, in which th winner gains great prestige and ofte material reward.

In some societies riddles retain strong magical or religious significanc for example as a means of addressin indirectly what would otherwise b **taboo**, particularly in the vicinity of corpse, in order to deceive the dange ous spirit. In ceremonies such as harves **initiation** or **marriage**, participants ma be asked riddles which they must answe correctly to ensure the success of th rites, and at other occasions riddle-tel ing is strictly forbidden. In contrast t the innocent riddles now associated wit children, such cultures often hav obscene riddles using words otherwis forbidden, which suggest that bot aboo words and riddles are bound up with belief in potent magic which must be carefully controlled. There is still a strong and ancient tradition in European folklore of the 'dirty joke', often told in riddle form, which recalls the time when riddles were an accepted part of the orgiastic festivals of the winter solstice.

One of the most widespread motifs of folklore is the riddle contest, in which the hero stakes his life, his reputation or his claim to the glittering prize upon his ability to answer the riddles set him. Sometimes he may triumph through his own cleverness, more usually he benefits from helpful animals or supernatural aid. The most famous classical example is the **Sphinx**'s riddle solved by **Oedipus**, who thus saved the city of Thebes, but in Biblical lore also Samson posed riddles and Solomon answered them. The princess of the fairy tale is often won by the peasant who can answer the riddle set by her father, and the **Devil** is well-known in Scandinavian lore for posing riddles about himself which a man must answer to save his soul.

> **conundrums**; **jokes**

Rip Van Winkle

LITERARY FIGURE PARTAKING OF THE MAGICAL SLEEP, a popular motif of folklore. Washington Irving's Rip Van Winkle, whose story was published in *The Sketch Book* in 1819–20, is a good-natured peasant from a Dutch colonial village in the Catskill Mountains, New York state. An easy-going man, helpful to others but hopeless at keeping his own affairs in order, Rip Van Winkle enjoys great popularity in the village, but has to endure the continual hectoring of a shrewish wife. Climbing in the Catskills one day he comes to the aid of a quaintly dressed traveller, labouring to carry a large keg up the mountain. They climb a gully in silence to a fissure where a group of sombre, similarly outlandish figures are playing nine-pins. There, overcome by thirst and curiosity, Rip drinks from the keg and soon falls into a deep sleep. He awakes to find his surroundings changed; the gully has become a stream, his gun is rusted and old, his dog no longer by his side. He sets off hastily down to the village, fearing the anger of his wife, and finds it and its inhabitants greatly changed.

The sleep has lasted not one night but 20 years, and Rip has much trouble establishing his identity. Finally he is accepted by his grown children and begins a new life of content and idleness free from his nagging wife, by now deceased. The strange crew he had met in the mountains is identified as Henrik Hudson and his men, one of the earliest explorers of the area after whom the river was named.

Irving was drawing on an ancient folk narrative when he wrote this legend; he had heard from Sir Walter Scott the legend of **Thomas the Rhymer** but the theme of the **sleeper** is far more ancient. Grimm records a tale in *Teutonic Mythology* of a blacksmith who loses his way in the mountains, encounters some

Rip Van Winkle

unworldly bowlers and is given a bowling ball which turns into gold. The German tale of Peter Klaus, a goatherd in Thuringia, is very similar to Irving's tale in many details, as is a Chinese version about Wang Chih, who stumbles across an unearthly chess game. In all these examples of the form, the consistent use of mountains and caves as scenes of the supernatural sleep is clearly significant.

The motif of the sleep outside time is a common one then, and its fascination is obvious, but what is characteristic of Rip Van Winkle and a significant few such as Peter Klaus is the witnessing of the enigmatic game ritual. This seems to be an element from ancient mythology, where thunder is caused by the sport of the gods; Rip has stumbled into an **otherworld** drawn from ancient Scandinavian and Teutonic mythologies via the traditions of fairy lore. In Irving's working of the ancient form, Hudson and the colonists take the place of the gods and of the kings and warriors of earlier legends.

▷ **sleepers**

rites de passage

CEREMONIAL EVENTS, charting the progress of the individual through all stages of life in the community, celebrated in some form in every society known to have existed. The French phrase has been widely accepted by anthropologists; it translates as 'rites of passage' or 'passage rites'.

The key life events regarded by most societies as *rites de passage* are **childbirth**, **initiation**/adulthood, **marriage** and **death**. In many societies the ceremonies associated with these involve a ritual separation from the former state, special instruction or teaching (for initiation particularly) and a welcome and celebration of the individual's new state in the community (or, in the case of death, beyond it). In highly developed societies such ceremonies remain central to societal life, although the literal interpretations of separation, death to the old life and rebirth to the new are generally portrayed in more symbolic terms, for example in the pictorial drowning and re-emergence of baptism, a form of initiation, or the lifting of the bride's veil at the wedding.

ritual

CHARM TO ENSURE PROTECTION, especiall at points of life-crisis such as birth marriage and death. Pregnant wome and babies are thought to be especiall susceptible to the **evil eye** and demons and the obvious dangers of birth i primitive societies have led to a wid variety of charms to ensure the safety c mother and child. The wedding ring ma well be a relic of a protective and bindin charm, as metal rings are found to be i other parts of the world. Ritual mark out and makes safe the transition from each stage of life to the next, and the us of charms is a natural means c expressing the need for protection from evil at these sensitive times. Ritual wa also a significant factor in the making c charms: to be fully effective, **amulets** c **talismans** were often made at certai propitious times with specific ceremo nies, such as sacrifices.

▷ **charm**; **childbirth**; **spell**

roane

GENTLE FAIRY-RACE, the seal people c the Scottish Highlands and Island Whereas their close cousins **selkies** ofte took revenge against their captors th roane seem to have held no suc grudges, desiring only peace and respectful privacy. Roane females some times come up to the shore, cast off the seal-skins and dance as human maiden and a fisherman who manages to steal skin can force the **seal maiden** to becom his wife; she will inevitably return to th sea eventually (see **fairy marriages**).

▷ **swan maiden**

Rob Roy properly Robert MacGre gor (1671–1734)

NOTORIOUS OUTLAW OF THE SCOTTIS HIGHLANDS, named for his dark red ha (his nickname means 'Red Rob'). H became a popular Scottish folk her especially after the romanticized view c his life promulgated by Sir Walter Sco (*Rob Roy*, 1818) and Wordsworth, aki to England's **Robin Hood**. He was even tually arrested and incarcerated, despi the friendly influence of John Campbe of Argyll which had protected him for s long, but was pardoned before depo tation and subsequently converted to pious Roman Catholicism.

robin

EUROPEAN BIRD WITH A DISTINCTIVE
RUSTY-ORANGE THROAT AND CHEST, *Erithacus rubeula*. The term is also applied
to a variety of similar-looking thrush-like birds around the world. It is known
affectionately in British lore as Robin
Redbreast, and a pious tradition tells
how the compassionate bird tried to
pluck the thorns from Christ's crown on
his way to Calvary; the blood from
Christ's head, or that from the injured
robin, stained its breast red. The bird
was traditionally said to provide a covering of leaves for the dead.

Robin Goodfellow see puck

Robin Hood

LEGENDARY ENGLISH FOLK HERO, the
noble outlaw. Said to have lived in
Sherwood Forest in the English North
Midlands, he protected the poor and
outwitted, robbed, or killed the wealthy
and unscrupulous officials of Church and
State. Since the only source we have for
the existence of Robin Hood is the
ballad cycle probably beginning in the
14th century, it seems likely that he is an
entirely fictitious character, in whom
was embodied the rebellious disquiet of
the northern peasants during the turbulent years from the end of the 12th
century, which culminated in the
Peasants' Revolt of 1381.

A Geste of Robyn Hode is the most
detailed and complex of all the early
ballads; it appears to be a collection of
tales circulating in oral tradition loosely
tied together in a 15th-century work.
Characteristically, it portrays Robin as a
brave, highly skilled archer, well-versed
in romance traditions and etiquette,
whose aim is to take money for the rich
and corrupt, not for his own benefit but
to help the poor and dispossessed. The
Geste also contains a fragmentary
account of Robin's death, treacherously
bled to death by a prioress, his
kinswoman.

That tales of Robin Hood were widespread among the peasantry (and viewed
with some suspicion by the gentry) is
evident however from earlier references, such as that of William Langland in
Piers Plowman, in which the negligent

priest Sloth prefers 'rymes of Robyn
hood' to his paternoster.

It seems clear that the original character Robin Hood was a folk hero of the
people, usually described as a yeoman,
who waged effective war on the local
government officials of Nottingham and
South Yorkshire (much of the action is
set in Barnsley, not Sherwood Forest).
His feats of archery were legendary, as
was the amazing strength of his followers
such as **Little John**. The medieval ballads, which most nearly portray this
early form of the legend, include *A Geste
of Robyn Hode*, *Robin Hode and the
Monk*, *Robin Hood and Guy of Guisborne* and *Robin Hood and the Potter*.

In later ballads and tales **Friar Tuck**
and, even later, Maid Marian joined the
band and they quickly became the most
popular characters after Robin himself.
As the legend developed a circulation
among the nobility, it was suggested and
quickly accepted that Robin Hood had
originally been a nobleman, dispossessed by treachery and living the life of
an outlaw. This lent the legend romance,
chivalry and literary appeal, but
removed it from its original context of

Robin Hood

peasant rebellion, and thereby lost much of the earlier vitality. The common belief that he lived during the absence of Richard I at the Crusades sprang from the misleading history written by Richard Stukey in the 18th century, but it has held much credence since its adoption in Walter Scott's *Ivanhoe* (1818). It has also been suggested, more plausibly, that the historical Robin Hood was a dispossessed follower of Simon de Montfort, who lived as an outlaw after the defeat of his leader at Evesham in 1265.

Robin Hood, Maid Marian and Friar Tuck became popular figures in May Day celebrations, and the marriage of Robin and Marian took the place of symbolic fertility rituals in some areas, replacing the usual May King and Queen.

roc

FABULOUS BIRD OF ARABIAN LORE, said to carry off **elephants** and other such improbable creatures to devour in its mountain nest. It appears primarily in the tale of **Sinbad** in the *Arabian Nights*, but the explorer Marco Polo mentions it; he tells how Kubla Khan, seeking sight of the roc in Madagascar, was presented with an alleged roc's feather. This is thought to have been a palm frond of the *Raphia* genus. It is associated with storms, but its enormous luminous **egg** is a symbol of the sun. It is said never to land on earth, except on the axis of the world, Mount Gaf.

Rock Candy Mountain

IMAGINARY OTHERWORLD, the object of quest for generations of American hobos. Like the Land of **Cockaigne**, it is a place of unending pleasure and plenty, where cool beer splashes in the streams, cigarettes grow on trees, ice-cream tops the mountains and fried breakfasts nestle among the undergrowth. Dollar bills grow in place of leaves, but these can cheerfully be left on the tree since no-one has need of any money. The Big Rock Candy Mountain has been celebrated in traditional hobos' songs.

rockfoil see saxifrage

Roderick (d.711)

SPANISH KING AND HERO, also known as Rodrigo, the last of the Visigoth kings slain by Muslims. He was elected king in preference to the infant son of his predecessor Witiza; Witiza's widow and family fomented revolt and conspired with the Muslims of North Africa to overthrow him. Tariq ibn Ziyad, governor of Tangier, defeated and killed Roderick at Rio Barbate and marched on to Toledo to take control of much of Spain.

Many legends grew up around the figure of Roderick. In some versions the Muslim troops attacked in revenge for Roderick's rape of Florinda, daughter of the count of Ceuta, and he survived the defeat to spend the rest of his days as a hermit doing penance before being eventually devoured by snakes. In some versions too he is a **sleeper**, a hero awaiting the call of his country in need to awaken him.

Roland

HERO OF OLD FRENCH LEGEND, one of the 12 paladins of **Charlemagne**, and central figure of what is generally considered the earliest and greatest *chanson de geste*, *La Chanson de Roland*.

He was portrayed in medieval legend as a tall, heroic nobleman, headstrong and reckless in danger. His step-father Ganelan, angered because of Roland's success or because the hero recommended him for the dangerous mission of negotiating peace with the Saracens conspired with the enemy to overthrow him. He revealed the route to be taken by the returning army and ensured that Roland would lead the rear guard. Roland's men were overpowered at the pass of Roncesvalles in the Pyrenees and massacred. Despite the urging of his friend Oliver, Roland refused to sound the **horn** that would bring Charlemagne to their aid until it was too late, and when Charlemagne arrived he could only avenge his dead heroes. In some versions Ganelan convinces Charlemagne that Roland is merely hunting deer when he sounds the horn and thus the hero is left to his fate.

Many folkloric elements are present in the tale, particularly in the figure of the hero of supernatural strength and stature. Roland's horn Olivant was said to have come from the giant Jutmundus when it was sounded for the third time birds fell from the sky and the horn cracked in two. His marvellous sword Durandel, or Durindana, which contained several saints' relics, including a tooth of St Peter's, Roland cast into a poisoned stream to prevent his enemies taking possession of it, and it is said to lie there still, imperishable.

In Italian legend, Roland becomes Orlando, hero of such literary works as Boiardo's *Orlando Innamorato* and Ariosto's *Orlando Furioso*, in which Orlando goes mad on being rejected by the king of Cathay's daughter until his wits are collected from the moon and brought back to him by Astolpho.

romancero

BALLAD FORM OF SPAIN. Although more historically-based than the ballads of England and Scotland, with much greater emphasis being placed on credibility, *romancero* show the same dramatic form and concentration on sensational incident. The old epics were reworked into ballad form, for example El **Cid** becomes by the 14th century a swash-buckling folk hero in an enormous number of ballads. Another important area is that of the 'frontier ballad', composed about and during the conquest of Granada and the Christian wars against the Moors. In Spain the literary and historical value of the ballads is unusually high; they have permeated the national spirit and culture for generations.

In the centuries of Spanish colonization these ballads were spread to much of the New World, where the form developed into the Hispanic ballads of South America, the Philippines and parts of Africa.

Romulus and Remus

LEGENDARY TWINS, THE FOUNDERS OF ROME. They were the sons of Rhea Silvia, daughter of King Numitor of Alba Longa and a Vestal Virgin by compulsion when her uncle Amulius usurped the throne. Amulius thus hoped to avoid legitimate heirs to the throne, but Rhea Silvia was impregnated by the war-god Mars. She was executed for breaking her vow of chastity and the

twins were abandoned; they were discovered and suckled by a she-wolf and taken in by a kindly herdsman, Faustulus.

The two grew up and eventually led a group to kill Amulius and restore Numitor to the throne; they then collaborated on a city to be built near the site by the Tiber where they had been saved, beside a sacred fig tree. They argued over the plans, however, and in anger Romulus killed his brother and became sole king of the new city, Rome. He invited the neighbouring Sabines for a feast and abducted and raped their wives; the women married their Roman captors and hence the population of Rome began to grow.

Romulus was said to have been swept up into heaven in Mars's chariot; he was subsequently worshipped by the Romans as Guirinus. After killing his brother, Romulus is said to have instigated the Lemuria in his memory.

The legend is an example of the preoccupation with providing eponymous heroes to account for important institutions and places, common in the classical world and many other cultures. It includes several key folkloric motifs, such as the **abandonment** of infants, the supernatural conception of twins, the **animal nurse** and the ascent to the sky by the hero.

Rónán

IRISH KING OF LEINSTER, whose tragic tale is recorded in the ***Book of Leinster***. After his first wife, the mother of his son Mael Fothartaig, died, Rónán takes as wife a young girl who falls in love with his son. Mael rejects her advances, but eventually the rebuffed queen, angered by his rejection, seeks revenge. She tells Rónán that Mael has tried to seduce her repeatedly, sending his foster-brother Congal as his pander, and Rónán is persuaded by her lies. He impales Mael and Congal with his spears as they sit, but as they die learns the truth. Congal's brother avenges himself on the queen's father, mother and brother, and when she sees their heads brought back she commits suicide. Mael's two sons kill their grandfather in revenge.

This tale is a characteristically Irish reworking of the Potiphar's wife motif, in which a repulsed woman revenges herself by accusing the object of her love of rape or attempted seduction, marked by a bloody preoccupation with revenge and elaborate laments for the dead.

rose

RENOWNED FOR THEIR COLOURFUL, FRA-GRANT BLOOMS, any of over 100 plant species of the genus *Rosa*, family Rosaceae. Most rose species are native to India; legend has it that the rose was brought to the West by Alexander the Great. It has a rich and varied folklore and has functioned as an emblem of beauty, secrecy, suffering and love.

The rose is said to have grown in Eden; it was originally white but blushed pink when Eve kissed its petals. An early Christian legend claimed that before the Fall the rose had no thorns. In classical myth it became red from the blood of Venus, whose feet were pricked by its thorns as she sought Adonis heedlessly, or from a cup of wine mischievously poured over the flower by Cupid. Another legend tells how Cupid shot an arrow into the flower after being stung by a **bee** as he bent to smell it; hence the sharp thorns of the rose. The **nightingale** is said to be enamoured of the rose, and the blood from its breast which it presses to a thorn stains the flower red. Similarly, the rose was used to make Christ's crown of thorns and its red colour comes from the divine blood. Several pious saints' legends relate how the flames that consumed martyrs turned afterwards into red roses, and when Zoroaster was placed in the fire as a baby he was saved when the flames turned immediately into roses.

Despite its consistent association in Western lore with female attributes—the rose is particularly associated in art with the Virgin **Mary** and other chaste female saints—in Arab lore it was an emblem of male beauty. The white rose was said to have sprung from the tears of Muhammad on his journey from heaven.

From classical times to the present, rose bushes have been associated particularly with the dead; a Swiss cemetery is commonly known as a Rosengarten. White roses were traditionally placed on a virgin's grave. The falling of the petals of the blown rose is often used as symbol

rose

of mortality. In a Turkish fable a rose and **butterfly** vie for supremacy, the rose boasting of its long life and beauty and the butterfly of its freedom to visit many different gardens. As they argue the lives of both are cut short; a woman stoops to pluck the rose while a bird swoops down on the butterfly. The moral is the uselessness of vanity. In Indo-European folktales the rose often appears as a **chastity test** (it loses its petals or changes colour in the presence of impurity) and a **life token**, which fades and dies with the hero.

To hang a rose in a room in ancient Greece meant that all conversation could be freely conducted and treated as confidential, hence *sub rosa*, in secret.

In Northern Europe the rose is widely believed to be a possession of the **little people**, and it is considered prudent to ask their permission before picking one. This is echoed in the tale of **Beauty and the Beast**, in which Beauty's father arouses the beast's wrath by plucking a rose for his daughter from the beast's garden. In some tales the rose has the power of restoring a transformed animal back to human shape.

Roses have been used extensively in folk medicine. The benefits of vitamin-rich rosehips have been recognized since ancient times and rosehip syrup is still commonly given to babies. A petal in the wine glass was thought by the Romans to guard against drunkenness; this may explain in part the lavish preponderance

of rose petals at banquets. In Britain a distillation of rose petals in wine was used as a compress for sprains. Greeks used the petals to treat wounds, especially the bite of a mad dog.
▷ **obstacle flight**

rosemary

PUNGENT HERB, *Rosmarinus officinalis* (family Laminaceae), widely used in seasoning and in folk medicine. It has been regarded as an emblem of remembrance and faithfulness since classical times—it was said to strengthen and improve the memory if consumed, and was a popular plant for funeral wreaths (for remembrance) and wedding bouquets (for fidelity). Greek scholars wore amulets of rosemary sprigs to enable them to memorize their lessons.

Rosemary is associated with rejuvenation, perhaps because of its benefits in keeping memory clear, and a bath in rosemary water is said to make the old young again. It is also regarded as a stimulant and aphrodisiac, and is associated particularly with female love; a girl wishing to see her future husband had only to take a mixture of rosemary and **thyme** on St **Agnes**'s Eve (20 January). An old English proverb claims that 'where rosemary thrives the mistress is master' but elsewhere in Europe rosemary will grow only in the garden of sinless folk. It is widely credited with the virtue of keeping evil spirits at bay, and a sprig placed under the pillow will protect the sleeper from a visit by the **nightmare**. In Christian lore it is blessed because it once opened its branches and enclosed the Holy Family on the flight to Egypt, since when its flowers have been tinged with the blue of the Virgin's cloak.

Apart from its uses in strengthening memory and as a tonic, rosemary is widely used to clear the complexion, soothe a sore throat and prevent baldness. Rosemary ash was used as a dentifrice in England, and rosemary tea is drunk to cure feverish colds.

Rosh Hashana

JEWISH NEW YEAR FESTIVAL, celebrated on the first two days of Tishri (September/October). It is a time of reflection and self-examination; the blowing of the ram's **horn**, the *shofar*, calls the people to spiritual wakefulness, before the celebrations of Yom Kippur, the feast of atonement. Like many New Year festivals, it may originally have been a feast of the dead, at which the ceremonial blowing of the horn dispelled evil spirits.

In Jewish legend, God is said to open three books at Rosh Hashana—the book of the blessed, the book of the damned, and the book of those who must decide their fate before Yom Kippur. The custom of Taschlich, casting, is associated with the festival; crumbs are thrown from the pocket into water to symbolize the rejection of sin. This reflects ancient folk practices of offering bread and other offerings to water-spirits by throwing them onto the water at important festivals.

Ross, Betsy (1752–1836)

UPHOLSTERER, who won a place in American folk history by making the first ever Stars and Stripes, the flag of the Union, in 1776. According to popular legend, George Washington, Robert Morris and General George Ross visited her workshop in Philadelphia with their design for the new flag, but Betsy rejected their six-pointed stars, insisting that stars with five points would look much better. She prevailed, and the flag has retained her design ever since.

Round Table

ARTHURIAN LEGEND. The table at the court of King **Arthur** and the focus for his chivalric fellowship of knights. The table first appears in the *Roman de Brut* of the Norman poet Wace of Jersey (1155). He explains that Arthur had it constructed to avoid contests over precedence among his knights—at a round table, nobody can claim the head. The English poet Layamon elaborated on this with a tale of a bloody battle fought by Arthur's barons over seating arrangements, in which seven nobles died, before the Round Table was built. This tradition may owe much to the Irish tale of **Bricriu's Feast** and the Last Supper, at which the disciples of Jesus quarrelled among themselves as to precedence; early Christian art traditionally portrayed the **thirteen** around a round table, and this identification sat well with the medieval portrayal of Arthur as an archetypal Christian ruler, and with his close association with the **Grail** legend. Robert de Borron in his *Joseph d'Arimathie* (c.1200) records how **Joseph of Arimathea** was instructed to make a table like that of the Last Supper, with a seat to be left eternally vacant, symbolizing the place of Judas. The seat left vacant by **Judas Iscariot** the betrayer translated to Arthur's table as the Siège Perilous, on which only a sinless knight could sit; all others (including **Merlin**) were swallowed by the earth. In later Arthurian legend Merlin was credited with the idea of the Round Table, in his role as advisor to **Uther Pendragon**.

The table was alleged in some versions to seat 1 600 persons comfortably; other sources give the number at a more modest 150 or even 13, as at the Last Supper. The great round table hanging on the wall in Winchester, said to be that of Arthur's court, is thought to date from the 13th century, and was probably designed with the Arthurian legend in mind; the painted figures of Arthur and the names of the knights probably date from 1486, and the reign of the Tudor king, Henry VII.

The Round Table became a central emblem in Arthurian literature and legend, and was influential in forming the popular image of a chivalric company centred in the court of a nobleman or ruler.

▷ **John o'Groat**

rowan

MOUNTAIN ASH, a favourite tree of the Druids. It is one of the many trees said to have been used to make Christ's cross, and is regarded as especially potent against **witchcraft** and evil spirits. Crosses of rowan wood were placed as **amulets** over the doors of houses and stables to protect the occupants, and in Scotland it was said that a witch touched by a rowan switch would instantly be carried off by the **Devil**.

ruby

PRECIOUS GEMSTONE, the colours of which range from pale rose to the most highly valued pigeon-blood red. True, or oriental, rubies are found mainly in Myanma (Burma), and occasionally in Thailand and Sri Lanka, but red gems throughout the world are commonly known as rubies; the rubies spoken of in the Bible are probably carbuncles.

In Islamic lore, the **Atlas**-like angel who supports the world himself stands on a cosmic ruby. Hindu lore asserts that the possessor of a ruby would enjoy a peaceful, secure and successful life, and here as in many cultures the ruby is a **charm** against the ill-will of enemies, sickness and damage to property. Its value has therefore been exceptionally high. Marco Polo reported that the king of Ceylon (Sri Lanka) possessed a ruby of extraordinary size and beauty, for which Kubla Kahn offered him the price of an entire city, in vain. Being blood-coloured, the gem was believed to be medicinally useful in treating diseases of the blood and haemorrhages, and its associated functions included the power to dispel anxiety, grief and fear and promote a sanguine temperament and to both stimulate and control sexual desire. Ancient Burmese inserted rubies into cuts in the skin to render themselves invulnerable to any weapon.

In **alchemy**, the perfect ruby is a term used to refer to the **philosopher's stone**.

rue

AROMATIC HERB, genus *Ruta* of the family Rutaceae. It was a herb of the sun in ancient lore, and has a mixed reputation in folklore. On the one hand it is associated with bitterness (because of its taste), hence grief and remorse, and the word is still used in English with this meaning. **Witches** were said to use the bitter herb in their brew, no doubt because of its mildly poisonous, narcotic effects as well as the bitter taste. However, the herb was also widely used as an antidote to pain (recommended by Pliny against snake-bites) and as an ingredient in **charms** against **witchcraft** and the **evil eye**. Medieval English herbals, followed by Culpeper, promote rue as a remedy for all human ills.

The herb is also closely associated with sexuality; it could be eaten when tempted by the fires of the flesh as a preserver of chastity, or kept as an index of the fidelity of an absent loved one; if it withered, the lover had been untrue (cf **chastity test**, **life token**). Couples experiencing problems in the marital bed used rue to sprinkle holy water in the bedroom, as a charm against mischievous demons.

rukhs see roc

Rumpelstiltskin

ANGRY DWARF OF EUROPEAN FOLKLORE. The tale of Rumpelstiltskin was collected by the Grimm brothers in their *Kinder und Hausmärchen*. In this version, a poor miller attempts to impress the king by boasting that his beautiful daughter can spin straw into gold. The king has the girl brought to him and locks her with a spinning wheel in a room full of straw, with the injunction to spin it into gold on pain of her life. As the terrified girl begins to cry at the hopelessness of her situation, a dwarf appears and offers to perform the impossible task for the price of her necklace.

When the king returns at daybreak the straw has vanished and the reels are full of spun gold. He is delighted, and takes the girl to another, larger room full of straw with the same instructions and the same threat. The dwarf appears again, and agrees to spin the straw into gold for the ring on the miller's daughter's hand. The king is again delighted when he returns the next morning to find the reels full of gold, and takes her to a third, even larger room. This time he promises that if she should spin the straw into gold he will make her his wife; if not, her life would be forfeit. The miller's daughter is in despair, but the dwarf appears again and offers to spin for her. This time the girl can offer nothing, and the dwarf demands instead the promise that when she becomes queen, her first child should be given to him. Not knowing what else to do, she reluctantly agrees.

So the king, finding the next morning a neat pile of gold as usual, marries the miller's daughter and a year later she bears him a child. The dwarf promptly reappears, demanding his payment, but moved by her tears he agrees to give her a chance: if she can discover his name in three days, she may keep the child. The

Rumpelstiltskin

queen sends messengers throughout the land to collect every name they can find, but none belong to the dwarf. On the third day however, one messenger tells how he has overheard a strange little man singing in glee a rhyme which included his name, Rumpelstiltskin. That night, the queen begins her meeting with the dwarf with the usual litany of wrong guesses, and when she finally tells the triumphant dwarf his name he is so enraged that he stamps his foot deep into the ground and tears himself in two trying to pull it out.

The tale is known only in Europe, and elsewhere through European influence, and it has been suggested that it originated in Britain and spread to the rest of the Continent. All the versions share a dependency on the ancient belief in the potency of names, that power can be exercised over an individual if his true name is known. In very many societies the names of gods or revered animals are taboo, and in European folklore ghosts can be exorcised and the **Devil** rendered powerless by the use of their true names.
▷ **Girle Guairle**; **name taboo**; **Tom-Tit-Tot**

rusalki

WATER-SPIRITS OF SLAVIC LORE, usually considered as the spirits of dead females. Northern rusalki are demonic beings, who lure men to their deaths with siren songs before drowning them. The rusalki of the south, however, are more gentle beings; although they too use sweet songs to lure men to them they can prove affectionate lovers, and their victims at least die happy. The rusalka is said in some areas to be the damned soul of a beautiful but wicked girl, in other areas, particularly in Bulgaria where rusalki are known as *samovily*, she is the spirit of an unbaptized baby girl, and elsewhere a bride who died on her wedding night.

▷ **vodyanik**

saffron

SPICE AND DYE, obtained from the dried orange stigmas of the purple crocus *Crocus sativus* (family Iridaceae). It has been prized since ancient times for its flavour, exotic aroma and deep golden colour; in India and Greece particularly it was regarded as an aphrodisiac so potent that it could corrupt any woman who came in contact with it. It was a popular stewing spice in classical times, and its heady aroma became particularly associated with the halls of the professional courtesans. The dye produced by saffron in India was adapted by Buddhist priests as the official colour for their robes soon after the death of Buddha himself. In some areas of China folk rub their bodies with saffron after taking a bath, partly because saffron is regarded round the world as a beneficial ointment for skin and partly to make themselves resemble gold statues of the Buddha. The Arabs used it as a **charm** to keep melancholy at bay and to drive out lizards from the house.

When the spice was introduced to Europe during the Crusades its medicinal value was quickly recognized and exploited; it was drunk in water to cheer the spirits and quicken the mind, carried to ward off the plague by its smell, and taken for gout, rheumatism and measles.

Saffron is still the most expensive of all spices by weight; it has frequently been valued at over its weight in gold. Despite this it has entered the lore of common folk, as colouring in rice and fish dishes in Oriental and Mediterranean cuisine, as well as in charms and medicine.

saga

PROSE WORK OF ICELANDIC LITERATURE, more specifically legendary–historical adventure tales and biographies of medieval Iceland and Scandinavia. Although the word derives from Icelandic *segja*, meaning 'what is told', it is no longer thought that the tales are an accumulated oral lore transmitted through generations before crystallizing in print, but rather consciously literary and artistic creations drawing heavily on oral traditions. The central themes of the saga are typically heroism, revenge (especially blood feuds), loyalty and, especially in the earliest forms, human rather than supernatural action.

Notable sagas include the early *Egils saga* attributed to Snorri Sturluson (1179–1241), the great *Njáls saga* (mid 13th century) and later, more mythologically-inclined works such as the late-13th-century *Volsungasaga*.

sage

AROMATIC HERB, *Salvia officinalis* (family Lamiaceae), native to the Mediterranean regions. It has been renowned in folk medicine for its effects as a stimulant; sage tea is widely drunk as a tonic, and the leaves are said to improve the memory, strengthen the muscles and prolong life.

sailors' lore

TALES AND CUSTOMS SURROUNDING SEAFARING. The unpredictable nature of the sea, hostile, beautiful and mysterious, has long been a refrain of mariners; although seafaring has been used since primitive times for transport, trading, war and fishing, the sense of venturing into an environment which is hostile to human life, and which may harbour unknown creatures in its mysterious depths, is always present. Those societies which depend upon sea travel or fishing usually develop a powerfully ambivalent relationship with the sea—the magnificent source of food and livelihood, but also the harsh 'grey widow-maker'—and this attitude is reflected in the folklore of sailors.

Before the days of sophisticated navigational aids, and even to some extent afterwards, the success of a journey by sea depended largely on external and elemental forces, beyond the control and understanding of the crew. The common response of the folk to danger has always been superstition and the primitive religious impulse of placating the supernatural forces. In Viking shipbuilding, human sacrifice was offered to ensure the true sailing of a longboat and throughout Europe **amulets** of some kind were incorporated into the framework; woods such as **ash** or rowan, powerful against **witches**, shoes, coins and horse-skulls were all used. The **figurehead** was a protective spirit, an animistic embodiment of the ship's spirit, and if it were damaged bad luck would surely follow. A primitive version, widespread in the ancient world, was the *oculus*, a staring eye painted onto the bow of the boat to defeat the **evil eye** and to enable the boat to 'see' its way across the ocean. The elaborate figureheads of the 18th and 19th centuries were often bare-breasted women, from a popular superstition that such a sight would calm a storm.

Once afloat, judicious use of amulets and the observance of taboos were thought to ensure safety. Individual sailors carried **charms** such as gold earrings or lucky coins, and one of the most potent and widespread amulets was the caul which covers the baby's head in the womb, presumably because it prevents it from drowning, and Chinese ships hung up nets to entangle evil spirits. In the 19th century the use of the **tattoo** as the ultimate personal amulet became almost inseparable from a naval career; a crucifix on the back was said to protect against the pain of flogging as well as the more general concern about drowning, and a star on the hand aid navigation. The 'ship-in-a-bottle' is descendant of ancient amulets depicting ships; enclosed in its protective bottle and left safely at home, it secures trouble-free voyage for the ship it represents.

The ship's **cat**, useful to control rats on the voyage, was also associated with good luck and various animal **mascot** were carried by ships until very recently their continued health was said to be connected to that of the ship. On the other hand, women were unwelcome aboard ships as bringers of bad luck until very recently, the exception being a pregnant woman who symbolized new life. A menstruating woman is particularly unlucky, and should not be allowed even to touch the ship or its crew.

The treatment of novices aboard ship traditionally shares many of the elements of primitive **initiation** rites including humiliation, physical pain or arduous effort, and final acceptance into a prestigious male community. Young sailors might be required to swim in the Arctic, or be threatened with flogging or keel-hauling (being dragged by rope under the ship and up the other side) unless they supplied their fellows with drink or money. More recently this has given way to teasing such as instructing the novitiate to collect eggs from the crow's nest. A special case for initiation was upon **crossing the line**, that is, the Equator. At this dangerous spot, when ships could easily become becalmed for days under a blazing sun, human sacrifice was originally practised to appease the god of the sea. The ducking of those who are crossing the line for the first

sailors' lore

time is a relic of such practices. Many reports of the 19th century describe the buffoonery of these ceremonies, which often involved being covered in paint and tar, a rough shave or haircut and dousing with salt water, all under the watchful eye of an august Neptune and his court. The scientist Charles Darwin underwent such a ceremony.

Death at sea was, understandably, regarded with unease, and the corpse was disposed of as soon as possible not merely for hygiene but because it was thought to attract evil spirits. To ensure that the corpse sank, and that it would be unable to follow the ship, it was sewn firmly into a weighted canvas sheet, and frequently the flesh was secured by stitches to the shroud, to ensure that it could not rise as a troublesome ghost. Such practices are reminiscent of burial customs in which scythes or heavy slabs of stone were placed over corpses to prevent them rising as **revenants**. The customary salute of gunfire may have originated as a means of frightening away evil spirits at the moment of burial.

The **mermaid**, beautiful siren, is one of the staple creatures of seafaring lore, but there are many others. There are many tales of snake-like creatures such as **Jormungandr** or the octopus-like **Kraken**, particularly but not exclusively around Scandinavia, and they were regarded as ill omens as well as zoological curiosities. **Dolphins** on the other hand escorted a ship in friendly company, and were said to escort human souls to heaven; it was taboo to harm them.

> **rat**

Saint-John's-wort

YELLOW-FLOWERING SHRUB FAMILY, Hypericaceae, in the tea order (Theales), and particularly the genus *Hypericum*. It is also known as devil's flight, from the properties of keeping evil at bay attributed to it by the crusaders who brought it back from the East. It is traditionally hung above doors to protect the house from evil, especially on feast-days; this may explain the common name for the plant since St John's feast-day (24 June) is **Mid-summer**'s Day and a crucial time for protecting and decorating the house in

such a way. In the witch mania of the 17th century St-John's-wort was widely used to divine **witches** and combat their power; it was also used in exorcisms of people or places possessed by evil spirits. Red spots were said to appear on the leaves on the anniversary of John's beheading at the behest of Salome (29 August).

In folk medicine, St-John's-wort can be used to treat festering wounds and chilblains, and in a wash for sore eyes or as a gargle for inflamed throats. The Meskwaki of North America use the plant to treat tuberculosis.

saints

HISTORICAL AND FICTITIOUS FIGURES OF PIOUS LEGEND, fertile ground for the tales and superstitions of the folk. During the persecutions of the early Christian church, the term 'saint', which had originally been applied to all baptized believers, came to denote the specific class of martyrs, commemorated for making the ultimate sacrifice for their faith. Since such believers were guaranteed a place in heaven because of their suffering, it became common for Christians to regard them as powerful intercessors with God as well as models of Christian life, and thus began the cults and their associated folklore. Later, as persecution ended, the qualifications for sanctity broadened to include any heroic form of piety, such as teaching, asceticism or, particularly for women, chastity.

In medieval Europe, under the influence of Christianity, saints largely replaced supernatural forces as beneficent and powerful protectors, interceding before God on behalf of those who honoured them. Legends of saints' lives proliferated and with the inclusion of supernatural details became almost folkloric (not entirely, since they were received as holy mysteries). Professions and groups claimed saints as their patrons, and those in trouble or danger could call upon a specific saint for protection and relief, for example having lost a valuable possession the peasant might pray to St Antony of Padua, patron saint of lost objects, for its restoration.

Whatever the established Church

might say about the theology of saint worship and its subordination to the worship of God, for the unlettered people the appeal of the saints lay in the magical legends of their lives and their efficacy as supernatural helpers for a variety of situations. Nearly all societies recognize supernatural forces, half-way between natural and divine, and folklore is especially concerned with those things that lie closer to the local and mundane than the purely cosmological aspects of myth. It seems clear that in many peasant societies the saints were accepted within a pre-existent framework of spiritual forces and pagan heroes, and certainly many pagan festivals and temples were later devoted to saint worship, and the distinction not made entirely clear in the popular imagination. In Ireland St Brigid, founder of Kildare Abbey, was conflated with the ancient Celtic deity Brigit in fertility rituals, and the Syrian saint, **George**, is now famously associated with a form of the **dragon-slaying** legend. He has also been renowned for his ability to fertilize barren women, in rituals evolved from ancient Syrian rites.

The practice of writing *Lives* of saints, the precursor of modern biography, led to a legend tradition characterized by a predictable stock-in-trade of motifs and morals. The most famous collection of saints' legends was made by Jacques de Voragine in the 13th century, the *Golden Legend*. These legends were told as *exempla*, to encourage the faithful and reprove the lax, rather than objective history, and hence certain features recur as shorthand expressions of sanctity. Common motifs include infant piety (St Elizabeth of Hungary at the age of five could not be torn away from chapel, and tithed her childish possessions), miraculous healing, and tortures undergone for **virginity**. Closer to the heart of the folk however were the tales of retrieval of lost objects, the power to bring about good crops and fair weather, or to punish horribly for the crime of blasphemy against them.

The relics of saints are invested with great potency also, and incorruptibility of the body after death is another motif of the saint's legend, usually coupled with tales of sweet odours, and this sits alongside the tradition of burial of the dead, in which the spirit or efficacy is said to be dissipated on dissolution of the body.

▷ **guardian spirits**; **Mary, Blessed Virgin**

salamander

A FABULOUS LIZARD-LIKE CREATURE. In ancient lore the salamander was said to dwell in fire, the flames of which were continually quenched by its icy body. It was regarded as the elemental being of fire (as **gnomes** were the elemental beings of earth). Its ability to quench fire led to its adoption by early Christians as a symbol of triumph over the desires of the flesh, and it became associated with the property of fire to consume dross and refine good metal; hence Francis I chose as his symbol the salamander in the flames, with the motto 'I nourish and extinguish'.

The salamander is in fact one of a group of amphibians in the order Urodela (or Candata). It is considered poisonous in many areas.

salt

HIGHLY PRIZED MINERAL, sodium chloride, usually produced by evaporating brine. Because of its fundamental place in human history as a preservative and seasoning, salt has been regarded with special significance in many cultures, as emblem of a binding covenant with God or others. In Hebrew lore it was used to signify a solemn binding agreement, 'a covenant of salt forever' (Numbers 18:19); to eat the salt of one's host in Arab lore meant that one was then bound never to harm or malign him, and Greeks recognized such a discourteous act as a serious crime, a 'sin against the salt'. In many areas, especially the Middle East, it is customary to offer bread and salt to a guest in token of such a goodwill covenant. Salt is commonly given to newly-weds, to preserve and season their happiness, and along with wine and bread to represent the staples of life. Roman soldiers were once paid their wages in salt, and this is the root of the English word salary (from Latin *salarium*). Salt Woman or Salt Mother is a key figure in Pueblo lore and features in the mythologies of several other Native American groups. She represents the vital principle of salt and must be honoured and propitiated if good salt is to be produced.

The modern superstition that spilling salt is unlucky almost certainly derives from this ancient significance. However, ill fortune can be avoided if a pinch of the salt is thrown over the left shoulder, some say to drive the **Devil** from his accustomed position. Certainly salt has long been credited with the power to banish evil influences, since it is an emblem of purity and incorruptibility; it was also commonly added to coffins to preserve the corpse, and thrown into fermenting mash by brewers to keep **witches** from it. Perhaps because of these associations, salt is said to be anathema to **fairy** folk, and a fairy's human disguise can be penetrated by one observant enough to spot this aversion.

Salt features in several folktales; in a version of the **King Lear judgement** motif the wronged princess, who has been banished for telling her father that she loves him more than meat loves salt, reveals herself by the identity token of preparing him a meal without salt. When he realizes how bland and savourless his food is, he appreciates his daughter's love. In another European tale, however, the soup becomes inedible when every member of the family separately remembers to add a handful of salt.
▷ **alomancy**

Samhain see Hallowe'en

Sand Man

CHARACTER OF NURSERY LORE, popular especially in western Europe. He is said to carry a sack of magical sand, which he sprinkles on the eyes of children to send them to sleep and happy dreams. Although he seems to have developed in the tradition of nursery **bogeys**, he is not a fearsome but a benevolent figure.

Santa Claus

PERSONIFICATION OF THE SPIRIT OF GIVING, the most famous figure of **Christmas**. Santa Claus or Father Christmas is a complex creaton drawn from many different threads of tradition. In Scandinavian mythology, Odin rode the winter skies distributing punishment to the wicked and rewards to the good. The Christianized figure is drawn from St **Nicholas**, a bishop of Myra, Asia Minor, in the 4th century whose legend recounts how he saved three sisters from enforced prostitution by secretly providing them with a **dowry** in the form of a bag of gold for each on three successive nights. The Dutch brought their 'Sante Klaas' to the New World, the English of New York took over from the Dutch the name and the present-giving custom, now transferred to Christmas Day, and the modern figure of Santa Claus (anglicized to Father Christmas) developed; a chubby, cheerful, sentimentalized character for children.

A rather morbid development of the Santa legend grew up in modern America; a father dresses up as Santa Claus and climbs down the chimney to surprise his children on Christmas Eve, but unfortunately gets stuck and suffers a heart attack (or asphyxiates) half-way down and dies. The family do not know what has happened until they try to light the fire some time later, or until the smell gives the hiding-place away.

sapphire

VALUABLE GEMSTONE, most characteristically blue in colour. Opaque sapphire, which is usually cut smooth and polished, is known as star sapphire and is prized especially in the Orient, where it is said to contain a captive spirit. The stone is widely credited with benevolent power; it drives away **witches** and demons, strengthens and soothes the eyes, brings health, strength and wealth to the wearer, and promotes goodwill and the indulgence of others.

Sasquatch see Bigfoot

sassafras

NORTH AMERICAN TREE, *Sassafras albidum* of the laurel family (Lauraceae), with aromatic leaves, bright yellow flowers and dark blue berries. It has traditionally been used by Native Americans to treat all manner of illnesses, particularly the ague (its other common name is ague tree). The roots are used to produce a tonic tea, given especially to mothers recovering from childbirth, and the shoots were used by Mohawks to produce an eyewash. Oil of sassafras, extracted from the roots, was the original flavouring for root beer. Among the Iroquois, the leaves were commonly used to treat wounds and purify the blood.

Satan see Devil

satire

POWERFUL CURSE. In old Irish lore, a satire was a rhyme with powerful magic effects; should one be satirized, usually for discourtesy, cowardice or treachery, it was not merely a humiliation but usually literally fatal. **Cuchulainn** was tricked into throwing away the **gae bulg** by one of **Medb**'s satirists, who threatened to denounce the hero and his country as ungiving if he did not. This blackmailing use of the satire is a popular device of Irish legend.

Saturnalia

ROMAN FESTIVAL, the riotous celebration in honour of the god of sowing and agriculture, Saturn. The feast was originally held on 17 December, but as it grew in popularity to become the central popular feast of the year it was extended to cover seven days. During this period all normal social conventions were overthrown; slaves dressed and acted like freemen, no work activities were conducted, and the usual moral and sexual codes were set aside while presents were exchanged and the entire population indulged in feasting, drinking and general merry-making. The festival has had enormous influence on the development of **Christmas** and **New Year** celebrations in Europe. The culmination of the extended festival was the celebration of the birth of the sun, *natalis invicti solis*, dedicated to the god Mithras, on 25 December.

satyrs

FABULOUS BEINGS OF GREEK MYTHOLOGY, half-man and half-goat. They were closely associated with licentiousness and debauchery and in early art were always portrayed in a state of sexual arousal. They pursued nymphs incessantly, but were cowards and generally fled from men. Satyrs and sileni were at first seemingly indistinguishable, but in later lore satyrs became more graceful, **faun**-like creatures while sileni were generally older and fatter, occasionally redeemed by a homely wisdom. Satyr plays, in which the chorus was dressed as a group of satyrs with the attendant liberty to satirize serious legends, were a feature of the great Athenian Dionysia, performed as relief after three tragedies in succession.

Many cultures have similar beings, for example, the goat-footed demons of the mountain passes in Arab lore.

saxifrage

SMALL FLOWERING PLANT, genus *Saxifraga* (family Saxifragaceae), native to Europe. As it typically grows in cracks on rocks, its common names are breakstone and rockfoil. Possibly by analogy with its growing situation, the juice of the plant is said to heal open wounds if dripped into them. It is regarded in many areas as a sterile plant—in Russia, for example, an infusion of saxifrage root is taken as a contraceptive—but in Italy it is said to increase a woman's loveliness. In the 16th century it was widely used by wet-nurses as a **charm** to increase the flow of milk. Perhaps because of its connection with rocks it is said to have the virtue of breaking up kidney stones and gall stones.

scarab

BEETLE, THE SYMBOL OF LIFE IN ANCIENT EGYPT. One of the most famous of ancient **amulets**, it was worn by the living to protect themselves from death and by the dead to ensure the restoration of their vital heat in the next world.

Scheherazade

NARRATOR OF THE TALES OF THE ARABIAN NIGHTS. The elder daughter of the Vizier, she agrees to marry King Shahryar despite his vengeful practice of killing each bride the day after the wedding, which has depopulated the kingdom of women. She saves herself by entrancing the king with a succession of stories, each broken off before the climax, which together form the tales of the 'thousand and one nights'.
▷ *Arabian Nights*

Schlaraffenland see **Cockaigne, Land of**

scorpion

STINGING ARACHNID, any one of approximately 800 species of the order Scorpionida with a venomous sac at the end of a segmented tail. In Roman myth the scorpion stung **Orion** to death, belying his boast of supremacy, and was raised by Jupiter to become the constellation Scorpio. The scorpion is frequently associated with evil and death; in ancient Egyptian myth the goddess of the dead is scorpion-headed and the evil god Set has a scorpion as an attribute. In Christian lore the scorpion represents evil and treachery, and hence is frequently associated with **Judas Iscariot** and, in medieval anti-Semitic fervour, with the Jewish race. Jesus gave his disciples authority over and immunity from scorpions (Luke 10:19), hence dominion over all evil forces. In Hebrew lore (eg 1 Kings 12:11) the scorpion was a symbol of desolation and wilderness. It was commonly believed that the scorpion's flesh contained an oily antidote to their sting, and hence scorpion flesh was given to its victims.

Scott, Michael (c.1175–c.1230)

SCOTTISH SCHOLAR AND ASTROLOGER, the 'wondrous wizard', born probably in Durham, of Border ancestry. He studied at Oxford, Paris and Padua, was tutor and astrologer at Palermo to Frederick II, the Great, settled at Toledo 1209–20 and translated Arabic versions of Aristotle's works and Averroës's commentaries. He wrote a learned work on astrology, *Quaestio curiosa de natura solis et lunae* (1622). Dante alludes to him in the Inferno in a way which proves that his fame as a magician had already spread over Europe, and he is also referred to by Albertus Magnus and Vincent de Beauvais. In Border folklore he is credited with having, in the words of Sir Walter Scott 'cleft the Eildon Hills in three and bridled the Tweed with a curb of stone'; and his alleged grave is shown in Melrose Abbey.

scraper

PRIMITIVE PERCUSSIVE INSTRUMENT, a notched or serrated surface across which a stick or hard implement is rasped. It has been popular in virtually all cultures since the Stone Age. Early uses of the scraper seem to have been consistently associated with magico-religious ceremonies of fertility and hence **rain**-making; as an emblem of the life force (from the phallic connotations of the stick) it is widely used also at funerals, to reinforce the continuation of life in the midst of death. Its use in rain ceremonies may also derive from the resemblance of the sound to the croak of the **frog**.

The Chinese *yü* is a wooden tiger with a notched backbone, scraped three times to mark the close of a Confucian service. A more sophisticated mechanism on the same principle is the cog **rattle** or ratchet, which can produce a continuous rasp by means of a tongue scraping over a revolving cog wheel. Such ratchets have been used as warning devices and particularly as noise-makers in festive parades or at rowdy gatherings (particularly football matches); this use almost certainly derives from ancient ritual practices of sounding scrapers to frighten away evil spirits.
▷ **folk instruments**

sea-serpent

LEGENDARY MONSTER, said to inhabit seas or, less frequently, large lakes, and usually portrayed as a giant snake. Many ancient mythologies record the existence of a primeval sea-serpent defeated by the gods; this seems to be a forerunner of the great **dragonslayer** motif of legend and folklore. Hence the Hebrew God as well as the Canaanite Baal overcomes **Leviathan**, while the Babylonian

sea-serpent

Morduk defeats the many-headed Timat.

Sailors' lore has reported so many sightings of monstrous marine creatures, and with such surprising consistency of detail, that such tales have traditionally been invested with great credibility in folklore. It seems probable, however, that most sightings of monsters can be accounted for by such creatures as the giant squid, with its two elongate arms trailing on the water's surface. These arms flailing around the bulk of a sperm whale as the whale dragged its hapless victim below the surface might easily suggest the reverse to the watcher; that a serpent had looped itself around the whale and was taking it down to devour it. Other possible explanations include a school of leaping porpoises, which might resemble at a glance one long undulating creature.

▷ **dragon**; **Loch Ness monster**; **Patrick, St**

seal maidens

SUPERNATURAL SEA-BEINGS. Like the **swan**, they can be captured and married by mortal men if their sealskins are stolen from them. Like swan maidens, seal maidens may have reasonably happy marriages and produce mortal offspring (often identifiable by webbing between the fingers and toes), but eventually they will almost certainly rediscover the lost sealskin and disappear forever.

▷ **roane**; **selkies**

Sedna

INUIT HEROINE, the mistress of the **underworld**. She disgraces her family by marrying a sea-bird or a dog in preference to all her human suitors, and she is sought by her outraged father. He kills the animal husband and throws Sedna from the boat on the way home. She refuses to release her hold on the side of the boat and he cuts off her **fingers**, which wriggle away with a life of their own to become all the creatures of the sea and eventually avenge Sedna by consuming her father. She is the chief god of the underworld, who is honoured annually with a great feast.

Although the tale is primarily mythological, an origin tale dealing with a god,

Sedna

it has a folkloric flavour, and contains common motifs such as the **Dog Husband** and the blocking father figure.

seelie court

THE BLESSED HOST, the benevolent and graceful race of **fairies** in Celtic lore, in contrast to their malicious kin, the **unseelie court**, or damned host. They should be treated with respect as must all fairies, since they can be easily offended by clumsy or prying humans, but to their favourites, usually needy honest farmers or old women, they can perform great kindnesses. A Scottish tale tells of an old peasant woman who gave some of her little grain to a fairy; afterwards, even in the harshest winter, her supply was never-failing (the inexhaustible pot is a characteristic fairy gift).

selkies

SEAL-FOLK OF THE ORKNEY AND SHETLAND ISLANDS, occasionally known as silkies. Although not strictly **mermaids**, they share many of their characteristics and are said to live harmoniously under the sea with the merpeople. Selkie folk, who live below water, appear naturally

selkie

in human form, but they don seal-skins to travel through the sea. The males often take human lovers and produce offspring with webbed hands and feet, and a selkie woman can be captured by the theft of her sealskin. A Shetland tale tells how a human male steals the sealskin of one such maiden as she dances with her companions at the edge of the sea and she is obliged to become his wife until one day her children discover the hiding place of the sealskin in their game; she pulls it on and disappears below the waves again.

It is a common feature of **mermaid** tales that the death of the mermaid causes a storm which wrecks the ship on which she was caught, and if the blood of a selkie drips into the sea it has the same effect.

▷ **ceasg**; **roane**; **swan maiden**

separable soul

AN ELEMENT OF MOST PRIMITIVE RELIGIONS, and of folktales the world over, is the concept of a person's life essence existing apart from the body it animates. The soul is conceived of as a concrete object, which can be hidden away for safe keeping, and as long as the soul itself is not found and destroyed the person is invulnerable. The most famous folktale to embody this belief is the Norwegian tale, 'The Giant who had no Heart in his Body'. The giant hides his heart, in other words his soul, in an **egg** which is within a duck which is in turn in a series of larger things. The giant (or magician) is killed when the hero, overcoming all obstacles, discovers the hiding place of the soul and destroys it. Frequently the giant gives himself away by telling his secret to a woman whom he wishes to marry, as in the Hindu tale of Punchkin the magician, or to his daughter. A classical legend on the same theme is that of King Nisus of Megara, whose soul was located in a single purple hair among the others on his head. When his daughter Scylla falls in love with the invading Minos, she treacherously pulls out this hair and destroys her father. Similar too is the Hebrew story of Samson, who reveals to Delilah that the source of his strength is in his uncut hair, although this is not strictly a story of separable soul since Samson lives after being sheared.

Where belief in the separable soul is strong, illness is usually regarded as the departure of the soul from the body. In healthy people the soul only quits the body in sleep, but if it leaves when the body is awake, illness, madness or death is inevitable. Among Australian tribes healing is performed by recapturing the wandering spirit before it can enter the underworld. In Asia too elaborate rituals have been recorded for the recalling of the strayed soul, with invocations and music. In many such cases an outward sign such as a cord knotted round the arm or wrist is used to sympathetically tether the soul to the body. One of the most common reasons for a soul to leave the body in this irregular way was the influence of another, recently-dead soul, which beckoned it to follow (see **death** and **soul**). If the soul had been captured by a demon, sacrifices were required to secure its liberation.

In North America, many native groups believe that the soul leaves the body during sleep, during which time its adventures are perceived as **dreams**. In such cultures it is considered dangerous to waken a sleeper suddenly, since the soul may not have time to return.

serpent see snake

sesame

A PLANT PROBABLY NATIVE TO INDIA OR EAST AFRICA, *Sesamum indicum*, of the family Pedaliaceae, prized since ancient times for its flavoursome seeds and their oil. Perhaps because of the single erect stalk of the sesame plant, its seeds have been widely credited with aphrodisiac properties; the *Kama Sutra* recommends a paste made largely from sesame seeds to impart sexual stamina, and Arabs traditionally used sesame seeds in a cure for impotence. Sesame cakes are traditionally provided for the dead at the Sraddha ceremony in Hindu lore; they are said to grant exemption from hell and to provide a new body for the **otherworld**. These mystical associations may underlie the most famous appearance of sesame in folklore today, in **Open Sesame**, the formula that opens the robbers' cave for **Ali Baba**.

Sesame oil is still used medicinally to treat both constipation and diarrhoea. According to Pliny it was useful too in settling an upset stomach after overindulgence.

seven

PARTICULARLY SIGNIFICANT ODD NUMBER, especially in Semitic, North African and European lore. Jacob was following an existing tradition when he worked for Laban seven years to gain a wife. Joshua marched round Jericho seven times, the seventh son of a seventh son is thought to have great magical and healing powers, and seven is central to many **witchcraft** rituals. Its significance may be due to **astrology**, the ancient knowledge of the seven planets. The Koran recognizes seven heavens, and Christians speak of the Seven Deadly Sins (matched in Langland's *Piers Plowman* by the seven virtues). In the Middle Ages, as numerical **divination** became a favourite pastime, a theory of critical periods in life was developed which featured especially the numbers **three**, seven and **nine**. Human life was thought to consist of a series of seven-year cycles; at seven one left infancy, at 14 puberty was reached, at 21 adulthood, and so on. So combinations of significant numbers were particularly critical for good or bad: 21 (3 x 7), 63 (7 x 9) and 81 (9 x 9). From Roman times it has been said that to pass the age

of 63 is to survive the most dangerous year and augurs a long life.

▷ **numbers**

Seven League Boots

MAGIC OBJECTS OF EUROPEAN FOLKLORE, said to allow the wearer to cover seven leagues (34km/21ml) in a single step. They are frequently stolen from **giants**, but obligingly shrink to fit the foot of every new owner.

shadow soul

THE VISIBLE SOUL. In many parts of the world the shadow or one's reflection in glass or water is thought of as the soul made visible. It is therefore unlucky to allow one's shadow to be trapped in a coffin or under a heavy object, or to let oneself be reflected in crocodile-infested water. Similarly, a photograph or portrait is thought to take away the vital soul and lead to death. An extension of the concept is the **fetch** or **doppelgänger**, a visible spirit double of a living person.

shaitans

EVIL SPIRITS OF ISLAMIC LORE, an infidel class of **jinn**. Ali-Shaitan, the demonic aspect of the devil, Iblis, was created by Allah and gave birth to numerous unbelieving progeny. Folk culture has expanded the role and function of the shaitans; they are said to be supernaturally ugly creatures, feeding on excrement and living in perpetual shade. Although they can assume human form, they can always be identified by their cloven hoofs (cf **defects**, **Devil**). They bring disease to humans, and tempt them to evil by incessantly whispering in their ears. In their earliest incarnations among pre-Islamic Arabs, shaitans do not appear as particularly evil, and they were formerly considered as familiar spirits or genii (see **genius**), giving inspiration to prophets and poets.

Shaka (c.1787–1828)

ZULU WARRIOR AND CHIEF, a key figure in the history of the Zulus and in the folklore of the region. He was born of an illicit union—his mother Nandi and his father, the Zulu chief Senzangakona, belonged to the same clan and therefore

Zulu sculpture of warrior, 19c

their marriage was incestuous—and was brought up away from his father as a despised child among his mother's people until they were finally driven away from the group (cf **abandonment**). He spent his early warrior years fighting for the group that sheltered him, the Mtetwa. After his father's death he asserted his authority over the small Zulu population, displaying from the beginning the harshness and absolutism that were to characterize his rule. He organized the men into a deadly fighting force, and beginning with revenge on the Langeni who had made his boyhood a misery he swept through coastal southern Africa, leaving the kraals of his enemies burnt and ruined and their occupants impaled on stakes as a warning to others. Clan structure throughout the country was devastated as groups fleeing before the Zulus attacked others in the scrabble for land and food. Shaka encountered European culture when members of the Farewell Trading Company settled in Port Natal (modern Durban), and although intrigued by their curious manners and marvellous

trinkets remained convinced of the superiority of his own rule.

After the death of his mother in 1827 Shaka's despotism turned to psychosis—he massacred his subjects in his grief and forbade the planting of crops, the use of milk and all procreation among his people. He was finally assassinated by a group of his own warriors, including his two half-brothers.

Shaka's undoubted stature as a leader and his remarkable life made him a natural subject for folk legend. He figures prominently in the popular African poetic form, the praise name, in which eulogizing epithets are attached to his name.

Shalott, Lady of see Elaine

shamanism

MYSTICAL PRIMITIVE RELIGION, characterized by a belief in the shaman's ability to communicate with the **otherworld**, heal or bring about disease and generally protect the group. The word derives ultimately from Sanskrit *šramana*, ascetic, or one who knows. The shaman was frequently termed the medicine man by early explorers, but this is misleading as it gives an incomplete picture of his role. Shamanism is especially prevalent among central Asian and Siberian peoples, but the word is commonly used to signify parallel aspects of Native American and African religions.

The shaman performs his vital roles while entranced in a state of ecstasy in which his soul migrates from the body or a powerful spirit takes possession (**epilepsy** and narcotics both feature in the selection and methodology of shamans). Most frequently the shaman effects a cure by sending his soul to fetch back that of the sick individual, and the tales of his adventures in the spirit realm often form an important part of the oral tradition of the group.

shamrock

TRIFOLIATE PLANT, any of a variety of similar small plants, particularly wood sorrel (*Oxalis acetosella*). It is the national symbol of Ireland, from the legend that St **Patrick** used it to explain

shamrock

the concept of the Trinity when he evangelized Ireland: one leaf in three parts, one God in three persons. It is traditionally sported by Irish folk, or those with even tenuous Irish ancestry, on St Patrick's day (17 March), and is said to have been taken on the long journey by the many emigrants leaving Ireland in the 19th century. 'To drown the shamrock' refers to the well-attested custom of downing drinks in honour of St Patrick's day.

shanty

TRADITIONAL SAILORS' SONG, characterized by a strongly rhythmical refrain interspersed with solo, often narrative, verses. Shanties were sung to aid in the coordinating of hard labour, and many of the refrains contain phrases that relate directly to such tasks (eg 'Heave ho my hearties'). They were sung unaccompanied, although the black slaves of the American South introduced complexity in the form of harmonies, the rhythm and tempo dependent upon that required for the job in hand.

Favourite themes for shanties include the harshness of the life at sea, the pleasures of drinking and womanizing, and the noble calling of the sailor. Shanty heroes and, more particularly, heroines developed; Sally Brown was particularly renowned as a charming and accommodating mistress, whose varied pleasures, whilst enjoyable, tend to leave the besotted sailor somewhat poorer. Manly heroes such as Stormalong were also celebrated in shanties portraying the ideal sailorly virtues; courage, strength and hearty appetites.

The word is thought to derive from French *chantez*, 'Sing!'.

shapeshifters and shape-shifting

WORLD-WIDE MOTIF OF FOLKTALES AND BELIEF. In addition to hybrids produced by **beast marriage**, human and beast are combined in the figure of the shapeshifter. Classic examples are found in **transformation** tales collected by Ovid in his *Metamorphoses*, an enormous influence on Western culture, but the concept of a human changing into a beast, whether permanently or temporarily, is found in virtually every culture. The **werewolf**, half man, half wolf, is a monster of European lore, and its equivalent is found in every continent. In South America it becomes the jaguarman, in West Africa the were-tiger and so on. In such stories a human being is bewitched into the shape of a ferocious animal by night, at certain phases of the moon, or may have the power to assume such a shape at will, but will usually return to human form in the daytime, or if wounded. Many Native American shamans are believed to be able to change shape in this way, often to become a jaguar.

Shapeshifters form a huge corpus of world folklore; the ability to assume another form, attributed to humans, animals or supernatural beings, is a universal theme. In China the *hu hsien*, fox-spirits, may appear as humans, but can always be discovered since when they are drunk they return to their true

shape-shifting

form. Zeus made much use of his shape-shifting abilities to seduce unwary human maidens, approaching **Leda** as a swan and Europa as a bull.
▷ **Proteus**

shark

SHARP-TOOTHED FISH, of the class Chondrichthyes, the largest species of which have been known to attack and kill humans. In Polynesian lore the shark is generally said to embody the spirits of the dead, or to represent divine beings, and it is therefore considered sacred.

sheitans see shaitans

shivaree see charivari

shoes

SYMBOLS OF SEXUALITY, and a significant element in mythology, folktales and proverbial lore. It is perhaps surprising that the shoe has proved such a focus for sexual imagery, but it is certainly true, particularly in the Middle and Far East, that footwear is consistently used in reference to female sexuality. The reasons can only be guessed at, but it seems to be closely linked with the idea of the feet, and therefore the shoes, representing subservience. Perhaps the most famous custom which illustrates this point is one practised until relatively recently in China, that of foot-binding. The feet of young well-to-do girls were tightly bound in cotton bandages, the toes bent beneath the foot and often beaten to prevent the bones springing back into shape. The result was a deformed, tiny club foot, which would fit into shoes of only a few inches in length but which rendered locomotion virtually impossible. The adult woman would be dependent on her husband or servants for support, and otherwise travelled in a sedan-chair or carriage.

Various reasons have been proposed for the origins of this painful and seemingly pointless tradition. One T'an-Ki, a semi-mythological figure, wife of the last Shang emperor in c.1100BC, was said to be a fairy **changeling** whose feet were those of a hind; she disguised them with dainty fairy shoes and bindings, and thus established a

pattern for female beauty. Another royal favourite P'an-Fei, loved by the emperor Ho-Ti, was said to be so lovely that golden lilies sprang up from the impressions of her tiny feet. In the same tradition but much later, around AD970, the wife of a Sung ruler was said to have dainty feet around which her besotted husband would wind satin ribbons. Clearly, small feet served as a potent symbol for ideal female beauty in Oriental lore. Alongside these mythological explanations are the inevitable cultural factors, the sexual politics which functioned to keep women as the male's ideal of beauty and to make infidelity or disobedience to the male physically impossible, a form of female circumcision.

In the **Cinderella** tale the shoe is used as a **recognition token**; only the beautiful heroine can slip her dainty feet into the glass slipper. Again, practicality is sacrificed for a mythic ideal of beauty and again the woman is willing to deform herself to conform to that standard; the Ugly Sisters hack off heels and toes to squeeze their feet into the shoe. A similar device is used in Egyptian mythology, when Rhodope's slipper is stolen by an **eagle** as she bathes and dropped into the hands of Psammetichos who sends servants throughout the land to find its owner. To enable Hermes to have his way with Aphrodite, Zeus sends an eagle to steal her shoe and thus send her questing after it.

In Indian folktales, the familiar **chastity test** is often rendered as a willingness by the bride to be beaten by her husband with a shoe. On a more pragmatic note, an Italian folktale tells of a prudent courtesan who charges her lovers a pair of shoes to enjoy her sexual favours. These she keeps, and uses them as currency in her old age to buy the attentions of others.

Shoes tend to denote ownership, adding credence to the conceptual link between footwear and subjugation; in the biblical story of Ruth, Boaz ratifies his purchase of her by ritually placing his sandal on the ground before the assembled men. An Arab divorce was accomplished by a formula in which the man claimed the woman was his shoe and that he now set it off. In Anglo-Saxon

England the shoe of the bride was passed from her father to her husband as a symbol of transferred ownership and responsibility.

The use of the shoe in the **marriage** ceremony still persists; shoes are tied behind the car of newly-weds as tokens of good luck, and, by extension, in Scotland it is customary to throw shoes after someone leaving on a journey or beginning a new venture. Queen Victoria reports in her journal that an old shoe was thrown into the house for luck behind her as she entered the house at Balmoral. The link here appears to be with prosperity; all is going well as long as one still has one's shoes. Conversely, mourners at funerals often wore old shoes or went barefoot to avoid arousing the envy of the dead. New shoes however are often regarded with suspicion; to have them in the house at Christmas, or to set them on the table, was considered particularly ominous in England, and in Japan, perhaps understandably, it is considered unlucky to wear new shoes to go to the lavatory. When receiving a pair of new shoes as a gift, it is advisable to give a token sum of money in exchange, lest the shoes walk away. Anyone wearing new shoes which creak would be suspected of not having paid the shoemaker for them. To put on the left shoe first is widely considered to portend bad luck, and in the Philippines it is considered unlucky to set a pair of slippers widely apart.

Interpreted correctly, shoes can also be used for **divination**. An old shoe thrown over the house was said to reveal by the way it lands whether a sick person will live or die. The girl who wishes to see her future husband in a dream has only to place her shoes at right angles and say 'Hoping this night my true love to see, I place my shoes in the form of a T'. Folk wisdom can assess character and destiny from the appearance of an old shoe:

Tread at the toe, live and see woe;

Tread at the heel, live and get a deal;

Tread at the side, friends will abide;

Tread at the ball, you lose them all

(reported in *Household Words*, September 1888).

An old English cure for cramp is to place one's shoes upside-down beneath the bed, or alternatively outside the bedroom door with one pointing towards the room and one away. More poetically, a sick child of the Omaha tribe in North America may be protected by a hole cut in the sole of his moccasin; when the spirits of death call him he will be unable to make the journey because his shoes have worn out. Similarly, shoes were buried with the bodies of Egyptian rulers and nobility, along with other provisions, to ease the long journey to the **otherworld**. This practice existed among Teutonic and Scandinavian peoples, and a Scottish ballad, *The Lyke-Wake Dirge*, tells how the gift of shoes to a beggar in life means that the giver will be provided with a pair of shoes at death, to walk the thorny path before him.

shvod

GUARDIAN SPIRIT, a house spirit of American folklore. Although generally benevolent, he is sometimes used as a nursery **bogey** to frighten children into obedience.

sidhe

PEOPLE OF THE MOUNDS, the **fairy** race of Irish folklore, also known as aes sidhe or daoine sidhe. They were originally the divine race, the full-size **Tuatha de Danann**, forced to take refuge in the *sidhe* (mounds or hills), when the **Milesians** conquered Ireland. They developed the art of **invisibility**, and thenceforth could never be seen by mortals except when they chose to reveal themselves or their **glamour** was defeated by magical ointments or second sight and the like. Even ordinary mortals, it is said, may see them once a year, on **Midsummer**'s Eve. In later lore they became demythologized into a diminutive race of **little people**, who hunt, dance, feast and may also steal human children (see **changelings**), take human lovers (see **fairy marriage**) and torment, help or abduct mortals. The *sluagh sidhe*, the fairy host, rides by on the wind and can only be perceived by the rushing noise and the tinkling of harness bells and laughter.

▷ **banshee**; **sluagh**

Siegfried see Sigurd

Sigurd

Sigurd

TEUTONIC HERO, appearing in Old Norse legends as Sigurd and in German as Siegfried. There are significant differences between the two traditions. In the Old Norse tales, as found in the *Volsungasaga*, Sigurd is the son of Sigmund and Hjordis, last of the Volsungs. He slays **Fafnir** the **dragon** on the prompting of his tutor, the **dwarf** smith Regin, but after eating the dragon's heart he receives the power of animal communication. Thus he learns of Regin's greed and treachery from the **birds** and, slaying Regin, obtains the Andvari treasure for himself. He goes on to waken **Brynhild** the Valkyrie from her exhausted sleep in the circle of fire and pledges himself to her with a magic ring. On his subsequent travels, however, he marries **Gudrun**, having drunk a potion that caused him to forget Brynhild, and aids her Nibelung brother Gunnar to win Brynhild for himself. Brynhild, discovering his trickery, incites Gunnar to kill Sigurd but later repents and is placed alongside him on his funeral pyre.

In German tradition, found primarily in the *Nibelungenlied*, Siegfried is the son of the king of the Netherlands, Siegmund. He slays the dragon Fafnir and is made invulnerable by bathing in its blood, except for one spot on his back that is covered by a fallen linden leaf. He obtains the Nibelung gold and with the help of his cloak of **invisibility** aids the Burgundian prince Gunther to win the hand of Brunhild. He weds Gunther's sister, Kriemhild, but the two queens' arguments reveal Siegfried's trickery and Brunhild persuades **Hagen** to murder the hero.

Despite the differences in detail in the two strands of tradition, it is clear that Sigurd is primarily a **dragon-slaying** hero—born of noble blood but brought up without his parents, proving himself and gaining treasure by defeating the dragon.

silkie see **selkie**

silver

PRECIOUS METAL, one of the earliest known and valued by humans. Ornaments crafted in silver have been discovered in tombs dating from early 4000BC, and it has been used for bullion and coins in many societies, usually as a slightly lower currency than **gold**. This reflects the association of gold and silver with sun and moon respectively; early alchemists referred to silver as Diana and gave it the symbol of the crescent moon.

In Greek lore, the Silver Age followed on from the earliest, most glorious Golden Age, marking the time when humans lost reverence for the gods and began killing one another, losing the simple piety that had brought them happiness. The second heaven of Islamic lore is of silver. In modern lore a gold anniversary is 50 years and its halfway point, 25 years, is a silver celebration, often celebrated by the giving of silver gifts.

Like **iron**, silver is renowned in folklore for its effectiveness against evil influences; a silver bullet is the recommended means of slaying a **vampire**, **witch** or **ghost** and silver nails may be used in a coffin to prevent the occupant rising should he or she become dissatisfied. Chinese parents tie a silver locket around their child's neck to ward off demonic spirits. Silver **bells** are associated with the **elves** and benevolent **fairy** races. Gypsy fortune-tellers have traditionally claimed to be unable to practise their art until their palm has been crossed with silver. The **dwarf** king of German lore illuminates his realm with a silver lantern that shines as brightly as the sun.

Simple Simon

NURSERY-RHYME CHARACTER, who attempts to buy pies from a pie man without the benefit of money. The term has passed from the nursery into general usage to denote a naive simpleton.

Simurgh

FABULOUS CREATURE OF PERSIAN LORE, half bird and half mammal, with a wingspread like storm clouds. It roosted in the **tree** of life, Gaokerena. It is a symbol of divinity in later Persian lore. In one version of the legend the bird lives for 1 700 years before plunging itself into flames, **phoenix**-like, to rise again.

Sinbad

HERO OF THE ARABIAN NIGHTS, called 'the Sailor' because of his seven marvellous voyages of discovery. He was a wealthy merchant of Baghdad who, having squandered his money, sets off on his first trading voyage. He and his crew visit an island which proves to be the back of an enormous **whale**. On his second voyage he discovers the nest of a **roc** and is carried to the Valley of Diamonds where he amasses a fortune. His third voyage recalls episodes in the *Odyssey*; captured by dwarfs, Sinbad and his companions are left on an island with a cannibalistic one-eyed monster. Sinbad puts out the monster's eye and he escapes with the two remaining crew members. He is captured by cannibals again on his fourth voyage, but thwarts their designs by remaining skinny and escaping from his cage. He finds himself in a land where bridles and stirrups have not been invented, and wins general acclaim and the hand of the princess for his marvellous innovation. According to the customs of the land, however, Sinbad is buried alive with his bride when she dies, but escapes from the

Sinbad

catacombs back to Baghdad with many of the costly ornaments of the dead.

On Sinbad's fifth voyage his ship is destroyed by rocs, and he is washed ashore to confront the frail-seeming **Old Man of the Sea**, whom he overcomes. He is shipwrecked on the next voyage too, but finds himself on a marvellous island whose king welcomes the voyager to his court at Serendib and sends his home with enormous wealth and a gift for Caliph Harun al-Rashid. Sinbad sets sail on his seventh and final voyage laden with gifts from Caliph Harun to the king of Serendib, but is captured by pirates on the way and sold into slavery as an elephant hunter. He discovers the secret elephants' burial ground, with its piles of ivory, buys his freedom and returns home.

One of the voyaging heroes, Sinbad has remained popular in modern culture through children, tales and films.

singing bone

FOLKLORE MOTIF, FOUND PARTICULARLY IN EURASIAN TALES. Most commonly, a part of a murdered person is incorporated into a musical instrument, for example, the bones make up a **harp** frame or the hair its strings, and when the instrument is played it sings the story of its victim's fate. In a tale collected by Grimm two brothers are seeking the wild boar, since whoever slays it will wed the princess. The younger defeats the beast, but his brother kills him and takes the boar's head to the king himself and marries the princess. Some years later a shepherd discovers a smooth bone in the forest and makes a pipe of it; when it is blown, the bone discloses the elder brother's treachery.

A similar motif, found in Grimm's *The Juniper Tree*, has a bird rising from the bones of the child victim and singing his story, and in other tales wood taken from a tree growing on the burial site is the mouthpiece for the song. A related tale is that of Midas who grew the ears of an ass; his barber could not keep the dreadful secret but whispered it to the reeds by the river, and whenever the wind blew through them they repeated the story.

siren

GREEK SEA-CREATURE, half woman and half bird, who lured sailors to their deaths by their irresistibly sweet singing. According to Homer there were only two, but later legends set their number at three, and in popular lore they were numerous. The earliest portrayals show them as almost entirely birds, with human heads, and this suggests a close connection with the soul birds of Asian lore, winged ghosts that envied the living and sought to take their precious life (cf **harpies**).

Despite their sweet songs, the sirens were cheated of their prey twice. Odysseus stopped the ears of his crew with wax so that they might sail safely by, and he had himself lashed to the mast so that he might hear their song without going to his ruin. **Orpheus** succeeded in drowning their music with his own sweeter song, entrancing the crew of the *Argo* until they had passed the danger. After one or other of these defeats, the sirens are said to have leaped into the sea in despair and become rocks.

The sirens are classical examples of the fatal supernatural lover motif so common in European and Asian lore. They also prefigure **mermaids**.

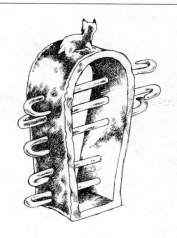

Egyptian sistrum, middle dynasty

sistrum

PERCUSSION INSTRUMENT, a type of **rattle** having a frame (usually wood or metal) enclosing loose cross-bars, often carrying jingles that make a noise when agitated. It was particularly associated with worship of the fertility goddess Hathor in ancient Egypt, and spread in popularity throughout the Mediterranean world as Hathor merged with the earth goddess Iris. Variants are found in India and Japan particularly and the sistrum was adopted by several Native American groups to supplement rattles in ritual dances and ceremonies.

Sita

CONSORT OF RAMA, the heroine of the *Ramayana*, and the incarnation of Vishnu's consort Laksmi. She was said to have sprung from a furrow ploughed by King Janaka and was raised by him. She is the archetypal devoted wife, who when abducted by Ravana kept herself chaste by concentrating on Rama throughout the ordeal, but Rama banished her to the forest on suspicion of infidelity, largely due to public opinion. She asserted her innocence by an **act of truth**, and was swallowed by her mother Earth, leaving behind her grief-stricken husband and their two sons, Kusa and Lava.

Skidbladnir

MARVELLOUS SHIP OF NORSE MYTHOLOGY, crafted by **dwarfs** for the weather god Freyr. On the sea it could comfortably carry the entire Norse pantheon (the Aesir) with all their arms and accoutrements, yet when required it could be folded up small enough to fit in a pocket (cf **magic carpet**). It was not limited to water but could fly through air, and had no need of favourable natural winds.

skritek

HOUSEHOLD SPIRIT OF SLAVIC LORE, usually dwelling behind the oven or in the stable. He appears in statues as a small boy, crowned and with crossed arms, and this statue is placed on the hearth to guard the house while the family is absent. If he is offended, however, perhaps because the family has neglected to leave him a portion of the meal, he may resort to destructive poltergeist activities.

sky people

INHABITANTS OF AN OTHERWORLD. A common device of Native American folktales, and indeed folktales world-wide, is an **otherworld** in the sky, inhabited by hostile sky people or the souls of the dead, to which the hero may ascend by a number of means. He may ride an **arrow** in flight, climb a magical tree or travel on a large feather. A long narrow road is more common in Africa and Asia. Another, more risky, method is to time precisely the jump between the sky and earth at the horizon; if he fails, the hero will be crushed between the two. In many tribal mythologies, especially those of the Iroquois, humans originate from the sky and came to earth when a Sky Woman fell through a hole, and the animals quickly spread out the earth on the back of **Turtle** to provide a home for her. The upperworld of Native American lore is often thought to be populated by star people, mortals caught up to the sky to become constellations.

sleepers

HEROES SLEEPING UNDERGROUND, making the heroic qualities of the past available to the present. This strong folkloric tradition is often invoked for the hero-king, said to be now asleep underground, to be roused when his people shall once more have need of him. **Arthur** of Britain, the Frankish king **Charlemagne** and Robert the Bruce of Scotland are all believed to be awaiting such a call, and various local folk traditions have developed concerning the whereabouts of their resting place, giving rise to names such as that given to the volcanic formation of Arthur's Seat in Edinburgh.

In classical legend Epimenides, a Cretan seer, was said to have slept for 57 years having crept into a cave to escape the sun's heat. Closer to the **Rip Van Winkle** legend is the famous tale of the Seven Sleepers, Ephesian Christians who fled to the mountains to escape the Decian persecutions. After what seemed a night's sleep, one risked the journey

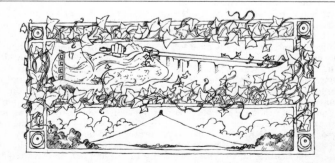

sleepers

into the town to buy bread and discovered that the Lord's name was being used freely, the sign of the cross was everywhere, and the coins he proffered were an archaic curiosity; they had slept for 360 years. A version of this story appears too in the Koran.
▷ **Blánik**; **kings**

Sleeping Beauty

EUROPEAN FOLKTALE TYPE, most famously found in the tale collected by Grimm, 'Little Briar Rose'. A childless queen eventually produces a baby daughter and the entire kingdom is invited to the castle to celebrate. However, since the king has only twelve gold plates he invites only twelve of the Wise Women. While the twelve are giving their gifts of beauty, happiness, etc, the slighted thirteenth bursts in to curse the child, saying that she will prick her finger and die in her fifteenth year. The curse is ameliorated by the last Wise Woman; not death, but a sleep of 100 years.

Despite the best efforts of her royal parents to banish spindles from the kingdom, in the course of time the princess discovers an old woman spinning in one of the castle towers, picks up the strange spindle and pricks herself. She falls asleep immediately, and the entire palace follows suit, from the king and queen to the servants in the kitchen and the very flies on the wall. An impermeable thorn hedge grows up around the palace, resisting the best efforts of the many adventurers trying to reach the princess whose legendary beauty has become well-known. Eventually, exactly 100 years later, a prince succeeds in finding a way through, journeys to the tower and awakes the sleeping princess with a kiss. The enchantment broken, the inhabitants of the castle come back to life and resume their normal activities, and the pair marry.

The tale contains several key folkloric motifs, most centrally that of the sleeping beauty or enchanted princess. The offended supernatural taking revenge is a universal preoccupation, underlying folklore throughout the world from primitive magic ceremonies and **funeral customs** to nursery lore. It is echoed by many myths of neglected deities bringing destruction on humans (see **Hippolytus**).

The waking of the princess can be seen as a restoration, akin to that of transformed humans by the love of another (cf **Beauty and the Beast**). The tale is found in various forms throughout Europe; another famous version is that of Perrault, *La Belle au Bois Dormant*.

sluagh

FAIRY RACE OF THE HIGHLANDS OF SCOTLAND, the host of the unforgiven souls of the dead. They are among the most feared of the little people, capable of drawing mortals into their company forever. Like **ghosts**, they are forced to haunt forever the scenes of their earthly misdemeanours.

snail

GASTROPOD, differing from the slug in its spiral protective shell. Its habit of withdrawing and emerging from this shell has earned it a connection with the cycles of the moon in many societies. It also represents **childbirth**, the emergence from the womb.

snake

SINUOUS REPTILE, whose most distinctive feature is its absence of limbs. In Judaeo-Christian tradition the snake is generally associated with evil, since it is the form taken by the **Devil** to tempt Eve in the garden. However, the tale recorded in Numbers 21:5–9, in which Moses lifts up a brass snake with power to heal all those that look upon it during a plague in the desert, indicates a more ancient symbolism. In ancient Egypt the snake, which sheds its skin and emerges anew, was a symbol of resurrection and two snakes twined around a wand was the emblem of the Greek god of medicine, Asklepius.

snake

Several Native American groups have snake dances, generally designed to tap the snake's magic powers by imitating its mimetic gesture or, in some cases, by involving live snakes in the dance. The snake's power is associated with rain-bringing and fertility.

If bitten by a snake, the best remedy is to compel the offending reptile to suck its own poison out again. In some folktales the serpent is said to have a golden crown, which imparts to any human who can come by it the power of animal communication. In some cases merely eating snake flesh will impart such knowledge.

sneeze

OMINOUS SIGN, regarded as having spiritual significance in many cultures. Since the **nose** is one of the body's main orifices, a sneeze is thought by many to be a sign of some demonic spirit within trying to get out. Certainly it leaves one vulnerable to spiritual influences, and hence it is widely considered not only polite but essential to ward off danger with a spoken charm: in Britain and the United States '[God] bless you', in Germany 'Geshundheit', and so on. To sneeze in one's sleep is a good sign among some groups, showing that the soul has come back to the body (see **separable soul**).

The variety of local customs and beliefs associated with sneezing is dizzying; in some areas a sneeze means that the last statement was true, in others a lie. To sneeze while putting on shoes or beginning a job is often considered an ill omen.

Surviving into modern lore in areas of Europe and America especially is a form of counting rhyme **divination** for sneezes: 'Two for a kiss, three for a letter, four for something better'.

Snegurotchka

THE SNOW MAIDEN, heroine of a Russian folktale. She is the offspring of Frost and Spring, who grows up protected from the **sun** in the coolness of the forest. When she discovers humanity, however, and wishes to receive the power of human emotions, she falls in love and is immediately destroyed by the fiery touch of the sun.

solstice

PIVOTAL SOLAR POINT, one of two occasions in the year when the sun is at its furthest point, either north or south, from the Equator. In the northern hemisphere the summer solstice takes place on 21 or 22 June and the winter solstice on 21 or 22 December; these dates are reversed in the southern hemisphere.

Many groups engage in rituals or celebrations to help the sun accomplish this change of course, especially in winter when the solstice marks the turnaround towards spring and new life. Actual practices differ, but typical features of such ceremonies are the lighting of new fires, the use of **masks** to impersonate supernatural powers, and noisy celebrations to frighten away evil spirits.

▷ **Christmas**; **Midsummer**

sortes see **bibliomancy**

soul

ESSENCE OF LIFE, widely considered in folk belief to be capable of existing apart from the body. Belief in the soul is widespread in primitive religion and folklore, and is usually closely linked to the cult of the dead, in which the souls of the deceased linger on after the death of the body. It is commonly assumed that the soul and the body are divisible, that both can continue to operate, for a limited time at least, when separated. Perhaps the most common example of belief in the soul leaving the body is during sleep. Many cultures explain **dreams** as the adventures of the soul, and it is considered highly dangerous to wake or disturb a sleeper. The soul may not find its way back in time, and without his soul the person will eventually sicken and die. Hence if a person is ill, the efforts of the shaman or medicine man will often be directed towards recalling the soul to the body, with the aid of special soul-catching instruments and incantations.

▷ **bush soul**; **separable soul**; **shadow soul**

South Asian folklore

THE LORE OF DIVERSE RACIAL GROUPS, from India, Pakistan and Bangladesh, to Sri Lanka, Nepal and Bhutan. A minority of the population live tribally, isolated from the main centres of civilization up in the hills, and the vast majority are peasants in village societies living by basic agriculture. Despite this diversity, the peoples are characterized by a fatalistic outlook on life and an emphasis on ritual and religious belief. The major religions of the area, Hinduism and Buddhism, may be very different to the Christian tradition familiar in the West, but as both cultures originate from a common Indo-European tradition there is much in the folklore that corresponds with European lore. These connections have been reinforced by centuries of trade between East and West. There is for example a continuity of moral tradition in which the beautiful and the good triumph over evil in the end, and the humble peasant wins the heart of the prince (or princess), which contrasts sharply with the unpunished triumph of the devious trickster in many African tales. Another common principle is the belief in a benevolent **otherworld**, but whereas in European lore this is usually perceived as distinct from the everyday world, in Asian lore it is inextricably mixed with it. The hero need not journey to the stars or to the enchanted island, the magic is all around him.

Despite the similarities however, Asian folktales are distinctive in their exotic, magical detail. The tales deal more naturally than does European lore with the fantastic and miraculous, so that ogres and jinn feature in place of the more earthy, less exotic **goblins** or **brownies** of Europe.

The earliest Sanskrit writings, over 3000 years old, demonstrate an enduring preoccupation with the fundamental conflict of good and evil, positive and negative, light and dark, which has fed into the tradition in both Asian and European lore of simplifying characters in simple dichotomies of good and evil.

sparrow

SMALL BIRD, usually of the Old World family Placeida (family order Passeriformes) and particularly the house sparrow, *Passer domesticus*. The bird was associated with eroticism and virility in classical times, and was sacred to Aphrodite. It is widely eaten as an aphrodisiac.

speaking head

MOTIF OF FOLKLORE, a common device in Celtic lore particularly. A disembodied head is able to converse sometimes for many years after its severing. Although the concept seems somewhat grisly, speaking heads are generally useful companions, given to prophecy and wise advice, as well as singing and telling tales. In classical lore the head of **Orpheus** is said to have predicted the death attending Cyrus's expedition into Scythia, among many other oracular pronouncements during its time on Lesbos. The head of **Bran the Blessed** entertained his followers and was finally buried to guard Britain from invasion, and numerous Islamic saints were said to have carried on speaking after beheading. In modern lore **ghosts** are popularly portrayed carrying their severed heads, which are still perfectly able to speak, under their arms. In Grimm's tale The **Little Goose Girl** the horse Faleda continues to speak and advise the goose girl even when its head is nailed over the gate.

Speewah, The

CATTLE-STATION OF AUSTRALIAN LORE, a fabulous place where men are stronger, cattle are bigger and everything is better than anywhere else.
▷ **tall tales**

spell

AN ENCHANTMENT LAID UPON ANOTHER TO TRANSFORM HIM, or render him subject to the chanter's will. This form of charm, closely related to the **chant**, is often used in fairy tales; generally it can only be broken by a specific event, such as the kiss of a virgin. As chants were often spoken over **amulets** to invest them with supernatural powers of protection, the two inevitably became conflated to an extent, and sometimes the chant itself would be written down and worn as an amulet.

The spell or incantation functions as the central part of all magical ritual. Such formulae have survived from ancient Egypt, Greece and Rome; they are more generally handed down orally to a select, initiated few. Such spells demonstrate belief in the mysterious power of words, and in many societies an individual's true name is revealed only to a few, a nickname being given for everyday use, lest .enemies should use the true name in spells.

Sphinx

FABULOUS CREATURE OF GREEK MYTH-OLOGY, a composite beast with the upper half of a woman, the body of a lion, the wings of an eagle and a serpent's tale. The Sphinx was stationed on the road to Thebes, sent by Hera as punishment for Laius's crimes, and she threw down from her high rock any passer-by who could not answer her **riddle**: 'What walks on four legs in the morning, two at noon and three in the evening?'. When **Oedipus** gave the correct answer (man, who crawls in infancy, walks in adulthood and leans on a stick in old age) she threw herself from the rock in disappointment.

The Egyptian Sphinx is an emblem of royal power, the body of a lion with a human face, and is always male. The magnificent sphinx at Gizeh is an emblem of the god Horus, searching the horizon for his father, the sun-god Rā.

Spartan Sphinx

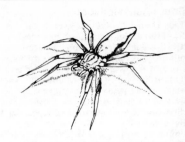

spider

spider

UBIQUITOUS ARACHNID GROUP, order Araneida. As a spinner of webs, producing silk from within itself, the spider has been associated in many mythologies with the fate principle or mother goddess, drawing out and patterning the thread of destiny. It was the emblem of Neith in ancient Egypt and Athene and the Fates in Greece, and in many Native American mythologies Spider is a creative female force bringing the world into being by her spinning. Spider can also be the male **trickster** figure and **culture hero**, Anansi, a quick-thinking and audacious being who taught many groups their skills and lore.

Although all spiders have venom glands, used to paralyze the prey they trap, very few are harmful to humans. There is however a widespread belief, which flourished particularly in late medieval Europe, that spiders are poisonous and they were thus considered vital ingredients in the noxious preparations of **witches**. The use of spiders in folk medicine around the world belies this squeamishness; spiders have long been regarded as cures for just about every ill, including the plague, leprosy, runny eyes and gout. The spider could be taken whole (often rolled in molasses or butter to aid their passage) or pulped, in pill-form, or applied live to draw the contagion into itself. A spider in a silk bag was carried as a **charm** for health. The cross pattern on the abdomen of certain spiders was regarded as a sign of sanctity, and therefore especial effectiveness. The web of the spider too was thought to have curative powers applied to a wound; this is actually quite logical, since it helps the blood to coagulate, although the web is sometimes rubbed into the wound rather than simply held against it, implying a belief in its intrinsic healing properties, encouraging the skin to knit and heal by **sympathetic magic**. A spider worn in a pouch or nutshell around one's neck was a charm against fever and contagion.

A common motif of folklore is the spider who saves a fugitive by spinning a web over his or her hiding-place: the pursuers pass by, thinking that no-one can have entered the cave recently. This tale is told of various heroes, including the Holy Family and Muhammad, and it reflects the ancient tendency to regard spiders favourably. A variant tale tells how the Scottish hero Robert Bruce, despondent in his cave, was encouraged to continue his fight against the English by watching the patient efforts of a small spider spinning its web.

Small spiders in England are still referred to as money-spiders or money-spinners, and to have one land on the person is a lucky omen, foretelling wealth and prosperity. In Tahitian lore spiders are sacred, the 'shadows of the gods', and in Polynesia generally it is especially lucky to have a spider drop from a line in front of one. To kill a spider is thought to be very unlucky.
▷ **tarantella**; **Tom Thumb**; **transformation**

spikenard

PERENNIAL HERB (*Aralia racemosa*), a member of the **ginseng** family, Araliaceae, characterized by its large, fragrant roots. The roots yield a heady ointment, held in high regard in ancient times both for its fragrance and its cost (the plants grew at high altitude in the Himalayas). It is with this perfume that **Mary Magdalene** was said to have anointed Jesus.

American spikenard (*Aralia racemosa*), also known as Life-of-Man, is widely used in folk medicine by Native Americans as a poultice, soothing vapour or purgative; it is said to be particularly effective in lifting depression and purifying the blood.

spirit

NON-CORPOREAL ESSENCE, a supernatural power, generally used to refer to supernatural beings such as **fairies**. A spirit differs from a **soul** because it is not connected with the human individual; it is a different class of being from humans and animals, composed of an entirely different essence and therefore capable of supernatural feats such as **invisibility** and the power of flight. Frequently this distinction between human and spirit is blurred, however, as with **ghosts** and particularly spirits such as **langsuir**, women who have died in childbirth. In earliest times, and still in many primitive societies, spirits were the essence of every inanimate thing—sun, moon, wind, stars, fire, water, stones, etc (cf **kachina**). Development of such basic principles leads to a proliferation of water-spirits, guardians of huts, corn spirits, and so on, giving the rich lore of fairies and spirits found throughout the world. In non-industrialized lore spirits live and go about their business alongside humans, often interfering in their affairs and always demanding their respect and attention. In modern lore communication between the spirit world and this one is still allowed by many, but spirits are generally taken to be the souls of the dead rather than fairy-like beings.

spiritual

FOLK HYMN, particularly those deriving from the songs of 19th-century dissenters in America. White spirituals have an ancient tradition, from the 'lined-out' psalms of the mid-17th century, where a leader would intone the line and the congregation would follow, often in harmony, singing to a well-known melody, and the similar but drearier chants of the Puritans. In the 18th century a more spirited type of hymn-singing (as opposed to psalm-recitation) came into vogue with the itinerant Methodist and Baptist preachers such as John and Charles Wesley, often sung to **ballad** tunes with original, more memorable lyrics that did not require lining out. Such hymns, based on traditional folk melodies, passed quickly into oral lore, and during the religious revivals of the late 18th and early 19th centuries mass meetings popularized and developed such forms, usually sung in unison, emphasizing such themes as the journey to the promised land and victory over the **Devil**.

In America, these revivalist hymns were absorbed and developed by the black tradition and resulted in a distinctive black spiritual style, marked by harmonies, complex rhythmic accompaniment and freer vocal effects. Since black performances of the hymns also affected the singing of whites at the same meetings, it is difficult to disentangle the two traditions and determine to what extent they are interdependent. Certainly black slaves developed the themes of emancipation, suffering and injustice in this life and final vindication, and worked them into a state of identity and a common lore, often focusing on biblical heroes delivered from hardship such as Daniel, Moses and Lazarus, or developing the theme of the joys and comforts to come in heaven. Spirituals were absorbed as work songs, and included references to day-to-day tasks and the plight of the workers in a direct way that would have been unthinkable in speech. Modern white spirituals have been heavily influenced by black developments, and incorporate the rhythms of **jazz** techniques such as syncopation and the use of folk instruments such as the **banjo**, **guitar** and accordion.

spitting

ANCIENT FORM OF MAGIC, a means of ensuring good luck or averting ill. The potency of spittle as a good-luck charm throughout the world and the consistency of the belief is remarkable, indicating an extremely ancient tradition. Spitting on hands before beginning work or battle, on a hook before one begins to fish, or on the first money received in trade that day all secure luck in the business ahead. An omen of ill-fortune can be turned by spitting, so if one walks unwittingly under a **ladder**, or meets someone with a squint (see **evil eye**), the curse can be offset.

The ancient power of spittle is also demonstrated in its widespread use as a seal on bargains. The ritual may simply consist of spitting together in a show of solidarity, or shaking hands that have been spat on, or it may involve a ritual

exchange of saliva, each spitting into the mouth of the other.

Perhaps because it is used to combat evil influences, and because it is a symbol of ridding oneself of something, spitting is also perceived as a mark of disgust in many areas. Hence it can be used as a challenge and gesture of defiance. The saliva of an angry man is said to be poisonous, and this contrasts sharply with the general belief in the medicinal powers of saliva (upheld by scientific research). In ancient Rome and the Orient spittle is used to soothe irritated eyes, and in the gospel accounts Jesus heals a blind man with the aid of a paste made from mud and spittle (John 9:6). In Britain it is said to be possible to spit one's toothache into a frog and politely request it to carry the pain away. Defects such as corns, warts and birthmarks may be removed by regular application of spittle; most effective is fasting spittle, produced before eating or drinking in the morning.

Spitting may also be used in **divination**. One technique is to spit on the palm of one hand and strike it with one finger of the other; the direction taken by the largest drop of spittle indicates the location of a lost object. A similar direction-finding technique is to spit on a hot shovel or iron and note which way the bubbles boil off.

spruce

EVERGREEN TREE, of the genus *Picea* (family Pinaceae), with a particularly resonant wood much used for musical instruments as well as in construction and ship-building. Several Native American groups use the gum of the tree as a poultice for open sores, and in Newfoundland the young buds are thought to cure toothache if chewed.

squirrel

RODENT OF THE FAMILY SCIURIDAE, order Rodentia, most commonly the bushy-tailed tree-dweller found throughout Europe, Asia and North America. It is the symbol of **Medb** in Celtic mythology, and perhaps appropriately is portrayed as a mischief-maker in Norse lore, setting the **eagle** and **snake** at odds. Its habit of storing and hoarding nuts in its nest has given it a double-edged symbolism, as both prudent husbander and avaricious miser.

A folktale of Finland tells how a man tricks an **ogre** into a tree-climbing contest, saying that the task is so easy he will get his young child (a squirrel) to climb in his place. A Russian **animal fable** tells how the wolf catches the squirrel and demands to know why he is so cheerful all the time; the squirrel begs to be set free before giving an answer, then dancing out of reach in the tree shouts down that the wolf will never be cheerful because his heart is so wicked.

star people see **sky people**

stars

INSPIRING A SENSE OF SIGNIFICANCE AND MYSTERY, the spectacle of the night sky has made a great impression on every society. Like most natural phenomena, stars have featured in human society as objects of magic, religion, folktales and superstitions, and, practically, as navigational aids. Primitive **astrology** may have begun with the recognition that the cycles of the sun and moon influenced human life directly, and from an instinctive reverence for the myriad, shifting points of light associated with the potent night. Quite early in human history people began to pick out fixed clusters or constellations in the constant shifting of the skies. Much primitive religion is animistic and anthropomorphic, and so the stars were attributed with power and purpose, and outlines of humans and animals.

Tales of humans and animals being caught up into the sky to become a constellation are widespread in Native American, African, Asian and European lore. One common Native American tale tells how a human girl falls in love with the stars and shuns a human husband; she is taken up to the sky and marries a star. In some versions she becomes homesick for earth and tries to escape with her new son, but often she is killed and the boy survives to become a great hero. Many **culture heroes** are said to enter the sky as constellations rather than die.

The folklore of stars is rich with such tales, and it seems likely that the names

stars

of heroes from folktales or myths were attached to constellations as a means of fixing the pattern in the cultural memory of a society, since with the exception of a few, such as **Orion**, Scorpio and Cygnus, the constellations do not automatically suggest any one shape. This becomes clear in comparative astrological study; although Taurus is recognized as a bull in Greek, Babylonian and Hebrew culture, it was portrayed as part of the Great White Tiger in ancient China.

A particularly interesting variation in star-gazing is found in Australia, where above the deserts the clear skies appear packed with stars. The Aborigines like most cultures projected pictures such as the figure of the emu onto the night sky, but they tended to use for these the gaps between the stars, the 'dark constellations', a sort of negative to the usual approach.

At a more primitive level than the systematized tenets of astrology, stars have traditionally been looked to as omens and portents. The **Pleiades** and Pisces are both considered rain-bringing constellations (although Pisces rains tend to be stormy) and they are therefore welcome ascendants in most cultures, although their influence is said to be malign in astrology. The brightness of the Pleiades and their association with weeping has led to a widespread folk belief that one who cannot see the cluster is fated to die shortly.

In **funeral customs** of ancient Egypt, the pyramid of the king was constructed so that one passage pointed directly at the constant North star to symbolize the ascent of the king to the heavenly, eternal world. Greek kings were judged by the behaviour of the stars; for one night every eight years the city's ephors gazed into the heavens, and if a shooting star was detected it was considered a sign that the king had offended the gods and should be removed. A rather more mundane use of shooting stars was made by the peasants of Europe; to be rid of spots one need only wait for a falling star, then as it falls wipe the spots with a cloth so that they too will fall away. This is an example of **sympathetic magic** in healing.

▷ **moon**; **sky people**; **sun**

stick dances

FORM OF FOLK DANCE, found throughout the world, in which dancers (almost invariably male) manipulate some form of staff or stick. The stick can be said in most forms to be, at least originally, a phallic symbol, often stuck vertically into the ground in fertility dances (eg the **Morris dance**'s 'dibbing') to represent the readying of the earth for conception and harvest. Often such sticks may combine this function with that of a **rattle**.

In combat dances and their derivatives sticks act as swords, struck against that of the opponent in carefully choreographed and stylized representation of a fight. Such dances are often performed in line formation; examples include the Spanish–Moorish *moriscas* and the Portuguese *dança des poulitos*. A variation on this theme has dancers stepping between sticks laid crossed on the ground.

The wide dissemination of stick dances with similar forms and functions suggests that it is a very early development.

▷ **dance**

Stone of Destiny see **Stone of Scone**

Stone of Scone

TRADITIONAL SEAT OF THE SCOTTISH KINGS, also called the Stone of Destiny (Gaelic *lia fail*). It is a block of sandstone 66cm/26in x 41cm/16in x 28cm/11in, marked only by a simple Latin **cross**. It was said in Celtic lore to have been the stone that Jacob used as a pillow when he saw his vision of angels at Bethel (Genesis 28:12) which found its way across Europe to Tara, the seat of the High Kings of Ireland, c.700BC. It was taken by invading Scots and in c.AD840 was removed from Dunstaffnage Castle by Kenneth McAlpin, first king of the united Scots and Picts, and installed at Scone, near Perth.

A coronation chair was built around it, and it saw the crowning of every Scottish king until John of Balliol in 1292. In 1296 Edward I of England invaded Scotland, and carried the stone away along with other Scottish treasures to London. He installed it in Westminster Abbey in 1307, under a specially-built coronation throne, symbolizing that the one crowned king in England would rule over Scotland too. In fact James VI of Scotland was crowned over the stone as James I of England in 1603, after Elizabeth I failed to produce an heir.

On Christmas Day 1950 a group of Scottish Nationalists stole the stone from Westminster Abbey and returned it to Scotland, placing it in Arbroath Abbey, scene of the Declaration of Arbroath in 1320; it was recovered and reinstated at Westminster four months later.

stork

LONG-LEGGED WADING BIRD, any species of the family Ciconiidae. Because of its association with water and hence fertility, the stork is widely portrayed in Western lore as a bringer of babies, and a German superstition says that a stork flying over a house foretells a birth in it. Another common belief, found in ancient Egypt and Greece, was that the stork's offspring cared for their parents in old age, feeding them and helping them to fly by supporting their frail wings on either side; this myth, largely propagated by Aristotle, made the stork a symbol of filial duty and devotion. Aristotle also tells how storks devoured a plague of snakes in Thessalonica, and the stork's antipathy to snakes has become proverbial. Storks are generally welcomed; in many areas it is considered unlucky to kill them, and their quitting is often seen as an omen of coming disaster. Moroccan peasants examine the arriving storks to see what the year ahead will hold; if the birds are clean and brilliant white the weather will be good, but if dusty and bedraggled, there is bad weather ahead.

In a folktale collected by Grimm, the stork king is sent by Zeus to terrorize the **frogs** dissatisfied with the log he has already provided. In an Indian version of the Snow White tale the abandoned child is brought up by two storks in the forest, who fulfil the role of the seven **dwarfs**. In some areas, migrating storks were said to arrive at their destination in human form (see **shape-shifting**).

Stormalong

HERO OF SAILORS' LORE, embodying the traditional ideals of strength, daring and virility. He features in several **tall tales**, for example, the claim that he had to soap the sides of his enormous ship *Courser* to squeeze through the English Channel; the cliffs of Dover testify to the tightness of the squeeze, since their white colour comes from the scraped-off soap. His ship was driven by a hurricane across the Isthmus of Panama, thereby creating the Panama canal. Naturally, Stormalong died at sea and was buried beneath the waves. The **shanty** *Stormalong*, recounting his exploits and celebrating the glories of the sailor, was sung to accompany heavy toil at the capstan, such as the weighing of a mud-stuck anchor.

strangleweed see dodder

strawberry

FRUIT PLANT, of the genus *Fragaria* (family Rosaceae). In Norse mythology the fruit was sacred to Frigga, goddess of married love and patron of housewives; she was said to hide the souls of dead children in strawberries to smuggle them into paradise. After the Christianizing of Europe, this association was transferred to the Virgin **Mary**. The strawberry is also associated with Venus, and is widely used in cures for venereal disease.

Strawberries are used in folk medicine wherever they are grown. They are an effective dentifrice, and are believed to make loose teeth firm in the gum. They restore a melancholic's spirits and control fainting and nervous disorders, and distilled strawberry water cools the liver and eyes, soothes palpitations and purifies the blood. Strawberries are used cosmetically to improve the complexion and lighten freckles.
▷ **berries in winter**

stroke

A SEIZURE OR FIT, the result of a reduced blood-flow to the brain or a rupture in the cranium. The characteristic paralysis, often down one side only, which may be transient, gave rise to the folk belief that the condition was caused by the touch of the **fairies**, hence fairy-stroke or elf-stroke. In some areas it signified that the soul of the individual had been stolen by the fairies and only a lifeless image, animated by **glamour**, left in its place.

succubus

A FEMALE NIGHT-DEMON, the counterpart of an **incubus**, who seduces men in their sleep so that she may conceive a demon child. Any man visited by a succubus should recite prayers or **charms** on wakening so that his seed might not produce demonic offspring.
▷ **hag**; **Lilith**; **nightmare**

Sukkoth

THE JEWISH FEAST OF TABERNACLES, or Booths, celebrated from 15 to 22 Tishri (September–October). It commemorates the period of wandering in the desert, when the Israelites lived in huts (*sukkot*), although in fact they would have slept in tents and not the structures of branches and leaves constructed for the festival. The festival developed from the old Feast of Ingathering, the storing of the crops after the summer harvest. Its origins are ancient, probably based on pagan rites of the autumn equinox, to reinvigorate the waning sun.

sukusendal

NIGHT DEMON OF FINNISH LORE, both **succubus** and **incubus** depending on the sex of the sleeper. It also engages in **changeling** activities, and preys on those who venture out to the bathhouse late at night alone. It can be kept from the bed or cradle by placing an **iron** implement under the bedclothes.

sukuyan

VAMPIRE WOMAN OF TRINIDAD, who gains power over her victims by persuading them to give her **salt**. Should one be deceived by her innocent appearance and fall into this trap, the sukuyan can be exorcised from the house by marking a **cross** on every door and window and hanging up a **mirror**; the creature will be so frightened by seeing herself, stripped of enchantment in her true form, that she will run away forever.

▷ **azeman**

sun

THE 'GREAT LIGHT', traditionally venerated as the source of heat and life. The sun features in the mythology and lore of every society, since not only is it vital for life and growth, but its brightness, power and locomotion all suggest great supernatural power to the animistic mind. Light is almost universally equated with wisdom and understanding, and the fierce heat of the sun, especially in tropical areas, suggested a powerful deity who must be placated to ensure the success of crops and the continuation of water supplies.

Although almost every magical or religious system uses the symbolism of the sun to express power or wisdom, some ancient civilizations developed solar ideology into a highly organized religion. In such cultures, such as Egyptian and Inca, the sun is usually associated with kingship, the ancestor and source of power of the royal line. The Egyptian sun god is Rā (or Rē), personification of the blazing midday sun, first king of Egypt, who created himself from nothingness and then castrated himself and engendered mankind from the blood. He is portrayed as a **scarab** beetle, symbol of self-generation and life, a serpent or a human with the head of a **hawk**, and his celestial eye represented all-seeing wisdom. The sun kings of India are a peaceful race, unlike their counterparts, the warring moon gods.

Where the sun is worshipped as a deity it is personified as all-seeing and usually male, although some Native American groups acknowledge a female sun who gave birth to the tribe (for example the Yuchi tribes of the South East). Often the sun deity is portrayed as male in contrast to that of the moon which is female, for example Apollo and Diana in Greek mythology. Several cultures worship the solar deity by a sun dance. The most famous is that of the Great Plains groups of North America, which is performed around a specially constructed, ornate pole with fasting, austerities such as laceration and hanging by strips of skin, and ritual, song and dance.

The daily course of the sun has aroused much folkloric interest; one Inuit tale, **Sun Sister, Moon Brother**, tells how a woman fled to the skies pursued by her brother after she had been tricked into an incestuous sexual relationship. She is turned into the sun and he, as the moon, continually pursues her. Phaeton drew his father's chariot across the sky (with disastrous results, owing to his inexperience), and Rā travelled his course in a great boat, which sailed back under the world to the east every night. At the start of his journey he is Kheper, the young god; he becomes Rā at midday, and in the evening he is the old god of the sun, Atum. In Polynesia it was said that the sun originally crossed the skies so quickly that man could do no work; a mythological hero ascended to the sky to break his leg and thereby slow him down.

The sun is said by some groups to have been put in position by a **culture hero**, often stolen from other supernatural powers for the benefit of humans. Such tales are closely related to that of the Greek trickster figure Prometheus, who stole fire from Zeus and brought it back to earth.

Absence of sun is a less common and less pressing concern for most primal societies than lack of **rain**, but rituals do exist to produce sunshine. Many ancient ceremonies of sacrifice, particularly in South America, are performed to rejuvenate the sun for his continued journey across the sky, since like any deity he will inevitably fail if left to wither and grow feeble. Round stones and fire, both meant to symbolize the sun, are common ingredients in sun-inducing rituals, and the letting of blood was believed to impart colour and strength to the sun as it climbed the sky.

sun dance

RITUAL DANCE, performed by many Native American groups in honour of the **sun**. The dance takes many forms, from the opposing lines and **stick dance** of the Iroquois and the elaborate gold **masks** of the Incas to the spectacular rituals of the Great Plains groups, involving self-mutilation and torture, including the Arapaho, Blackfoot, Crow, Cheyenne and others. The most characteristic form is the circular dance, reflecting the form of the sun itself, and there is widespread use of the phallic stick, often supplemented by ritual intercourse, to communicate the life principle.

sunflower

TALL, SINGLE-STEMMED PLANT, genus *Helianthus*, family Asheraceae, found mainly in North and South America and introduced to Europe by Spanish explorers. In Inca religion the flower was worshipped as an emblem of the **sun** with its large circular flower and ray-like golden petals. Sunflower seeds contain a useful oil, good for eating, cooking and burning, or may be eaten as they are or

sunflower

toasted; because of this high oil content they are often recommended for colds and coughs. The Meskwaki of North America use the roots of certain sunflowers to yield a poultice for sores and burns.

In Greek mythology, the sea nymph Clytie was transformed into a sunflower because she constantly sought out her lover Helios, the sun god; she still turns her face to follow his path.

Sun Sister, Moon Brother

TALE-TYPE OF INUIT LORE, an origin tale of the sun and moon involving the ancient motif and **taboo** of brother–sister incest. A brother becomes his sister's lover, visiting her only at night so that she remains unaware of his identity. Consumed by curiosity, she coats her palms with soot one night to discover his identity (see **recognition token**). Discovering the truth, she mutilates herself by cutting off her breasts and giving them to him, then flees to the sky and is transformed into the sun. Her brother pursues her and becomes the moon, doomed to follow her through the sky forever.

svartálfar

THE DARK ELVES, the **dwarfs** of Norse Lore who inhabit Svartalfheim. If they emerge from their underground kingdom in sunlight they are transformed into stone. They will sometimes mischievously echo a traveller's words as he walks through rocky, lonely places.
▷ **alfar**

swallow

SMALL AGILE BIRD, of the family Hirundinidae (order Passeriformes). It was sacred to the great mother-goddess Isis in Egyptian lore, and in classical myth to Venus/Aphrodite. Because it is a migratory bird, its return to northern areas in March is welcomed with general celebrations as a sign that spring has arrived; in Greece particularly swallow songs are sung in their honour. In Christian lore, this migratory habit led to the bird's being identified with Christ and resurrection; a swallow was frequently portrayed hovering by the suffering Christ on the cross in token of resurrection and consolation. A Jewish tradition ascribes the swallow's characteristic forked tale to a dispute with the snake, during which the bird escaped but his tail feathers were ripped.

Because of its habit of nesting in house eaves rather than perching in trees, it was popularly believed that swallows had no feet, and thus they are occasionally represented in art, especially heraldry, with legs ending in feathers.

To have a swallow nest in the eaves is widely held to be a good omen; in Rome the bird was sacred to the **penates** and represented their guardianship, and in some areas swallows were the spirits of dead children of the family, come back to visit the house. It was considered very bad luck to kill one.

swallowing

COMMON DEVICE OF FOLKTALES, forming a tale-type known as the 'swallow story'. Typically the hero or another is swallowed whole by a monster but survives and is later regurgitated or emerges from the gullet once the beast has been slain (eg the biblical tale of Jonah, **Little Red Riding Hood**). Sometimes the hero discovers others alive in the monster's belly, and liberates them, as in a Baron **Münchausen** tale. Occasionally the swallower is a human glutton, who consumes his or her own children, neighbours, animals and so on until killed, whereupon the victims emerge unharmed.

In etiological tales explaining **eclipses**, a monster swallowing the sun or moon frequently appears, who must be driven away by the people.

swan

GRACEFUL WATER BIRD, particularly the genus *Cygnus* (family Anatidae, order Anseriformes). In Greek myth Zeus assumed swan form to ravish **Leda** and the bird was associated with Venus/Aphrodite; it remains an erotic symbol in Western folklore. In Celtic lore the swan was a solar symbol, associated with water and therefore healing and fertility. Since the swan moves in the three elements earth, water and air, it has traditionally been associated with **shape-shifting**, especially with the form of a beautiful young woman (see **swan**

maiden). Like **storks**, swans were sometimes thought to assume human form when they migrated to other lands.

One of the most popular folk beliefs about swans is that of the death song; the swan is said to be silent all its life and sing its unbearably sweet song just before it dies. This superstition, propagated by Plato and Aristotle and beloved of poets, is doubly inaccurate—the swan does not sing before it dies, and neither is it absolutely mute during its life; it has a wide repertoire of grunts, shrieks and nasal sounds.

The use of swans as **figureheads** on boats is widespread, and stems not merely from their graceful form but from the fact that they never dive beneath the surface of the water for food (as ducks do) but only dabble; they are therefore able to keep the boat from sinking.

▷ **Angus Og**; **crow**; **Lir, Children of**; **Lohengrin**; **ugly duckling**

swan maiden

SUPERNATURAL ANIMAL-WIFE. Tales of this type occur universally, telling of a lover lost when she resumes her animal form. In the basic swan maiden tale, the hero sees a flock of swans land by a lake and creeps up to watch them, only to find he has in fact stumbled upon a group of beautiful women bathing. He sees their white feather dresses piled by the lakeshore and contrives to steal one of them; when the maidens take fright they all pull on their dresses and fly away as swans except for the one whose dress has been stolen, whom the hunter marries. All goes well for some time, and the couple even have children, but one day the wife happens upon the old feathery dress which her husband has kept hidden; she resumes her swan form and flies away, never to be seen again. Alternatively, the husband breaks a **taboo**, typically of not striking the woman or referring to her origins, and she disappears in her original form. Versions of this tale are found throughout Europe and Asia and also in Polynesia, Melanesia, Africa and South America.

In Native American versions of the tale (probably adapted from European colonists) the maiden may take the form of a **goose** or **vulture** rather than a swan, and in Shetland the swan maiden is replaced by a **seal maiden**, the **selkie**. In some of these tales, especially in Europe, the swan maiden figure retains much affection for her human husband and children, in others she merely disappears silently back into her supernatural life. In a very few versions she is pursued and killed by her irate husband.

A familiar tale type builds on the basic swan maiden story to tell how the hero is challenged to do various impossible tasks by a king envious of his beautiful wife. The swan maiden lends her husband supernatural aid, and the plots of the king are frustrated.

▷ **beast marriage**; **fox maiden**

swastika

FORM OF CROSS, also known as the crux gammata (as it is composed of four Greek gammas joined together) or the **fylfot**. It was widely regarded as a symbol of good fortune in ancient and more recent civilizations; the word derives from Sanskrit *svastika*, 'of well-being'. Cultures other than Christian utilizing it include Mesopotamian, Cretan, Mayan, Navajo, Celtic, Hindu, Jain and Buddhist. Its clockwise direction is held to represent the movement of the sun through the heavens, and therefore embody the solar principle, or it may, especially in Native American lore, represent all the directions and their winds. The swastika with cross-arms pointing to the left, so the rotary motion appears counter-clockwise, is frequently regarded as negative symbol, representing night, dark powers and evil magic, for example in Hindu lore. Scholars have hotly debated the significance of the swastika in each society, and the reasons behind its undisputed popularity and potency, but with no conclusive results.

The most outstanding use of the symbol in recent times was that of Hitler's Nazi party, who adopted the swastika as a national emblem and a rallying standard for anti-Semitism.

Swithin, St (c.800–62)

BISHOP OF WINCHESTER, whose feast of translation has entered popular weatherlore as the day on which rainfall signals

unceasing rain for 40 days. In 852 he was appointed bishop of Winchester, the capital of Wessex, one of the most significant posts in the Anglo-Saxon church. In the course of the next 10 years Wessex became recognized as the most powerful English kingdom; Swithin was energetic in founding new churches throughout his diocese and was renowned for his compassion and charity towards the needy. Before his death on 2 July he had asked to be buried in the cemetery of the Old Minster, and his grave was placed by the west door of the cathedral and marked by a tomb.

When Ethelwold succeeded to the episcopate of Winchester in 964, it was planned that Swithin's relics should be translated to a shrine inside the cathedral. The translation was scheduled to take place on 15 July 971, but it was delayed by an exceptionally heavy rainfall, which was perceived as further manifestation of the saint's power. When finally accomplished, it was accompanied by a number of miraculous cures. This is probably the origin of the famous superstition which states that rain on St Swithin's translation feast on 15 July means rain for the following 40 days.

sword

HAND-HELD BLADE, the preferred weapon of many Asian and European cultures for centuries until overtaken by the firearm. In Eurasian folktales it is often traditional for a warrior hero to have a highly personal sword, one so big that only he can lift it, or, as in the case of **Arthur**'s **Excalibur**, destined for him alone and lost from the world after his death. This tradition was especially popular among medieval romance writers in Western Europe.

Frequently such a sword is a gift from a supernatural helper, a **talisman** with the power of never missing its mark, or of bestowing **invisibility** on its possessor. In Celtic lore swords often have the power of speech, and in China they may enable the hero to travel great distances or summon the winds. In Europe especially, where justice and revenge are powerful themes, villains generally die by their own sword (see **Amleth**).

The mystical link between man and

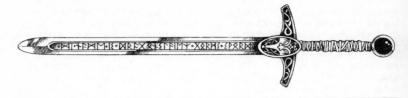

sword

sword is so strong that the sword can function as a **life token**, rusting or weeping blood when its master dies (cf **sword of chastity**).

Some of the most famous swords of folklore and legend are **Balmung** or Gram (owned by Siegfried), Durandel (**Roland**), Excalibur (Arthur), Tizona (the **Cid**) and Joyeuse (the sword of **Charlemagne** that was buried with him).

sword dances

TYPE OF FOLK DANCE, performed exclusively by men, using actual weapons or sticks to represent swords. There are various forms of the dance. Solo dances performed especially in Scotland, such as *Gillie Callum*, involve nimble steps over a crossed sword and scabbard, and are thought to derive from ancient victory dances (see **Highland Fling**). Stylized battle mime, such as that found in Greece, Turkey and the Balkans, in which participants flourish their swords and feign attacks and parries, suggest that this form may have developed from military training exercises. A third form is the tilt-and-point dance found throughout Europe, in which dancers form complex figures, linked to each other by holding the handle of their own sword and the point of the one behind. Such dances often incorporate a mock beheading, with all swords locked in a 'rose' around a central figure's neck, and may suggest ancient rituals of vegetation involving sacrifice. The supposition that this form has its origins in vegetation magic is supported by the phallic connotations of the sword, and the fact that tilt-and-point dances are frequently performed as an element in drama, reflecting the classical tradition of the Dionysian play cycle (battle, death, resurrection). Some such dances devel-oped into **stick dances**, or the members of the trade guild that made them their own substituted implements of their trade.

sword of chastity

MOTIF OF FOLKTALES, found in Germanic legend and in medieval romances. A man sleeps with a woman who is not his wife, but to guard himself against sin and demonstrate his honour he lays his sharp sword between them. It gained widespread currency in Europe after the popular dissemination of **Amis and Amiles**, but this romance in turn drew the motif from its folkloric ancestor, the ancient tale of the **Two Brothers**. In this tale the hero sleeps every night with the wife of his missing twin, hoping to discover his fate, although she is unaware of the change, and he places his sword between them as a token of continence and faithfulness to his missing brother.

Anthropologists have recorded widespread use of some separating object serving as a symbol of sexual continence, often used during periods in which intercourse is **taboo**, for example, in preparation for hunting, after **childbirth** or before an important ritual. The nature of the object seems in all cases to be insignificant—there is little or no use of **charms** or magical plants. The important issue then is that some object serves as a concrete symbol of the couple's intention to practise continence. With the development of the **sword** as a chivalric and heroic attribute and the popularity of the Two Brothers tale-type, this became the standard form of the motif in Western tales. Similar tales developed around **saints**, as demonstrations of their self-control and asceticism; in such cases the appropriate

symbol was a **cross** laid in the bed between the saint and the temptress.
▷ **bundling**

sympathetic magic

SIMPLE FORM OF MAGIC, depending upon the perceived similarity between two objects or operations. By altering or performing one, the magician hopes to influence the other. Hence if an image of one's own enemy modelled in wood, wax or even drawn in sand is injured, a corresponding injury will afflict that enemy. Similarly, doors are opened in the house of confinement to ease the child's delivery. Such practices, which are widespread and varied, are also known as imitative magic. Sometimes the sympathetic link between objects is one of proximity or possession—contagious magic. An object closely connected to a person, such as a lock of hair or an article of clothing, can be used in spells against them.
▷ **childbirth**; **spell**

taboo

NEGATIVE MAGIC, the principle of social prohibition. The taboo is a type of **curse**, with the condition attached that misfortune or death will befall anyone who neglects to heed it. The ill-fortune is not thought to be brought about by humans, but by the power of the taboo or violated object itself. The interdictions and unmentionables of each culture reveal its deepest preoccupations.

Although the word 'taboo' itself is from Polynesia, adopted into English by Captain James Cook, virtually every culture has a similar if less fully developed system of prohibition. Taboos may include actions, words, names or even syllables contained in names, sexual relationships, food and social contact; the object or action is forbidden because it is considered ritually unclean, or too sacred to profane by use. Usually the punishment for breaking a taboo is thought to be divinely or magically effected, but in some cases, notably incest, the community itself may punish the offender.

The taboo system is so ancient and widespread that it is impossible to do more than speculate on its origins. Since its two applications are to the seemingly contradictory areas of the sacred and the unclean, it seems clear that its original meaning was unapproachable or dangerous, as opposed to common and everyday. Its origins seem to predate even religion, going back to primitive magic; objects themselves are invested with magical power, which may harm or defile the one who touches them, and the taboo will avenge itself if broken. In such societies the power is neither good nor evil, merely mysterious and dangerous, and this explains the apparent inconsistency by which the chief could not be touched because of his sacredness while a corpse could not be touched because of its uncleanness.

As religion developed, the taboos were assigned to the commands of the gods, and failure to observe them would be divinely punished. In modern Western societies taboos have become socially restrictive patterns of behaviour and the consequences of disregarding them social reprehension. Although its origin is in magic, the taboo in practice is always a method of social control, establishing the permitted bounds of behaviour and the consequences of transgression. Among some primitive peoples family bonds are complicated by avoidance taboos (often between a man and his mother-in-law, who are not permitted to speak with or sometimes even to see one another). The taboos of a people shed as much light on the values of their society as upon their system of belief.

The most fundamental taboos then are those associated with the most basic human experiences, such as death and sex. This primitive class of taboos includes prohibitions against incest (astonishingly widespread), touching corpses or menstruating women, and scratching oneself with the fingers in puberty or **initiation**. **Menstruation**, initiation, sickness and to a lesser extent puberty are special states in which the individual is thought to be particularly susceptible to the influence of supernatural power; the most dangerous of all such states from the point of view of the community is death. To observe the taboo is to avoid provoking the demonic power associated with such states.

Incest, the general sense of constraint against the sexual act with those closely related to oneself, is particularly interesting because although it is the most universal taboo, the exact relationships prohibited vary from culture to culture, and the empirical reasons for such rules are obscure. Freud suggests that taboo here represents the power perceived in orbidden actions which the unconscious desires, resulting in temptation, renunciation and therefore an ambivalent ension.

> **food taboo**; **name taboo**

Tahmūrath

IRANIAN HERO, brother of Yima in the Avesta (or Zend-Avesta), the sacred book of Zoroastrianism. He is a **culture hero**, who teaches the people how to spin wool and raise animals. After defeating his enemy, Angra Mainyu, he rides him like a horse in triumph thereafter, in best **trickster** fashion, but Angra Mainyu revenges himself for this humiliation after learning from Tahmūrath's wife that his one vulnerable spot was on the mountain Alburz. Angra Mainyu turned on his rider on this mountain and devoured him; the body was recovered by Yima and so the skills he had taught were not lost.

Tailor, The Valiant Little

GERMAN FOLKTALE, collected by Grimm, corresponding to the English tale of **Jack the Giant-killer** and sharing many identical motifs. The tailor fools giants into fearing his immense strength by ruses such as squeezing water from a stone (a piece of cheese), and finally marries the king's daughter.

Táin Bó Cuailnge

THE CATTLE RAID OF COOLEY, the central tale of the Old Irish **Ulster cycle** and its longest text. This is thought to be the oldest heroic epic of Europe, traditionally believed to have been recited by **Fergus Mac Roich** himself, summoned from the grave. The tale was supposedly transcribed on the hide of a dun cow, hence the name of the early 12th century manuscript, the *Book of the Dun Cow*. It tells how Queen **Medb** of Connaght, jealous of a particularly fine bull of her husband's, requests the loan of the celebrated Dun Bull owned by **Daire Mac Fiachna**, a chieftain of Louth. Her envoys imprudently insult Daire however, who returns them empty-handed, and Medb indignantly amasses an army to march against Ulster which numbers in its ranks old enemies of **Conchobar**'s such as Fergus Mac Roich, and the

warriors who had left when Conchobar slew the Sons of Usnech. Medb's army advances, despite prophecies of disaster, but **Cuchulainn** stalks them secretly and kills a hundred each time the army camps. One day, overcome by a **berserk** fury, Cuchulainn faces the entire army and slaughters many, and then dispatches another every day in single combat, until Medb sends against him his half-brother **Ferdiad**, forced unwillingly into the combat by her threats and reproaches. The duel rages on for days, and the narration is among the finest in the cycle, but finally Cuchulainn overcomes Ferdiad. Meanwhile Medb's duplicity in promising her daughter **Findabair** to 12 Munster chiefs is discovered and slaughter breaks out in her own camp. Finally Conchobar, who has been ill, rallies, and brings his men to the fight. In the great battle of the Táin the invaders are driven back to Connaght. Medb succeeds in carrying off the Dun Bull, only to have it kill Ailill's bull and escape back to Louth.

Taliesin

WELSH BARD, believed to have flourished in the latter half of the sixth century. The oldest extant copy of his work is the *Book of Taliesin* (c.1275) which contains a wide variety of poems, from sacred verse to eulogy to heroic tales. He himself became a focus for much popular lore, and among the non-authentic elements in the 13th-century book are ten prophetic poems and tales in which Taliesin claims to have transformed himself into a variety of marvellous forms. In one tale, 'The Spoils of Annwn', he tells of his journey with the followers of **Arthur** to raid the palace of the Welsh **underworld**.

A collection of tales attributed to Taliesin but unknown before the 16th century are included in Lady Charlotte Guest's *Mabinogion*.

talisman

POWERFUL MAGICAL OBJECT. Whereas an **amulet** is a passive, protective **charm**, a talisman is one which is believed to possess of itself certain powers and characteristics. Hence in medieval Christendom holy relics were carried by pilgrims and believed to effect cures, as was the **philosopher's stone**, which was said to transmute base metals into gold and to empower the one who held it. Talismans are common not only in superstition but as central elements of folktales, especially Märchen. Items such as **Aladdin**'s lamp, the wand of Cinderella's fairy godmother and the cloak of **invisibility** all give their possessors special powers, and contain power within themselves. Such charms may be organic too, for example the **goose** that laid golden eggs, or Jack's amazing beanstalk. However in the common practice of folk belief the talisman is generally small and carried on the person like an amulet.

tall tales

TYPE OF FOLK NARRATIVE, an extravagant and exaggerated tale usually portraying the attributes or adventures of some larger-than-life hero. The genre is almost exclusively a form of imaginative oral entertainment, with little or no didactic or traditional burden; the emphasis is on the inventiveness and humour of the tale-teller. The tall tale is associated especially with the pioneers of the Western frontier, peopled with marvellous heroes such as Paul **Bunyan** and **Stormalong**. Tall talk is characterized by vivid vernacular idioms, dialect and fanciful metaphor—a bombastic and often fiercely nationalistic rhetorical vehicle for the tales.

There are several consistent conventions in all these forms of tall tale. First is the traditional presentation of an exceptional circumstance in which the hero cannot be expected to offer verification; the marvellous event may have occurred at night with no one else present, or in a foreign land while the narrator was travelling. The burden of proof is often further shifted (especially where the narrator is the tale-teller himself and not a fictional character) by attributing the tale to another, now dead, far away or otherwise unavailable for verification. Tall tales most commonly deal with hunting ('the one that got away' of fishermen's lore, the sudden attack of a seemingly dead bear) and agriculture (there is a world-wide folk tale motif of giant vegetables) or marvellous feats of

strength or speed, or they relate the astonishing virtues of a place (the prairie wind bringing corpses back to life) or its shortcomings (insect plagues that invade houses and carry off all the occupants and so on). Tall tales thrived especially in the pioneering days of the American West, but they have been an intrinsic part of world folklore from earliest times.

▷ **fabulous creatures**; **lying tale**; **Münchausen, Baron**; **travellers' folklore**

Tam Lin

SCOTTISH BALLAD HERO, whose tale 'Young Tam Lin', is collected by Child in his *English and Scottish Popular Ballads*. The ballad is noteworthy because it contains so many features of popular fairy lore.

Janet, daughter of the king, is with child by her fairy lover, Tam Lin. She discovers that he was once a human knight, stolen by the queen of the fairies when he fell from his horse while hunting one day, and that she can restore him to the human world on **Hallowe'en** night by holding fast to him as the fairy host ride by. Tam Lin warns her that the fairies will transform him into terrifying forms to shake her off, 'But hold me fast, and fear me not, I'll do to you nae harm'.

The ballad's motifs include the summoning of a supernatural by the breaking of a sacred branch (Janet plucks a **rose** from a certain bush to summon her lover), the ride of the fairy host with their jingling bridles, the rescue by holding fast despite magical **shape-shifting**, and the malevolence of the fairy court. A characteristic feature of Scottish fairy lore is the *teind* or tithe, the tribute, often a human captive, paid by the fairies to the **Devil** every seven years. Tam Lin fears that he will be the teind if he is not rescued.

tangie

WATER-SPIRIT OF ORKNEY, named from Danish *tang*, seaweed, since it is said to appear as a shaggy horse covered in seaweed. It can also assume the form of an old man. Tangies, although mischievous and given to ducking their unwary riders, are less malicious than **kelpies**.

Tannhäuser

Tannhäuser (c.1200–c.1270)

GERMAN MINNESINGER, or professional lyric poet, known to have travelled extensively and to have taken part in the Crusade of 1228–9. A few of his poems, such as six *Leiche* (lyric songs) survive, but he is best remembered for the traditions that grew up around his name after his death. He became identified with an adventurous knight, hero of a 13th-century legend, and his name is associated with the tale in a ballad dating from the early 16th century.

According to this legend, Tannhäuser is captivated by the songs and blandishments of Venus (Frau Holde), whom he sees as a beautiful woman in Hörselberg, Thuringia. He enters her court, and devotes his life to hedonism and sensual appetite. Eventually however he becomes sated and remorseful, and goes on pilgrimage to Rome to seek forgiveness from the pope. The pope, outraged at his tale of debauchery, declares that Tannhäuser has as much chance of receiving absolution as the papal staff (or in some versions Tannhäuser's own pilgrim's staff, which he throws down in his grief) has of bearing blossom. Tannhäuser leaves Rome distraught, and since he can do nothing else heads back to Venus's dissolute court. Three days later the staff does indeed break into bud, and the pope realizes his mistake; messengers are sent after Tannhäuser but he cannot be found.

The legend was especially popular with 19th-century Romantics in Europe. In Wagner's musical drama *Tannhäuser* (1845) the hero does in fact return to his home and his faithful fiancée Elizabeth, and rejects the siren call of Venus. Tragically however, Elizabeth has just died; Tannhäuser dies when he sees her funeral procession, and the blossoming papal staff arrives too late to save him.

▷ **act of truth**; **Eckhardt**

tansy

SPICY, AROMATIC PLANT, *Tanacetum vulgare* or *Chrysanthemum vulgare*, family Asteraceae. It is often known by its folk name, golden buttons. Its fragrance is said to clear headaches, and a distillation in water is believed to promote a clear complexion and soothe inflamed eyes. Tansy tea is used throughout the northern hemisphere as a general tonic, and to treat upset stomachs and cramps. Opinions are divided, however, on whether tansies aid conception or induce abortion. Some Native Americans chew the root to ease sore throats and fevers, and others use the flowers and leaves in poultices for sprains, bruises, bites and inflammation. In parts of England tansy flowers worn in the shoes are a **charm** against ague.

tarantella

FOLK DANCE OF ITALY, named from the popular belief that frenzied dancing was the only way to survive the bite of the tarantula spider. A form of hysteria known as tarantism in 16th-century Italy was connected with both the spider's bite and incessant dancing. In its present form however it is not particularly frenzied; a couple act out with light, lively steps and the aid of ribbons and tambourine the process of attraction and flirtation. Many steps resemble those of the Irish jig, with much hopping and foot-pointing.

tar baby

STICKY FIGURE, playful motif of folklore common to many trickster cycles. The basic tar baby plot, as used by Joel Chandler Harris in Uncle Remus's **Brer Rabbit** tales, involves a figure made from some sticky substance such as pitch, wax or gum erected by an enemy of the trickster-figure hero. When the trickster passes the doll he salutes it, and is discomfited by the stranger's silence. When his threats have no effect and the tar baby will not return his greeting, he becomes angry and hits out. His hand sticks firmly to the sticky figure, and in rage he hits it with the other. Now with both hands stuck he threatens to kick the tar baby if it will not release him. Finally, stuck by both hands, both feet and frequently the head or stomach too, the trickster figure is found by the one who set the trap and endures his punishment or humiliation helplessly.

The Brer Rabbit tales were examples of those told by blacks in the south of the USA, and it seems clear that the tale is most widely known throughout Africa and especially in the west. In much African folklore the trickster caught by the tar baby is **Spider**, known as Anansi in the West Indies and West Africa. In this version the tar baby is set up by the owner of a field from which Anansi has been pilfering, and when the owner (a man, king or another animal) discovers the thief's identity he beats him into the flat shape which spiders still have today.

Although the most familiar form of the tale clearly travelled from Africa to America along with the slave trade, there appears to be a strong tradition of sticky figure tales in Native American lore. The Apaches tell how their trickster figure **Coyote** became stuck to a pitch figure, and in Navajo lore the thieving skunk is similarly trapped. Slightly different but related tales tell of creatures such as **buffalo** becoming stuck in a tree while pursuing their prey. It seems likely that the tar baby motif originated in Africa or possibly in India or Europe and was widely accepted into Native American lore because of its similarity to existing trickster tale motifs.

The enduring popularity of the tale is attested by its survival in modern urban lore, slightly adapted, as any one of a number of 'superglue' tales. Most of these incorporate the key elements of the original—the trickster (often an adulterer) is tricked by the victim of his own tricks (usually the outraged wife) and rendered helpless and humiliated, usually in a compromising position.

Tarzan

LITERARY CHARACTER, the creation of Edgar Rice Burroughs (1875–1950), who first appeared in 1912. He has become one of the most durable heroes of modern Western culture, and one of the key reasons for his popularity may be the echoing of the basic folkloric motifs, **abandonment** and the **animal nurse**. Tarzan is the son of an English nobleman abandoned in an African jungle and raised by apes. After many marvellous and improbable adventures Tarzan become civilized, falls in love with Jane, daughter of an American scientist, and claims his English title.

tasē

EVIL SPIRITS OF BURMA (MYANMA), the souls of the dead who desire revenge on the living. The **ghosts** of the recently dead are those most feared; they can take the shape of wild animals or grotesque monsters, and are particularly active during their own funeral. They can be kept at bay by loud noises and disturbance, and so at funerals and times of epidemic or disaster they must be frightened away by shouting, dancing and banging **drums**, **cymbals** and tin pots.
▷ **death**; **funeral customs**

tasks and tests

MOTIFS OF FOLKLORE, the means by which the hero secures the prize. A common motif of folktales from around the world is the supernatural task, in which the hero must perform the seemingly impossible in order to secure his bride or save his life (or frequently both). This differs slightly from the quest, in which he or she is enjoined to search for a mysterious person or object, and from the test, in which various **riddles** and unknowable questions are put to the hero, but all three share much common ground and frequently overlap in folktales. The motifs are usually accompanied by that of the supernatural helper, who enables the hero to perform the tasks, find the objects and answer the questions.

In European fairy tales especially, tasks often come in threes. One of the best-known of such multiple task motifs is that in some Eastern European versions of **Cinderella**, in which the heroine is ordered to sort out a mixture of **lentils** and ashes. This is an example of the tedious task; other such tasks include counting the hairs on a pig's back, bailing out a lake with a thimble or small cup, or walking until a pair of iron shoes are worn out. Another famous example of a tedious task is the punishment of Sisyphus in the **underworld**; he is doomed to push a heavy stone up a hill only to have it endlessly roll back down as he reaches the top.

Often such tasks are imposed at the suggestion of wicked counsellors (usually the king's barber in Indian tales) or jealous rivals, especially in tales where the hero is suitor to the king's daughter. In many such suitor tales the tasks are set by an unwilling father-in-law, and occasionally by the bride herself. In some matrilineal societies the tasks are assigned by the mother-in-law.

Sometimes it is the hero's own boast that provokes the assignment of the task, or the boast of a foolish parent or wife. Thus in the **Rumpelstiltskin** tale-type the heroine is set to spin a quantity of flax into gold because of the bragging of her father. The motive of the person setting the task may be simply credulous greed, as in the Rumpelstiltskin tale itself, or more usually an envious desire to be rid of the hero. It may also be a test to secure the hand of the longed-for bride. In such cases the hero often triumphs unexpectedly with supernatural aid; hence **Aladdin** finally overcomes the objections of the Sultan to win the hand of Badr al-Budur by building a magnificent pavilion outside his palace in the space of one night, aided by the jinni of the lamp. With the rise of Christianity magical helpers were often replaced by **saints**; hence, in a reworking of a familiar tale-type, St **Kentigern** (or Mungo) recovers from a fish's belly the ring of the queen, who had been threatened with death for its loss.

Stories of numbskulls who set out to do impossible tasks are common, and one Scottish tale tells how a young woman baffled the designs of a **kelpie** by requiring him to bring her water in a sieve, urging him to stop the leaks with fog. Not all tasks are accomplished by supernatural helpers; in one famous European tale collected by Grimm, *All Stick Together*, a foolish peasant wins the hand of the princess when he succeeds in making her laugh with the ludicrous procession of people stuck to each other and to his magic **goose**.

Similar to the impossible task is the challenge to the hero or heroine to answer a series of questions or riddles, usually for similar stakes, the saving of one's own or somebody else's life, or the hand of a bride. The Rumpelstiltskin tale neatly combines both task and test motifs; the heroine accomplishes the impossible task of spinning flax into gold with the aid of the dwarf, who then demands her first child as payment. She saves her child by learning his name and thus answering his question. The **Sphinx** can only be defeated by one who can answer his riddle, which **Oedipus** does. In one European tale a clever woman ensures justice for her people by satisfying the king's challenge that she approach him neither naked nor clothed, neither mounted nor walking, and neither on nor off the road. All these conditions she fulfils by arriving wrapped in a fishing net, tied behind a horse and dragged in a rut.

In Native American and other lores, tests are a means of proving one's hardiness, courage and endurance as well as intelligence. So the hero may have to hunt rare prey, or submit to tortures such as being roasted or eating red-hot stones, or, in China, hot metal objects. In Icelandic and Indian tales he has to endure severe cold, in England he must keep up with a woman who tires out a succession of dancing partners. In fairy tales the test is often moral, so the heroine, like Griselda in the *Canterbury Tales*, must practise patience and forbearance, and chivalric heroes are tempted to break their vows of chastity and fidelity. Many tales tell of tests of

tattoos

friendship either failed or fulfilled; a common deception is to appear as Death to see whether the spouse or parent who protested sacrificial love will be prepared to exercise it. In one African tale a chief discovers which of his four wives truly loves him when she is the only one to offer herself to Death in his place.

In tests of identity the hero may prove himself by performing a deed only he could do, such as drawing a sword from a stone (**Arthur** and others), bending a marvellous bow (Shiva), or fitting into magical clothes, such as Cinderella's glass slipper. The princess proves herself royal by her inability to sleep when a pea is placed beneath her mattresses (the **Princess on the Pea**), and there are many tales in which the heroine or hero produces a token such as a ring to prove identity.

Very many European tales tell how the **Devil** attempts to ensnare humans with seemingly impossible questions. The heroes of such stories trick the Devil by guessing successfully, for example, the nature of his horse (a he-goat) or food (dead dog), and thus benefit from the Devil's help while evading his claim on their soul.

tattoos

BODY ORNAMENTATION, an indelible design made by puncturing the skin and introducing coloured dyes into the ruptures. In primitive societies throughout the world, and in ancient civilization such as Egypt and Greece, tattooing believed to impart magical propertie eyes tattooed on the buttocks, fo example, will enable the hunter to se behind him. Such beliefs persisted unt relatively recent times; the popula anchor tattooed on a sailor's arm wa intended to keep him close to the boa should he fall overboard. Other tattoo functioned as **charms** to ward off sick ness or evil spirits, or to identify th bearer by rank or caste. Often th painful process of tattooing is part of th **initiation** rite, a visible and incontrover ible proof of manhood.

Various methods are used to produc tattoos, from simple pricking rubbe with pigment to slashing, scratching needle punctures and grooving. Th word comes from Polynesia—it was fir recorded in Tahiti in 1769 by Captai Cook's crew—and this exotic decor ation became a fashionable vogue i areas of Europe as well as a hallmark sailors. Tattooing has been used fo identification since it cannot b removed; prisoners in Siberian prison and Nazi concentrations camps wer among those permanently stigmatize by a tattoo. The practice continues int the 20th century, particularly amon members of motorcycle gangs and so or and has enjoyed a recent revival as form of body art. Designs range from th common heart bearing the name of loved one to intricate and highly artist abstract patterning, and from a discree mark to whole-body coverage.

taxims

REVENANTS OF EASTERN EUROPE, th animated corpse of a restless sou Unlike **vampires**, taxims generally hav a decomposing body and hence the approach is often signalled by a stencl Such physical revenants are almost cer tainly motivated by specific revenge, an will generally not cause harm to any bu the one they seek.

tengu

MISCHIEVOUS SPIRITS OF JAPANESE LOR dwelling in trees in mountainous area They are said to be born from eggs, an may be portrayed either as winge

Moko tattoo

beaked creatures with human limbs or larger beings with long noses, feather fans and a threatening, aggressive mien. The more human tengu are chiefs, and the smaller *koppa tengu* his retainers. They are sometimes said to be master swordsmen, the ghosts of those who were arrogant in life.

tennin

BEAUTIFUL SUPERNATURAL MAIDENS, the lovely inhabitants of the Buddhist **Paradise**. In one Japanese tale Hagoromo was a tennin who visited earth and, delighted by the beauty of the sea and sand, hung up her feathery robe and began to dance. When she realized that she was being watched by a fisherman however she fled, leaving her beautiful robe behind. The episode forms the plot of a popular No play.

thabet

SPIRITS OF BURMESE (MYANMA) LORE, grotesque monsters with long flickering tongues, who wish to avenge themselves particularly on men.

Thanksgiving

NATIONAL HOLIDAY OF THE UNITED STATES AND CANADA, said to have originated in 1621 when the governor of Plymouth William Bradford led a joint celebration of Native Americans and Puritan settlers to give thanks for the harvest. In the mid 19th century the festival extended beyond New England, and in 1863 was officially proclaimed a national holiday by Abraham Lincoln. It was originally celebrated on the last Thursday in November, but in 1941 was set as the fourth Thursday in that month. In Canada it is celebrated on the second Monday in October.

Among the traditions associated with Thanksgiving is the family meal, usually roast **turkey** followed by **pumpkin** pie.

thayè

IN BURMESE (MYANMA) LORE, the ghost of the victim of a violent death, similar in appearance to the **thabet** but not confining its animosity to men alone.

thirteen

NUMBER OF SUPERSTITION. Thirteen is considered an especially unlucky number in Christian societies, traditionally because of the Last Supper at which 13 were present, including the traitor **Judas Iscariot** who later hung himself. A very common English superstition holds that if 13 people sit down for dinner one will die before the year is out. Thirteen is the 'Devil's dozen', a number traditionally used by **witches** as a parody of the 12 disciples of Jesus, but it is also the baker's dozen, a custom said to have developed among bakers fearful of being prosecuted for giving short measures of bread.
▷ **numbers**

thistle

PRICKLY WEED, most commonly species of *Carduus* and *Cirsium* of the family Asteraceae, with their dense round purple or pinky flowers and characteristically spiky leaves. It is the national emblem of Scotland, from a tradition that in the mid-10th century a raiding party of Danes gave themselves away by their screams as they tried to wade barefoot through the moat of Staines Castle in the dark; the moat was dry and full of thistles. Emulating several Scottish kings before him, James VII of Scotland and II of England established a chivalric brotherhood of Scottish knights known as the Order of the Thistle in 1687. A medieval French chivalric order, also named the Order of the

thistle

Thistle, was founded in honour of the Virgin **Mary**.

Mary is closely associated with the plant; the sacred thistle (*Carduus benedictus*) is said to have grown from a nail from Christ's cross that he planted in the ground. On the other hand, because of its prickles it is often known as the Devil's vegetable. It is most commonly regarded as a healthful plant, however, and may be hung on door-posts to protect the inhabitants from malignant spirits. It is said to cure toothache, jaundice and side stitches; as a decoction in water it is a restorative tonic, and in wine it improves melancholic spirits.

▷ **nettle**

Thomas the Rhymer (c.1220–c.1297)

SCOTTISH VISIONARY POET, also known as Thomas Rymour of Erceldoune or True Thomas, from his correct prediction in 1286 of the death of Alexander III and the battle of Bannockburn. He was said in **ballad** lore to have dwelt for seven years in **fairyland** bewitched by the fairy queen (such a sojourn is a common feature of Celtic fairy lore). His 'prophecies' were collected and published in 1603.

three

NUMBER OF MYSTICAL SIGNIFICANCE. With the introduction of the number three into the sequence of one and **two**, self and other, the decisive step was taken towards a potentially infinite system. Many societies did not progress beyond this triple distinction: the single, the double and the plural.

Three is a traditional emblem of deity in many religions; the Brahmin god is three-headed, the classical gods ruled the threefold world (heaven, sea and earth) in a trinity of figures, Zeus (Jupiter), Poseidon (Neptune) and Hades (Pluto), and the Norse **Asgard** contained three high thrones. Ancient scholars were quick to draw the parallels with tripartite mankind—body, soul and spirit. In Christian symbolism three came to be regarded as a sacred number representing the Trinity; St Barbara infuriated her pagan father by changing the plans for his wash house to include three windows—'to truly admit light'.

In folktales too, especially i European **fairy tales**, the number three is very significant. The threefold repe tition of an action is one of the fairy tale' most characteristic motifs. It works b establishing a pattern in the first tw tellings, usually one of failure, which i broken by the success of the hero on th third repetition. So in the **Lear** story, th two older sisters give flattering answer when asked by their father to give th measure of their love, but the younges gives a modest, more sincere one. The pattern of the two older sisters o brothers and the younger child wh proves the hero is a parallel motif, as i the triple-task and the three-night vigil i the enchanted castle. This technique i common too in **ballads** and loca legends.

▷ **numbers**

Three Bears

POPULAR NURSERY TALE, now known a *Goldilocks and the Three Bears*, which first appeared in the early 19th century i a collection of Robert Southey's, *Th Little Doctor*. In Southey's version th intruder is a little old woman; she late developed into Silverhair and finally th young girl Goldilocks. Elements of th tale are drawn from folk tradition—th empty house in the woods in which th protagonist takes refuge and the puz zlement of its inhabitants when the return are found in *Schneewittchen* collected by Grimm, and the identifica tion of the occupants as porridge-eatin bears may derive from a Norwegian tale Although simplified for children, th structure of the tale typifies the three fold repetition common to man folktales: Goldilocks tries out thre bowls of porridge, and settles on the last three chairs and three beds, alway choosing that belonging to the bab bear. When she is discovered, she flee or is chased from the house.

Three Golden Sons

FOLKTALE TYPE FOUND THROUGHOUT TH WORLD, with countless variations and i conjunction with many other tales. I the basic tale, a king overhears thre sisters boasting what they would do i they were to marry him. He weds th oungest, who has promised to bear him riplet sons with stars on their foreheads. The jealous sisters however throw the abies into the river and replace them with an animal, whereupon the queen is unished or banished. The children are ound and brought up by a kindly easant, and when grown the first sets ff on a quest to find the **bird** of truth, he singing **tree** and the **water of life**, and hereby discover his father. He fails and s turned to stone. The second triplet kewise fails, but the last and youngest ucceeds with the aid of a supernatural elper (usually an old woman to whom e shows kindness) and releases his rothers. The king learns the truth, the ueen is restored, and the treacherous sters punished.

Primarily a European tale drawing eavily on familiar folkloric motifs, this ale and its derivatives are found mainly a Europe and areas of the world olonized by European settlers.

hree Old Women

OLKTALE COLLECTED BY GRIMM, found lmost exclusively in Western Europe. A beautiful girl who cannot spin is ummoned to the palace after her nother foolishly boasts of her profiency, or through the machinations of nvious rivals, to spin three roomfuls of ax into thread. The prize is the hand of ne prince in marriage, but the girl is in espair since she does not even know ow to begin. Three supernatural help-

Three Old Women

ers appear, old women with peculiar deformities; one has an enormous foot, another an enormous lower lip, and the third an enormous thumb. They offer to spin the flax, asking in return only that they be invited to the wedding. To this the girl readily agrees, and the job is soon completed. When the prince sees them at the bridal feast, he cannot help but ask how they received their deformities, and when he learns that they came from working the treadle, moistening the flax and twisting the thread he vows that his lovely bride shall never spin again. The couple are therefore able to live happily ever after.

Three Ravens

ENGLISH BALLAD, telling of the faithful companions of a slain knight through the conversation of three birds of prey. The ravens are debating how best to obtain the carrion, but are thwarted by the knight's hounds, who keep watch around their master's feet, his hawks, which faithfully circle his head, and his sweetheart, who comes to give him burial. Although heavily pregnant with his child, she carries her dead lover unaided on her back to the churchyard and buries him, before dying herself. The ballad was first printed in London in 1611.

An interesting variation on this theme is the Scottish ballad, *The Twa Corbies*, collected by Scott in 1803. Here the crows are luckier in their meal; the slain knight's hounds have left to join the hunt, his hawks have vanished, and his lady has already found another sweetheart, so they can feed undisturbed. The tone is stark and bitter rather than chivalric. A modern song of the United States, having many variants, is clearly a descendant of this ballad but much degenerated—three old crows caw and bicker over the carcass of a cow.

thunder

METEOROLOGICAL PHENOMENON, a crashing or rumbling sound from a compression wave formed by a **lightning** discharge. Most cultures have evolved explanations for this dramatic occurrence. It is most commonly attributed to fighting in the sky, usually between gods, accompanied naturally by fallen divine arrows and spears (lightning). It may also be an indication of divine displeasure, accompanied by a strike of lightning at a guilty individual or community. Many mythologies assign a god specifically to the task of creating thunder, for example Thor in Norse lore, Lei Kung in China, and Thunderbird among Native North Americans. In central Australia, thunder is said to be the laughter of Mamaragon. These spirits, since they control both thunderbolts and rain, and are renowned for their volatility, must be constantly appeased. In some Native American societies thunder is attributed not to a god but to cosmic beings—the rattle of a snake's tail, the voices of **sky people**, the beating wings of a bird (usually Thunderbird, or the **eagle**) or **bat**. During rain-making ceremonies, the **bull-roarer** is often used to simulate thunder, in the hope of bringing on a storm by **sympathetic magic** or by arousing the slumbering spirit Thunder. In modern nursery lore, children are often told that thunder is the rumbling stomachs of hungry angels, or God's bathwater draining away.

thyme

AROMATIC HERB, *Thymus vulgaris*, of the mint family (Lamiaceae). It has been used as a flavouring for centuries, particularly in the traditional English dish jugged hare and in Benedictine liqueur. It is a favourite plant of bees, and thyme honey is a renowned delicacy in Sicily. Fairies too are believed to frequent thyme shrubs, especially in the north of England. In the Middle Ages in Europe it was an emblem of strength, and sprigs of thyme were given to jousting knights by their ladies, both as a token of favour and a **charm** to increase strength. It was used in England particularly in love **divination**, often in conjunction with **rosemary**.

tiger

GREAT CAT OF ASIA, *Leo tigris*, a hunter of strength, grace and ferocity rivalling the traditional king of the beasts, the **lion**. Like the lion, it has traditionally been associated with nobility, royalty, courage and particularly war. Those who

hunt or live in close proximity to the tiger must observe careful rituals and formulae to avoid incurring the displeasure of this sensitive creature. In Sumatra particularly villagers are careful to speak respectfully of the tiger and to explain to the prey exactly why its death is necessary whenever they hunt one. In Malaysia and other areas **euphemisms** are used to avoid mentioning the tiger directly by its name—it is 'the striped one', 'the hairy face' or simply 'Lord'.

Tiger-meat is said to impart strength and bravery (and is therefore seldom given to women). The gallbladder of the beast is especially potent, as the seat of the tiger's ferocity. Other parts of the beast—claws, whiskers or bones—are widely used as **charms** to impart strength and sap the courage of enemies. Eating of the tiger is also believed to impart virility to men and to act as a potent aphrodisiac.

In Asian folktales the tiger often appears as a **shapeshifter**, particularly in central and southern China (the fox largely replaces him in the north). In Malaysia were-tigers are greatly feared; they are said to embody the spirits of shamans or the vengeful dead.

Tilleulenspiegel

MISCHIEVOUS TRICKSTER FIGURE of GERMAN LEGEND, whose adventures were first collected in a 16th-century chapbook, compiled by the Franciscan monk Thomas Murner. He was a peasant, born in Brunswick, who died in 1350 after a life engaged in plotting dastardly practical jokes and pranks on the townsfolk. His jokes consisted largely in taking figuratively-expressed commands literally. Among those who suffered particularly under his often brutal jesting were the innkeepers, tradesmen and shopkeepers. The popularity of the tales is due to the ancient formula of the witty underdog besting the more powerful, duller beings, but this tradition is given additional piquancy by the emphasis on class divisions and the narrow-minded lumpishness of the bourgeois classes. He was celebrated in an epic poem by Gerhard Hauptmann (1928) and a tone poem by Richard Strauss (1894).

Tir Nan Og

'THE LAND OF THE YOUNG', the magical **otherworld** of Irish lore. It was said to lie to the west, across the sea, but although this is an earthly paradise it is not subject to mortal constraints. Many of the **Tuatha de Danann** retreated there after the invasion of the **Milesians**, and the place is now a **fairyland** where centuries pass in what seems only a day, and the inhabitants never grow old or die but feast, hunt and make merry without ceasing. As with all otherworlds, Tir Nan Og is occasionally visited by mortals, such as **Oisín**, but if they return to the mortal world they will find it changed beyond recognition in the intervening centuries. Those who return in this way are invariable charged with a **taboo**, such as not dismounting from the fairy horse, or not disembarking from the coracle; if they disobey, the mortal years will overtake them and they may crumble into dust.

Titania

QUEEN OF THE FAIRIES, consort of **Oberon**, in Shakespeare's *A Midsummer Night's Dream*. The name was originally an epithet of Diana, the virgin goddess of hunting, and it is seldom used in popular lore to refer to the fairy queen; she is more commonly the less ethereal figure, **Mab**.

toad

ROUGH-SKINNED TAILLESS AMPHIBIAN, particularly the true toad (genus *Bufo*), found in most areas of the world, although not in Australasia. Many toads secrete an irritating poison from their skin, and particularly the glands behind the eyes, if molested, and in ancient tradition were believed to spit venom. Its poisonous associations and its unprepossessing appearance have given the toad a generally bad reputation in folklore around the world; it is the familiar of **witches** and an important ingredient in their evil potions, a form assumed by the **Devil**, an emblem of evil and the epitome of ugliness. In popular folk belief contact with a toad produces warts. Its reputation is higher in Japan however, where dried toad-venom is a highly prized ingredient in medicinal

toad

preparations and the toad is an emblem of gods (eg the Taoist immortal Lin-hai) and sorcerers. It is a lunar being in Chinese lore, associated with the yin principle, and lunar **eclipses** are explained as the cosmic toad devouring the moon.

Like the **snake**, the toad is sometimes said to contain a precious and powerful jewel in its head, which is efficacious as an antidote to poison (see **jewel in serpent's head**). An old European tradition holds that the toad and **nightingale** (or **lark**) exchanged eyes, since the eyes of the toad are thought to be too large and liquid to belong to such an ugly creature.

The toad is a favourite form for transformations; although princes are more commonly manifested as **frogs**, witches are often said to turn those who offend them into toads. A Polish folktale has a princess transformed into a toad and restored to human form by the kiss of a prince.

tobacco

PLANT OF THE NIGHTSHADE FAMILY, any species of the genus *Nicotiana*, native to the Americas and the West Indies. The leaves, which contain the narcotic nicotine, have traditionally been smoked, sniffed or chewed by Native Americans after a process of drying or curing. The plant and the habit were introduced into the Old World by explorers in the 16th century and cultivation quickly developed.

Among Native Americans tobacco is regarded with reverence as a sacred plant, often given to the group by a **culture hero**, who explained its use. It is widely used in magical and religious ceremonies, as sacrifice and in consumable form (snuff, pellets or cigarettes), and among some groups serves as a form of currency. Smoking induces a trance-like state conducive to communication with the spirits; in some groups only shamans or initiated members are allowed to smoke ceremonially, although all members of the group might do so recreationally. Important treaties or agreements between group were frequently ratified during a smoking ceremony, in which the pipe would be shared among the elders.

Tom Thumb

DIMINUTIVE FOLK HERO, whose adventures are first recorded in an English pamphlet of 1621 but whose legend appears to be much older. He is linked to Arthurian legend; **Merlin** aids a childless couple to bear a baby after they beg him for a child, 'even if he be no bigger than my thumb'. Tom never grows beyond this size; he is dressed by the obliging **fairies** and undergoes various perils and performs many pranks associated with his size such as falling into pudding mix and being part-baked and taking a mouse as a steed. He eventually finds his way to **Arthur**'s court in the belly of a salmon destined for the king's table, and quickly becomes a royal favourite.

Similar tales are found in German, Japanese and Indian lore; here too the narrative structure tends to be a loosely connected series of episodes and esca-

Tom Thumb

pades, without a definite conclusion, although in some versions Tom meets his end in a duel with a spider. The name became proverbial for any diminutive person, and was assumed by the dwarf Charles Sherwood Stratton (1838–83) when he became an exhibit at P T Barnum's circus.

Tom-Tit-Tot

DWARF OF ENGLISH FOLKLORE, central figure of a **Rumpelstiltskin** tale-type.

tongue twisters

FORM OF ORAL TRADITION, a phrase, sentence or rhyme contrived to challenge the elocution of the speaker, especially in repetition, by difficult successions of consonants or tricky changes in otherwise constant consonant occurrences. An example of the former is the well-known 'Peter Piper picked a peck of pickled peppers', while 'Red lorry, yellow lorry' illustrates the latter (the liquid consonants 'l' and 'r' become hopelessly confused in repetition). Although their primary focus is not narrative, tongue twisters may give the appearance of something tantalizingly close to a plot, as in the intriguing American rhyme 'She thrusts her fists against the posts And still insists she sees the ghosts', which is a fragment of a more ancient rhyme. Neither are such rhymes didactic, although they have been used in alphabet books for children (this is the origin of the Peter Piper rhyme), and they seldom serve to communicate the value system or cultural heritage of a group. They do occasionally function in folk medicine, as a cure for hiccups; this is usually however not a superstitious belief in the power of the rhyme as a **charm**, although this is not unknown, but a means of controlling the breath and hence quieting the diaphragm, akin to the other simple folk remedy of holding one's breath as long as possible. The fact that certain rhymes are considered especially effective however suggests that the folk practice is based on less than purely functional foundations. Tongue twisters are also recommended for curing stammers and other speech defects, particularly lisping; many tongue twisters turn on the horny th/sh/s alternation, eg 'The Leith police dismisseth us', or 'The sixth sheik's sixth sheep's sick'. The s/sh alternation is particularly useful as a test for sobriety; anecdotal evidence suggests that British police formerly required a suspected drunk to intone the phrase 'The precedents and associations of the British constitution'.

The true value of such rhymes to the folklorist is their stature as almost purely oral lore passed on with intriguing variations but remarkable consistency, through generations and geographical boundaries. They rank alongside **jokes** (especially dirty jokes seldom collected in print, and interestingly there are many obscene tongue twisters too) and **riddles** as one of the primary repositories of the oral tradition in the modern West.

> **alphabet rhymes**

Tonttu

FINNISH HOUSEHOLD SPIRIT, who rewards the family that provides him with suitable offerings with wealth and a successful harvest.

Topaz

SILICATE MINERAL, valued for centuries as a precious stone, although the name has frequently been given to chrysolite, for example in ancient Egypt. It is the **birthstone** of November. In Hindu lore it is a **charm** ensuring long life, beauty and success, and in Christian tradition it is a symbol of righteousness, perhaps because it is listed as one of the two stones on the breastplate of the High Priest in Exodus, and forms part of the vision of the New Jerusalem described in Revelation. In medieval folk medicine it was worn to raise the spirits and sharpen the intellect, and it was said to cure the plague, flatulence, haemorrhoids and temper tantrums.

Tortoise

LAND-DWELLING TURTLE, characterized by its hard domed shell, scaly forelegs and back legs resembling those of an **elephant** in miniature. It is associated in folklore throughout the world with longevity, patience, slowness and persistence. Ancient cultures seldom distinguished between marine turtles and

tortoise

terrestrial turtles, hence the common belief in the cosmic turtle as **Atlas** figure, supporting the world, is often associated too with the tortoise in Chinese, Hindu, Native American and other cultures. In Chinese lore this identification has led to the development of the tortoise as an emblem of the yin principle and of water. The tortoise embodies the female principle in West Africa too, and is widely invoked in fertility rites. In China it was regarded as a warrior and emblem of invincibility, because of its uncrushable shell. Among the Aztecs however the creature symbolized cowardice and empty boasts, displaying a hard outside but a soft underbelly.

One of the most common motifs in tales about the tortoise is its attempts to fly; such fables generally illustrate the inadvisability of attempting something for which one is not suited by nature, or the dangers of rising above one's station. A fable of **Aesop**'s tells how the tortoise persuaded a reluctant **eagle** to teach him how to fly; the bird flew with the tortoise to a great height and then let him go as he was bid, and the foolish creature was dashed to death on the rocks beneath. This fable may be the source of the popular anecdote that the Greek playwright Aeschylus was killed by a tortoise dropped on his head by an eagle, or both may refer to the practice of the eagle, which smashes its hard-shelled prey on rocks to get more readily at the meat. A similar fable appears in Indian lore, collected in the *Kacchapa Jataka*; a tortoise is carried through the air by means of a stick clamped in its mouth, held on either side by two birds, but it falls to its death when it opens its mouth to answer back the taunts of the birds.

Buddha uses the fable to illustrate the wisdom of holding one's peace.

Another famous fable associated with the tortoise is the race against the **hare**, again collected by Aesop. The hare is complacent at what it thinks will be an easy victory and takes a nap before reaching the finishing line; the slowly plodding tortoise overtakes him and wins the race. This is an unusual example of the tortoise coming out on top in folktales; more frequently he is the thwarted **trickster** or the dupe.

▷ **turtle**

totemism

THE MYSTICAL BOND. Although notoriously difficult to define, totemism demonstrates a clear principle of sympathy between humans and nature. Among the Algonquin groups in the north west of North America, *ototeman* denotes brother–sister kinship by blood. Totemism is derived from this word; it is a system of beliefs and practices based on the central principle that there exists a mystical kinship between individuals or groups within the community and various natural objects, usually animals and occasionally plants. Since it is such a widespread belief system, found in Africa, North and South America, Melanesia, Australia, India and central Asia, totemism is associated with many different forms of behaviour, but there are several characteristic features. The totem is generally regarded as a protective, benevolent being, although its supernatural power may also arouse fear, and it is taboo to touch, eat or kill the totem, except in ritual sacrificial ceremonies, in which the animal is elaborately praised and lamented. In itself totemism is not a religion, although its practice produces certain rituals of observance and prohibition, neither is it magic, but it often coexists along with religion and magic- and may exhibit magico-religious characteristics.

In the most common form of totemism, the revered species is attached to a clan within the group, as progenitor or sustainer. Often such clans practise exogamy or endogamy, marrying only outside or within the clan respectively. Exogamy is more frequent, on the grounds that since the clan shares common supernatural ancestor, marry within it would be incest. The totems may be handed down patrilineally or matrilineally, depending of the social structure of the group; occasionally, as for example among the Nor-Papua of New Guinea, an individual chooses between the two system at **initiation**.

In the system of individual totemism found especially among Australia Aborigines, each individual is believe to enjoy an intimate mystical relationship with a particular animal (occasionally the whole species of that animal or a natural object. Individual totemism is often closely related to beliefs in the **bush soul**, ie that the death of one of the pair means the death of the other. Even in societies with group totemism, the shaman or chief often has an individual totem. It has been suggested that individual totemism, which implies a more direct and literal relationship between the human and the totem, may be the older form and that clans developed among people who shared the same totemic species. This is suggested too by the common practice of assigning totem by heredity, although in some societies more idiosyncratic means are used, such as scattering **ashes** around the new baby and checking to see by its tracks which animal has visited in the night.

Since John Ferguson McLennan, who argued in *The Worship of Animals and Plants* (1869–70) that totemism was stage in all cultural development, many theories of totemism have been advanced. Sir James George Frazer (*Totemism and Exogamy*, 1910) claimed it may have originated in an attempt to explain the mysterious process of conception. Freud saw in the prohibition against killing and sexual activity parallels with the Oedipal dilemma (*Totem and Taboo*, 1950). However late writers, especially Claude Lévi Strauss have doubted the validity of totem theory since the beliefs and behaviour patterns associated with it vary so widely between societies.

The common usage of the name 'totem poles' is misleading; the tall carved poles of the Native North Americans do not represent totem spirits but re grave markers, depicting heraldic animals or actual events.

ouchstone

BLACK SILICEOUS STONE, used since ncient times as a means of testing the urity of **gold** or, less effectively, **silver**. 'he metal to be tested is rubbed against he stone alongside a sample of known urity, and the streaks made by the two re treated with nitric acid, which dissoles impurities, and compared to establsh the purity of the metal under trial. 'he word has come to represent any test f worth, hence a criterion or standard, /hich exposes fraud and reveals true uality. It was a vital part of the lchemist's equipment.
> **alchemy**

ransference healing

MEANS OF CURING A PATIENT, involving he transference of the sickness into nother object. Illnesses can be transfered from one person to another by the imple expedient of rubbing the patient /ith leaves which absorb the illness and re then buried; the first person to walk ver them will then fall sick. A similar echnique is used to transfer disease into nimals; an individual may touch or beat beast (often a goat or sheep) to rid imself of illness and the animal is then illed. This is especially common in ases of community sickness such as lagues and epidemics, when a scapeoat is chosen to take the pestilence pon itself and then driven away or tually slaughtered. In Europe, scorion stings were commonly treated by he simple remedy of mounting an **ass** nd whispering into its ear 'a scorpion as stung me', whereupon the animal /as thought to take the pain upon itself. 'rees', especially willow, were used in a imilar way.

Sufferers from fatigue would take a tone or stick from the path and strike hemselves with it to transfer their reariness, and it is thought that this may ave given rise to the wayside **cairns** een in many countries, to which each raveller adds another stone.

ransformation

A CHANGE OF SHAPE, usually imposed by nother, as opposed to voluntary **shape-**

shifting. It is usually the result of enchantment, caused in European lore by **witches**, in mythology by gods, and by sorcerers in Asian tales. In early tales such transformations may be a punishment for breaking a **taboo**—hence Lot's wife is turned into a pillar of salt in Hebrew lore for looking back at the destruction of Sodom and Gomorrah— or challenging the gods (as in the case of Arachne who was transformed into a **spider** by the irate Athena when she rivalled the goddess's skill in weaving). These transformations are generally permanent. In fairy-tales however the interest shifts from the act of transformation itself to the breaking of the enchantment, the restoration of the prince or princess by the fulfilling of various conditions (often a kiss), and the transformation, as in the tale of the **Sleeping Beauty**, may be modified to a supernatural sleep.

travellers' folklore

VERY FEW EUROPEAN GROUPS WERE OR ARE NOMADIC, and they tend to be regarded with suspicion or scorn by their settled counterparts. A few Lapp communities live nomadically, the whole community following the herd, and there are a few semi-nomadic communities in Scandinavia and northern Spain. The most striking example of a semi-nomadic European culture is that of the Romany community, or the gypsies, as they are commonly known, from the mistaken early belief that they originated in Egypt, or travellers. Their origins are obscure; they probably began as nomads but many have now settled to form communities and travel only occasionally. They have a wealth of distinctive folklore and are unique in having attracted to themselves a body of lore, for example it is commonly believed that gypsies possess second sight (hence the popularity of the gypsy fortune-teller), and the power to curse or to heal.

Their own folklore combines elements of many traditions, for example the **separable soul**, the **evil eye** and the taboos against **menstruation** and the use of a person's true name (see **name taboo**). Their culture, which tends to be based on oral rather than literary tradition, has preserved an astonishing body of tales, superstitions, songs and dances, and they are renowned for their skill in traditional crafts such as tinkering, which require few tools and will therefore travel easily. The Romany community has its own language, of Indo-European origin, and also a special sign language known as Patteran which enables them to leave messages for later travellers.

trees

SYMBOLS OF LIFE AND REGENERATION, featuring in mythical and folkloric thought world-wide. Trees are a central aspect of almost every world religion and mythology, from the great world-tree of Norse mythology, **Yggdrasil**, to the Banyan tree under which Vishnu was born in Hinduism and the Hebrew trees of life and of knowledge in the Garden of Eden. In the primitive religions of Europe and elsewhere trees were themselves objects of worship, and rituals were performed in sacred groves, and in Native American and African lore trees were believed to be inhabited by powerful supernatural beings or the spirits of the dead. In folktales such as **Cinderella** too a tree planted over a grave is often endowed with the spirit of the deceased.

Trees have universally been accepted as symbols of life and sacred knowledge; in Greek legend **Jason** incorporated a log from the oracular oak of Zeus at Dodona into his ship to ensure that the Argonauts would receive wise counsel, and Buddha sat under a pipul tree to gain enlightenment. **Finn Mac Cumhal** gained the gift of inspiration from tasting a salmon which had fed on the nuts of the five **hazel** trees of wisdom.

In many mythologies humans are created from trees, for example the Teutonic belief that men were formed from the oak. Often too the tree is portrayed as the support of the world, upon whose branches the sky rests, providing a link between earth and the otherworlds. In addition to the many sacred trees and mythological World Trees, however, there is a vast body of folkloric tradition associated with the origin, nature and use of various species of tree.

Since trees have long been invested with animate spirits and sensibility many cultures practise customs to placate, encourage or even frighten trees into productivity. Throughout the world pardon is begged of a tree before it is felled, and it is widely believed that the tree feels the bite of an axe as keenly as a human feels a wound. This is also used to promote fertility however; if a tree fails to bear sufficient fruit in Asia and Europe it may be threatened by a villager swinging an axe, while another hidden among its branches, answers on behalf of the tree that if spared it will certainly produce much fruit next year. Another means of ensuring a good crop is to 'marry' two trees, usually by linking them together with ropes or, as in Hindu tradition, by observing a lavish wedding celebration. In *The Golden Bough* Frazer tells how, as the natural successor to this, blossoming clove trees in the Moluccas are treated with the care and consideration extended to pregnant women, that they may not be alarmed into miscarriage.

'Bringing back the May', a custom widely practised in Europe, derives from ancient belief in the beneficent power of tree spirits; on May morning the villagers brought branches from the wood back to the village and fastened them as protective charms on every door. The erection of the May Pole is also a relic of tree worship, a celebration of the return of the vegetative spirit.

trees

Many legends are associated with trees, for example the famous Glastonbury thorn, said to have grown from the staff of **Joseph of Arimathea** and to bud without fail on old Christmas Eve, 5 January, or the oak which concealed **Robin Hood**. Trees feature prominently too in folktales. The innumerable transformations of maidens into trees described by Ovid in his *Metamorphoses* (the nymph Daphne became a laurel when pursued by Apollo, for example) are echoed by the Indian tale of Parizataco's daughter, who pined for love of the sun and eventually killed herself because of his harsh treatment. From her grave grew the Tree of Sorrow, the night jasmine, whose fragrant leaves open only at night and never see the sun. Fabulous trees are also a motif of folktales, such as the marvellous beanstalk which grew from Jack's dearly-bought beans, or the mythical Arabian tree, the only one of its kind, in which nested the **phoenix**.

Trees have also been used in **divination**. A popular means of testing love was for a couple to place two **acorns** in water: if they floated together, the love was true; if they drifted apart, there could be a separation. To dream of a fig tree is a sure sign of wealth, happiness and a comfortable old age, but to dream of a **pine** tree is considered very unlucky. Hazel rods are the most popular and effective for **dowsing**, and have also been used to detect thieves, liars and treasure.

trickster

WILY AMORAL HERO, whose adventures form the most characteristic tale-type of African lore. Animal trickster tales are among the most characteristic, but in many the hero is human or even semi-divine. He is often regarded as the **culture hero** of a tribe, who in mythology either created them or taught them their knowledge. In these tales the hero usually overcomes a more powerful adversary by using cunning and deceit, often motivated by nothing more than sheer mischievousness, but sometimes his plans backfire and he himself is duped. In a common type of this tale, the trickster figure, by feigning weakness, fools a stronger animal into bearing him like a horse and then humiliates him.

Another commonly recurring idea is the tug-of-war between two strong animals, hidden from each other, who each believe they are tugging against the trickster. The purpose of these tales is primarily entertainment; to the European listener they often appear amoral. In a Western version of a trickster tale, **Tortoise** wins against **Hare** by slow persistence rather than complacency; in the African version the trickster wins by a brilliant deceit.

The tales are not devoid of moral content, however. Often they are used to demonstrate injustice: instead of miraculously performing Herculean labours, a trickster will often agree to do the task on a fantastical condition to show the unreasonableness of the request. So when Tortoise, primary trickster figure among several Nigerian tribes, is asked by his prospective father-in-law to carry water in a basket, he agrees on condition that he can have a strap of smoke by which to carry the basket. This may show a difference in the attitude towards unreasonable authority in tribal leaders than has traditionally been the case for monarchs in the West. Alternatively, a tale will often serve as explanation for a particular belief or custom of the group, and thus justify the society's value system, or the trickster's behaviour may be held up to children as unacceptable. Trickster tales are often grouped loosely in cycles, but with no underlying unity of character or purpose.

Tristam and Isolde

MEDIEVAL ROMANCE, deriving from Celtic legend and subsequently incorporated into the Arthurian cycle. The protagonists are also known as Tristan and Iseult or Isolt. Tristam is an orphaned noble, nephew of King Mark of Cornwall. He fights for Mark against the Irish giant Morholt and slays him, but the giant's poisoned sword has pierced his side and the wound will not heal. He finds his way to the only one who can heal him, Isolde, sister of Morholt, who nurses him back to health. She discovers by a tell-tale notch in his sword that he is her brother's killer, but is persuaded to withhold her vengeance because Tristam has killed a **dragon** that was terrorizing the country.

Tristam returns to Cornwall; Mark is led by his tales of Isolde's beauty to woo her as his queen, and sends Tristam to bring her to him. On the voyage however the two inadvertently drink the potion prepared by Isolde's mother for the newly-weds, and fall deeply and immovably in love. Isolde substitutes a maid in her bridal bed, and Mark remains unaware of the passionate relationship between his wife and his nephew until reports of their clandestine trysts reach him from the lips of envious courtiers. He follows the lovers into the forest but discovers them asleep with Tristam's unsheathed sword between them (cf **sword of chastity**) and, taking this as proof of innocence, merely replaces it with his own in reproof and leaves them still sleeping. The rumours continue however, and Isolde is finally submitted to **ordeal** by fire. Tristam, disguised as a beggar, carries her across a stream to the place of trial, and she is thus able to honestly claim that she has never been in the arms of another man, saving the one who has just borne her across the stream in their sight, and passes the ordeal.

The two are tortured by their clandestine love, however, and finally Tristam can bear it no longer and sails for Brittany. There Isolde of the White Hands falls in love with him and, hearing him sing of his love for Isolde, believes he reciprocates her affection. The two wed, but Tristam is unable to bring himself to consummate the marriage. When Tristam is wounded by a poisoned arrow he sends for Isolde of Ireland, the only one who can save him, but Isolde of the White Hands is livid with jealousy. Tristam has arranged a signal with the captain of the ship that is to brings Isolde to him; if she agrees to come it will fly a white sail, but if she refuses it will be black. Isolde of the White Hands falsely reports that the sail is black, whereupon Tristam dies of grief and despair, and Isolde of Ireland, reaching him too late, dies in his lifeless arms. After their burial, two trees grow from their graves and intertwine their branches.

The origins of the story may lie with the Picts—Tristam has been identified as the Pictish king Drostan or Drust—

and although the earliest forms of the tale have been lost the first surviving versions suggest that they were in fact quite coarse and violent. From the late 12th century however reworkings of the legend softened the original tone and followed the Celtic pattern of the elopement tale (cf **Deirdre**) and later the chivalric conventions of medieval French romance. In the 13th century the tale became absorbed into Arthurian prose romances, and Tristam became a virtuous and chivalrous knight rivalling Sir **Lancelot of the Lake** himself. This is the form of the legend utilized by Malory in his *Morte d'Arthur*.

tritons

GREEK SEA BEINGS. Triton was the son of Poseidon and Amphitrite, the archetype of the merman—human above the waist, fish below. He carried a conch shell, which he blew to summon or calm storms. In later classical lore the name was given to an entire class of such creatures (cf **fauns**).

trolls

SCANDINAVIAN MONSTERS, powerful and gigantic beings (although in later lore, particularly in southern Scandinavia,

trolls

conceived of as **dwarf**-like). They were implacable enemies of humans, but folktale heroes often dare to tackle them because of the treasure stored in their castles or, more altruistically, to rescue others kidnapped by trolls. They have many similarities to the **ogres**, and like them are generally slow-witted and thus defeated by an inferior force with superior intelligence. Their characteristic weakness is that they cannot survive direct sunlight, and will either burst or turn to stone if they have not gained their mountain homes or castles by daybreak. In European **fairy tales** trolls frequently live under bridges, and demand heavy tolls (often the life) of any that pass. They are without exception an ugly, heavy-set race.
▷ **trows**

trows

MALICIOUS BEINGS OF ORKNEY AND SHETLAND, folkloric descendants of the **troll** beliefs of Scandinavian settlers. Although occasionally gigantic, trows are more generally portrayed as dwarfish creatures, found as often in caves by the sea and amongst sand dunes as in their more traditional haunts among the hills. They are greatly feared and generally said to be inimical to humans, although some folk anecdotes tell of humans on relatively friendly terms with trows.

trumpet

INSTRUMENT SOUNDED BY LIP VIBRATION, a narrow tube or cane that amplifies the vibrating column of air. In modern usage the word denotes a brass instrument, but in primitive cultures trumpets have been made from wood, conch shells, horn, bone and bark. Because of their long slender shape, primitive trumpets were associated with the male principle and hence with fertilization, the renewal of life, war and **initiation**. Among many groups it is **taboo** for a woman to play or even to hear the trumpet; often its harsh rasping sound was said to be the voice of the spirits (cf **bull-roarer**) attending the boys undergoing initiation, the ritual death and rebirth. The loud sound produced was also considered useful by many groups for terrifying the enemy in battle or for signalling over long distances.

Since longer tubes produce deeper pitches, several groups have produced straight trumpets of such length that they have to be rested on the ground when played, or held aloft by one or two supporters. Other groups, especially those with skill in metal-working, have overcome this problem by coiling a length of tube (as in the modern instrument). The valved trumpet is a very late development, introduced in the 19th century.

Tuatha de Danann

'PEOPLE OF THE GODDESS DANU', the divine race of Celtic mythology spoken of in early Irish history as a human race. They were said to have been banished from heaven because of their wisdom and knowledge, or else to have sailed to Ireland from the east, in either case arriving in a cloud of mist in about the 15th century BC, and defeated the **Fomorians**. They were a tall, strong, beautiful race, skilled in magic, hunting and poetry.

The Tuatha were eventually defeated by the **Milesians** however, and retreated into the hills or mounds (*sidhe*) which became their kingdom, or across the water to the wonderful Land of Youth, **Tir Nan Og**. They developed in time into the **sidhe**, the fairies of modern Irish folklore.

Although scholars regarded the Tuatha as a human warrior race for centuries, it is now thought that they may represent early deities euhemerized into legendary folk, or primitive earth spirits. In the **Mythological cycle** they are portrayed as a marvellous but baffling composite of human, god and supernatural being.

turkey

BIRD NATIVE TO NORTH AMERICA, *Meleagris gallopavo*, or the related Central American species *Agriocharis ocellata*, the smaller ocellated turkey. Turkey features as a benevolent character often a **culture hero**, in much Native American lore. It was one of the earliest creatures of the continent to be domesticated, and was highly valued as a source of food. The turkey dance of many Native Americans underlines the significance of the turkey, but demonstrates also an appreciation of its quirky and ungainly gait; dancers imitate its erratic changes in direction coupled with a strutting toe-heel walk and vigorous to-and-fro movements of the head. The dance seems to have no sacred import or magical content. Interestingly, similar movements and an equally humorous mood characterized the early 20th-century ballroom dance, the turkey trot, founded on ragtime music.

Settlers in America quickly developed a taste for turkey, and it became part of the traditional **Thanksgiving** feast; explorers took the bird back to Europe and it quickly replaced the traditional **goose** at **Christmas** dinner in many parts of Britain.

turmeric

ORANGE-YELLOW SPICE, prepared from the root of a plant of the **ginger** family (Zingiberaceae), *Curcuma longa*, native to south and east India and Indonesia. It has been used in various cultures as perfume, dye, flavouring, medicine and cosmetic. It is also burned in many areas as its fumes are thought to keep away evil spirits.

turmeric

Because of its orange-yellow colour, turmeric is closely associated with love and marriage in Hindu lore. The bridal dress is dyed with turmeric, and the body of the bride rubbed with turmeric water both to beautify her and to prepare her for her conjugal duty. Turmeric powder may also be sprinkled over the bridal contract, and smeared on the walls of the bridegroom's house. Young girls throughout Asia use turmeric water for a radiant complexion.

Turpin, Dick (1705–39)

ENGLISH ROBBER, HIGHWAYMAN AND HORSE-THIEF, hanged for his crimes. He is best known in legend for his astonishing one-day ride from London to York on his horse, Black Bess. This version of Turpin's life, together with the figure of Black Bess, only began with the tale fabricated by William Harrison Ainsworth in his romance *Rookwood* (1834); the legend may properly belong to 'Swift John Nevison', who in 1676 is said to have robbed a sailor at Gadshill at 4am and established an 'alibi' by reaching York at 7.45pm. Nevison's legend is related by Daniel Defoe in his *A Tour Thro' the Whole Island of Great Britain*.

turquoise

MINERAL DEPOSIT, hydrated copper and aluminium phosphate, valued as a gemstone for its beautiful greeny-blue colour. In Tibet particularly it is venerated as an **amulet** bringing good fortune, health and happiness, and a protection against the **evil eye**, in much the same way as jade is regarded in China. It is widely held in Asia and parts of Europe to protect the bearer against falls (especially from horseback), and was often given as a token of friendship or love, since it is believed to promote good relationships. Turquoise served as a favourite unit of currency among many Native American groups.

turtle

SLOW-MOVING SHELLED REPTILE, particularly aquatic species (terrestrial turtles are commonly known as **tortoises**). Found throughout the world, turtle species have changed little over the last

200 million years or so. They are generally regarded as benevolent creatures, often credited with enormous wisdom because of their aged, wrinkled appearance, and feature as **Atlas** figures in several mythologies. Turtle is a popular figure in animal fables, particularly among Native North Americans; he demonstrates the superiority of quick-wittedness over brute force, often personified by **Jaguar**. In a typical tale, Turtle defeats his stronger opponent in a tug-of-war by taking his end of the rope and tying it around an even stronger creature.

As a water-creature the turtle is emblem of the female essence and fertility in many cultures, and North American turtle dances often invoke these attributes, with dancers bearing turtle shells and **rattles**. Since it is a symbol of persistence and perseverance, and therefore long life, the turtle is widely used in folk medicine.

Twa Sisters

SCOTTISH BALLAD, found also in England, collected by Child. It tells of a beautiful young girl drowned by her jealous elder sister, and the discovery of the crime when the girl's hair is used to string a **harp** and the instrument sings her fate. This is a key example of the **singing bone** motif in folklore. In other versions of the ballad other parts of her body are used, eg her bones become a harp frame, and the truth is made known at the elder sister's wedding. The ballad is found widely in northern Europe, and became popular in the United States, often in corrupted form as a dancing song.

Twelfth Night see Epiphany

twins

PRODUCTS OF A PORTENTOUS BIRTH, regarded with equal measures of fear and reverence in primitive lore. Attitudes to twins are ambivalent in most early societies. Sometimes they are regarded as ill omens, an unclean mutation, destroyed at birth, and sometimes they are said to be especially lucky. Almost always they are invested with supernatural powers, such as second sight or control of the weather.

Much of the disquiet associated with the birth of twins comes from a misunderstanding of the biological mechanics of conception. Thus the birth of twins is regarded in many cultures as proof of infidelity, and the mother might undergo punishment or enforced ritual cleansing. In such cases, one or both of the babies would probably be killed. An example of such a belief in Greek mythology is the birth of **Heracles**, sired by Zeus, whose twin Iphicles was fathered by the mortal Amphitryon. The two were conceived on the same night when Zeus seduced Alcmene by assuming her husband's form. Surprisingly, this persists as a half-belief in modern times. One urban legend tells how, after a bachelorette (or hen) party gets rather out of hand, the bride-to-be ends up in bed with a black stripper the night before her wedding. Nine months later she gives birth to twins, one of whom is black.

Women are discouraged from eating paired fruits such as cherries or bananas, or twin nuts or grains, during pregnancy, lest by **sympathetic magic** they produce multiple offspring. One Native American group believed that twins were the offspring of a grizzly **bear**. Some later societies however saw in the birth of twins proof of the unusual virility of the father, hence the children were considered especially gifted, and the parents may be called upon to perform the customary rituals of fertility for the crops.

In classical myth, Castor and Pollux were twins worshipped throughout the Mediterranean world but especially in their native Sparta. They appear to be examples of a peculiarly widespread tendency to acknowledge heavenly twins which ranges from prehistoric times through virtually all civilizations. The Dioscuri (Caster and Pollux) were transported to the sky as the constellation Gemini, and the two main stars have been associated with twins in other cultures, including ancient Egypt, or, as in China, with the twin principles yin and yang. In South American lore particularly, and also in the North, Twins feature as culture heroes, for example the War Brothers of the Pueblo. Often the pair are diametrically opposed, one brave and clever, the other weak, stupid and malicious and they may be associated with sun and moon respectively. Thus the twin motif typically illustrates the concept of mortals becoming heavenly bodies and of the dualism inherent in many systems of religion and philosophy. In many Native American tales however this dualism is not rigorously applied; both twins bring knowledge and benefits to the tribe, and both may act as trickster.

In modern society, much anecdotal lore has developed concerning the mystical 'bond' which twins are popularly supposed to share. Reports of long-separated twins dressing and behaving in identical ways, and of psychic links between remote twins, have stimulated popular and scientific interest in the phenomenon and preserved the ancient sense of the supernatural in the twin relationship.

Twm Shon Catti

WELSH FOLK HERO, born around 1530, an adventurous outlaw in the mould of **Robin Hood**. He was eventually said to have married an heiress and ended his life as a squire.

two

NUMBER OF GREAT SYMBOLIC SIGNIFICANCE, marking the beginning of plurality and otherness. The impulse to organize the world into binary elements is universally powerful: day and night, male and female, hot and cold. One of the greatest and earliest advances in babyhood is the separation of the self from the non-self. So in much folklore two is regarded as symbolic of a dichotomy, often (especially in European lore) of good and evil, as in the two spirits prompting **Faust**.
▷ **numbers**

Two Brothers

MOTIF OF FOLKTALES. A widespread form telling of two brothers, or two friends, in which the suffering of one is relieved by the intervention (usually the voluntary death) of the other.
▷ **Amis and Amiles**; **Damon and Pythias**; **Faithful John**

tylwyth teg

'THE FAIR FAMILY', most common **euphemism** used to refer to the Welsh **fairy** race (alternatives include *bendith y mamau*, 'Mother's blessing'). The tylwyth teg are mischievous but generally friendly; they are an unattractive, stunted race whose main occupation is stealing healthy, good-looking human children and leaving **changelings** in their place. Unlike other fairy folk, they take not only new-born children but also older infants, and the ugly child they leave in return is known as a crimbil. It is possible to regain a child stolen by the tylwyth teg by performing exactly certain powerful spells, such as the roasting of a black chicken, and a child returned to its parents in this way remembers nothing of his experiences among the fairies except a vague recollection of lovely music. The fairy maidens will often consent to marry human husbands and bear them children. They demonstrate many typical **fairy** characteristics, but are unusual in that they do not speak but communicate only by signs.

type

A MORE COMPLEX STRUCTURE THAN A MOTIF, a 'type' generally refers to any tale told as an independent narrative, which will probably be composed of several motifs, and is found in several varying but similar forms.

Tyrfing

SWORD OF SCANDINAVIAN LEGEND, crafted by **dwarfs** and having the remarkable power of fighting on its own. Although it could never be defeated, it would eventually bring about the death of its owner, and once unsheathed it could not be replaced until it had drawn blood.

tzitsimine

SPIRITS OF AZTEC LORE, emaciated beings with skull faces, the restless and vengeful spirits of women who have died in childbirth. They cause illness and contagion amongst other women's children.

UFOs

UNIDENTIFIED FLYING OBJECTS, commonly known as 'flying saucers'. With the development of aeronautics and space travel in the 20th century came a popular wave of interest in the hypothesis that other forms of life on other planets, whose space technology had outstripped our own, might themselves make exploratory trips in space craft. Early instances of unidentified aerial phenomena or radar sightings covered enthusiastically by the press gave rise to an enormous and enduring popular interest in the subject, and despite the fact that the vast majority of such phenomena have been adequately explained by scientists (as cloud formations, ion clouds, meteors, balloons,

auroras etc) the few remaining unsolved cases have fuelled interest in the subject. Anecdotes of such sightings are common—in some versions contact is made between the human observer and the extra-terrestrial beings, often of an intimate nature—and the tale-type has proved a rich source of oral lore as well as the basis for a genre of science-fiction literature and film-making. In some senses such extra-terrestrials have replaced the supernatural races of earlier folk belief: they are invested with great wisdom and (technological) knowledge which, like ancient **culture heroes**, they may desire to share with humans; they are feared and yet simultaneously eagerly sought; they come from an **otherworld** in uncharted territory (now that we know what lies beyond the western sea); and they are frequently credited with supernatural powers of levitation, **invisibility** and so on.

ugly duckling

TYPE OF FOLKTALE MOTIF, named after the well-known tale of Hans Christian Andersen in which a swan's egg is hatched by a duck. The grey cygnet looks ridiculous beside his golden duckling siblings, and undergoes much humiliation, but he grows up to become a magnificent swan. The tale illustrates one of the key themes in folktales throughout the world—the unpromising and derided protagonist triumphing against the odds (see **hero**).

uldra

FAIRY RACE OF LAPLAND, who dwell beneath the ground and emerge in winter to take care of hibernating animals. They are a shy race and generally well-disposed towards humans, but if angered they may retaliate by poisoning the reindeer or stealing human children, replacing them with uldra **changelings**.

UFOs

435

Ulster cycle

OLD IRISH EPIC AND ROMANCE, 'the saga of the Red Branch'. The oldest and the greatest of the great Irish cycles, it tells of the reign of **Conchobar** and the knights of the **Red Branch**. Most of the events of the Ulster cycle are set in the heroic age of the Ulaids of North East Ireland, the first century BC, and were probably transcribed in manuscript form from the seventh century AD, after long circulation in oral form among the bards and the peasants themselves. The surviving manuscripts date from the 12th century, the *Book of the Dun Cow* (c.1100) and the *Book of Leinster* (c.1160).

King Conchobar rules over Ulster, having overcome **Fergus Mac Roich**, and at his great palace at Emain Macha is a building called 'the Red Branch', in which the arms and heads of his defeated enemies are stored. He is served by the Knights of the Red Branch, most prominent of whom is his nephew **Cuchulainn**, whose father was either **Lugh** or Conchobar himself in some versions. In Connaght is the hostile court of King **Ailill Mac Matach** and Queen **Medb** (or Maeve). The loosely-structured cycle contains numerous episodic stories, brought together from oral tradition, such as the tragedy of **Deirdre** and the sons of Usnech, the marriage of Cuchulainn with Aoife and his subsequent inadvertent slaying of his son, and the heroic death of Cuchulainn himself, strapped upright against a rock.
▷ **Táin Bó Cuailnge**

Ulysses see *Odyssey*

Uncle Remus

TALE-TELLING CHARACTER, a literary creation of Joel Chandler Harris. Uncle Remus was a black slave in the American South, whose tales featuring **Brer Rabbit** and his companions are drawn from the African tradition of animal tales and **trickster** lore. Harris tried to convey the idiom and dialect of the black slaves in his characterization, in an ambitious and at least partly successful attempt to fuse folktales and folk narrative patterns into the literary genre. His popular success can be gauged from the enthusiastic reception given to Uncle Remus himself, who has become one of the best-loved characters in children's literature for his gentle humour, homely philosophy and narrative skill.

Uncle Sam

PERSONIFICATION OF THE UNITED STATES, portrayed as a lean Yankee figure clad in tall star-spangled plug hat, striped trousers and swallow-tail coat, with long white hair and whiskers. He replaced **Brother Jonathan** during the 19th century as the symbol of the new Union in popular cartoons, both in the States and in Britain (notably in *Punch* magazine). The name itself has passed into folk tradition; it is said to derive from 'Uncle Sam' Wilson, a businessman who sup-

Uncle Sam

plied beef to the US army in the War of 1812. The barrels were stamped with the initials US to mark them as government property, and were facetiously identified with Wilson's nickname. Congress recognized this etymology in 1961. The cartoon figure of Uncle Sam became an ineradicable part of the national psyche after James Montgomery Flagg's famous recruitment poster for World War I, subsequently used in World War II, in which Uncle Sam points sternly at the observer above the legend 'I want you'.

Uncle Tom Cobleigh

FIGURE OF A DEVON BALLAD, whose name

has passed into English folk speech as a means of saying 'pretty much everybody': 'Uncle Tom Cobleigh and all'. The phrase is in fact the last line of the ballad, which tells how seven men borrowed the poor grey mare of Tom Pearce to take them to Widecombe Fair.

undead

REVENANT, risen bodily from its grave to trouble the living. If all the precautions of the **funeral customs** failed, and the body escaped the grave, it would often attempt to wreak havoc among the living. A dismembered or decomposed body is thought to be less dangerous; in some European countries exhumation was carried out to check whether a corpse had decomposed or not, and there are several reports of bodies found in a non-putrified state with fresh blood around the mouth. This is now known to be connected with the natural process of decomposition, but for centuries it was taken as an infallible sign that the corpse was a **vampire**, a body reanimated by its own or another spirit, which left its grave at nights hungry for the blood of the living. (The lust of the dead for blood is almost universally acknowledged, hence blood and red wine are their most common sacrifices; blood is the symbol of life *par excellence*.) Wherever a spate of unexplained deaths occurred, the anxious citizens would tend to look for the cause in the jealousy of the recently dead, and corpses would often be dug up for investigation. Vampires had to be killed again with a stake through the heart or by burning to destroy the blood and release the spirit. To prevent the corpse rising from the grave in this way, many Central European cultures took precautions such as burying the body face down or placing a scythe, sickle or other sharp object with it, often over the heart or neck, to stop it walking abroad. It may well be that our most famous image of death as the Grim Reaper, a cloaked skeleton carrying a scythe, comes from the early discovery of the decomposed figure in its funeral shroud with a sickle to hand.

▷ **death**; **funeral customs**; **ghosts**

underworld

THE LAND OF THE DEAD, a type of otherworld found in many cultures. It may be a place of torment, as the Christian Hell, of reward, as the Egyptian Fields of Aalu, or neutral, as was the underworld of the ancient Greeks. This world is usually forbidden to mortals, although there is frequently a way of access and the most daring can find their way, past obstacles such as a river of forgetfulness (often with the aid of a guide) to the ruler of the underworld, and still return to the land of the living. In many cultures the route into the underworld was considered a long and arduous one, and the dead were supplied with shoes and nourishment to sustain them on the journey, and coins to pay the ferryman (see **death**).

Undine

WATER SPIRIT, an elemental being who, though created without a soul as all such supernatural spirits are, could obtain a soul by choosing to marry a human and bear his child. She thus became subject to all the pains and limitations of mortality. Her tale was told by Friedrich de la Motte Fouqué in his *Undine* (1811), and she is more closely linked with literary rather than oral tradition.

unicorn

FABULOUS ANIMAL, a symbol of strength and purity. There has been much debate over the centuries as to whether the unicorn was a fictional or factual beast; some scholars have suggested that the term may have referred to the rhinoceros, who shares the characteristic of the single horn. The unicorn is mentioned in the Bible and by Herodotus, but the first detailed description comes from the Greek physician Ctesias in his *Indica* (fourth century BC). He claimed that it is of similar build to a horse but capable of running much faster, with a white body and purple head in the centre of which grew a long, single horn, white at its base, black in the middle, and with a dark red tip. Since then travellers down the centuries have given conflicting accounts of the unicorn's appearance and behaviour, some speaking of its ferocity and others of its astonishing timidity. One common belief was that, while aggressive towards other unicorns and therefore generally solitary, the

unicorn

unicorn became gentle in mating season, and this is one of the reasons for its association with chastity. Hunting the unicorn, with its fierce and powerful horn, was notoriously difficult, and bestiaries of the Middle Ages are unanimous in their conviction that the only infallible method is to use a virgin as bait. The unicorn would instantly become placid and move to place its head adoringly in her lap, at which point he could easily be killed by the intrepid hunter. As a particularly picturesque symbol of purity, the unicorn came to be portrayed with various female saints, including the Virgin **Mary**. Alongside this reputation for revering purity, however, the unicorn appears to have attracted speculation in some medieval accounts as to the exact nature of its attraction to the virgins, and there are hints of bestiality in the ancient traditions of animal–lover folklore; in some cases the maiden is portrayed nude, for example.

The other recommended way to catch the unicorn was to stand in front of a sturdy tree and taunt the animal until it charged. The hunter could then step nimbly to one side at the last moment and at his leisure cut off the head of the unicorn, stuck fast by its deeply embedded horn.

The horn of the unicorn was widely believed to be efficacious against poison, and hence it was often used as a drinking-horn by prudent monarchs, and was a popular item in apothecaries' shops. It was in great demand in the 16th and 17th centuries, although a growing body of sceptics argued against its existence. From the third century AD writings of Aelian developed the tradition that the unicorn's horn was twisted, and the horns of the narwhal (or sea-unicorn), rhinoceros and other animals were often peddled either mistakenly or fraudulently as those of unicorns.

Because of its reputation for purity, nobility and strength, the unicorn was frequently featured in heraldry, and came to be regarded as a symbol of royalty in Britain in the time of James I.

unseelie court

MALIGNANT SCOTTISH FAIRY TROOP, the counterpart of their more affable cousins, the **seelie court**. They comprise the souls of the dead (**sluagh**) who died unsanctified and intend harm to the envied living, and various solitary fairy types such as **Redcap** who delights only in causing mischief to humans.

Urashima Taro

HERO OF A POPULAR JAPANESE FOLKTALE, who marries the daughter of the Dragon

Urashima Taro

King of the Sea and lives happily with her in her father's kingdom. He returns to pay a visit to his home and finds everything altered, his friends dead and his village beyond recognition; what had seemed to him just a short time had been over three hundred mortal years. In his perturbation he opens a box (in some versions a bottle) given to him by his wife, who had solemnly charged him to keep it sealed if he wished to see her again. His life-essence escapes as a wisp of smoke, the magic preserving him disperses, and he withers and dies on the sand.

▷ **fairyland**; **Rip Van Winkle**; **taboo**

urban legends

TALES CIRCULATED WIDELY IN MODERN SOCIETY, considered as folk narratives by many folklorists. Urban legends display many features characteristic of folklore. They are generally transmitted orally (although some are also picked up and disseminated, usually unattributed, by mass media), and told as 'true stories', often attributed to a 'friend of a friend' (in fact, Jan Harold Brunvand, a prominent researcher on American urban legends, coined the acronym *foaf* to denote this mysterious personage). The teller and recipient may demonstrate full belief or express reservations about details of the tale, but the true urban legend, though it may be fantastic, grotesque or supernatural, is always plausible. Like all forms of folk narrative, the tales are recreated in each telling, with new details added, geographical or historical references given to strengthen the impression of veracity ('This happened a couple of years ago, in a lane about four miles out of town, heading west . . .'). Thus one identifiable legend, while preserving its essential motifs and sequence of events, exists in a myriad of variant forms in different areas, much like, say, the **Cinderella** tale. Interestingly, this very feature, which marks the legends so clearly as folk narrative to the folklorist, serves to confirm the truth of the tale among many people, who assume that the news of the historical event they reported has spread and become a little confused. Although systematic attempts, usually fruitless, have been made to trace certain urban

legends back to an actual 'true' incident, their historical veracity or otherwise is not their most interesting feature. What is more relevant for the folklorist is the means by which they circulate, the reasons behind their popularity and staying power, and what they reveal about the communities in which they spread.

In common with most folk narrative forms, the urban legend serves a specific, often didactic, social purpose. So for example the widespread tale of the girl whose elaborate unwashed hairstyle housed a colony of spiders serves as a graphic illustration of the importance of personal hygiene. Couched as an anecdote, it catches the imagination and impresses itself on the memory, and is therefore infinitely more effective than a straightforward admonition to keep oneself clean. A similar principle lies behind the growing number of chilling 'AIDS tales'; typically, a man meets an attractive woman in a bar, they dance, flirt, and finally he takes her back to his house and they make passionate love. In the morning he wakes to find the woman gone and scrawled across his mirror in lipstick the words 'Welcome to the world of AIDS'. Such tales are vivid reminders of the dangers of sleeping around, more effective than any government campaign. Urban legends feed off society's most basic fears and preoccupations, and although some of these are of their essence modern, others are more ancient than we realize. AIDS, for example, is a recent condition, but the tale above is drawn from a well-established tradition of contagion tales; in Daniel Defoe's *Journal of the Plague Year* (1722), an infected woman kisses a man and says 'As I have the plague, why should not you?'. Notice here too the details drawn from folk tradition: the woman seducing and destroying the man, the doom-laden writing (paralleling the Biblical writing on the wall, Daniel 5:1–30) in red, in this case lipstick, symbol of seduction, but traditionally **blood**.

Although fear of **bogies** and malevolent spirits has receded in the modern world, their place in the communal psyche has been filled by non-specific 'maniacs' or 'axe-men', embodiment of the general fears generated by what many see as an increasingly violent, fragmented society. Real-life tales of abductions, rapes and murders lend credence to a vast body of 'maniac tales'. Among the best-documented from urban American lore is that of the couple who, out for a drive one night, hear on the car radio of an escaped maniac in the area. At that moment the car breaks down, and despite the protests of the terrified woman the man gets out to walk to the nearest motel or petrol station. The woman locks herself in the car, or in some versions hides beneath a rug in the back. Some time later her boyfriend has still not returned, and the woman hears a strange scraping on the roof of the car. This continues all night, until dawn breaks and the woman, by now hysterical with terror, is rescued by policemen. In some versions she is told over a loudspeaker to walk slowly away from the car and not to look back, under any circumstances. Of course, **Orpheus**-like, she does so, and sees the decapitated body of her boyfriend swinging from a tree above the car, his hands (or boots) brushing against its roof. Another tale tells of the two young babysitters, both girls, who received disturbing telephone calls late one night after they have put the children to bed. Panicked, they telephone the police and arrange to have a trace put on the next call. The threatening caller duly calls again, and immediately afterwards the police call back, shouting at the two to leave the house as they have traced the call to the upstairs line. In some versions, one girl goes upstairs to check on the children and her companion later hears a dull thumping coming down the stairs followed by a moaning at the door that goes on until dawn; her friend has had all her limbs cut off and dragged herself downstairs with her chin, trying to get help before dying. Grotesque mutilation, the doomed attempt to attract attention and the frantic telephone call that saves another intended victim are all popular motifs of urban legends. The helplessness of the female and the role of the male as rescuer as well as attacker is often emphasized; in some cases this lends an almost erotic tone to the tale, and by fuelling women's fears it may

function, in the same way as ancient **bogie** tales, as a form of social control.

Often urban legends contain a satisfyingly ironic twist. In this they correspond to the fairy tale, which constructs an orderly universe in which the evil get their recompense. So for example the two men out in the bush who get their sport tying sticks of dynamite to rabbits then releasing the terrified creatures and watching them explode are neatly punished when one poor beast hops off to take refuge under their truck. This tale draws on ancient traditions; when **Hanuman** has his tail set alight by Ravana, for example, he runs throughout the city, torching and destroying it.

Ancient **taboos** such as incest also feature. In one tale a boy and girl camping illegally are accosted by two policemen, one of whom sticks his head inside their tent. After conferring with his colleague, he agrees to the couple's proposal that in exchange for the girl's sexual favours they will let the matter drop. After the first policeman has enjoyed his part of the bargain, the second enters the tent in some haste, preparing to disrobe himself, and is brought up short in horror by the sight of his own daughter. Cannibalism is also hinted at; during the hippie era a tale circulated in the United States about a spaced-out babysitter who reassured the anxious mother over the telephone that 'Everything's fine, I've just stuffed the turkey and put it in the oven.' The mother, uneasy, rushes home to find the baby just beginning to brown and crisp. **Abandonment** is another popular theme; a couple leave their two-year-old son in his high chair awaiting the arrival of nanny, who has been delayed by a flat tyre, while they leave to catch their flight. Unfortunately nanny is knocked down and killed on the walk to the house, and the couple return tanned and healthy to find their starved son still strapped in his chair.

Like **jokes**, urban legends sometimes operate to feed prejudice where cultural tensions exist. Tales of human bones recognized by doctors in Indian takeaway meals, or domestic cats and dogs disappearing near Chinese restaurants, are frequently repeated and believed in the USA and Britain, but the folklorist who tries to trace the tale to an authenticated case is doomed to disappointment. Such tales are rather an expression of distrust and resentment, often motivated by economic pressures such as immigration and increasing unemployment.

Perhaps the most entertaining form of urban legend is that which feeds off the modern fear of social embarrassment. These tend to rely on plausible scenarios which all listeners can identify with, and the laughter and winces they provoke are a means of both exorcising the listener's own anxieties and confirming their superiority (see **laughter**). A typical example is the college girl out on her first date, who spends hours preparing herself but finds when her escort arrives that she desperately needs to break wind. She manages to contain herself until they reach the car, then lets it out in a resounding blast and fans the smell out of the window as he walks around the car to the driver's seat, and is composed by the time he opens his door. As he gets in, however, he says 'I don't think you've met Bob and Ruth', and indicates the couple on the back seat. A variant on this theme has the victim blindfolded and led into a room where, believing himself to be alone, he breaks wind noisily, then discovers dozens of friends and colleagues congregated to wish him happy birthday. The fart has, it seems, become a taboo of the 20th century. In another surprise party tale, the man is taken out to lunch by his attractive secretary, and they return together to his house. She leads him into a dark room and leaves him for a minute, telling her she has a surprise for him, and the man undresses hastily in anticipation. The lights go on, and the naked man is confronted by his secretary bearing a birthday cake, followed by his stunned wife, children, friends and colleagues. Such tales demonstrate the link between dreams and folklore as an index of societal preoccupations; dreams about **nudity** in public are generally interpreted as denoting anxiety or insecurity.

Many tales include a supernatural element, and these are often referred to as ghost tales. A classic example of one such popular tale common in America is that of the 'vanishing hitchhiker'; two boys (sometimes only one) pick up a girl who tells them where she lives. They take her home but she has vanished from the back seat, and when they ask at the house they discover that the girl they saw died several years ago. In some versions the girl does not speak, merely points to each turning and finally to her house, and sometimes she leaves her jacket in the car, and it is later confirmed as hers by her parents. In another ghostly hitchhiker tale, a man stops to pick up an elderly man and they discover a mutual enthusiasm for chess in the course of their conversation. The hitchhiker invites the man to look at a particularly interesting chess problem next time he is in the area; if he is out, the man is to tell his wife that the problem is kept in a pot on the mantelpiece. Some time later the man visits the house he was directed to, to find that the old man died years ago but the problem has lain since then undiscovered in the jar he had described.

The urban legend is a thriving, unselfconscious repository of folklore in the modern world, more authentic than much of the pseudo-folk culture (or 'fakelore', as Richard Dorson terms it) that many people understand by the term. It demonstrates that the mechanics and functions of folk narrative remain largely unchanged, and that the skill of tale-tellers and the universal delight in hearing and repeating, are still very much alive.

Ursula, St

VIRGIN MARTYR, a romantic heroine whose fanciful legend set ablaze the medieval imagination. A Latin inscription of c.400 discovered in Cologne refers to a number of virgin martyrs. The inscription gives no details of names, numbers or date, but the enigma caught the popular imagination and a strong local cult grew up. By the ninth century the tradition declared that the women were numerous, originated from Britain and had suffered under Maximian. Martyrologies of the late ninth century name Ursula as the leader of a group of up to 11 virgins, but by the 11th century the number had become fixed at 11 000. It seems unlikely that this exorbitant inflation can be explained by the normal processes of exaggeration; it is probably due to a misreading of a manuscript in which the M denoting 'martyres' was interpreted as the Roman numeral M, and the figure was multiplied by a thousand.

From then on the legend gained popularity and after several elaborations reached its final form, which appears in Voragine's *Golden Legend*. According to this version, Ursula was the daughter of a Christian king in Britain who was betrothed against her will to a pagan prince and managed to secure a delay of three years in which to enjoy her virginity. She spent the reprise sailing the oceans with 10 companions; each had a ship and 1 000 virgin companions. They were believed to have sailed up the Rhine to Switzerland and then on to Rome for pilgrimage. On their return to Cologne they were massacred by the pagan Huns, enraged because Ursula refused to marry their chief.

The legend displays the common folkloric themes of the marvellous voyage and the all-female race (cf **Albion**).
▷ **virginity**

Uther Ben

'WONDERFUL HEAD', the head of the Celtic hero **Bran the Blessed** buried to protect England after his death. It was dug up by **Arthur**, who wished his subjects to rely on their own strength alone, not magical protection.

Uther Pendragon

FATHER OF ARTHUR, according to a popular tradition apparently begun by Geoffrey of Monmouth in his *History of the Kings of Britain* (c.1136). He seems to have played little part in authentic tradition before this. According to Geoffrey, Uther Pendragon was the brother of Aurelius Ambrosius and took the throne after his death; he seduced Igranie, wife of the Duke of Tintagel, by appearing to her in the form of her husband Gorlois and later killed the duke in battle and married his widow. **Arthur** was born of their union. He was finally overcome by treachery, poisoned by the Saxons, and was buried at Stonehenge. Later elaborations had Uther instituting the **Round Table** on the advice of **Merlin**.

utukku

DEMONS, a generic term of ancient Babylonian and Assyrian mythology. Individual utukku had specific characteristics and individual names (see for example **Lilith**). The utukku were portrayed as armed and terrifying monsters, usually having roughly human bodies with animal heads and limbs or wings.

Väinämöinen

FINNISH EPIC HERO, chief figure of the *Kalevala*. He is a **culture hero**, the inventor of the **harp** and of poetry, a powerful magician, a builder of ships and a sower of seed, who protects his people from harm. He is born in the sea, and his name (derived from a word meaning 'mouth of a river') suggests that the connection with water has some ancient mythological significance. Although slain by one of his implacable enemies, the Lapps, he is pieced together and resurrected by his mother.

He defeats the Laplander Joukohainen in a singing contest and is promised his sister, Aino, in marriage; Väinämöinen is perpetually old however, and his bride-to-be rejects her wrinkled suitor. Väinämöinen goes to Pohjola in the north and attempts to win the hand of the Maiden of Pohjola by making the magic sampo (mill) her mother demands, but Ilmarinen makes the sampo, and wins the hand of the Maiden of Pohjola. Despite his lack of success in love, Väinämöinen is held in great affection by the Finns. His departure at the end of the epic, when the new king of Karelia is crowned, is interpreted by many scholars as a reference to the supplanting of the pagan gods by Christianity.

Valentine, St (d. c.269)

THE PATRON SAINT OF LOVERS. There are in fact two Valentines, whose feasts are both celebrated on 14 February in the Roman martyrology, neither of whom has any obvious connection with courting couples. One was a Roman priest and doctor who is believed to have been martyred under Claudius II on the Flaminian Way where a basilica was erected in his honour in 350. The other was a bishop of Turni (about 60 miles distant from Rome) who was brought to Rome and tortured and executed there in c.273 at the command of Placidus, the ruling prefect. Some believe that the two Valentines are in fact one person, that the Roman priest became bishop of Turni, was condemned there and brought to Rome for execution of his sentence. Since the *Acts* of both are equally unreliable, the final verdict may never be more than conjecture.

The present popularity of Valentine's day has little to do with the historical saint or saints. It was a commonly held belief, attested from the time of Chaucer, that birds began to choose their mates on Valentine's feast-day, the very beginning of Spring, and this is thought by many to be the origin of the tradition of choosing one's object of love as a 'Valentine'. Some scholars believe that Chaucer was actually referring to the feast-day of the bishop Valentine of Genoa, celebrated on 2 May, and that he may have had in mind the betrothal of Richard II to Anne of Bohemia on 3 May 1381. If this is the case, the conflation of the various Valentines on to a single feast-day probably occurred some time after the death of Chaucer.

Many folklorists believe that there may also be surviving elements of the Roman Lupercalia festival, celebrated mid-February. The subsequent commercialism of his feast and its removal both from historical fact and the observance of piety has been distrusted by the Catholic church, and his cult has recently been reduced. Valentine is often represented in art with a crippled or epileptic child at his feet whom he is believed to have cured. For this reason too he is often invoked against epilepsy. Other depictions show his beheading, or his refusal to worship idols, which led to his martyrdom. His feast-day is 14 February, and he is the patron saint of beekeepers, betrothed couples, travellers and the young, invoked against epilepsy, fainting and plague and for a happy marriage.

valerian

TEASEL PLANT, most commonly of the genus *Valeriana* (order Dipsacales). The best-known is common valerian (also known as garden heliotrope because of its sweet smell), *Valeriana officinalis*. Its name, derived from Latin *valere* (to be strong), suggests the high regard the plant has traditionally enjoyed in folklore. In the Arab world it was it was widely used as an aphrodisiac (perhaps because of its exceptionally long, straight stem) while in Greece and Rome it was used to staunch bleeding, scent linen and drive away pests and as an incense. The roots produce a spicy perfume, often used as a substitute for **spikenard**. In European folk medicine its general effects as a sedative and restorative were exploited, and it was used for almost all complaints. It was said to be particularly effective in the treatment of lung disorders and rickets as well as nervous conditions. The state of relaxation and well-being that it promoted was often sought by **magic**-workers, either of love spells or more general supernatural activity. Native North Americans too use the plant as a sedative, to stop excessive bleeding, and as a soaking poultice for sprains, bruising and rheumatic joints.

Valhalla

NORSE OTHERWORLD, the destiny of the bravest warriors. Viking warrior heroes would be caught up from their battlefield graves by the **Valkyries** and taken to Valhalla, a great hall made of spears and polished shields and the favourite home of Odin, where they battle without injury, feast and drink, and spend their evenings hearing the songs of their great battles, waited on by the Valkyries dressed in becoming white dresses.

Valkyries

NORSE BATTLE MAIDEN, attendant spirits of Odin who accompany heroes slain on the battlefield to the afterworld reserved for the worthiest, **Valhalla**. They are beautiful maidens dressed entirely in white, with golden hair, a magnificent

Valkyries

sight mounted on white steeds as they ride to the battlefield with their burnished helmets and shields through the sky and across the sea. To see this troop is an omen of battle. In some versions they could appear as **ravens** or **wolves**, but in Valhalla itself they waited on the warriors at table in their white robes, despite their warlike nature.

Valkyries seem to have been of two types, either entirely supernatural (as with most equivalent attendant spirits in world folklore) or Amazonian human women (see for example **Brynhild**).

Valmiki

THE AUTHOR OF THE RAMAYANA, an ex-thief who became a poet and hermit.

vampire

REVENANT GHOST, which returns from the grave to prey on human blood, the most famous of the **undead** monsters. The vampire proper belongs to the lore of Eastern Europe, and especially Hungary, but it is descended from a long line of ghostly predators in the folklore of Asia and Europe in particular. The

vampire

lamia of ancient Greece and the Roman *striges* or *mormos* were ghosts with similar characteristics; they returned from their burial place, usually in bodily form but sometimes, as Ovid asserts, as fierce birds, to visit humans by night and devour them or drink their blood. The lamia was generally portrayed as a beautiful woman who would lure an unsuspecting, rosy-cheeked youth into her clutches and then devour him. This illustrates another principle of vampires, particularly female vampires; they are traditionally thought to be insatiably amorous and sensual.

In primitive belief, **blood** is potent and often sacred since it is regarded as the essence of life, sacrificed to deities to empower them and envied by the spirits of the dead. It is natural then that vampires should be thought to feed on the life force that they themselves lack, and natural too that the victims should then be left drained and sickening, to die soon afterwards and become blood-thirsty vampires in turn. In popular belief the vampire appears bloodless and pallid, with pointed incisors to enable him to puncture his victim's throat. Such creatures were soulless, living on blood rather than the vital force of the spirit. Misunderstanding of the Christian doctrine of transubstantiation, by which the faithful believed they actually drank Christ's blood and ate his body in the Mass, led to vampire-related beliefs and practices in newly Christianized lands where paganism still held sway. In the medieval Church, it was commonly believed that suicides and the unbaptized, unshriven or excommunicated would be forced to return as vampires.

Vampirism in Eastern Europe especially was thought to be closely related to **lycanthropy**; in life the person satisfied his blood lust in the shape of a **wolf**, and after death he or she became a revenant vampire.

If suspected of vampirism, a person's grave would be investigated. If the body was found undecomposed, with fresh blood staining the lips, the case was proven and the body would either be burned or a stake driven through its heart to pin it into the grave. Many legends tell of bodies writhing and screaming in agony as they are dispatched. The vampire can be recognized by the fact that it casts no reflection in a **mirror**, nor a shadow, and if threatened by a vampire one would ward it off with the sign of the **cross**, **iron**, light or **garlic**, and if by such means the vampire could be delayed until dawn it would be obliged to return unsatisfied to its grave, or to a coffin containing its native soil. If bitten, the only means of preventing oneself from becoming a vampire after death was to kill the vampire by transfixing it with a stake or nail then smearing oneself with its blood and eating some of the earth from its grave.

Vampire bats, shy brown mammals of the Desmodontidae family, earned their name by their eating habits; they alight on their sleeping prey and make a small incision with their teeth, then lap up the blood as it flows out. Often the victim is not even aware of their presence.

Veronica, St

A COMPASSIONATE WOMAN, who stopped to wipe the anguished face of Christ as he stumbled beneath his cross on the way to Calvary. The features of his face were said to have been imprinted on the cloth which she used for her act of simple charity. Despite the lack of evidence or collaboration the legend has appealed to popular devotion for centuries, especially as interest in the human and physical aspects of Christ developed, and a cloth known as 'St Veronica's veil' has been kept at St Peter's in Rome from the eighth century. Although devotion to the relic peaked in the late medieval period, it was exhibited as recently as 1933.

Much debate has arisen over the derivation of her name, which many believe to be derived from 'vera icon', true image. According to this theory, the name arose as a means of explaining the relic itself, and was then attached to a fictional character to create a charming legend. (It is worth noting however that the woman who suffered from internal bleeding, often identified with the saint, was known in the East as Berenike long before she was associated with the image on the cloth.)

Several legends purport to record the acts of Veronica after her encounter with Christ; some claim she used the cloth to cure the emperor Tiberius in Rome, others that she accompanied her ex-tax-collector husband Zacchaeus in his evangelism of France. She is frequently represented in art, either wiping Christ's face or holding the imprinted veil. Her feast-day is 12 July, and she is the patron saint of washerwomen

vervain

FLOWERING PLANT, genus *Verbena* (family Verbenaceae), particularly *verbera officinalis*, almost universally renowned for its healing properties. It was a herb sacred to Venus (Aphrodite) in the classical world, and traditionally held by brides (this use survived until quite recently in Germany). Because its leaves resemble those of the **oak** somewhat, it was a sacred plant too in Druid lore, and when crusaders returned from the Holy Land claiming that vervain had sprung from the blood that fell from Christ at his crucifixion, continued veneration of the plant in Europe was assured. It was therefore widely accepted as a **charm** against all forms of evil, including **witches**, **nightmares**, the **incubus** and the **evil eye**. Paradoxically, it was also regarded as a potent magical plant in **witchcraft**, a common ingredient in spells and potions. The juice of vervain could impart to the one who bathed in it the gift of prophecy and

invulnerability. Its many beneficial properties led to its traditional use, in England especially, as a strewing herb to give a healthful and happy atmosphere, and not just a pleasant fragrance, to the house.

The ancient association with Venus led many folk healers to regard the plant as especially efficacious for women's complaints—to keep the womb healthy, regulate **menstruation** and ease childbirth (this association is prominent too in Native American lore, for example among the Meskwaki). An infusion of the leaves in vinegar was said to be good for the eyes, while a **charm** of vervain around the neck cured ulcers, jaundice and a whole range of other complaints. Native Americans took it internally to promote pleasant dreams and calm upset stomachs, and it is used in many areas in preparations to arouse love in another. The herb is sometimes known as pigeons' grass, from the old superstition that pigeons would eat it to strengthen their eyes.

vetàla

SPIRIT OF HINDU LORE, a terrifying **ghoul** that haunts burial grounds and can take possession of corpses. He is instantly identifiable by the way his hands and feet point backwards (see **defects**). In folktales he is less terrifying, taking the aspect of a mischievous prankster rather than a terrifying monster.

vila

SLAVIC GHOSTLY SPIRIT, also known as veela or willi, the spirit of an unbaptized child or a virgin doomed to remain on earth and, naturally, hostile to the living. The vile are said to dance in circles, and any mortal who happens upon them or breaks their circle is condemned to dance with them to death. They occasionally appeared to lure men into the grave, but they could also be benevolent supernatural helpers for those on a **quest**, and some were said to take human husbands and bear them offspring, after the manner of the **swan maiden**.

violet

FLOWERING PLANT, any of the genus *Viola*, family Violaceae. The petals are typically purple, violet or blue. The plant is variously said to have sprung from the blood of Attis or to have been created by Zeus to feed Io, whom he had transformed into a cow. In Christian lore the violet droops because the shadow of Christ on the cross fell over it, and it is considered sacred to the Virgin **Mary**. It is generally associated with humility, suffering and mourning, and because of the double attribution is often said to grow over the graves of virgins.

In folk medicine, violet petals were used to treat epilepsy and liver-related complaints such as jaundice. The plant was believed to induce restful sleep and pleasant dreams. It has a soothing, cooling influence on heated tempers, grief-stricken hearts and tired feet alike.

virginity

OF GREAT MYSTICAL AND ECONOMIC SIGNIFICANCE, the virginity of the bride (almost never the groom) has traditionally been considered to be of great importance in the **marriage** ceremony. In China and other Oriental cultures her virginity is considered a vital part of the marriage contract, and blood-stained sheets are traditionally displayed after the wedding night as proof of the bride's purity. This concern is shared by some aboriginal groups, for example some Nigerian tribes who, interestingly, are little concerned about sexual activity after defloration. Among other groups, such as the Thanga of South Africa, virginity is considered an embarrassment. The bride price for women who have already borne children is higher than that for virgins among some groups in Nigeria, which does seem to make practical sense from a procreational point of view.

▷ **dowry**; **droit de seigneur**; **marriage**

Vitus, St (d.c.300)

A MARTYR UNDER DIOCLETIAN, patron saint of nervous disorders. Along with his nurse Crescentia and her husband (Vitus's tutor) Modestus, the 12-year-old Christian refused to recant his faith in Sicily and fled to Rome. There he cast an evil spirit out of the son of Emperor Diocletian. Awed by the miracle, the Roman authorities demanded that Vitus offer sacrifices to pagan gods, and when he refused to do so his miracle was construed as sorcery and the three were subjected to torture and executed. Some more fanciful legends record that they emerged unharmed from their tortures, and were freed from captivity amidst a violent storm, under cover of which an angel guided them back to Luciana.

Vitus's relics have been claimed by Saint-Denis and by Corvey in Saxony, where they were believed to have been translated in 836. It seems possible that two different groups of saints have been collapsed together in popular veneration; there is some evidence to suggest that there was an ancient cult of Vitus alone in Luciana, pre-dating that of Vitus, Modestus and Crescentia in Sicily.

Because he was reputed to have cured the emperor's child of demonic possession, Vitus came to be regarded as patron of those suffering from epilepsy and nervous disorders (hence the popular name for Sydenham's chorea, St Vitus's Dance). Similarly, he was invoked against the effects of bites from snakes or rabid dogs. It is interesting that his patronage was later extended to include dancers, actors and comedians. His cult was especially strong in Germany after the supposed translation of 836, and he was named one of the Fourteen Holy Helpers. In art Vitus's emblem is a cock, and he is frequently associated with the palm of martyrdom, a sword, a book or a dog. His feast-day is 15 June, and he is the patron saint of dogs, dancers, actors and comedians, invoked against epilepsy, St Vitus's dance and snakebites.

Vivien see Lady of the Lake

vodyanik

SLAVIK WATER SPIRIT, male counterpart of the **rusalki**. He is an unpredictable spirit, who may aid the fishermen one day and tangle their nets or upturn their boat the next. He can appear in human form, appearing as a portly old man with a cap made of water-reeds; he can be known by his green hair and by the water oozing from the hem of his coat. He is responsible for many deaths by drowning. (See illustration on p448.)

vodyanik

Volkh

HERO OF RUSSIAN FOLKTALES, appearing also in several **byliny**. He is an epic hero with great powers of **shape-shifting** and supernatural strength. His name may be rendered as the more familiar Volga.

Volsungasaga

A TEUTONIC PROSE EPIC, dating from the 13th century, which derives in part from the Norse **Eddas**. It tells the story of the dynasty of the Volsungs, a tale parallel with that of the Nibelungs (see **Nibelungenlied**).

voodoo

FOLK RELIGION OF HAITI, fusing Roman Catholic elements introduced by French colonists and magico-religious African tradition. The practice of voodoo focuses mainly on the *loa*, a general term for divinities, ancestral spirits, supernatural beings and saints, who are propitiated by ritual and sacrifice and who will give guidance and healing to their devotees. The **zombi** is a central feature of voodoo lore.

vulture

LARGE SCAVENGING BIRD, any of several species of the order Falconiformes. In ancient Egyptian mythology the bird is an emblem of the goddess Isis and Nekhebet, and is associated with the female principle (an ancient superstition holds that all are female, and are fertilized by the south wind in flight). Since they haunt battlefields they were associated in classical myth with the gods of war, Ares and Mars. The bird was also sacred to **Heracles**, who killed the vulture that incessantly tore at the liver of Prometheus. To have a vulture hover over one's head during battle boded extremely ill.

Because of the vulture's habitual association with rotting flesh, perfume is held to be anathema to it, myrrh especially is fatal. Its reputation is much higher in many cultures than its somewhat repulsive image in Western lore—its claw was widely used in classical times to detect poison (as was the horn of the **unicorn**), and in Zoroastrian tradition the vulture is regarded as a cleansing force, the 'Compassionate Purifier'.

vultures

wagtail

SMALL BIRD, any species of the genus *Motacilla*, characterized by a long tail that bobs up and down. In popular belief, this motion is said to be an attempt to shake off three drops of the Devil's blood. The Ainu of Japan claim that the world was beaten into its present contours by the wings and tails of cosmic wagtails. In general Japanese lore they are powerful emblems of love. The bird is sacred in Hindu lore, and its movements and behaviour are studied in a form of **divination**.

walnut

DECIDUOUS TREE, genus *Juglans* of the family Juglandeceae, and its woody nut. The nuts are regarded as a symbol of fertility in the classical world, and were traditional wedding fare. **Witches** are said to gather beneath walnut trees in European folk belief, but this has not reflected badly on the walnut tree itself, which is generally regarded as a useful and beneficial nut. A whole nut was frequently carried as a general **charm** to ward off illness and especially rheumatism, and because of its brain-like appearance the walnut was said to be useful for all diseases of the head. The leaves of the black walnut (*J. nigra*) are said in popular US belief to keep ants and flies from the house.

Walpurgisnacht

SHROVETIDE FESTIVAL, the eve of **May Day**, a night of revelry for European **witches**. The day is named after St Walpurga (or Walburga), an eighth-century English abbess who with her brothers established a Benedictine convent at Heidenheim, near Munich (1 May is the feast of her translation). The cult that grew up after her death, centring mainly on the miraculous healing balm said to age from the rock housing her relics, led to a confusion with the pagan fertility goddess Waldborg and her feast was attached to the pre-existing pagan celebrations of spring and the witches' sabbat.

On Walpurgisnacht witches are said to carouse on the Brocken, the highest point of the Harz Mountains in Germany. The **Devil** leads the celebrations, attended by a host of demons.

Wandering Jew

FIGURE OF CHRISTIAN LEGEND, a Jew who taunted Jesus on the way to Calvary and who is now doomed to wander unceasingly until the Second Coming. Widespread anti-Semitism in Europe from the Middle Ages on ensured the popularity of the legend. The Wandering Jew has many identities. The medieval English chronicler Roger of Wendover names him as Cartaphilus, who struck Jesus and urged him to press on when he stopped for a rest; Jesus cursed him saying 'I go, and you will wait until I return'. This version goes on to tell how Cartaphilus is baptized by Ananias as Joseph, in the hope of receiving salvation. A German pamphlet of 1602 purports to give 'A brief description and narration regarding a Jew named Ahasuerus', and this name became widely popular. In an Italian version the Jew was known as Giovanni Buttadeo ('strike God'). Credulous Christians throughout Europe and beyond reported sightings of this endlessly roaming figure as late as the 19th century, and he became a staple figure of both oral and literary tradition.

The motif of the human granted immortality and longing for the release of death is found elsewhere in myth and legend, for example King **Herla**, forever unable to dismount from his horse.

wandjinas

WEATHER SPIRITS OF AUSTRALIAN LORE, who dwell in the ground or mountains and emerge to bring on rain or storms and to ensure the transition from season to season.

war dances

HIGHLY SPECIALIZED FORM OF DANCE, intended as a stimulus to fighting passion in the dancers and to arouse the spirits of battle and the group's protectors, or else a celebration of victory over a fallen enemy. The most common form taken by such dances is the combat mime, usually performed with weapons and occasionally demanding bloodshed; such mimes may be more or less stylized. In Japan they are particularly elaborate and non-naturalistic, in China the emphasis is on acrobatics, in the Americas many native groups use weapons and realistic combat techniques. Women may play a role in some dances, especially in Central America, but in most areas the dances are performed exclusively by men. They can also function as displays of virility (hence courting dances) and to induce fertility.
▷ **dance**; **stick dance**

Washer of the Ford

SPECTRE OF CELTIC LORE, known as *bean nighe*, found mainly in Ireland and the Scottish Highlands. She is generally portrayed as an ugly **hag** washing blood-stained clothes in a stream, and to see her portends one's own death. Some authorities claim that she can be compelled to grant three wishes to anyone quick-witted enough to see her before being seen and get between her and the water. She sometimes appears as a beautiful young woman, wailing and weeping, and is often said to be the ghost of a woman who has died in childbirth and must now haunt the earth until her rightful time to die has come.
▷ **banshee**

Washer of the Ford

Washington, George

FIRST PRESIDENT OF THE USA. The most famous legend associated with George Washington tells how, as a boy of six, he chopped down his father's prize cherry tree with his new axe. When confronted by his irate parent, he supposedly confessed 'I can't tell a lie, Pa; you know I can't tell a lie. I did cut it down with my hatchet.' Whereupon his father, more delighted at such honesty than angered at the loss of his tree, clasped his errant son to his breast. This confession comes from the account of Mason Locke Weems (known as Parson Weems) in his *Life of George Washington* (1810). He claimed to have heard the tale 20 years earlier from an elderly lady, a distant relation of Washington's. In his version George does not chop the tree down, but merely damages it so badly that it dies.

wasps

STINGING WINGED INSECTS, related to but distinct from **bees**, of the suborder Apocrita, particularly those of the species *Vespa* and *Vespula* (family Vespinae). Like **ants**, they are widely used as an endurance test, part of the **initiation** rite. Several Native American groups regard the wasp as a **culture hero** and it is a favourite form assumed by **shape-shifting** shamans. It is widely regarded as a symbol of aggression and masculinity, hence a wasp swallowed by a pregnant woman will ensure the child is a boy, and warriors in many areas undergo wasp stings or rub wasp ashes on themselves to absorb by **sympathetic magic** the war-like attributes of the insect. In European lore the wasp is often regarded as the **separable soul** of a witch, going about her evil purposes.

A wasps' nest frequently functions as pitfall or punishment in folktales. A trickster tale told in India and Indonesia has two animals stealing food together, but the clever animal eats the lot. When he is chased by his companion he sits beside a wasps' nest and claims that it is the king's new **drum**, which he has been entrusted to guard; the dupe insists on banging it and is badly stung. In a common European tale **fox** tricks **bear** into blundering into a wasps' nest in search of honey. A Romanian tale tells how the greedy gypsy was persuaded to swap his **bee** for the wasp of the Romanian when the latter assured him that the wasp produced more honey (or alternatively gold). He was well stung for his greed and stupidity, and since then the wasp has been the gypsies' bee.

wassailling

RITE OF CELEBRATION, a drinking to the communal health. Wassail derives from Old Norse *ves heill*, 'be well and healthy', through Old English *waes hael*, be whole'. The eve of Twelfth Night was the most popular time for wassaillers in Germanic Europe, although any time during the Twelve Days of Christmas was appropriate. Revellers toured the village, raising wassail bowls (usually of wood, sometimes mounted on silver) full of hot spiced ale or cider to their neighbours. In the south of England, orchards were often wassailled; the trees were beaten amid much carousing, a relic of ancient rites to ward off evil spirits and impart renewed fertility, and cider was poured as a libation at the foot of the trees (see **Apple-Tree Man**).

wasted food

MOTIF OF EUROPEAN FOLKTALES PARTICU-LARLY, generally regarded as a dire crime and always punished. The heroine of the **fairy tale** is frequently distinguished by her thriftiness, while the elder sisters are profligate. This is a good example of the practical moral code enshrined in much folklore, and it seems to recall an ancient belief in the sinfulness of wastage. The Israelites in the desert were forbidden by God to collect more manna than they

needed, and in Tyrolean legend Frau Hütt is turned into stone by God when she wastes good food. The folk maxim 'waste not, want not' survives in common use today.

water divination see dowsing

water of life

ALSO KNOWN AS THE WATER OF YOUTH, object of quest in folktales around the world. It is generally found in a far-off well, spring or lake, and has the power to restore youth, health and wholeness, or to confer immortality. As in most quest tales, the water is generally secured with the aid of an animal or supernatural helpers. The concept of the water of life has passed from mythology (Ishtar took the water of life into the **underworld** to restore Tammuz to life in a Babylonian myth) into folk narrative and folk belief; several of the adventurers exploring the New World searched in all earnestness for the Fountain of Youth thought to be sited in South America.

Wayland the Smith

A MARVELLOUS BLACKSMITH, also known as Weland, hero of Norse, German and Anglo-Saxon legend. He was said in some version of the tale to be king of the **elves**, renowned for his skill in crafting

Wayland the Smith

magic objects—a feather boat, amuletic jewellery, magic **swords** and winged cloaks. He was captured by King Nidud of Sweden and compelled to work in his smithy, lamed so that he could not escape. Wayland took his revenge by killing two of Nidud's sons and setting their skulls in gold as drinking bowls, which he presented to their father. He also raped Bödvid, their sister, when she came to him with a ring to be mended. He made his escape with the marvellous wings he had made, and travelled to **Valhalla**.

In English folklore, he is said to inhabit a cove named Wayland's Smithy near Lambourn, Berkshire; if a traveller leaves his horse tethered there with a coin on a stone and takes himself out of sight, he will return to find his horse newly shod and the money gone. Should he try to peek, however, his horse will remain unshod. This type of tale occurs too in areas of Germany, Belgium and Denmark.

Wayland's tale is told in the *Völundarkuida*, a poem in the Icelandic *Poetic Edda* and reappears in the mid-13th-century prose work *Thidriks saga*, but he is mentioned much earlier, in *Beowulf*.

weasel

LITHE LONG-TAILED CARNIVORE, any of a number of species belonging to the family Mustelidae. The weasel has an intriguingly mixed reputation in world folklore. It was said in classical times to be the only creature, apart from the **cock**, to be capable of killing the **basilisk**, and hence in medieval Christian lore could serve as an emblem of Christ overcoming the **Devil**. It was also thought to be immune to snakebites, and its flesh was taken medicinally as a cure for bitten humans. More generally however the weasel has been renowned for its stealth and viciousness, in Ireland and old Bohemia it is a bad omen, and in Greece even its name is to be avoided. Native Americans attribute great shrewdness and insight to the weasel.

Several folktales deal with the reasons why the weasel's tail has a dark tip, generally attributing it to singeing in a fire at the prompting of a **trickster**. **Witches** are said in European lore to transform themselves into weasels, and in China weasels were attributed with the power to bewitch humans.
▷ **ermine**

weather

ELEMENTS FOR LIFE AND GROWTH. A vast body of folklore deals with the problem of controlling or predicting weather patterns, since the vagaries of sun, rain and storm, despite their enormous significance for human existence, are in scientific terms at least beyond human control, and it is only with the development of sophisticated meteorological equipment that we have been able to predict weather patterns with any degree of accuracy. Man's preoccupation with the weather however is as ancient as society itself; primitive weather lore consists mainly of strategies for producing rain or sun or abating storms as required, while peasant lore is generally concerned with superstitions rather than magical techniques for predicting weather changes from atmospheric and other indications, some of which are surprisingly accurate.

Weather is often explained as a result of supernatural forces, so **thunder** is the anger or laughter of the gods, and **rain** is water spilt from a great cosmic jug. Hence deities are generally held responsible for weather and credited with the power to change it. Alongside these widely held beliefs however are the more purely folkloric observations of animal behaviour and superstitions such as the belief that rain on St **Swithin**'s day foretells rain for 40 days.

The wisdom of the folk contains much accumulated commentary on the prediction of weather patterns from observed signs in the environment, and the accuracy of such predictions has often surprised more conventional meteorologists of recent years. There are many methods of forecasting rain, one of the most common being observation of animal behaviour. If ants, for example, retreat into their burrows rain cannot be far behind, and in Ireland the call of the curlew is said to herald a downpour. European peasants swear they can predict rain by the condition of their corns or rheumatism. One of the most famous pieces of weather lore, 'Red sky at night shepherd's delight, Red sky in morning shepherd's warning', is found in various forms across the world and has been shown to have a passable degree of accuracy, since the scattering of light rays is linked to thermal stratification. The various types of clouds now associated with particular weather fronts have been observed by the folk eye for generations, and predictions formulated on the basis of experience, hence 'a round-topped cloud with flattened base [ie cumulus] Carries rainfall in its face'. Observations of plant behaviour can also indicate weather changes; several plants fold leaves or petals before stormy or cold weather, and trees such as the poplar and silver maple are said to turn up their leaves to greet rain.

Natural phenomena of the sky—**rainbows**, **aurora** or **eclipses**—are often regarded as omens, either good or evil. Many groups have developed elaborate rituals to preserve the sun or moon during an eclipse, to frighten off the devouring monsters. Rainbows are often seen as serpents, or as a bridge to the upper world or the road along which the dead travel. In much European lore, it marks the spot at which is buried a crock of fairy gold.

The traditional 'white Christmas' is said to portend a happy and prosperous year ahead, and if the sun shines clearly it portends peace and plenty, but if Christmas is cloudy and stormy then sickness is in store.

wedding annniversary

ANNUAL CELEBRATION, a minor **rite of passage** commemorating a couple's marriage. Although it is primarily a personal celebration, certain anniversaries (particularly the 25th and 50th) are held to be particularly significant and are marked by wider family and community celebrations. Each anniversary is traditionally associated with a different material and gifts made of this material are considered especially appropriate. These are some of the most widely observed, although there are variations between countries:

1st	cotton
2nd	paper
3rd	leather
4th	fruit/flowers
5th	wood
10th	tin
15th	crystal
20th	china
25th	silver
30th	pearl
40th	ruby
50th	gold
60th	diamond
70th	platinum

Wenceslas, St (c.907–29)

'GOOD KING WENCESLAS', Wenceslaus Duke of Bohemia, who promoted the spread of Christianity in the country by inviting German missionaries to enter on evangelistic missions. He acknowledged the overlordship of Henry the Fowler, king of Germany, whom he recognized as successor to **Charlemagne**. These political and religious policies provoked a strong reaction among some of the more hardline pagan Bohemians, and especially the dissatisfied nobles. Among those opposed to the new ruler was his own brother Boleslav, whose resentment was increased at the birth of Wenceslas's son and heir.

Wenceslas was murdered at the hands of Boleslav and his followers on 20 September, traditionally believed to have been attacked and overcome on his way to Mass during a visit to his brother's estate. He was immediately venerated as a martyr, and Boleslav had his relics translated to the church of St Vitus in Prague, an astute political move given the immense popularity of Wenceslas's memory, whether spurred by personal remorse or not.

The church quickly became established as a popular destination for pilgrims and Wenceslas himself was soon regarded as the patron saint of Bohemia, with his image stamped on the country's coins. The crown of Wenceslas came to be regarded as a potent symbol of nationalism for the Czechs. Because of the region's reputation for producing fine beer, its patron naturally became associated with the brewing industry, although in life he was in fact more closely associated with the wine trade; he used to produce the wine for Mass from his own vineyards. In Britain, the familiarity of his name is due mainly to the famous **carol** by J M Neale, *Good King Wenceslas*, a reworking of the medieval carol *Tempus adest floridum*. The story which it tells however has little to do with historical fact and everything to do with Victorian ideals of charity and social responsibility. His feast-day is 28 September, and he is the patron saint of Czechoslovakia and brewers.

wendigo see windigo

werewolf

SHAPE-SHIFTING MONSTER. Belief in lycanthropy was widespread in the ancient and medieval worlds, and is a popular superstition today. The werewolf is a human who is either bewitched into animal form (often for specific periods, such as a full moon) or has the ability to transform him or herself into the ferocious form at will.

Although the word werewolf comes from Old English (meaning man-wolf), the scientific term for such a disorder, lycanthropy, comes from the Greek and the condition was known in Ancient Greece, as evinced by Ovid in his *Metamorphoses* with the story of Lycaeon, who attempted to feed human flesh to Zeus and was punished by transformation. Belief in werewolves exists in every continent of the world.

Werewolves are traditionally associated with cannibalism and blood lust; they may prey on animals such as sheep or goats but generally they prefer human flesh. They are immensely savage and strong, but they may be fought with and if wounded or killed will generally revert to their human shape. Any wound sustained in animal form will be found on the human, and a legend from Auvergne tells how a female werewolf was discovered when the paw cut from a ferocious wolf by a huntsman turned into a human hand bearing the lady's ring, and she herself was discovered to have lost a hand. Sometimes shedding the blood of a werewolf in animal form will break the enchantment and the human will be restored. This is particularly true of the loup-garou of France and French Canada. Another method of removing the werewolf threat is to find and destroy the wolfskin donned on the creature's nightly excursions, perhaps by coating it with pepper to make it impossible to wear. This is not always possible how-

werewolf

ever, as many werewolves are thought to sprout their own hair and fangs under the influence of the full moon.

Belief in the werewolf flourishes where wolves are feared as dangerous beasts such as Europe and North America; in various parts of the world they are replaced by other animals. In West Africa the weretiger is particularly common, together with the werefox in China and Japan, while in other areas of Africa **leopard**, **lion** or **crocodile** are common variants, as is the **jaguar** in South America.

Werewolf lore belongs to the tradition of **shape-shifting**, a central concept of folklore world-wide. A shapeshifter is a creature who can assume the form of another, either at will or under compulsion, and who is attributed with supernatural powers which may be used for good or, more commonly, evil purposes. The **swan maidens** or animal-wives of folktales belong to this tradition, but werewolves and their like are part of the demon or monster lore concentrated in myth and anecdote rather than folktale.
▷ **wolf**

whale

MARINE MAMMAL, one of the larger member of the order Cetacea. Its enormous bulk (blue whales may reach 30m/100ft in length) has made it a favourite staple of **sailors' lore**. In mythology the whale appears as the cosmic fish on which the world is supported (see **Atlas motif**), replacing the more common **turtle**. One of the most common whale tales, found in the adventures of **Sinbad** in the *Arabian Nights*, tells how a ship's crew mistake the back of a whale for a island, and disembark onto it to prepare their meal. After they light a fire, the whale disappears below the waves, taking the unfortunate sailors with it. Medieval Christian writers utilized such tales as warnings against the cunning of the **Devil**, who lures men to sin and then destroys them. This identification was strengthened by the popular belief that the whale lured fish into its mouth by its sweet breath (cf **leopard**). Another common motif of the whale lore, fuelled by the fact that the animal swallows its prey whole and digests it in its capacious, multi-chambered stomach, was the human swallowed by a whale discovered whole within it (this motif occurs in a tale of Baron **Münchausen**, for example). The biblical tale of Jonah, who was swallowed by a whale as he attempted to free God's directive to preach to sinful Nineveh, was interpreted by Christian writers (following St Matthew) as an emblem of Christ's three days in the tomb before resurrection, and hence the whale's jaws were identified as the gates of Hell.

▷ **sea-serpent**

wheat

CEREAL CROP, genus *Triticum* of the Gramineae (Poaceae) family, one of the oldest known to humans. It has formed the staple of the European diet in the same way as **rice** in the East. Wheat goddesses existed in many cultures, eg Ceres in ancient Greece, and in Christian lore one of the epithets attached to the virgin **Mary** in France was *panetière*, the 'bread-giver'.

The production of wheat like that of any crop is hedged around with numerous rites for fertility and harvest, for example the making of the final sheaf into a decorated figure (cf **harvest doll**). Before mechanized and highly efficient collection of wheat, peasants benefited from the ancient folk custom of gleaning, following the harvesters and taking any grain that is left. Giving a sheaf of wheat to a beggar in Holy Week was considered a **charm** to ensure an abundant harvest that year.

▷ **harvest celebrations**

whirlwind

VERTICALLY CIRCULATING MASS OF AIR, often made visible by the dust or sand it carries. Among native Americans whirlwinds are usually regarded with suspicion, as an emblem of dead spirits and evil power. They bring sickness and bad dreams to humans, and if conjured by an evil-minded shaman may bring about death or madness. One should avoid a whirlwind whenever possible, or try to avert its ill effect by talking to it and directing it elsewhere. Several groups personify whirlwinds as a character in their tales, often as a messenger of the gods or a dead spirit.

▷ **anchanchu**; **wind**

Whitsunday

PENTECOST, a festival of the Christian church commemorating the dramatic descent of the Holy Spirit on the disciples (Acts 2:1–4), celebrated 50 days after **Easter**. It derives from the Jewish festival of the giving of the law, held 50 days after the second day of **Passover**. It is marked by different folk customs throughout Europe, but the common theme is one of celebration that the summer has arrived and new life is burgeoning; the festival was almost certainly grafted on to pre-existent pagan festivals. In many areas of Europe **May Day**-type celebrations prevail, with the bringing back of green boughs, the election of a child ruler and processions led by a figure clothed in vegetation (see **Jack-in-the-Green**).

Wild Hunt

IN ANCIENT TEUTONIC MYTHOLOGY, the riotous hunt of the spirits of the dead, led by Woden on his white horse, accompanied by fearsome ghostly dogs. Mortals can hear the hunt thundering across the sky, and dogs will often begin to howl at the noise of the ghost hounds, but to see the procession is to invite death or disaster, perhaps even to be caught up with it and swept away.

Wild Hunt

Similar are the hell-hounds of Europe, the Devil's hunting dogs, whose ghostly howling foretells death.

▷ **ghosts**

wili

SLAVIC NIGHT SPIRIT, the ghost of a young woman who was engaged to be married but died before her wedding day. Wilis were said to haunt roadsides, and any young man who travelled alone at night might fall prey to their power and be forced to dance with the wilis until he dropped dead from exhaustion. This belief reflects several widespread traditions; the dangerous ghost having been frustrated or left with unfinished business in life, the danger to men from women's **virginity**, and the compulsive fairy dance. The wilis feature in the ballet *Giselle* by Théophile Gautier.

William of Cloudesly

ENGLISH BALLAD HERO, an outlaw with remarkable skill in archery, companion of **Adam Bell** and **Clym of the Clough**. William makes a clandestine visit to the town to see his wife and is captured by the authorities; he is rescued from hanging by his two friends and then journeys with them to London to seek the favour of the king. William impresses his sovereign by shooting an **apple** from his son's head, but unlike **William Tell**, who also famously performed this feat, he did so voluntarily to demonstrate his skill.

William Tell

LEGENDARY FOLK HERO OF SWITZERLAND, whose name became a rallying call for Swiss independence and nationalism. According to the *Chronicon Helveticum* (1734–6) of Gilg Tschudi, William Tell performed his daring deeds in 1307, the year before the liberation of Switzerland from Austrian rule. Despite this precise dating, however, there is little to suggest that such a man actually existed, or even that a legend developed around a historical William Tell, although his existence is popularly accepted. It seems likely that, like **Robin Hood**, Tell is a largely fictional figure around whom the legends of the fight for liberation and tales of superlative skill and strength grew up. His tale was circulating in **ballad** form (again like that of Robin Hood) for two centuries before its inclusion in historical literature.

Tell was a peasant in Bürglen in the province of Uri, in Switzerland under Habsburg rule. The local governor, Herman Gessler, erected a pole in the market-place atop which he placed his hat, commanding the villagers to bow to it as they passed. When Tell refused this humiliation, the governor used his reputation as a marksman to mock him. Tell's son was placed against a distant tree with an **apple** on his head; Tell was to hit the apple as punishment. He accomplished this feat, but when the governor asked why he had taken two bolts from his quiver, Tell said that had he killed his son the second arrow was meant for Gessler himself. At this Gessler's men seized him, and he was taken in chains aboard ship for the prison at Küssnacht. In the confusion of a storm however, he managed to jump from the ship (the rock on which he landed is called Tell's Leap) and later ambushed and killed Gessler. His defiance signalled the uprising of Swiss resistance and eventually the overthrow of Austrian rule and the formation of the Confederation.

Many elements of the tale are motifs familiar in folklore, particularly the central episode of the **arrow** in the apple. In ancient Greek legend Alcon, one of the companions of **Heracles**, was famed for his ability to shoot rings from peoples' heads and once killed a snake twined round his son without harming the child. In a Teutonic saga, one of the heroes is compelled to shoot an apple from his son's head and he, like Tell, prepares a second arrow for the king should he miss. Another close parallel is found in the Danish chronicle of Saxo Grammaticus (c.1200), in which Tokko (whose name, like Tell's, is derived from the word for 'senseless') is forced to perform the same feat by Harold Bluetooth in c.950. An English ballad tells of the great archer **William of Cloudesly**, who was sentenced to death for his crimes, but who managed to convince the king that he was too valuable to lose by shooting an arrow from a child's head at 120 paces. Other similar tales can be found throughout Northern Europe.

The popularity of William Tell is largely due to the great play of Schiller, *Wilhelm Tell* (1804). Tell caught the imagination of the people in that era of Romantic nationalism.

will o' the wisp

MYSTERIOUS MOVING LIGHT, usually seen over marshes at night, caused by the spontaneous ignition of methane (produced by decomposing organic matter). It goes under many other folk names—ignis fatuus ('foolish fire'), jack-o'-lantern, corpse light, friar's lantern and fox-fire are some of the most common. The light is almost universally regarded as an ill omen, often signifying death to the one who sees it or to his loved ones. A popular folk belief identifies it as a wandering soul rejected from both heaven and hell, or the spirit of an unbaptized child. It is also interpreted as a **witch** going about her nocturnal business, or a **mischievous spirit** whose delight it is to lead travellers astray. In Ireland it is often said to lead a spectral funeral procession, and in areas of North America it is called fire creature and is said to bring death and destruction in its wake.

Will Scarlett

ONE OF THE 'MERRY MEN', a companion of **Robin Hood**.

wind

PERSONIFIED WEATHER CONDITION. Winds were thought in early Christian cosmology to be controlled by four angels standing at the four corners of the world. In Native American lore Wind frequently appears in folktales, a capricious character who is brought under control by the cunning of the **culture hero**. In Apache and South West lore the winds are frequently associated not only with direction but also with their distinctive colour. Winds from particular directions may be thought to carry pestilence, and whirlwinds especially are thought to house evil spirits, or to be the vehicle for **witches** and ghosts. To avoid having one's soul sucked into its vortex, a number of precautions could be taken, ranging from simple avoidance (running and hiding) to confidence tricks such as chatting to the whirlwind, clapping at it or stamping one's feet. A common folktale motif is that of the winds being contained within a cave or a bag, to be freed by a mischievous or benign spirit. This is found in ancient Greek mythology (in the *Odyssey*, Aeolus gives Odysseus a bag containing the winds), and in Native American tales.

▷ **rain**; **sun**; **weather**; **whirlwind**

windigo

CANNIBALISTIC MONSTER, also known as wendigo, who roams the forests and ice wastes of northern North America. In Algonquian lore the windigo was once a human but, having preyed on human flesh, became an insatiable monster; however, among the Ojibwa the windigo is generally portrayed as a nursery **ogre**.

wintergreen

EVERGREEN HEATH, any of the several species in the order Ericales, particularly the genus *Pyrola*, typically having glossy leaves and bright red berries. Wintergreen oil, extracted from the leaves, has been widely used in folk medicine of Native Americans and others to treat aches and pains, particularly lumbago and rheumatism. In British lore the leaves were said to have a cooling, drying effect, and hence were much used for blood disorders and open wounds. It is also known as Deerberry, from the common belief that its berries give venison its pungent, distinctive taste.

witch hazel

FLOWERING SHRUB, a native of North America and eastern areas of Asia, of the genus *Hamamelis* (family Hamamelidaceae). It is renowned for its medicinal properties; the astringent liniment known as witch hazel, produced from dried leaves and occasionally bark, is widely used for clearing the complexion and removing blemishes such as varicose veins, and soothing eyes and inflammations. Witch hazel tea is taken to stop intestinal bleeding. Its potency was said to be due to the fact that its thin twisted petals resembled the snakes of Aesculapius.

The name derives from the traditional use of the forked twigs in **dowsing**.

witches and witchcraft

'BLACK MAGIC', the application of supernatural power for harmful or evil ends. Belief in witchcraft is found in almost every society. A witch is one, male or female, who possesses such powers either from birth or by communion with a devil or demon, as opposed to the magician or sorcerer, whose power is derived from certain magical techniques and invocations. Unlike sorcerers too, witches tend to gather in groups to perform their rites. Known as the companions of the **Devil**, witches have traditionally been feared and often hunted.

The universality of witch-lore suggests that it fulfils an important social function; just as magic or religion is invoked to explain seemingly inexplicable events, or those which cause particular unhappiness or suffering, so witches provide a conveniently local point on which to place responsibility for such happenings. In this sense witchcraft belongs to the folk in a much more immediate sense than does religion, since witches usually belong to the community itself, and their activities are in the field of everyday occurrences; bread or milk spoiling, sickness, death of family or livestock, disease and so forth. In practice of course folk beliefs about witchcraft and religion are inextricably linked.

Witches are described variously in different societies; they are often thought of as female (although individual men may be charged with witchcraft), usually as gaunt and ugly, although some may deceive by a beautiful appearance and others (especially in Africa) are said to be fattened on human flesh. A witch is often a shapeshifter, with the ability to transform others, hence the witch of the Grimms' tale who transforms the hero into a **frog**, and she may be able to render herself invisible, to creep through impossibly small openings or assume fearful supernatural strength. Most witches are credited with the power of flight, often on a broom, and they are usually accompanied by familiars, demons in the form of animals, which aid them in their nefarious work or prompt them to greater atrocities. Thus any old woman in medieval Europe who kept a **cat** for company, especially if it were black, might be a target for accusations of witchcraft. If she were a skilled herbalist this would intensify suspicion, since witches were credited with knowledge of potions of healing, fertility, love and magical transformation, usually concocted from repulsive or irreligious ingredients such as human parts. In Native American lore too witchcraft is closely related to cannibalism and human sacrifice.

Witch-lore in Europe derives partly from heresy rather than the 'natural realism' of more primitive cultures. Ancient heresies such as Gnosticism, Manicheaism and Catharism were dualist, emphasizing the power of evil as well as of good, and these heretics were accused of cannibalism, Devil worship and licentiousness by orthodox Christians in much the same way that the Romans had accused the early church. Medieval concepts of witchcraft therefore focused on Devil-worship, perversions of Christian rites such as the Witches' Sabbath, prayers spoken backwards or cannibalistic communal meals. The standard way for a witch to greet her master, the Devil, was with an obscene kiss under the tail, the *osculum infame*, and female witches were widely believed to copulate with the Devil or with an **incubus** (demon lover). One became a witch by selling one's soul to the Devil, who generally appeared as an animal (often a **goat**), a black man or a horned figure with cloven feet and a tail. In return for her soul, a witch received satanic powers and often a familiar or helper, which she fed by means of a 'third nipple', a wart or pimple on the body concealed from view.

The witches' sabbat, or Sabbath, was the regular obscene satanic gathering to which all witches were believed to fly, and where they swore allegiance to the Devil. The term is clearly anti-Semitic in origin, coined as it was amid the prejudices of the Middle Ages. The established church sometimes denounced witchcraft as mere superstition, but on other occasions it appeared to sanction such superstitions by formally denouncing witches.

The great witch mania of the late Middle Ages began in c.1450, as the belief in witchcraft as a pact with the Devil grew stronger and legal sanctions were introduced in Europe making it a crime against the Church to be a witch (although in Britain it generally remained a civil offence). The enormously influential *Malleus Maleficarum* (Hammer of the Witches) was published in 1486 by Heinrich Institoris, one of the German Dominican Inquisitors, and its denunciation of demonology and superstition was regarded for centuries as authoritative, and so witch mania was sanctioned in the courts and in the Church.

One of the features of these trials was the belief that the guilt or innocence of the accused would be proved by divine intervention, with the burden of proof being heavily on the side of innocence. Hence suspects might be poisoned, and if innocent would necessarily vomit up the poison. A witch might use her

witch

powers to save herself however, and so an impossible logic was born; if a witch, bound and thrown into the river, were to float, her guilt was proven and she would be burned at the stake, but if she sank, accepted by God's creation, water, her innocence was established but her life usually forfeit. The driving force and justification behind such trials, in which many thousands lost their lives, was zeal to fulfil the biblical injunction, 'Thou shalt not permit a witch to live'. Superstition, tensions within communities, and the fear of being accused oneself if one did not join the witch hunt with vigour all combined to fan the flame of hysteria. Confessions were extracted by torture, and each new confession added to the impetus of the cause. Protestant and Catholic churches pursued witch hunts with equal vigour throughout Europe over the next three hundred years.

The witch mania reached its peak in Europe in the early part of the 17th century, but its spread to European colonies was marked by the infamous Salem witch trials of 1692. Among a puritanical Massachusetts community, social and religious tensions burst into hysteria with the accusations of a number of adolescent girls who had dabbled in the occult. The panic led to the deaths of many within the community, with neighbour accusing neighbour.

The persistence of belief in witchcraft even up to the present day is an indication of its social and psychological function, as a means of transferring responsibility for the apparent malevolence of fate onto visible and comprehensible objects. Unless institutionalized persecution is present, witches are generally regarded with fear and respect among the community, and may even be called upon to perform white magic such as healing or concocting love potions.

In folktales, witches are invariably villainous. They may take the place of the cannibalistic **ogre** as in **Hansel and Gretel**, originate the enchantment by which the prince is turned into the beast or frog, or imprison the heroine in a tower (**Rapunzel**) or a deep sleep (**Sleeping Beauty**), but her power can always be

defeated by stronger magic, or by the virtue or cunning of the hero.

More recently, witchcraft has been regarded as a science rather than a superstition, a form of natural magic, and the practices of self-professed witches of modern society bear little resemblance to the jumble of superstition loaded upon witches in folklore.

wivern

HERALDIC CREATURE, a **dragon** with the barbed tail of a **snake**.

wizards

A PRACTITIONER OF MAGIC, in popular usage the male equivalent of the **witch**. The wizard is not however identified with malignant purposes and the employment of evil spirits, familiars, and the lordship of the **Devil**. Wizardry is generally a learnt craft, and wizards are portrayed as elderly, bookish individuals. They may, as in the case of **Merlin**, occupy influential positions as advisors, and although they may be regarded with awe and even suspicion they are seldom subject to the persecution undergone by their female counterparts.

wolf

WILD DOG-LIKE ANIMAL, particularly the grey wolf (*Canis Lupus*), regarded with equal measures of fear and reverence by many societies. In Celtic lore the wolf, like the **dog**, often functions as a **helpful beast** or a guide for lost travellers, and among some Native American groups Wolf is a **culture hero** and pathfinder, brother of the culture hero Nanabozho, or associated with the Dog Star, Sirius. In many accounts he is portrayed as the ruler of the land of the dead, and this accords with the role prescribed for him in Egyptian mythology as the guide for the souls of the dead at the gates of Osiris's western domain. In Roman tradition a she-wolf suckled **Romulus and Remus**, and in North America several groups claim descent from the wolf.

The wolf is a common figure in innumerable **animal fables**, generally

wolf

-presenting ferocity and untrust-
orthiness, and frequently bested by the
uick-witted **trickster**. In a typical tale,
ollected by Grimm, the **fox** persuades
ιe wolf to break into a cellar to steal
ιod, but the greedy wolf eats so much
ιat he cannot get back through the hole
ιd is taken and killed. A fable of
esop's, found throughout the world in
ιrious forms, tells how the wolf gets a
ɔne stuck in its throat and implores the
ιher animals to aid him. Most of the
ιimals, realising that the bone could
ιsily have been one of their own,
·fuse, but the **crane** is persuaded by his
ιight and by his promise of great reward
ɔ stretch his long neck down his throat
ιd remove the bone. Her only reward
ɔwever is that the wolf permits her to
ιthdraw her head intact—the moral is
ιat one should not expect gratitude
ɔm those incapable of it. The tale
ɔpears in Buddhist lore with Buddha as
ιe crane and Devaddatta as the
ιgrateful creature, in this case a lion.

Another moralistic tale of Aesop's,
ιhich has passed into modern proverbial
ιre, is that of the young shepherd who
ɔuld amuse himself by shouting 'Wolf!'
ɔ see his neighbours come lumbering up
ιe hill to his aid for no reason. He did
ιis once too often, however, and when
ιe day a wolf actually did attack his
ɔck nobody believed his cries, hence
ɔ cry wolf' is to raise a false alarm
ιschievously.

Fenrir; firebird; kornwolf; werewolf

wolfbane see aconite

woodpecker

ONE OF THE MANY SPECIES OF FOREST BIRD,
subfamily Picinae (order Piciformes),
that feed by probing for insects in the
bark of trees. In classical lore the bird
was ascribed magical and prophetic
powers, and was an emblem of Zeus
(Jupiter) and Ares (Mars). Like Zeus,
the Hindu god Indra was said to transform himself into a woodpecker to
pursue his amorous adventures. In
Christian lore the bird was associated
with the **Devil**, although, under the name
Yaffle, it is regarded in parts of England
as a weather prophet.

work song

FOLK SONG TYPE, in which form and often
content are shaped primarily to facilitate
the communal labour. In some cases the
aim may be no more than to pass the
time during tedious tasks, but especially
in hard manual labour the song is
designed to set a rhythm both to sustain
the effort of each individual and to
maximise their combined efficacy by
synchronizing the work stroke. This
form is especially used by sailors and
oarsmen (see **shanty**), agricultural
labourers and those engaged in repetitive construction (eg navvies on the
railroad). Almost every group of
workers has devised its own songs,
however, from spinners and weavers to
fishermen and goatherds.

The most basic type of work song is
built around the shouts already required
by the task—'Heave ho', or 'Pull
away!'—but in many cases narrative
content is enlarged and the songs may
deal overtly with the pleasures and
sorrows of the workers or any subject
found in general folksong, such as love
and betrayal, topical events or religious
spirituals. Typically, however, the song
will be firmly associated with one task or
group of workers in the community. The
plaintive solo French song the *chanson
de toile* was usually a love song sung to
accompany the rhythms of spinning and
weaving linen.

Although the refrain of work songs at
least is generally sung in unison, in many
cases a leader will sing each verse, or will

sing a line which is then answered by his fellows in a call-and-response pattern.

The work song of enforced labourers was often used as a vehicle for expressing sentiments that would otherwise not be tolerated; this is especially notable in the songs of black slaves in North America. Such songs deal with resentment at the attitude of the masters, complaints at the harshness of the work, and the hope of liberation and recompense in the next world (see **spirituals**). Working songs of women, which frequently deal with the themes of the hard lot of women and the fickleness of men, may be included in the same class.

Although most work songs have died out of practical use in the West, made redundant by machinery, a related form of song still survives and is even developed into new forms. The cry of the street vendor, while it lacks the sustained interest and narrative of many work songs, is nevertheless a folk form, and survives in areas today in the call of the rag-and-bone man, newspaper sellers and those purveying refreshments at many events such as circuses and sports matches.

▷ **spiritual**

wraith

THE GHOSTLY DOUBLE OF A PERSON, a **dopplegänger** or **fetch**, the appearance of which is generally taken to indicate that the person has just died or is about to do so. Although it usually has a insubstantial, ghostly quality, it may sometimes appear so life-like that the observer mistakes it for the person in flesh.

wren

SMALL BIRD, family Troglodytidae, of the Western hemisphere; in Europe and Asia the name refers specifically to what North Americans know as the winter wren, *Troglodytes troglodytes*. In Danish version of the tale-type, the wren gains the title of King of the Birds by hiding itself on the back of the eagle since the contest is to see which bird can fly nearest the sun, the wren wins. It was the king of the birds too among the Druids, and is regarded in Celtic lore generally as a prophetic bird. In Britain especially it is closely associated with **witches**, although its feathers can be used to make a **charm** against **witchcraft**. In many areas throughout the world it is regarded as a lucky omen, and in Scotland, Brittany and Japan in particular it was considered very unlucky to kill a wren.

xylophone

TUNED PERCUSSION INSTRUMENT, a set of graduated bars laid across a frame and struck with padded beaters. It is of Neolithic origins, thought to have been developed first in south-east Asia or Oceania. In its simplest form it consists of two or three pieces of wood laid across the legs of the player, but many highly sophisticated versions are crafted by primitive groups, with gourds beneath the bars to aid resonance, finely tuned keys, and table-like supports or cradles that can be suspended from the neck. The Indonesian *gambong*, known since the 8th century, has bars attached to the edges of a resonating wooden trough, while the *marimba* of Latin America, derived from African models, has bars cut from the best hardwoods with great ceremony. In the late Middle Ages the instrument reached central Europe, where it was widely known as *Strokfiedel* (straw fiddle). It became a fashionable member of the orchestra in Europe in the 19th century. Some modern versions having metal bars are the glockenspiel and metallophone.

Cambodian Ronéat-ek xylophone

yakkus

NATIVE AMERICAN SPIRITS OF DISEASE, **shape-shifting** demonic beings who prey on humans by causing all kinds of sickness. They can be propitiated by sacrifice.

yakshas

SPIRITS OF EARLY INDIAN LORE, generally regarded as benevolent. They are nature spirits, closely associated with a particular mountain or well, but were also credited with guardianship of a city or district. They are often the guardians of treasure hidden in the earth, and female yakshas are often portrayed nude but heavily bejewelled. Although they were considered generally harmless, they were worshipped in popular cults and it was sometimes said that discontented female yakshas might steal a human child as a meal. Chief among the yakshas is Kubera, ruler of the mythical kingdom of Alakā in the Himalayas.

Yama-uba

MOUNTAIN SPIRIT OF JAPAN, a terrifying demon who appears as a woman with long tendrils of hair. This hair transforms into writhing serpents, which catch her human prey and draw her victim into the mouth on top of her head.
▷ **Gorgon**

Yankee Doodle

CITIZEN OF THE NORTHERN UNITED STATES, and more precisely of the New England states. The term gained popularity as a derisory epithet used by Southern forces to refer to Federal and Northern troops during the Civil War (1861–5), and its early connotations of cheating were modified by the northerners themselves into a comic portrayal of a shrewd rogue, a **trickster**-type figure, adept at bargaining and trading, master story-teller and witty, womaniz ing, likeable crook. The name is c dubious and much-contested etymology It was claimed that a tribe of nativ Yankos (meaning 'invincible') wa defeated by New England settlers wh then took the name, or that it derive from a mythical Cherokee word *eankee* meaning 'coward'. It seems more likel however that it derives from Dutc *Janke* (John) or *Jan Kees* (John Corne lius), nicknames given by Dutch settler of New England to their Englis neighbours.

yarrow

PUNGENT HERB, any species of the genu *Achillea* (family Asteraceae), als known as milfoil. It is named fc Achilles, who is said to have used it t cure the wounds of Telephus, and i medicinal properties were widely used i North America and Europe before th discovery of the New World. The leave of *A. ptarmica*, known as sneezewor were dried to produce a snuff.

The plant was a favourite of Europea **witches**, probably because of its clos association with graveyards and there fore death. It can be used in mor innocent forms of magic, such as lov **divination**; a sprig of yarrow plucke from the grave of a young man wa widely used in Britain and North Ame ica as a **charm** to bring about dreams of girl's future husband. In areas of Europ it was hung in the house on St John's Ev to preserve the occupants from sickne in the coming year.

Native North Americans took yarro as snuff, and drank yarrow tea to sooth nervous disorders (Chippewa) and cui fevers and colds (Meskwaki). It is wide used for rheumatism, usually as a con press, and in England it was taken in c to prevent hair-loss and encourage luxuriant **beard**.

eck

SHAPE-SHIFTING DEMON, a mischievous spirit of Indian folklore. It frequently takes the form of a small furry animal, wearing a distinctive white cap, and delights in leading travellers astray. Its cap has the power to confer **invisibility** on any mortal who succeeds in stealing it, and if the human can remove the cap and hide it beneath a millstone (no other hiding place will suffice) the yeck will be bound to him as his servant. Since yecks are powerful beings, able to lift mountains (though not millstones), this is a prize well worth risking the creatures' pranks for.

eti

FABULOUS CREATURE, believed to inhabit the snow-line of the Himalayas. In 1951, Shipley's Everest expedition popularized the common alternative name, *Abominable snowman*. Accounts of sightings of this shy creature are rare; most descriptions are based on the evidence of tracks which appear similar to a bear's hind feet but with four humanoid toes, and which indicate a lengthy two-footed stride and, by their depth, a remarkable bulk. Those who claim to have encountered a yeti speak of it as a non-aggressive creature,

Yeti

although capable of causing harm if surprised, but most travellers remain in their tents when they hear the snuffling of a yeti around them.

It has been suggested that a loping **bear** may be responsible for some of the alleged yeti tracks; the hind foot landing just before the print of the front paw creates a human-looking footprint pointing in the opposite direction. Other explanations have included falling rocks and snow balls bouncing down the mountainside.

▷ **Bigfoot**

yew

EVERGREEN TREE, any species of the genus *Taxus* (family Taxaceae) in the Northern Hemisphere. It is closely associated with graveyards in Europe, as it was planted alongside the dead to keep **witches** and demons away from the holy ground, and to thwart any intentions they might have of turning the corpses into **revenants**.

Yggdrasil

WORLD TREE OF NORSE MYTHOLOGY, an evergreen **ash** that links and supports the universe. Its three roots extend into Niflheim (the **underworld**), Jötunheim or Midgard (the home of the **giants**) and **Asgard** (land of the gods), and the gods meet daily at its base to pass judgement. Each root is fed by a spring: Hvergelmir in Niflheim, where the monster Nidhagg gnaws eternally at the root, Mimir's well in Midgard, and the Well of Fate (Urdarbrunnr) in Asgard. The three Norns, or Fates, water the root from this last well. The highest branches of the tree shade **Valhalla**, and the world of mortals is contained within its lower branches. Four stags feed on its upper branches, and dew falls onto the world from their antlers. At the very top sits the golden **cock**, Vithofnir, with the **hawk** Vedfolnir perched on his head; these two see all things and make report to the gods.

Yggdrasil is a striking example of the cosmic **tree** motif found throughout the world.

youngest son

HERO OF FOLKTALES, particularly the

fairy tale. The success of the youngest child (usually of three) after the failure of his or her siblings is a stock **motif** of folktales around the world. Typically he performs an impossible **task**, or fulfils a **quest**, having won by his good qualities the necessary aid of supernatural or animal helpers. In many cases the youngest son is despised, or considered a simpleton, but he is invariably practically minded and kind-hearted. Frequently the elder brothers are treacherous, but the youngest invariably triumphs in the end.

▷ **Bear's Son cycle**; **hero**

yuki onna

'SNOW WOMAN', a female demon of Japanese lore who inhabits the snow storm and is responsible for causing travellers to lose their way, become exhausted, and freeze to death.

Yule see **Christmas**

zodiac

DIVISION OF THE HEAVENS, a belt extending 9° to either side of the ecliptic plane, containing the orbits of the moon and the major planets. It is divided into 12 zones, originally representing the 12 constellations through which the sun passes in the year (although this no longer holds true). Most of these constellations were named after animals by ancient astronomers, and so the circle was named *zodiakos kyklos*, 'circle of animals'. Each sign is ascribed a symbol, and those born beneath it are said to partake of certain character traits and to share to some extent a common destiny. The reading of horoscopes in the West is an avid passion for many, and demonstrates the tenacity of superstition even in a materialistic age.

Several other astrological systems have developed zodiacs, for example the Chinese zodiac, in which 12 animals—Rat, Ox, Tiger, Hare, Dragon, Snake, Horse, Goat, Monkey, Cock, Dog and Boar—stand beneath the 12 branches of the Year Tree. They embody cosmic balance: six are yin, six yang; six wild and six domestic. A similar principle underlies the Islamic zodiac, where the constellations are balanced between North and South, wet and dry, and the four elements air, fire, earth and water. In the Arabian zodiac too a tree stands at the centre; each of its 12 branches bears its respective constellations as a fruit.

zodiac

zombi

REVENANT MONSTER, a being of Haitian **voodoo** lore. A zombi is a human whose **soul** is stolen by black magic and thus becomes lifeless and is buried. His murderer then exhumes the body and gains a useful slave with no will except that of its master, which he imposes on it. In some versions of the belief the zombi is the disembodied spirit of a dead human, but this is less common.

It is thought that voodoo priests may actually perform such an operation, effectively at least, by giving their victims a strong poison which results in a death-like coma. The 'corpse' is exhumed some hours after burial, before he or she can suffocate, and when the effects of the poison wear off may be given a hallucinogenic plant to eat before being used for slave labour. Such practices are recognized in Haitian law by strong strictures against them. The zombi has become a staple figure of horror films and literature, and is probably the most widely known element of voodoo.

Further Reading

General Reference

Aarne, A *The Types of the Folktale* (2nd rev, translated and enlarged by Stith Thompson, Helsinki Soumalainen Tiedeakatemia, 1964)

Baumann, Hans *Hero Legends of the World* (translated by Stella Humphries, Dent, London, 1975)

Brace, C Loring et al *Atlas of Human Evolution* (Holt, Reinhart & Winston, 1979)

Briggs, Katharine M *A Dictionary of Fairies, Hobgoblins, Brownies, Bogies and Other Supernatural Creatures* (Penguin, Harmondsworth, 1977)

Campbell, Joseph *The Hero with a Thousand Faces* (Pantheon Books, New York, 1949)

Cavendish, Richard (ed.) *Legends of the World* (Orbis Publishing, London 1982)

Dorson, R M (ed) *Folktales Told Around the World* (University of Chicago Press, Chicago, 1975)

Frazer, James George *The Golden Bough: A Study in Magic and Religion* (Macmillan and Co Ltd, London, 1912)

Hunter, David E and Philip Whitten (eds) *Encyclopedia of Anthropology* (Harper & Row, 1976)

Leach, Maria (ed.) *Standard Dictionary of Folklore, Mythology and Legend* (Funk & Wagnalls, New York, 1972)

Mercatante, Anthony S *The Facts on File Encyclopedia of World Mythology and Legend* (Facts on File, New York and Oxford, 1988)

Robinson, Herbert Spencer *The Encyclopedia of Myths and Legends of All Nations* (Kaye & Ward, London, 1972)

Thompson, Stith *Motif-Index of Folk Literature* (Copenhagen, 1955–8)

Walker, Barbara H *The Women's Encyclopedia of Myths and Secrets* (Harper & Row, San Francisco, 1983)

Scholarship

Brunvand, Jan Harold *The Study of American Folklore: An Introduction* (W W Norton, New York and London, 1968, new edition 1986)

Campbell, Joseph *The Masks of God* (4 vols, Penguin, Harmondsworth, 1976)

Cox, M R *Cinderella* (1893)

Dorson, R M (ed) *Folklore and Folklife: an introduction* (University of Chicago Press, Chicago, 1972)

Dorson, R M *American Folklore and the Historian* (University of Chicago Press, Chicago/London, 1971)

Dundes, Alan *The Study of Folklore* (Prentice-Hall, Englewoods Cliffs, N. J., 1965)

Gennep, Arnold Van *The Rites of Passage* (translated by Monica B Vizedom and Gabrielle L Caffee, London, 1960)

Honko, Lauri (ed) *Religion, Myth and Folklore in the World's Epics: the Kalevala and its Predecessors* (Mouton de Gruyter, Berlin, 1990)

Krappe, Alexander H *The Science of Folklore* (Methuen, London, 1974)

Lévi-Strauss, Claude *The Savage Mind* (Wiedenfeld & Nicolson, London, 1974)

The Raw and the Cooked (Cape, London, 1970)

The Origin of Table Manners (Cape, London, 1978)

The Naked Man (Cape, London, 1981)

Myth and Meaning (Routledge & Kegan Paul, London, 1978)

Lord, Albert *The Singer of Tales* (Harvard University Press, Cambridge, Mass., 1960)

Thompson, Stith *The Folktale* (University of California Press, Berkeley/London, 1977)

Methodology

Dorson, R M *Folklore and Fakelore: essays towards a discipline of folk studies* (Harvard University Press, Cambridge. Mass./London, 1976)

Further Reading

Dundes, Alan *Interpreting Folklore* (Indiana University Press, Bloomington, 1980)

Fine, Elizabeth C *The Folklore Text from Performance to Print* (Indiana University Press, Bloomington, 1984)

Jackson, Bruce *Fieldwork* (University of Illinois Press, Urbana, 1987)

Africa

Abrahams, R D *African Folktales: traditional stories of the black world* (Pantheon Books, New York, 1983)

Bascom, W R *African Dilemma Tales* (Mouton Publishers, The Hague, 1975)

Carey, Margaret *Myths and Legends of Africa* (Hamlyn, Feltham, 1970)

Finnegan, Ruth *Oral Literature in Africa* (Oxford University Press, Oxford/Nairobi, 1970)

Murray, John A (ed) *Wild Africa: three centuries of nature writing from Africa* (Oxford University Press, Oxford/New York, 1993)

Ancient Near East

Gibson, J C L (ed) *Canaanite Myths and Legends* (Clark, Edinburgh, 1978. First edition edited by G R Driver, 1956)

Pritchard, J B (ed) *Ancient Near Eastern Texts Relating to the Old Testament* (Princeton University Press, Princeton, 1969)

Sandars, N K (trans) *The Epic of Gilgamesh* (Penguin, Baltimore, 1960)

Spence, Lewis *Myths and Legends of Babylonia and Assyria* (Harrap and Co, London, 1916)
    Myths and Legends of Ancient Egypt (Dover, New York, 1990)

Arthurian

Goetinck, Glenys *Peredur: a study of Welsh traditions in the Grail legends* (University of Wales Press, Cardiff, 1975)

Loomis, Roger Sherman (ed) *The Grail: from Celtic myth to Christian symbol* (Constable, London, 1993))

Topsfield, L T *Chrétien de Troyes: a study of the Arthurian Romances* (Cambridge University Press, Cambridge, 1981)

Australia

Bishop, Amanda *The Gucci Kangaroo and Other Australian Urban Legends* (The Australian Publishing Company, Hornsby, 1988)

Edwards, Ron *The Australian Yarn* (Rigby, Adelaide, 1977)
    Yarns and Ballads of the Australian Bush (Rigby, Adelaide, 1981), reprinted as *The Wealthy Roo and Other Bush Yarns* (Rams Skull Press, 1988)

British

Alexander, Marc *British Folklore, Myths and Legends* (Wiedenfeld & Nicolson, London, 1982)

Briggs, Katharine M *British Folktales* (Pantheon Books, New York, 1977)
    The Fairies in English Tradition and Literature (Bellew, London, 1989)

Chambers, Robert (ed) *Popular Rhymes of Scotland* (W & R Chambers, Edinburgh, 1870)

Child, Francis James (ed.) *The English and Scottish Popular Ballads* (Houghton, Mifflin & Co, New York, 1884–98)

Geoffrey of Monmouth *The History of the Kings of Britain* (translated by Lewis Thorpe, Penguin, Harmondsworth, 1973)

Hartland, E S (ed) *English Fairy and Other Folk Tales* (Walter Scott Publishing Co, London, 1894)

Jones, Gwyn and Thomas Jones (trans) *The Mabinongion* (J M Dent & Sons, London, 1989)
    Mabinogion (translated by Charlotte Guest, Bernard Quaritch, London, 1877; reissued by Academy Press Ltd, Chicago, 1978)

Malory, Sir Thomas *Le Morte D'Arthur* (2 vols, edited by Janet Cowen, Penguin, Harmondsworth, 1969)

Percy, Thomas (ed.) *Reliques of Ancient English Poetry* (ed J V Prichard) (Thomas Y Cromwell & Co, New York, 1875)

Swanton, Michael (trans.) *Beowulf* (Manchester University Press, Manchester, 1978)

Westwood, Jennifer *Albion: a guide to legendary Britain* (Granada, London, 1985)

Buddhist

Amore, Ray C *Lustful Maidens and Ascetic Kings: Buddhist and Hindu stories of life* (Oxford University Press, Oxford, 1981)

Celtic

Bruford, Alan *Gaelic Folk-Tales and Mediaeval Romances: a study of the Early Modern Irish 'Romantic tales' and their oral derivatives* (Folklore of Ireland Society, Dublin, 1969)

Glassie, H (ed.) *Irish Folktales* (Pantheon Books, New York, 1985)

Mac Cana, Proinsias *Celtic Mythology* (Newnes, Feltham, 1970)

O'Hogain, Daithi *Myth, Legend and Romance: an encyclopedia of the Irish folk tradition* (Ryan Publishing, London, 1990)

O'Suilleabhain, S and R T Christiansen *Types of the Irish Folktale* (1963)

Rees, Alwyn and Brinley Rees *Celtic Heritage: ancient traditions in Ireland and Wales* (Thames & Hudson, London, 1973)

Yeats, W B *Fairy and Folk Tales of Ireland* (Colin Smythe, Gerard Cross, 1992)

Christian

Bauer, Walter *Orthodoxy and Heresy in Earliest Christianity* (SCM Press, London, 1972)

Jones, Alison *Saints* (Chambers Harrap, Edinburgh, 1992)

Metford, J C J *Dictionary of Christian Lore and Legend* (Thames & Hudson Ltd, London, 1983)

Voragine, Jacques de *The Golden Legend* (translated by William Granger Ryan, Princeton University Press, Princeton, 1993)

Wilson, Stephen (ed) *Saints and Their Cults: studies in religious sociology, folklore and history* (Cambridge University Press, Cambridge, 1983)

Classical

Grant, Michael *Myths of the Greeks and Romans* (Wiedenfeld & Nicolson, London, 1989)

Graves, Robert *The Greek Myths* (illustrated edn., Cassell, London, 1981)

Homer *Odyssey* (translated by Walter Shewring, Oxford University Press, Oxford, 1980)

Lattimore, Richmond (trans) *The Iliad of Homer* (1951)

Lines, Kathleen *The Faber Book of Greek Legends* (Faber & Faber, London, 1973)

Norton, Dan S and Peters Rushton *Classical Myths in English Literature* (Rinehard & Company, Inc., 1952)

Ovid *Metamorphoses* (translated by A D Melvill, Oxford University Press, Oxford, 1986)

Far East

Hanan, Patrick *The Chinese Vernacular Story* (Harvard University Press, Cambridge, Mass., 1981)

In-Sŏp Chŏng (ed/trans) *Folk Tales from Korea* (1952)

Kyoko Motomochi Nakamura *Miraculous Stories from the Japanese Buddhist Tradition: the Nihon Ryōiki of the Monk Kyōkai* (1973)

Ma, Y W and Joseph S M Lau (eds) *Traditional Chinese Stories; Themes and Variations* (1978)

Werner, E T C *Myths and Legends of China* (Sinclair Browne, London, 1984)

France

Duggan, Joseph J *A Guide to Studies on the Chanson de Roland* (Grant & Cutler, London, 1976)

Massignon, G *Folktales of France* (University of Chicago Press, Chicago, 1968)

Perrault, Charles *Histories or Tales of Past Times* (translated by G M Gent, Fortune Press, London, 1928)

Further Reading

Germany

Crossley-Holland, Kevin (ed) *The Faber Book of Northern Legends* (Faber & Faber, London, 1977)

Grimm, Jakob *Kinder und Hausmärchen* (translated by Peter Carter, Oxford University Press, Oxford, 1982)

Raspe, R E *The Surprising Adventures of Baron Munchausen* (Falkirk, c.1820)

Greece

Beaton, Roderick *Folk Poetry of Modern Greece* (Cambridge University Press, Cambridge, 1980)

Dawkins, R M *Modern Greek Folktales* (Clarendon Press, Oxford, 1953)

South Asia

Beck, Brenda E F et al (eds) *Folktales of India* (University of Chicago Press, Chicago, 1987)

Blackburn, Stuart H and A K Ramanujan (eds) *Another Harmony: new essays on the folklore of India* (University of California Press, Berkeley, 1986)

Goldman, Robert P *The Ramayana of Valmiki: an epic of Ancient India* (translated by William Buck, University of California Press, Berkeley/London, 1976)

Gray, J E B *Indian Tales and Legends* (Oxford University Press, Oxford, 1979)

Jacobs, J (ed) *Indian Fairy Tales* (Dover, New York, 1969)

Maung Myint Thein *Burmese Folk Songs* (Oxford Asoka Society, London, 1970)

O'Flaherty, Wendy Doniger *Hindu Myths: a sourcebook* (Penguin, Harmondsworth, 1975)
   The Rig Veda: an anthology (Penguin, Harmondsworth, 1981)

Van Buitenen, J A B (ed/trans) *The Mahabharata* (University of Chicago Press, Chicago, 1973–   )

Islamic

Bushnaq, I (ed) *Arab Folktales* (Pantheon, New York, 1986)

Dawood, N J (ed) *Tales from the 1001 Nights* (Penguin, Harmondsworth, 1983)

Italy

Boccaccio, Giovanni *Decameron* (translated by Guido Waldman, Oxford University Press, Oxford, 1993)

Calvino, I *Italian Folktales* (Pantheon Books, New York, 1980)

Croce, Benedetto *The Pentamerone of Giambattista Basile* (translated by N M Penzer, 2 vols, 1932)

Jewish

Garter, T H *Myth, Legends, and Custom in the Old Testament* (1969)

Ginzberg, Louis *Legends of the Jews* (7 vol, 1909–39)

Noy, D and D Ben-Amos (eds) *Folktales of Israel* (1962)

Sadeh, Pinhas (ed) *Jewish Folktales* (translated by Hillel Halkin, Collins, London, 1990)

Schwartz, H *Elijah's Violin and Other Jewish Fairy Tales* (Penguin, Harmondsworth, 1987)

Native American

Collaer, Paul (ed) *Music of the Americas: an illustrated music ethnology of the Eskimos and North American Indian Peoples* (Curzon Press, London, 1973)

Erdoes, R and A Ortiz (eds) *American Indian Myths and Legends (Pantheon Books, New York, 1984)

Gyles, Anna Benson and Chlöe Sayers *Of Gods and Men; Mexico and the Mexican Indian* (BBC, London, 1980)

Thompson, Stith *Tales of the North American Indians* (Indiana University Press, Bloomington/London, 1966)

North America

Abrahams, R D (ed) *Afro-American Folk Tales* (Pantheon Books, New York, 1985)

Botkin, B A *A Treasury of American Folklore* (Crown Publishers, New York, 1944)

Further Reading

Cohen, Hennig and Tristam Potter (eds) *The Folklore of American Holidays* (Gale Research Co, Detroit, 1987)

Dorson, Richard M *America in Legend* (Pantheon Books, New York, 1973)

Buying the Wind: Regional Folklore in the US (University of Chicago Press, Chicago, 1964)

Fowke, Edith *Folklore of Canada* (McClelland and Stewart, Toronto, 1976)

Harris, Joel Chandler *The Complete Tales of Uncle Remus* (Houghton Mifflin & Co, Boston, 1955)

Rozzetta, Hans *Folklore, Culture, and the Immigrant Mind* (Garland, New York/London, 1991)

Oceanic

Andersen, Johannes C *Myths and Legends of the Polynesians* (1928)

Barrow, Terence *Art and Life in Polynesia* (Pall Mall Press, London, 1972)

Lessa, W A *Tales from Ulithi Atoll: a comparative study in Oceanic folklore* (1961)

Oliver, Douglas L *Oceania: the native cultures of Australia and the Pacific Islands* (2 vols, University of Hawaii Press, Honolulu, 1989)

Simms, Norman *Silence and Invisibility: a study of the literature of the Pacific, Australia and New Zealand* (Three Continents Press, Washington D.C., 1986)

Wolkstein, D *The Magic Orange Tree and Other Haitian Folktales* (Alfred A Knopf, New York, 1978)

Scandinavia

Asbjørnsen, P C and Moe, J *Norwegian Folk Tales* (Dreyers Forlag, Oslo, 1978)

Popular Tales from the Norse (David Douglass, Edinburgh, 1888)

Clover, Carol J and John Lindow (eds) *Old Norse-Icelandic Literature: a critical guide* (Cornell University Press, Ithaca, 1985)

Glendinning, Robert J and Haraldur Bessason (eds) *Edda: a collection of essays* (University of Manitoba Press, Winnipeg, 1983)

Lindon, J *Swedish Legends and Folktales* (University of California, Berkeley, 1978)

Slavic

Afanasyer, A *Russian Fairy Tales* (Pantheon Books, New York, 1945)

Alexander, Alex E (trans and ed) *Russian Folklore; an anthology in English* (Nordland Publishing Co., Belmot, Mass., 1975)

Dégh, L *Folktales of Hungary* (University of Chicago Press, 1965)

Folktales and Society (Indiana University Press, Bloomington/London, 1969)

Ivanits, Linda *Russian Folk Belief* (M E Sharpe, Armonk, NY, 1989)

Modern Folklore

Bronner, Simon J *Piled Higher and Deeper: The Folklore of Campus Life* (August House, Little Rock, 1990)

Brunvand, Jan Harold *The Vanishing Hitchhiker: American Urban Legends and their Meanings* (W W Norton, New York and London, 1981)

The Choking Doberman and Other 'New' Urban Legends (W W Norton, New York and London, 1984)

The Mexican Pet: More 'New' Urban Legends and Some Old Favorites (W W Norton, New York and London, 1986)

Curses! Broiled Again! The Hottest Urban Legends Going (W W Norton, New York and London, 1989)

Dickson, Paul and Goulden, Joseph C *There are Alligators in Our Sewers and Other American Credos: A Collection of Bunk, Nonsense and Fables We Believe* (Delacorte, New York, 1983)

Dorson, R M (ed) *Folklore in the Modern World* (Mouton, The Hague, 1978)

Children's lore

Bronner, Simon (ed) *American Children's Folklore* (August House, Little Rock, 1988)

Further Reading

Gomme, Alice Bertha *The Traditional Games of England, Scotland and Ireland, with Tunes, Singing-Rhymes and Methods of Playing According to the Variants Extant and Recorded in Different Parts of the Kingdom* (2 vols, D Nutt, London, 1894–8)

Opie, Iona and Peter *The Lore and Language of Schoolchildren* (Clarendon Press, Oxford, 1959)

The Oxford Dictionary of Nursery Rhymes (Clarendon Press, Oxford, 1951)

Opie, Iona *The People in the Playground* (Clarendon Press, Oxford, 1993)

Turner, Ian (ed) *Cinderella Dressed in Yella* (Heinemann, Melbourne, 1969)

Folk art

Griaule, Marcel *Folk Art of Black Africa* (Tudor, New York, 1950)

Layton, Robert *The Anthropology of Art* (1981)

Vlack, John Michael and Simon J Bronner (eds) *Folk Art and Art Worlds* (UMI Research Press, Ann Arbor, 1986)

Folk dance

Alford, Violet and Rodney Gallop *The Traditional Dance* (Methuen, London, 1935)

Haskins, James *Black Dance in America* (Crowell, New York, 1990)

Lawson, Joan *European Folk Dance* (1953)

Nevell, Richard *A Time to Dance: American Country Dancing from Hornpipes to Hot Hash* (St Martin's Press, New York, 1977)

Sacks, Curt *World History of the Dance* (W W Norton, New York, 1963)

Spencer, Paul (ed) *Society and the Dance: the social anthropology of process and performance* (1985)

Folk music

Charters, Samuel Barclay *The Roots of the Blues: an African search* (M Boyars, Boston, 1981)

Jenkins, Jean *Man and Music: a survey of traditional non-European musical instruments* (Royal Museum of Scotland, Edinburgh, 1983)

Jones, Le Roi *Blues People; Negro Music in White America* (Morrow, New York, 1963)

Lomax, Alan *Folk Song Style and Culture* (1968)

Oliver, Paul et al *The New Grove Gospel, Blues and Jazz* (W W Norton, New York, 1986)

Sacks, Curt *The History of Musical Instruments* (W W Norton, New York, 1940)

Widdess, D R and R F Wolpert (eds) *Music and Tradition* (Cambridge University Press, Cambridge, 1981)

Biographical Notes
on Prominent Folklorists

esop

abulist and moralist, whose name has been
extricably linked with the form of the animal
ble for centuries. In the fifth century BC the
istorian Herodotus wrote of him as a historical
gure of the previous century. Various tradi-
ons purport to tell his history; Aesop was
idely believed to have been born on the island
' Samos, or alternatively in Lycia, Thrace or
hrygia, and to have become a slave in Samos.
is first master was called Xanthos; his second,
dmon, was so delighted with his slave's wit
at he freed him.

As a freedman, Aesop was believed to have
sited Pisistratus in Athens and, according to
lutarch, to have served in Sardis as adviser to
ing Croesus of Lydia. He met his death at
elphi while on a mission to distribute money
om Croesus; disgusted by the bickering and
reed of the citizens he refused to give them the
oney and the furious townsmen threw him off
cliff. It was said that they were later visited by a
ague and were obliged to offer a sum of money
• atone for the murder. This offering was
ccepted by Iadmon, grandson of Aesop's old
aster. Another tradition says that Aesop
rved in the court of Lycurgus in Babylon as the
ng's personal riddle-solver.

These legendary accretions have so overlaid
e historical figure of Aesop that some modern
holars have doubted his very existence. It
ems quite possible that the name served as a
eneric label for collections of animal fables
lled from ancient Greek folklore, perhaps the
ame of the first such collection to be made.

ndersen, Hans Christian (1805–75)

anish writer and folklorist, one of the greatest
orytellers in the world. He was the son of a
oor shoemaker who took a job in a factory after
s father's death but soon displayed a talent for
oetry. He left for Copenhagen, hoping to find
ork in the theatre, but was rejected because of
s lack of education. With the aid of generous
iends however and the intervention of the king
mself he was placed in an advanced school and
egan to make a name as a writer. He is best
nown for such fairy tales as 'The Tin Soldier',
he Emperor's New Clothes', 'The Tinderbox',
he Snow Queen' and 'The Ugly Ducking'.

sbjørnsen, Peter Christian (1812–85)

orwegian folklorist, born in Christiania (now
slo). He studied at the university there, then
r four years was a tutor in the country. In long
urneys on foot he collected a rich store of

popular poetry and folklore, and, with his
lifelong friend Jørgen Moe, bishop of Christiansand, published the famous collection of Norwegian folk tales, *Norske Folkeeventyr* (Norwegian Folk Tales, 1841–4), followed in 1845–8
by *Norske Huldreeventyr og Folkesagn* (Norwegian Fairy Tales and Folk Tales) which he
brought out alone.

Aubrey, John (1626–97)

English writer and antiquary. Although Aubrey
produced little sustained literary output, his
natural curiosity suited him ideally to the
collection of 'antiquities', fragments of oral lore
and folk customs drawn largely from conver-
sations with the Wiltshire folk. His *Miscellanies*
(1696), the only work published during his life, is
an uncritical compilation of folk items and ghost
stories. His *Brief Lives* (published posthum-
ously, 2 vols, 1898) is characterized by anecdote
and a taste for the marvellous and supernatural.
Aubrey observed too the threat of modern
innovations such as printing to the traditional
tales and the folk way of life; '. . . the many good
Bookes, and variety of Turnes of Affaires, have
putt all the old Fables out of doors: and the
divine art of Printing and Gunpowder have
frighted away Robin-goodfellow and the
Fayries'.

Brand, John (1744–1806)

English clergyman and antiquary. In 1777 he
published *Observations on Popular Antiquities*,
a heavily annotated edition of the *Antiquitates
Vulgares* of John Bourne (1725). In it Brand
draws out the key distinctions that were to
underpin the science of folklore: that between
'the People' and 'men of learning', and between
'the written Word' and 'oral Tradition'. Like
Bourne, he demonstrated the pagan roots of
many Christian traditions, and he laid the roots
of modern field-work in his advocacy of ques-
tioning elderly village folk. He began an
expanded edition of the work, supplemented by
numerous jottings and clippings, but this was not
published until after his death, when Sir Henry
Ellis edited and produced the work as *Observations on Popular Antiquities: chiefly illustrating
the origin of our Vulgar Customs, Ceremonies
and Superstitions* (2 vols, 1813). This monumental work has been considered the foundation of
folklore scholarship in Britain and beyond.

Brinton, Daniel Garrison (1839–99)

American medic, folklorist and linguist, who
wrote extensively on North American ethno-

Biographical Notes

logy. He was an influential advocate of polygenesis, the doctrine that cultural similarities are due to independent invention rather than borrowing or diffusion.

Brunvand, Jan Harold (1933–)
American folklorist and scholar, professor of English at the University of Utah. As a fellow of the Folklore Society, editor of the *Journal of American Folklore* (1976–80), and a regular newspaper columnist since 1987, his extensive research on urban legends has contributed enormously to popular awareness of folklore in the modern world. His writings include *The Study of American Folklore; an introduction* (1980), *The Vanishing Hitchhiker: American Urban Legends and their meanings* (1981), *The Choking Doberman and Other 'New' Urban Legends* (1984), *The Mexican Pet: More 'New' Urban Legends and Some Old Favorites* (1986), and *Curses! Broiled Again! The Hottest Urban Legends Going* (1989).

Chambers, Robert (1802–71)
Scottish writer and publisher. At the age of 22 he published the first part of his *Traditions of Edinburgh*, which so impressed Sir Walter **Scott** that he supplied the young bookseller with material for the subsequent volumes. His further works in the field include *Popular Rhymes of Scotland* (1826), *The Scottish Ballads* (1829), *The Scottish Song* (2 vols, 1829), and *Scottish Jests and Anecdotes* (1832). After this point Robert concentrated on his career as a publisher, with his brother William, and only returned to the field of folklore with his *Book of Days: a Miscellany of Popular Antiquities in Connection with the Calendar*, which broke his health. His significance lies particularly in his work on Scottish traditions, the volume of material he collected and faithfully reproduced, and his own perceptive insights into its nature and value, but his technique remained essentially that of the collector of miscellanies rather than the serious scholar and theorist.

Cosquin, Emmanuel (1841–1922)
French folklorist. In his *Contes Populaires de Lorraine* (2 vols, 1886), he argued for the transmission of European folk tales from India within the historical period.

Cox, George William (1827–1902)
English historian and mythologist, born in India. Educated at Rugby School and Trinity College, Oxford, he took holy orders in 1850. Among his works were *Tales of Ancient Greece* (1886), *Aryan Mythology* (1870), *History of Greece* (1874), *Comparative Mythology and Folklore* (1881), *Lives of Greek Statesmen* (1886), and *Life of Colenso* (1888).

Croker, Thomas Crofton (1798–1854)
Irish antiquary and folklorist, born in Cork. A a boy of 14 he began to collect songs and legen of the Irish peasantry and in 1818 he se Thomas Moore nearly 40 old Irish melodies. 1825, as a clerk in the Admiralty, he publishe anonymously his *Fairy Legends and Tradition of the South of Ireland*, a work which caught th public imagination, charmed Sir Walter Sco and was translated into German by the brothe **Grimm** (1826). A second and third serie followed (1827–8). The book was significant the first serious collection from the field Britain, paralleling the work of the Grimms Germany, and although his collections a certainly not free from editorial intervention, won a respected place in the canon of folklo scholarship by his informative and detaile collection notes. Of nearly 20 more works th best were *Researches in the South of Irelan* (1824), *Legends of the Lakes* (1829), *Th Adventures of Barney Mahoney* (1832), an *Popular Songs of Ireland* (1839).

Culpeper, Nicholas (1616–54)
English physician and herbalist, who began practise astrology and physic in Spitalfields London in 1640. His *English Physic Enlarged, or the Herbal* (1653) enjoyed eno mous sales, and formed the basis of subseque herbalism in the English-speaking world.

Dasent, Sir George Webbe (1817–96)
English scholar of Scandinavian studies ar folklorist. During his varied career as barriste journalist, civil servant and professor, he pr duced his best-known works, popular transl tions of classical Icelandic literature, includir *The Prose or Younger Edda* (1842), *The Saga Burnt Njal* (1861), and the *Story of Gisli t Outlaw* (1866). He also published *Popular Tal from the Norse* (1859) and *Tales from the Fje* (1874), both from the Norwegian of **Asbjørnse**

Dorson, Richard M (1916–)
American historian and folkorist, born in Ne York City. After studying American history Harvard he taught there (1943–4) then Michigan State University (1944–56), befo moving to Indiana University (1957), becomi Distinguished Professor of History and Folklo (1971). He organized the Folklore Institute ar became its first director in 1963. He was gene editor of the series *Folktales of the World* Chicago University Press, and has produc numerous books, articles and essays, do much to raise awareness of folklore both as field of study and as a continuing feature of t modern world. His publications include *Buyi the Wind: Regional Folklore in the US* (196 *American Folklore and the Historian* (197 *Folklore and Folklife: an introduction* (1972

America in Legend (1973), *Folktales Told Around the World* (1975), *Folklore and Fakelore: essays towards a discipline of folk studies* (1976), and *Folklore in the Modern World* (1978).

Frazer, Sir James George (1854–1941)

Scottish anthropologist and folklorist, whose most crucial work was *The Golden Bough: a Study in Magic and Religion*, named after the golden bough in the sacred grove at Nemi, near Rome. The work was first published in two volumes in 1890 and it was reissued in an expanded version of twelve volumes between 1907 and 1915. This monumental work aimed to provide a coherent view of the development of human society, moving from the magical to the religious to, finally, the scientific mode. Magic he defined as the attempt to control the environment by indirect activities based on flawed reasoning, and religion as the invocation of external supernatural forces for help. This sweeping anthropological and psychological framework, while its main thrust has since been discredited, enabled Frazer to bring together an enormous amount of hitherto unknown material concerning primitive civilizations for comparative study, and this breadth of conception has proved invaluable in later folkloric study.

One of the central contentions of *The Golden Bough* was the magical, sacred nature of kingship; the vitality of the king represented the life of the community, and this kingship could legitimately be challenged and wrested by a stronger contender; a king with failing powers would be killed by his subjects and a younger, fitter successor appointed.

Frazer's other works include *Totemism* (1884), *Totemism and Exogamy* (1911), *Belief in Immortality and the Worship of the Dead* (1913–22) and *Magic and Religion* (1944).

Gennep, Charles-Arnold Kurr van 1873–1957)

French ethnographer and folklorist, born in Württemberg, Germany, of a Dutch father and French mother and brought up in France. A civil servant and academic, he became an energetic collector and publisher of folklore material, including the *Manuel de Folklore Français Contemporaine* (1937–58). His best-known work however is the seminal *Les Rites de Passage* (1909), a comparative study of rituals marking transitions of social status. He argued persuasively that such rituals have a tripartite structure, in which a stage of separation is followed by stages of transition and reincorporation into the group. His other publications include *Religions, Murs et Légends* (1908–14).

Gezelle, Guido (1830–99)

Flemish poet, born in Bruges. Ordained in 1854, he was for 28 years a curé in Courtrai. He published many volumes of verse, wrote on philology and folklore, founded literary magazines, and is regarded as the founder of the West Flemish school.

Gilmore, Dame Mary Jane (1865–1962)

Australian poet and author, born in New South Wales. In 1896 she left to join William Lane's Utopian 'New Australia' settlement in Paraguay, South America. There she met and married a shearer, William Gilmore, and they returned to Australia in 1902. Her socialist sympathies were now harnessed to campaigning for the betterment of the sick and the helpless, through the women's column which she edited for over 20 years in the Sydney *Worker* newspaper, but also in her six volumes of poetry published between 1910 and 1954. Three books of recollections illustrate her lifelong efforts to preserve early Australian traditions and folklore. She was created DBE in 1937.

Gomme, George Laurence (1853–1916)

British folklorist, founder member and subsequently president of the Folklore Society (1890–4). His first publication, *Primitive Folk Moots; or Open-Air Assemblies in Britain* (1880), revealed his approach to folklore, not as relic of myth but as the vehicle for preserved 'remnants of archaic social existence'; thus for him the proper field of folklore was untutored classes in a civilized society, not primitive societies themselves. A member of the same group as Andrew **Lang** and Alfred Nutt, he was the most crusading in his desire to see folklore recognized as a scientific discipline. He expanded these issues in *Ethnology in Folklore* (1892) and *Folklore as an Historical Science* (1908). In 1890 he produced a *Handbook of Folklore*, the first fieldwork guide for amateur collectors.

Grimm, Jakob (1785–1863) and Wilhelm (1786–1859)

German folklorists, the 'Fathers of modern folklore'. In the cultural ferment of 18th- and 19th-century Germany, which had until then been relatively undeveloped in this field compared to its European neighbours, a strong emergent nationalism began to make itself felt. Along with German pre-eminence in music, literature and philosophy in the 19th century and the strongly nationalistic Romantic movement came an awakening of interest in German heritage, and hence in Germanic folklore.

The two men who were to lead this field of scholarship were Jakob Grimm and his brother Wilhelm. They were well respected as scholars of language and linguistics, but it was as collectors of German legend and folklore that they achieved their most widespread acclaim.

The first volume of *Kinder und Hausmärchen*

Biographical Notes

was published in Berlin in 1812, followed by a second volume in 1815. An English translation, *Household Tales*, was published in 1884. The work differed from preceding collections in its claim to be taken unchanged from authentic folk narrators, retaining the roughness and simplicity of the original telling, and details about the individual peasants who had supplied the material were given. Folklorists have traditionally recognized in this approach the beginnings of the science of folklore, in which narratives are transcribed to preserve as closely as possible the exact form of the original and details of narrator and context are added by the collector. It seems clear, however, from the discrepancies between their original manuscripts and the 1812 edition, that the Grimms did make several alterations, not all of them minor, to the tales. Some tales, for example, are almost doubled in length, and stories such as Bluebeard, admittedly dropped after the first edition, drew more heavily on French literary tradition than German peasant lore. In all, seven editions of *Kinder und Hausmärchen* were edited by the brothers Grimm between 1812 and 1857, and there are quite significant changes in all of them. Other works on folklore include their collection of legends, *Deutsche Sagen* (1816–18) and Jakob's *Deutsche Mythologie* (1835) which clearly set out his scientific principles.

The Grimms produced a great work which quickly became a classic of German literature, but it is not a wholly objective one; their strong nationalistic and artistic motives must be acknowledged. Wilhelm Grimm suggested in 1856 that folktales can only be understood as degenerate myth; this supposition has now largely been discredited. The brothers held that similar tales must have originated in one common Indo-European form, whereas later folklorists recognized the phenomenon of separate genesis.

Although the claims of authenticity made by the brothers in the preface to the first edition of *Kinder und Hausmärchen* are severely compromised by the evidence of alterations between manuscript and finished work, the principles which they professed have had an enormous influence on the development of folklore research. Before the Grimms, writers such as Perrault had used folktales as material for their literary art. *Volksmärchen der Deutschen* by Johann Musäus was published in 1782–6, but its preface spoke of the peasants' tales as rough raw material which the writer had shaped into a work of art suitable for his readership. The Grimms articulated the ideals by which later folklorists stood, although they themselves fell short of these standards. The development of folklore as a recognized and respected area of scholarship owes much to the prestige of the highly successful *Kinder und Hausmärchen*. Modern folklore study has emphasized the importance of accurate collecting, the context of a tale and the identity of the narrator, and also the necessity of determining his or her cultural origins, and has rejected the literary style and free addition of detail which still characterizes the tales told by the Brothers Grimm.

Harris, Joel Chandler (1848–1908)

American author, in turn printer, lawyer, and journalist on the staff of the *Atlanta Constitution* (1876–1900). His *Uncle Remus* (1880) made him internationally famous, at once to children and to students of folklore. In Uncle Remus, Harris used the idiom and dialect of the plantation slaves as a vehicle for the tales of Brer Rabbit, Brer Fox and others, based on traditional African trickster tales. Later works are *Nights with Uncle Remus* (1883), *Mingo, Daddy Jake, Aaron in the Wildwoods, Sister Jane, Tales of the Home Folks, Plantation Pageants, Minervy Ann* (1899), and a history of Georgia (1899).

Jacobs, Joseph (1854–1916)

Australian scholar and folklorist, born in Sydney. He spent much of his life collecting folk fables and myths, and compiled and published several collections. He was the editor of the *Jewish Encyclopedia* in America (from 1900).

Keightley, Thomas (1789–1872)

Irish writer and folklorist. Inspired by his friend Thomas Crofton **Croker**, and following on from his own work as a writer of history text-books he compiled *The Fairy Mythology* (1828 expanded 1850). Here and in his *Tales and Popular Fictions* (1834), he demonstrates a respect for the preservation of actual form that marks a significant advance in folklore fieldwork. Unlike previous British folklorists he touches upon non-native lore, and in his comments on recurring themes and motifs he anticipates the theories of diffusion and polygenesis of the 20th century: ' . . . some tales and legends are transmitted; others are, to speak geologically, independent formations. When, in a tale of some length, a number of circumstance are the same, and follow in the same order, I would term it transmitted.' (from *The Fairy Mythology*).

Khun, (Franz Felix) Adalbert (1812–81)

German philologist and folklorist, born in Knigsberg. A teacher and director (from 1870 of the Kollnisches Gymnasium in Berlin, he founded a new school of comparative mythology based on comparative philology. He published collections of German folktales, but is best known for his work on the Indo-European languages. He was founder and editor (from 1851) of the *Zeitschrift für vergleichende Sprachforschung*, now entitled *Historische Sprachforschung*.

La Fontaine, Jean de (1621–95)

French poet and fable writer. He is best known for his *Contes et nouvelles en vers* (1665) and *Fables choisies mises en vers* (1668), lively and original poetry inspired by traditional tales. Many of his fables are based on the collection of **Aesop**, and despite their polished style they did much to popularize the *conte* or fable form.

Lang, Andrew (1844–1912)

Scottish writer and folklorist. A scholar of prodigious literary output, he took part in a celebrated controversy with Max **Müller** over the interpretation of folktales, arguing that ethnology and folklore were the key to mythology. His works include *Custom and Myth* (1884), *Myth, Ritual and Religion* (1887), *Modern Mythology* (1897) and *The Making of Religion* (1898). He enlarged the province of folklore from the European peasant traditions Tylor had intended by the term to the oral traditions of all cultures, and gave respectability to the field of psycho-folklore in his writings on ghost stories; in *Cock Lane and Common Sense* (1894) he refuses to reject altogether the supernatural.

Lönnrot, Elias (1802–84)

Finnish philologist and folklorist, born in Sammatti in Nyland. He studied medicine, and was district medical officer for 20 years in Kajana. As a result of his folklore researches there, he was appointed professor of Finnish at Helsingfors (now Helsinki) (1853–62). His major achievement was the collection of oral popular lays, which he organized into a long, connected epic poem of ancient life in the far north, the *Kalevala* (the shorter *Old Kalevala* in 1835, the longer version in 1849). He also compiled a great Finnish–Swedish dictionary (1866–80), which helped to establish a literary Finnish language.

McNeill, Florence Marian (1885–1973)

Folklorist, born in Saint Mary's Holm, Orkney. Educated there and at the universities of Glasgow and Edinburgh, she spent two years travelling before returning to take up a position as Secretary to the Association for Moral and Social Hygiene. She was busy in these years as a suffragette and, after the breakdown of her health, as a tutor in Athens and a freelance journalist in London. Returning to Scotland in 1926 she worked for the Scottish National Dictionary. Best known for her work as a folklorist, her reputation is based upon *The Scots Kitchen* (1929), which examines Scottish culinary history, and its links to France, and includes many traditional recipes. Her comprehensive *The Silver Bough* (1957–68) is a four-volume study of the folklore, festivals and traditions of Scotland. In a similar vein, her work *Hallowe'en* (1970) uses photographs and illustrations to explore the origins of the rites and ceremonies associated with this occasion in Scotland.

Marett, Robert Ranulph (1866–1943)

British anthropologist. He studied classics and philosophy at Balliol College, Oxford and German philosophy at Berlin. He was admitted to the Bar in Jersey in 1891 but he had already developed an interest in anthropology and, after becoming a fellow of Exeter College, Oxford in 1891, he progressively pursued this line of enquiry. He obtained his doctorate in 1909 and in 1910 he became Reader in Anthropology at Oxford, where he founded the Department of Anthropology. He wrote a number of influential books, including *The Threshold of Religion* (1909), *The Birth of Humility* (1910), *Anthropology* (1912), *Psychology and Folklore* (1920), *Man in the Making* (1928), *The Raw Material of Religion* (1929), *Faith, Hope and Charity in Primitive Religion* (1932), *Sacraments of Simple Folk* (1933), *Head, Heart and Hands in Human Evolution* (1935), and *Tylor* (1936). Marett became famous for his theory of pre-animism or dynamism in which he went beyond Tylor's theory of animism and Frazer's theory of magic. He argued that religion begins with a sense of awe in the face of a religious force that is felt and experienced rather than thought about and reasoned out. Thus religion starts with a supernatural stage, and before long Marett was using the Melanesian term *mana* as a useful word to describe the religious force at work.

Moe, Jørgen Engebretsen (1813–82)

Norwegian folklorist and poet, bishop of Christiansand (1875–81). With Peter Christian **Asbjørnsen** he collected and edited *Norwegian Folk Stories* (1841–4). He also published a children's classic, *I brønden og i kjærnet* (1851).

Müller, (Friedrich) Max (1823–1900)

German-born British philologist and orientalist, born in Dessau, where his father, the poet Wilhelm Müller (1794–1827), was ducal librarian. He studied at Dessau, Leipzig and Berlin, and took up the then novel subject of Sanskrit and its kindred sciences of philology and religion. In Paris, under Eugène Burnouf, he began to prepare an edition of the *Rig-Veda*, the sacred hymns of the Hindus; he came to England in 1846 to examine the MSS, and the East India Company commissioned him (1847) to edit and publish it at their expense (1849–74). He was appointed Taylorian professor of modern languages at Oxford (1854) and professor of comparative philology (1868 onwards), a study he did more than anyone else to promote in Britain. Among his most popular works were *Lectures on the Science of Language* (1861–4), *Auld Lang Syne* (1898) and *My Indian Friends*

Biographical Notes

(1898), and he edited the *Sacred Books of the East* (51 vols, 1879–1910). He was a proponent of the mythological school of folklore scholarship attacked by **Lang** and his fellows, and emphasized the function of solar myth as the origin of folk tales.

Opie, Peter Mason (1918–82) and Iona (1923–)

Children's literature specialists. They married in 1943 and the birth of their first child prompted them to study the folklore of childhood. This culminated in *The Oxford Book of Nursery Rhymes* (1951), acknowleged widely for its scholarship as well as its sense of humour. Through their work on this they amassed the peerless Opie Collection of children's books which is now housed in the Bodleian Library. Further research into the folklore of children led to the classic text *The Lore and Language of Schoolchildren* (1959). In 1993 Iona published *The People in the Playground*, based on the research she had done with her husband for their earlier books.

Scott, Sir Walter (1771–1832)

Scottish novelist, poet and man of letters. Born in Edinburgh, he contracted polio as a child and was sent to his grandfather's Borders farm to recuperate; this is the country that figures so prominently in his works. His first publication was rhymed versions of ballads by Bürger in 1796, and he subsequently published *The Border Minstrelsy* (3 vols, 1802–3) and *The Border Antiquities of England and Scotland* (1814–17). Because of his strongly literary bent, Scott cannot be regarded as a pure folklorist, but his passion for oral tradition and traditional forms and themes even in his historical romances did much to popularize interest in the field in the early 19th century thanks to his phenomenal personal influence.

Sébillot, Paul (1843–1918)

French folklorist, born in Matignon. He abandoned law for painting, and from 1870 to 1883 exhibited in the Salon. He then held a post in the ministry of public works, and devoting himself to the study of Breton folktales, published the standard reference work *Le Folklore de France* (1907).

Spence, (James) Lewis Thomas Chalmers (1874–1955)

Scottish poet and anthropologist. He studied dentistry at Edinburgh, but turned to writing and in 1899 became a sub-editor on *The Scotsman* newspaper, and subsequently *The British Weekly* (1906–09). He became an authority on the folklore and mythology of central and South America, and elsewhere, with numerous books including *Mythologies of Mexico and Peru* (1907), *Dictionary of Mythology* (1913), *Encyclopaedia of Occultism* (1920), and *The Magic Arts in Celtic Britain* (1945). As a poet he was a pioneer of the use of archaic Scots language, in such collections as *The Phoenix* (1924) and *Weirds and Vanities* (1927). An ardent nationalist, he was one of the founder members of the National Party of Scotland in 1928, and the first nationalist to contest a parliamentary seat.

Thoms, William John (1803–85)

English antiquary. His *Collection of Early Prose Romances* (3 vols, 1828), drew on the rich traditions of oral lore and marvellous tales in medieval literature, and he began a series of *Lays and Legends of Various Nations*, of which the most notable was that for Germany, published 1834. His most enduring contribution to folk scholarship however was his coining of the term 'folklore', which he advanced in a letter to the weekly *Athenaeum* on 22 August, 1846. He wrote: 'What we in England designate as Popular Antiquities . . . would be most aptly described by a good Saxon compound, Folk-Lore.' His innovation quickly found common currency, and although the term's exact field of reference has been energetically disputed, the connotations of serious academic study that Thoms intended have been retained.

Tylor, Sir Edward Burnet (1832–1917)

English anthropologist, widely regarded as the founder of the systematic study of human culture. In his seminal *Researches into the Early History of Mankind* (1865), Tylor distinguished between folklore and mythology (in answer to the prevailing school of mythological folklorists) and argued that human culture is governed by definite laws of evolutionary development, such that the beliefs and practices of primitive nations may be taken as representing earlier stages in the progress of developed cultures. In *Primitive Culture* (2 vols, 1871), Tylor introduced his concept of 'survival in culture', in which folk customs and tales were seen as preserved fragments of a more primitive stage of cultural development, hence investing folk items with new scholarly significance and respectability. His material also illustrated the similarity of traditions throughout the world. The anthropological school of folklore, championed by Andrew **Lang** and his fellow members of the Folklore Society, was largely built on his research.

List of
Ethnographical and Folklore Museums
throughout the World

The following museums are a selection of those given over entirely or for the most part to ethnographical or folklore studies. Many of the world's large museums contain excellent ethnographical sections, and although these are omitted here for reasons of space they should not be disregarded by the folklorist.

Albania
Tirana
Museum of Archaeology and Ethnography, Institute of Scientific Research in History and Linguistics, State University of Tirana, Tirana

Algeria
Algiers
Bardo Museum of Ethnography and Prehistory (*Musée d'Ethnographie et de Préhistoire du Bardo*), 3 rue F. D. Roosevelt, Alger

Argentina
Buenos Aires
José Hernandez Museum of Argentine Decorative Art (*Museo de Motivos Populares Argentinos 'José Hernandez'*), Avenida del Libertador 2373, Buenos Aires

National Museum of Man (*Museo Nacional del Hombre*), 3 de Febrero 1370–1378, Buenos Aires

Juan B. Ambrosetti Museum of Ethnography (*Museo Etnográfico 'Juan B. Ambrosetti'*), Moreno 350, Buenos Aires

Austria
Grossgmain
Salzburg Open-Air Museum (*Salzburger Freilichtmuseum*), Hasenweg, A-5084 Grossgmain, Salzburgerland
Innsbruck
Museum of Tyrolean Folk Art (*Tiroler Volkskunstmuseum*), Universitätsstraße 2, A-6020 Innsbruck, Tirol

Vienna
Austrian Folklore Museum (*Österreichisches Museum für Volkskunde*), Palais Schönborn, Laudangasse 15–18, A-1080 Wien

Belgium
Antwerp
Folklore Museum (*Volkskundemuseum*), Gildekamersstraat 2–6, B-2000 Antwerpen
Binche
Museum of the Carnival and the Mask (*Musée International du Carnaval et du Masque*), rue de l'Eglise, B-7130 Binche, Hainaut-Mons
Brugge
Folklore Museum (*Museum voor Volkskunde*), Rolweg 40, B-8000 Brugge, West-Vlaanderen
Gent
Museum of Folklore (*Museum voor Volkskunde*), Kraanlei 65, B-9000 Gent, Oost-Vlaanderen

Bolivia
La Paz
National Museum of Folklore (*Museo Folklórico Nacional*), Calle Ingavi 942, La Paz

Brazil
Pôrto Alegre
Museum of the Institute of Folklore (*Museo do Instituto de Folclore*), Rua Carlos Chagas, Esquina Avenida Júlio de Castilhos, Pôrto Alegre, Rio Grande do Sul

Rio de Janeiro
Museum of Folklore (*Museu de Folclore*), Rua do Catete 179, Rio de Janeiro, Guanabara

Museum of Popular Art (*Museu de Arte Popular*), Parque do Flamengo, Avenida Rui Barbosa, Rio de Janeiro, Guanabara

Museum of the Indian (*Museu do Indio*), Rua Mata Machado 127, Maracaña, Rio de Janeiro, Guanabara

Bulgaria
Sofia
National Ethnographic Museum of the Bulgarian Academy of Sciences (*Nacionalen Etnografski Muzej na Bălgarskata Akademija na Naukite*), ul. Moskovska 6a, Sofija

Cameroon
Yaoundé
Museum of Negro Art (*Musée d'Art Nègre*), Aumonerie Catholique Universitaire, Njoag-Malen, B. P. 876, Yaoundé

Canada
Ontario
National Museum of Man (*Musée National de l'Homme*), Victoria Memorial Building, Metcalfe and McLeod Streets, Ottawa, Ontario, K1A 0M8
Vancouver
University of British Columbia Museum of Anthropology, 6393 Northwest Marine Drive, Vancouver, British Columbia, V6T 1W5

Ethnographical and Folklore Museums

Sainte-Foy
Museum of Anthropology
(*Musée d'Anthropologie*),
Université Laval, Sainte-
Foy, Québec G1K 7P4

Saskatoon
Vigfusson Museum, Room
69, Arts Building, University
Campus, Saskatoon,
Saskatchewan S7N 0W0

Waterloo
Museum of Games,
University of Waterloo, 415
Philip Street, Waterloo,
Ontario N2L 3G1

Chile
Santiago
Museum of American
Popular Art (*Museo de Arte
Popular Americano*),
Facultad de Bellas Artes,
Universidad de Chile, Cerro
Santa Lucia, Santiago

China
Beijing
China Museum of Buddhist
Literature and Heritage,
Fa Yuan Si Hou Jie Street,
Xuan Wu District, Beijing

Colombia
Bogotá
Colombian Museum of
Ethnography (*Museo
Etnográfico de Colombia*),
Calle 34, No. 6–61 piso 30,
Apdo. Aéro 10511, Bogotá
Museum of Popular Arts and
Traditions (*Museo de Arte y
Tradiciones Populares*),
Carrera 8 No. 7–21, Bogotá

Cuba
Havana
Museum of Ethnography
(*Museo de Etnologia*),
Palacio Aldama Reina y
Amistad, La Habana

Cyprus
Limassol
Municipal Folk Art Museum,
Heroes Square, Limassol

Nicosia
Museum of Folk Art,
P.O. Box 1436, Archbishop
Kyprianos Square, Nicosia

Czech Republic
Prague
Ethnographical Department
of the Historical Museum
(*Národopisné Oddělení*),
Petřinske sady 97–98,
Letohrádek Kinskych,
150 00 Praha 5
National Museum: Naprstek
Museum of Asian, African
and American Cultures
(*Národni Múzeum v Praze:
Náprstkovo Múzeum
Asijských, Afrických a
Amerických Kultur*),
Betlémske náměski 1, Staré
Město, 110 00 Praha 1

Denmark
Skørping
Spillemand Museum
(*Spillemands-Jagt-og
Skovbrugsmuseet*),
Cimbrervej 2, Rebild,
DK-9520 Skørping, N.
Jylland

Ecuador
Quito
Museum of Ethnography
(*Museo de Etnografia*), Casa
de la Cultura Ecuatoriana,
Avenida 6 de Diciembre
332, Apartado 67, Quito

Egypt
Cairo
Arabic Museum, Midal
Babel-Hkalk, Cairo

Germany
Bad Oeynhausen
Museum of Fairytales and
Weser Legends (*Märchen-
und Wesersagen-Museum*),
Am Kurpark 3, D-4970 Bad
Oeynhausen, Nordrhein-
Westfalen

Berlin
Museum of German
Ethnology (*Museum für
Deutsche Volkskunde SMPK
Berlin*), Im Winkel 6–8,
D-1000 Berlin 33

Bodenwerder
Baron Münchausen Museum
(*Baron-Münchausen-
Museum*), Rathaus,
D-3452 Bodenwerder,
Niedersachsen

Kassel
Kassel Museum (*Hessisches
Landesmuseum*), Brüder-
Grimm-Platz 5,
D-3500 Kassel, Hessen
Museum of the Brothers
Grimm (*Brüder-Grimm-
Museum*), Schöne
Aussicht 2, D-3500 Kassel,
Hessen

Kitzingen
German Carnival Museum
(*Deutsches
Fastnachtmuseum*),
Alemannenstraße 76,
D-8710 Kitzingen, Bayern

Greece
Athens
Museum of Anthropology
and Ethnology, University
of Athens,
Papadiamandopoulou
Street, Goudi, Athinai
Museum of Greek Folk Art,
17 Kydathineon, Plaka,
Athinai

Mykonos
Folklore Museum
(*Laographiko Mouseio*),
GR-846 00, Mykonos

Salonica
Macedonian Folk Art
Museum (*Mouseio
Ethnologiko Laografiko
Makedonias*), Vassi lissis
Olgas 68, GR-546 42
Thessaloniki

Guatemala
Guatemala City
National Museum of Arts and
Handicrafts (*Museo
Nacional de Artes y
Industrias Populares*),
Avenida 10 No. 10–70,
Ciudad de Guatemala

Hungary
Budapest
Ethnographical Museum
(*Néprajzi Múzeum*), Kossuth
Lajos tér 12, 1055 Budapest

Iceland
Reykjavik
Árbær Folk Museum
(*Árbæjarsafn*), Árbær, 110
Reykjavík

India

Calcutta

Ethnographic Museum of the
Cultural Research Institute,
Tribal Welfare Department,
New Secretariat Buildings,
1st Floor, Block B,
1 K. S. Roy Road, Calcutta
700001, West Bengal

Hyderabad

Tribal Cultural Research and
Training Institute Museum,
Road No. 1 Banjara Hills,
Hyderabad, Andhra Pradesh

Mysore

Folklore Museum, University
of Mysore, Manasagangotri,
Mysore 6, Karnataka

Iran

Tehran

Museum of Anthropology
(*Muséyé Mardom Shenassi*),
Golestan Palace, Eydane
Panzdhe Khordad, Tehran
Museum of Decorative Arts
(*Muséyé Honarhayé
Tazymi*), Karim Khan Zand
Avenue, Tehran

Iraq

Baghdad

Museum of Costume and
Ethnography, Bab-al-Shargi,
Baghdad

Ireland

Glencolumbkille

Folk Museum,
Glencolumbkille,
Co. Donegal

Israel

Haifa

Haifa Museum: Ethnological
Museum and Folklore
Archives, Rehov Shabtai
Levi 26, Haifa

Jerusalem

Sir Isaac and Lady Wolfson
Museum, Heichal Shelomo,
Rehov Hamelekh
George 58, Jerusalem

Tel Aviv

Historical Folk Museum of
the Land of Israel, Rehov
Beeri 14, Tel Aviv
Museum Ha'Aretz: Museum
of Ethnography and
Folklore, Tel Qasile, Tel
Aviv

Italy

Florence

National Museum of
Anthropology and
Ethnology (*Museo Nazionale
di Antropologia ed
Entologia*), Via del
Proconsolo 12, Firenze

Lunigiana

Lunigiana Ethnographic
Museum (*Museo
Etnografiko della Luni-
giana*), Via dei Mulini 71,
I-54028 Villafranca
Lunigiana, Massa Carrara

Naples

Museum of Anthropology
(*Museo di Antropologia*),
Via Mezzocannone 8, Napoli

Rome

National Museum of Popular
Art (*Museo Nazionale delle
Arte e Tradizioni Popolari*),
Piazza Marconi 10,
I–00144 Roma

Sardinia

Sardinian Museum of
Ethnology (*Museo Sardo di
Antropologia e Etnografia*),
Via G. T. Porcell 2, I-09100
Cagliari, Sardegna

Sicily

Pitrè Museum of Sicilian
Ethnography (*Museo
Etnografico Siciliano
Giuseppe Pitrè*), Casina
Cinese, Via Duca degli
Abruzzi 1, I-90144 Palermo,
Sicily

Japan

Matsumoto

Japan Folklore Museum
(*Nippon Minzoku
Shivyōkan*), 1, Marunouchi
4-chōme, Matsumoto-shi,
Nagano-ken

Nara

Oriental Folk Museum
(*Touyō Minzōkukan*),
Ayameike-machi, Nara-shi,
Nara-ken

Osaka

Japan Handicrafts Museum
(*Nippon Mingeikan*),
3–619 Shinkawa, Naniwa-ku,
Osaka-shi, Osaka
National Museum of Ethnology
(*Kokuritsu Minzokugaku
Hakubutsukan*), Expo
Memorial Park, Senri,
Suitashi, Osaka

Tokyo

Ethnographical Museum of
Hoya (*Hoya Minzokugaku
Hakubutsukan*), Shimhoya,
Hoya-machi, Kitatama-gun,
Tokyo

Jordan

Amman

Folklore Museum,
Department of Antiquities,
PO Box 88, Amman

Korea, South

Seoul

National Folklore Museum,
Kyonbok Palace, Seoul

Libya

Tripoli

Ethnographical Museum,
Essaraya El-Hamra, Tripoli

Madagascar

Tananarive

Museum of Folklore,
Archaeology, Palaeontology
and Fauna (*Musée
Folklorique, Archéologique,
Paléontologique et
Faunistique*), Parc de
Tsimbazaza, PO Box 434,
Tananarive

Mexico

Mexico City

Ethnographical Museum of
Wax Figures (*Museo
Etnográfico de Esculturas de
Cera*), Guatemala y
Seminario, México City
National Museum of
Anthropology (*Museo
Nacional de Antropologia*),
Chapultepec Park, México
City
National Museum of Arts and
Crafts (*Museo Nacional de
Artes e Industrias
Populares*), Avenida
Juárez 44, México City

Morocco

Tetouan

Museum of Art and Folklore
(*Musée d'Art et de Folklore*),
Bab al-Uqla, Tetouan
Museum of Moroccan
Popular Art (*Musée d'Art
Populaire Marocain*),
30 boulevard Mohamed V,
Tetouan

Ethnographical and Folklore Museums

Netherlands

Delft

Nusantara Ethnographic Museum (*Volkenkundig Museum Nusantara*), St Agathaplein 4, 2611 HR Delft

Nigeria

Ibadan

Museum of the Institute of African Studies, Univesity of Ife, Oyo State

Norway

Lillehammer

Maihaugen Open-Air Museum (*de Sandvigske Samlinger*), Lillehammer 2600, Oppland

Molde

Romsdal Museum (*Romsdalsmuseet*), 6400 Molde, Møre og Romsdal

Oslo

Norwegian Folk Museum (*Norsk Folkemuseum*), Museumsveien. 10, Bygdøy, N-0287 Oslo

Trondheim

Trøndelag Folk Museum (*Trøndelag Folkemuseum*), Postboks 1107, Sverresborg, N-7002 Trondheim, SørTrøndelag

Pakistan

Islamabad

Folk Heritage Museum, Islamabad, Punjab

Lahore

Museum of Folk Arts of the Punjab, Lahore, Punjab

Paraguay

Asunción

Ethnographical Collection (*Colección Enográfica*), Calle Don Bosco 323, Asunción

Peru

Lima

Museum of Archaeology and Ethnology (*Museo de Arqueología y Etnología*), Azangaro 931, Lima National Museum of Peruvian Culture (*Museo Nacional de la Cultura Peruana*), Avenida Alfonso Ugarte 650, Apdo. 3048, Lima

Philippines

Manila

Bayanihan Folk Arts Centre, Philippine Women's University, Taft Avenue, Manila 2801

Pasay City

Panamin Museum of Philippine Traditional Cultures, Pasay City 3129

Poland

Warsaw

National Ethnographical Museum (*Państwowe Muzeum Etnograficzne*), ul. Kredytowa 1, Warszawa, woj. warszawskie

Wrocław

Ethnographical Museum (*Muzeum Etnograficzne*), ul. Kazimierza Wielkiego 33, Wrocława, woj. wrocławskie

Portugal

Lisbon

Museum of Archaeology and Ethnology (*Museu Nacional de Arqueologia et Etnologia*), Mosteiro dos Jerónimos, Praça do Império, 1400 Lisboa

Nazaré

Manso Museum of Ethnography and Archaeology (*Museu Etnográfico e Arqueológico do Dr Joaquim Manso*), Rua D. Fuas Roupinho, Sitio, 2450 Nazaré

Saudi Arabia

Riyadh

Museum of Archaeology and Ethnography, Riyadh

Senegal

Dakar

Museum of African Art (*Musée d'Art Africain*), Institut Fondamental d'Afrique Noire, Place Tascher, B. P. 206, Dakar

South Africa

Johannesburg

Africana Museum, Public Library, Market Square, Johannesburg 2001, Transvaal
Ethnological Museum of the Department of Social Anthropology, University of Witwatersrand, Jan Smuts Avenue, Johannesburg 2001, Transvaal

Stellenbosch

Ethnology Museum, C. L. Marais Library, University of Stellenbosch, Crozier Street, Stellenbosch 7600, Cape Province

Spain

Barcelona

Ethnological Museum (*Musée Etnològic*), Avinguda Santa Madrona, Parc du Montjuîc, 08004 Barcelona

Madrid

National Museum of Ethnology (*Museo Nacional de Etnología*), Alfonso XII No. 68 and Paseo Infanta Isabel No. 11, 28014 Madrid
Museum of Popular Arts (*Museo de Artes y Tradiciones Populares*), Canto Blanco, 28049 Madrid

Sri Lanka

Ratnapura

Museum of Ethnography and Folk Art, Ratnapura Gem Bureau and Laboratory, Ratnapura, Sabaragamuwa Province

Sudan

Khartoum

Ethnographical Museum (*Mathaf al Ethnografia*), University Avenue, PO Box 178, Khartoum

Sweden

Stockholm

Nordic Museum (*Nordiska Museet*), Djurgårdsvaågen 6–16, S-115 21 Stockholm
Skansen, Djurgården, 115 21 Stockholm

Switzerland

Bürglen
William Tell Museum (*Tell-Museum Uri*), Pastplatz, CH-6463 Bürglen, Uri

Lucerne
Museum of Costume and Folk Life (*Schweizerisches Trachten- und Heimatmuseum Utenberg*), Dietschibergstraße, CH-6006 Luzern

Zurich
University Ethnological Museum (*Völkerkundemeuseum der Universität*), Universität, Pelikanstrasse 40, 8001 Zürich

Syria

Damascus
Museum of Popular Arts and Traditions, Rue Bzourich, Palais Azem, Damascus

Tanzania

Dar es Salaam
Village Museum, Bagamoyo Road, Dar es Salaam

Thailand

Bangkok
Hill Tribes Museum, Commissioner's Office of the Border Patrol Police, Phaholyothin Road, Bangkok

Tunisia

Tunis
Dar Ben Abdallah Museum (Musée Dar Ben Abdallah), 1000 Tunis
Museum of Popular Arts and Traditions (*Musée des Arts et Traditions Populaires de la Ville de Tunis*), Dar Ben Abdallah, 1000 Tunis

Turkey

Ankara
Ethnographical Museum (Etnoğrafya Müzesi), Atatürk Bulvari, Ankara

United Kingdom

Bath
Museum of English Native Art, Countess of Huntingdon Chapel, The Vineyard, Paragon, Bath BA1 5NA

Birmingham
Danford Collection of West African Art and Artefacts, Centre for West African Studies, University of Birmingham, Birmingham B15 2TT

Cambridge
Cambridge and County Folk Museum, 2/3 Castle Street, Cambridge CB3 0AQ
University Museum of Archaeology and Anthropology, Downing Street, Cambridge CB2 3DZ

Cardiff
Welsh Folk Museum, St Fagans, Cardiff, South Glamorgan CF5 6XB

Gloucester
Folk Museum, 99–103 Westgate Street, Gloucester GL1 2PG

Holywood
Ulster Folk and Transport Museum, Cultra, Holywood, Co. Down, BT18 0EU

London
Commonwealth Institute, Kensington High Street, London W8 6NQ
Horniman Museum, London Road, Forest Hill, London SE23 3PQ
Museum of Mankind (Ethnography Department of the British Museum), 6 Burlington Gardens, London W1X 2EX
The London Museum of Jewish Life, The Sternberg Centre, 80 East End Road, Finchley, London N3 2SY

Manchester
Manchester Jewish Museum, 190 Cheetham Hill Road, Manchester M8 8LW

Omagh
Ulster–American Folk Park, Mellon Road, Castletown, Omagh, Co. Tyrone BT78 5QY

Oxford
Pitt Rivers Museum, South Parks Road, Oxford OX1 3PP

United States of America

Alaska
Alaska Indian Arts, 23 Fort Seward Drive, Haines, Alaska 99827
Sheldon Jackson Museum, 104 College Drive, Sitka, Alaska 99835

Arizona
Heard Museum, 22 E. Monte Vista Road, Phoenix, Arizona 85004
Museum of Anthropology, Eastern Arizona College, 626 Church Street, Thatcher, Arizona
Navajo Tribal Museum, Highway 264, Window Rock, Arizona 86515

California
Malki Museum, Marongo Indian Reservation, 11-795 Fields Road, Banning, California 92220
Robert H Lowie Museum of Anthropology, 103 Kroeber Hall, University of California, Berkeley, California 94720
Craft and Folk Art Museum, 5800 Wilshire Boulevard, Los Angeles, California 90036
Museum of Cultural History, Haines Hall, University of California, Los Angeles, California 90024
Southwest Museum, 234 Museum Drive, Highland Park, Los Angeles, California 90065
Merritt College Anthropology Museum, 12500 Campus Drive, Oakland, California 94619
Pacific Asia Museum, 46 N. Los Robles Avenue, Pasadena, California 91101
California State Indian Museum, 2618 K Street, Sacramento, California 95816
San Diego Museum of Man, 1350 El Prado, Balboa Park, San Diego, California 92101
Museum of Russian Culture, 2450 Sutter Street, San Francisco, California 94115
San Francisco African-American Historical and Cultural Society Museum, Fort Mason Center,

Ethnographical and Folklore Museums

California cont.
Building C, Room 165, San Francisco, California 94123

American Indian Historical Society Museum of Indian Arts, 1451 Masonic Avenue at Frederick, San Francisco, California 94100

Colorado
Adams State College Museums, ES Building, Alamosa, Colorado 81102

Connecticut
American Indian Archaeological Institute Museum, Route 199, Washington, Connecticut 06793

Florida
Museum of the Americas, 105 W. Gonzalez Street, Pensacola, Florida 32501

Stephen Foster State Folk Culture Center, White Springs, Florida 32096

Hawaii
Bernice P. Bishop Museum, 1525 Bernice Street, Honolulu, Hawaii 96817

Illinois
Du Sable Museum of African-American History, 740 E. 56th Place, Chicago, Illinois 60637

Maurice Spertus Museum of Judaica, 618 S. Michigan Avenue, Chicago, Illinois 60605

Anthropology Museum, Northern Illinois University, DeKalb, Illinois 60115

Indiana
Museum of Indian Heritage, 6040 De Long Road, Eagle Creek Park, Indianapolis, Indiana 46254

Kansas
Museum of Anthropology, University of Kansas, Lawrence, Kansas 66044

Massachusetts
Peabody Museum of Archaeology and Ethnology, 11 Divinity Avenue, Cambridge, Massachusetts 02138

Michigan
University of Michigan Museum of Anthropology, 4009 Ruthven Museums Building, Ann Arbor, Michigan 48109

Museum of Anthropology, Merrick and Anthony Wayne Drive, Detroit, Michigan 48202

Wayne State University Museum of Anthropology, 6001 Cass Avenue, Detroit, Michigan 48202

Minnesota
African-American Cultural Center, 2429 S. 8th Street, Minneapolis, Minnesota 55454

Evelyn Payne Hatcher Museum of Anthropology, Stewart Hall, St. Cloud State University, St. Cloud, Minnesota 56301

Missouri
Museum of Anthropology, University of Missouri, 104 Swallow Hall, Columbia, Missouri 65211

Museum of Art and Archaeology, University of Missouri, 1 Pickard Hall, Columbia, Missouri 65211

New Mexico
Maxwell Museum of Anthropology, University of New Mexico, Albuquerque, New Mexico 87131

Museum of International Folk Art, Camino Lejo, Santa Fé, New Mexico 87501

Wheelwright Museum of the American Indian, 704 Camino Lejo, POB 5153, Santa Fé, New Mexico 87502

New York
Brooklyn Children's Museum, 145 Brooklyn Avenue, Brooklyn, New York, New York 11225

Chinese Museum, 7 Mott Street, New York, New York

Jewish Museum, 1109 Fifth Avenue at 92nd Street, New York, New York 10128

National Museum of the American Indian, Smithsonian Institution, 3753 Broadway, New York, New York 10032

Museum of American Folk Art, 2 Lincoln Square, New York, New York 10023

Museum of Courtship, Love and Marriage, 50 W. 57th Street, New York, New York 10019

Museum of Primitive Art, 15 W. 54th Street, New York, New York 10019

Museum of the American Indian, Heye Foundation, Broadway at 155th Street, New York, New York 10032

Ukrainian Museum, 203 Second Avenue, New York, New York 10003

Native American Center for the Living Arts, 25 Rainbow Boulevard South, Niagara Falls, New York 14303

North Carolina
Catawba Museum of Anthropology, 2113 Brenner Avenue, Heath Hill Forest, Salisbury, North Carolina 28144

Museum of Man, Wake Forest University, 114 Reynolda Village, Winston-Salem, North Carolina 27106

Ohio
St Mary's Ethnic Museum, 3256 Warren Road, Cleveland, Ohio 44111

Pennsylvania
Afro-American Historical and Cultural Museum, 701 Arch Street, Philadelphia, Pennsylvania 19106

Balch Institute for Ethnic Studies, 18 S. 7th Street, Philadelphia, Pennsylvania 19106

The University Museum of Archaeology and Anthropology, The University of Pennsylvania, 33rd and Spruce Streets, Philadelphia, Pennsylvania 19104

Rhode Island
Haffenreffer Museum of Anthropology, Brown University, Mount Hope Street, Bristol, Rhode Island 02809

Museum of Primitive Culture, 604 Kingstown Road, Peace Dale, Rhode Island 02883

South Carolina
Avery Institute of Afro-American History and Culture, 66 George Street, Charleston, South Carolina 29424

South Dakota
American Indian Culture
  Research Center
  Collections, Blue Cloud
  Abbey, Marvin, South
  Dakota 57251

Texas
International Museum of
  Cultures, 7500 W. Camp
  Wisdom Road, Dallas,
  Texas 75236

Utah
Museum of Peoples and
  Cultures, Allen Building,
  Brigham Young University,
  710 N. 100 East, Provo,
  Utah 84602
University of Utah, Museum
  of Anthropology,
  East Bench, Salt Lake City,
  Utah 84102

Washington
Museum of Anthropology,
  Department of
  Anthropology, Washington
  State University, Pullman,
  Washington 99164

Washington D.C.
Gallery of African Art, 1621
  21st Street N.W.,
  Washington D.C. 20009
National Museum of African
  Art, 316–8 A Street N.E.,
  Washington D.C. 20002

Wisconsin
Logan Museum of
  Anthropology, Beloit
  College, Beloit, Wisconsin
  53511

Wyoming
University of Wyoming
  Anthropology Museum,
  Anthropology Building,
  Laramie, Wyoming 82070

Venezuala

Caracas
Folklore Museum (*Museo de
  Folklore*), Avenida Avila,
  Quinta Silueta, Los Chorros,
  Caracas

Yemen

Aden
National Ethnographic
  Museum, Taweela, Aden

Zaire

Kinshasa
Museum of Ethnology and
  Archaeology (*Musée
  Ethnologique et
  Archéologique*), Université
  National du Zaïre,
  B. P. 127, Kinshasa

Kinsangani
Museum of Local Life (*Musée
  de la Vie Indigène*),
  B. P. 1118, Kisangani

A Calendar of
Festivals and Folkloric Events
throughout the World

The following is just a sample of the enormous variety of feasts, festivals and commemorations observed by communities around the world. For ease of reference, the Gregorian calendar, that most common in the West, has been used throughout, but it should be noted that many cultures operate on different calendars, for example agricultural or lunar. This means that many festivals cannot be fixed in the Gregorian month, and in such cases their specific dates are given after their approximate placing in the Gregorian calendar. Many cultures organize their festivals around specific events, such as drought, the birth, marriage or death of an important figure, the beginning of the fishing season and so on. Such festivals have largely been omitted from this calendar. On the other hand, many religious festivals, which would not usually be classed as folklore, have been included here because of the folk customs that have grown up around them.

January

1
New Year's Day
Emancipation Day
Feast of the Circumcision; Christian
Solemnity of Mary; Christian (Roman Catholic)
1–3
Oshogatsu; Japan (New Year celebrations)
2
Second New Year; South Africa (carnival)
3
Genshi-Sai (First Beginning); Japan
5
Twelfth Night; Christian
Eve of Epiphany; Christian
Wassail Eve; Europe
George Washington Carver Day; USA
6
Old Christmas Day; Julian calendar (pre-1752) and Eastern Orthodox Church Epiphany; Christian
Día de Los Tres Reyes (Day of the Three Kings); Spain, South America
7
Distaff Day; Britain (marking the return of the women to their spinning work)
Genna; Ethiopia (Christmas celebration with traditional games of *genna*, similar to hockey)
13
Tivondag Knut (St Knut's Day); Sweden (marking the end of Christmas celebrations and the removal of the tree)

Old Silvester; Switzerland (old New Year celebration marked by *Silvesterklausen*, a form of wassailling)
14
Ratification Day; USA (commemorating official end of American Revolution)
St Kentigern's (Mungo's) Day; Scotland and Northern England
15
Sein-No-Hi (Adults' Day); Japan (day of tribute to those who have turned 20)
19
Timkat; Eastern Orthodox Church (equivalent of Western Epiphany)
Confederate Heroes' Day; USA
20
St Agnes's Eve; Britain (propitious for love divination)
Día de San Sebastián (St Sebastian's Day); Mexico
22
St Dominique's Day, or Midwives' Day; Greece (celebrated by women of child-bearing age)
25
Burns Night; Scotland (honouring the poet Robert Burns with recitals of poetry and eating of haggis)
26
Australia Day; Australia
30
Holy Day of the Three Hierarchs; Eastern Orthodox Church (honouring SS Basil, Gregory and John Chrysostom)

first Monday in Jan
Handsel Monday; Scotland
first Monday after Twelfth Night
Plough Monday; Europe (the return to agricultural work after the festive season)
last Tuesday in Jan
Up Hally A'; Shetland (fire festival culminating in the torching of a Viking ship)
1st day of the lunar month of Muharram
Islamic New Year
1–4 Tagu
Thingyan; Buddhist (Festival of throwing water)
Jan 21–Feb 19 (1st day of 1st moon)
Chinese New Year
Tet (Tet Nguyen-Dan); Vietnamese New Year
Jan–Feb (7th day of 1st moon)
Nanakusa (Festival of the Seven Grasses); Japan (in which young herbs are pounded into a stew)
Jan–Feb (14th–19th days of 1st moon)
Butter Festival; Tibet (climax of New Year celebrations, with elaborate large-scale sculptures made from coloured butter)
Jan–Feb (15th day of first moon)
Feast of Lanterns; China (culmination of New Year celebrations)

February

1
Imbolc; Celtic
St Brigid's Day; Ireland

February *cont.*

2

Candlemas (or Presentation of the Lord, or Purification of the Virgin Mary, or the Wives' Feast); Christian (Western Church)

Hypapante; Christian (Greek Church)

Groundhog Day; USA

3

Powamû Festival; Hopi, USA

Setsubun (Bean-Throwing Festival); Japan

5

Spring Festival; Mauritius

St Agatha's Day; Christian

8

Narvik Sun Pageant; Norway

11

Empire Day; Japan

14

St Valentine's Day

Fjartende Februar; Denmark

22

Mother's Day; India (established in tribute to Mrs M K Gandhi)

George Washington's Birthday; USA

25

St George's Day; Georgia

28

Kalevala Day; Finland

29

Leap year day (or Batchelors' Day); Europe

30*

Job's birthday; USA

first Sunday in Feb

Hamstrom; Switzerland

four days before Ash Wednesday

Carnival; Rio de Janeiro, Brazil

Feb–Mar (at the flooding of the Zambezi)

Ku-omboku; Zambia (ritual removal to higher ground in a river procession)

late Feb–early Mar

Shrove Monday; Christian (when cheese and eggs are used up in preparation for Lent)

late Feb–early Mar

Shrove Tuesday; Christian

Mardi Gras; New Orleans (canival)

late Feb–early Mar

Ash Wednesday; Christian (first day of Lent)

19th day of 1st moon

Rats' Wedding Day; China (feasts to propitiate the household rats)

1st day of 2nd moon

Yungdeung Mama (Wind Festival); Korea

Feb–Mar (13th day of Adar)

Taanit Esther (Fast of Esther); Jewish

Feb–Mar (14th–15th days of Adar)

Purim (Feast of Lots); Jewish

Feb–Mar (14th day of waxing fortnight of Phalguna)

Holi (Festival of Fire); Hindu

Feb–Mar (15th day of waxing fortnight of Phalguna)

Dolayatra (Swing Festival); Hindu (Bengal)

March

1

St David's Day; Wales

3

Ohinamatsuri (Dolls' or Girls' Festival); Japan

4

Constitution Day; USA (commemorating the inauguration of the US Constitution, 4 March 1789)

17

St Patrick's Day; Ireland (also celebrated Chicago and New York)

Noah's entry into the Ark; medieval Europe

19

St Joseph's Day; Christian

Swallow Day; California, USA (celebrating the return of the swallows to the Mission of San Juan Capistrano)

c.20

Ibū Afo Festival; Nigeria (Igbo New Year)

21

Vernal Equinox

23

Shunki-Koreisan (Spring Imperial Festival); Japan

25

Annunciation, or Lady Day (New Year in Julian calendar); Christian (feast of the Virgin Mary celebrating the Incarnation)

first week in March

National Festival of the Grape Harvest: Mendoza, Argentina

Mar–Apr (9th day of the dark half of Chaitra)

Ramanavami; Hindu (birthday of Rama)

late Mar–Apr (Saturday before Palm Sunday)

St Lazar's (or Lazarus's) Day; Eastern Europe

late Mar–April (Sunday before Easter)

Palm Sunday: Christian (commemorating Christ's entry into Jerusalem, the beginning of Holy Week)

late Mar–April (Thursday before Easter)

Maundy Thursday

late Mar–April (Friday before Easter)

Good Friday; Christian

22 Mar–25 Apr

Easter Sunday

end Mar–late Apr (second Monday and Tuesday after Easter)

Hocktide; England (medieval festival in which women imprisoned men on Monday and vice versa on Tuesday, for ransoms paid to church funds)

Mar–Apr

Festival of St Aphrodise, the Procession du Camel; Béziers, France

Mar–Apr (Chaitra)

Hanuman Jayanti; India (in honour of Hanuman, the monkey-god)

Mar–Apr (5th day of San Yue)

Ch'ing Ming; China, Hong Kong and Taiwan (festival of the dead)

Han Sik-il; Korea (festival of the dead)

late Mar–Apr (15–22 Nisan)

Passover or Pesach; Jewish

April

1

April Fools' Day (All Fools' Day); Europe and North America

8

Hana Matsuri (Birthday of the Buddha), or Flower Festival; Buddhist

12 or 13

New Year; South-East Asia

Festivals and Folkloric Events

April *cont.*

13

Baisakhi; Sikh (New Year celebrations, also commemorating the founding of the Khalsa order in 1699)

15

Bengali New Year; Bangladesh

17

New Year's Day; Myanma (Burma)

first Thursday after 19 Apr

Sumarda gurinn-fyrsti (first day of summer); Iceland

23

St George's Day; England

Peppercorn Day; Bermuda (commemorating the payment of one peppercorn given to the governor for the use of the Old State House by the Masonic Lodge, 1816)

Apr–May (full moon of Vaisakha)

Buddha Jayanti; Buddhist (Buddha's birth, enlightenment and death)

late April–early May (1 week)

Toonik Tyme; Frobisher Bay, Canada (early spring carnival named in honour of a pre-Inuit race)

late Apr–May (28th day after Easter)

Repotine; Romania (women's festival, in which they assume authority)

30

Walpurgisnacht; Teutonic

Beltane; Celtic

May

1

May Day; Europe

Workers' Day; socialist

2–3

Tane Matsuri (Rice Planting); Japan

3

Día de la Cruz (Day of the Cross); Spain and South America

5

Tango no Sekku (Boys' Festival); Japan

8

Furry (or Floral) Dance; Cornwall, England

9

Ploughing Ceremony; Thailand

9, 11, 12

Lemuria; Ancient Rome

24 (often celebrated on fourth Monday)

Victoria Day; Britain and Commonwealth (the birthday of Queen Victoria)

29

Oak-apple Day; England (commemorating the Restoration of Charles II, 1660)

30

Memorial Day (originally Decoration Day); USA

31

Visitation of the Virgin Mary; Christian (Episcopal Church)

first Tuesday

Ffair Ffyliaid (Fools' Fair); Llanerfyl, Wales

second Saturday

Windmill Day; The Netherlands

second Sunday

Mother's Day; USA

Cat Festival and Parade; Ypres, Belgium (based on a custom dating from 962 of throwing a cat from the castle tower to symbolize the renunciation of pagan superstitions)

May–June (Monday, Tuesday and Wednesday preceding Ascension Day)

Rogationtide or Rogation Days; Britain (marked by the beating of the bounds)

May–June (40 days after Easter)

Ascension Day; Christian

May–June (6–7 Sivan)

Shavout (Feast of Weeks); Jewish

May–June (month of Ramadan)

Ramadan; Islamic (month of fasting)

late May–June (50 days after Easter)

Whitsunday or Pentecost; Christian

late May–June (7th Thursday after Easter)

Semik; Russian (flirtatious spring festival)

late May–June (first Sunday after Whitsunday)

Trinity Sunday; Christian

late May–June (Thursday after Trinity Sunday)

Feast of Corpus Christi

end May–late June (1st Thursday after Corpus Christi)

Lajkonik; Krakow, Poland (pageant and dancing)

May–June (Jaistha)

Ganga Dussehra; India (bathing festival)

May–June (Jaistha)

Vata Savitri; India (intercession of married women for husband's longevity)

late May–June (10th day of Dhu 'l-Hijja)

Id al-Adha (Feast of the Sacrifice); Islamic (commemorating Abraham's willingness to sacrifice Isaac, the favourite time to undertake pilgrimage to Mecca)

June

first three weeks

Holland Festival; The Netherlands

13

St Anthony of Padua's Day; celebrated New York

13–29

Fiestas Juninas; Brazil

14

Flag Day; USA (commemorating the adoption of the Stars and Stripes design by the Continental Congress, 1777)

21/22

Summer Solstice

Geshi; Japan (purification festival)

23

Midsummer's Eve

24

St John the Baptist's Day; Christian

Midsummer's Day

29

Feast of SS Peter and Paul; Christian (especially South America)

30

Fandroana; Madagascar (feasting)

June *cont.*
June (variable)
Egungun Festival; Nigeria
(Yoruba, masked festival of
ancestral spirits)

first Satuday
Festival of São Gonalo
(patron saint of married
couples and lovers);
celebrated in Amarante,
Portugal, with the baking of
phallic cakes

first Sunday
Rose Harvest Festival;
Bulgaria

3rd Sunday
Father's Day; USA

June (1st day of Shawwal)
Id al-Fitr (Feast of Breaking
the Fast); Islamic (the end of
fasting when the new moon
is sighted)

late June (3 days)
Miramichi Folk Song Festival;
Newcastle, Canada

**June–July (5th day of the 5th
moon)**
Dragon Boat Festival; China,
Hong Kong, Malaysia (an
inauspicious day)

June–July (for 1 month)
June Crop-Over Festival;
Barbados (celebrating the
harvesting of the sugar-cane)

**June–July (5th day after full
moon of Asarka)**
Naga panchami; Hindu
(propitiation of the nagas)

**June–July (1st–10th days of
Muharram)**
Muharram; Shi'ite Muslim
(commemorating the
martyrdom of Husayn)

**late June–July (24th day of 6th
moon)**
Birthday of the Lotus; China

July

1
Dominion Day; Canada

2
Il Palio; Siena, Italy
(medieval games)

4
Independence Day; USA

7
Ommegang Pageant; Belgium
(commemorating the
medieval entertainment of
Charles V)

Hoshi matsuri or Tanabata;
Japan (star festival)

11
Naadam Festival; Mongolia
(celebrated with horse-
racing, archery and
wrestling)

13–31
Obon (Festival of the Dead);
Japan

14
Bastille Day; France
(commemorating the start of
the French Revolution in
1789)

15
St Swithin's Day; Christian

17 (celebrated on 3rd Sunday)
Il Redentore (Feast of the
Redeemer); Venice
(gondola races and
procession commemorating
deliverance from an
epidemic, 1575)

22
St Mary Magdalene's Day;
Christian

23
Birthday of Haile Selassie I;
Rastafarian

24
Bolívar's birthday; much of
South America

25
St James's Day (Fiesta de
Santiago); Spain

29
Ólavsoka (St Olaf's Wake);
Faroe Islands

1st Monday
Caribbean Day

last Sunday
Procession of the Witches;
Beselare, Belgium

July (variable, for 3 days)
Winnipeg Folk Festival;
Winnipeg, Canada

early July
Schrulblha (Festival of the
Ears of Grain); Tibet

mid-July (4 days)
Northern Games; Northwest
Territories, Canada (Inuit)

**Jul–Aug (11th–15th days of the
dark half of Sravana)**
Jhulanayatra (Swinging of the
Lord Krishna); Hindu

**Jul–Aug (15th day of the waxing
part of Sravana)**
Rakshabandhana (Festival of
Tying on Lucky Threads);
Hindu

July–Aug (7th day of 7th moon)
Chhit Sek or Chilsuk; China,
Hong Kong and Taiwan (the
meeting of the Heavenly
Spinning Lady [Vega] and
her lover the Cowherd
[Altair])

late July–early August (1 week)
Caribana; Toronto, Canada
(festival of Caribbean
culture)

August

1
Lammas (Harvest Festival);
Celtic
Lughnasa; Ireland

4–6
San Salvador's Feast; El
Salvador

5–15
Acadian Festival; Caraquet,
Canada

6
Transfiguration; Christian

10–12
Puck's Fair; Killorglin, Co.
Kerry, Ireland

13–15
Three Glorious Days; Congo

15
Assumption or Falling Asleep
of the Blessed Virgin Mary;
Christian

22
Queenship of Mary; Christian
(formerly 31 May)

24
St Bartholomew's Day;
Christian (the occasion of an
annual fair at Smithfield,
London from 1133 to the
19th century)

Aug (variable, for 10 days)
Asala Parahara (Festival of
the Tooth); Buddhist
(procession of the Buddha's
tooth in Kandy)

first week in August
Tortola Festival; British
Virgin Islands
(commemorating the end of
slavery in 1834)

first full week in August
Gaelic Mod; St Ann's,
Canada (festival of Scottish
heritage in Nova Scotia)

second Tuesday in August
Fox Hill Day; Bahamas
(celebrating the end of
slavery)

Festivals and Folkloric Events

August *cont.*
mid-August (1 week)
Folklorama; Winnipeg, Canada (multi-ethnic event)
Aug (at the first ripening of the corn, 3 days)
Green Corn Festival; Native North-East Americans
Aug–Sep (15th day of 8th moon)
Moon Festival; China, Hong Kong, Korea, Taiwan Vietnam
Aug–Sep (7th day of the waxing half of Bhādrapada)
Krishna Jayanti (Krishna's Birthday); Hindu
Aug–Sep (12th day of the waxing half of Sravana)
Paryushana Parva; Jain (end of year celebrations, marked by fasting, penitence and reconciliation)
late Aug (1 week)
Umhlanga (Reed Dance Day); Swaziland (coming-of-age ceremony for girls)

September

1
Abbots Bromley Horn Dance; Abbots Bromley, England
8
Nativity of the Blessed Virgin Mary; Christian
11
Coptic New Year; Christian (Coptic Orthodox Church)
Enkutatash; Ethiopia
14
Exaltation of the Holy Cross, or Holy Rood Day; Christian
15
Our Lady of Sorrows, or The Compassion of our Lady; Christian
21/22
Autumn Equinox; Northern hemisphere
27
Feast of the Finding of the True Cross; Christian (Eastern Orthodox)
28
St Wenceslas's Day; Christian
29
St Michael's Day or Michaelmas; Christian
first Monday
Labor Day; USA, Canada, South Africa

early Sep
Rose of Tralee Festival; Tralee, Ireland
Sep–Oct (12th day of Rabi'al Awwal)
Ma-ulid; Islamic (birthday of Muhammad)
Sep–Oct (1st–2nd days of Tishri)
Rosh Hashana; Jewish (New Year celebrations)
Sep–Oct (10th day of Tishri)
Yom Kippur (Day of Atonement); Jewish
Sep–Oct (15th–21st days of Tishri)
Sukkot (Feast of Tabernacles); Jewish
Sep–Oct (23rd day of Tishri)
Simkhath Torah (Rejoicing of the Law); Jewish (the end of one reading cycle of the Torah and the start of another)
Sep–Oct (1st–10th days of the waxing fortnight of Asvina)
Navaratri (Festival of the Nine Nights); Hindu
Sep–Oct (7th–10th days of the waxing fortnight of Asvina)
Durga-Puja (or Dassehra); Hindu (celebrating the goddess Durga's defeat of the demon buffalo Mahishasura)
Sep–Oct (9th day of the 9th moon)
Kiku no Sekku (Chrysanthemum Festival); Japan

October

2
Mahatma Gandhi's Birthday; India
Guardian Angels' Day; Christian
12
Columbus Day; some parts of Central, South and North America (celebrating the discovery of the so-called New World)
17
Mother's Day; Malawi
23
Chulalongkorn Day; Thailand
31
Hallowe'en (or All Hallows' Eve); Europe
Samhain; Celtic

Oct (variable)
Lisdoonvarna Fair; County Clare, Ireland (at which shy batchelors take the opportunity to hunt for a wife during the mating game)
first Sunday
Mikkelin Paiva (St Michael's Day); Finland
second Monday in Oct
Thanksgiving (Canada)
Oct (20 days before Diwali)
Ram Lila; Hindu (commemorating the abduction and rescue of Sita)
Oct (15th day of the waning fortnight of Avsina)
Diwali, or Dewali; Hindu (festival of lights)
late Oct–Nov (Kartika)
Karwachath; India (festival of married women)

November

1
All Saints' (or Hallows') Day; Christian
2
All Souls' Day, or Memorial Day; Christian
Día de Muertos (Day of the Dead); Mexico
Anniversary of the Crowning of Haile Selassie; Rastafarianism
5
Guy Fawkes or Bonfire Night; Britain and Commonwealth, USA
11
St Martin's Day, or Martinmas; Christian
15
Shichi-go-san (Seven-five-three); Japan (festival of blessing for children of 7, 5 and 3 years old)
21
Presentation of the Blessed Virgin Mary; Christian
22
St Cecilia's Day; Christian
23
Kinro Kansha No Hi (Labour Thanksgiving Day); Japan
30
St Andrew's Day; Scotland
fourth Thursday in Nov
Thanksgiving (USA)

November *cont.*
Nov–Dec (Rabi I)
Birthday of Muhammad;
Islamic

late Nov–early Dec (last Sunday before Advent)
Stir-up Sunday; England (traditionally the days for stirring and wishing upon the Christmas pudding, but the name derives from the first words of the collect for this day, 'Stir up, we beseech thee, . . .')

end Nov–Christmas (4 weeks before Christmas beginning on a Sunday)
Advent; Christian

December

6
St Nicholas's Day; Christian

7
La Quema del Diablo (Burning the Devil); Guatemala**8**
Immaculate Conception of the Blessed Virgin Mary; Christian (Roman Catholic)
Mother's Day; Panama

Blessing of the Waters; Paraguay

12
Sada; Zoroastrian (fire festival of Iran)

17–25
Saturnalia (Ancient Rome)

21
Forefathers' Day; USA

21/22
Winter Solstice; Northern hemisphere

22
Toji; Japan (marking beginning of new solar year)
Pongal; Hindu (Tamil new year festival, ending the inauspicious month of Poh. The traditional greeting, 'Has the rice boiled?', is answered 'It has boiled.')

23
St Thorlak's Day; Iceland

24
Christmas Eve

25
Christmas Day

26 (not Sunday)
Boxing Day; UK (thought to have been the day for emptying the poor boxes in churches)

26 (and 1 January)
Junkanoo Parade and Festival; Bahamas

26–28
Feast of Fools; medieval Europe

27
St John's Day; Christian

28
Holy Innocents' Day, or Childermas; Christian (commemorating the infants slain by Herod)

31
New Year's Eve
Hogmanay; Scotland

early Dec (25th day of Kislev– 2/3rd day of Tevet)
Hanukkah (Feast of Dedication); Jewish (commemorating the rededication of the Temple after the Maccabean victory over the Syrians, 165 BC)

Dec (1st day of Muharram)
Hirja; Islamic (commemorating the emigration of Muhammad from Mecca to Medina)